The Law of Trusts

The Law of Trusts

Fourth Edition

J. G. Riddall MA (TCD)
of the Inner Temple, Barrister at Law
Formerly Senior Lecturer in Law, University of Leeds

Butterworths
London, Dublin & Edinburgh
1992

United Kingdom	Butterworth & Co (Publishers) Ltd, 88 Kingsway, LONDON WC2B 6AB and 4 Hill Street, EDINBURGH EH2 3LJ
Australia	Butterworths SYDNEY, MELBOURNE, BRISBANE, ADELAIDE, PERTH, CANBERRA and HOBART
Belgium	Butterworth & Co (Publishers) Ltd, BRUSSELS
Canada	Butterworths. A division of Reed Inc., TORONTO and VANCOUVER
Ireland	Butterworth (Ireland) Ltd, DUBLIN
Malaysia	Malayan Law Journal Sdn Bhd, KUALA LUMPUR
New Zealand	Butterworths of New Zealand Ltd, WELLINGTON and AUCKLAND
Puerto Rico	Equity de Puerto Rico, Inc, HATO REY
Singapore	Butterworth Asia, SINGAPORE
USA	Butterworth Legal Publishers, AUSTIN, Texas; BOSTON, Massachusetts; CLEARWATER, Florida (D&S Publishers); ORFORD, New Hampshire (Equity Publishing); ST PAUL, Minnesota; and SEATTLE, Washington

First published 1977
Second edition 1982
Reprinted 1985
Third edition 1987
Fourth edition 1992

© J. G. Riddall 1992

A CIP Catalogue record for this book is available from the British Library

ISBN 0 406 51840 8

Filmset in Times by
Selwood Systems, Midsomer Norton
Printed and bound in Great Britain by
Butler & Tanner Ltd, Frome and London

Preface

The principal changes in the sphere of legislation since the last edition have been those made by the Charities Act 1992. This Act has brought about much needed reform of the controls exercisable by the public authorities over the administration of charities. (Whether the reforms will prove to be adequate remains to be seen.) The occasion of the new Act has prompted a division of the single chapter on Charities in the last edition into two in this. Chapter 7 now deals with charitable status, Chapter 8 with the control and administration of charities (including *cy près*).

No case has required the same revision of the law as did *McPhail v Doulton* in the last edition but a wide range of cases have added to our knowledge: the pattern (with one exception) has stayed the same but many interstices have been filled in. The exception was *Sen v Headley* in which it was held that *donatio mortis causae* could apply to gifts of land. Among other cases of interest have been *Re Hetherington* concerning the status of gifts for the saying of Masses, *Sekhon v Alissa* and *Lloyds Bank plc v Rossett* which threw light on the acquisition of beneficial interests, *Gibbon v Mitchell* on protective trusts, *Harries v Church Commissioners for England*, which dealt with the ethical considerations that were relevant in making investments by trustees, *Lloyds Bank plc v Duker* on the duty to act equitably between beneficiaries, *Stevenson v Wishart* on the nature for tax purposes of money advanced by trustees, *Guinness plc v Saunders* on conflicts of duty, and *Lipkin Gorman v Karpnale Ltd* and *Re Montagu's Settlement Trusts* on the knowledge needed to incur liability, through the imposition of a constructive trust.

Re Beatty produced no change in the law but it prompted me to think afresh about the nature of what in the last edition were termed 'trust powers' and in this edition 'fiduciary powers', and a substantial amount of the chapter on Trusts and Powers (Chapter 11) has been rewritten as a result. Other sections that have been rewritten or amplified include those dealing with the rules relating to certainty as they affect gifts to a class, the effect of section 53(1)(b) of the Law of Property Act 1925, trusts for political purposes, and (in the light of *Re Montagu's Settlement Trust*) constructive trusts. An appendix, on the rule against inalienability, has been added to Chapter 9.

Trusts law since the last edition in 1987 progressed in an unruffled manner. Cases were heard that raised interesting points but nothing occurred of outstanding significance. Equity dozed. Nothing of significance happened that is, until in the early hours of the morning of 6 November 1991, Robert Maxwell, chairman of Maxwell Communications, fell from the deck of his yacht *The Lady Ghislaine*, near Tenerife, and was drowned. Following closely on his death came the disclosure that Maxwell had been responsible for the theft of approximately £4m from the funds of Mirror Group Newspapers' employees' pension trust.

A select committee of the House of Commons[1] found that 'Robert Maxwell's looting of the pension funds for which he had responsibility makes ... reform urgent'[2], and the committee made recommendations for ensuring that pension funds were protected by a legal framework that would prevent future thefts. In addition to attaching blame to the trustees' accountants and other advisers, the trusts' auditors, and the existing regulatory machinery (principally the Occupational Pensions Board), the committee attached blame also to the fact that pension funds had been permitted to operate under what the committee referred to as 'medieval trust law'. Much was made of the archaic nature of trust law and its inappropriateness as a basis for modern pensions schemes.

It is submitted that the committee's comments on the fitness of trust law for the purpose of pension schemes is misconceived. It is not the nature of a trust that enabled Maxwell to steal the pension funds, and certainly not the fact that the trust has its origins in medieval law. The notion of a corporation of which the modern public limited company is one manifestation, has a long history also. But companies have been subject to regulation, increasingly tight regulation, for over a century and a half. The tragic fiasco of the Maxwell depredations was made possible by the failure of those with responsibilities in the pensions sphere to draw to public attention the need for regulation of pension fund trusts of the kind that successive Companies Acts have provided in the case of companies, and which the Charities Act 1992 seeks to provide in the case of charities. (The committee wrote 'Pontius Pilate would have blushed at the spectacle of so many witnesses washing their hands in public before the committee of their responsibilites in this affair[3]'.) Legislation is promised. But whatever its details it seems likely that the essence of its machinery cannot be other than that of a trust – the device by which a group of people hold and manage property for the benefit of certain others.

The cross-referencing to Maudsley and Burn's *Trusts and Trustees: Cases and Materials* (indicated after case references by '(M&B)') has been brought into line with the most recent (fourth) edition of that book.

My thanks go to the publishers for all the work behind the scenes that goes into the preparation of a book on law, and to my wife for checking the text and the proofs, and for things too numerous to mention here.

My aim has been to present the law as it stood at 31 March 1992.

Hills View Cottage,   J. G. Riddall
Bradwell,
Derbyshire

---

1 HC 61–II.
2 Para 285.
3 Para 173.

Contents

Table of statutes

References in this Table to *Statutes* are to Halsbury's Statutes of England (Fourth Edition) showing the volume and page at which the annotated text of the Act will be found.

List of cases

Chapter 1

Introduction

Those who approach the study of trusts after having first studied land law will have already learned several things about trusts. They will know, for example, that:

1. if A holds a legal interest in property and he transfers it to T on trust for B, then the legal interest is vested in T and the equitable (beneficial) interest in B;

2. the subject matter of a trust may be legal or an equitable interest in property, in the latter case the trustees holding an equitable (not legal) interest in the property (and the beneficiaries an equitable interest also, a sub-trust, as it were, having come into existence);

3. the subject matter of a trust may be real property or personal property; and further, that the form which the trust property takes may change during the life of a trust, as where land is settled under a strict settlement, and the tenant for life exercises his power of sale and sells the settled land (thus converting the trust property from land to money); and the trustees then invest the money in shares (thus converting the trust property from one kind of personal property to another);

4. when we speak of a 'gift' of property this can refer to an outright gift by A to B, or the creation of a trust, by a transfer to trustees on trust for B;

5. the equitable interests of beneficiaries under a trust may be of various durations—including any of the durations or 'estates' which came to be accepted in the context of land law, eg a fee simple absolute in possession, a life interest, conditional and determinable forms of these, a fee tail, interests in remainder and reversion and so on;

6. where a legal interest in land is held on trust, the interest which the trustees hold, since 1925, can be only either a fee simple absolute in possession or a term of years (since no other form of interest in land may exist in a legal form since the end of 1925);

7. since the end of 1925 a settlement of land can exist only under one or other of two forms of trust—a 'strict settlement' under the Settled Land Act 1925, or a trust for sale;

8. under the rule in *Saunders v Vautier*[1] where a beneficiary is of full age and absolutely entitled he may call on the trustees to convey the legal interest to him and that when they have done this the trust comes to an end;

---

1 (1841) 4 Beav 115.

9. if trustees dispose of trust property in breach of trust to X, then whether X takes the property free from or subject to the equitable interests of the beneficiaries depends, under the basic rule, on whether or not X is a bona fide purchaser for value of the legal estate without notice, actual or constructive, of the equitable interests;

10. the bona fide purchaser rule is subject to a number of modifications introduced by statute, in particular by the Land Charges Acts 1925 and 1972, under which various interests, in order to bind a purchaser, must be registered in a register of Land Charges;

11. the trust emerged under the name of 'use' in the later middle ages; that the development of trusts was checked by the Statute of Uses 1535; that ways of evading the Statute were devised in the following two centuries, until, by the eighteenth century, the effects of the Statute had for most purposes been eliminated; that the Statute of Uses was repealed in 1925, thus bringing the law into line with what had long been the reality.

12. earlier terms for beneficiary were 'cestui que use', or 'cestui que trust'.

All these, and many other facts, a student of land law will have learned about trusts. What more, it might be asked, is there to know? Well, there is much to be considered in connection with the position and duties of a trustee. Suppose that A conveys property to T_1 and T_2 on trust for B: what are the duties of T_1 and T_2 with regard to the property? Can T_1 and T_2 appoint an additional trustee? And if so, how? What say, if any, does B have over the management of the trust? What is the position if one trustee makes off with the property? Is the other trustee liable? What remedies does B have against T_1 or T_2 if they act in breach of trust? What defences are open to T_1 and T_2 in an action against them by B? What is the position if a trustee wishes to resign? Can he do so? And if so, how? These are all matters which are treated in the second part of this book.

In the first part we consider various aspects of the nature of trusts, beginning with a matter that constantly has a bearing on legal issues affecting a trust – succession to property on a person's death.

Chapter 2

Succession on death

Introduction

Much of the law relating to trusts is concerned with the question as to whether a valid trust has been created. Trusts are commonly created by a testator in his will. It is thus upon the death of a testator that questions regarding the validity of a trust often arise. Because of this, principles of law relating to trusts are much interlinked with principles of law that govern the devolution of a person's property on his death—the principles of law relating to succession. And terms of law which form part of the law of succession—revocation, partial intestacy, lapse, administration, *per stirpes*— lie scattered through the judgments on cases concerning trusts. Because of the interrelation of the law of trusts and the law of succession, a student of the law of trusts may in some instances not be able fully to grasp the reason for the outcome of a particular court decision unless he has a knowledge of the elements of the law relating to succession. It may therefore be helpful, before launching out into the law of trusts, to consider briefly the main principles of law relating to succession.

When a person dies it may be found that he has died without making a will, or that he has died after having made a will—that he has died intestate, or that he has died testate.

The ability to direct to whom one's property is to pass on one's death— to dispose of property by will—is an innovation. Originally, on a person's death, his property went to persons determined according to certain set principles of law: devolution was not according to the wish of the deceased, but according to operation of law. Only gradually did it come about that a person came to be able to leave his property on his death to one or more persons other than those whom the law prescribed as otherwise being entitled.

Thus we can[1] say that intestate succession came before testate succession. At present the tendency is to treat testate succession as representing the norm, and intestacy as constituting an exception. But the nature of the law, and its operation, will best be understood if intestacy is treated as the starting point and disposition by will as constituting the exception.

We shall therefore deal first with the position where a person dies intestate.

---

1   If we are prepared to ignore the fact that one could logically demur at the use of the term 'intestate succession' when no such thing as testate succession existed.

Intestate succession

The devolution of property on the death of a person intestate after 1925 is governed by the Administration of Estates Act 1925, as subsequently amended, in particular by the Intestates' Estates Act 1952.

Before the 1925 Act, if a person died intestate leaving real property, then this passed to his heir ascertained under the old common law canons of descent. If he left personalty then this passed to the next of kin as ascertained under the Statute of Distribution 1670.[2] Thus if an intestate person died before 1926, and his estate (ie the whole of his property at his death) included both land and personalty, the two types of property devolved according to different rules. For example, if he died a widower leaving three daughters and two sons, his land would pass to the elder of the two sons; his personalty would be divided equally between all five children. These archaic and trouble-some arrangements the 1925 Act swept away and, in their stead, provided that on a death intestate after 1925 all of an intestate person's property should (subject to two exceptions[3]) devolve in the same way. As to the person entitled, it was the aim of the Act to secure that an intestate's property should pass to the person or persons whom the intestate might be presumed to have wished to receive it had he given his mind to the matter. Accordingly, the persons entitled[4] begin with members of the intestate's family closest to him and from them extend outwards, as it were, to relations less and less closely related. At the top of the list are the intestate's wife and children, next come his parents, then his brothers and sisters, followed by grandparents and ending with uncles and aunts. Subject to what is said later, if persons exist in any one category they take to the exclusion of others in categories below. For example, if at his death an intestate had no wife, children or parents, and had one brother, one grandfather and three aunts, then the brother would take the whole.

We shall need to consider the workings of the statutory list more closely but first we shall consider how the intestate's property is passed to the person or persons entitled under the Act. The reader may know that when a person dies leaving a will it is normal for the will to appoint an executor and that it is the executor's responsibility to assemble the deceased's property, pay any debts outstanding at his death, and distribute what is left according to the terms of the will—to *administer* the estate. In the case of a death intestate, since there is no will, no executor exists. In order to overcome the difficulty, the 1925 Act provides for the appointment by the court (in what are termed *letters of administration*) of an official (the *administrator*) to administer the distribution of the intestate's estate.

The court, being unaware of the death, can appoint an administrator only on an application being made to it. Who is entitled to apply to the court to be appointed administrator—*to apply for letters of administration*? The answer, broadly, is that the persons so entitled are determined according to the same

2 As amended, and explained, by the Statute of Frauds 1677, and the Statute of Distribution 1685.
3 (i) If at his death the intestate holds land by an unbarred fee tail, the land devolves upon his heir ascertained under the old canons of descent. (ii) Where at 1 January 1926 a lunatic was of age and he later dies intestate without having recovered his senses, his realty passes similarly.
4 Subject to what is said below.

list as that which sets out those entitled to receive the intestate's property. Letters of administration may be granted to two or more administrators, up to a maximum of four.

On his appointment, it is the administrator's duty to assemble the intestate's property, pay his debts, funeral expenses, and the cost of applying for letters of administration and other expenses arising from the winding up of the estate, and divide what remains (what is termed the *residuary estate*) among those entitled (including, normally, himself or herself).

In case the intestate's debts amount to more than the money available (eg in cash and in the bank), the Act empowers the administrator to sell the intestate's property in order to raise cash. This is achieved by the provision of the Act[5] that all[6] the intestate's property is to be held by the administrator on trust for sale, with power to postpone sale for such period as he may think proper. Thus a death intestate is an occasion on which a statutory trust for sale arises.

On the grant of letters of administration, the title to the intestate's property vests in the administrator. Between the intestate's death and the grant, the title to the property is made by statute to vest (because it has got to vest somewhere, there can be no vacuum) in the President of the Family Division of the High Court.

The persons entitled are set out in the table on page 8. This table shows the position after the amendments made to the Administration of Estates Act 1925 by the Intestates' Estate Act 1952[7] and applies to deaths occurring after 1952[8]. The persons entitled under the 1925 Act, as amended, are by convention referred to as the *next of kin*. This term does not, however, appear in the legislation.

In the explanation that follows we shall assume that the intestate was a man. Hence the references to 'widow'. The provisions of the Act apply equally, however, to a spouse of either sex. Thus, where we refer to 'widow', a full statement of the law would require the words 'surviving spouse'.

Consider the table on page 8. A number of matters call for attention.

1. It will be readily apparent that what we have is not a simple list of relatives, but a given number of circumstances, in two of which the property is shared; in number one between the widow and children, and in number two between the widow and either the intestate's parents or, if none, his brothers and sisters of the whole blood.

2. The term 'widow' denotes the intestate's former *wife* and therefore excludes a divorced wife. (Where the intestate was a woman, a divorced husband is similarly excluded[9].)

3. In numbers 1 and 2 the widow takes the 'personal chattels'. These are defined in detail by the Act[10] and broadly include furniture, household articles (including plate, linen, china, glass), books, pictures, jewellery, domestic

---

5 Administration of Estates Act 1925, s 33(1).
6 Subject to what is said below with regard to the personal chattels (see infra) and the matrimonial home (see p 6).
7 Section 1 and Sch 1.
8 For deaths occurring between 1925 and 1953 see Administration of Estates Act 1925, s 46, summarised in Megarry and Wade, *The Law of Real Property*, 5th ed, p 549, n 42.
9 Where spouses are judicially separated, the property of a spouse who dies intestate devolves as if the other were dead. Matrimonial Causes Act 1973, s 18(2), replacing Matrimonial Proceedings and Property Act 1970, s 40.
10 Section 55(1)(x).

animals, cars, and consumable stores. Personal chattels do not include money, securities, or chattels used for business purposes.

Although all the intestate's property is held on trust for sale, the Act lays down that personal chattels are not to be sold without special reason, unless sale is required in order to pay the costs of administration. We may add here that reversionary interests (eg the interest that arises on the death of the holder of a life interest[11]) are similarly not to be sold without special reason.

4. Instead of receiving a life interest in half the residue, the widow is entitled to elect to receive a lump sum representing the value of her life interest[12]. (Where a widow makes this election, the entire residuary estate can be distributed between the widow and children forthwith.)

5. In number 1 the widow takes a statutory legacy of one amount (£75,000), and in number 2 a statutory legacy of another, higher, amount (£125,000)[13]. The amounts of each level of statutory legacy are revised from time to time by Order made by the Lord Chancellor under the authority of the Family Provision Act 1966[14]. (Prior to 1 June 1987 and after 1 March 1981 the statutory legacies were £40,000 and £85,000 respectively). The widow takes the statutory legacy free of inheritance tax, and with interest at 4% from the date of the intestate's death.

6. Several matters arise concerning the matrimonial home.

(i) Where the house is in the name of the husband (H) alone (ie and the wife (W) has no interest, legal or equitable, in the property) and H dies intestate, and W wishes to have the house, then she can require the administrator to appropriate the home to her as part of the property to which she is entitled (ie out of the statutory legacy and the one half of the residue to which she is entitled absolutely).[15]

(ii) where the house is in the joint names of H and W, holding in equity as joint tenants, and H dies intestate, then H's half share passes to W under the *jus accrescendi* (and thus no part of W's statutory legacy will need to be used towards the cost of the house).

(iii) Where the house is in the joint names of H and W, holding in equity as tenants in common, and H dies intestate, and W wishes to retain the house, the value of H's half share will count as part of the property to which she is entitled under his intestacy.

The seriousness of the implications of the varying outcomes in (i), (ii) and (iii) will be appreciated.

7. Under the Family Law Reform Act 1969[16], where the intestate's death occurred after 1959, 'children' (and, under the *per stirpes* rule[17], 'issue') include illegitimate children (or illegitimate issue as the case may be); and 'parents' include the parents of an illegitimate child. The Family Law Reform Act 1987,[18] continuing the policy and extending the scope of the 1969 Act, provides that (after 3 April 1988) when identifying relationships for the

---

11 The nature of reversionary interests is considered later, in Chap 16.
12 Administration of Estates Act 1925, s 47A (added by the Intestates' Estates Act 1952, s 2(b)). The method of reckoning the capital value of the life interest is prescribed in the Intestate Succession (Interest and Capitalisation) Order 1977 (No 1491).
13 The Family Provision (Intestate Succession) Order 1987, SI 1987/799.
14 Section 1.
15 Intestates' Estates Act 1952, s 5, Sch 2; *Re Collins* [1975] 1 WLR 309.
16 Section 14.
17 See below, p 7.
18 Sections 1, 19.

purpose of the intestacy rules, no distinction is to be made between people whose parents are or were married to each other and people whose parents are or were not.

8. Adopted children rank as the children of their adopting parents (for the purposes of the death intestate of the child, or of the parents).[19]

9. As mentioned earlier, if one or more relatives exist in one class, he or they take to the exclusion of all others.

10. It will be noted that children, brothers and sisters (of the whole and the half blood) and uncles and aunts (of the whole and the half blood) are stated to take 'on the statutory trusts'. Where a relative takes on the statutory trusts (which are distinct from, and in no way connected with, the statutory trust for sale on which the administrator holds the deceased's entire estate), then the following consequences ensue:

(a) No relative in the class takes unless and until he attains the age of 18[20] or marries under that age.[1] If such a relative dies before attaining the age of 18 or marrying under that age, then his share, which will have been held on trust for him pending his satisfying either condition, must be dealt with as if he had never been born. For example, where an intestate widower leaves five children, and one dies under 18, his share would go to the other four. If he had died leaving only one child, and that child died under 18, the intestate's property would go to his parents.

(b) If a person who would otherwise have been entitled to a share of the intestate's property dies before the intestate, and that person left issue who are living at the intestate's death, then the issue take their dead parent's share (they take *per stirpes*), provided that they attain a vested interest (by attaining 18 or marrying under that age).[2] For example, supposing that an intestate had three children A, B, and C. B has two children D and E. D has two children, G and H. C has one child, F. B, C and D pre-decease the intestate. A will takes one third. G and H will take a one twelfth share; E a sixth share; and F a one third share (assuming that each of these attains a vested interest).

11. A person under 18 does not[3] have legal capacity to make a will.[4] Thus on the death of a person under 18 his property necessarily devolves upon his next of kin under the Administration of Estates Act 1925.

Testate succession

Formalities

Suppose that T, who is a widower, infirm and of advanced age, has been looked after for several years by a housekeeper. T has a son and grandchildren who live in another part of the country. On T's death, it is found that in his will he has left his house and all the rest of his property to the housekeeper. 'Is this in fact my father's signature?' the son may wonder, 'or has the

---

19 Adoption Act 1976, ss 38–46.
20 Family Law Reform Act 1969, s 3(2). Prior to 1970 the age prescribed was 21.
1 Administration of Estates Act 1925, s 47.
2 Administration of Estates Act 1925, s 47(1), (2).
3 Unless he is a *privileged testator*. See p 10, n 16.
4 Wills Act 1837, s 7.

Distribution of property on an intestacy

The intestate dies leaving	Distribution	
1. A widow and children	Widow receives	(i) The personal chattels; (ii) Statutory legacy of £75,000; (iii) a life interest in half the residue.
	Children receive	(i) Half the residue absolutely, on the statutory trusts; (ii) Half the residue in remainder, on the widow's death, on the statutory trusts.
2. A widow and either parents or brothers and sisters of the whole blood	Widow receives	(i) Personal chattels; (ii) Statutory legacy of £125,000; (iii) Half the residue.
	Other half of residue goes to	(a) Parents or, if none (b) Brothers and sisters of the whole blood, on the statutory trusts.
3. A widow, and no children, no parents, no brothers and sisters of the whole blood	Widow receives entire estate.	
4. Children, and no widow	Children receive the entire estate on the statutory trusts.	
5. No widow and no children	Entire estate passes to— (a) Parents (b) Brothers and sisters of the whole blood on the statutory trusts (c) Brothers and sisters of the half blood on the statutory trusts (d) Grandparents (e) Uncles and aunts of the whole blood on the statutory trusts (f) Uncles and aunts of the half blood on the statutory trusts (g) The Crown, the Duchy of Lancaster or the Duchy of Cornwall. (Of its grace the Crown etc, may provide out of the estate for dependants of the deceased who are not on the statutory list.)	

signature been forged? And if the signature is genuinely that of my father, has he been unfairly induced, or perhaps even cajoled, into giving his signature?' Clearly, if the signature on the will was forged, or if the will was signed under some form of undue influence, or duress, then the will should be set aside as being invalid. But the testator, being dead, is no longer available to give evidence as to whether the signature is his; or, if the signature is his, as to the circumstances in which he signed the will.[5]

It has been with the aim of ensuring that a signature on a will is genuinely that of the testator, and that the will expresses the wishes of the testator, free from pressures brought to bear by persons seeking to benefit from the will, that statute has for long provided that certain requirements must be met for a will to be valid. The present law on the execution of a will is contained in s 9 of the Wills Act 1837 as substituted by the Administration of Justice Act 1982.[6] By this section no will is valid unless:

'(a) it is in writing[7], and signed[8] by the testator or by some other person in his presence and by his direction; and,

(b) it appears that the testator intended by his signature to give effect to the will[9]; and,

(c) the signature is made or acknowledged[10] by the testator in the presence of two or more witnesses present at the same time; and,

(d) each witness either (i) attests and signs the will, or (ii) acknowledges his signature, in the presence of the testator (but not necessarily in the presence of any other witness),[11] but no form of attestation shall be necessary.'

An alteration (including a deletion) to a will is effective only if the making of the alteration is executed in the same manner in which a new will would be required to be executed in accordance with section 9 of the Wills Act 1837[12]; ie each alteration must be signed[13] by the testator and witnessed by two witnesses[14] (though not necessarily the same witnesses that attested the original will).

---

5   For an example of alleged undue influence, see *Re Brocklehurst* [1978] Ch 14, [1978] 1 All ER 767.
6   Section 17. On the changes made by the 1982 Act, see [1983] Conv 21 (A. Samuels); (1983) 133 NLJ 859 (R. D. Mackay).
7   Any form of writing (handwriting, typing, printing) may be used.
8   Any mark by the testator suffices if it is intended to constitute the execution of the will (eg a thumb mark, see *Re Finn* (1935) 52 TLR 153).
9   Ie, even if the signature is not (as will normally be the case) at the foot of the will. *Re Mann's Goods* [1942] P 146, [1942] 2 All ER 193 (signature on envelope containing will held to be intended to give effect to the will); cf *Re Bean* [1944] P 83, [1944] 2 All ER 348; *Wood v Smith* [1991] 2 All ER 939, [1991] 3 WLR 514.
10 Eg by the testator saying to a witness, 'This is my signature.'
11 Thus if the testator signs the will (or acknowledges his signature) in the presence of witness 1 and witness 2; witness 1 leaves the room; witness 2 attests the will and leaves the room; witness 1 returns and attests the will, then the section is satisfied. But if the testator signs the will in the presence of witness 1; witness 2 enters the room; the testator acknowledges his signature; witness 2 attests the will, then the section is not satisfied and the will is void.
12 Wills Act 1837 s 21. *Re Martin's Goods* (1849) 1 Rob Eccl 712; *Re White* [1991] Ch 1.
13 See n 8.
14 Ie in accordance with (c) and (d) above.

Gifts to witnesses

In order to seek to ensure that the testimony of witnesses to a will can be relied on as truthful (ie that a witness has no incentive to lie as to the circumstances in which the testator made his signature) the Wills Act 1837[15] provides that any gift in a will to a witness, or to the spouse of a witness, is void.[16] Thus if X induces a testator to sign a will which leaves X or his spouse certain property, and then X (with another) signs as witness, the gift concerned is void. The will itself, be it noted, is valid; it is only the gift to X (or his spouse) which fails. (This is so even if it can be shown that the will expressed the testator's genuine intention, free of any undue influence.)

There is no reason why an executor should not witness a will, provided, of course, that it is borne in mind that any gift in the will to the executor will be void.

Revocation

Nothing in the law prevents a testator who has made a will from changing his mind and cancelling the will: a will can be *revoked*. Where a testator wishes to revoke a will he may do so by executing (in accordance with the Wills Act 1837) a fresh will which contains words that revoke the earlier will. Such words of revocation (eg 'I hereby revoke all previous wills and testamentary dispositions') are customarily inserted in all professionally drawn wills. (Such words as, 'This is the last will and testament of me, X . . .' are not sufficient to revoke an earlier will.)

Where a testator makes will 1, and then later makes another will, will 2, which does not contain a clause revoking will 1, then will 1 is not revoked. The two wills are read together; will 1 is revoked only to the extent that provisions in it are inconsistent with will 2. (Where the second will disposes of *all* the testator's property, then the second will impliedly revokes the whole of the first will.)

A will may also be revoked by the presumed intention of the testator. This will be the result where a testator destroys the will, for example by burning it, or tearing it up, provided that the destruction is carried out by the testator

---

15 Section 15.
16 There are certain exceptions. The following gifts are not invalidated by the rule:
(i) A gift to the spouse of a witness where the marriage took place after the execution of the will.
(ii) A gift to a witness as a trustee on trust for another.
(iii) A gift which is confirmed by a later will which is not witnessed by the beneficiary.
(iv) A gift in a will made by a 'privileged testator', ie a person who, under the Wills Act 1837, s 11, extended by the Wills (Soldiers and Sailors) Act 1918, may make a valid will without the will being attested under s 15 of the 1837 Act. Privileged testators include, broadly, a soldier or member of the Air Force in actual military service, or a member of the Royal Navy or merchant marine at sea.
(v) A gift in a will which would be validly witnessed without the signature of the beneficiary, ie where the will is witnessed by two other persons and the beneficiary's signature as witness is therefore superfluous. Wills Act 1968, s 1 reversing *Re Bravda* [1968] 2 All ER 217, [1968] 1 WLR 479, CA.

himself or by someone else at his direction and in his presence[17] and is carried out with the intention that the will should be revoked.[18]

Where only part of a will is destroyed (eg by a part being cut out by scissors) or words are obliterated in such a manner[19] that they are no longer 'apparent'[20], then only that part (or those words) are revoked unless the part destroyed or the words obliterated are vital to the validity of the will[1], in which case the whole will is revoked.

A will is also revoked, under the Wills Act 1837,[2] by the subsequent marriage of the testator. The reason for the provision is this: a testator makes a will leaving all his property to his friend X; many years later he marries Y; he forgets about the will he has made and makes no new will in favour of his wife; some years later the testator dies. Without the existence of the Act all his property would pass to X, none to his widow. As a result of the Act, on the testator's marriage the will is revoked and on the testator's death his property passes under his intestacy to Y. (If the testator wishes to make a fresh will after his marriage, making such provision for Y as he chooses, then he is free to do so.) However, where it appears from a will that at the time it was made the testator was expecting to be married to a particular person and that he intended that the will should not be revoked, then the will is not revoked by his marriage to that person.[3] (Eg where a testator left property 'to my fiancée, Z', and he later married Z, the will was not revoked by the marriage.[4])

The subsequent divorce of a testator does not cause the revocation of a will, notwithstanding 'that in almost all cases a will made during the subsistence of the marriage ... will no longer be appropriate in the changed circumstances produced by the divorce'.[5] But on a testator's divorce, any gift by will to the former spouse lapses.[6]

It will be appreciated that the revocation of a will alters the course of devolution of property even where no fresh will is made: before the revocation, the property would have passed on the testator's death to those named in the will; after the revocation, the property passes to his next of kin. For this reason, where a testator wishes to revoke a will, the document revoking the will must be signed and attested in accordance with s 9 of the Wills Act

---

17 Where a will was in the custody of the testator's solicitor, the testator telephoned the solicitor and instructed him, there and then, to destroy the will, and the solicitor did so, the conditions required for revocation of the will were not satisfied, and the will was not revoked. (The contents of the will would be proved from, eg, a carbon copy.) See *Re De Kremer* (1965) 110 Sol Jo 18.
18 Wills Act 1837, s 20.
19 Eg by heavy scoring with ball-point pen. *Re Adams* [1990] Ch 601, [1990] 2 All ER 97.
20 Wills Act 1837, s 21; 'Apparent' means decipherable by experts using magnifying glasses when necessary (but not, eg, chemical aids).
1 Eg the signatures of the testator or witnesses. *Re Adams* [1990] Ch 601, [1990] 2 All ER 97.
2 Section 18(3), replaced for wills made after 1982 by the Administration of Justice Act 1982, s 18.
3 Wills Act 1837, s 18(3), as replaced by the Administration of Justice Act 1982, s 18, replacing Law of Property Act 1925, s 177.
4 *Re Langston* [1953] P 100, [1953] 1 All ER 928.
5 Law Reform Committee, Report on the Making and Revocation of Wills (Cmnd 5301) para 3.32.
6 Wills Act 1837, s 18A, added by the Administration of Justice Act 1982. See 129 SJ 646 (R. T. Oerton). On the meaning here of 'lapse', see *Re Sinclair* [1985] Ch 446, [1985] 1 All ER 1066, CA overruling *Re Cherrington* [1984] 2 All ER 285, [1984] 1 WLR 772.

1837.[7] (Thus where a testator drew a line across the front of a will and wrote 'All these revoked', and kicked it into the corner, the will was not revoked.[8])

A will that has been revoked by the marriage of the testator or by written instrument (duly attested) can be expressly revived by either re-execution of the will, or execution of a fresh will showing an intention to revive the revoked will.[9] But a will that has been revoked by destruction cannot (even if the pieces of a torn up will still exist) be revived by any means.

If T (a) makes Will 1; (b) makes Will 2, which revokes Will 1; (c) makes Will 3, which revokes Will 2, then the revocation of Will 2 does not revive Will 1.[10] (Thus if Will 3 did no more than revoke Will 2, T would die intestate.)

Specific gifts; gifts of residue

A testator can, if he so wishes, make a gift of *all* his property to one, or several, persons. But where a testator singles out one item of land or personalty for one particular recipient (where he makes a *specific devise* or a *specific bequest*) then the question arises as to how the remainder of his property (the *residue*) is disposed of. (It would be rare for a testator to succeed in making specific gifts of every item of his property; he will be likely to overlook at least some items of his property—perhaps the pen he is writing with.) Commonly, where a testator wishes to make specific gifts, the will concludes with a gift by which the residue of all his property is given to a named beneficiary (a gift of residue), or with a gift by which all the residue of his land is made to one person (a *residuary devise*) and the remainder of his personalty to another (a *residuary bequest*). Where a testator, after making specific gifts, fails to make a gift of residue, then the residue is not disposed of by the will. The devolution of the residue therefore takes place outside the will and passes to the person entitled according to the law of intestacy—to the testator's next of kin. When this happens it will be seen that the deceased has died partially testate (with regard to the specific gifts) and partially intestate (with regard to the residue). Thus a person may die testate; or intestate; or partially testate and partially intestate.

Lapse

Suppose that a testator (T), a widower, in his will leaves £1,000 to his friend A; £2,000 to his son B; £3,000 to his son C; and the residue to his daughter, D. On T's death it is found that A is already dead. The general rule here is that where a beneficiary named in a will predeceases the testator the gift fails to take effect: the gift *lapses*. Where a specific gift lapses, the property falls into residue. Where a gift of residue lapses the property passes to the next of kin. (Note that where the residuary gift is to two or more persons, and one of them predeceases the testator, then the lapsed share does not pass to the other residuary beneficiary or beneficiaries, it passes to the testator's next of

7   Wills Act 1837, s 20.
8   *Cheese v Lovejoy* (1877) 2 PD 251.
9   Wills Act 1837, s 22. *Re Davis* [1952] P 279, [1952] 2 All ER 509.
10   *Powell v Powell* (1866) LR 1 P & D 209.

kin. This is the meaning of the dictum 'A lapsed share of residue does not fall into residue'—it passes as on intestacy.)

The general rule stated above is subject to certain exceptions. The most important of these, under s 33 of the Wills Act 1837 (as amended by the Administration of Justice Act 1982[11]) is that where in the case of the death of a testator after 1982 (i) property is given by will to a child or remoter descendant; and, (ii) the intended beneficiary dies before the testator, leaving issue[12]; and, (iii) issue[13] of the intended beneficiary are living at the date of the death of the testator, then (subject to any contrary intention in the will) the gift does not lapse but takes effect as a gift directly to the issue of the intended beneficiary, who take *per stirpes*.[14] The section operates to save not only a specific bequest or devise but also a gift of residue, or a share of residue.

For example, suppose that a testator, T, has three sons, A, B, and C. A has two children, D and E. E has one child, F. B has one child, I, who has a child, J. C has one child, G, who has a child, H. At T's death D, F, B, J, and H are living. In his will T makes bequests to A, I and C. The gift to A is saved by s 33 and takes effect as a gift to D and E. Since E is dead, F takes his father's share *per stirpes*. The gift to I is similarly saved and takes effect as a gift to J. The gift to C is also saved and takes effect as a gift to H.

Where the death of the testator occurred before 1983, then under the original s 33 of the Wills Act (ie prior to the substitution made by the Administration of Justice Act 1982), then (subject to the conditions at (i)–(iii) above being satisfied) the gift took effect as if the death of the intended beneficiary happened immediately after the death of the testator, with the consequence that the gift passed under the intended beneficiary's will or intestacy.[15] For example, a testator, T, has one son, A, who has a child, B. A predeceases T leaving a will in which all his property is given to his secretary, S. T's will contains a gift of £1,000 to A. T dies in 1980. The gift to A is saved from lapsing, under s 33, by the fact that there is issue of A (B) living at T's death. But the £1,000 does not (as it would if T had died after 1982) go to B. It passes under A's will and therefore goes to S. (If S were dead at the time of T's death, the gift would pass under S's will, ie to those entitled to the residue, or under her intestacy.)

Commorientes

It is possible that in some circumstances it is necessary, in order to determine the course of devolution property left by will, to know which of two persons died first. For example, T leaves a specific gift to his son, A. A has a daughter, D. A dies. T and his granddaughter die in an accident. If the evidence shows that D died after T, the gift to A is saved by s 33 of the Wills Act 1837[16], and

---

11 Section 19.
12 Children or remoter descendants. *Mower v Orr* (1849) 7 Hare 473; *Wisden v Wisden* (1854) 2 Sm & G 396.
13 Not necessarily the same issue as that referred to in (ii), *Mower v Orr*, *Wisden v Wisden*, supra.
14 See p 7.
15 The next of kin being determined according to the law at the date of the intended beneficiary's real, not notional, death. *Re Hurd* [1941] Ch 196, [1941] 1 All ER 238.
16 See supra.

on T's death the property passes to D; on D's death (perhaps only minutes later) the property passes under D's will or (as will necessarily be the case if D is under 18) under D's intestacy (eg to D's mother if she is then living). If the evidence shows that D died before T, then the gift to A lapses and falls into residue.

However, it may happen that two people die in circumstances in which it is uncertain which of them died first. In such a case, s 184 of the Law of Property Act 1925 provides that, for all purposes affecting the title to property, the deaths shall be presumed to have occurred in the order of seniority, the younger accordingly being presumed to have survived the older. In the example above, if it were uncertain whether it was T or D who died first (eg if they both died at the moment of the accident), then D would be presumed to have survived T, the gift would therefore be saved from lapsing by s 33, and, after 1982, the property would pass under D's will or intestacy.

Parties

Later in this book we shall meet many instances in which a party to legal proceedings seeks to have a gift in a will set aside, for example on the ground of uncertainty.[17] From what has been explained, it will be appreciated that where the gift concerned is a specific one, the person who stands to benefit if the gift is declared void is the residuary legatee; where the gift is a gift of residue, the person who stands to benefit is the next of kin. It is for this reason that in cases concerning trusts the adversaries are often found to be the specific legatee and the residuary legatee; or the residuary legatee and the next of kin.

Where a gift is given for a purpose that may or may not be charitable, one party to the proceedings will be the Attorney General, one of whose functions it is to seek to uphold gifts to charity. The other party will be the person who will obtain the property if the purpose is not charitable and the gift therefore is void—if the gift is specific, the residuary legatee, if the gift is of residue, the next of kin.

17   See Chap 4.

Chapter 3

Creation and classification of trusts

A. Creation of trusts

A trust may be created expressly, as where S executes a deed transferring property to trustees on trust for a named beneficiary.

In other situations a trust may arise, not as a result of a person's expressed intention, but as a result of what the law infers as having been a person's intention: a trust which arises in this manner is termed an implied trust. For example, suppose that V is selling Blackacre. B purchases the land and hands over the purchase money to V, but instructs him that the deed of conveyance is to convey the land not to him, B, but to T. V conveys the land to T. In this situation the law infers that it is B's intention that T should hold the legal title not beneficially, but as trustee, on trust for himself, B. T holds on an implied trust for B. We shall see later that where an implied trust arises there is a presumption that, in our example, T should hold on trust for B. We shall also see that the presumption, like any other presumption in law, can be rebutted. For example, if T can show that B intended to make him a gift of the land, then no trust will arise, and T will take the land beneficially.

In other situations there may have been no intention, express or implied, that a trust should be created, but the law nevertheless imposes a trust, ie requires that whoever holds certain property should hold it, not beneficially, but on trust for a beneficiary or beneficiaries. A trust which arises in this way is termed a constructive trust; the law, as it were, constructing a trust. For example, suppose that T_1 and T_2 hold property on trust for B. T_1 and T_2, in breach of trust, sell the property to P. If P fails to show that he is a bona fide purchaser for value of the legal estate without notice of B's interest, he will hold the property subject to B's interest, ie he will hold the property on trust for B. The law imposes the trust on P. P thus holds on a constructive trust for B.

In other situations a statute may provide that a trust shall come into existence. For example, if G grants Blackacre to A, B, C and D then, under ss 34 and 36 of the Law of Property Act 1925, a trust (in this case a trust for sale) arises. As a result of the provisions of the Act A, B, C and D hold the legal estate as trustees on trust for sale for A, B, C and D, the beneficiaries under the trust. A trust which comes into existence as a result of the provision of a statute is termed a statutory trust.

B. Classification of trusts

Trusts may therefore be classified according to how they come into existence
under these four heads, viz:

    Express trusts
    Implied trusts
    Constructive trusts
    Statutory trusts

Trusts may also be classified according to whether their object is to benefit
private individuals (private trusts) or certain public purposes (public trusts).
An alternative name for a public trust is a charitable trust. Since a public (ie
charitable) trust can arise only as a result of the express intention of the
settlor, the classification into private and public can be regarded as a sub-
classification of express trusts. Implied, constructive and statutory trusts exist
as private trusts only.

In order to pave the way for a matter contained in the next chapter, we
must mention at this point one other means of classification; namely a sub-
division of express private trusts into discretionary and non-discretionary
trusts. By way of explanation let us suppose that a testator leaves certain
property to trustees on trust for 'my sons A, B and C'. Here the trustees are
not required to exercise any discretion as to which beneficiary should receive
the property. Nor do they have any discretion as to what share each should
have: each is entitled to one-third. Such a trust is a non-discretionary trust.
On the other hand, if S leaves the property to trustees on trust for such of
his sons A, B and C, and in such shares, as the trustees should decide, the
trust is discretionary. Under a discretionary trust, if the trustees fail to
exercise their discretion the beneficiaries can seek the aid of the court[1]. The
court will generally carry out the trust, not by exercising the discretion
conferred on the trustees, but by dividing the property between the beneficiaries equally.

There are certain other subsidiary ways of classifying trusts and these will
be met at various points later.

C. Trusts and powers of appointment

At many points in the law of trusts the reader will meet references to a form
of disposition termed a *power of appointment*, and there will be occasions
when a comparison is drawn between a trust and a power of appointment. The
various distinctions that exist between a trust and a power of appointment are
dealt with in some detail in Chapter 11. But it will be useful, to pave the way
for certain matters in the next chapter, to explain here the essential differences
between the two forms of disposition.

In the case of a trust, trustees hold the title to property on trust for one or
more beneficiaries. The trustees are under a duty to administer the trust
property on behalf of the beneficiaries and to distribute the property accord-

1   Subject to what is said later, see Chap 11.

ing to the beneficial interests laid down by the settlor. Where the trust is a discretionary one, the trustees are under a duty to consider which beneficiary or beneficiaries should receive the trust property.

In the case of a power of appointment, one person (termed the *donor of the power*) confers power on another (termed the *donee of the power*) to direct (in an *exercise* of the power) that property should go to one (or more) out of a group of persons (the *objects* of the power) specified by the donor. But the donee of the power is under no duty to exercise the power. Indeed, he is in breach of no legal obligation if he never even gives his mind to the matter, and dies without exercising the power. (If a donee does die without exercising the power, then the property passes to the person whom the donor directed should receive the property in this circumstance (the person entitled *in default of appointment*). If the donor made no such direction, the property reverts to the donor or his estate.)

A power of appointment has formed a useful piece of machinery in family settlements. For example, suppose that a husband (H) wishes to leave property to his widow (W), with remainder to his children. It would be possible for him to leave the property to W for life with remainder to the children equally. But when he makes his will, H cannot foresee which of his children will, perhaps many years later, be in the greatest need (or which of his children are most deserving, with regard to care for their mother, of their father's benefaction). So in his will H can leave his estate to W for life with remainder to such of his children as W should (by deed, during her lifetime, or by her will) appoint, with a gift over in default of appointment to—say—all his grandchildren living at his widow's death. In this way, by conferring a power of appointment on W, and making the children the objects of the power, H can in effect delegate to his widow which (if any) of his children should inherit.

It will therefore be seen that in the case of a trust there is an intention that it is the beneficiaries (or one or more out of them) who should benefit. In the case of a power of appointment there is no necessary intention of this kind. Further, a trust is mandatory in nature; a power of appointment lacks this quality.

Chapter 4

Conditions for an express private trust

INTRODUCTION

In this chapter we shall consider the conditions which must be satisfied for a valid express private trust to come into existence. (We shall also deal, at the end of the chapter, with secret and half secret trusts.) But first, we may ask: why does it matter whether a valid trust has come into existence? Who is likely to dispute the validity of the creation of a trust? If A gives money to T_1 and T_2 on trust for B, the only person who might be thought likely to dispute the validity of the trust would be A, in the event of his changing his mind about making the gift. But it often happens that, in our example, it is neither A, nor the trustees, nor B who question the validity of the trust, but the Inland Revenue. For example, suppose that trust property consists of shares in X Ltd. X Ltd pay dividends on the shares. Income tax is payable on the dividends. Who should pay the tax? If a valid trust has been created, T_1 and T_2 (as trustees) are liable (thus reducing the benefit to B); if no valid trust has been created, A is liable (notwithstanding that the dividends may in fact have been paid to T_1 and T_2, and perhaps used for the benefit of B). It might seem that it is immaterial to the Inland Revenue who pays the tax, provided it is paid. But this is not necessarily so. Suppose that A has a high income (even without the dividends), and that B's income (both under the trust and otherwise) is lower. In this situation, A will pay income tax at a higher rate than B. Thus more tax will be payable if no valid trust has been created (and thus the shares in law remain the property of A) than if a trust has been created (and the title to the shares effectively vested in the trustees).

Suppose that A takes steps to transfer £90,000 to T_1 and T_2 on trust for B. A then makes a will leaving all his property to Z. When A dies, if the trust has been validly created, Z will have no claim to the £90,000. But if Z can show that a valid trust had not been created, then the £90,000 will constitute part of A's estate and on A's death will pass to him.

Having considered some of the reasons why it may be of consequence whether a valid trust has been created, we may now proceed to examine the conditions which must be satisfied for valid express private trusts to come into existence. The conditions are as follows:

1. There must be an intention to create a trust.

2. There must be certainty as to the property forming the subject matter of the trust.

3. The trust must have beneficiaries.

4. There must be certainty as to the identity of the beneficiaries.

5. There must be certainty as to the share of property each beneficiary is entitled to receive.

6. The correct formalities must be observed.

7. The trust must not infringe the rule against perpetuities.

8. The trust must not infringe the rule against inalienability.

9. The trust must not infringe the rule against accumulations.

10. The trust must not be designed to defraud creditors.

We shall consider each of these requirements in turn.

1 INTENTION

The settlor must intend to create a trust. For example, if S states in his will, 'I devise Blackacre to T to hold as trustee on trust for my nephew B', the necessary intention is clearly present. But suppose that S stated 'I devise Blackacre to T in the fullest confidence that on his death he will leave the land to B', the question arises, does T take the property as a trustee (ie holding on trust for himself for life with remainder to B), or does T take the property beneficially, free of any trust, the words 'in the fullest confidence ...' having no legal effect, and amounting to no more than an expression of hope by S, which T may comply with or not as he chooses?

The same question would arise if, instead of using the words 'in the fullest confidence', S had used words such as 'in the hope', 'desiring', 'wishing', 'requesting', 'begging', 'in full belief', 'recommending', 'entreating', 'beseeching'. Words such as these are termed *precatory* words. The question we must answer, then, is: are precatory words sufficient to create a trust? Many cases have come before the courts in which this question has been at issue. Consider those set out below, listed according to whether or not a trust was created. (The italics have been added.)

Trust created	*No trust created*
A gift by will to a wife, adding 'I make no provision expressly for my dear daughter knowing that it is my dear wife's happiness as well as mine to see her comfortably provided for; but in case of death happening to my said wife ... I hereby *request*' (two named friends) 'to take care of and manage ... for my lovely daughter ... all I may die possessed of'. (1785)[1]	
A gift by will which included the words 'hereby *recommending* to my said wife, in case my said daughter shall have any more children, to provide ... for such child'. (1803)[2]	

---

1 *Nowlan v Nelligan* (1785) 1 Bro CC 489.
2 *Paul v Compton* (1803) 8 Ves 375.

Trust created

A gift by will to a wife 'to be used for her own and the children's benefit *as she shall in her judgment and conscience think fit*, being convinced that it will be disposed of conscientiously and properly by her for the purpose mentioned ...'. (It was held that there was a trust for the children in remainder on the death of the widow.) (1854)[3]

A gift by will to a wife 'to and for her own sole use and benefit for ever, *feeling assured* and *having every confidence* that she will hereafter dispose of the same ... amongst my two daughters and their children'. (It was held that the widow took a life interest with remainder to the beneficiaries named as she should appoint.) (1857)[4]

A gift by will to a wife 'for her sole use and benefit, in the *full confidence* that she will so bestow it on her decease to my children ...'. (It was held that the widow took a life interest, with a power to appoint among the children.) (1874)[6]

No trust created

A gift by will to a wife 'to be at her disposal in any way she may think best, *for the benefit of herself* and her family'. (1871)[5]

A gift by will to a wife 'feeling *confident* that she will act justly to our children in dividing the same when no longer required by her'. (1882)[7]

A gift by will to a wife 'in *full confidence* that she will do what is right as to the disposal thereof between my children ...'. (1884)[8]

A gift by will to a daughter, adding 'And it is my *desire* that she allows

3   *Hart v Tribe* (1854) 18 Beav 215.
4   *Gully v Cregoe* (1857) 24 Beav 185.
5   *Lambe v Eames* (1871) 6 Ch App 597.
6   *Le Marchant v Le Marchant* (1874) LR 18 Eq 414; *Curnick v Tucker* (1874) LR 17 Eq 320.
7   *Mussoorie Bank Ltd v Raynor* (1882) 7 App Cas 321.
8   *Re Adams and Kensington Vestry* (1884) 27 Ch D 394; (M & B).

Trust created

No trust created

to A.G. an annuity of £25 during her life'. (1888)[9]

After giving legacies to two nieces, a testator stated 'I *wish* them to bequeath them equally between the families of O and P in such mode as they shall consider right'. (1895)[10]

A gift by will: 'As to all the ... residue of my estate ... I bequeath the same unto my wife Lucy ... *absolutely, in the fullest confidence* that she will carry out my wishes in the following particulars; namely ...'. (1897)[11]

A gift by will to a wife '*absolutely in full confidence* that she will make such use of it as I should have done myself and that at her death she will devise it to such one or more of my nieces as she may think fit and in default to be divided equally between the nieces'. (1905)[12]

A gift by will, with the statement 'I specifically *desire* that the sums herewith bequeathed shall ... be specifically left by the legatees to such charitable institutions ... as my sisters may select'. (1910)[13]

A gift by will to five named persons '*for the benefit* of themselves and their respective families'. (It was held that there was no trust for the families.) (1923)[14]

It will be seen that originally precatory words generally created a trust, but that during the latter half of the nineteenth century the attitude of the courts changed with the result that today precatory words are unlikely to create a trust.

The changes in attitude towards the effect of precatory words was expressed in 1895 by Lopes LJ when he said '... it seems to me perfectly clear that the current of decisions with regard to precatory trusts is now changed, and that the result of the change is this, that the court will not allow a precatory trust

9   *Re Diggles* (1888) 39 Ch D 253.
10   *Re Hamilton* [1895] 2 Ch 370.
11   *Re Williams* [1897] 2 Ch 12.
12   *Comiskey v Bowring-Hanbury* [1905] AC 84.
13   *Re Conolly* [1910] 1 Ch 219.
14   *Re Eyre-Williams* [1923] 2 Ch 533; see also, *Re Johnson* [1939] 2 All ER 458.

to be raised unless on the consideration of all the words employed it comes to the conclusion that it was the intention of the testator to create a trust'[15]. (The phrase 'precatory trust' is misleading[16], since if precatory words are construed as showing an intention to create a trust, the trust is no different from any other trust.)

The modern view, then, is that it is the intention of the donor which should prevail[17]. The matter is thus one of construction. 'You must take the will which you have to construe and see what it means ...'[18]. If the words used are imperative in form, and indicate an intention to create a binding obligation, then a trust is to be construed as having been created. On the other hand, if the words leave any measure of freedom to the donee to decide whether or not the property should be applied as indicated, then they are likely to be construed as being insufficient to create a trust. It was on the basis of this principle that the decision in *Comiskey v Bowring-Hanbury*[19] was reached. 'To my mind it is clear that he [the testator] is contemplating that she [his widow] shall have the full use of the property during her lifetime, and that after her death one or more of his nieces is to be the object of his bounty, and if his widow does not select one or more, then they are all to share alike. That, to my mind, is the meaning of the language. I do not stop to bring in any rules of law or any canons of construction. I look at the words merely as they stand in the will, and I think the natural and ordinary meaning of those words is what I have suggested.'

From what has been said it will be clear that no form of technical words is needed in order to create a trust. There is no need even for the word 'trust' to be employed[20], although the use of the word is usually likely to be the surest indication that a trust is intended. But since it is intention that is the overriding factor, even if this word is used, the result will not be the creation of a trust where there is evidence that this had not been the intention. For example, in *Tito v Waddell (No 2)*[1], the use of the word 'trust' was held to refer not to a trust as recognised by law but merely to a governmental obligation, not enforceable in law.

It is relevant at this point to ask whether, if a particular form of wording has been held by the court to produce a certain result (ie that a trust exists, or that it does not), the use of the same words on a later occasion necessarily produces the same result. In 1948 Wynn-Parry J[2] indicated that he would answer this queston in the affirmative. But such a position would run counter to the modern view that the proper course is to ascertain a testator's intention in each case. It therefore seems that today the view of Wynn-Parry J would be unlikely to be followed, and that the courts would prefer the view of Lindley LJ when he said '... if you come to the conclusion that no trust was

15 *Re Hamilton* [1895] 2 Ch 370 at 374.
16 The phrase is a 'misleading nickname'. Per Rigby LJ, *Re Williams* [1897] 2 Ch 12 at 27.
17 See *Universe Tankships Inc of Monrovia v International Transport Workers Federation, The Universe Sentinel* [1983] 1 AC 366, [1982] 2 All ER 67, HL (payment by shipowners to trade union to form welfare fund not intended to create trust).
18 Lindley LJ, *Re Hamilton*, ante, at 373.
19 [1905] AC 84 at 88.
20 See *Re Kayford* [1975] 1 All ER 604, [1975] 1 WLR 279.
1   [1977] Ch 106, [1977] 3 All ER 129. See also *Re Bond Worth* [1980] Ch 228, [1979] 3 All ER 919.
2   *Re Steele's Will Trusts* [1948] Ch 603, [1948] 2 All ER 193; (M & B).

intended you say so, although previous judges have said the contrary on some wills more or less similar to the one you have to construe'[3].

Finally, we must ask what result ensues if no intention to create a trust is found to exist. The answer is that if the necessary intention is absent, the donee (ie the person who would have been the trustee if a trust had been created) takes the property beneficially, free of any trust.

2 CERTAINTY AS TO THE PROPERTY FORMING THE SUBJECT MATTER OF THE TRUST

It is a principle of English law that a transaction may be void due to lack of sufficient certainty. Thus if V contracted to sell P 'the greater part of Black-acre', the contract would be void for uncertainty as to the subject matter of the contract. The same principle applies in the creation of a trust: in order to create a valid trust the description of the trust property must be sufficiently certain. If there is not sufficient certainty the disposition is ineffective and no transfer of property to the trustee takes place. Thus where a settlor purported to settle 'the bulk of my said residuary estate'[4], this requirement was not met and no trust was created.

If the purported settlement is added to a valid gift to a named donee then, since no trust arises, the donee takes absolutely. For example in *Sprange v Barnard*[5] a testatrix bequeathed stock to her husband for his lifetime and added the direction that 'at his death, the remaining part of what is left, that he does not want for his own . . . use' should be held for specified beneficiaries. The property comprised in 'the remaining part . . .' was uncertain. Therefore no trust arose and the husband took the property absolutely.

3 THE TRUST MUST HAVE BENEFICIARIES (THE TRUST MUST BE OF 'PERFECT OBLIGATION')

For a private trust to be valid, there must be one or more legal persons (ie either human beings or corporations) as beneficiaries[6]. 'No principle perhaps has greater sanction of authority behind it than the general proposition that a trust by English law, not being a charitable trust, in order to be effective, must have ascertained or ascertainable beneficiaries'[7].

But, it might be asked, how could there be a trust without any beneficiary? The answer is that a trust for a *purpose* does not necessarily have a beneficiary. For example, if T left property to trustees on trust for the purpose of teaching poodles to dance[8], there are no beneficiaries. The trust is therefore void[9]. It should be noted, however, that if a settlor sets up a trust to benefit a beneficiary in a particular way, and indicates the purpose of the trust accord-

---

3 *Re Hamilton* [1895] 2 Ch 370 at 373.
4 *Palmer v Simmonds* (1854) 2 Drew 221.
5 (1789) 2 Bro CC 585.
6 *Bowman v Secular Society* [1917] AC 406 at 441, HL. ('A trust to be valid must be for the benefit of individuals.') *Re Astor's Settlement Trusts* [1952] Ch 534, [1952] 1 All ER 1067; *Re Wood* [1949] Ch 498, 501, [1949] 1 All ER 1100.
7 Per Lord Evershed MR, *Re Endacott* [1960] Ch 232, [1959] 3 All ER 562, CA; (M & B).
8 Russell J, *Re Hummeltenberg* [1923] 1 Ch 237 at 242.
9 *Leahy v A-G for New South Wales* [1959] AC 457, 478, [1959] 2 All ER 300, PC.

ingly, eg 'on trust for the purpose of educating my grandsons', this does not render the trust void, since the trust does have beneficiaries, ie the grandsons.

The reason for the requirement that there must be beneficiaries is that the courts hold it to be essential that there must be persons who are able to enforce the trust[10], ie to compel the trustees to carry out the trust. 'There must be somebody in whose favour the Court can decree performance'[11].

We are speaking here of private trusts. We shall see in a later chapter[12] that if a trust is for a charitable purpose, responsibility for enforcing the trust rests with the Attorney General. In the case of a charitable trust, therefore, the fact that the trust has no beneficiaries is no bar to its validity.

If someone exists who has standing to enforce a trust, the trust is termed a trust of *perfect obligation*. If a trust is charitable it is thus necessarily of perfect obligation. If a trust is private and there are no beneficiaries, it is a trust of *imperfect obligation'*. As we have said, a trust of imperfect obligation is void[13]. The requirement that for a private trust to be valid there must be one or more beneficiaries is sometimes expressed by saying that the trust must be of perfect obligation.

If a settlor transfers property to trustees under a trust which is of imperfect obligation, the transfer to the trustees is effective but, the trust being void, the trustees hold the property on trust for the settlor. If the attempt to create the trust is by will, the property falls into residue (or, if itself residue, passes to the testator's next of kin[14]).

We saw earlier[15] that express trusts can be classified into private trusts and charitable (ie public) trusts. We have now seen that a private trust may be of perfect obligation or may be of imperfect obligation (in which case it is void[16]); and that a charitable trust is necessarily of perfect obligation.

4 CERTAINTY AS TO THE IDENTITY OF BENEFICIARIES[17]

Gifts to specified beneficiaries

The identity of the beneficiaries must be sufficiently certain. If a settlor names the beneficiary or beneficiaries ('on trust for A, B and C', or 'on trust for A Ltd') then there is sufficient certainty as to the identity of the beneficiaries. If the settlor does not name individual beneficiaries, but describes them, in such terms as 'on trust for my eldest son living at my death', or 'for my first daughter to marry', here too there is sufficient certainty even though the identity of the beneficiary entitled may not be immediately known. Special considerations apply, however, in the case of a gift in favour of a class.

It should be noted that what matters here is certainty as to the identity of the beneficiaries, not certainty as to their existence, ie whether they are still

---

10   Or persons (eg infants or unborn persons) on whose behalf the trust can be enforced.
11   Per Sir William Grant MR, *Morice v Bishop of Durham* (1804) 9 Ves 399 at 404.
12   Chap 7.
13   We shall see in Chap 9 that there are a limited number of exceptions to this rule.
14   As in *Re Pugh's Will Trusts* [1967] 3 All ER 337, [1967] 1 WLR 1262.
15   See Chap 3.
16   Subject to what is said in Chap 9.
17   (1982) 98 LQR 551 (C. T. Emery).

alive at the date of the gift. (Uncertainty as to the latter can be overcome by applying to the court for what is termed a *Benjamin* order.[18])

Gifts to a class

If a settlor gives property on trust for a class of persons then it is necessary, in determining whether the trust is valid under this head of certainty, to know whether the trust is discretionary or non-discretionary[19] (ie whether the trust is one under which the trustees have discretion as to which beneficiaries should be entitled; or one, sometimes termed a 'fixed trust', under which all the beneficiaries are entitled, equally).

NON-DISCRETIONARY TRUSTS

In the case of a non-discretionary (ie 'fixed') trust, the class must be ascertained (ie known) or ascertainable no later than the time when the interest of the last beneficiary entitled under the trust falls into possession[20]. A class of persons is ascertainable if it is possible for the trustees to draw up a list of all the beneficiaries, and when they have completed the list to be sure that the name of every beneficiary entitled to be on the list appears on it, and that the name of no one is on the list which should not be there. Ascertainable thus means 'listable'. Examples of a class which is ascertainable would be: 'all the employees of X Ltd at 1 January 1987'; or 'the sisters for the time being of the aural department of the Ear Nose and Throat Infirmary, Myrtle Street, Liverpool'[1]. The reason why the beneficiaries of a non-discretionary trust must be ascertained or ascertainable is plain: 'there cannot be equal division among a class unless all the members are known'[2].

In *Re Eden*[3], Wynn-Parry J indicated that if the class is ascertainable, then the width of the class is no bar to the validity of the trust. It was irrelevant that a large part, or even the whole, of the property concerned might be consumed in locating the members entitled. That this principle has no limits is, however, it is submitted, open to question. For a trust to be valid it must be capable of being subject to the control of the court: 'a trust shall be under the controul of the Court, it must be of such a nature, that it can be under that controul; so that the administration of it can be reviewed by the Court; or, if the trustee dies, the Court itself can execute the trust: a trust therefore ... [must be of such a nature that] mal-administration could be reformed; and due administration directed'[4]. So if a class is, although ascertainable, so wide that it would be impossible for the court to ensure that the property was correctly distributed between all members entitled, then, it is submitted, the trust would fail, not for uncertainty of beneficiaries, but because it is

---

18 See p 339
19 See p 16, ante.
20 For an argument that the test of certainty for a non-discretionary trust is the same as that that now applies in the case of a discretionary trust, see P. Matthews [1984] Conv 22. For replies, see J. Martin [1984] Conv 304; D. J. Hayton [1984] Conv 307.
1 *Re Bernstein's Will Trusts* (1971) 115 Sol Jo 808.
2 Per Lord Wilberforce, *McPhail v Doulton* [1970] 2 WLR 1110 at 1130, HL.
3 [1957] 2 All ER 430 at 435.
4 Per Lord Eldon, *Morice v Bishop of Durham* (1805) 10 Ves Jun 522 at 542.

'administratively unworkable'. For example, a trust in which property was directed to be divided equally between 'all living individuals who have, or in the past have had, a telephone number listed in the London telephone directories', would, it is suggested, be likely to be void for the reason given. The phrase 'administratively unworkable' was used by Lord Wilberforce in *McPhail v Doulton*[5] with reference to discretionary trusts for the benefit of a class which was unduly wide. The submission here is that the principle that the width of a class can render a trust void applies also to a non-discretionary trust,[6] though, as will be seen later when dealing with discretionary trusts, the reason for the invalidity differs between the two types of trust.

DISCRETIONARY TRUSTS

Before McPhail v Doulton
If the trust is discretionary, then formerly, before a major change in the law made by the House of Lords in 1970 in *McPhail v Doulton*[7], the position was the same as that just described for a non-discretionary trust: unless the class was ascertainable the trust failed for uncertainty. The reasoning behind this rested on the fact that for such a trust to be valid it must (like a trust for an ascertained class) be capable of being controlled by the court. To control a trust the court had to be in a position to carry out the trust in the event of the trustees failing to do so. Where trustees of a discretionary trust failed to carry out their duty, then it had long been accepted that the court would execute the trust by ordering an equal division of the property among all the members of the class. In order to make this division, the beneficiaries entitled had to be ascertained or ascertainable. For example, in *Re Ogden*[8] a testator left property to a trustee to be distributed 'amongst such political federations or bodies in the United Kingdom having as their objects or one of their objects the promotion of Liberal principles in politics as he shall in his absolute discretion select and in such shares and proportions as he shall in the like discretion think fit'. The trustee gave evidence that he was able to ascertain all the bodies in the United Kingdom which fell within the description in the bequest, and the trust was held to be valid. On the other hand, in *Re Saxone*[9], where the trust was to provide pensions for employees or former

5   [1971] AC 424 at 457.
6   For support for this view, see [1990] Conv 24 (I. M. Hardcastle).
7   [1971] AC 424, [1970] 2 All ER 228; (M & B). The case was heard at first instance (by Goff J) under the name of *Re Baden's Deed Trusts* [1967] 3 All ER 159, [1967] 1 WLR 1457. It went to the Court of Appeal [1969] 2 Ch 388, [1969] 1 All ER 1016 under the same name. It was heard by the House of Lords under the name of *McPhail v Doulton* [1971] AC 424, [1970] 2 All ER 228. It was referred by the House of Lords back to the Chancery Division for the new test enunciated by the House of Lords to be applied. There it was heard (by Brightman J) under the name of *Re Baden's Deed Trusts (No 2)* [1972] Ch 607, [1971] 3 All ER 985. The appeal from Brightman J's decision was heard by the Court of Appeal ([1973] Ch 9, [1972] 2 All ER 1304) under the same name. (1970) 34 Conv (NS) 287 (F. R. Crane); (1971) CLJ 68 (J. Hopkins); (1971) CLP 133 (H. Cohen); (1971) 87 LQR 31 (J. W. Harris); (1973) 5 NZ ULR 348; (1974) 37 MLR 643 (Y. Grbich); (1973) 7 VUWLR 258 (L. McKay); (1975) 4 Anglo-American LR 442 (S. Fradley); (1982) 98 LQR 551 (C. T. Emery). Law Commission 8th Annual Report 1972–1973 (Law Com 1973 No 58), para 68.
8   [1933] Ch 678.
9   *Re Saxone Shoe Co's Trust Deed* [1962] 2 All ER 904, [1962] 1 WLR 943.

employees and the provision of benefits for employees or their dependants, because of the impossibility of drawing up a precise, definitive, list of 'dependants', the trust was held to be void.

Thus the law, as it had long stood, and as it was confirmed in 1954 in *IRC v Broadway Cottages Trust*[10], was that a discretionary trust 'is void for uncertainty unless the whole range of objects eligible for selection is ascertained or capable of ascertainment'[11].

After McPhail v Doulton

In *McPhail v Doulton*[12], however, the chain of reasoning that had been thought to make it necessary that the beneficiaries under a discretionary trust should be ascertained (or ascertainable) was rejected. It did not follow, Lord Wilberforce said, 'that execution is impossible unless there can be equal division'[13]. In explaining his rejection of the requirement that equal division must be possible he said, 'As a matter of reason, to hold that a principle of equal division applies to trusts such as the present is certainly paradoxical. Equal division is surely the last thing the settlor ever intended: equal division among all may, probably would, produce a result beneficial to none. Why suppose that the court would lend itself to a whimsical execution? And as regards authority, I do not find that the nature of the trust, and of the court's powers over trusts, calls for any such rigid rule. Equal division may be sensible and has been decreed in cases of family trusts for a limited class, here there is life in the maxim "equality is equity", but the cases provide numerous examples where this has not been so, and a different type of execution has been ordered, appropriate to the circumstances'[14]. He then proceeded to cite cases[15] in which the court had executed discretionary trusts not by ordering equal division but by seeking to give effect to the 'perceived intention' of the settlor. In later cases he noted the introduction of the practice of ordering equal division. 'But', he said, 'I do not think that this change of attitude, or practice, affects the principle that a discretionary trust can, in a suitable case, be executed according to its merits and otherwise than by equal division. I prefer not to suppose that the great masters of equity, if faced with the modern trust for employees, would have failed to adapt their creation to its practical and commercial character'[16]. The cases he had cited, he held, at least 'seem to prove that the supposed rule as to equal division does not rest on any principle inherent in the nature of a trust'[16].

10　[1955] Ch 20, [1954] 3 All ER 120. Followed in *Re Sayer* [1957] Ch 423, [1956] 3 All ER 600.
11　Per Jenkins LJ, at 449, following Tomlin J in *Re Ogden* [1933] Ch 678. Cf P. Matthews [1984] Conv 22. In *IRC v Broadway Cottages Trust* the beneficiaries within the class consisted of certain named individuals together with those employed, within a specified period, by certain named individuals and by certain ascertainable companies. Thus the class *was* capable of ascertainment and therefore *complied* with the test for certainty accepted by Jenkins LJ. The court was therefore wrong in its decision that the trust was void for uncertainty. This was accepted by the House of Lords in *McPhail v Doulton* [1971] AC 424, 456, [1970] 2 All ER 228.
12　Ante.
13　[1970] 2 WLR 1110 at 1127.
14　At 1127.
15　*Mosely v Mosely* (1673) Cas temp Finch 53; *Clarke v Turner* (1694) Freem Ch 198; *Warburton v Warburton* (1702) 4 Bro Parl Cas 1, HL; *Richardson v Chapman* (1760) 7 Bro Parl Cas 318, HL.
16　At 1128.

His conclusion was that since there was no reason for the existence of the rule that for a discretionary trust to be valid the class must be ascertained or ascertainable, the rule should be discarded, and that the test for the validity of discretionary trusts should in future be the same as that accepted by the House of Lords for powers of appointment (the nature of which were mentioned in Chapter 3 and will be treated more fully in Chapter 11), namely, that the trust is valid if it can be said with certainty that any given individual is or is not a member of the class.

The House, albeit by a majority of three to two, concurred with Lord Wilberforce's view. Thus, by the decision in *McPhail v Doulton*, the tests for certainty in the case of discretionary and non-discretionary trusts ceased to be the same. The test for a non-discretionary trust remained unaffected. The old test for certainty in a discretionary trust was abandoned[17] and in its stead was adopted the test for certainty that had long applied (and still applies) in the case of the objects of a power of appointment—to be valid it must be possible to say 'with certainty whether any given individual is or is not a member of the class and the [disposition] does not fail because it is impossible to ascertain every member of the class[18].'

In order to be able to say whether any given individual is or is not a member of the class, the meaning of the word or words used by the donor to describe the class must be sufficiently clear to enable the trustees to know whether any individual can properly be regarded as falling within the description. This is what is meant by the requirement that there must be *linguistic*[19], or *semantic*[19], or *conceptual* certainty. We shall see shortly that the word 'relative' was held to satisfy the requirement. A discretionary trust for 'my friends' might possibly satisfy the test. But a discretionary trust for 'such of my acquaintances as have a tendency towards supporting fringe activities' would be unlikely to do so. *McPhail v Doulton* lowered the certainty hurdle, but it did not remove it.

With regard to the exercise by trustees of their discretion, Lord Wilberforce said in his speech in the House of Lords that trustees should 'make such a survey of the range of objects or possible beneficiaries as will enable them to carry out their fiduciary duty'[20]. In this connection he explained that the mere fact that the trustees might be faced with difficulties over 'ascertaining the existence or whereabouts of members of the class' was no bar to the validity of the trust. Uncertainties such as these, he said, could be resolved by an application to the court for directions.

With regard to the way in which the court should, if required to do so by the trustees' failure, execute a discretionary trust, Lord Wilberforce explained that the court would 'do so in the manner best calculated to give effect to the settlor's or testator's intentions. It may do so by appointing new trustees, or by authorising or directing representative persons of the classes of beneficiaries to prepare a scheme of distribution, or even, should the proper basis for distribution appear, by itself directing the trustees so to distribute. The books give many instances where this has been done, and I see no reason in

---

17   *Re Gestetner's Settlement* [1953] Ch 672, [1953] 1 All ER 1150; *Re Wootton's Will Trusts* [1968] 2 All ER 618, [1968] 1 WLR 681; *Re Whishaw v Stephens* [1970] AC 508, [1968] 3 All ER 785, HL.
18   Per Lord Wilberforce in *McPhail v Doulton* [1971] AC 424 at 450.
19   At 1133.
20   At 1132.

principle why they should not do so in the modern field of discretionary trusts ...'[20]

Width of the class—administrative unworkability[1]

At the end of his speech Lord Wilberforce said that another factor which could render a discretionary trust void was the width of the class of beneficiaries. It might be the case, he said, that the meaning of the words used was clear but 'the definition of beneficiaries is so hopelessly wide as not to form "anything like a class" so that the trust is administratively unworkable or in Lord Eldon's words one that cannot be executed (*Morice v Bishop of Durham* (1805) 10 Ves 522 at 527). I hesitate', he said, 'to give examples that may prejudice future cases but perhaps "all the residents of Greater London" will serve'. In *R v District Auditor No 3 Audit District of West Yorkshire Metropolitan County Council, ex p West Yorkshire Metropolitan County Council*[2] a trust in favour of 'any or all or some of the inhabitants' of West Yorkshire was declared void, evidently on the ground of the width of the class of potential beneficiaries.

We have suggested[3] a non-discretionary trust for a class such as the one cited by Lord Wilberforce is void, because it will be administratively impossible to carry it out. But why should a discretionary trust for such a class be void? Lord Wilberforce did not say, but it would seem that the reason rests on the fact that trustees of a discretionary trust must (as noted above) 'make such a survey of the range of objects or possible beneficiaries as will enable them to carry out their fiduciary duty'[4] (ie with regard to deciding how their discretion should be exercised). (As Stamp LJ was later to express the point: 'It is not enough that trustees should do nothing but distribute the fund among those objects of the trust who happen to be at hand or present themselves'[5].) If the class is so wide as to make it impracticable to survey adequately the range of possible beneficiaries, then it is impossible for the trustees to carry out their function. Thus, because the trust cannot properly be executed, it is void.

It is suggested, however, that valid discretionary trusts for a very wide range of beneficiaries may nonetheless exist, without infringing the principle to which Lord Wilberforce seems to have been adverting, if means exist by which trustees are able to obtain information as to the circumstances of individual members of the class. This might well be the case where the class was described by reference to membership of an existing organisation (eg the British Legion, the Scout Association), through the administrative machinery of which trustees could obtain recommendations as to individuals in whose favour their discretion might sensibly be exercised.

The case of McPhail v Doulton

McPhail v Doulton[6] concerned a case in which property had been given on

---

1 (1974) 38 Conv (NS) 269 (L. McKay); [1990] Conv 24 (I. M. Hardcastle).
2 [1986] RVR 24; (M & B).
3 See p 25, ante.
4 Per Lord Wilberforce, at 1133.
5 *Re Baden's Deed Trusts (No 2)* [1972] 3 WLR 250 at 262, HL. See also *Re Manisty's Settlement* [1974] Ch 17, 27, [1973] 2 All ER 1203. (A 'sensible consideration by the trustees of the exercise' of their discretion must be possible.)
6 See n 7, p 26, supra.

discretionary trusts for 'relatives or dependants' of employees or ex-employees of a certain limited company. The Lords did not decide whether the words 'relatives or dependants' satisfied the new test that they had laid down, but referred the matter to the Chancery Division. There, Brightman J held that the new test was satisfied and the trust therefore valid. The Court of Appeal (in *Re Baden's Deed Trusts (No 2)*[7]) upheld the decision, but the judgments showed the difficulties that could arise in seeking to apply the new test.

With regard to the word 'relative' it was argued before the Court of Appeal that the test laid down in *McPhail v Doulton* ('can it be said with certainty that any individual is or is not a member of the class'[8]) was not satisfied since, whilst proof could be adduced that one person *was* a relative of another, it could never be proved that one person was *not* a relative of another. Megaw LJ rejected this argument, pointing out that if it had to be possible to say of every person whether he was or was not within the class, this would mean that it would have to be possible to draw up a list of all the members of the class, the requirement (under the *IRC v Broadway Cottages Trust* test) that the House of Lords had rejected. Furthermore, he pointed out, to give the meaning to the words 'or are not' claimed by the executors (who were contesting the validity of the trust) would be inconsistent with the latter part of the formulation of the test, that the trust 'does not fail simply because it is impossible to ascertain every member'[9]. Sachs LJ concurred in rejecting the executors' argument that the word 'relative' failed the *McPhail v Doulton* test. The field was narrowed, he said, by the need to produce evidence of relationship and, in practice, the trustees 'would presumably select those whom a reasonable and honest employee or ex-employee would introduce as "relative" rather than "kinsman" or as a "distant relative"'[10]. Stamp LJ, whilst not rejecting the executors' argument, held that in order to give effect to the settlor's probable intention to benefit his 'nearest blood relations'[11], the word 'relatives' could validly be construed as 'next of kin', and since there was no difficulty in determining whether a given individual came within this description, the trust did not fail for uncertainty by reason of the use of the word in question.[12]

In considering the word 'dependant', Sachs LJ stressed the distinction drawn by the House of Lords between conceptual (ie linguistic, semantic) uncertainty and 'evidential difficulties'[13]. It was in relation to conceptual uncertainty that a trust stood or fell. What matters is whether the *meaning* of the words used is clear. 'Once the class of persons to be benefited is conceptually certain it then becomes a question of fact to be determined on the evidence whether any postulant has on inquiry been proved to be within

7   [1973] Ch 9, [1972] 2 All ER 1304; (M & B); (1973) 36 Conv (NS) 351 (D. J. Hayton); [1973] CLJ 36 (J. A. Hopkins); *Re Bethel* (1971) 17 DLR (3d) 652; (1971) ASCL 377; (1981) 9 Syd LR 58 (R. P. Austin).
8   Per Sachs LJ, [1972] 3 WLR 250 at 254.
9   At 259.
10   At 257.
11   At 264.
12   In *Re Poultons' Will Trusts* [1987] 1 All ER 1068, [1987] 1 WLR 795 it was held that no uncertainty arose from the use of the word 'relatives' and that use of the word did not confine the beneficiaries intended to a testator's statutory next of kin. (The case concerned a power of appointment but the decision would seem likely to be the same in the case of a discretionary trust.)
13   At 255.

it: if he is not so proved, then he is not in it'[14]. If in doubt, the trustees could, if they wished, ask the court for directions.

There was, Lord Sachs held, no conceptual uncertainty inherent in the word 'dependant'. A 'dependant' was 'any one wholly or partly dependent on the means of another'[15]. The word 'conjures up a sufficiently distinct picture'[16] for the trustees, or if necessary, the court, to be '... quite capable of coming to a conclusion in any given case as to whether or not a particular candidate could properly be described as a dependant...'[17]. Stamp LJ agreed. After dealing with the word 'relative', he said: 'The only other challenge to the validity of the trust is directed against the use of the word "dependants" which it is said introduces a linguistic or semantic uncertainty. That in the context the word connotes financial dependence I do not doubt, and although in a given case there may be a doubt whether there be a sufficient degree of dependence to satisfy the qualification of being a "dependant", that is a question which can be determined by the court and does not introduce linguistic uncertainty'[18]. Megaw LJ also agreed that the word 'dependant' satisfied the test laid down by the House of Lords in *McPhail v Doulton*. To his mind, he said, 'the test is satisfied if, as regards at least a substantial number of objects, it can be said with certainty that they fall within the trust; even though, as regards a substantial number of other persons, if they ever for some fanciful reason fell to be considered, the answer would have to be, not "they are outside the trust", but "it is not proven whether they are in or out". What is a "substantial number" may well be a question of common sense and of degree in relation to the particular trust: particularly where, as here, it would be fantasy, to use a mild word, to suggest that any practical difficulty would arise in the fair, proper and sensible administration of this trust in respect of relatives and dependants'[19].

CONDITIONS PRECEDENT AND SUBSEQUENT

It may be helpful to note here that the rules relating to certainty as to the identity of beneficiaries must be distinguished from the rules relating to certainty in connection with conditions precedent and conditions subsequent. In the case of a condition precedent the test is that the condition is certain if it is possible to show of one person that he satisfies the condition[20]. (In *Re Allen*[1] the Court of Appeal held that a devise 'to the eldest of the sons of (X) who shall be a member of the Church of England and an adherent of the doctrine of that church' satisfied the test and was therefore valid.) In the case

14 At 255.
15 At 257.
16 At 257, adopting the phrase of Brightman J [1971] 3 WLR 475 at 485.
17 At 257.
18 At 264.
19 At 259.
20 *Re Allen* [1953] Ch 810, [1953] 2 All ER 898; *Re Barlow's Will Trusts* [1979] 1 All ER 296, [1979] 1 WLR 278; (M & B). (Grant of options exercisable by any persons who answered the description of 'friend' held not to be void for uncertainty.) See L. McKay [1980] Conv 263. In *Whishaw v Stephens* [1970] AC 508, [1968] 3 All ER 785, HL, the House of Lords held (overruling *Re Gibbard* [1966] 1 All ER 273, [1967] 1 WLR 42) that this was not the test applicable in determining the validity of a power of appointment. See Chap 10.
1 Supra.

of a condition subsequent, it is necessary that the words used should indicate precisely what event will constitute the occurrence of the condition specified[2].

POWER TO CURE UNCERTAINTY

In some circumstances an element of uncertainty that might otherwise be sufficient to render a disposition void may be removed by giving power to determine a certain matter to one or more persons, eg to the trustees. For example, in *Re Coxen*[3] a testator gave a house to his trustees with a direction that his wife was to be permitted to 'reside there in her life, or as long as she shall desire to reside therein', and declared that 'from and after her death or if in the opinion of the trustees she shall have ceased to permanently reside therein' the house was to fall into his residuary estate. It was held that the power of decision conferred on the trustees in relation to the meaning of 'reside' cured any defect of uncertainty that might exist and so enabled the gift to take effect. And in *Re Tuck's Settlement Trusts*[4] the court accepted the validity of a declaration that any dispute as to whether a person 'continued to worship according to the Jewish faith' was to be determined by 'the Chief Rabbi in London of either the Portuguese or Anglo-German Community'. But a power to adjudicate can only validly be given in relation to matters of fact, not of law, since to direct that, eg trustees, are to be the arbiters on a matter of law would be to oust the jurisdiction of the court and hence contrary to public policy. A fortiori, any direction that would directly have the effect of ousting the jurisdiction of the court is void. For example, in *Re Raven*[5], a testator gave money to 'The National Association for the Prevention of Consumption' and directed that 'if any doubt shall arise ... to the identity of the institution intended to benefit, the question shall be decided by my trustees whose decision shall be final and binding on all parties'. It was held that the direction was void.

It would seem, however, that if a trust failed the test in *McPhail v Doulton*, the addition of a direction giving a power to arbitrate would be unlikely to save the gift, since if the description of the class was conceptually uncertain, then it would be no more possible for a private person to make a rational decision in relation to the description given by the settlor than it would be for the court to do so. And if the class is conceptually certain, then the trust is valid without the inclusion of a power to arbitrate. An advantage of a power to arbitrate might, though, be that it could obviate any need to seek directions from the court over whether any person was to be regarded as coming within the class.

If a trust fails owing to uncertainty as to identity of the beneficiaries then the trustees hold the trust property on trust for the settlor or, if the trust was created by will, for his estate[6].

---

2   *Sifton v Sifton* [1938] AC 656, [1938] 3 All ER 435 ('reside in Canada' uncertain).
3   [1948] Ch 747, [1948] 2 All ER 492.
4   [1978] Ch 49, [1978] 1 All ER 1047, CA; (M & B) (disapproving *Re Jones* [1953] Ch 125, [1953] 1 All ER 357). See also *Dundee General Hospitals Board of Management v Walker* [1952] 1 All ER 896; (M & B).
5   [1915] 1 Ch 673. See also *Re Wynn* [1952] Ch 271, [1952] 1 All ER 341; (M & B).
6   As in *Re Pugh's Will Trusts* [1967] 3 All ER 337, [1967] 1 WLR 1262.

5 CERTAINTY AS TO THE INTEREST TO WHICH EACH BENEFICIARY IS ENTITLED

If there is more than one beneficiary, the trustees must know how the settlor intends the trust property to be distributed between the various beneficiaries. If the settlor directs that the property is to be divided equally between all the beneficiaries (or if the construction placed by the court on the words used by the settlor is that he intended equal division[7]), no problem arises. If he gives property on trust for 'A, B and C', or 'for all my cousins', again no problem arises as the presumption is that the property is to be divided equally. Alternatively, the settlor may give the trustees discretion as to the amount which is to go to each beneficiary, eg 'on trust for such of my grandsons, and in such shares, as my trustees shall at their discretion decide'. Here too the condition we are speaking of is satisfied. (It is usual under a discretionary trust for trustees to have discretion both with regard to the selection of the beneficiaries to benefit out of the class specified, and with regard to the share of trust property which each beneficiary selected should receive.)

However, if the terms of the trust preclude the trust property being divided equally, and discretion is not conferred on the trustees to decide how the distribution should be made, then if the terms of the trust do not make clear what share each beneficiary is to take, the trust fails, and the trustees hold the trust property on trust for the settlor; or, if the trust was created by will, for his estate.[8] For example, in *Boyce v Boyce*[9], a testator devised all his houses in Southwold to trustees on trust to convey to his daughter Maria whichever one 'she might think proper to choose' and all the others to his daughter Charlotte. Maria died before the testator. On the testator's death Charlotte claimed all the houses. It was held that the property held on trust for Charlotte consisted of all the houses other than that chosen by Maria. Maria had made no choice. So the property to be held on trust for Charlotte was uncertain and the trust therefore failed.

We have stated the general position with regard to certainty regarding the share in the trust property. There are certain exceptions. The first is that where the quantum of the gift is not certain (eg where a testator directed that a beneficiary was to receive a 'reasonable income'[10] from certain properties) but the words used 'provide an effective determinant of what he intends so that the court in applying that determinant can give effect to the testator's intention',[11] then the gift will not fail for uncertainty.

Second, where the whole of the beneficial interest is given to one beneficiary, subject to the right of other beneficiaries to an uncertain part of it, the direction as to the uncertain part fails, and leaves the principal beneficiary entitled to the whole. For example in *Curtis v Rippon*[12] a testator stated in his will 'I give my real and personal estates to my said wife Elizabeth, trusting that she will, in fear of God and in love to the children committed to her

---

7 As in *Re Steel* [1979] Ch 218, [1978] 2 All ER 1026.
8 *Re Flavel's Will Trusts* [1969] 2 All ER 232, [1969] 1 WLR 444.
9 (1849) 16 Sim 476.
10 As in *Re Golay* [1965] 2 All ER 660, [1965] 1 WLR 969; (M & B); R. E. Megarry (1965) 81 LQR 481.
11 Per Ungoed-Thomas J, *Re Golay* [1965] 1 WLR 969 at 971.
12 (1820) 5 Madd 434. See also *Watson v Holland (Inspector of Taxes)* [1985] 1 All ER 290, [1984] STC 372; cf *Re Last* [1958] P 137, [1958] 1 All ER 316. (Words added to absolute gift had effect of reducing absolute interest to a life interest.)

care, make such use of it as shall be for her own and their spiritual and temporal good, remembering always, according to circumstances, the Church of God and the poor'. It was held that, 'there being no ascertained part of it provided for the children' (or for the Church, or the poor), the trust failed leaving the wife absolutely entitled.

The principle illustrated in *Curtis v Rippon* is, however, merely one application of a wider rule (the rule in *Lassence v Tierney*[13]) that where the whole of the beneficial interest in property (real or personal) is given (inter vivos or by will) absolutely[14] to one person, subject to the interests of other persons (eg by trusts being engrafted or imposed on the absolute interest), and these interests fail for any reason (ie not merely by reason of uncertainty) then the principal gift takes effect absolutely. For example, in *Hancock v Watson*[15], in his will a testator gave certain property 'to SD' (ie he gave it to SD absolutely). Later in the will he stated, 'But it is my will and mind that the [property] allotted to the said SD shall remain in trust' for her for life. The remainder was left on trusts which were void for remoteness. It was held that, the trusts in remainder having failed, SD took the property absolutely. (The result in *Sprange v Barnard*[16], a case which we considered when dealing with certainty as to the identity of the trust property[17], may be regarded as having been reached by the application of the same principle).

Uncertainty under this head may relate not to a beneficiary's share of the trust property, but to the interest in the property granted to him, 'interest' here being used in the technical sense of duration of time of entitlement, as in 'life interest'. For example, where a trust was established 'for the longest period allowed by law, that is to say, until the period of 21 years from the death of the last survivor of all persons living at my death', it was held that as the duration of the trust could not be determined with sufficient certainty, the trust was therefore void[18].

THE 'THREE CERTAINTIES'

We have said that for a valid private trust to exist,

1. there must be an intention to create a trust;

2. there must be certainty as to the property forming the subject matter of the trust;

3. the trust must have beneficiaries;

4. there must be certainty as to the identity of the beneficiaries;

5. there must be certainty as to the interest in the property to which each beneficiary is entitled.

These requirements are sometimes grouped under three heads of

13   (1849) 1 Mac & G 551.
14   See *Re Goold's Will Trusts* [1967] 3 All ER 652.
15   [1902] AC 14.
16   (1789) 2 Bro CC 585.
17   See p 23, ante.
18   *Re Moore* [1901] 1 Ch 936.

certainty—certainty of words, certainty of subject matter and certainty of objects[19].

Certainty of words refers to the requirement that the words used by the settlor must indicate an intention to create a trust (1 above). Certainty of subject matter refers to the requirements set out at 2 and 5 above. Certainty of objects refers to the requirements set out at 3 and 4 above, ie that there must be one or more beneficiaries, and that their identity must be sufficiently certain.

The phrase 'certainty of objects' can be misunderstood, owing to the possibility that the word 'objects' may be taken to mean 'objectives' or 'purposes', rather than 'beneficiaries'. Since, as we have seen, a private trust cannot exist for a purpose alone, the word 'objects' in the phrase 'certainty of objects' must therefore connote 'beneficiaries'. It should therefore be understood that the word 'objects' in the statement 'a private trust must have certainty of objects', refers to the persons who are the objects of the settlor's benefaction, and does not carry the meaning of 'objectives', or 'purposes'.

6 THE CORRECT FORMALITIES MUST BE OBSERVED

Methods of creating a trust

Let us begin by supposing that S wishes to establish a trust for the benefit of B. One way in which this can be done is for S to transfer the property concerned to trustees on trust for B. This means of creating a trust is represented at 1 on page 401. In this situation S holds the legal title to the property to be transferred to the trustees (eg he holds the legal fee simple in land; he is the registered owner of shares; or he has money of his own in a bank account).

On the other hand, it may be that S's property consists of an equitable interest. For example suppose that t_1 and t_2 hold land on trust for sale for S for life with remainder to Z. S wishes the income which he receives under the trust for sale to be held on trust for B.[20] S therefore transfers his equitable life interest to T_1 and T_2 on trust for B. This is represented at 2 on page 401. It will be noted that in both 1 and 2 there is a transfer of the trust property from the settlor to the trustees (in 1 of a legal interest, in 2 of an equitable interest).

It may be, however, that S, whilst wishing to create a trust for B, does not wish to transfer property to trustees, but wishes instead to constitute himself

---

19 This three-fold analysis of the conditions necessary for a valid private trust to exist was put forward by Lord Eldon in 1823 in *Wright v Atkyns* (1823) Turn & R 143, 157, and followed by Lord Langdale in 1840 in *Knight v Knight* (1840) 3 Beav 148, 173. The words used by the two judges in setting out the three conditions were as follows:

Lord Eldon	*Lord Langdale*
'... the words must be imperative ...'	'... the words are so used, that upon the whole, they ought to be construed as imperative'.
'... the subject must be certain ...'	'... the subject ... (must) be certain';
'... the object must be ... certain ...'	'... the objects or persons intended to have the benefit ... (must) be also certain ...'

20 In *Kekewich v Manning* (1851) 1 De GM & G 176 the assignment was of an equitable interest in remainder.

trustee of the property, holding it no longer beneficially, but on trust for B. Where S holds a legal title to the property concerned, this means of creating a trust is represented at 3 on page 401.

Where S constitutes himself trustee in this way and the interest which he holds is equitable (eg the equitable life interest under a trust for sale cited above), then the creation of the trust is represented at 4 on page 401.

It will be noted that in the case of 2 and 4, sub-trusts have come into existence[1]. The legal title continues to be held by T_1 and T_2, who continue to hold on trust for S, who now holds the equitable interest, no longer beneficially, but as a trustee on trust for B.

One final transaction remains to be mentioned. If S holds an equitable interest in the property which he wishes to be held on trust for B, then instead of either transferring the interest to T_1 and T_2 on trust for B (Situation 2 on page 401), or constituting himself trustee of the interest for B (Situation 4), S may direct T_1 and T_2 to hold the property on trust in future, not for himself, but for B. This is represented at 5 on page 401. Before the event T_1 and T_2 held on trust for S; after the event they hold on trust for B. It will be seen that the same result would be achieved if S (without necessarily informing T_1 and T_2) made a transfer of his equitable interest to B. Such a transaction (which is represented at 6 on page 401), does not constitute the *creation* of a trust, and consists merely of a disposition of an existing equitable interest. The transaction represented at 5 should probably not be regarded as creating a trust either, but in considering what formalities must be observed in order to create a trust, it will be convenient to consider also the formalities needed to carry out transactions represented at both 5 and 6. (Situation 7 on page 401, is considered later in this chapter.)

Formalities required

DECLARATION

Consider Situation 1 on page 401. It is clear that this transaction has two parts: (a) the transfer of the property to T_1 and T_2, and (b) the creation of the trust. If (a) was carried out but not (b), T_1 and T_2 would take the property beneficially, free of any trust. If (b) was carried out but not (a), this would establish that if the transfer did later take place, T_1 and T_2 were to take the property as trustees (on trust for B), and not beneficially. But for the trust to be constituted completely both (a) and (b) above must be carried out. In the case of 2 on page 401, the position is the same; the transaction has two parts, viz, the transfer of the trust property (ie the equitable interest) to T_1 and T_2, and the creation of the trust.

In the case of 3, however, the transaction has only one part, namely, S making himself a trustee of the property. Similarly in the case of 4, the transaction has only the one, same, part.

In Situations 1 and 2, when S makes T_1 and T_2 trustees of the property (for B), we speak of S making a *declaration of trust*, ie he declares that T_1 and T_2 are to hold the property as trustees (on trust for B). Thus it is the transfer which vests the title to the property in T_1 and T_2; it is the declaration

---

1   Subject to what is said later.

of trust which creates the trust. (If S had transferred the property without making a declaration of trust, then T_1 and T_2 would take beneficially.)

In Situations 3 and 4, the trust is similarly created by S making a declaration of trust, ie he declares that from thenceforward he holds the property, no longer beneficially, but as a trustee, on trust for B[2]. (As we have seen, in these two situations no transfer to trustees is involved.)

It will be noted that in all of the first four situations there is a declaration of trust. In explaining what formalities are required for the creation of a trust, let us therefore begin by considering what formalities are needed in order to make a valid declaration of trust.

Land

Section 53(1)(b) of the Law of Property Act 1925[3] provides that 'A declaration of trust respecting any land or any interest therein must be manifested and proved by some writing[4] signed by some person[5] who is able to declare the trust or by his will.' Thus if the trust property is land or an interest in land, the declaration of trust need not be in writing, but must be *evidenced*[6] by some writing, signed by the settlor. It should be noted that the section applies to the creation of a trust in any interest in land (eg a lease), and applies regardless of whether the interest in the land is legal or equitable. Whether the section applies to the interest of a beneficiary under a trust for sale of land is uncertain. Strictly, since the interest of such a beneficiary is (by reason of the doctrine of conversion) personalty, the section should have no application. On the other hand, there are affinities between s 53(1)(b) and, before its repeal,[7] s 40(1) of the same Act (which required contracts for the disposition of land or any interest in land to be evidenced in writing) and as it was held[8] that an 'interest in land' in the context of the latter section included the interest of a beneficiary under a trust for sale, it may be that the interest of such a beneficiary is subject to s 53(1)(b).

Thus in the case of Situations 1, 2, 3 and 4, if the trust property is land, the declaration of trust must, under s 53(1)(b), be evidenced in writing signed by S. It should be noted that it does not matter if the declaration itself is oral, provided that there is evidence in writing (signed by S) that the declaration was made. For example, suppose that S tells B[9] 'From today I am holding Blackacre on trust for you,' and the following day he writes a letter to B saying 'You remember that yesterday I told you that I was holding Blackacre on trust for you, well I should explain that the house needs redecorating . . .' The declaration, although oral, is valid because it is 'manifested and proved' by the letter signed by S.

---

2 Or on trust for, eg himself and B equally. See *Paul v Constance* [1977] 1 All ER 195, [1977] 1 WLR 527, CA.
3 Replacing s 7 of the Statute of Frauds 1677, with certain changes of wording.
4 The declaration and the writing need not be contemporaneous. *Rochefoucauld v Boustead* [1897] 1 Ch 196, CA.
5 The signature of an agent is not sufficient. *Re Northcliffe* [1925] Ch 651.
6 See *Forster v Hale* (1798) 3 Ves 696; affd (1800) 5 Ves 308. On the desirability of reform of the section possibly requiring the declaration to be *in* writing, see [1990] Conv 539 (J. D. Davies)
7 Law of Property (Miscellaneous Provisions) Act 1989, s 4, Sch 2.
8 *Cooper v Critchley* [1955] Ch 431, [1955] 1 All ER 520, CA.
9 *Smith v Matthews* (1861) 3 De GF & J 139, 151; *Re Tyler's Fund Trusts* [1967] 3 All ER 389, [1967] 1 WLR 1269.

The evidence in writing must show both that a trust is intended to exist and the nature of the beneficial interests. But the writing need not contain all the terms of the trust. It is sufficient if the writing shows 'the nature' of the trust: the terms and conditions must 'sufficiently appear'[9]. Nor is there a requirement that the declaration must be communicated to the beneficiary.[10]

The statute not permitted to be an instrument of fraud[11]

If S executes a conveyance transferring the legal title in land to T, with the intention, which is known to T, that T shall hold the land on trust for B, but there is no statement that T is to hold as trustee in the conveyance, and no other evidence in writing exists of S's intention, then, without more, since s 53(1)(b) has not been complied with, T could take the property absolutely. For this to occur, however, would mean that the section (and its predecessor, s 7 of the Statute of Frauds 1677) had been the means by which T had been enabled to commit fraud (ie taking the land, with knowledge of S's intention, and then relying on the section to defeat this intention). Where the section would in such a way as this enable fraud to be committed, equity exercised jurisdiction to prevent the fraud, notwithstanding that by so doing it enabled the application of the section to be sidestepped[12]. As the matter was expressed (in relation to s 7 of the 1677 Act) by Lindley LJ in *Rochefoucauld v Boustead*[13] in 1897, '... not withstanding the statute, it is competent for a person claiming land conveyed to another to prove by parol evidence that it was so conveyed upon trust for the claimant, and that the grantee, knowing the facts, is denying the trust and relying upon the form of conveyance and the statute, in order to keep the land himself'. The decision of the court was, in the terms of our example, that T held on an express trust for B. In *Bannister v Bannister*[14], however, in 1948, the Court of Appeal held that equity's means of preventing the statute from being an instrument of fraud entailed the imposition of a constructive trust. The facts were that S, a woman who owned two cottages in Essex, made an oral contract for the sale of the properties to T, subject to S being allowed to live rent free for as long as she wished in one of them. The conveyance made no mention of the latter arrangement. Later T claimed possession of the cottage in which S was living. T claimed that s 53(1)(b) prevented S claiming that he held the property on trust for her. It was held that T held the property as a constructive trustee for S. It has been pointed out that 'it is at least a little curious to say, in effect, that the express trust being unenforceable because it is not in writing, the court will impose a constructive trust to carry out the terms of the express trust ...' and, further, that it 'would be much better in these cases to reach the same result by a straightforward application of the principle in fact laid down in *Rochefoucauld v Boustead*, namely that in a case of fraud equity will allow an express trust to be established by parol evidence notwithstanding the statute'.

10   *Middleton v Pollock* (1876) 2 Ch D 104 (M & B).
11   T. G. Youdan, 'Formalities for Trusts of Land; and the doctrine in Rouchefoucauld v Boustead' [1984] CLJ 307.
12   *Montacute v Maxwell* (1719) 1 P Wms 618; *Re Duke of Marlborough* [1894] 2 Ch 133.
13   [1897] 1 Ch 196 at 206.
14   [1948] 2 All ER 133.

In 1971, in *Hodgson v Marks*[15], the Court of Appeal prevented s 53(1)(b) from being an instrument of fraud by finding that a resulting trust had come into existence, and that since s 53(2) provided that s 53 was to have no application to resulting trusts, the section was no bar to the validity of the trust. Resulting trusts, and the case, are treated in Chapter 10.

It is clear that over the application of section 53(1)(b) the courts have been torn in two directions. On the one hand the courts have seen the statute in front of them and recognised their duty to give effect to it. On the other hand, the courts, conscious of the principles of equity, have wrestled against allowing a person to get away with fraud. Where S conveys land to T in circumstances in which it is held that T holds the land on a resulting trust for S then since (as mentioned above) s 53(1)(b) has no application to resulting trusts, no problem arises: T holds under the resulting trust for S. But where S conveys land to T with a declaration that T is to hold the land for B (and the transaction does not fall within limited categories in which equity will aid B[16]) it seems that B is precluded by the section from enforcing the trust against T.[17]

Personalty
No statute or rule of law requires a declaration of trust concerning any form of property other than land (and interests in land) to comply with any particular formality, and declarations of trust concerning any other property can therefore validly be made orally.

TRANSFER TO THE TRUSTEES

So much, for the present, for the declaration of trust. Now let us consider that part of the setting up of a trust in Situations 1 and 2 which consists of the transfer of the property from S to the trustees. What formalities are required for the valid transfer of the property from S to T_1 and T_2? The answer is that the same formality must be observed as for any other transfer of property from one person to another. The formality required therefore depends on the type of property concerned. By way of illustration we shall set out certain items which we shall suppose S wishes to transfer to T_1 and T_2 and state against each the formality required.

Item	*Type of property*	*Formality needed*	*Authority*
Greenacre Farm	Legal fee simple	S must execute a deed conveying the land to T_1 and T_2.	LPA 1925, s 52
A lease by deed of Flat 22, High Borough Mansions	Legal lease	S must execute a deed assigning the lease to T_1 and T_2.	LPA 1925, s 52

---

15 [1971] Ch 892, [1971] 2 All ER 684.
16 Eg a secret trust (qv see page 52 post). For a review of these categories see [1987] Conv 246 (J. D. Feltham).
17 See J. D. Feltham [1987] Conv 246; *contra* T. G. Youdan [1988] Conv 627.

Item	Type of property	Formality needed	Authority
1,000 shares in I.C.I.	Chose in action requiring a special formality provided by statute	S must execute a share transfer form and lodge it (with the share certificates) with the company, which will then register T_1 and T_2 as the legal owners of the shares.	Companies Act 1985[18]
A debt of £100 which Z owes to S.	Chose in action	The transfer must be in writing signed by S.	LPA 1925, s 136
A Fresian cow	Chose in possession	S must either (a) physically transfer the cow to T_1 and T_2, with the intention of transferring the legal title to them (and not merely with some lesser intention, eg of lending them the cow); or (b) execute a deed of gift transferring the legal title to T_1 and T_2.	Common law

In all the above examples we have assumed that S held the legal title to the property, as in Situation 1. If S held an equitable interest in any of the above items (ie the legal title was held by trustees on trust for him, as in Situation 2) then in each case the formality required is the same, the transfer must be in writing signed by S[19]. This is because s 53(1)(c) of the Law of Property Act 1925 provides that *any* disposition of *any* equitable interest in *any* form of property must be in writing signed by S[20]. The written disposition may consist of two or more documents which, when read together, dispose of the equitable interest[1]. 'Disposition' includes the release of an interest[2] (eg where a tenant for life releases his interest to the remainderman) but not a disclaimer (which 'operates by way of avoidance and not by way of disposition'[3]).

Thus, whereas the formality needed for the transfer of the trust property in Situation 1 will depend on the nature of the property concerned, the

---

18   Section 183.
19   Or by his agent authorised in writing to sign the transfer or authorised to do so by S in his will.
20   On the scope of the section, see B. Green (1984) 47 MLR 385.
 1   *Re Danish Bacon Co Ltd Staff Pension Fund* [1971] 1 All ER 486, [1971] 1 WLR 248; (M & B). See also *Re Tyler's Fund Trusts* [1967] 3 All ER 389, [1967] 1 WLR 1269; (M & B) (evidence admissible of details of the trust communicated orally to the trustee before the written assignment).
 2   *Oughtred v IRC* [1960] AC 206, [1959] 3 All ER 623; (M & B); B. Green (1984) 47 MLR 385.
 3   Per Danckwerts LJ, *Re Paradise Motor Co Ltd* [1968] 1 WLR 1125 at 1143.

formality needed for the transfer in Situation 2 is always the same—s 53(1)(c) must be complied with[4].

Now consider Situations 5 and 6. In Situation 6 S transfers his equitable interest to B. So the transaction must comply with s 53(1)(c) and thus be in writing signed by S. In the case of Situation 5, it has been held that a direction by a beneficiary to trustees that they are to hold trust property on trust for some other person constitutes a disposition of the equitable interest to that other person, and that s 53(1)(c) must therefore be complied with.[5] Thus the direction to the trustees must be in writing, as required by the section. And, since the transaction constitutes a disposition of property, liability to stamp duty arises[6].

GENERAL

1 Situation 7

Where T_1 and T_2 hold property on a bare trust for B (so that B is entitled under the rule in *Saunders v Vautier*[7] to call on T_1 and T_2 to transfer the legal title to him), then B is entitled to require T_1 and T_2 to transfer the legal title to whomsoever B names, eg X. (It is logical that this should be so. If it were not, B would first have to assign his equitable interest to X and X would then have to call on T_1 and T_2 to transfer the legal title to him.) When X receives the legal title from T_1 and T_2 he holds it beneficially, the legal and equitable titles, which previously were in different hands (those of T_1 and T_2, and B, respectively) being merged. This is represented at 7 on page 401. For T_1 and T_2 to transfer the legal title to X they must observe any formality required (eg land must be conveyed by deed). Since B is in effect transferring his equitable interest to X, it might be thought that B would need to make an assignment in writing (signed by B) sufficient to satisfy s 53(1)(c) of the Law of Property Act 1925. It was held, however, in *Vandervell v IRC*[8], that s 53(1)(c) has no application in this situation. (X would of course, in practice, be wise to obtain a signed copy of B's instruction to T_1 and T_2 directing them to transfer the legal title to him beneficially.)

It will be noted that here we are speaking of a way in which a trust may be ended, not of a way in which a trust may be created.

The facts, and the decision, in *Vandervell v IRC* may conveniently be given at this point. V wished to give £150,000 to the Royal College of Surgeons in order to found a chair of pharmacology. He planned to give this sum to the College by allowing the College to receive dividends on 100,000 shares in the engineering company which V controlled, until the sum of £150,000 had been provided. The shares were held by a bank, as nominee, on trust for V. Therefore, in 1958, at V's direction, the bank transferred the shares to the College. As part of the arrangement, the College granted to the trustees of a trust set up in 1949 for V's children (VT Ltd), an option to

---

4 An example of Situation 2 is provided by *Kekewich v Manning* (1851) 1 De GM & G 176.
5 *Grey v IRC* [1960] AC 1, [1959] 3 All ER 603, HL; B. Green (1984) 47 MLR 385.
6 *Oughtred v IRC*, ante.
7 (1841) 4 Beav 115.
8 *Vandervell v IRC* [1967] 2 AC 291, [1967] 1 All ER 1, HL; (M & B); (1966) 24 CLJ 19 (G. Jones); (1967) 31 Conv 175 (S. M. Spencer); (1967) 3 MLR 461 (N. Straus); [1979] Conv 17 (G. Battersby).

acquire the shares for £5,000 (far less than the market value of the shares) at any time within five years. But the terms of the arrangement did not make clear for whom, in the event of VT Ltd exercising the option and acquiring the shares, it was to hold the shares on trust. During the tax years 1958–59 and 1959–60 dividends totalling £150,000 were paid to the College. In 1961 VT Ltd exercised the option and paid £5,000 (out of the funds of the children's settlement) to the College, which thereupon transferred the shares to VT Ltd.

Later, the Inland Revenue claimed surtax from V on the dividends paid to the College on the ground that by reason of the existence of the option, V had not absolutely divested himself of the shares and that, under s 415 of the Income Tax Act 1952, the dividends fell for surtax purposes to be treated as his income (ie and not that of the College). The Commissioners argued, inter alia, that when V (who had held an equitable interest in the shares under a bare trust) directed the bank to transfer the shares to the College, he was disposing of his equitable interest to the College. Section 53(1)(c) of the Law of Property Act 1925 required a disposition of an equitable interest to be in writing signed by the person disposing of the interest, or his agent. There had been no such written disposition by V of the equitable interest, which therefore remained with him. Thus V had not absolutely divested himself of the shares.

The House of Lords rejected this argument. It held that s 53(1)(c) 'refers to the disposition of an equitable interest as such. If, owning the entire estate, legal and beneficial in a piece of property, and desiring to transfer that entire estate to another, I do so by means of a disposition which *ex facie* deals only with the legal estate it would be ridiculous to argue that s 53(1)(c) had not been complied with, and that therefore the legal estate alone passed. The present case, it is true, is different in its facts in that the legal and equitable estates in the shares were in separate ownership: but when V instructed the bank to transfer the shares to the College, and made it abundantly clear that he wanted to pass, by means of that transfer, his own beneficial, or equitable, interest, plus the bank's legal interest, he achieved the same result as if there had been no separation of interests. The transfer thus made ... was a disposition not of the equitable interest alone, but of the entire estate in the shares. In such case I see no room for the operation of s 53(1)(c)'[9]. Thus no equitable interest in the shares remained in V by reason of his failing to dispose of it (together with the legal title) by a valid transfer to the College. However, the Lords went on to hold that, under the arrangement made in 1958, the option to purchase the shares was vested in VT Ltd not beneficially, but on trust. The trusts on which VT Ltd were intended to hold the option had not been defined. Thus VT Ltd held the option on a resulting trust for V. For this reason V had not absolutely divested himself of the property, and he was therefore liable for the surtax on the dividends paid to the College.

2 Creation of trusts by will

It has been suggested that, except where a settlor declares himself trustee, the creation of a trust can be regarded as having two parts, the declaration of trust and the transfer to the trustees. Where a trust is created by will, then the declaration of trust is contained in the will. Under the Wills Act 1837[10],

---

9 Per Lord Donovan, at p 11.
10 Section 9, as substituted by s 17 of the Administration of Justice Act 1982.

to be valid a will must be signed by the testator, or by some other person in his presence and at his direction; and the signature must be made or acknowledged by the testator in the presence of two or more witnesses present at the same time, who must sign the will as witnesses in the presence of the testator. The transfer of the trust property to the trustees occurs on the testator's death when the trust property vests in his executor, who holds it in a fiduciary capacity pending the transfer to the testator's trustees[11]. Where the property is land, then the transfer must be by way of written assent[12].

3 Sub-trust or drop out
We have seen that in Situation 2, S transfers his equitable interest to T_1 and T_2 to hold on trust for B, and that a sub-trust then comes into existence. This, at any rate, is the position where S imposes any form of duty on T_1 and T_2[13] (for example, by making the trust a trust for sale or where the trust was for B and others and was discretionary). But where S imposes no duties on T_1 and T_2, then the result is that T_1 and T_2 drop out and t_1 and t_2 hold directly on trust for B[14] (or, at any rate, T_1 and T_2 cease to be of any significance in the structure or administration of the trust).

Similarly, in Situation 4 if, when S declares himself trustee for B, he imposes no duties on himself with regard to the trust, he drops out of the picture, and t_1 and t_2 hold directly on trust for B. (It is necessary 'to look through [S] as a nobody'[15].) It will be seen that the result (ie that previously t_1 and t_2 held on trust for S, and after the transaction t_1 and t_2 hold on trust for B) corresponds with that (in Situation 5) where t_1 and t_2 held on trust for S, and S directed that thenceforth they were to hold on trust for B. Since in this latter situation it has been held[16] that for the transaction to be effective the direction by S to t_1 and t_2 must comply with s 53(1)(c), it has been suggested[17] that where S declares himself a trustee for B and (imposing no duties on himself) drops out, here too, for the transaction to be effective, s 53(1)(c) must be complied with. It is submitted, however, that such a proposition ignores the distinction between a declaration of trust, and a disposition of an existing equitable interest. It is true that in Situation 4, where S drops out, the end result is the same as in Situation 5, but the result is produced by operation of a principle of law, and ought not to be permitted to obscure the nature of S's ·act, one of declaration of trust, to which s 53(1)(b) may be applicable, but not s 53(1)(c). To hold otherwise would be to introduce an anomaly into the law because the result would be that if S declared orally that he held certain shares on trust for sale for B (ie imposing a duty on himself), B would acquire the beneficial interest in the shares; if S declared orally that he held the shares merely on trust for B (imposing no duty on himself), B would acquire nothing (since s 53(1)(c) had not been complied with).

11 Administration of Estates Act 1925, s 1.
12 See *Re King's Will Trusts* [1964] Ch 542, [1964] 1 All ER 833.
13 *Re Lashmar* [1891] 1 Ch 258 at 270, following *Onslow v Wallis* (1849) 1 Mac & G 506.
14 *Grainge v Wilberforce* (1889) 5 TLR 436 at 437.
15 Per Lindley LJ, *Re Lashmar* [1891] 1 Ch 258 at 268.
16 *Grey v IRC* [1960] AC 1, [1959] 3 All ER 603, HL.
17 Underhill, *Law of Trusts and Trustees* (12th edn) p 124; Pettit, *Equity and the Law of Trusts* (5th edn) p 74.

4   Transfer outside s 53(1)(c) of an equitable interest for consideration
Where V purports to convey the legal estate in land to P, but fails (as required by s 52 of the Law of Property Act 1925) to execute a deed for this purpose, and P has contracted to give consideration to V for the land, then under the rule in *Walsh v Lonsdale*[18], P acquires an equitable fee simple, the legal title being held by V as a constructive trustee for P. Since failure to comply with a formality (the deed) required by statute coupled with consideration from the would-be transferee results in the transferor, V, holding on trust for P, who holds an equitable title, should it, by the same principle, be the case that if S purports to assign his equitable interest to B, in return for consideration from B, but makes the assignment orally (thus failing to comply with the requirement of writing imposed by s 53(1)(c)) the result is that S holds the interest as a constructive trustee for B, who holds, as it were, an interest that is doubly equitable? (Equitable, first, because it was an equitable interest that S held; equitable, second, because the interest reaches B by the application of an equitable principle.) The matter is undecided[19]. Section 53(2) provides that s 53(1) is not to apply to the creation of constructive trusts, so there is no statutory bar (from the lack of writing) to S holding as constructive trustee. In *Re Holt's Settlement*[20], Megarry J accepted (albeit with no great certainty and albeit in a context[1] other than that concerning a direct assignment) that consideration from the transferee of an equitable interest would, as a result of the application of the principle in *Walsh v Lonsdale*[2], enable him to enforce his interest notwithstanding that s 53(1)(c) had not been complied with by the transferor.

5   Transfer within s 53(1)(c)
Where S transfers property to T on trust for purposes that will be communicated to him, then pending the communication T holds the property on trust for S. When S notifies T that the property is to be held for, say, B, this constitutes an assignment by S of his equitable interest to B. The notification by S to T must therefore comply with s 53(1)(c)[3].

6   Implied and constructive trusts
The requirements covering formalities with which we have been dealing are applicable only where a trust is created expressly. Formalities for the creation of a trust have no place where a trust arises as a result of what is inferred by the court as having been the parties' intention (an implied, including a resulting, trust), nor where the court imposes a trust (a constructive trust). This fact is given statutory confirmation in s 53(2) of the Law of Property Act 1925 which provides that s 53 'does not affect the creation or operation of resulting, implied, or constructive trusts'.

---

18   (1882) 21 Ch D 9, CA.
19   The issue arose in *Oughtred v IRC* [1960] AC 206, [1959] 3 All ER 603, HL (see (1959) 17 CLJ (J. C. Hall)), but the majority decision of the House of Lords was reached by a route other than one requiring a decision on the matter of compliance with s 53(1)(c).
20   [1969] 1 Ch 100 at 116.
1   See Chap 18.
2   *Ante.*
3   *Re Tyler's Fund Trusts* [1967] 3 All ER 389, [1967] 1 WLR 1269.

Summary

We can summarise the formalities we have referred to in this chapter as follows:

DECLARATION OF TRUST

Inter vivos
Land and interests in land	Evidenced in writing under LPA 1925, s 53(1)(b).
Other forms of property	No special requirement; oral declaration sufficient.

By will
Any form of property	Signed and attested under Wills Act 1837, s 9.

TRANSFER TO TRUSTEES

Inter vivos
Legal interests	The formality varies according to the type of property to be transferred. See pp 39–40, ante.
Equitable interests	In writing under LPA 1925, s 53(1)(c).

By will
All forms of property	Signed and attested under Wills Act 1837, s 9.

7 THE TRUST MUST NOT INFRINGE THE RULE AGAINST PERPETUITIES

The trust must comply with the rule against perpetuities[4]. This is so with regard both to the vesting of the trust property in the trustees, and the vesting of the interests of the beneficiaries.

The rule against perpetuities, it will be recalled, is concerned with the initial vesting of property. It is not concerned with the duration of time during which a person holds property, once he has received it. (This latter matter is the subject of the rule considered next.)

---

4 *Re Bushnell* [1975] 1 All ER 721, [1975] 1 WLR 1596. *Re Lord Stratheden and Campbell* [1894] 3 Ch 265, a case concerning a charitable trust, but the principle is the same whether the trust is private or charitable.

8 THE TRUST MUST NOT INFRINGE THE RULE AGAINST INALIENABILITY

A trust is void if, by the terms of the trust, the capital is incapable of being alienated for a period longer than the common law perpetuity period. This is the rule against inalienability, sometimes termed the rule against perpetual trusts. The rule is concerned, it will be noted, not with the initial vesting of the property (ie not with the commencement of the beneficial interest), but with the duration of the trust once it has come into existence. The matter is considered further in Chapter 9.

9 THE TRUST MUST NOT INFRINGE THE RULE AGAINST ACCUMULATIONS

In his will Peter Thellusson, who died in 1797, left property to the value of about £700,000 for the benefit of certain of his descendants. He directed that the capital should be invested and the income added to the capital (that the income should be 'accumulated') during the lives of his sons, grandsons and great-grandchildren living at his death, and that on the death of the survivor of all these, the fund should be divided among certain descendants whom he specified. Was the gift valid? It did not infringe the rule against perpetuities, as the gift was bound to vest within the life or lives in being at his death. Nor did the gift infringe the rule against inalienability, as the capital was not made inalienable for longer than the lives in being specified in the gift. But what about the direction that the income should be accumulated? If the youngest great-grandchild living at Mr Thellusson's death lived until the age of 80, the original sum would, at compound interest, have mounted up to £140,000,000. Was it in the public interest that a sum of such magnitude should be amassed in this way? At common law a direction to accumulate income was valid if the period of accumulation specified did not exceed the period for which property could validly be made inalienable, ie for the perpetuity period[5]. Mr Thellusson's direction complied with this requirement and when the direction was challenged the House of Lords upheld its validity[6].

The testator had feared that the legislature might intervene and prevent the will taking effect as he had directed, and a clause in the will expressed his apprehension: 'As I have earned the fortune which I now possess with industry and honesty I trust and hope that the legislature will not in any manner alter my will or the limitations thereby created but permit my property to go in the manner which I hereby dispose of it'. Parliament did not intervene by passing retrospective legislation, and the will took effect as the testator had prescribed. In the event, because of mismanagement and the costs of further litigation, when the last great-grandson died in 1856 those entitled succeeded to only a modest fortune[7]. The case demonstrated, however, the unsatisfactory state of the law, and in 1800 to remedy the position for the future the Accumulations Act (the 'Thellusson Act') was

---

5   *Thellusson v Woodford* (1798) 4 Ves 227 at 317, 318.
6   (1805) 11 Ves 112.
7   *Dictionary of National Biography.*

passed. The purpose of the Act was to prevent accumulations being directed for undue lengths of time.

The Act of 1800 was repealed by the Law of Property Act 1925 which, together with the Perpetuities and Accumulations Act 1964, contains the present law. The effect of the combined provisions of the two Acts[8] is that a settlor may not direct that income should be accumulated for longer than one (and one only) of the periods set out below.

In the case of an inter vivos settlement:

1. 21 years from the date of the settlement[9].

2. The life of the settlor.

3. 21 years from the death of the settlor.

4. The minority of any person (or the minorities of any persons) living *en ventre sa mère* at the date of the settlement[10].

5. The minority of any person (or the minorities of any persons) living or *en ventre sa mère* at the death of the settlor.

6. The minority of any person (or the minorities of any persons) who, under the terms of the settlement would, if he were of full age, be entitled to the income directed to be accumulated. (There is no requirement that this person should be alive or *en ventre sa mère* at the time of the settlement.)

In the case of a settlement created by will:

A. 21 years from the death of the testator.

B. The minority of any person (or minorities of any persons) living or *en ventre sa mère* at the death of the testator.

C. The minority of any person (or minorities of any persons) who, under the terms of the will, would, if he were of full age, be entitled to the income directed to be accumulated. (There is no requirement that this person should be alive or *en ventre sa mère* at the time of the testator's death.)

The following matters should be noted:

(a) Since the Family Law Reform Act 1969[11], minority ends on the attainment of age of 18.

(b) In the case of periods 4, 5, and B, the minority may be that of any person specified by the settlor or testator, and need not be that of a person upon whom some benefit is conferred.

(c) Periods 1 and 4 above were added by the Perpetuities and Accumulations Act 1964. Thus in the case of dispositions taking effect after 1925 but before the 1964 Act took effect on 16 July 1964, only the other periods may be used.

If a settlor directs that income should be accumulated for one of the statutory periods, or for a shorter time (eg 15 years from the date of the settlement) then the direction is valid[12]. What is the position if he fails to

---

8 LPA 1925, ss 164–166; PAA 1964, s 13.
9 This period was added by the Perpetuities and Accumulations Act 1964, s 13.
10 Ibid.
11 Section 1.
12 See *Re Sharp's Settlement Trusts* [1973] Ch 331, [1972] 3 All ER 151. (Period of accumulation could not exceed minorities of settlor's children.)

limit a period of accumulation to one specified by statute? Suppose that a
testator directs that income from certain capital should be accumulated for
40 years from his death, and the accumulation and the capital then divided
among his children living at that date. It might be supposed that since
the terms of the disposition infringe the rule against accumulations (since
accumulation has been directed for other than a statutory period) then the
result (following the same principle as in the rule against perpetuities) would
be that the gift is void. This is not the case. The gift itself, ie to the children,
is valid; what infringes the law is the direction to accumulate. The gift and
the direction to accumulate are therefore treated separately. As we have said,
the gift is valid. As to the direction to accumulate, the position is as follows:

1. If a period of accumulation prescribed by a settlor *may* extend beyond
the expiry of the common law perpetuity period, then the direction to accumulate is wholly void, and no accumulation is made[13].

2. If the period of accumulation which has been directed[14] cannot extend
beyond the expiry of the common law perpetuity period, but could extend
beyond any period of accumulation permitted by statute, then the direction[15]
to accumulate is valid until the expiry of whatever is held by the court in the
circumstances to be the appropriate statutory period. At that point the
direction becomes void and accumulation ceases. If the period prescribed by
the settlor in fact expires before the end of the statutory period, the accumulation ceases at that point. For example, suppose that a testator directs that
income from certain capital should be accumulated during A's life, and that
on A's death the capital and the accumulated income should be divided
between A's children living at his death. The period of accumulation prescribed by the testator cannot exceed the common law perpetuity period and
so is not wholly void. But it could last longer than any period permitted by
statute. The direction to accumulate is therefore void as to the excess over
whatever is held by the court to be the appropriate statutory period. The
court decides, let us suppose, that the appropriate period is that at A above,
ie 21 years from the death of the testator.[16] Income will therefore continue
to be accumulated until the expiry of 21 years from the testator's death, or
until the death of A, whichever occurs sooner.

How does the court determine what period is appropriate? The court looks
in the first place to see whether it appears that the settlor had a particular
period in mind[17]. If it considers that he did, then this is the period which the
court selects. The court will by this means select whichever period appears
to come closest to the settlor's intentions[18]. If the period prescribed by the
settlor does not point to the selection of any particular statutory period[19],
then the court will select whichever period it considers in the circumstances

---

13 As in *Curtis v Lukin* (1842) 5 Beav 147; a direction to accumulate income until a lease with
    over 60 years to run had 'nearly expired'.
14 Or the period during which the trustees have been given *power* to accumulate income (ie
    accumulate it or distribute it). *Baird v Lord Advocate* [1979] AC 666, [1979] 2 All ER 28.
15 Or power. *Baird v Lord Advocate*, ante.
16 As in *Re Green's Will Trusts* [1985] 3 All ER 455.
17 *Re Watt's Will Trusts* [1936] 2 All ER 1555 at 1562.
18 *Re Lady Rosslyn's Trust* (1848) 16 Sim 391.
19 This will generally be the case. 'The trouble in ... most cases dealing with the rule against
    accumulations is that the (settlor) has given directions clearly not having the rule in mind
    at all.' Per Upjohn J, *Re Ransome* [1957] Ch 348 at 361.

to be appropriate. For example, where a testator directed that income should be accumulated during the lifetime of X, the court held that the appropriate period was that at A above, ie 21 years from the death of the testator (the accumulation to end at X's death if this occurred sooner)[20]. This period was also selected as being appropriate where it was directed by will that accumulation should continue until Y was 25[1]; until Z's death[2]; and during the minority of certain persons whose minorities were not within the statutory list[3]. Where a settlor directed that trustees should have power to accumulate income during the lifetimes of his children, the court held that the appropriate period was the lifetime of the settlor[4].

If a direction to accumulate income is void, either wholly void or partially void (ie after the expiry of a statutory period of accumulation prescribed by the court), then the income concerned passes to the person who would be entitled if the direction to accumulate had not been made[5]. Who this person is will depend on the circumstances. If the income is found to be undisposed of, it will fall into a testator's residuary estate, or, if the trust property is residue, pass as on his intestacy. In other circumstances the income may revert to the trust fund out of which the gift in question has been made[6]. But the income cannot go to the beneficiary for whose benefit the direction to accumulate was made, since the statutory provision which would otherwise require the trustees to pay the income to that person (s 31(1)(ii) of the Trustee Act 1925[7]) is excluded by a contrary intention, and the direction to accumulate (notwithstanding that the direction ceases to be effective after the end of the statutory period) constitutes such an intention[8].

10 THE TRUST MUST NOT HAVE BEEN MADE VOID BY REASON OF IT BEING DESIGNED TO DEFRAUD CREDITORS

Suppose that A has incurred more debts than he can pay, and thinks that he is likely to be declared bankrupt. He knows that if this happens his property[9] will vest in his trustee in bankruptcy who will distribute it among his creditors. Suppose that, in order to save what property he has left from falling into the hands of his creditors, A transfers his property to his wife. She, he thinks, will then be the sole owner of their home; she will be the owner of their car, and their money, and so on. So, he thinks, there will be nothing of his for the trustee in bankruptcy to take. If this result were allowed to ensue it would be an easy matter for a debtor to escape from the claims of his creditors, by off-loading his ship before it sank. To close up this avenue of escape, the

20 *Griffiths v Vere* (1803) 9 Ves 127; *Re McGeorge* [1963] Ch 544, [1963] 1 All ER 519.
1 *Crawley v Crawley* (1835) 7 Sim 427.
2 *Weatherall v Thornburgh* (1878) 8 Ch D 261.
3 *Re Ransome* [1957] Ch 348, [1957] 1 All ER 690.
4 *Baird v Lord Advocate* [1979] AC 666, [1979] 2 All ER 28, HL.
5 LPA 1925, s 164(1). But if the accumulation is for the purpose of establishing a fund the income from which is to be applied for a charitable purpose, and if a general charitable intention is present, then at the end of the appropriate period, the income is applied *cy près*. (See Chap 8.) *Re Bradwell* [1952] Ch 575, [1952] 2 All ER 286.
6 As in *Re Ransome* [1957] Ch 348, [1957] 1 All ER 690.
7 See Chap 17.
8 *Re Ransome*, ante; [1979] Conv 423 (J. G. Riddall).
9 With certain exceptions set out in s 283 of the Insolvency Act 1986, replacing Bankruptcy Act 1914, s 38.

Insolvency Act 1986[10] provides[11] that where an individual, being insolvent (where he is unable to pay his debts or where his liabilities exceed his assets), enters into a transaction 'at an undervalue' or has 'given a preference' to another during a prescribed[12] period before the presenting of a bankruptcy petition against him, and he is subsequently adjudged bankrupt, then the court can make an order restoring the position to what it would have been if the transaction had not been entered into or the preference not given. A transaction 'at an undervalue' includes a gift, or a transfer for which the consideration is significantly less than that supplied by the transferee. (Marriage does not constitute consideration.) An individual gives a 'preference' to another when he does anything that puts a creditor of his into a position which, in the event of the individual's bankruptcy, will be better than the position would have been if that thing had not been done, and he does the thing with the intention of achieving this end.

Further, where an individual who is later adjudged bankrupt makes a gift to another (including a gift for which the consideration is marriage) with the object of putting assets beyond the reach of a person who is making a claim against him, then (irrespective of how long before the bankruptcy the gift was made), the court may make an order restoring the position to what it would have been if the gift had not been made.

EFFECT OF NON-COMPLIANCE WITH THE CONDITIONS REQUIRED

It may be helpful, by way of recapitulation, to state the result which ensues if the first eight conditions set out above are not fulfilled.

1. If there is no intention to create a trust, the transferee takes the property beneficially.

2. If there is not sufficient certainty as to the subject matter of the trust, no transfer to the trustees takes place and the property remains in the settlor.

3. If the trust does not have beneficiaries, the trustees hold the property on a resulting trust for the settlor.

4. If there is not sufficient certainty as to the identity of the beneficiaries, the result is the same.

5. If there is not sufficient certainty as to the share of property each beneficiary is entitled to, the result is the same.

6. If there is no declaration of trust, the transferee takes the property beneficially. If there is a declaration of trust but no transfer to the trustees the trust is 'incompletely constituted'. The effects of this are considered in the next chapter.

7. If the limitation of the beneficial interests under the trust infringes the rule against perpetuities, the trustees hold the property on a resulting trust for the settlor.

8. If the trust infringes the rule against inalienability, the result is the same.

---

10   Replacing Law of Property Act 1925, s 172(1) and Bankruptcy Act 1914, s 42.
11   Sections 339–342, 423–425.
12   The maximum period is five years. Section 341(1), (2).

Trust or debt

At this point it will be convenient to mention that a dispute concerning the existence of a trust may take the form of a dispute, not over whether there is or there is not a trust, but over whether an obligation is fiduciary in nature or contractual in nature, eg whether X holds £1000 on *trust* for Y; or whether he *owes* the £1000 to Y: whether it is a trust, or a debt.[13]

It may happen that it is immaterial to Y whether his entitlement to the £1000 arises under a trust or exists as a debt. If he receives the £1000 from X, that will be the end of the matter. But suppose that X becomes insolvent, with assets of £100,000 and creditors claiming £200,000. If X holds the £1000 on trust for Y, then since a beneficiary has a proprietary interest under the trust, he can claim the £1000 out of X's assets as *his* money. He will therefore take the £1000 in priority to Y's creditors, who will have the remaining £99,000 shared among them in proportion to the sums they are owed. On the other hand, if X owes the £1000 to Y, then Y ranks merely as a creditor, and ranks *pari passu* (in equal step) with the other creditors (in this case receiving only £497.51, ie £100,000[14]÷£201,000[15]×£1000[16]).

There is another reason why it is beneficial for Y if X's obligation is fiduciary, not contractual. If X holds money on trust for Y, X is under a duty to invest it, with the result that the money produces income for Y. If X owes the money to Y then, in the absence of an agreement, express or implied, X is under no duty to invest the money.

In some, exceptional, circumstances an obligation may in one respect carry the characteristics of a debt, and in another the characteristics of a trust. For example, in *Barclays Bank Ltd v Quistclose Investments Ltd*,[17] a company, R Ltd, declared a dividend on its shares. It transpired that it did not have enough money to pay the dividend, and sought to borrow money in order to be able to do so (in order to avoid the collapse that would have followed if the dividend were not paid). A loan was obtained from Q Ltd (which had an interest in keeping R Ltd afloat), subject to an agreement by R Ltd that the money would be used only for the purpose of paying the dividend. Q Ltd paid the money into a separate account at Barclays Bank, which received the money with notice of the arrangement. Before the dividend was paid, R Ltd went into liquidation. What was to happen to the money held by the bank? If the money was to be regarded as having been loaned by Q Ltd to R Ltd, then Q Ltd would rank with R Ltd's other creditors; if, on the other hand, it was found that R Ltd held the money as trustee, on trust for the purpose of paying the dividend, then, if the purpose was regarded as having failed, the result would be (as considered in more detail in Chapter 9) that R Ltd would hold the money on trust for Q Ltd, and that Q Ltd would be able to

---

13 See *Re Kayford Ltd* [1975] 1 All ER 604, [1975] 1 WLR 279; *Paul v Constance* [1977] 1 All ER 195, [1977] 1 WLR 527, CA; *Alimand Computer Systems v Radcliffes & Co* (1991) Times, 6 November (solicitors holding funds for client as stakeholder did so as trustees, not in a contractual capacity).
14 The assets.
15 The total claims, including Y's.
16 Y's claim.
17 [1970] AC 567, [1968] 3 All ER 651, HL; (M & B); following *Re Rogers* (1891) 8 Morr 243, CA; *Re Northern Developments (Holdings) Ltd* (6 October 1978, unreported); see (1985) 101 LQR 269 (P. J. Millett).

claim the money in priority to R Ltd's creditors. The House of Lords held unanimously that, notwithstanding that the transaction had been entered into as a loan, because of the arrangement regarding the purpose for which the money was to be applied, the money was held on trust to be applied for that purpose. The purpose had failed[18] and the money was therefore held on trust for Q Ltd. Thus what may be initiated as a debt may, in certain (limited and exceptional) circumstances, result in the creation of a trust, with the characteristics of a trust prevailing over those of a debt in the event of the recipient's bankruptcy.[19]

It is possible that what has the appearance of the reverse may also exceptionally happen; what begins as a fiduciary relationship may assume the characteristics of a contractual one. An example is provided by *Space Investments Ltd v Canadian Imperial Bank of Commerce Trust Co (Bahamas) Ltd.*[20] A bank held money as trustee. Under the terms of the settlement the bank was empowered to deposit money in the savings account (ie thereby earning interest) of any bank, including itself. The bank, as trustee, deposited trust money in its own savings account. Later, the bank went into liquidation. The beneficiaries claimed that the money in the savings account was held on trust for them, and that they therefore took priority over the bank's creditors. The Privy Council rejected the claim. Customers who placed money in a bank savings account were entitled in contract to the money they had deposited (together with any interest due); the money in such an account was not held on trust for them. The bank as trustee was not in any better a position than other depositors in the savings account. Therefore in their claim the beneficiaries ranked *pari passu* with the other creditors.

Secret and half secret trusts

SECRET TRUSTS

In dealing with the formalities required for setting up a trust we saw[1] that the creation of a trust may be regarded as having two parts: the declaration of trust and the transfer to the trustee. Frequently the two will occur contemporaneously, but it is not necessary that this should be so: the declaration of trust may come first, the transfer later. For example, A may declare[2] that T is to hold Blackacre on trust for B. If, later, he transfers Blackacre to T then, irrespective of whether there is any mention of T holding as trustee for B in the conveyance, T holds the land as trustee for B. Or it may be that a testator, T, tells someone, D, that he intends to leave him certain property in his will and that, although there will be no mention of this in the will, he wishes the donee, D, to hold the property on trust for a certain beneficiary, B. D agrees so to hold it. Later T dies leaving the property to D. A trust has

---

18   But see P. J. Millett (1985) 101 LQR 269, 275.
19   See also *Carreras Rothmans Ltd v Freeman Mathews Treasure Ltd* [1985] Ch 207, [1985] 1 All ER 155; (M & B); (1985) 101 LQR 269 (P. J. Millett); [1985] All ER Review 316 (P. J. Clarke); *Re EVTR* [1987] BCLC 646; (M & B).
20   [1986] 1 WLR 1072, PC.
 1   See ante.
 2   In compliance with LPA 1925, s 53(1)(b).

been created. T's arrangement with D constitutes a declaration of trust; the leaving of the property to D constitutes the transfer to the trustee. A trust which comes into existence in this way is termed a secret trust: the will reveals neither the fact that the property is to be held by D as trustee; nor the identity of the person for whom it is held. On the face of the will, it appears that D takes the property beneficially. The fact that he holds it as trustee is kept secret. For D to attempt to keep the property in these circumstances would be a fraud on T, and it was on the basis that a fraud of this kind should not be countenanced that equity first began to enforce secret trusts[3]. 'It has long been settled that if a gift be made to a person or persons in terms absolutely but in fact upon a trust communicated to the legatee and accepted by him, the legatee would be bound to give effect to the trust, on the principle that the gift may be presumed to have been made on the faith of his acceptance of the trust, and a refusal after the death of the testator to give effect to it would be a fraud on the part of the legatee'[4].

Of course, the existence of the trust may in fact be published to the world by T, by D or by B. But the will itself does not disclose the existence of the trust. Unless the parties so wish, no one, apart from themselves, need know that B, not D, is the real beneficiary. The secret trust has therefore been a convenient means for a testator to provide for persons whose existence he did not wish publicly to recognise, for example, his mistress or his illegitimate children or both[5]. Later[6] we shall be seeing another, and perhaps more common, purpose which a secret trust may serve.

Where B claims that property left by T in his will to D is held by him subject to a secret trust in his, B's, favour, then the onus is on B to prove the existence of the trust[7] (ie that the necessary conditions are satisfied). In the absence of fraud on D's part, the standard of proof is no different from that required for the establishment of an ordinary trust[8]. It may happen that B's claim will stand or fall on the evidence produced to the court of T's intention. In this case it must be shown that T imposed a trust on D. If it is found that T imposed no more than a moral obligation on D to deal with the property concerned in the way that T specified, then T takes the property absolutely[9].

A secret trust may come into existence not by T leaving property to D, but by T refraining from making a will, where D is the person entitled under T's intestacy. Here T will say 'If I refrain from making any will, when you get my property will you promise to hold it (or a certain part of it) on trust for B?' If D agrees, a secret trust arises. A secret trust may come into existence also by T revoking a will. For example, D is entitled in the event of T's intestacy. T makes a will leaving his property to X. T says to D 'If I revoke my will, with the result that all my property will come to you, will you hold it (or a certain part) on trust for B?' If D agrees a secret trust arises.

A secret trust will arise notwithstanding that when D makes his promise to T, T has not yet told him of the identity of the person for whom D is to

---

3 *Drakeford v Wilks* (1747) 3 Atk 539.
4 Per Lord Warrington of Clyffe, *Blackwell v Blackwell* [1929] AC 318 at 341, HL. For the view that the basis of secret trusts is to be found in the principles relating to the admissibility of evidence to explain the meaning of a will, see B. Perrins [1986] Conv 248.
5 As in *Blackwell v Blackwell* [1929] AC 318, HL; (M & B).
6 See p 54, post.
7 *Jones v Badley* (1868) 3 Ch App 362, CA.
8 *McCormick v Grogan* (1867) 1 IR Eq 313 at 328, 329, CA.
9 *Re Snowden* [1979] Ch 528, [1979] 2 All ER 172; (M & B); [1979] CLJ 260 (C. E .F. Rickett).

hold on trust: T may ask D whether, if he receives certain property under his, T's, will, he will hold it on trust for a person whose identity T will, at some later date, communicate to him. If D agrees, and the identity of the beneficiary is communicated to him, then a secret trust arises. It is essential, however, that the communication should take place before T's death. It is not sufficient if, for example, the identity of the beneficiary is discovered from an examination of T's papers after his death. In *Re Keen's Estate*[10] T named the beneficiary in a paper which he placed in a sealed envelope, marked 'Not to be opened until my death'. He passed the envelope to D, who knew that it contained the terms of the trust (which he had agreed to observe). It was held that the communication was to be treated as having occurred at the time of the delivery of the envelope and thus during T's lifetime[11].

We have referred, and shall be referring, to property being held under a secret trust for a particular beneficiary, B. A secret trust can also arise for a charitable purpose[12]. A secret trust has also taken the form of a promise by D that if T leaves him certain property in his will, then he, D, will leave that property in his own will to a person specified by T. The effect here will be that on T's death D will take a life interest in the property, and will be bound to leave it in his will to the beneficiary specified[13].

It will be seen that there are three elements necessary for the creation of a secret trust: the promise by D; the communication of the identity of B; the making of the will by T (or the revoking of a will, or refraining from making a will) which results in D receiving the property. Provided that the communication occurs before T's death, it is immaterial in which order these three events occur. Thus T could say to D 'I have made my will leaving x to you. Will you promise to hold it on trust for B?' Or, 'I am thinking of leaving x to you when I make my will. If I do, will you hold it on trust for someone whose name I shall tell you at some later date?'

We have referred to D promising T that the property he receives will be held on trust. This promise may be expressed (orally or in writing), or it may be implied from D's silence, as where D fails to inform T that he declines to accept the property on the terms which T has indicated.

If the property is left in the will to two or more persons as co-owners and only one or some of them gave the required promise, then the general rule is that only those who promised will be bound and the others will take their share beneficially[14]. There is one exception—if the gift is to the owners as joint tenants (ie not as tenants in common) and if the promise was given before the will was made, then those who did not promise will be bound as well as those who did[15].

We can now set out the conditions for a secret trust to exist.

1. Before or after[16] the making of a will[17] (or refraining from making a will[18],

---

10 [1937] Ch 236, [1937] 1 All ER 452, CA; (M & B).
11 This case concerned a half secret trust but it seems that the principle is the same in a secret trust. See Snell, *Principles of Equity* (28th edn) p 113.
12 See *Re Pitt Rivers* [1902] 1 Ch 403; *Re Tyler's Fund Trusts* [1967] 3 All ER 389, [1967] 1 WLR 1269.
13 *Ottaway v Norman* [1972] Ch 698, [1971] 3 All ER 1325; (M & B).
14 *Moss v Cooper* (1861) 1 John & H 352; *Tee v Ferris* (1856) 2 K & J 357.
15 *Re Stead* [1900] 1 Ch 237.
16 *Blackwell v Blackwell* [1929] AC 318 at 341, HL.
17 *Drakeford v Wilks* (1747) 3 Atk 539.
18 *Re Gardner* [1920] 2 Ch 523.

or revoking a will[19]), a donee must expressly promise a testator, or by his silence imply[19], that he will hold specified property to be given to him in the will on trust for a beneficiary whose identity has been or will be communicated to him[20];

2. the identity of the beneficiary and the terms of the trust must be communicated to the donee during the testator's lifetime by the testator or by an agent authorised by him[1].

3. the terms of the trust must not be rejected by the donee;

4. the property is given to the donee in the will.

What is the result if one of these conditions is not satisfied? If it cannot be proved that D gave the necessary promise, either express or implied (as where D can show that he only learnt of T's intention after T's death[2]) then D takes the property beneficially. If it is shown that D gave the necessary promise, but that the communication of B's identity did not occur until after T's death, then D will hold the property on a resulting trust for T's estate[3].

It might seem that the use of a secret trust can enable a testator to avoid the requirements of s 9 of the Wills Act 1837. By virtue of this section, if T wishes to leave £100 on his death to B, then the will under which this money is bequeathed to B must be signed by T and attested by two witnesses. Yet under a secret trust T can leave the property to D in his will and then later communicate B's identity to D in a letter which is signed by him, but not attested; or even communicate B's identity to D orally. The result will be that on T's death, B will get £100. Has T therefore not effectively left B £100 without complying with s 9? Has he not effectively altered his will by an unattested codicil? The answer is that s 9 is not sidestepped: it is not given 'the go-by'[4]. The reason is that the benefit was conferred on B, not by T's will, but by the creation[5] of the trust, and this occurred during T's life: '... what is enforced is not a trust imposed by the will, but one arising from the acceptance by the legatee of a trust, communicated to him by the testator, on the faith of which acceptance the will was made or left unrevoked, as the case might be'[6]. T's will, which complies with s 9, merely completely constitutes the trust by transferring the property to the trustee. Thus '... the Wills Act has nothing to do with the matter ... since the persons do not take by virtue of the gift in the will, but by virtue of the secret trusts imposed upon the donee: the benefit is conferred on B *dehors* the will'[7].

Since no special formality is needed for a declaration of a trust of personalty, the fact that D's promise and the communication of B's identity were merely oral (or written, but not attested) does not affect the validity of the trust. In the case of land we have seen that a declaration of trust, to be valid, must be evidenced in writing under s 53(1)(b) of the Law of Property Act 1925. In the light of this requirement it would seem that where the property which is the subject of the secret trust is land, then there would have

19 *Moss v Cooper* (1861) 1 John & H 352; *Tee v Ferris* (1856) 2 K & J 357.
20 *Moss v Cooper*, ante.
1 *Moss v Cooper*, ante.
2 *Wallgrave v Tebbs* (1855) 2 K & J 313.
3 *Re Boyes* (1884) 26 Ch D 531.
4 Per Vaughan Williams LJ, *Re Pitt Rivers* [1902] 1 Ch 403 at 407, CA.
5 *Re Young* [1951] Ch 344 at 350; (M & B).
6 Per Lord Warrington of Clyffe, *Blackwell v Blackwell* [1929] AC 318 at 342, HL.
7 Per Dankwerts J, *Re Young* [1951] Ch 344 at 350.

to be evidence in writing signed by T, of T's intention that D should hold on trust, and of the communication of B's identity. In *Ottaway v Norman*[8], where the property included land, this aspect was not considered and not-withstanding that there was no evidence in writing, a valid secret trust was held to have come into existence. If the lack of writing was raised as an objection to the validity of a secret trust of land, it might, however, be held that this defect would not be a bar to the existence of the trust by reason of the application of the principle that equity will not allow the statute to be used as an instrument of fraud[9].

Suppose that T makes a will leaving £10,000 to his son, D. Some years later T approaches D and says 'I've been thinking about the £10,000 I've left you in my will. You have been so successful that you don't really need the money now. And you know that your cousin has had this accident which has put her in a wheelchair for life. She needs the money more than you. If I leave my will as it stands, will you let her have the money?' D agrees. T dies leaving the money to D. D holds the money under a secret trust for the cousin. This illustrates that the device of a secret trust may be employed by a testator to alter the effect of his will without altering the will itself.

We have said that a secret trust is established inter vivos, and not by will, the will merely transferring the property to the trustee. Two consequences flow from this. If T had left B property in his will and B had signed the will as a witness, then he would lose his interest under the will[10]. But if B is the beneficiary under a secret trust, then the fact that he attests T's will will not disentitle him—his entitlement being under the trust, not the will[11]. Second, if T had left B property in his will, and B had died before T, then the gift to B would lapse. But it has been held that if B is a beneficiary under a secret trust, and B dies before T, then B's interest under the trust does not lapse on his death but passes (on T's death) to whoever is entitled under B's will or intestacy[12]. The soundness of this has however been questioned[13].

We may note here that if D predeceases T, then B receives nothing, since the existence of the trust in B's favour is regarded as being conditional on the property vesting in D[14]. On the other hand, if D survives T but disclaims the trusteeship (as he is entitled to do[15]) then it is uncertain whether or not the secret trust will survive[16] (eg by T's personal representative being required to hold on trust for B).

It is uncertain whether a secret trust can exist where the transfer of property to the donee is made not by will but inter vivos. In *Re Tyler's Fund Trusts*[17] Pennycuick J indicated that in his view secret trusts could arise only where the transfer was by will. There would seem, however, to be no grounds in logic why a secret trust should not exist in relation to an inter vivos dis-

---

8   [1972] Ch 698, [1971] 3 All ER 1325; (M & B).
9   See p 38, ante.
10   Wills Act 1837, s 15.
11   *Re Young* [1951] Ch 185, [1950] 2 All ER 1040.
12   *Re Gardner* [1923] 2 Ch 230.
13   Hayton and Marshall, *Cases and Commentary on the Law of Trusts* (8th edn) p 103. See p 85, post.
14   *Re Maddock* [1902] 2 Ch 220 at 231.
15   See Chap 12.
16   Cf *Blackwell v Blackwell* [1929] AC 318 at 341, HL; (M & B) (trust survives); *Re Maddock* [1902] 2 Ch 220 at 231 (trust fails).
17   [1967] 3 All ER 389 at 392.

position[18]. After all, the fraud which the doctrine of secret trusts exists to combat is as much present if a transferee denies the basis on which he has received property inter vivos as it is if a donee under a will does the same.

HALF SECRET TRUSTS

In a secret trust neither the identity of the beneficiary nor the very existence of the trust can be detected from the testator's will. Such a trust is sometimes termed a fully secret trust in order to distinguish it from another creature, the half secret, or semi-secret, trust. Under the latter, T's will will state that the donee, D, is to take the property as trustee, but does not state the name of the beneficiary. For a half secret trust to arise the following conditions must be satisfied:

1. T must communicate to D the fact that he is to hold the property on trust before the will is made.
2. T must communicate to D the identity of B before the will is made[19].
3. D must indicate his acceptance before or at the time the will is made.
4. The will must state that D holds the property as trustee and must indicate that the identity of the beneficiary has been communicated to him (ie before the execution of the will)[20].

It has been suggested that there is no rational basis for the second requirement listed above, and that there is no reason why the communication of the trust at any time before the testator's death should not suffice for half secret trusts[1]. Nevertheless, in *Re Bateman's Will Trusts*[2] in 1970 a half secret trust was invalidated on the ground that this requirement was not met[3].

If the will refers to a specific mode of communication (eg 'whose identity I have communicated to him by letter') and any communication had not been in the form referred to (eg it had been merely oral), then the half secret trust fails[4].

As in the case of a secret trust, the onus of proof is on the beneficiary claiming entitlement under the trust. Evidence is admissible from the trustee as to the identity of the beneficiaries for whom the property is held, but the trustee is not permitted to adduce evidence that the property, or part of it, was intended to pass to himself beneficially. For example, in *Re Rees' Will Trusts*[5], a testator left his residuary estate 'unto my trustees absolutely, they well knowing my wishes concerning the same'. When making the will the

---

18 In *Nichols v IRC* [1973] 3 All ER 632, [1974] 1 WLR 296 counsel conceded that the principle of secret trusts applied to inter vivos dispositions.
19 Communication includes the method (paper in a sealed envelope) used in *Re Keen's Estate* [1937] Ch 236, [1937] 1 All ER 452, CA.
20 *Blackwell v Blackwell* [1929] AC 318, HL; (M & B).
1 See Snell, *Principles of Equity* (28th edn) p 112.
2 [1970] 3 All ER 817, [1970] 1 WLR 1463.
3 For a justification for the existence of the requirement, see B. Perrins [1986] Conv 248, at 252–3.
4 *Johnson v Ball* (1851) 5 De G & Sm 85.
5 [1950] Ch 204, [1949] 2 All ER 1003 following *Re Baillie* (1886) 2 TLR 660. See also *Re Tyler's Fund Trusts* [1967] 3 All ER 389, [1967] 1 WLR 1269.

testator told his trustees that he wished them to make payments to certain people and to retain any surplus for their own use. The trustees sought to show that the gift was conditional, ie a gift to them subject to the condition precedent of their making the payments the testator had specified. It was held that evidence was not admissible to contradict the express imposition of trust on them. Thus the trustees held on a half secret trust for the purposes indicated by the testator. The surplus, being undisposed of, passed to the testator's next of kin.

If B is made a beneficiary under a half secret trust, and the donee pre-deceases the testator, then it seems that the trust is not affected, by reason of the principle that equity will not allow a trust to fail for want of a trustee.

If T wishes to create a half secret trust of land, then it seems that s 53(1)(b) must be complied with[6]. (Since there can be no question of D retaining the property beneficially, the principle that equity will not allow a statute to be used as an instrument of fraud is not available to enable the section to be sidestepped[7].)

Since the will states that D is to take as a trustee, if any condition for a valid half secret trust is not satisfied, D holds the property on a resulting trust for T's estate. He can never take the property beneficially[8].

ARE SECRET AND HALF SECRET TRUSTS EXPRESS OR CONSTRUCTIVE?[9]

There has been discussion over whether secret and half secret trusts are properly to be regarded as forms of express trust, or forms of constructive trust.

In the case of a secret trust it is pointed out that the reason why equity came to enforce a secret trust was that it would have been fraudulent for E to take the property beneficially and, to prevent this fraud, equity imposed trusteeship on him. Since the trust is imposed by equity, the trust, it is argued, is therefore a constructive trust[10]. The fallacy in this line of reasoning, it is suggested, is that it overlooks the fact that originally every form of trust was imposed by equity to avoid fraud. When S conveyed the legal title in property to T expressly on trust for B, equity required T to hold as trustee since it would be fraudulent for him to rely on his legal title and ignore S's intention. But the fact that trusts originated when equity began to require those to whom property had been conveyed expressly on trust to carry out the trust, has never been treated as a reason for saying that all express trusts are therefore constructive trusts. The better view therefore, it is submitted, is that secret trusts are merely one form of express trust[11].

It has been argued also that a half secret trust exists as a constructive trust[12]. This view, however, seems even less convincing than that which regards a fully secret trust as a constructve trust. Since in the case of a half

6   *Re Baillie* (1886) 2 TLR 660, at 661.
7   *Blackwell v Blackwell* [1929] AC 318 at 320, HL.
8   *Johnson v Ball,* supra; *Re Collin Cooper* [1939] Ch 580.
9   [1980] Conv 341 (D. R. Hodge); [1985] Conv 248 at 253 (B. Perrins).
10 Scott, *Trusts* (3rd edn) p i, 55.8; 67 LQR 314, 323 (L. A. Sheridan).
11 D. W. M. Waters, *The Constructive Trust,* pp 57 et seq; A. J. Oakley, *Constructive Trusts,* p 100; Pettit, *Equity and the Law of Trusts* (5th edn), and Snell, *Principles of Equity* (28th edn), place secret trusts under the heading of express trusts.
12 Scott, *Trusts* (3rd edn) p i, 55.8.

secret trust the testator states expressly in his will that D is to hold as a trustee, the only tenable view would appear to be that as between an express and a constructive trust, a half secret trust cannot be anything but an express trust[13].

---

13   D. W. M. Waters, *The Constructive Trust*, pp 57 et seq; A. J. Oakley, *Constructive Trusts*, p 100; (1951) 67 LQR 314, 323 (L. A. Sheridan); Pettit, op cit, p 99. For an alternative view, that the basis of a secret trust rests on an application of the probate doctrine relating to the incorporation of a document into a will by reference to it in the will, see P. Matthews (1979) 43 Conv (NS) 360. Cf D. R. Hodge [1980] Conv 341.

Chapter 5

Choses in action[1]

Introduction: the nature of a chose in action

The next main topic to be considered is the subject of completely and incompletely constituted trusts. In dealing with this topic the reader will meet a form of property termed a 'chose in action'. This chapter is set aside for the purpose of explaining the nature of choses in action, and the means by which they may be assigned.

Let us imagine that a builder, R, who is worried about getting into debt, is assessing his financial position. He says to himself, 'I owe the building society £40,000 for the loan on my house; I have an overdraft at the bank of £30,000; and I owe a finance company £20,000 for the purchase of equipment—my debts amount to £90,000. On the credit side I have £6,000 in shares, plant and equipment worth £14,000, my house and personal effects, say £50,000, and there is £30,000 due from D for the house which I have just completed for him. So, in all, my assets come to £100,000. I am still solvent'. It will be noted that without the inclusion of the £30,000 which R is owed by D, R would be in the red. Clearly it is correct for R to include the £30,000 owed to him by D in reckoning his financial position. But is the debt owed by D correctly regarded as an item of R's *property*—in the same way that his house and his other physical possessions are his property?

In English law for something to constitute property it must have two characteristics: it must be of value, and it must be capable of being assigned. (Not all things which are of value are assignable—a person's salary is of value, but it cannot be assigned[2].) The £30,000 is certainly of value and by means that we shall consider shortly, it is assignable. Thus the debt owed by D to R is an item of R's property. Being intangible, it is of a different nature from those items of R's property that are of a tangible, physical nature, for example his car. And the difference between the character of the two types of property is reflected in a legal difference. In the case of a physical asset, if R is deprived of the asset, for example if his car is stolen, the nature of the asset is such that title to it is capable of legally being asserted by physical means—if R finds the car outside the thief's house he can get in and drive it away. But in the case of the debt owed to him by R, there are no physical means by which R can legally assert his entitlement to receive the money: the

---

1 Snell, *Principles of Equity*, 28th edn, Chap 5; G. H. Treitel, *Law of Contract*, 6th edn, Chap 16; Crossley-Vaines, *Personal Property*, 5th edn, Chap 11; O. R. Marshall, *The Assignment of Choses in Action*.
2 For other instances, see Treitel, *Law of Contract*, 6th edn, p 513.

only legal course open to him is to sue D[3]. Items of property of a physical kind are termed *choses* (the French, 'things') *in possession*, meaning *things* the legal title to which is capable of being asserted by taking physical *possession* of them. Items of property of an intangible kind, such as the debt, are termed *choses in action*, meaning things (ie items of property) the title to which can be asserted only by taking legal *action* in the courts.

A debt (ie the benefit of a debt) is merely one kind of chose in action. There are many others[4]. R may hold the copyright[5] in a book, a play, or a song; or a patent[6] in some new invention; or he may have a right to receive rent[7]. Or R may hold shares in a company[8]. These last will entitle him to a proportion of the assets on the company's dissolution, and to dividends that the company has declared. These rights cannot be enforced by means of taking physical possession of anything, only by taking legal proceedings. The shares, like the copyright and the patent, are therefore choses in action. The same applies in the case of the right to receive a certain sum at a certain age under a contract with an insurance company, ie the benefit of a life insurance policy. And the same applies also with regard to rights conferred by documents of a commercial nature such as bills of lading. All these are choses in action. Finally, it should be noted that a chose in action includes the right to a benefit under a contract[9] other than the right to receive a sum of money[10]. For example, if R contracts with D for the purchase of 1,000 bricks, in D's hands the bricks are choses in possession, but the right to receive the bricks is a chose in action held by R. (R's obligation to pay for them is a chose in action held by D.)

ASSIGNMENT OF CHOSES

How are choses in action assigned? In the case of some types of chose the matter is straightforward: statute lays down the manner (eg the observance of a particular formality) in which a particular type of chose is to be assigned. Thus the Companies Act 1985[11] lays down that for shares to be transferred the owner must execute a share transfer form and send this, with the share certificate, to the company which must amend the register of shareholders by deleting the name of the previous owner and inserting the name of the new one. The Copyright Act 1956[12] provides that copyrights are assignable in writing.

But what of a debt, such as that of £30,000 owed in our example by D to

---

3 A chose in action, not withstanding its intangible nature, is, as an item of property, capable of being stolen within the terms of the Hong Kong 1980 Theft Ordinance. *Chan Man-Sin v The Queen* [1988] 1 WLR 196, PC (accountant who withdrew sums from companies' accounts by forged cheque held to have dishonestly appropriated companies' property and so to have properly been convicted of theft) [1988] Conv 157.

4 For a detailed account, see Halsbury, *Laws of England*, vol 6.

5 *Chaplin v Leslie Frewin (Publishers) Ltd* [1966] Ch 71, [1965] 3 All ER 764, CA.

6 *Re Heath's Patent* (1912) 56 Sol Jo 538.

7 *Knill v Prowse* (1884) 33 WR 163, DC.

8 *Humble v Mitchell* (1839) 11 Ad & El 205, 208.

9 Including rights under a contract of hire purchase. *Spellman v Spellman* [1961] 2 All ER 498, [1961] 1 WLR 921, CA.

10 *Torkington v Magee* [1902] 2 KB 427.

11 Section 183.

12 Section 36(3).

R? How can he transfer the benefit of this to, say E? ie, with the result that
D then owes the money to E, not R; and E (not R) can take steps to recover
the money from D, a transaction that can be visualised like this:

In considering this matter the starting point is to explain that at common
law (we shall explain how equity became involved later) the assignment of a
chose in action was not possible. That is to say, if R purported to transfer
the debt to E, and E attempted to sue D, the courts of common law would
not entertain the action[13]. The only circumstances in which the common law
would assist E were these. (In this chapter, the letter 'D' represents d̲ebtor;
'R' represents transfero̲r; and 'E' represents transfere̲e.)

(1) If R asked D to pay the debt to E, and D agreed to do so, and notified
    E of this fact (if D *acknowledged*[14] that the debt had become payable to
    E), then E could sue D[15].
(2) If D, R, and E entered into a fresh contract under which, in consideration
    from E to D, it was agreed by all three that henceforth the debt is owed
    to E (when *novation* occurs), then E could sue D[16].
(3) If on, or after, a purported assignment of the debt from R to E, R
    authorised E, by a power of attorney[17], to bring an action for the debt
    in his, R's, name, and to retain the money so obtained, then E could
    proceed accordingly.

Only by these indirect means could the common law be employed for the
assignment of choses. The position was clearly unsatisfactory, and there were
strong pressures from the worlds of commerce, banking and industry for

13 The reason was originally due to the common lawyers' difficulty in conceiving the transfer
    of something intangible, together also with the fear that allowing assignment of choses
    might lead to maintenance (a crime and a tort). See *Fitzroy v Cave* [1905] 2 KB 364, 371–
    372, CA. Later more practical grounds for the policy were recognised to exist. Suppose
    that, at a time when it was still possible for a creditor to have a debtor thrown into prison
    for failure to pay a debt, D was considering asking for a loan. Because of the consequence
    of non-payment by him, the character of the creditor was important. 'If I borrow from
    X', D might think, 'and if I am not able to repay on time, X is unlikely to secure my
    immediate imprisonment. I know him well. He won't be too hard. But I wouldn't like to
    be in Z's clutches. He'd get me imprisoned without compunction. No, I'll seek a loan
    from X.' If debts were assignable, the thinking of the common law was, then D could
    borrow from X only to find that shortly afterwards the debt had been transferred, and
    that he now owed the money to the merciless Z.
14 On acknowledgement, see (1959) 75 LQR 220 (J. D. Davies); (1977) 41 Conv (NS) 49 (D.
    Yates).
15 It is uncertain whether consideration is necessary from E to R. See *Shamia v Joory* [1958]
    1 QB 448, [1958] 1 All ER 111 (consideration not required).
16 See *Rasbora Ltd v JCL Marine Ltd* [1977] 1 Lloyd's Rep 645.
17 On powers of attorney, and the circumstances in which they are revocable, and those in
    which they are revoked, see Powers of Attorney Act 1971; Enduring Powers of Attorney
    Act 1985; S. Cretney, *Enduring Powers of Attorney* (1985); Treitel, *Law of Contract* (6th
    edn), p 564.

choses to be fully assignable at common law. To place matters on a rational footing the legislature intervened. The change was made in the Judicature Act 1873[18]. The relevant provision was replaced by s 136 of the Law of Property Act 1925.

Legal choses

LEGAL ASSIGNMENT

Section 136 enacts that a chose in action may be assigned on three conditions being satisfied. But even if the conditions are satisfied, no assignment will occur if the terms of the contract between D and R expressly or implied preclude an assignment[19].

The conditions are these:

1. The assignment must be in writing, signed by the assignor or by his agent 'thereunto lawfully authorised'. (No particular form of wording is required; and a deed need not be used. But the signature of an agent is not sufficient.)
2. The assignment must be 'absolute'. This has two meanings. (a) R must assign to E the whole of the debt owed to him by D, (not merely part of it)[20]. (b) The assignment to E must not be by way of 'charge'[1], ie by way of security for a loan from E to R[2].
3. Notice in writing must be given to the debtor (D)[3]. The Act does not state that the notice must be given by the assignee, E. So, the notice could be given by R. (It may happen that—and it will be sufficient if—the notice received by D takes the form of a claim by E for payment of the debt.)

The assignment occurs not when R executes the written assignment to E, but at the moment when D receives notice of the assignment. (Thus it may be that the assignment takes place after the death of the assignor[4].)

Suppose that R assigns a debt owed to him by D to E. E then wishes to assign the chose to F, and F wishes to assign the chose to G, like this:

D

R→E→F→G

In this situation, in order that the assignments should be effective under s 136,

18 Section 25(6).
19 [1979] Conv 133 (D. M. Kloss).
20 *Forster v Baker* [1910] 2 KB 636, CA.
1 *Durham Bros v Robertson* [1898] 1 QB 765, CA; *Bank of Liverpool and Martins Ltd v Holland* (1926) 43 TLR 29; cf *Fitzroy v Cave* [1905] 2 KB 364, CA.
2 Eg, under an arrangement by which E lent R money and as security R charged the chose to E (with the effect that if R failed to repay the loan, E would have a first charge on the chose and could require R to transfer it to him. However, where, as security for a loan from E to R, R transfers the chose to E subject to an agreement that on repayment of the loan, E will transfer the chose back to R, ie where R mortgages the chose to E, the assignment will be absolute and therefore within the section). *Tancred v Delagoa Bay and East Africa Rly Co* (1889) 23 QBD 239, DC.
3 *Holt v Heatherfield Trust Ltd* [1942] 2 KB 1, [1942] 1 All ER 404.
4 *Re Westerton* [1919] 2 Ch 104.

notice to D must be given on the occasion of each assignment. If, when G claims the money from D, it is found that either E or F had failed to give notice, then the requirements of the section are not complied with and no assignment under the section takes place. (If E but not F had given notice to D, then the assignment to E would be effective under s 136, but not the two subsequent assignments.)

If the requirements of s 136 are complied with at each step in the chain of assignments, then if D fails to pay G, and G sues him, G is able to do so in his own name. He is not required to bring R, E or F into the proceedings. (There will be no need for him to do so. Evidence of the assignments will be provided by the earlier written assignments, which G will produce to the court.)

The assignment we have been considering has been of a debt owed by D to R. It may be however that D disputes his liability to R. D may claim, for example, that (1) the debt is statute barred[5] (more than six years having elapsed since the debt was incurred and no claim having been made in the meantime); or (2) that the contract under which the debt arose is voidable as a result of undue influence or misrepresentation, or is void as a result of duress; or (3) that R owes him, D, money (under some transaction other than the contract that gives rise to the debt assigned) and that D is entitled to set this off against the sum he owes to R (that he has a right of *set-off*). If D is in a position to raise one (or more) of these defences against R, it is only right that he should be able to raise the same defences in the event of a claim for the money from E after an assignment to him of the debt by R. Otherwise the assignee of a chose would obtain a stronger title than the assignor. Thus E takes subject to the same defences (referred to, confusingly and misleadingly, in s 136 as 'equities'[6]) that would have been available to D in an action brought against him by R[7]. On the assignment by R, E, we say, 'takes subject to equities'. He does so irrespective of whether or not he knew of their existence at the time of the assignment[8].

There is no requirement that, for a valid assignment under s 136 to take place, consideration must move from E to R[9].

Note that the item of property which we have been dealing with, the debt owed by D to R, was a debt which R could have enforced at common law. The chose in action held by R was thus a *legal* chose, and since the provisions of statutes take effect in law (as opposed to taking effect in equity), we can say that s 136 provides for the assignment of a *legal* chose by *legal* means.

EQUITABLE ASSIGNMENT

The legal assignment of legal choses became possible (ie without the need for recourse to the devices noted above) after 1873. Long before this, however, equity—in keeping with its tradition of flexibility—had been prepared to recognise the assignment of legal choses[10]. That is to say, legal choses could

---

5   Under the Limitation Act 1980, s 5.
6   Which are nothing to do with equity, or any equitable principles.
7   *Ord v White* (1840) 3 Beav 357.
8   *Athenaeum Life Assurance Society v Pooley* (1858) 3 De G & J 294.
9   *Walker v Bradford Old Bank Ltd* (1884) 12 QBD 511, DC.
10   *Crouch v Martin and Harris* (1707) 2 Vern 595; *Ryall v Rowles* (1749) 1 Ves Sen 349; *Re Row, ex p South* (1818) 3 Swan 392.

be assigned in equity, ie when R assigned the legal chose to E, and E sued D, equity would entertain the action, and, if satisfied that the chose had been intended to be transferred to E, would give E a remedy against D. Equity achieved this by enabling R to use proceedings at common law. What happened was this: E went to the Chancellor's court and produced evidence of the debt owed by D to R, and of the assignment of the debt by R to E. The court did not require that the assignment must have been in writing (nor that it had been absolute). All that equity required was to be satisfied that R had *intended* that the debt should be assigned to E. On being satisfied on this score the court granted E an injunction restraining R from objecting to E bringing an action in his, R's, name against D. Armed with this injunction, E crossed Westminster Hall and commenced proceedings in a court of common law (usually the court of Common Pleas), in R's name, against D. On E, under the name of R, satisfying the court as to the debt owed by D, judgment was entered by the court in favour of 'R', and D was thereby compelled to pay 'R'. All the way through, E's injunction prevented the real R from intervening (or claiming the money when judgment was entered in his, R's, name)[11].

Today it is no longer necessary for E to commence two sets of proceedings, one in equity and then one at common law. Instead, E commences proceedings in his own name directly against D. However, since the court needs proof of R's intention with regard to the assignment, E must join R as a party to the proceedings, so bringing R into the action, and enabling the court to hear what R has to say. If R agrees that he intended to assign the chose to E, E joins him as a co-plaintiff (and the action is therefore E and R v D); if R denies intending to assign the chose, E joins him as a co-defendant (and the action is E v R and D).

Originally equity would only assist E (by granting the injunction that enabled him to bring proceedings at common law) if E had given consideration to R for the assignment to him of the chose. (It was the injustice that would be done to E if, having given consideration for the assignment, he had no remedy, that was the ground on which equity first came to assist E.) By early in the last century, however, equity began to uphold assignments of legal choses without consideration having been given by E[12]. All that equity came to require was (and all that equity still requires is[13]) proof of *intention* by R to assign the chose to E. But equity dispensed with consideration from E only if it was shown that R intended to make an immediate, outright, assignment to E. If it were shown that R had intended to assign the chose at some future time, then equity would only assist E on proof of consideration from him to R. The position is unchanged today: if R *assigns* the chose, no consideration from E is required[14]; if R *promises* that he will assign the chose, E must have provided consideration for the promise if equity is to assist him[15].

The usefulness of a legal chose being capable of being assigned in equity will be appreciated. Suppose that when R assigned the chose to E, he did so

---

11 Equity compelled E to indemnify R in the event of the action by 'R' failing, costs being awarded against the plaintiff, and the real R having to pay these.
12 *Ex p Pye* (1811) 18 Ves 140; *Fortescue v Barnett* (1834) 3 My & K 36.
13 *Palmer v Carey* [1926] AC 703, PC.
14 *Walker v Bradford Old Bank Ltd* (1884) 12 QBD 511, DC.
15 *Re McArdle* [1951] Ch 669, [1951] 1 All ER 905, CA.

orally, then the assignment, not being in writing, cannot take place at common law (under s 136) but can take place in equity. Or suppose that D owes R £2,000. R wishes to assign £1,500 out of the debt to E (perhaps in payment of a debt that he, R, owes to E). He cannot make a legal assignment, as the assignment is not absolute (and so outside s 136), but the assignment can take place in equity. Or suppose that there is a chain of assignments, as considered earlier, to E, to F, to G, and suppose that E or F failed to give notice to D. There will be no assignment to G at common law. But if it is shown that R, E and F each intended to assign the chose, then an assignment in equity takes place, and G can bring proceedings against D[16].

In the light of the advantages of an assignment in equity, is there any advantage, it might be asked, in making a legal assignment under s 136? The advantage is procedural, but may be crucial. Suppose that there is a chain of assignments as before, from R, through E, and F, to G. If G is to bring an action against D in equity (because at some stage s 136 has not been complied with), he must join R, E and F as parties to the proceedings, as co-plaintiffs or co-defendants as the case may be, as explained above. But what hope will G have of succeeding, in practice, if he finds that R has gone to live in New Zealand; E is a limited company that has been wound up; and F declines to answer letters? Not much. If the assignments along the chain had all taken place at law (by complying at each step with s 136) G would have no problem: he could commence proceedings immediately, in his own name alone.

We have said that the only requirement for a valid equitable assignment of a legal chose is proof that the assignor intended[17] to make the assignment. Thus it follows that there is no requirement that for an equitable assignment to be made, notice of the assignment must be given to the debtor. There are, however, a number of reasons why it is in the assignee's interest[18] that notice of the assignment should be given to the debtor. What these reasons are we shall consider shortly.

Assignment of equitable choses

If a settlor transfers property to a trustee on trust for a beneficiary, B, then B acquires an equitable interest in the property. The beneficiary is able to enforce his rights under the trust against the trustee before the courts. He has no right to assert his equitable title by taking physical possession of any property. He can do so only by taking action against the trustee before the courts. Thus a beneficiary's interest under a trust is a chose in action. Since his interest is equitable, he holds an equitable chose in action. (The right of a beneficiary under a will to have estate duty administered by the personal representative is a form of equitable chose in action[19].)

---

16 *Holt v Heatherfield Trust Ltd* [1942] 2 KB 1, [1942] 1 All ER 404.
17 'The language is immaterial if the meaning is plain.' Per Lord Macnaghten, *William Brandt's Sons & Co v Dunlop Rubber Co* [1905] AC 454 at 462, HL.
18 Where R and D are in dispute over a debt claimed by R from D, and R and D submit to arbitration, and R then transfers the debt to E by an equitable assignment, E must give notice to D of the assignment and submit to the jurisdiction of the arbitrator before he can become a party to the arbitration proceedings. *Baytur SA v Finagro Holdings SA* [1991] 4 All ER 129, CA.
19 *Deeks v Strutt* (1794) 5 Term Rep 690. See [1992] Conv 92 (J. K. Maxton).

From early times equity has permitted a beneficiary under a trust to assign his equitable interest to another. (And provided that a beneficiary's interest is vested, and is not determinable at his death, an equitable interest, eg an equitable interest in remainder, will pass under the beneficiary's will or intestacy.) Originally no particular formality was required for the assignment of an equitable interest. The Statute of Frauds 1677 introduced the require-ment that, for an assignment of an equitable interest to be valid, it must be in writing and signed by the assignor. The requirement is now contained in s 53(1)(c) of the Law of Property Act 1925. It should be noted that under this section *any* assignment (of whatever kind) of *any* equitable interest (for whatever reason the interest is equitable) in *any* form of property (whether realty or personalty, and in the latter case, whether a chose in possession or a chose in action) must be *in* writing (and not merely evidenced by writing[20]), and signed by the assignor.

We have used the interest of a beneficiary under a trust as an instance of an equitable interest. There is another way, which concerns us directly, in which an interest may be equitable, with the result that an assignment of the interest must comply with s 53(1)(c). Suppose that R is owed £1,000 by D. R holds a chose in action. It is a legal chose (because it is enforceable by R against D at common law—and there is nothing about the matter—no trust— to make it equitable). R assigns part of the debt, £700, to E. The assignment cannot come within s 136. The assignment operates in equity only. The nature of the chose held by E (the right to claim £700 from D) now takes on the colour of the assignment. Thus the chose that E holds is equitable. This need cause a student of land law no surprise. If A holds the legal fee simple in Blackacre, and he purports to assign his interest to B, but fails to use a deed, then, provided there is consideration from B, under the doctrine in *Walsh v Lonsdale*, equity recognises the transfer, and B obtains an equitable fee simple. The assignment of a legal chose in action outside s 136 occurs in an analogous manner (but with the important difference, it will be noted, that for the assignment of a legal chose in equity, consideration is not needed from E.)

Since, if R transfers a legal chose to E in equity, the chose held by E is an equitable chose, it follows that if E is to assign the chose to F, then E can only make the assignment by complying with s 53(1)(c) (ie by making the assignment in writing).

Where R transfers an equitable chose to E, and the assignment is of the whole of R's interest, E can bring an action against the trustees in his own name alone[1]. Where R retains some interest in the chose (eg if only part of the value of the chose is assigned) E must join R as a party to the action (as co-plaintiff if R is willing, as co-defendant if he is unwilling).

Desirability of notice

Section 53(1)(c) does not stipulate that notice of the assignment must be given to D. It is, however, in E's interests that notice to D should be given. The reasons for this are the same as the reasons why it is in the interests of

---

20 As under s 53(1)(b). See p 37.
1 *Cator v Croydon Canal Co* (1841) 4 Y & C Ex 405.

the assignee of a legal chose that (as mentioned earlier) notice should be given to a debtor. The reasons are as follows:

1. If the debtor (in the case of an equitable assignment of a legal chose) or the trustees (in the case of an assignment of an equitable chose) pay the assignor (ie the creditor or the beneficiary, as the case may be) without having received notice of the assignment, they get a good discharge, ie they need not pay the assignee over again[2]. (What is the assignee's position in this case? If he gave consideration, he can sue the assignor for breach of contract; if he gave no consideration, he has no remedy.)

2. The assignee takes subject not only to equities[3] existing at the time of the assignment, but also to any equities (eg the expiry of the limitation period) that arise between the time of the assignment and the time that notice was given to the debtor or the trustees, as the case may be, but not to equities that arise after that time.

3. Suppose that a beneficiary (R) assigns his equitable interest in Blackacre to E_1 for, say, £5,000. R then (deciding that this is an easy way to make money) assigns the same interest to E_2, this time for, say, £6,000. For whom do the trustees hold Blackacre—E_1 or E_2? The same question arises where the holder of a legal chose makes successive equitable assignments of the chose—to E_1 and to E_2. To whom must the debtor pay the money, E_1 or E_2? The answer is that in the case of such successive assignments, priority follows the order that notice[4] was received by the trustees, or the debtor, as the case may be. As regards the successive assignments of equitable interests this is the rule[5] in *Dearle v Hall*[6]. The priority of successive assignments of a legal chose is governed by a corresponding rule: priority follows the order that notice is given to the debtor[7].

Thus suppose that a beneficiary assigns his interest in Blackacre successively to E_1 and to E_2. E_2 gives notice of the assignment to the trustees. The trustees hold Blackacre on trust for E_2. The assignment to E_1 was not in itself defective for want of notice to the trustees; but by reason of E_1's failure to give notice to the trustees before E_2 did so, he loses priority to E_2, with the result that the assignment to him becomes a nullity. (Whether in this case he has any remedy against the beneficiary depends on whether or not he gave consideration for the assignment.)

However, a subsequent assignee cannot obtain priority by giving notice to the trustees (or the debtor) if he had notice, actual or constructive, of the prior assignment at the time of the assignment to him. (But if E_2 learns of the assignment to E_1 after the assignment to him, then there is nothing to prevent him gaining priority over E_1 by getting in his notice first.)

---

2 *Jones v Farrell* (1857) 1 De G & J 208; *Brice v Bannister* (1878) 3 QBD 569, CA.
3 See p 64.
4 To protect an assignee's priority, notice to the trustees must be in writing. LPA 1925, s 137(3).
5 Students of land law will recall that it is the rule in *Dearle v Hall* that governs priority in the case of successive mortgages of an equitable interest in land.
6 (1823–28) 3 Russ 1. See *Ellerman Lines Ltd v Lancaster Maritime Co Ltd, The Lancaster* [1980] 2 Lloyd's Rep 497, 503; *Pfeiffer Weinkellerie-Weineinkauf GmbH & Co v Arbuthnot Factors Ltd* [1988] 1 WLR 150; *Rhodes v Allied Dunbar Pension Services Ltd* [1988] 1 All ER 524, [1987] 1 WLR 1703. (Successive assignments, first equitable, second statutory under s 6 of Law of Distress Amendment Act 1908. First in time prevailed.)
7 *Marchant v Morton, Down & Co Ltd* [1901] 2 KB 829.

For all these reasons it will be appreciated that the moral with regard to the giving of notice is—hurry.

We have been speaking of successive assignments, first to E_1 and then to E_2. The term successive assignments as used here should be distinguished from the entirely different meaning of the term when it is used to refer to a chain of assignments—from R to E, from E to F, from F to G, and so on. In the case of a chain of assignments of a legal chose, notice may be relevant, not as regards determining any question of priority, but as regards determining whether s 136 is complied with (and thus whether the assignment is a *legal* assignment).

Expectancies

We have learned that a chose in action is a form of property. It is something in which the owner has an interest, *now*. If a person may, possibly, acquire an interest in something, at some date in the future, he cannot be regarded as having any interest, any proprietary interest, whatsoever. For example, T makes a will leaving Blackacre to his friend, A. A has no interest in Blackacre. T may revoke his will and leave Blackacre to B (or revoke the will and be content to die intestate so that the land passes to his next of kin). A has no more than a hope that T will leave his will unchanged. In such a case, A is said to have an *expectancy*. Or if A is the object of a power of appointment with the result that, whilst he has no property now, if the power is exercised in his favour he will do so, then A, as an object of the power, has an expectancy[8]. Or suppose that A holds shares in a company that may or may not declare a dividend at the coming year end. A's present right to receive a dividend, if one is declared, is a chose in action which can be assigned[9]. But if he purports to assign a dividend that has not yet been declared, he will be seeking to assign what is no more than an expectancy[10].

The word 'expectancy' is used in the older sense, the sense in which the word appears in the title *Great Expectations*, 'expectations' indicating 'prospects', a word which, when used by itself, is, of course, neutral.

The term 'after-acquired property' is used to refer to any property which a person may receive (by gift or by will) at a future date. An expectancy is thus a specific form of after-acquired property. The term 'future property' is a generic term which covers both expectancies and after-acquired property. Care should be taken to distinguish between future property (which is not property) and a future interest[11] (which is).

The question that now arises for consideration is—can future property be assigned? For example, suppose that T has made a will leaving Greenacre to his son, R. T is still living. R purports to assign the expectancy under his father's will to E. What is the effect of this? The answer is none: the assignment is void, and this is so even if the assignment was by deed[12]. Neither in equity

---

8 *Re Brooks* [1939] Ch 993, [1939] 3 All ER 920.
9 *Shepherd v Federal Taxation Comr* (1965) 113 CLR 385, [1966] ALR 969 (Aust HC).
10 *Norman v Federal Comr of Taxation* (1963) 109 CLR 9 (Aust HC).
11 Eg an interest in remainder.
12 *Meek v Kettlewell* (1842) 1 Hare 464; *Re Ellenborough* [1903] 1 Ch 697; (M & B); *Norman v Federal Comr of Taxation* (1963) 109 CLR 9; (M & B).

nor at common law[13] can an expectancy be assigned, and what we say of expectancies applies to any future property. The reason is that '... to make a grant or assignment valid the thing which is the subject of it must have an existence ... at the time of such grant or assignment ...'[14] and an expectancy has no such existence; and '... what may not be owned may not be effectively assigned.'[15] However, the transaction may not be without effect. If E gave consideration to R for the purported assignment, then equity will treat the transaction, not as a present assignment, but as a contract[16] by R that if he receives Greenacre under his father's will, he will transfer the land to E[17]. If R receives the property and declines to convey it to E then E may obtain a decree of specific performance to compel R to transfer the property to him. Further, from the moment of R's receipt of the property, he holds it on trust for E who therefore has an equitable interest in it.

Instead of a purported assignment of an expectancy, there may be a promise to assign it. For example, R may promise that if he is devised Blackacre by his father, he will transfer the land to E. Here, be it noted, there is not a (purported) immediate assignment, but a promise that if R receives Blackacre he *will* transfer it to E. Here the ordinary rules of contract come into play. If E gave no consideration, R's promise has no effect. (If R receives Blackacre, he can keep it.) If R's promise was made for consideration from E, then equity will compel R to abide by his promise: the promise is specifically enforceable. Further, if R receives Blackacre, from the moment of receipt he holds it on trust for E. If the promise was not for consideration, but was under seal (ie if R covenanted to transfer the land if he received it) then although equity will not enforce the covenant, at common law E is entitled to damages from R for his breach of the covenant by failing to convey the land to E[18]. We shall see that this last point is important in a matter to be discussed in the chapter that follows.

13   *Holroyd v Marshall* (1862) 10 HL Cas 191, 220.
14   Per Lord Ellenborough CJ, *Robinson v Macdonnell* (1816) 5 M & S 228, 236.
15   Per Turner J, *Williams v IRC* [1965] NZLR 395; (M & B); (1965) ASCL 328 (J. D. Davies).
16   *Re Burton's Settlements* [1955] Ch 82, [1954] All ER 193.
17   *Holroyd v Marshall* (1862) 10 HL Cas 191, 220; *Re Tilt* (1896) 74 LT 163.
18   *Cannon v Hartley* [1949] Ch 213, [1949] 1 All ER 50.

Chapter 6

Completely and incompletely constituted trusts

Introduction

The territory that we now enter overlaps the boundaries of the law of trusts, of choses in action, of contract and of gifts. The main principles that are of relevance in the latter two fields are as follows:

1. Where A agrees to confer a benefit on B, the arrangement becomes a valid contract, enforceable at common law by B against A, only where either (i) B provides consideration; or (ii) the contract is by deed, ie is under A's seal. (Where a person contracts under seal he is said to *covenant*.)

2. Where A covenants that he will transfer property to B and declines to observe the covenant then (i) if B provided consideration, he can proceed against A at common law and recover damages for the breach; or he can seek from equity a decree of specific performance requiring A to transfer the property to him (provided that the covenant is not one in respect of which equity regards specific performance as not being appropriate, for example, and in particular, a covenant to pay a certain sum of money[1]— for a breach of which the only remedy is an action at common law[2]); (ii) if B provided no consideration (if B is a *volunteer*), equity will not grant him the remedy of specific performance (the contract is not *specifically enforceable*) since equity will not aid a volunteer; but he can fall back on his right to sue at common law for damages for breach of contract, and recover damages equivalent to the value of the property.

3. For A to make a gift of property to B (ie so that the title moves from A to B) then either (i) (a) A must transfer the property to B[3]. How this must be done depends on the type of property concerned, eg a legal title in land to which the title is unregistered must be conveyed by deed, land to which the title is registered can be conveyed only by the execution of transfer, which must be passed, with the land certificate, to the transferee,[4] a chattel can be transferred only by physical delivery[5]; and (b) A must make the transfer to B with the intention of making an irrevocable gift (and not with any other intention, eg that of making a loan), or (except where, as in the case of registered land, execution of a deed is not sufficient to

---

1 If a covenant is to transfer a specific *fund* of money, specific performance may be granted. *Pullan v Koe* [1913] 1 Ch 9.
2 *Stone v Stone* (1869) 5 Ch App 74.
3 *Cochrane v Moore* (1890) 25 QBD 57, CA; *Dewar v Dewar* [1975] 2 All ER 728, [1975] 1 WLR 1532.
4 *Mascall v Mascall* (1984) 50 P & CR 119, CA.
5 Or, in some instances by an act that symbolises physical delivery, eg the delivery of a key to a safe may constitute delivery of the contents of the safe.

transfer a legal title) (ii) A must execute a deed ('a deed of gift') that conveys the title in the property expressly by way of a gift to B[6].

Completely and incompletely constituted trusts

A trust is 'completely constituted' when the settlor has done all in his power (according to the nature of the property concerned) to vest the trust property in the person or persons who are to hold it as trustee or trustees. In Chapter 4 we saw that a trust is created either by a transfer of trust property to trustees or by the settlor declaring himself trustee of property which hitherto he had held as beneficial owner. Thus a trust becomes completely constituted *either* by a valid transfer by S to trustees, *or* by a valid declaration of trust by S. Until this time is reached the trust is incompletely constituted.

It follows that a trust becomes completely constituted when the appropriate formality has been observed by S, either to declare himself trustee or to transfer the property to trustees. Thus, in the case of a transfer to trustees, if the trust property is land the title to which is unregistered, the trust is completely constituted when S has sealed, signed and delivered the deed of conveyance which vests the legal estate in T_1 and T_2. If the trust property is land the title to which is registered, the trust is completely constituted when S has signed a transfer and passed this with the Land Certificate to T_1 and T_2.[7] If the trust property is a chose in possession (ie an item of personalty capable of transfer by delivery, eg a pen, a horse, a ship) then the trust is completely constituted when S has either delivered the item to T, or executed a deed of gift[8] in his favour. (A deed of gift vests the title in the transferee notwithstanding that the property has not left the possession of the donor.) If the property consists of an equitable interest, then S must assign the interest to the trustees under s 53(1)(c)[9] of the Law of Property Act 1925[10]. (If the trustees have no specific functions to perform they will 'drop-out'[11].)

Consider the position if the trust property consists of shares[12]. S executes a share transfer form and posts it to the company. Until the company has received the form and entered the names of T_1 and T_2 in the register in place of S, the title to the shares remains in S. When does the trust become completely constituted? When S signs the form, or when the company registers T_1 and T_2 as owners of the shares? The answer is at neither of these times. The trust becomes completely constituted when S has signed *and posted* the form (together with the share certificate)[13], for at that moment S has done

---

6 If the gift is of an equitable interest, the gift is effective if the instrument is merely in writing (and not by deed). LPA 1925, s 53(1)(c). See p 40.
7 See *Mascall v Mascall* (1984) 50 P & CR 119, CA.
8 *Re Cole* [1964] Ch 175, [1963] 3 All ER 433, CA; *Thomas v Times Book Co Ltd* [1966] 2 All ER 241, [1966] 1 WLR 911.
9 See p 40, ante.
10 *Kekewich v Manning* (1851) 1 De GM & G 176; *Gilbert v Overton* (1864) 22 Hem & M 110.
11 See p 43, ante.
12 As in *Milroy v Lord* (1862) 4 De GF & J 264; (M & B).
13 Or handed the executed transfer form and share certificate to the trustees. *Re Rose* [1952] Ch 499, [1952] 1 All ER 1217, CA; (M & B). Irregularities in the transfer relating to minor matters of detail will not prevent the trust from being treated as completely constituted. *Re Paradise Motor Co Ltd* [1968] 2 All ER 625, [1968] 1 WLR 1125, CA.

all in his power to vest the trust property in the trustees[14]. Pending the registration of the trustees as owners of the shares, S holds the legal title to the shares on the trusts that he has declared.[15]

If a settlor transfers property to a trustee, but the trustee disclaims the trusteeship[16] the trust is nevertheless completely constituted, since the transfer (which is effective until the time of disclaimer) has taken place. When the trustee disclaims, the property revests by operation of law in the settlor who holds the property on the trusts that he has declared[17]. Where a settlor has completed the necessary formalities to effect the transfer of the property, but the trustees are dead at the date of the transfer (or have ceased to exist, eg by the winding up of a company), or are not sufficiently identified, then the trust is incompletely constituted.

Where a settlor declares himself a trustee (ie as opposed to transferring the property to trustees) then in the case of land or any interest in land, the trust will become completely constituted when the settlor complies with the formality required for a declaration of trust of such property, namely that the declaration is 'manifested or proved by some writing' signed by the settlor, as required by s 53(1)(b) of the Law of Property Act 1925. No particular formality is required for a declaration of trust of any other form of property, and the declaration can therefore be merely oral.

There is no requirement that, for a trust to be completely constituted, the beneficiaries must be aware of the creation of the trust[18].

Why does it matter whether a trust is completely or incompletely constituted? The principal reason (with one important exception we shall be meeting shortly) is that if a trust is incompletely constituted, the settlor need not complete it[19]. As long as the trust is incompletely constituted it is not too late for the settlor to change his mind, draw back, and decline to transfer the property to the trustees (or to make a declaration of trust). Once the trust is completely constituted it is too late for the settlor to seek to recover the beneficial interest in the property for himself[20].

Two important consequences follow. (1) Suppose that S takes some step to create a trust and then goes bankrupt. If the step was sufficient to completely constitute the trust[1], then the property belongs beneficially to the beneficiaries under the trust[2]; if it was not, the property will be held by S's trustee in bankruptcy and will be available for distribution to S's creditors. (2) Suppose that S takes some step to create a trust and then dies leaving all his property to X. If the step was sufficient to completely constitute the trust, the property

---

14 *Re Rose* [1949] Ch 78, [1948] 2 All ER 971; cf *Re Fry* [1946] Ch 312, [1946] 2 All ER 106 (would-be transferor of shares, resident abroad, executed share transfer, but had not obtained, as was necessary for the transfer, consent from the Treasury). See L. McKay, 'Share Transfers and the Completely Perfect Rule', (1976) 40 Conv (NS) 139.

15 *Re Rose* [1952] Ch 499, [1952] 1 All ER 1217, CA. *Mascall v Mascall* (1984) 50 P & CR 119, CA.

16 See pp 237, post.

17 *Mallott v Wilson* [1903] 2 Ch 494. But see [1981] Conv 141 (P. Matthews).

18 *Middleton v Pollock, ex p Elliott* (1876) 2 Ch D 104; (M & B); *Standing v Bowring* (1885) 31 Ch D 282, CA.

19 *Jefferys v Jefferys* (1841) Cr & Ph 138; *Re Bowden* [1936] Ch 71.

20 *Paul v Paul* (1880) 15 Ch D 580; on appeal (1882) 20 Ch D 742.

1 And provided that the creation of the trust was not void as being to defraud creditors. See p 49.

2 As in *Middleton v Pollock, ex p Elliott* (1876) 2 Ch D 104; (M & B).

belongs beneficially to the beneficiaries under the trust;[3] if it was not, the property would pass under S's will to X (if S died intestate, it would pass to his next of kin).

Gifts

If a donor, R, intends to make a gift to a donee, E, then, as noted above, for the gift to be complete or, as we say, *perfect*, (1) R must transfer the property to E; and (2) R must do so with the intention of making a gift.

Thus if R passes some article to E, 1 above is satisfied. But if it is shown that R intended a loan not a gift, 2 above is not satisfied and E will hold the article as bailee for R. If R promises to make E a gift of say, a pen, on the following day, but overnight he changes his mind, and the next day declines to hand over the pen, since 1 above is not satisfied, the gift is *imperfect*. E cannot[4] compel R to hand over the pen since '... there is no equity ... to perfect an imperfect gift'.[5]

An imperfect gift thus bears a close resemblance to an incompletely constituted trust: in the former the donor need not hand over the property to the person who hoped to be donee; in the latter, the settlor need not transfer the property to the trustees (or constitute himself trustee). (Further, the consequences with regard to bankruptcy and death explained above in connection with the creation of trusts follow equally in the case of gifts.)

Now, suppose, in the above example, that R had taken hold of his pen and said to E, 'I give you this pen. From now on it is yours', and that R had then put it back in his pocket. The gift is imperfect and E cannot compel R to hand over the pen.[6] On the other hand, suppose that R had said to E 'From now on I am holding this pen as trustee, on trust for you', and then put the pen back in his pocket. In this case R would have made a valid declaration of trust and would have constituted himself trustee of the pen for E. If E were of full age he could require R to hand over the pen to him.[7] Thus where property has not been delivered, this fact will invalidate[8] a gift, but not a declaration of trust. Would-be donees of property who have not received delivery of the property may therefore seek to show that the imperfect gift was a valid declaration of trust. But the courts are on their guard against attempts to construe an imperfect gift as a perfect declaration of trust, and a heavy burden of proof rests on any would-be beneficiary seeking to establish such a construction.[9]

---

3   As in *Re Rose* [1949] Ch 78, [1948] 2 All ER 971.
4   *Richards v Delbridge* (1874) LR 18 Eq 11; *Antrobus v Smith* (1805) 12 Ves 39; *Jones v Lock* (1865) 1 Ch App 25; (M & B).
5   Per Turner LJ, *Milroy v Lord* (1862) 4 De GF & J 264, 274.
6   *Jones v Lock* (1865) 1 Ch App 25; (M & B).
7   Under the rule in *Saunders v Vautier* (1841) 4 Beav 115.
8   Except in a few situations where 'constructive delivery' occurs. See Crossley–Vaines, *Personal Property* (5th edn) pp 307–310.
9   *Milroy v Lord* (1862) 4 De GF & J 264, 275; *Richards v Delbridge* (1874) LR 18 Eq 11; (M & B).

Consideration

Let us revert to the example where R promised to let E have the pen the following day, and then changed his mind. What would be the position if E had given consideration to R for his promise of the pen? This circumstance would convert the transaction from that of an (imperfect) gift to that of a valid contract. For example, suppose that R had promised to let E have the pen in return for a promise by E to let R have £10 for it. If, the next day, R had declined to hand over the pen, it would be open to E to apply to the court for a decree of specific performance compelling R to carry out his side of what had in fact been a contract, even if the word 'contract' had not been used.

The same principle operates in the sphere of trusts. Suppose that in return for some promise by B, S undertakes that he will convey certain property to T_1 and T_2 on specified trusts for B. S later declines to transfer the property to T_1 and T_2. The trust is incompletely constituted. But notwithstanding this fact, since there is consideration from B, equity will compel S to carry out his undertaking and transfer the property to the trustees: we say, the trust 'can be enforced' against S. Equity treats the undertaking by S and the consideration by B as constituting a contract, and will see that S carries it out.

Further, not only will equity compel S to transfer the property to the trustee, it will also (acting under the maxim 'Equity regards as done that which ought to be done'[10]) constitute S trustee of the property pending the transfer to the trustees.[11] Thus the trust is, in this respect, as good as completely constituted from the moment of the promise; from that moment equity compels S to hold the property on trust for B. The consequences explained above with regard to S's bankruptcy, or his death, therefore follow (ie the property belongs beneficially to B, and in the event of S's bankruptcy, the property is not available for S's creditors, and in the event of S's death, the property does not pass under his will or intestacy). Further, since from the moment of the promise, S holds the property on trust for B, if S disposes of the property to P, then unless P can show that he is a bona fide purchaser of the legal estate without notice of the circumstances that have rendered S a trustee of the property for B, he holds the property on trust for B. These consequences, with regard to the obligation to transfer the property to the trustees, S's bankruptcy, S's death, and S's disposition of the property to some other person, all follow from the fact that the trust is enforceable in equity against S.

The reasoning that leads equity to treat the trust as being enforceable harks back to that which lies behind the decision in *Walsh v Lonsdale*.[12] Since consideration was given, S would have been able to seek a decree of specific performance compelling S to convey the property to the trustees and to hold it in the meantime as a trustee; such a decree ought to be granted; equity looks upon that which ought to be done as having been done; therefore equity treats S as trustee from the moment of the covenant. But a reservation must be made. The chain of reasoning only follows through if a decree of

---

10 *Smith v Lucas* (1881) 18 Ch D 531; *Collyer v Isaacs* (1881) 19 Ch D 342, CA.
11 *Pullan v Koe* [1913] 1 Ch 9; (M & B).
12 (1882) 21 Ch D 9, CA.

specific performance ought to be granted. We noted earlier[13] that equity does not regard as appropriate a decree of specific performance of a contract to pay a specific sum of money. Thus if S covenants to pay £1,000 to trustees on trust for B, who gave consideration, S does not become trustee of £1,000 of his money to B. The only remedy against S in this case is an action by the trustees at common law for damages[14]. In such a case it may be that damages may provide the same result as a decree of specific performance (ie £1,000 in the trustees' hands, held for B) but we must remember the disadvantages of an action at common law in the event of S's bankruptcy, or death, or the lapse of a period of time before the commencement of the action.

For a trust to be enforceable against S due to consideration having been given for S's promise, the consideration must be valuable consideration, ie consideration which has some value in the eyes of the law, such as money or a promise of marriage.

MARRIAGE CONSIDERATION

When S undertakes to settle property on B (and perhaps on any children of the marriage) in consideration of B's promise to marry him, we speak of this as an ante-nuptial settlement. As part of the settlement, B, for his or her part, may undertake to settle property on S in consideration of S's promise of marriage. Such an arrangement would provide a means for S and B to share their property during their lifetimes, and to provide for their property to pass to their children on their death.

Suppose that as part of an ante-nuptial settlement S undertakes to settle (a) certain shares and (b) any land which he receives under the will of his father, F, on B for life with remainder to their first son for life, with remainder to his first son absolutely. The marriage takes place. S declines to transfer the shares to the trustees of the settlement. Since B gave consideration for S's undertaking, S can be compelled to transfer the shares to the trustees. Later F dies leaving Blackacre to S. S declines to convey the land to the trustees. Since the undertaking by S that he would settle the land, if he got it, was made in consideration of B's promise of marriage, here too S can be compelled to transfer the land to the trustees of the settlement.

If, after his marriage to B, S covenants that he will settle certain property on his wife, B, then since the marriage has taken place, no consideration exists, and if S fails to carry out the covenant, the covenant is not enforceable against him. (But if the post-nuptial covenant by S is made in pursuance of a pre-nuptial agreement[15] then the covenant is enforceable against S[16].)

Issue of the marriage
Now suppose that, before the transfer of either the shares or the land, B died, after having given birth to a son, C. C gave no consideration to S in return for the undertaking which S made. This being so, can S be compelled to settle the property for the benefit of C? The answer is, Yes. S can be compelled to

13   See p 71.
14   *Stone v Stone* (1869) 5 Ch App 74.
15   The post-nuptial settlement should contain a recital that it is made in pursuance of the pre-marriage agreement.
16   *Re Holland* [1902] 2 Ch 360, CA.

settle the property for the benefit of C, or any other issue of the marriage on whom S had undertaken that the property would be settled. The reason for this is that in the case of an ante-nuptial settlement, any issue of the marriage (children[17], and possibly also grandchildren[18]), although they have not given any actual consideration to the settlor, are deemed to have given consideration to the settlor. This is expressed by saying that the issue of the marriage are 'within the marriage consideration'.

We have stated that in an ante-nuptial settlement, children of the marriage are within the marriage consideration. Are children of a former marriage (of S or B) within the marriage consideration? In *A-G v Jacobs-Smith*[19] it was held, on the facts of that case, that they were not. But the view, expressed in an earlier case[20], was supported that where the children of a wife by a former marriage had interests 'so complicated and mixed up with the interests of the possible issue of the marriage then contemplated that they could not well be separated, they were to be treated as persons who were entitled to come to the Court to have the articles of settlement enforced, and were treated as being brought in that way within the marriage consideration or at least entitled to have the benefit of it, because otherwise the settlement would be or might be defeated, even as to the children of the contemplated marriage, who were undoubtedly within the marriage consideration'. (No example was given in the judgment of a situation in which the interests were so entwined as to entitle children by a former marriage to be treated as being within the marriage consideration.) Illegitimate children are not now[1] within the marriage consideration unless, it would seem (as in the case of children of a former marriage), their interests are so entwined with the interests of children of the marriage that the interests could not well be separated.

We may note here that if in a marriage settlement S undertakes to settle property on his wife, W, with remainder to any children of the marriage, and in default of children to S's cousin, Z; the property is not transferred to the trustees; W enforces the trust (and the property is accordingly transferred to the trustees), then, in default of children, on W's death the benefit of W having enforced the trust will accrue to Z, notwithstanding that he is a volunteer[2]. But, not being within the marriage consideration, it is not open to Z to enforce the trust against S[3] if W fails to do so. (Of course, if the trust had been completely constituted, it would have been irrelevant that Z was not within the marriage consideration and his entitlement under the trust would be secure[4].)

Marriage settlement by a third party

In speaking of marriage settlements we have envisaged S undertaking to transfer property to trustees on trust for his future wife, B, and their issue.

---

17 *Harvey v Ashley* (1748) 3 Atk 607, 610.
18 *Macdonald v Scott* [1893] AC 642 at 650, HL.
19 [1895] 2 QB 341. See also *Rennell v IRC* [1962] Ch 329, 341; affd sub nom *IRC v Lord Rennell* [1964] AC 173, [1963] 1 All ER 803, HL.
20 *Newstead v Searles* (1737) 1 Atk 265. Per Lord Hardwicke LC.
1 Old cases to the contrary.
2 *Davenport v Bishopp* (1843) 2 Y & C Ch Cas 451.
3 *Re D'Angibau* (1879) 15 Ch D 228, CA.
4 *Paul v Paul* (1882) 20 Ch D 742, CA.

But it may be that the undertaking to settle property is made by some other person. For example, suppose that B's father, F, undertakes to settle property on S and B and their issue. In this case can S or B (or their issue) enforce the trust against F? Does S or B provide consideration to F? Perhaps S provides consideration to F by agreeing to take B off his hands; perhaps B does so by agreeing to marry S and so taking herself off her father's hands. If marriage is a 'detriment'[5] then perhaps each provides consideration, and the trust is enforceable against F. In *Shadwell v Shadwell*[6] an uncle wrote to his nephew 'I am glad to hear of your intended marriage with Ellen Nicholl; and, as I promised to assist you at starting, I am happy to tell you that I will pay to you [£]150 yearly during my life . . .'. After paying the annuity for some years, the uncle fell into arrears, and died. The nephew brought an action against the uncle's executors to recover the arrears. It was held that the promise by the uncle was enforceable since, it was held, consideration moved from the nephew to the uncle in that (1) the nephew might 'have made a most material change in his position, and . . . may have incurred pecuniary liabilities . . . which would be in every sense a loss . . .'; and (2) the marriage might 'be an object of interest' to the uncle 'and in that sense a benefit to him'[7]. '. . . the importance', it was mentioned, 'of enforcing promises which have been made to induce parties to marry has been often recognised . . .'[7]. This was the decision of Erle CJ, with which Keating J concurred. In his judgment Byles J held that the promise was not enforceable since no consideration moved from the nephew to the uncle as the nephew was not marrying at the request of the uncle, the engagement having already been made. In *Tweddle v Atkinson*[8], A contracted with X that on the marriage of A's son B to X's daughter Y, A and X would each pay certain sums of money to B. A and X died. B claimed the money from X's executor. It was held that as no consideration moved from B to X, B had no action. But this case differed, of course, from *Shadwell v Shadwell* in that the promise was not made with a party to the marriage. With regard to the enforcement of a covenant made by a third party with a party to a marriage, the present law, it is submitted, is represented by the majority decision in *Shadwell v Shadwell*[9].

Covenants

We have spoken of S entering into an undertaking that certain property would be transferred to trustees on specified trusts. It is customary for such an undertaking to be made under seal and to be made with the trustees. Thus when a settlement is created we commonly read that 'S covenanted with trustees that—' such and such property would be settled on specified trusts. By entering into a covenant with the trustees, at common law a contract comes into existence between S and the trustees. (Since the contract is under S's seal, no consideration by the trustees is needed for the validity of the contract between them and the settlor.)

If the beneficiary gave (or is deemed to have given) consideration for S's

5   *Currie v Misa* (1875) LR 10 Ex Ch 153.
6   (1860) 9 CBNS 159.
7   Per Erle CJ, at 173.
8   (1861) 1 B & S 393.
9   *Ante.*

covenant, then the fact that a contract exists between S and the trustees is irrelevant since the trust can be enforced in equity against S (with the various important consequences that we have noted). But what if there was no consideration for S's covenant? Does any action against S accrue from the fact that his undertaking was under seal? One circumstance can be disposed of at the outset. If, when S covenanted that he would settle property, the covenant was made not only with the trustees but also with B (ie B was a party to the covenant) then on S's failure to settle the property, an action lies against him by B at common law for damages for breach of the covenant.[10] But what if the covenant was between S and the trustees only? (Be warned, we enter shark-infested waters.) Does an action lie against S for his breach of covenant in failing to convey the property to the trustees? In seeking an answer to this question, it is necessary to distinguish between the position (a) where S covenants to settle existing property, ie property in his possession at the date of the covenant; and (b) where S covenants to settle after-acquired (or 'future') property (including, in particular, an expectancy).

COVENANTS TO SETTLE EXISTING PROPERTY[11]

The position here is that an action will lie against S if there exists what has come to be termed a 'trust of the chose'. The nature of a trust of the chose can be explained like this: (1) The contract between S and the trustees, being under seal, is enforceable against S without the need for consideration. (2) The right to sue at common law on the contract constitutes a chose in action[12] held by the trustees. (3) The chose in action is an item of property. (4) The chose in action is held—if such is S's intention—by the trustees on trust for B. (5) Thus from the moment of the covenant, B holds an equitable interest in property—there is a 'trust of the chose'[13]. (6) The trust of the chose is (the right to sue being vested in the trustees) completely constituted. It follows that the trustees are entitled—indeed, are under a duty—to exercise the right to sue S, and will succeed in an action at common law against S for damages for breach of the covenant.

Originally, where S covenanted to settle property on a (volunteer) beneficiary, equity presumed that S intended that the chose in action created by the covenant should be held by trustees on trust for the beneficiary. For example, damages were recovered by trustees in *Watson v Parker*[14] (a covenant to settle a specific sum); in *Williamson v Codrington*[15] (a covenant to settle land); in *Clough v Lambert*[16] (a covenant to pay an annuity); in *Cox v Barnard*[17] (a covenant to settle existing debts); and in *Re Cavendish Browne's Settlement*[18] (a covenant to settle various assets). In none of these cases did

10   *Cannon v Hartley* [1949] Ch 213, [1949] 1 All ER 50; (M & B).
11   [1988] Conv 19 (D. Goddard)
12   See Chap 5.
13   The phrase 'trust of the promise', sometimes used as an alternative, is best avoided, since, whilst there can be a trust of a chose (which is an item of property), there can be no such thing as a trust of a mere promise (which is not).
14   (1843) 6 Beav 283.
15   (1750) 1 Ves Sen 511.
16   (1839) 10 Sim 174.
17   (1850) 8 Hare 310.
18   [1916] WN 341, 61 Sol Jo 27. See also *Synge v Synge* [1894] 1 QB 466, CA; *Ward v Audland* (1847) 16 M & W 862.

the court concern itself with the question as to whether the settlor intended that the trustees should hold the chose on trust for the beneficiary. More recently, however, in this century, the cases indicate that damages will be recoverable from S for breach of the covenant only where S intended to render himself liable to an action for damages, by creating a trust of the chose.[19]

Where a trust of a chose does exist, and the trustees fail to proceed against S, then B can bring proceedings to compel them to carry out their duty. Alternatively, if the trustees decline to sue, B can sue S directly[20]. It should be noted, however, that whether the action against S is brought by the trustees, or by B, the action will rise to the remedy of damages only. Thus if B sues S, he sues him in equity, as a beneficiary of a completely constituted trust. But the trust property which he is seeking equity's aid to obtain is the common law right to damages for S's breach of the covenant. What B cannot obtain in his action against S is the property which S covenanted to settle. With regard to *that* property the trust is incompletely constituted, and with regard to that property, B, being a volunteer, can obtain no assistance from equity.

Since an action against S by the trustees or by B is to enforce a common law right, the action will give rise to none of the consequences in the event of S's bankruptcy, or his death, that are (as seen earlier) so advantageous to B in the case of an action against S in equity. Further, an action on the covenant will, since it lies in contract, be subject to the Limitation Act 1980[1] (ie a delay of 12 years will render the action statute barred).

An early example of a trust of the chose is provided by *Fletcher v Fletcher*[2]. EF entered into a covenant with trustees to pay them £60,000 to be held (on the occurrence of specified events that happened) on trust for his natural son, Jacob. Jacob was a volunteer. The money was not paid over. The court held that Jacob was entitled to claim the money from EF (either by suing EF at common law in the name of the trustee, or by suing EF directly, in equity). Counsel for EF urged that since Jacob was a volunteer he was not entitled to equity's aid. But Wigram V-C stated, 'According to the authorities, I cannot, I admit, do anything to perfect the liability of the author of the trust, if it is not already perfect. This covenant however, is already perfect. The covenantor is liable at law, and the Court is not called upon to do any act to perfect it. One question made in argument has been, whether there can be a trust of a covenant the benefit of which shall belong to a third party; but I cannot think there is any difficulty in that.'

It will be noted that, in earlier times, having addressed the question, 'Can there be a trust of the benefit of a covenant?', and having given an answer in the affirmative, the court assumed, from the mere fact that a covenant had been made, that the settlor intended the trustees to hold the benefit of the

19   D.J. Hayton (Hayton and Marshall, *Cases and Commentary on the Law of Trusts* (8th edn, p 163) contends that where S covenants to settle existing property on B, then a presumption arises that S intended to create a trust of the chose, since without such an intention the making of the covenant would be pointless; but that where the covenant is to settle after-acquired property (see infra, p 83) on a volunteer, an intention to create a trust of the covenant must be shown).

20   He will be required to join the trustees as co-defendants in the action. *Vandepitte v Preferred Accident Insurance Corpn of New York* [1933] AC 70, 79, PC.

1   Section 8(1). See *Stone v Stone* (1869) 5 Ch App 74.

2   (1844) 4 Hare 67; (M & B).

covenant *on trust for the beneficiary*[3]. As stated earlier, this assumption is no longer made and today clear evidence of an intention to create a trust of the chose for the beneficiaries is required before any right of action against the settlor arises[4].

The notion of a trust of a chose has been employed in certain circumstances (circumstances strictly limited in scope) to give a remedy to a third party, outside the realm of settlements, in a contract of insurance. Suppose that A contracts with an insurance company that, in consideration of annual premiums by A to the company, on his death the company will pay a certain sum to his niece, X. A pays the premiums and then dies. Is the sum due under the policy the property of A's estate (and as such will pass under his will or intestacy) or is it the property of X? If it is found that the contract between A and the company showed an intention that A should hold the benefit of the contract for X, then A and, after his death, his personal representative, holds the chose created by the contract as trustee for X[5]. The company must[6] pay the money to X. If it fails to do so, and A's personal representative declines to enforce the contract on X's behalf, then X has a right of action against the company. But for the notion of a trust of chose to give a remedy to a third party to a contract, there must (as in the case of a covenant to settle property) be clear, unequivocal, evidence of an intention to create a trust of the chose. The burden on the plaintiff to show this intention is a heavy one[7]. (If it were otherwise, the notion of a trust of a chose would provide a simple means of breaching the principle of privity of contract.)

The question of privity arose before the House of Lords in *Beswick v Beswick*[8] in 1967. By an agreement in writing, P assigned his coal business to his nephew, J. By way of consideration J agreed to employ P as a consultant for an agreed weekly sum for the rest of P's life, and on P's death to pay his widow an annuity of £5 a week for her lifetime. P died. J declined to pay the annuity to the widow. Could the widow compel J to do so? No evidence existed that P had entered into the contract as a trustee for the widow, and the court held that s 56 of the Law of Property Act 1925 had no application. But the contract by P was enforceable by P's personal representative who, it happened, was the widow. The fact that the enforcement of the contract would be for her personal benefit was no bar to the action. (The decision, it will be noted, constituted no departure from the rule of privity of contract.)

An important question remains. Suppose that S covenants with trustees to settle property on a volunteer, B. He fails to do so. No intention to create a trust of the chose can be shown to exist. B has no remedy to compel the

3 Eg *Lamb v Vice* (1840) 6 M & W 467, and see p 79.
4 *Royal Exchange Assurance v Hope* [1928] Ch 179, CA; *Re Gordon* [1940] Ch 851; *Re Webb* [1941] Ch 225, [1941] 1 All ER 321; *Re Foster's Policy* [1966] 1 All ER 432, [1966] 1 WLR 222.
5 Where one spouse takes out a policy of insurance on his or her own life and the policy is expressed to be for the benefit of the other spouse (and/or their children), then the Married Women's Property Act 1882, s 11, provides that the policy creates a trust of the sum assured in favour of the objects named in the policy.
6 Assuming that X is of full age.
7 *Vandepitte v Preferred Accident Insurance Corpn of New York* [1933] AC 70, 79–80, PC; *Harmer v Armstrong* [1934] Ch 65, CA; *Re Schebsman* [1944] Ch 83, [1943] 2 All ER 768, CA; *Green v Russell* [1959] 2 QB 226, [1959] 2 All ER 525, CA.
8 [1968] AC 58, [1967] 2 All ER 1197, HL.

trustees to sue S, or to sue S directly himself. But could the trustees, if they so chose, sue S? After all, a contract exists between themselves and S, and S is in breach. Is there anything to prevent them suing S at common law for damages? No case has arisen (concerning a covenant to settle existing property) in which the courts have been asked to decide the matter[9]. It has been strongly argued, however, that an action by the trustees would fail. The arguments[10] are these: (A) (i) Since no trust of the chose was intended, if the trustees sued S and recovered damages, the money would not be held by them on trust for the beneficiary. (ii) Since the settlor could not have intended that the money should be held by the trustees beneficially, they will hold it for the settlor. (iii) Since the settlor would, under the rule in *Sanders v Vautier*, be entitled to recover the money from the trustees, the action by the trustees would be without purpose. (iv) The trustees would be unlikely to contemplate proceedings because of the likelihood that they would be required to pay the costs of the action. If, nevertheless[11], they commenced an action against S, they would, it is argued[12], be directed by the court not to proceed, on the grounds of the action's futility. (B) If the trustees were entitled to sue S, then whether the beneficiaries obtained any benefit would depend, not upon whether they were legally entitled to the beneficial interest, but on the chance of whether the trustees happened to decide to sue. Such a position would run counter to the principle that proprietary interests are to be determined according to principles of law, and are not to be affected by the manner in which trustees happen to decide to act.

What has been said in this section may have caused the reader to realise the paradoxes involved in the notion of a trust of a chose. If an intention to create a trust of the chose exists, and B sues S, then he is enforcing an equitable right as a beneficiary of a completely constituted trust of the chose to sue S to recover the benefit of the contract (ie damages)—a contract that, not being for consideration, equity would, if made between two parties, decline to enforce. As the matter has been expressed, '... the underlying paradox is that Equity is able to say there is a trust of the common law contract when Equity is not able itself to admit there is a contract'[13].

Further, if B compels the trustees to sue S, he will be able to do so by obtaining the equitable remedy of an injunction—an injunction compelling the trustees to sue on a common law contract that, as we have said, equity does not see. Any disquiet that these reflections may cause can, however, be eased if we remember that where a trust of a chose exists, what we are dealing with is a completely constituted trust of the *chose*, and that equity treats the trust as it would any other completely constituted trust, regardless of what the subject matter of the trust happens to be.

9   Cf cases concerning covenants to settle after-acquired property, infra, pp 83.
10 See, in particular, Hayton and Marshall, *Cases and Commentaries on the Law of Trusts*, (8th edn) pp 219–227; (1969) 85 LQR 213 (L. A. Lee).
11 Eg, being indemnified against costs of the action by the would-be beneficiary.
12 See n 10, supra.
13 B. Perrins [1986] Conv 146.

AFTER-ACQUIRED PROPERTY

So far we have considered the position where S covenants that he will settle property in his possession on a volunteer, B. We must now turn to consider the position where S covenants that he will settle after-acquired property on a volunteer. For example, on S's engagement to B, S may covenant with the trustees of the marriage settlement that he will transfer to the trustees certain specified property on trust for himself and B for their joint lives, with remainder to any children of the marriage, and in default of issue, with remainder to S's next of kin; and coupled with this he may covenant with the trustees that he will convey to them, on the same trusts, any property of a value over a specified sum that he subsequently receives under the will of his father. The marriage takes place. S conveys to the trustees the property specified. He later receives Greenacre under his father's will. He does not transfer the land to the trustees. B dies, without having borne issue. S dies leaving all his property to X. S's next of kin is his brother, Y. If S had transferred Greenacre to the trustees, as he had covenanted to do, they would hold the land on trust for Y, the remainderman under the settlement[14]. But he has failed to do so, with the result that Greenacre passes to X. Can the trustees sue S's executors for damages for S's breach of covenant? Put generally, can trustees sue at common law for damages for breach of a covenant to settle after-acquired property, where the beneficiary is a volunteer?

Here, important, and more recent, cases exist. In 1892, in *Re Parkin*[15] it was held that an action did lie for damages for breach of covenant to settle after-acquired property. And in 1910, in *Re Plumptre's Marriage Settlement*[16], it was held that trustees were not able to obtain this remedy because the action was statute barred—the implication being that if it had not been statute barred, they could have obtained damages for breach of the covenant. In 1917, however, in *Re Pryce*[17] the compass needle swung to the opposite pole. In this case there was a covenant in a marriage settlement by H to settle certain after-acquired property on W for life with an ultimate remainder to her statutory next of kin. H acquired the property but did not settle it. In his will he left his estate in part to W absolutely and in part to her for life with remainder to his two brothers. W thus received under H's will no less than she would have received under the settlement. The losers, under the will, were W's next of kin. The trustees took out a summons to determine whether they should enforce the trust. It was held that the next of kin, being volunteers, could not enforce the covenant. Further, since the court would not give the next of kin by indirect means what they could not obtain directly by suing H themselves, the court declared that the trustees 'ought not to take any steps to compel the transfer or payment to them'.[18] This decision has been interpreted as meaning that the trustees were not entitled to pursue any action based on the covenant. The decision in *Re Kay's Settlement* in 1939 was more specific. There having been a failure to transfer after-acquired

---

14 This also would be the case if S had authorised the trustees to receive the after-acquired property, and S's father's executors had transferred Greenacre directly to the trustees, the trust thus becoming completely constituted. *Re Bowden* [1936] Ch 71.
15 [1892] 3 Ch 510.
16 [1910] 1 Ch 609.
17 [1917] 1 Ch 234; (M & B).
18 At 242.

property in accordance with a covenant to settle such property, the court directed that the trustees should not take any step either by way of compelling performance of the covenant, or by suing for damages for breach of the covenant.

The same issue arose in *Re Cook's Settlement Trusts*[19]. As part of the redistribution of various items of property between a father and a son in 1934, certain valuable pictures were transferred to the son. The son covenanted with the father and with trustees that if the pictures were sold during his lifetime, the proceeds of sale would be paid to the trustees to be held by them on trust for various members of the son's family (not including the father). The father died in 1939. In 1962 the son gave one of the pictures to his wife and she proposed to sell it. The trustees took out a summons asking what steps they ought to take if the picture was sold and the proceeds not paid to them. It will be seen that there had been a declaration of trust (by the son, in the covenant) but no transfer of trust property to the trustees. The trust was thus incompletely constituted. Since the pictures had not been sold, no transfer to the trustees was yet due. But, the court had to decide, if the pictures were sold, what would be the position then? It was clear (and it was held) that it would not be open to the beneficiaries to enforce the trust since they were volunteers. (It would seem that the father, if he had still been alive, would have been able to enforce the trust, since the son had covenanted with him, and the father had provided consideration to the son. But the father was dead.) Could the trustees enforce the trust, relying on the covenant with them made by the son? It was held that the fact that consideration had been provided by the father to the son did not entitle the beneficiaries to require the trustees to take proceedings to enforce the covenant and a declaration was made that the trustees ought not to take proceedings against the settlor to enforce his covenant. In argument before the court, counsel for the volunteer beneficiary sought to employ the notion of a trust of a chose in support of his client's claim for damages for breach of the covenant; the covenant to settle after-acquired property resulted, he claimed, in a chose in action which was held by the trustees from the moment of the covenant. Therefore they should be allowed to sue on the strength of this chose for damages. Buckley J dismissed the argument. The covenant, he said, 'upon its true construction is, in my opinion, an executory contract to settle a particular fund ... which at the date of the covenant did not exist and might never come into existence. It is analogous to a covenant to settle an expectation or to settle after-acquired property'[20]. The covenant did not 'create a debt enforceable at law, that is to say, a property right'[1]. The covenant therefore did not bring into existence anything 'capable of being made the subject of an immediate trust'[2].

The decisions in *Re Pryce*, *Re Kay's Settlement*, and *Re Cook's Settlement*

19   [1965] Ch 902, [1964] 3 All ER 898; (M & B); (1965) 24 CLJ 46 (G. H. Jones); (1966) 29 MLR 397 (D. Matteson).
20   At 914.
 1   At 913.
 2   At 914.

Trusts have been both strongly criticised[3] and stoutly defended[4] (albeit sometimes with reservations[5]). As the law stands, however, it seems now to be firmly established that where there is a covenant to settle after-acquired property, trustees will not be permitted to sue for damages at common law for breach of the covenant[6].

SECRET TRUSTS AND *RE GARDNER*[7]

Seen in the light of the contents of this chapter it will be appreciated that a secret trust (and a half secret trust) is, until the death of the testator, an incompletely constituted trust, since there has been a declaration of trust, but no transfer to the trustee. If, as has been postulated, a beneficiary under an incompletely constituted trust who dies before the trust becomes completely constituted receives nothing, then it would seem that *Re Gardner*[8] was wrongly decided. In that case, as mentioned in Chapter 4, it was held that the interest of a beneficiary under a secret trust did not lapse in the event of the beneficiary predeceasing the testator, on the ground that the trust had been created, and the beneficiary's interest had vested, at the date that the arrangement between the testator and the donee had been concluded.

---

3 D. W. Elliott, (1960) 76 LQR 100. (The maxim 'Equity will not aid a volunteer' is not to be extended to mean that equity will prevent a common law remedy from being pursued. The trustees should therefore not be prevented from suing the settlor at common law on the covenant; though the volunteer beneficiary cannot compel the trustees to sue.) J. A. Hornby, (1962) 78 LQR 228. (The trustees should not be prevented from suing at common law. The court should direct them to sue. A volunteer beneficiary has a right to compel them to do so; otherwise the existence of the beneficiary's proprietary interest would hinge on the whim of the trustees.) Gareth Jones, (1965) 24 CLJ 46. (The reasoning in *Re Cooke* is correct with regard to enforcing the trust in equity against S, but no equity exists to prevent the trustees from exercising their common law right to sue for damages.) D. Matheson, (1966) 29 MLR 397. J. L. Barton, (1975) 91 LQR 236. (*Re Pryce* founded neither upon principle nor upon authority. Should be treated as anomalous and not taken as application of a wider principle. Attempts to provide a rational justification should be abandoned.) R. P. Meagher and J. P. F. Lehane, (1976) 92 LQR 427. (The argument that there cannot be a trust of a promise to settle after-acquired property because the promise cannot form the subject matter of a trust cannot be correct because a covenant to settle such property on a non-volunteer is enforceable and so forms the subject matter of a trust. *Re Pryce* should not be accepted as beyond challenge.) J. D. Feltham, (1982) 98 LQR 17. (In covenanting, S must have intended, irrespective of whether the settlement was of existing or after-acquired property, to bind himself legally to his undertaking, otherwise he would not have gone through the ritual of sealing. So he must have intended to create a trust of the chose for the benefit of the beneficiary, whether a volunteer or not.) M. W. Friend, [1982] Conv 280. (A covenant to settle after-acquired property on a volunteer probably generates a proprietary chose in action. No reason why this should not be capable of being held on trust.) S. Lindsay and P. Ziegler, (1986) 60 ALJ 387.
4 L. A. Lee, (1969) 85 LQR 213. Cf H. A. J. Ford and W. A. Lee, *Principles of the Law of Trusts* (1983), para 329, pp 117, 118.
5 C. E. F. Rickett, (1979) 32 CLP 1; (1981) 34 CLP 189. S. Smith, [1982] Conv 352.
6 It is argued by D. J. Hayton, op cit, that since a covenant to assign existing property to a volunteer (although not specifically enforceable in equity) gives the volunteer covenantee an action at common law for damages for breach of the covenant, there is no reason why a trust of a covenant to settle after-acquired property should not exist, and that if an intention is clearly shown that such a trust is intended, the trust will exist and give rise to the same remedies as in the case of a trust of a chose relating to existing property. See also (1988) 8 Legal Studies 172 (M. R. T. Macnair).
7 [1923] 2 Ch 230.
8 Ibid.

However, if a secret trust is viewed as an incompletely constituted trust, then a beneficiary under a secret trust must (assuming he is a volunteer) be regarded as having no interest in the trust property until the property passes to the donee under the will. Thus the correct conclusion, it is submitted, is that in the facts in *Re Gardner* the property should not have passed to the secret beneficiary's estate. This leaves to be resolved the question—to whom should it have passed? It might seem contrary to the principles of equity that the donee, having agreed to accept the property as trustee, should be permitted to take the property beneficially. But there would be no objection to this being the result if, as seems reasonable, the arrangement made by the testator is considered as being impliedly subject to the conditions (1) that the existence of the trust for the secret beneficiary is to be subject to the condition precedent of the beneficiary being alive at the time of the testator's death; and (2) that, if he is not so living, the property should be held by the donee beneficially.

THE RULE IN *STRONG v BIRD*[9]

In this chapter we have seen that in determining whether a trust is completely or incompletely constituted equity adopts certain of the principles of the law relating to gifts. This is logical since in creating a trust, if there is no consideration, the settlor is making a form of gift. (We have seen also that if a trust is incompletely constituted, in determining whether the trust should be enforceable, equity adopts certain of the principles of contract. This too is logical since, if consideration is present, the settlor is entering into a form of contract.) We must now explain another instance in which the law of trusts borrows from the law relating to gifts.

Suppose that R makes E a gift of a ring, but for some reason does not hand the ring over to him. Since there has been no delivery, the gift is imperfect[10]. In his will R appoints E his executor[11]. On R's death the legal title to all his property, including the ring, vests automatically in E as R's executor. Before R's death, the gift was imperfect since, although the necessary intention was present, the title had not been transferred to E. On R's death the second requirement is satisfied and the gift becomes perfect. E therefore holds the ring beneficially. This principle is known as the rule in *Strong v Bird*[12].

For the rule to operate, R must have intended to make an immediate, out-and-out, gift of the ring to E. Such an intention would be excluded if it was shown that R wished first to apply the ring for some purpose of his own, eg to lend the ring to Z[13]. Nor does the necessary intention exist if R merely promised that he would, at some time in the future, give the ring to E[14].

Further, for the rule to operate, R's intention that the ring should be E's must have continued up until the time of his (R's) death. If R ceases to

---

9   (1874) LR 18 Eq 315; [1982] Conv 14 (G. Kodilinye).
10   See ante, p 74.
11   In *Re James* [1935] Ch 449 it was held that the rule applied also where R dies intestate and E is appointed his administrator. This was doubted in *Re Gonin* [1979] Ch 16, [1977] 2 All ER 720.
12   (1874) LR 18 Eq 315.
13   *Re Freeland* [1952] Ch 110, [1952] 1 All ER 16.
14   See *Re Gonin* [1979] Ch 16, [1977] 2 All ER 720.

manifest this intention (eg by treating the ring as still being his own) the rule does not apply and no gift to E takes place. (The ring would then form part of R's estate and pass under his will.)

If these conditions are satisfied, then it is immaterial that R appointed other executors in addition to E, since the whole of the estate is regarded as vesting in each personal representative[15]. (The nature of the property is also immaterial, the rule applying to realty[16] and personalty, and to the release of a debt[17]).

The rule in *Strong v Bird*, which we have seen may cause an imperfect gift to be perfected, may also cause an incompletely constituted trust to become completely constituted[18]. For example, S purports to transfer Blackacre to T_1 and T_2 on trust for B, a volunteer. S fails to execute a deed of conveyance, and so fails to convey the title of Blackacre to T_1 and T_2. On S's death, it is found that he has appointed T_1 and T_2 his executors. Provided that the necessary requirements are satisfied (eg that S's intention that the land should be held by T_1 and T_2 on trust for B continued until his death[19]), the legal estate vests in T_1 and T_2 as trustees on trust for B.

DONATIO MORTIS CAUSA[20]

If R is ill and expecting to die and he hands a watch to E saying 'Take this, I want you to have it if I die', the gift is imperfect since although delivery has occurred, there is no intention, at that time, that the title should pass to E. The watch remains R's property until, if he dies, the condition precedent is fulfilled, and the necessary intention comes into existence. The gift to E is then perfected. A gift which takes effect in this way is termed a *'donatio mortis causa'*. Four conditions must be satisfied for a gift in this form to take effect.[1]

1. The gift must have been made by a donor who is expecting to die shortly,[2] as where a donor is seriously ill. He must believe his death 'to be impending'[3], not merely that he will die sometime, or that a coming event, eg travel by air,[4] or a surgical operation[5], carries a risk of his dying.

2. The gift must have been made expressly or (commonly) impliedly[6] on the condition that it would only take effect on the donor's death. Until his death, the donor can require the property to be returned to him. On his death the gift becomes effective. The property becomes that of the donee without the need of an assent from the donor's personal representatives.[7] The condition ceases to operate if the donor ceases to expect his impending death, eg if he recovers from a serious illness, or he resumes control of the property or, it seems, if he informs the transferee that he has reversed his intention.

15 *Re Stewart* [1908] 2 Ch 251.
16 *Re James* [1935] Ch 449, [1935] All ER Rep 235.
17 As in *Strong v Bird*.
18 *Re Ralli's Will Trusts* [1964] Ch 288, [1963] 3 All ER 940.
19 *Re Wale* [1956] 3 All ER 280, [1956] 1 WLR 1346.
20 [1989] Conv 184 (C. E. F. Rickett).
 1 *Re Craven's Estate* [1937] Ch 423, 426.
 2 *Duffield v Elwes* (1827) 1 Bli NS 497 at 530.
 3 *Re Craven's Estate* [1937] Ch 423 at 426.
 4 *Thompson v Mechan* [1958] OR 357.
 5 *Agnew v Belfast Banking Co* [1896] 2 IR 204 at 221.
 6 *Re Lillingston* [1952] 2 All ER 184.
 7 *Tate v Hilbert* (1793) 2 Ves 111 at 120.

3.   There must be delivery of the property (or something, eg the keys of a safe, that conveys control to the transferee and removes control from the donor[8]).

4.   The property must be such that it is capable of being transferred by mere delivery (eg a chattel) or be within a class of forms of property that have been held to be capable of being the subject of a donatio mortis causa (eg money in a Post Office savings bank acount). A formerly long established rule that land could not form the subject matter of a donatio mortis causa was recently rejected by the court.[9]

It is unusual for an incompletely constituted trust to become completely constituted by being a *donatio mortis causa*. This result might ensue if R said to E 'Take this, I want you to hold it on trust for B if I die', but there are no reported cases of this happening.

It will be seen that where the rule in *Strong v Bird* and the principle of *donatio mortis causa* operate, an initially imperfect gift (or incompletely constituted trust) subsequently becomes perfect (or completely constituted)[10].

CONCERNING TIME

In some situations the date on which a transaction occurs may be of significance. For example, if, before the abolition of estate duty, S gave property to B, and S later died, the gift to B was liable to estate duty unless S lived for seven years after the date of the gift. The length of the interval of time between the gift and S's death thus determined whether duty was payable. So the date of the gift was crucial.

If a gift takes the form of a gift to trustees on trust for B, then the transaction is treated as having occurred on the date when the trust becomes completely constituted. Thus the question is sometimes not *whether* a trust has been completely constituted, but at what point in time it becomes completely constituted.

RE RALLI AND *RE WALE*

In conclusion, the facts will be given of two cases which illustrate well a number of matters which have arisen in this chapter. In *Re Ralli's Will Trusts*[11], T, in 1892, made a will leaving his residue on trust for his wife for life and then to his children absolutely. T died in March 1899, leaving a widow and two daughters, H and I. In 1924, H covenanted in her marriage settlement to settle all her 'existing and after-acquired property' on certain trusts which, in the event, failed, and ultimately on trust for the children of

---

8   *Re Mustapha* (1891) 8 TLR 160.

9   *Sen v Headley* [1991] Ch 425, [1991] 2 All ER 638. (Donor, during last illness: 'The house is yours Margaret. You have the keys. They are in your bag. The deeds are in the steel box.'); [1991] Conv 307 (M. Halliwell). See also *Woodard v Woodard* [1991] Fam Law 470, CA; [1992] Conv 53.

10   Two other examples of apparently imperfect gifts or incompletely constituted trusts which are not ineffective arise under the Settled Land Act 1925. One concerns a purported conveyance of a legal estate in land to an infant (LPA 1925, ss 1(6) and 19(6); SLA 1925, s 27(1)); the other concerns a settlement made in a form which fails to comply with the requirements of the Act (SLA, s 4 and s 9).

11   [1964] Ch 288, [1963] 3 All ER 940; (M & B).

I. The settlement declared that all the property comprised within the terms of the covenant to settle existing and after-acquired property should 'become subject in equity to the settlement hereby covenanted to be made'. I's husband, P, was appointed one of the trustees of the settlement. In 1946, P was also appointed a trustee of T's will. In 1956, H died and in 1961, T's widow died. P was the sole surviving trustee of both T's will and H's settlement. The question before the court was whether P held H's half share of T's residue on trust for H's estate, or on the trusts of H's settlement.

The issue hinged, therefore, on whether the trust constituted by H's marriage settlement was completely constituted. If it was, then H's half share was to be held by P on trust for I's (ie and his) children. If it was not, then, since these children were volunteers, the trust was not enforceable, and the property passed to those entitled under H's will. It was held that whilst there had been no transfer of the trust property (H's interest in remainder under T's will) to the trustees of her settlement, and that from this viewpoint the trust had not been completely constituted, the trust was nevertheless enforceable for two reasons. First, the effect of H's declaration that the property within the settlement was to 'become subject in equity to the settlement covenanted to be made' was that she constituted herself trustee of the property from the date of the declaration[12]. Thus the trust in favour of the children existed from that time, and so prevailed over the claim of the residuary legatees under H's will. Second, when T died and the legal title to T's estate vested in P as T's personal representative, by the application of the rule in *Strong v Bird*[13], H's settlement became completely constituted. And, in accordance with the rule, it was immaterial that it had vested in him, not in his capacity as trustee of H's settlement, but in his capacity as T's executor. If it had not been for the fortuitous event that P was executor of T's will (and if there had been no declaration by H which had the effect already explained) then the trust in favour of the children would not have been enforceable, and the property would have passed under H's will.

In *Re Wale*[14], W was entitled to certain 'B' investments under her husband's will. These were registered in the names of the executors of her husband's will. She was also the absolute owner of certain 'A' shares, registered in her own name. In a voluntary settlement, executed in 1939, W settled the 'A' and the 'B' shares on her daughter, but did not take any steps to transfer the shares to the trustees of the settlement, and during the rest of her life showed no indication of remembering the creation of the settlement. In her will she left her property to her two sons. The two sons and the daughter were appointed her executors. When she died in 1953 the family solicitor produced the 1939 settlement. The question arose as to whether the shares should go to the daughter under the settlement or to the sons under the will. Regarding the 'B' shares, it was held that as, at the time of the settlement in 1939, W held an equitable interest in the shares, and as an assignment of an equitable interest in property need not be in any particular form, and since the execution of the settlement in 1939 satisfied the requirement of s 53(1)(c) that an assignment of an equitable interest must be in writing, there had been a valid assignment of W's interest in the shares to the trustees. Thus the daughter was entitled to the 'B' shares under the 1939 settlement. Regarding the 'A'

12 *Re Anstis* (1886) 31 Ch D 596 distinguished.
13 See p 86, ante.
14 [1956] 3 All ER 280, [1956] 1 WLR 1346.

shares, as W held the legal title to these, the property in them had not passed
to the trustees. The court considered whether the appointment of the daughter
as one of the executors of her mother's will brought the case within the rule
in *Strong v Bird*, but found that the requirement that the donor's intention
to make the gift must have continued until the donor's death was not satisfied.
The gift to trustees on trust for the daughter therefore remained ineffective
and the 'A' shares passed to the sons under the will. (Thus the trust of the
'B' shares was completely constituted, and the trust of the 'A' shares was
incompletely constituted.)

Chapter 7

Charitable trusts[1] I: charitable status

The background: why does it matter whether a trust is charitable?

In medieval England property was given on trust for many purposes which would today be classified in law as being charitable, for example, the maintenance of hospitals and almshouses, the distribution of doles (in the form of money or supplies) to the poor, the building of churches and chapels, and the building and endowing of schools and colleges. Originally, whilst the word 'charity' might have an everyday and a theological meaning, the word had no legal significance, the law drawing no distinction between charitable bodies and others. It was in the context of the Mortmain legislation that charities became subject to legal restrictions. This legislation can be explained by supposing that in 1200 A held Blackacre in fee simple. When A died incidents of tenure such as wardship, marriage and relief could prove lucrative sources of income to A's feudal lord. But suppose that during his lifetime A granted Blackacre to a corporation, say the Priory of St Cross at Hardham. As a corporation the priory had a life which, unless the corporation were dissolved, would continue for ever. Thus from the time of A's grant, although feudal services would continue to be due to the superior lord, no profit would accrue to him from the incidents of tenure accruing on a tenant's death. A grant of land to a corporation thus caused loss to the grantor's lord. The land passed into the 'dead hand' of the corporation.

It is natural that the accumulation of lands in the hands of corporations, in particular ecclesiastical corporations, should have been viewed with hostility by those holding seignories, and in particular by the Crown, the ultimate superior feudal lord and thus the ultimate loser.

After tentative moves made in Magna Carta (1216) and the Provisions of Westminster (1259), in 1279 the statute De Viris Religiosis, the first Statute of Mortmain, prohibited all sales or gifts to religious houses without a licence from the Crown. Since licences were granted for a fee the Crown was to some extent compensated for the loss of the value of incidents of tenure. If no licence was obtained the land was liable to forfeiture to the Crown. The

---

1 *Tudor on Charities* (7th edn), S. G. Maurice and D. Parker; H. A. P. Picarda, *The Law and practice relating to charities*; E. Cairns, *Charities: Law and Practice.* For charities in their social context, see B. Nightingale, *Charities*; M. Chesterman, *Charities, Trusts and Social Welfare*; F. Gladstone, *Charity, Law and Social Justice*; *Report of the Goodman Committee: Law and Voluntary Organisations* (1976). See also the annual Reports of Charity Commissioners for England and Wales; I. Williams, *The Alms Trade: Charities, Past, Present and Future.*

prohibition was extended to municipal corporations in 1392 and to unincorporated bodies in 1531.

In medieval and Tudor times what was significant in law was thus not
whether a body had charitable objects, but whether it had corporate status,
in the latter event the Mortmain statutes being applicable.

Only with the passing of the statute 43 Eliz 1 c 4, usually referred to as the
Charitable Uses Act 1601, did it become significant in law whether a body
was or was not *charitable*.

The 1601 Act was passed, its title states, 'to redress the misemployment of
Lands, Goods and Stocks of Money heretofore given to certain charitable
Uses'. Prior to the passing of the Act there had been no machinery for enquiry
into possible abuses in the way in which charities were administered. The Act
was intended to provide such a machinery. The principal provision of the
Act is set out below. The words of the preamble have been arranged in the
form of a list, and the numbering added.

'1 WHEREAS Lands ... Goods ... Chattels ... and Money, have been ...
given ... by sundry ... well-disposed Persons ...
  (i) for Relief of aged, impotent and poor People,
  (ii) for Maintenance of sick and maimed Soldiers and Mariners,
  (iii) (for maintenance of) Schools of Learning, Free Schools, and Sch-
       olars in Universities, ...
  (iv) for Repair of Bridges, Ports, Havens, Causeways, Churches, Sea-
       Banks and Highways, ...
  (v) for Education and Preferment of Orphans, ...
  (vi) for ... Relief, Stock or Maintenance for Houses of Correction, ...
  (vii) for Marriages of poor Maids, ...
  (viii) for Supportation, Aid and Help of young Tradesmen, Handi-
         craftmen and Persons decayed, ...
  (ix) for Relief or Redemption of Prisoners or Captives, ...
  (x) for Aid or Ease of any poor Inhabitants concerning payment of
      Fifteens, setting out Soldiers and other Taxes;
which Lands ... Goods ... Chattels ... and Money, nevertheless have not
been employed according to the charitable Intent of the Givers ... by reason
of Frauds, Breaches of Trust and Negligence in those that should ... employ
the same:

2 For Redress ... whereof, Be it enacted ... That it shall ... be lawful ...
for the Lord Chancellor ... to award Commissions ... to the Bishop of every
... diocese ... and to other Persons of good ... Behaviour,

3 authorising them ... to enquire ... of all ... such gifts ... aforesaid, and
of the Abuses, Breaches of Trust, Negligences ... of any Lands ... Goods
... Chattels ... and Money ... given ... for any charitable and godly

4 ... Uses before rehearsed ...

5 and upon such Enquiry ... set down such Orders ... as the said Lands ...
Goods ... Chattels ... and Money, may be duly and faithfully employed. ...
for such of the charitable Uses ... for which they were given'.

We shall have occasion to refer to the words of the statute later in this
chapter, but for the present we need merely note that the Act introduced
machinery for enquiry into abuses in the administration of charities.

In 1736 an Act[2] 'to distrain the Disposition of Lands, whereby the same become unalienable' (sometimes referred to as the Mortmain Act 1736[3], sometimes as the Charitable Uses Act 1735[4]) provided that any gift of land which was to be held on trust for any charitable purpose was valid only if the gift was made inter vivos, by deed, at least one year before the donor's death. Any other gift of land for a charitable purpose (eg one by will) was void. The Act thus extended the Mortmain restrictions to charitable trusts.

By the middle of the eighteenth century the question whether a body was charitable in law was therefore significant because, if it were charitable (a) it was subject to the Charitable Uses Act 1601 and (b) if it were not a corporation (ie merely a set of trustees) it was subject to the Mortmain Act of 1736. If it was a corporation, then it was subject to the earlier Mortmain statutes, which applied to corporations generally irrespective of whether or not they were charitable.

During the nineteenth century, various Acts[5] were passed with the purpose of controlling the administration of charities (the old machinery, provided by the 1601 Act, having fallen into desuetude). If a body was charitable, it was subject to these Acts. During the same century various amendments were made to the Mortmain laws, and if a charitable body was a corporation, these modifications applied. The restriction on gifts of land on trust for charitable purposes contained in the 1736 Act was modified in 1891[6].

During the nineteenth century two further reasons developed why it was significant in law whether a body was charitable. Most important of these was the emergence of the rule that a trust for a non-charitable purpose was void as a private trust, on the ground that there were no beneficiaries available to enforce the trust[7]. As a result of this rule, a trust for a purpose could only be valid if the purpose was charitable. A trust for a purpose was therefore either charitable or it was nothing[8]. Thus the question whether a trust does or does not have charitable status can today affect its very existence.

It was also in the nineteenth century that statute first conferred fiscal advantages on a body which had charitable status, in the form of relief from income tax on income earned, from estate duty on gifts received and, in certain circumstances, from rates.

The Charities Act 1960 (in this chapter referred to as the Act) swept away a great mass of earlier legislation concerned with the control of the administration of charities, and removed the last vestiges of the Mortmain laws[9]. The Act established a fresh system for the regulation of charities and their activities, under the supervision of the Charity Commissioners, a statutory[10] body[11] which forms a department of State, within the Home Office. The Commissioners are charged with the general duty of 'promoting the effective use of charitable resources by encouraging the development of better

---

2 Geo 2 c 36.
3 Megarry and Wade, *The Law of Real Property* (5th edn) p cix.
4 Snell, *Principles of Equity* (28th edn) p cxxxix.
5 Eg the Charitable Trusts Acts of 1853, 1860, 1862, 1869, 1887.
6 Mortmain and Charitable Uses Act 1891, s 5.
7 See Chap 9.
8 Subject to what is said in Chap 9.
9 Section 48(1).
10 Charities Act 1960, s 1.
11 Originally established by the Charitable Trusts Act 1853. The duties of the Commissioners had previously been carried out by the Chancery Court.

methods of administration, by giving charity trustees information or advice[12] on any matter affecting a charity and by investigating and checking abuses'[13].

From what has been said so far it will be seen that at the present day the reasons why it matters whether or not a body is charitable may be grouped under three heads:

1. Administration: if a body is a 'charity'[14] it is subject to the Charities Act of 1960.

2. Legal existence: unless a trust is charitable, it may be void.

3. Finance: if a body is charitable fiscal advantages result.[14a]

At the present day these are of much importance. With regard to a gift to a charity, benefits accrue in the field of inheritance tax, capital gains tax and corporation tax, and in relation to gifts that are covenanted to be made to a charity for a period that may last more than three years[15]. With regard to a charity's current operations benefits accrue in the field of income tax, the community charge, and capital gains tax (on disposals of property).

In addition to the benefits arising from specific tax exemptions, there is the financial benefit gained from the fact that a body with charitable status may be more likely to be successful in attracting donations than one without what, in the eyes of some, may appear to be a badge of respectability.

It will have been noted that in former times charitable status conferred no special advantage, and might indeed be disadvantageous. For example, in *Re Allsop*[16] a legacy given to the Nottingham School of Art failed because it was charitable and so was subject to the Mortmain laws[17]. A legacy to the Nottingham Sacred Harmonic Society was not charitable and so was not subject to the Mortmain laws and thus was valid. At the present day, on the other hand, if a body has charitable status considerable advantages accrue.

We have outlined the evolution of the significance in law of the word 'charity'. In a book of this size it is not possible to give an account of the development of charities themselves from their beginnings until the present day—of predominance of the ecclesiastical institutions in medieval philanthropy; of the breakdown of the old order during the fifteenth century; the diversion of donations from religious to secular objectives, in particular schools and colleges, during the sixteenth century; the emergence during the same century of new social needs produced by the economic (and, in particular, agrarian) changes, and the rise of a wealthy merchant class who tended to channel their benevolence directly to their chosen ends rather than, as formerly, through the medium of the church; the part played by the

---

12 Section 24. Whilst the Commission in giving advice must exercise reasonable care, no action for damages at common law lies against the Commission in respect of advice that proves to have been given negligently, proved false, and occasioned loss. *Mills v Winchester Diocesan Board of Finance* [1989] Ch 428, [1989] 2 All ER 317.

13 Section 1(3).

14 As defined by s 45(1) of the Act: 'any institution, corporate or not, which is established for charitable purposes and is subject to the control of the High Court in the exercise of the court's jurisdiction with respect to charities'. See *Construction Industry Training Board v A-G* [1973] Ch 173, [1972] 2 All ER 1339. 'Charitable purposes' are defined as 'purposes which are exclusively charitable according to the law of England and Wales' (s 46).

14a M. Norton, *A Guide to the Benefits of Charitable Status.*

15 [1989] Conv 321 (D. Morris).

16 (1884) 1 TLR 4.

17 There was a corresponding outcome in *Re Lacy* [1899] 2 Ch 149.

influence of Protestantism in producing the distinction that came increasingly to be drawn between the 'deserving' and the 'undeserving' poor, the introduction of statutory provision for relief of the poor—administered by the parish, and paid for out of local rates—by the Act of 1572 and the beginning that this marked of the separate but intertwined stories of State and private provision for the relief of destitution; the decline in the older, paternalistic, attitudes of the rich towards the poor that followed the growing acceptance of laissez-faire principles during the eighteenth century; the emergence of new needs following the changes of the industrial revolution; the growth in size and scope of private philanthropy during the nineteenth century (and the moralistic attitude of many charities founded during this period); the increasing use of appeals for subscriptions from the public to support charities, and the changes made in the statutory regulation of charities during the second half of the last century; the emergence in the twentieth century of the State as the principal provider in the field of social welfare, and the consequent relegation of charities in this field to a supplementary rôle; the increase in the range of charitable objects pursued in the present century; the adoption by many charities, as a means of achieving their aims, of activities in some respects characteristic of a 'pressure group', and the problems that this development has posed in view of the principle that a body which pursues political objectives cannot be charitable—these, and many other themes, cannot be explored in the detail that their interest warrants. All that can be done is draw the reader's attention to the importance of seeing the present law against the background of the development of private philanthropy and of State provision in this country over previous centuries and to refer him to the accounts given of these matters in other books[18].

Charitable status

Having outlined why it matters whether a trust has charitable status, we must now consider the question of what constitutes charitable status.

It might be thought that a trust set up for one of the purposes mentioned in the preamble to the 1601 Act would unquestionably have the status of a charity. After the passing of the Act this was probably so. But it has subsequently become established that in order to have charitable status in law (and so be entitled to the various advantages attaching to charitable status) a trust must not only be for a charitable purpose (ie for a purpose mentioned in the preamble or a purpose which in later times has since been accepted by the courts as being a charitable purpose) but (subject to certain exceptions) must also be for what is termed the *public benefit*. We shall be examining the meaning of the term public benefit later, but for the present it can be taken as indicating the benefit of a sufficiently large group of people.

We shall first consider what purposes are in law charitable, and then the meaning of the term 'public benefit'.

---

18 See M. Chesterman, *Charities, Trusts and Social Welfare* (1979) Chaps 1–5; G. H. Jones, *History of Charity Laws 1550–1827* (1969); G. W. Keeton and L. A. Sheridon, *The Modern Law of Charities* (2nd edn, 1971); Annual Reports of the Charity Commissioners.

Charitable purposes

THE PREAMBLE OF THE ACT OF 1601

What, in law, is a charitable purpose? Consider the list of purposes in the preamble to the Act of 1601, set out on page 92.

It will be seen that the preamble does not give a definition of 'charity'. The Act does, however, indicate (in s 3) that the purposes listed were regarded as being charitable. But what if a purpose is not included in the list? It has long been accepted that the list is not exclusive: 'no catalogue of illustrations, however long, can exhaust or confine charity's scope[19]'. Thus the categories of charitable purpose are not closed, and a purpose not on the list may be charitable nonetheless, provided it is within the 'spirit and intendment'[20] of the Act. As the matter has been expressed 'In deciding the case we must fall back upon the Statute of Elizabeth, not upon the strict or narrow words of it, but upon what has been called the spirit of it, or the intention of it'[1]. Whether or not a purpose satisfies this condition is for the courts to decide and over the years a great volume of case law has accumulated on the question.

With regard to the legal status of the preamble today, the whole of the 1601 Act was repealed by the Mortmain and Charitable Uses Act 1888[2], but the 1888 Act, after reciting the words of the preamble, provided[3] that 'references to such charities shall be construed as references to charities within the meaning, purview, and interpretation of the said preamble'. The whole of the 1888 Act was repealed by the Charities Act 1960[4], which in turn provided[5]

> 'Any reference in any enactment or document to a charity within the meaning, purview and interpretation of the Charitable Uses Act 1601, or of the preamble to it, shall be construed as a reference to a charity within the meaning which the word bears as a legal term according to the law of England and Wales'.

The precise effect of these words on the status of the preamble is not entirely clear[6], but whatever the position of the preamble may be in the context of the statute law, its influence as a guide to what in law is a charitable purpose continues to operate by virtue of the fact that the courts have themselves accepted[7], as noted above, that in order to be charitable, a purpose must be within the 'spirit and intendment'[8] of the preamble. Thus the

---

19   Per Lord Evershed MR, *Re Cole* [1958] Ch 877 at 891.
20   Per Grant MR, *Morice v Bishop of Durham* (1804) 9 Ves 399, 405.
1   Per Lindley LJ, *Re Macduff* [1896] 2 Ch 451 at 467.
2   Section 13(1) and Schedule.
3   Section 13(2).
4   Section 38(1).
5   Section 38(4).
6   See O. R. Marshall (1961) 24 MLR 444; Picarda, op cit, p 9.
7   *Gilmour v Coats* [1949] AC 426, 442–3, per Lord Simmonds.
8   *Morice v Bishop of Durham* (1804) 9 Ves 399 at 405; *Re Macduff*, ante. *Scottish Burial Reform and Cremation Society Ltd v Glasgow City Corpn* [1968] AC 138, [1967] 3 All ER 215, HL; (M & B); *Incorporated Council of Law Reporting for England and Wales v A-G* [1971] Ch 626, [1971] 1 All ER 436; (M & B).

authority of the preamble, though born in a statute, continues its life in case law[9].

On the subject of the relevance of the Preamble to the 1601 Act the Charity Commissioners have commented[10], 'There is also a misconception about the state of charity law. The modern concept of what purposes are charitable in law is based on a list of examples set out in the Preamble to the Elizabethan Statute of 1601. This fact is often mentioned with derision by those who criticise the existing law, allege that it is out of date, and would like to see it altered to accommodate their own ideas. The fact is, however, that over the centuries the Courts have developed and extended by analogy the law relating to charitable purposes thus enabling the concept of charity to evolve with the changing needs of Society ... (We do not wish to argue that the present position is free from anomalies—no system is. But the idea that charity law has not altered since the mists of time is misplaced[11].)'

LORD MACNAGHTEN'S SUMMARY

In *Income Tax Special Purposes Comrs v Pemsel*[12], Lord Macnaghten said:

'How far then, it may be asked, does the popular meaning of the word "charity" correspond with its legal meaning? "Charity" in the legal sense comprises four principal divisions: trusts for the relief of poverty; trusts for the advancement of education; trusts for the advancement of religion; and trusts for other purposes beneficial to the community, not falling under any of the preceding heads'[13].

It will be noted that Lord Macnaghten said that charity *comprised*, ie included, the divisions he gave. He did not attempt to define charity, nor did he purport to classify charitable purposes. This is as well, because, as a classification, his system is unsatisfactory, since any classification with more than two heads which includes a group headed, in effect, 'others', is not a valid system of a classification. Nor are the categories mutually exclusive; some purposes could fall under two or more heads, eg a trust for the provision of religious education to poor orphans. Further, as a classification, it is without a point: a purpose under, say, the second head is in no different a position in law from one under the third. The only category of purpose which in law stands apart from all others is Lord Macnaghten's first head, trusts for the relief of poverty. In what way it stands apart we shall see later. But the fact that it does stand apart means that one classification which serves some purpose in law is:

9   *Re Hopkins* [1965] Ch 669 at 678. On the criteria by reference to which the courts today determine whether a purpose is in law charitable, see H. Cohen, *Charities—A Utilitarian Perspective* [1983] CLP 241.

10 Report of the Charity Commissioners for England and Wales for 1982, para 5. On the Commissioners' awareness of the need to take account of change in social conditions in their application of the law, see their Report for 1985, paras 5–7. (In 1985 the Commissioners accepted as charitable trusts for providing advice and facilities concerning contraception; for providing family conciliation services; and for the promotion of good community relations.)

11 For the case for reform of the definition, see [1989] Conv 28 (S. Bright).

12 [1891] AC 531 at 583.

13 Lord Macnaghten's divisions were based on those put forward in argument by Sir (then Mr) Samuel Romilly in *Morice v Bishop of Durham* (1805) 10 Ves 522 at 532.

1. Trusts for the relief of poverty.

2. Trusts for purposes other than the relief of poverty.

Lord Macnaghten's summary has, however, been referred to, relied on and confirmed in numerous subsequent cases. And it has become customary when giving examples of purposes which are charitable to group them under Lord Macnaghten's four headings, a course which we shall follow here.

1 Trusts for the relief of poverty

Trusts for the relief of poverty are one of the oldest forms of charitable trust and this object is referred to in the preamble both expressly (as at (i), (vii) and (x)[14]) and impliedly (as at (viii)).

What is 'poverty' today? In the law of charities the word is used in two senses. In the first place, it is used in an absolute sense, to indicate the condition of those who live at so low an economic level as to have reached the point when, for example, they stand in need of soup dispensed free at a soup kitchen[15]. An intention to relieve poverty can be inferred also from a stipulation that to be eligible persons must have an income below a specified level[16]. But, using the word 'poverty' in an absolute sense, a trust will not necessarily be for the relief of poverty if it is merely for the relief of those who happen to have relatively low incomes. Thus in 1954 a trust for the provision of housing for 'the working classes' (which might have been thought to be intended to benefit those who were, at any rate in 1954, financially not well off) was held not to be for the relief of poverty[17].

On the other hand in 1978, in *Re Niyazi's Will Trusts*[18], Megarry V-C held that a gift for the purpose of constructing a 'working men's hostel' in Famagusta, Cyprus, was, although 'desperately near the border-line', charitable. He said, 'The connotation of "lower income" is, I think, emphasised by the word "hostel". No doubt there are a number of hostels of superior quality; and one day, perhaps, I may even encounter the expression "luxury hostel". But without any such laudatory adjective the word "hostel" has to my mind a strong flavour of a building which provides somewhat modest accommodation for those who have some temporary need for it and are willing to accept accommodation of that standard in order to meet the need. When "hostel" is prefixed by the expression "working men's", then the further restriction is introduced of the hostel being intended for those with a relatively low income who work for their living, especially as manual workers. ... Furthermore, the need will not be the need of the better paid working men who can afford something superior to mere hostel accommodation, but the need of the lower end of the financial scale of working men, who cannot compete for the better accommodation but have to content

---

14 See p 92, ante.

15 *Biscoe v Jackson* (1887) 35 Ch D 460.

16 *Re De Carteret* [1933] 1 Ch 103. On the difficulties inherent in attempting to define poverty by reference to a minimum datum line, see Chesterman, op cit, pp 141–144.

17 *Re Sander's Will Trusts* [1954] Ch 265, [1954] 1 All ER 667. See also *Re Drummond* [1914] 2 Ch 90.

18 [1978] 3 All ER 785, [1978] 1 WLR 910; (M & B).

themselves with the economies and shortcomings of hostel life'. Thus the gift was charitable, though 'by no great margin'[19].

In recent times housing associations have been accorded charitable status when their objects have been in such terms as: 'to carry on for the benefit of the community the business of providing housing and any associated amenities for persons in necessitous circumstances upon terms appropriate to their means'.

In the second sense of 'poverty', the word is used relatively and indicates the condition of those who for some reason stand in some special need, or who are less well off than they were. In this sense a trust is for the relief of poverty if it is for the benefit of those who have come down in the world; who have fallen upon 'evil days'[20]; 'who have to "go short" in the ordinary acceptation of that term, due regard being had to their status in life and so forth'[1]. Trusts for 'decayed actors'[2], for 'ladies of limited means'[3], for relatives 'in special need'[4], for 'ladies in reduced circumstances'[5] and for 'distressed gentle folk'[6] were held to be charitable on this ground. Under this head of special need may be placed also trusts for the relief of those who have suffered as a result of some natural[7] or man made[8] disaster.

The fact that a trust is for the relief of poverty may be indicated expressly or may be inferred, as for example in a trust for the assistance of young women having their first baby in a Salvation Army home[9]; in a trust to assist persons who resided in a certain borough to emigrate to any of the Dominions of the British Empire[10]; and in a trust for 'widows and children of seamen belonging to the town of Liverpool'[11]. An intention to relieve poverty will not, however, be inferred from use of the word 'deserving' (as in a trust to provide dowries 'for deserving Jewish girls'[12]) unless the context shows the relief of poverty to be the intention.

Trusts for the relief of poverty may be in general terms or may specify the particular means by which the end is to be achieved; for example, the provision of almshouses, soup kitchens, hospitals, dispensaries, orphanages, 'homes' of various kinds, flats, allotments, interest-free loans, apprenticeships, clothing, fuel, food, or money, in each case with or without specification of the category of persons (eg clergymen, working girls, railwaymen, policemen, inhabitants of a locality) entitled to benefit.

We shall see later[13] that a trust is charitable only if it is exclusively for charitable purposes. This rule has a special relevance in the case of trusts for

19 [1978] 1 WLR 910 at 915.
20 *Spiller v Maude* (1881) 32 Ch D 158n.
 1 Per Evershed MR, *Re Coulthurst's Will Trusts* [1951] 1 All ER 774 at 776.
 2 *Spiller v Maude* (1881) 32 Ch D 158n.
 3 *Re Gardom* [1914] 1 Ch 662.
 4 *Re Cohen* [1973] 1 All ER 889, [1973] 1 WLR 415.
 5 *Mary Clark Home Trustees v Anderson* [1904] 2 KB 645.
 6 *Re Young* [1951] Ch 344, [1950] 2 All ER 1245. See also *Re Clarke* [1923] 2 Ch 407 (a trust 'for persons of moderate means such as clerks, governesses and others who may not be able or eligible to benefit under the National Insurance Act' held to be charitable).
 7 *Re North Devon and West Somerset Relief Fund Trusts* [1953] 2 All ER 1032, [1953] 1 WLR 1260.
 8 *Hobourn Aero Components Ltd's Air Raid Distress Fund* [1946] Ch 86, [1945] 2 All ER 711.
 9 *Re Mitchell* [1963] NZLR 934.
10 *Re Tree* [1945] Ch 325, [1945] 2 All ER 65.
11 *Powell v A-G* (1817) 3 Mer 48.
12 *Re Cohen* (1919) 36 TLR 16.
13 See p 128, post.

the relief of poverty; if a trust can benefit others besides those who are poor, it is not charitable. For example, in *Re Gwyon*[14] property was left on trust to establish a foundation to provide knickers for boys of a specified age, the sons of parents resident in the district of Farnham. It was held that as other than the poor could benefit, the trust was not charitable.

The preamble refers to the relief of the 'aged, impotent and poor'. It has been held[15] that this phrase may be read disjunctively. Thus trusts for the 'aged' or for the 'impotent' may be charitable. Trusts for these objects are considered below[16].

2 Advancement of education

Trusts falling under this head are mentioned at (iii) and (v) in the preamble.

'Education' has been interpreted widely and extends far beyond the encouragement of the teaching in schools and colleges of subjects customarily taught in such institutions. 'Education' connotes, inter alia, the imparting and dissemination of knowledge (eg of the decisions of the courts[17]); the encouragement of the study of conventional academic[18] and commercial subjects[19], the carrying out of technical or industrial training[20]; the establishment or maintenance of museums or libraries[1], and the promotion of practices considered to be of educational benefit (eg chess[2], choral singing[3], and musical appreciation[4]).

The encouragement of sport for its own sake (eg the provision of prizes for yachting[5]) is not for the 'advancement of education', but the encouragement of a sport at an educational establishment (eg by providing a fives court at a public school[6]) may be for this purpose if it incidentally assists the purpose of education as where a trust was created for the encouragement of the playing of football and other sports at schools and universities 'to assist in ensuring that due attention is given to the physical education and developments and occupation of [the] minds' of those who would benefit[7]. So also may be a students' union if it provides the physical, cultural and social outlets

---

14 [1930] 1 Ch 255; (M & B); see also *Re Drummond* [1914] 2 Ch 90, and *Re Ward's Estate* (1937) 81 Sol Jo 397 (gift to provide sweets every Bank Holiday for children under 14 resident in a certain parish held not to be charitable).
15 *Re Fraser* (1883) 22 Ch D 827.
16 See p 105, post.
17 *Incorporated Council of Law Reporting for England and Wales v A-G* [1972] Ch 73, [1971] 3 All ER 1029, CA.
18 Eg by the provision of books for prizes in classics. *Re Mariette* [1915] 2 Ch 284.
19 *Re Koettgens Will Trusts* [1954] Ch 252, [1954] 1 All ER 581.
20 *Construction Industry Training Board v A-G* [1971] 3 All ER 449, [1971] 1 WLR 1303; *Reeve v A-G* (1843) 3 Hare 191 and *Loscombe v Wintringham* (1850) 13 Beav 87 (training for domestic service).
1 *A-G v Marchant* (1866) LR 3 Eq 424.
2 *Re Dupree's Deed Trusts* [1945] Ch 16, [1944] 2 All ER 443; (M & B).
3 *Royal Choral Society v IRC* [1943] 2 All ER 101, CA.
4 *Re Delius* [1957] Ch 299, [1957] 1 All ER 854; (M & B).
5 *Re Nottage* [1895] 2 Ch 649.
6 *Re Mariette* [1915] 2 Ch 284. See also *Re Geere's Will Trusts (No 2)* [1954] CLY 388 (gift to provide a swimming pool at a public school).
7 *IRC v McMullen* [1981] AC 1, [1980] 1 All ER 884, HL; (M & B).

which are necessary if a college is efficiently to perform its educational function[8].

'Education' has also included augmenting the stipends of fellows and scholars of a college[9], building and endowing a theatre for the performance of Shakespeare's plays and other English classical drama and promoting good acting[10], providing an annual field day or treat for school children (as tending to encourage nature study)[11], the purchase of works of art for public display[12]; the teaching of 'self-control, elocution, oratory, deportment, the arts of personal contact, of social intercourse, and the other acts of public, private, professional and business life'[13]; the provision of a playground for children in a city[14]; the endowment of prizes[15]; gifts to learned institutions (eg the Royal Geographical Society[16]); assisting the publication of books likely to be of educational value (eg a dictionary[17]), and promoting certain forms of research.

What forms of research would be charitable (either under the head of education or under Lord Macnaghten's fourth head) was considered in *Re Hopkins Will Trusts*[18] where it was held (obiter) that for a gift for research to be charitable it must,

   (i) be of educational value to the researcher; or
   (ii) be so directed as to lead to something which would pass into the store of educational material; or
   (iii) be so directed as to improve the sum of communicable knowledge in an area which education (including the formation of literary taste and appreciation) might cover.

Since 'education' consists of the imparting of knowledge to others, a gift to be applied for the mere acquisition of knowledge by research, without any diffusion of such knowledge when acquired, will not be charitable[19]. However, in the absence of any indication to the contrary, the court will be readily inclined to construe a trust for research as importing subsequent dissemination of the results, either by publication, or by being made available to others researching in the same field[20].

There is no requirement that a trust for the advancement of education must, to be charitable, be confined to the advancement of the education of the poor[1]. Thus schools or colleges, the level of whose fees, in practice, restrict

---

8 *London Hospital Medical College v IRC* [1976] 2 All ER 113, [1976] 1 WLR 613; *Baldry v Feintuck* [1972] 2 All ER 81, [1972] 1 WLR 552; *A-G v Ross* [1985] 3 All ER 334, [1986] 1 WLR 252.
9 *Christ's College, Cambridge Case* (1757) 1 Wm Bl 90.
10 *Re Shakespeare Memorial Trust* [1923] 2 Ch 398.
11 *Re Mellody* [1918] 1 Ch 228.
12 *Re Shaw's Will Trusts* [1952] Ch 163, [1952] 1 All ER 49; (M & B).
13 *Re Shaw's Will Trusts*, supra.
14 *Re Chesters* [1935] Ch 77, cited in *IRC v Baddeley* [1955] AC 572, [1955] 1 All ER 525, HL.
15 *Re Mariette* [1915] 2 Ch 284.
16 *Beaumont v Oliveira* (1869) 4 Ch App 309.
17 *Re Stanford* [1924] 1 Ch 73.
18 [1965] Ch 669, [1964] 3 All ER 46; (M & B); (1965) 29 Conv (NS) 368 (M. Newark).
19 *Whicker v Hume* (1858) 7 HL Cas 124; *Re Besterman* (1980) unreported.
20 *Re Besterman*, supra.
1 *A-G v Lord Lonsdale* (1827) 1 Sim 105 (school for 'the sons of gentlemen' held to be charitable).

admission to the children of the relatively well off, are not precluded[2] from having charitable status.

That a line exists beyond which the courts will decline to accept that a purpose will have the effect of advancing education, is illustrated by *Re Pinion*[3], in which a testator left his studio and its contents (which included paintings by himself, furniture, china and bric-à-brac) to his trustees to form a museum, to be endowed by the residuary estate. It was held that there was overwhelming evidence that the 'haphazard assembly'[4] was worthless as a means of education, and that no useful purpose would be served by foisting on the public a 'mass of junk'[4]. (The specific and the residuary gifts thus both failed.)

3 Advancement of religion[5]

Although trusts for the advancement of religion are amongst the oldest forms of charitable trust, religion is referred to only indirectly in the preamble. But it was only shortly after the Act that the court accepted that a trust for the advancement of religion in the form of a gift to maintain a preaching minister was charitable 'though this is no charitable use mentioned in the Statute'[6]. The process of extending the sphere of trusts associated with religion has continued down to modern times, and at the present day trusts for the advancement of religion embrace a wide field and extend as regards religions and denominations, (i) to all Christian denominations (eg the established church[7], Roman Catholics[8], Baptists[9], Unitarians[10], Exclusive (formerly Plymouth) Brethren[11], the Salvation Army[12],) and the followers of a sect founded by a particular person[13] (notwithstanding that the court 'might consider the opinions sought to be propagated foolish or even devoid of foundation'[14]); (ii) to the Jewish faith[15]; (iii) and possibly to other religions, though there is no judicial authority on this point. When Sir John Romilly said in 1862, 'I am of the opinion that the Court of Chancery makes no distinction between one sort of religion and another'[16], it is not clear whether he was speaking of one sort of Christian religion and another or whether he intended to be taken literally. Today the literal sense of his words would probably be regarded as representing the accepted view. In 1961 Cross J said, 'As between different religions the law stands neutral, but it assumes that

2   For discussion of the argument as to whether independent schools should continue to be entitled to charitable status, see Chesterman, op cit, pp 332–339.
3   [1965] Ch 85, [1964] 1 All ER 890; (M & B). See also *Re Ward's Estate*, ante.
4   Per Harman LJ [1965] Ch 85 at 107.
5   *Religious Trusts*, C. E. Crowther; *Religion and the Law*, St. J. A. Robilliard (Chap 4).
6   *Pember v Inhabitants of Kington* (1639) Toth 34, Duke 82.
7   *Re Eighmie* [1935] Ch 524.
8   *Re Flinn* [1948] Ch 241, [1948] 1 All ER 541.
9   *Re Strickland's Will Trusts* [1936] 3 All ER 1027.
10 *Re Nesbitt's Will Trusts* [1953] 1 All ER 936, [1953] 1 WLR 595.
11 *Holmes v A-G* (1981) *Times*, 12 February.
12 *Re Fowler* (1914) 31 TLR 102, CA.
13 *Thornton v Howe* (1862) 31 Beav 14; *Re Watson* [1973] 3 All ER 678, [1973] 1 WLR 1472; (M & B).
14 Per Sir John Romilly MR, *Thornton v Howe*, ante, at 19.
15 *Neville Estates Ltd v Madden* [1962] Ch 832, [1961] 3 All ER 769; (M & B).
16 *Thornton v Howe* (1862) 31 Beav 14, 19.

any religion is at least likely to be better than none'[17]. (Regulations[18] made under the Charities Act 1960 assume that trusts for the advancement of religions other than Christianity are for a charitable purpose, and organisations associated with the Muslims, Sikh and Hindu faiths have been registered.) It has been held, however, that a body, the Free Masons, which did not hold religious services or carry out religious instruction and whose members, whilst required to believe in a Supreme Being and lead a moral life, did not need to practise any religion, was not for the advancement of religion[19].

As regards organisations within a religion or denomination, trusts for the advancement of religion have been held to include organisations which exist to propagate the tenets of a faith, either at home[20] or abroad[1] and communities which exist for the observance of a particular form of religious life[2].

As regards the physical accoutrements of religion, trusts for the advancement of religion have included trusts for the erection or maintenance of the fabric of a church[3] or chapel or synagogue[4]; or part of such a building, eg a window[5], a chancel[5], or a tomb or monument forming part of the fabric of a church[5]; and to the upkeep of a whole churchyard or burial ground[6] and to the erection and maintenance of a particular set of headstones (those of the graves of pensioners of certain almshouses), since this would tend to the improvement of the appearance of the whole churchyard[7].

As regards religious observances, trusts under this head have included trusts for the promotion of choral singing[8]; for the ringing of bells on the anniversary of the Restoration each year[9]; for the preaching of an annual sermon[10], for the provision of prizes at a Sunday school[11]; and for the saying of Masses for the dead (this practice enabling a ritual act to be performed which is central to the religion of a large proportion of Christian people and assisting in the endowment of priests whose duty it is to perform the act[12]). In *Re Hetherington*[13], in 1989, it was held that in a gift for the saying of Masses there was a sufficient element of public benefit if the Masses were said in public, and the moneys used for the provision of stipends for the priests who said the Masses, so relieving the church funds *pro tanto*.

---

17 *Neville Estates Ltd v Madden, ante,* at 781. *Re Watson* [1973] 3 All ER 678, [1973] 1 WLR 1472.
18 S.I. 1962 (No 1421); S.I. 1963 (No 2074).
19 *United Grand Lodge of Ancient Free and Accepted Masons of England v Holborn Borough Council* [1957] 3 All ER 281, [1957] 1 WLR 1080; (M & B).
20 *Re Smith* (1938) 54 TLR 851.
1 *Re Maguire* (1870) LR 9 Eq 632.
2 *Re Banfield* [1968] 2 All ER 276, [1968] 1 WLR 846.
3 *Re Eighmie* [1935] Ch 524.
4 *Neville Estates Ltd v Madden* [1962] Ch 832, [1961] 3 All ER 769; (M & B).
5 *Hoare v Osborne* (1866) LR 1 Eq 585.
6 *Re Eighmie, ante. Re Douglas* [1905] 1 Ch 279.
7 *Re Pardoe* [1906] 2 Ch 184.
8 *Re Royce* [1940] Ch 514, [1940] 2 All ER 291.
9 *Re Pardoe* [1906] 2 Ch 184.
10 *Re Parker's Charity* (1863) 32 Beav 654.
11 *Re Strickland's Will Trusts* [1936] 3 All ER 1027.
12 *Re Caus* [1934] Ch 162; *Bourne v Keane* [1919] AC 815, HL (gift for the saying of Masses held not to be illegal as being for superstitious uses). See Brady, *Religion and the Law of Charities in Ireland* (1976) pp 66–119; Picarda, op cit, pp 65–68.
13 [1990] Ch 1, [1989] 2 All ER 129; (M & B); (1989) CLJ 373 (J. Hopkins); (1989) Conv 453 (N. D. M. Parry).

As regards the support of ministers of religion, trusts have been held to be charitable when they were for the payment of ministers, either generally[14], or for a particular purpose, eg to pay an incumbent for preaching an annual sermon in commemoration of the testatrix[15], and for the relief of infirm, aged and sick ministers[16].

As regards the framing of the gift, trusts have been held to be charitable under this head where the purpose is stated expressly and where it is impliedly for the advancement of religion, eg a gift 'for God's work'[17].

As regards religious communities and organisations associated with a particular religious denomination the courts have accepted that these are charitable if the purpose of their existence is to advance, ie to 'promote'[18], religion. Thus a Sunday school has been held to be charitable[19]. In the case of a religious community, if the members undertake work, pastoral or social, outside the walls of the house, or offer services of a spiritual[20] or eleemosynary character to members of the public who visit the house—if in some way the work of the community 'opens out to reach the public'[1]—then the community will have charitable status[2]. On the other hand, it has been held that a community whose members live a purely cloistered life and undertake no outside work is not charitable. For this reason, (and also on the grounds of lack of public benefit) a gift to a Carmelite Convent which consisted of a cloistered community of nuns who contemplated and prayed but did no outside work[3], and a gift to a Dominican Convent which consisted of a celibate community of females who lived together under a common superior, for the purpose of sanctifying their own souls by prayer and pious meditation[4], were held not to be charitable[5].

So wide a field does 'religion' today embrace that a trust that in any way advances religion (as opposed to a gift which could be for purely secular purposes, eg 'for good works'[6]) is only likely to fail to be for the advancement of religion if the religion or sect concerned is one which 'inculcates doctrines adverse to the very foundations of all religion', or is 'subversive of all morality'[7], or is one whose belief is atheism or agnosticism[8]. Further a society will not be for the advancement of religion if its objects are 'the study and dissemination of ethical principles and the cultivation of a rational religious

---

14   *Pember v Inhabitants of Kington* (1639) Toth 34.
15   *Re Parker's Charity* (1863) 32 Beav 654.
16   *Re Forster* [1939] Ch 22, [1938] 3 All ER 767.
17   *Re Barker's Will Trusts* (1948) 64 TLR 273.
18   Per Rigby LJ, *Re Macduff* [1896] 2 Ch 451 at 474.
19   *Re Strickland's Will Trusts* [1936] 3 All ER 1027.
20   *Re Banfield* [1968] 2 All ER 276, [1968] 1 WLR 846.
1   Per Goff J, *Re Banfield,* ante, at p 852.
2   A decision which is difficult to reconcile with others in this field is *Re Warre's Will Trusts* [1953] 2 All ER 99, [1953] 1 WLR 725 in which an Anglican 'retreat house' (a house devoted to a form of religious exercise known as a 'retreat', by which persons retired for a time from the activities of the world for religious contemplation and cleansing of the soul) was held not to be charitable. See Picarda, op cit, p 71.
3   *Gilmour v Coats* [1949] AC 426, [1949] 1 All ER 848, HL; (M & B).
4   *Cocks v Manners* (1871) LR 12 Eq 574.
5   Cf *Holmes v A-G* (1981) *Times,* 12 February.
6   *Re How* [1930] 1 Ch 66.
7   Per Sir John Romilly, *Thornton v Howe* (1862) 31 Beav 14 at 19.
8   *Barralet v A-G* [1980] 3 All ER 918, [1980] 1 WLR 1565, [1981] Conv 150 (St. J. Robilliard).

sentiment'[9]. ('Religion, as I see it, is concerned with man's relations with God, and ethics are concerned with man's relations with man'[10].)

If the terms of the trust extend beyond religious (or other charitable) purposes, then the trust will not be charitable by reason of the rule (to be considered in more detail later[11]) that, in order to be charitable, a trust must be exclusively charitable. It was for this reason that a gift to establish 'a Catholic daily newspaper' was held not to be charitable[12].

4 Other purposes beneficial to the community

To be charitable, trusts falling under this head must (like those under Lord Macnaghten's other three heads) be 'within the spirit and intendment' of the preamble of the 1601 Act. Trusts which have been held to satisfy this requirement may be grouped for convenience under the following sub-headings. The range of objects, however, is so wide that no classification is likely to be entirely satisfactory or exhaustive. We shall begin by considering purposes authority for which may be traced to the preamble of the Act of 1601.

RELIEF OF THE 'AGED'

We have seen[13] that the words 'aged, impotent and poor' in the preamble may be read disjunctively. Thus relief of the aged is a charitable purpose. Trusts for this purpose have taken the form of trusts for the old or the aged, *simpliciter,* or for those over a specified age[14], or in a certain condition or in a particular place (eg in a nursing home[15]), trusts to provide direct financial aid[16], or to provide accommodation (eg flats[17] or bungalows[18], with[18] or without additional services such as a warden) for the aged, or to maintain such accommodation[19]. Thus housing associations have been accorded charitable status where their objects have been in such terms as 'for providing for aged persons in need thereof housing and any associated amenities specially designed or adapted to meet the disabilities and requirements of such persons'.

In some instances it is to be inferred that the intention is to aid elderly persons who are in need of assistance by virtue of their limited means[20]. Here the relief of poverty reinforces the charitable character of the trust. But it

---

9 *Barralet v A-G* [1980] 3 All ER 918, [1980] 1 WLR 1565; (M & B). (The society was, however, held to be charitable as being for the advancement of education.)
10 Per Dillon J, *Re South Place Ethical Society,* supra, 1571, 924.
11 See p 121, post.
12 *Roman Catholic Archbishop of Melbourne v Lawlor* (1934) 51 CLR 1.
13 See p 95, ante.
14 *Re Glyn's Will Trusts* [1950] 2 All ER 1150n.
15 *Re Bradbury* [1950] 2 All ER 1150n.
16 *Re Robinson* [1951] Ch 198, [1950] 2 All ER 1148.
17 *Re Cottam's Will Trusts* [1955] 3 All ER 704, [1955] 1 WLR 1299.
18 *Joseph Rowntree Memorial Trust Housing Association Ltd v A-G* [1983] Ch 159, [1983] 1 All ER 288; (M & B); (1983) 46 MLR 782 (R. Nobles).
19 *Re Payling's Will Trusts* [1969] 3 All ER 698, [1969] 1 WLR 1595.
20 See *Re Lucas* [1922] 2 Ch 52.

has never been held that in order to be charitable a trust for the relief of the elderly must be for the relief of the elderly who are also poor[1].

RELIEF OF THE 'IMPOTENT'

Relief of the 'impotent' is a charitable purpose for the same reason as is relief of the 'aged'. Today 'impotent' includes the condition of those suffering as a result of sickness, injury or disease, or of physical or mental disability, or who are in special need of rest (eg by reason of the stress caused by the conditions in which they live or work)[2]. Trusts for these purposes have included trusts for establishing and endowing non-profit-making[3] hospitals[4], nursing homes, and homes of rest (eg for 'lady teachers'[5], and for 'the Sisters of the Epiphany at Truro'[6]); providing additional amenities or facilities for patients in hospitals (eg accommodation for relatives visiting the critically ill[7], flowers[8]); providing a nurses' home (as tending to increase the efficiency of a hospital[9]); providing aid for those suffering from a particular disease, disability (eg blindness[10]) or conditions (eg alcoholism or drug addiction[11]); the furtherance of the use of a particular form of treatment (eg 'psychological healing in accordance with the teaching of Jesus Christ'[12]) promoting the science and art of nursing[13], and the training of doctors and nurses; providing for the care of sick or wounded members of a branch of the armed forces[14]; promoting research to find the cause of, or treatment for, a particular disease (which could also be a charitable purpose under the head of education[15]); and for the impotent generally, as is a gift for 'the sick and wounded'[16].

PUBLIC WORKS AND BUILDINGS

The preamble refers to 'the repair of bridges, ports, havens, causeways, ... sea-banks and highways, ... the relief, stock or maintenance of houses of correction'.

1   See *Re Glyn's Will Trusts* [1950] 2 All ER 1150n in which Dankwerts J held that the elderly need not be poor to be the subject of charity. For the difficulties raised by this proposition, and, for example, as to whether trusts for 'aged peers' or 'impotent millionaires' would be charitable, see R. E. Megarry (1951) 67 LQR 164, (1955) 71 LQR 16; Picarda, op cit p 79.
2   *Re Chaplin* [1933] Ch 115; *Re James* [1932] 2 Ch 25.
3   *Re Smith's Will Trusts* [1962] 2 All ER 563, [1962] 1 WLR 763.
4   *Re Resch's Will Trusts* [1969] 1 AC 514, [1967] 3 All ER 915, PC; (M & B); *Re Bradwell* [1952] Ch 575, [1952] 2 All ER 286.
5   *Re Estlin* (1903) 72 LJ Ch 687.
6   *Re James* [1932] 2 Ch 25.
7   *Re Dean's Will Trusts* [1950] 1 All ER 882.
8   *Re Adams* [1968] Ch 80, [1967] 3 All ER 285.
9   *Re White's Will Trusts* [1951] 1 All ER 528; see also *Re Bernstein's Will Trusts* (1971) 115 Sol Jo 808 (gift to form fund to provide extra comforts for nurses of a particular hospital at Christmas).
10 *Re Lewis* [1955] Ch 104, [1954] 3 All ER 257.
11 *Re Banfield* [1968] 2 All ER 276, [1968] 1 WLR 846.
12 *Re Osmund* [1944] Ch 206, [1944] 1 All ER 262.
13 *Royal College of Nursing v St Marylebone Corpn* [1959] 3 All ER 663, [1959] 1 WLR 1077.
14 *Re Welsh Hospital (Netley) Fund* [1921] 1 Ch 655.
15 See p 100, ante.
16 *Re Hillier* [1944] 1 All ER 480.

Trusts for the provision[17] as well as the maintenance[18] of these and other public works (eg the supply of water for Chepstow[19]) and facilities (eg a village club and reading room[20], a museum[1]; a hall 'for public purposes'[2]; a memorial hall[3]; a zoo[4]; a public library[5]; a park[6]; a cemetery[7]) have been held to be for charitable purposes. And the Charity Commissioners have treated maintenance of monuments to certain famous men as being charitable[8].

Whether a war memorial, in the form of, eg, a cross (unrelated to any purpose for the betterment of the living, such as a village hall) is charitable is undecided[9]. In *Murray v Thomas*[10] Clauson J indicated that he considered that to collect money for such a memorial was to collect money for a charitable purpose, 'particularly when those to be commemorated are particularly connected with a certain limited area.' But the view was obiter.

PUBLIC SERVICES

The preamble refers to 'the education and preferment of orphans; the relief, stock or maintenance for houses of correction'. Trusts for the provision or improvement of many forms of public service, both national and local, have been held to be charitable. Under this sub-heading can be included trusts for founding a children's home[11]; providing facilities for cremation[12]; promoting the efficiency of the police[13]; and the provision of a fire brigade[14].

RELIEF FROM NATIONAL OR LOCAL TAXATION

The preamble refers to 'the Aid or Ease of any poor Inhabitants concerning payment of Fifteens, ... and other Taxes', but it does not seem that in order to be charitable a gift under this sub-heading need relieve only the poor from taxation.

17 *Forbes v Forbes* (1854) 18 Beav 552 (bridge).
18 *A-G v Governors of Harrow School* (1754) 2 Ves Sen 551 (highway).
19 *Jones v Williams* (1767) Amb 651.
20 *Re Scowcroft* [1898] 2 Ch 638.
 1 *Re Allsop* (1884) 1 TLR 4.
 2 *Re Spence* [1938] Ch 96, [1937] 3 All ER 684.
 3 *Murray v Thomas* [1937] 4 All ER 545.
 4 *North of England Zoological Society v Chester RDC* [1959] 3 All ER 116, [1959] 1 WLR 773, CA.
 5 *Re Jones* [1898] 2 Ch 83.
 6 *Re Hadden* [1932] 1 Ch 133.
 7 *A-G v Blizard* (1855) 21 Beav 233.
 8 Eg the Wellington monument in Somerset and the Cobden obelisk at Midhurst, Sussex. In 1984 the Charity Commissioners accepted as being charitable a fund to erect a monument to a murdered woman police officer on the ground that the provision of such memorials served the public benefit in promoting good citizenship by inculcating in the public an awareness of the hazards constantly undertaken by the police service. *Report of the Charity Commissioners for 1984*, para 17.
 9 See H. Picarda (1983) 133 NLJ 1107.
10 [1937] 4 All ER 545.
11 *Re Sahal's Will Trusts* [1958] 3 All ER 428, [1958] 1 WLR 1243.
12 *Scottish Burial Reform and Cremation Society Ltd v Glasgow City Corpn* [1968] AC 138, [1967] 3 All ER 215, HL; (M & B).
13 *IRC v City of Glasgow Police Athletic Association* [1953] AC 380, 391.
14 *Re Wokingham Fire Brigade Trusts* [1951] Ch 373, [1951] 1 All ER 454.

Gifts under this sub-heading which have been held to be charitable have included a contribution to a fund raised by levying a tax or rate (eg the poor rate[15]); a gift designed to reduce a debt which would otherwise have to be paid out of public money[16]; and a gift designed to pay a tax or rate on behalf of those who would otherwise have to pay it[17].

AIDING NATIONAL SECURITY AND INCREASING EFFICIENCY IN THE ARMED FORCES AND THE MERCHANT MARINE

Where the preamble refers to the 'Aide or Ease of any poor Inhabitants concerning Payment of Fifteens, setting out Soldiers and other Taxes', it might seem that the intention was to relieve only the poor of taxes concerned with, inter alia, 'setting out Soldiers'. Trusts connected with 'setting out Soldiers' have, however, been accepted as forming a separate head of charity. Examples include a gift of an annuity of £100 to the 22nd Middlesex Rifle Volunteer Regiment[18]; a gift for 'the teaching of shooting at moving objects ... so as to prevent as far as possible a catastrophe similar to that at Majuba Hill'[19]; a gift of personalty to maintain a library and purchase plate for the officers' mess of the 2nd battalion of H.M. West Yorkshire Regiment (formerly the 14th Regiment of York)[20], a gift 'to promote the defence of the United Kingdom from attack by hostile aircraft'[1], a gift for the training of boys as officers in the Mercantile Marine and for the provision of an allowance for those who had qualified[2], and a gift 'for the promotion of sport (including in that term only shooting, fishing, cricket, football and polo)' in the 6th Dragoon Guards[3].

FOR RECREATION

A trust for public recreation generally may be charitable as where property is given 'for the provision of playing fields, parks, gymnasiums or other places which will give recreation to as many people as possible[4]' or where land is set aside for 'park and recreation purposes[5]'. But it is well established that a trust to promote a particular form of recreation (eg yachting[6], cricket[7],

---

15   *Doe d Preece v Howells* (1831) 2 B & Ad 744.
16   *Newland v A-G* (1809) 3 Mer 684.
17   *A-G v Bushby* (1857) 24 Beav 299.
18   *Re Lord Stratheden and Campbell* [1894] 3 Ch 265.
19   *Re Stephens* (1892) 8 TLR 792.
20   *Re Good* [1905] 2 Ch 60.
 1   *Re Driffill* [1950] Ch 92, [1949] 2 All ER 933.
 2   *Re Corbyn* [1941] Ch 400, [1941] 2 All ER 160.
 3   *Re Gray* [1925] Ch 362; (M & B).
 4   *Re Hadden* [1932] 1 Ch 133.
 5   *Brisbane City Council v A-G for Queensland* [1979] AC 411, [1978] 3 All ER 30, PC; see
     also *Re Morgan* [1955] 2 All ER 632, [1955] 1 WLR 738. Cf *A-G (ex rel Scotland) v Barratt
     (Manchester) Ltd* (1990) 60 P & CR 475 (agreement under seal between local authority
     and landowner in 1934 under Town and Country Planning Act 1932, s 34 that certain
     land should be preserved as an open space 'for the benefit and amenity of the district' did
     not operate to create a charitable trust of the benefit of the covenant given by the 1934
     agreement to the local authority.
 6   *Re Nottage* [1895] 2 Ch 649.
 7   *Re Patten* [1929] 2 Ch 276.

angling[8] or athletics[9]) is not charitable, unless the recreation is of educational value (eg chess[10]) or the promotion of the recreation is the means adopted to further some object which is charitable in itself (eg the advancement of education[11] or the increase in efficiency of the armed forces[12]).

In *IRC v Baddeley*[13] a trust whose object was 'to establish a community centre in which social intercourse and discreet festivity may go hand in hand with religious observance and instruction' was held not to be charitable (on the ground, inter alia, that the objects of the trust were not exclusively charitable). The decision suggested that the trusts under which many village halls and memorial and other similar institutes operated, trusts which had been accepted as being charitable[14], were in fact not charitable. In order to remove uncertainty the Recreational Charities Act 1958 was passed. Under s 1 of this Act the provision of facilities for 'recreation or other leisure-time occupation' is charitable provided that the facilities are provided 'in the interests of social welfare', and the trust is for the public benefit. In order to satisfy the requirement that the facilities must be provided 'in the interests of social welfare', the Act provides[15] that:

1. The facilities must be provided with the object of *improving the conditions of life* of the person for whom the facilities are primarily intended[15a]; and

2. The facilities must be either

(a) needed by those for whom they are primarily intended by reason of those persons' *youth, age, infirmity or disablement, poverty or social and economic circumstances*; or

(b) available to *members of the public at large*.

The Act provides[16] that subject to these conditions being satisfied, s 1 is to apply in particular 'to the provision of facilities at village halls, community centres and women's institutes, and to the provision and maintenance of grounds and buildings to be used for purposes of recreation and leisure-time occupation and extends to the provision of these facilities by the organising of any activity'.

An example of compliance with conditions 1 and 2(a) above is provided by *Wynn v Skegness UDC*[17], in which a scheme to provide a convalescent home and holiday centre for Derbyshire miners and their wives and families who were in need of a change of air was held to be charitable by virtue of the Act. An example of failure to satisfy the conditions in the Act is provided by the decision of the Court of Appeal in *IRC v McMullen*[18] that a trust

---

8   *Re Clifford* (1911) 106 LT 14.
9   *IRC v City of Glasgow Police Athletic Association* [1953] AC 380, [1953] 1 All ER 747, HL; (M & B).
10 *Re Dupree's Deed Trusts* [1945] Ch 16, [1944] 2 All ER 443; (M & B).
11 *Re Mariette* [1915] 2 Ch 284; *IRC v McMullen* [1981] AC 1, [1980] 1 All ER 884; (M & B).
12 *Re Gray* [1925] Ch 362; (M & B).
13 [1955] AC 572, [1955] 1 All ER 525; (M & B).
14 *Murray v Thomas* [1937] 4 All ER 545.
15 Section 1(2). The italics are added.
15a *Guild v IRC* [1992] 2 All ER 10, [1992] 2 WLR 397, HL. (No requirement that persons to whom facilities provided must be in a position of relative social disadvantage, or suffering from some degree of deprivation.)
16 Section 1(3).
17 [1966] 3 All ER 336, [1967] 1 WLR 52.
18 [1979] 1 All ER 588, [1979] 1 WLR 130; (M & B); [1980] Conv 173 (J. Warburton).

established by the Football Association to provide facilities for, and to encourage the playing of, football and other sports and games by pupils at schools and universities could not be regarded as being 'in the interests of social welfare' within s 1. (The trust was, however, held on appeal by the House of Lords[19] to be charitable as being for the advancement of education[20].)

FOR SAFEGUARDING HUMAN LIFE

Examples are provided by gifts to the Royal National Lifeboat Institution[1] and to the Royal Humane Society for Saving Life[2].

FURTHERANCE OF NATIONAL POLICIES

Under this head may be placed a gift to assist the repatriation of Australian soldiers after the First World War to their country and to help give them a fresh start in life[3], and gifts which have the effect of increasing national prosperity by the promotion of agriculture[4], or industry and commerce[5], or which have the effect of promoting the preservation of law and order[6].

CONSERVATION OF THE NATIONAL HERITAGE

Examples are provided by a gift to the National Trust[7], and a gift of two ancient cottages to the Royal Society of Arts, with a bequest to enable the cottages to be preserved in their existing condition[8].

FOR RELIEF AFTER DISASTERS

Trusts have been held to be charitable where the trust property was money raised by an appeal after a particular disaster (eg the flood which destroyed part of Lynmouth in 1952[9]) or after a certain type of disaster (eg air-raids[10]).

It sometimes happens that the object of an appeal is not framed with any precision at the time when the appeal is launched. In one such case[11], the court being 'unable ... to discover ... any intention to benefit this part of the community in any way which the law would not regard as charitable',

19 [1980] 1 All ER 884, [1980] 2 WLR 416.
20 See p 100, ante.
 1 *Thomas v Howell* (1874) LR 18 Eq 198.
 2 *Beaumont v Oliveira* (1869) 4 Ch App 309.
 3 *Verge v Somerville* [1924] AC 496.
 4 *IRC v Yorkshire Agricultural Society* [1928] 1 KB 611; (M & B).
 5 *Crystal Palace Trustees v Minister of Town and Country Planning* [1951] Ch 132, [1950] 2 All ER 857n. *IRC v White, Re Clerkenwell Green Association for Craftsmen* [1980] TR 155 (preservation and improvement of craftsmanship).
 6 *IRC v City of Glasgow Police Athletic Association* [1953] AC 380, [1953] 1 All ER 747, HL. See also *Re Koeppler Will Trusts* [1986] Ch 423, [1985] 2 All ER 869, CA.
 7 *Re Verrall* [1916] 1 Ch 100.
 8 *Re Cranstoun* [1932] 1 Ch 537.
 9 *Re North Devon and West Somerset Relief Fund Trusts* [1953] 2 All ER 1032, [1953] 1 WLR 1260.
10 *Re Hobourn Aero Components Ltd's Air Raid Distress Fund* [1946] Ch 194, [1946] 1 All ER 501.
11 *North Devon and West Somerset Relief Fund Trusts*, ante.

held that the trust was for a charitable purpose. But where the terms of an appeal are not exclusively for charitable purposes, the trust is not charitable[12].

ENCOURAGING GOOD CITIZENSHIP AND THE PROMOTION OF THE MORAL WELFARE OF MANKIND

Trusts for animals
It is a charitable purpose to 'elevate the human race', and to do so by promoting 'feelings of humanity and morality generally'; and to achieve this by, inter alia, stimulating 'humane and generous sentiments in man towards the lower animals'[13], and to attain this end by promoting kindness towards animals and discouraging cruelty to them. It is on these grounds that trusts for the protection or benefit of animals are today held to be charitable.

Formerly, certain trusts for animals were held to be charitable on the grounds of the utility of animals to mankind[14]. However, although the ground for holding trusts for animals to be charitable has changed, the notion of utility of animals to mankind arises in another context. If the moral benefit to mankind of preventing pain and suffering to animals is held on the evidence to be outweighed by the advantages to mankind of carrying out experiments on animals for the purpose of medical research, experiments which cannot be done without inflicting a degree of pain and suffering on the animals concerned, then the latter advantage will be held to prevail over the former. This was one reason why the abolition of animal vivisection was held not to be a charitable purpose[15].

Trusts for animals have taken the form of trusts for establishing, endowing or maintaining homes for lost, unwanted or elderly animals, either generally or of a particular species (eg dogs[16]), and dispensaries and hospitals for sick animals[17], campaigning for humane treatment of animals[18], either generally or in a particular respect (eg humane slaughter-houses[19]); promoting vegetarianism[20]; and providing for the welfare of animals, either generally[1] or of a particular species (eg cats[2]).

In *Re Grove Grady*[3] property was given to provide 'a refuge or refuges for the preservation of all animals, birds or other creatures . . . so that [they] shall there be safe from molestation and destruction by man'. It was held that the trust was not charitable as it afforded no advantage to man (eg by protecting animals useful to man; or by permitting observation or research) and did not

12 *Re Gillingham Bus Disaster Fund* [1959] Ch 62, [1958] 2 All ER 749; (M & B).
13 Per Swinfen Eady LJ, *Re Wedgwood* [1915] 1 Ch 113 at 122.
14 *London University v Yarrow* (1857) 1 De G & J 72.
15 *National Anti-Vivisection Society v IRC* [1948] AC 31, [1947] 2 All ER 217, HL; (M & B), (reversing the decision in *Re Foveaux* [1895] 2 Ch 501, that a trust for the suppression of vivisection was charitable); *Re Jenkin's Will Trusts* [1966] Ch 249, [1966] 1 All ER 926. (For the other reason, see p 119, post.)
16 *Re Douglas* (1887) 35 Ch D 472.
17 *London University v Yarrow* (1857) 1 De G & J 72.
18 *Re Green's Will Trusts* [1985] 3 All ER 455 (for the rescue, maintenance and benefit of cruelly treated animals).
19 *Tatham v Drummond* (1864) 4 De GJ & Sm 484.
20 *Re Slatter* (1905) 21 TLR 295.
 1 *Re Wedgwood* [1915] 1 Ch 113, CA.
 2 *Re Moss* [1949] 1 All ER 495.
 3 [1929] 1 Ch 557; (M & B).

have the effect of preventing cruelty to animals generally.

It should be noted that only trusts for animals generally or animals of a particular species are charitable. Trusts for specific animals are not charitable. In what form such trusts may exist we shall see later[4].

Other purposes under this head

Examples of trusts for encouraging good citizenship and promoting the moral welfare of mankind other than trusts for the welfare of animals include a gift to provide prizes for the best-kept gardens in a certain parish[5]; a gift to 'aid active steps to minimise and extinguish the drink traffic'[6]; a gift to assist the Boy Scout movement by helping to buy camp sites[7], a gift to the Anthroposophical Society to be used for carrying on the teaching of its founder, Dr Rudolf Steiner, who desired 'to further the life of the soul on the basis of a true knowledge of the spiritual world'[8] and a gift to a society the objects of which, whilst agnostic in character, were directed, through the dissemination of ethical principles, towards the mental and moral improvement of man[9].

With regard to matters under Lord Macnaghten's fourth head generally, it has been suggested that, whilst purposes under the first three heads may relate to the attainment of the objectives specified anywhere in the world[10], a purpose will only be charitable under the fourth head if it provides some benefit to the community of the United Kingdom[11].

IMPLIED CHARITABLE INTENT

So far we have considered instances where the purpose of a charitable trust has been stated expressly. In two situations the courts will infer from the terms of the gift that the donor impliedly intended that the property should be applied for charitable purposes.

Gifts to officials *virtute officii*

If a gift is made to an official who by virtue of his office carries out charitable functions (eg to clergy or churchwardens, who carry out religious functions; or to the head of a college or school, who carries out educational functions[12]) and there is nothing to indicate that the official is intended to take beneficially, then it will be inferred that the donor intended that the official should take the property as trustee on trust to apply it for the purpose of his official functions, religious or educational, as the case may be. The gift will thus be charitable.

---

4 See Chap 8.
5 *Re Pleasants* (1923) 39 TLR 675.
6 *Re Hood* [1931] 1 Ch 240.
7 *Re Webber* [1954] 3 All ER 712, [1954] 1 WLR 1500.
8 *Re Price* [1943] Ch 422, [1943] 2 All ER 505.
9 *Barralet v A-G* [1980] 3 All ER 918, [1980] 1 WLR 1565.
10 *Re Geck* (1893) 69 LT 819; *Re Redish* (1909) 26 TLR 42.
11 See *Camille and Henry Dreyfus Foundation Inc v IRC* [1954] Ch 672, [1954] 2 All ER 466; and the Report of the Charity Commissioners for 1963, para 72. But cf *Re Jacobs* (1970) 114 Sol Jo 515 (gift for planting a grove of trees in Israel held to be charitable).
12 *See Re Norman* [1947] Ch 349, [1947] 1 All ER 400.

The result will be the same where the gift to the official is followed by words conferring on him absolute discretion as to the disposition of the property. For example, gifts to the Archbishop of Westminster 'to be used by him for such purposes as he in his absolute discretion thinks fit'[13], to the vicar and churchwardens of Kingston, 'to be applied by them in such manner as they ... think fit'[14], and to the Bishop of the Windward Islands 'to be used by him as he thinks fit in his diocese'[15], were all held to be charitable.

If the gift to the official is followed by words giving some indication of the manner in which the property is to be applied, then the matter ceases to be one of implied charitable intention and falls to be considered under the principles relating to trusts where the purpose is expressly stated. If the words added indicate that the trust is for a charitable purpose, then a charitable trust arises[16]. For example, gifts to a vicar and churchwardens 'for any purpose in connection with the said church which they may select'[17], and to a vicar 'to be used for his work in the parish'[18] were held to be charitable. On the other hand, if the words used indicate a purpose other than a charitable one, or if the words would permit the property to be applied for purposes beyond those which are charitable (with the result that the trust is not exclusively charitable) then the trust is not charitable[19]. For example, gifts 'for such objects of benevolence and liberality as the Bishop of Durham in his own discretion shall approve of'[20]; to a vicar to be 'distributed at his discretion among such parochial institutions and purposes as he shall select'[1]; to the vicars and church-wardens of two parishes 'for parish work'[2], and to the Archbishop of Brisbane 'to be used ... as such Archbishop may judge conducive to the good of religion in this diocese'[3] were all held not to be charitable. (Regarding the last gift, it was held that this was not charitable as there might be things which the Archbishop regarded as being conducive to the good of religion which were not necessarily in law charitable.)

Gifts for the benefit of a locality

Where a gift is made to a locality[4], or to trustees for the benefit of a locality, then the courts will infer that the donor intended that the property should be held on trust for charitable purposes within the locality named. Trusts have been created in this form for the benefit of a parish[5], a town[6] and for 'my country England'[7].

---

13 *Re Flinn* [1948] Ch 241, [1948] 1 All ER 541.
14 *Re Garrard* [1907] 1 Ch 382.
15 *Re Rumball* [1956] Ch 105, [1955] 3 All ER 71.
16 *Re Pipe* [1937] 3 All ER 536.
17 *Re Eastes* [1948] Ch 257, [1948] 1 All ER 536. See also *Re Bain* [1930] 1 Ch 224.
18 *Re Simson* [1946] Ch 299, [1946] 2 All ER 220.
19 *Re Spensley's Will Trusts* [1954] Ch 233, [1954] 1 All ER 178.
20 *Morice v Bishop of Durham* (1804) 9 Ves 399.
 1 *Re Stratton* [1931] 1 Ch 197; see also *Re Davidson* [1909] 1 Ch 567; *Re Jackson* [1930] 2 Ch 389.
 2 *Farley v Westminster Bank Ltd* [1939] AC 430, [1939] 3 All ER 491, HL.
 3 *Dunne v Byrne* [1912] AC 407.
 4 *Re Smith* [1932] 1 Ch 153.
 5 *Re Norton's Will Trusts* [1948] 2 All ER 842.
 6 *Re Allen* [1905] 2 Ch 400.
 7 *Re Smith,* ante.

Where words are added indicating the means of benefiting the locality, then the matter falls to be dealt with under the principles relating to trusts where the purpose is expressly stated. If the purpose stated is charitable, the trust is for a charitable purpose[8], and vice versa[9]. The restriction of the benefit to a particular locality thus does not affect the outcome either way[10].

Public benefit[11]

We have seen that in order that a trust may have charitable status, it must not only be for a charitable purpose, but it must also be for the public benefit. The term 'public benefit' has in law a narrow meaning and a wider, more general, meaning. In order to have charitable status, a trust must[12] be for the public benefit in both senses in which the term is used.

PUBLIC BENEFIT IN THE NARROW SENSE

We saw in Chapter 3 that, in order to be valid, a private trust must have one or more beneficiaries. We have seen in this chapter that a charitable trust need have no beneficiaries and may be merely for an abstract purpose, eg promoting temperance. We have also seen, however, that in the case of some charitable trusts there may, nevertheless, be people in whose interests the trust is likely to operate. For example, in *Re Wokingham Fire Brigade Trusts*[13] the provision of the fire brigade would be of benefit to the inhabitants of Wokingham. But such a group of people are not beneficiaries in the sense that the word is used in the context of private trusts. They are merely people who may derive benefit. In this respect they resemble beneficiaries under a private discretionary trust. But here the resemblance ends. Beneficiaries under a discretionary trust are entitled to bring proceedings against the trustees to compel the proper administration of the trust. But persons who may benefit from a charitable trust have no such standing. It may happen that they receive benefits; but they are not 'beneficiaries'.

It was indicated earlier[14] that the requirement of public benefit related to the question for *whose* benefit the charitable purpose was to be carried out. The statement that a charitable trust must be for the *public* benefit would therefore seem to indicate that the trust must be for the benefit of the whole public throughout the kingdom. How then can it be that a trust can have charitable status notwithstanding that, as we have seen, the trust is for the benefit of some limited group within the kingdom, eg the inhabitants of Wokingham? The answer is that a trust may be deemed to be for the public

8   *Re Lewis* [1955] Ch 104, [1954] 3 All ER 257; *Re Tree* [1945] Ch 325, [1945] 2 All ER 65.
9   *Re Gwyon* [1930] 1 Ch 255; (M & B).
10   Provided, it would seem, that the locality is not so restricted (eg a certain row of houses) that the trust is not for the public benefit; see infra.
11   See G. S. Plowright, 'Public Benefit in Charitable Trusts' (1975) 39 Conv (NS) 183.
12   Subject to what is said later.
13   [1951] Ch 373, [1951] 1 All ER 454.
14   See p 95, ante.

benefit (in the narrow sense of which we are now speaking) if it benefits a particular, limited, *section* of the public.

The question as to whether a particular group constitutes a sufficiently wide section of the public for a trust for the benefit of that group to be accepted as being for the 'public' benefit has been one that has received considerable attention, and various attempts have been made by the courts to define what constitutes a section of the public for the purpose of the rule. For example, it has been stated that 'It is the extensiveness which will constitute [a trust] a public one'[15]; that 'the salient point to be considered ... is whether the class is one which extends to a substantial body of the public'[16]; and a trust is sufficiently wide if it is for 'an appreciably important class of the community'[17], that a trust is not for the public benefit if it is for the benefit of merely 'a fluctuating body of private individuals'[18]. These formulations, although no doubt going some way towards conveying the notion the courts are seeking to apply, do not provide us with any effective test, since we are left with the question as to, for example, what is 'substantial', or 'appreciably important'?

Another attempt to define the distinction between those trusts which are and those which are not sufficiently 'public' to satisfy the public benefit rule was that made by Lord Simonds in *IRC v Baddeley*[19] when he distinguished between 'a form of relief extended to the whole community, yet by its nature advantageous only to the few [which satisfies the rule, eg a sea wall] and a form of relief accorded to a selected few out of a larger number equally willing and able to take advantage of it' (which does not satisfy the rule). Yet, as has been pointed out[20], this formula does not provide a water-tight test since instances can be found which disprove the validity of each limb of the formulation.

If Lord Simonds's dictum cannot be accepted as providing a satisfactory test, is it, we may pause to consider, possible to find any common factor shared by those sections of the public which the courts have held to be sufficiently wide to satisfy the rule? Consider sections of the public in respect of benefit for which a trust has been held to be charitable and so the section wide enough to satisfy the rule with regard to public benefit: nurses, clergymen, railwaymen and their families, boys and young men under 21 resident in a certain town, decayed actors, working men, ladies of limited means, the blind, or those suffering from some other form of disability, widows and children of seamen belonging to Liverpool, the sons of gentlemen, children attending a particular Sunday school, daughters of missionaries, pregnant women, the inhabitants of a manor, a parish, a ward, a town, a county, rate payers of a certain borough, those who have suffered as a result of some disaster, those who wish to avail themselves of some public facility, such as the Long Bridge at Bideford, members of the drapery and allied trades. It is difficult to see any common denominator shared by such disparate groups and, indeed, so numerous are the types of sections of the community that have been accepted as forming a sufficient section of the public to satisfy

15 Per Lord Hardwicke, *A-G v Pearce* (1740) 2 Atk 87.
16 Per Buckley LJ, *Shaw v Halifax Corpn* [1915] 2 KB 170 at 181, CA.
17 Per Lord Wrenbury, *Verge v Somerville* [1924] AC 496 at 499.
18 Ibid.
19 [1955] AC 572, [1955] 1 All ER 525, HL; (M & B).
20 See G. S. Plowright, op cit, p 184.

the rule that it might be thought that *any* section would be so accepted.

Yet this is not so. Trusts for some types of sections of the public have been held not to be for the public benefit. For example, in *Oppenheim v Tobacco Securities Trust Co Ltd*[1] a trust to provide education for children of employees or former employees of a certain company, whose existing employees numbered over 110,000, was held to fail the test of public benefit. According to what principle, then, have the courts distinguished between those sections that are and those sections that are not to be regarded as constituting a sufficiently wide section to comply with the public benefit rule? The answer is that the courts have resolved the matter not by laying down a requirement with regard to sections that satisfy the rule but, from the other direction, negatively, by laying down that certain forms of sections of the public are *not* wide enough to comply with the requirement of public benefit; with the result that if a section does not fall within the proscribed class, then it passes the public benefit test. Subject to an important exception to be mentioned shortly, the courts have held, under what has become known as the *Re Compton*[2] test, that two types of section of the public are too restricted to entitle a trust for their benefit to be regarded as being for the public benefit. The first is a group the membership of which is determined by relationship to a particular individual (or particular individuals)[3]. This type of group would include a testator's relatives, his family, his descendants. The second type of section which is too restricted to be accepted as being for the public benefit is a group the membership of which is based on the existence of a contract, either between the members of the group themselves, or between the members of the group and some other person or body. Under this head come groups determined by relationship based on a contract of employment, eg all the employees of X Ltd, or a contract of membership of an association or club, or a contract of membership of a trade union, or a contract by which persons join together for the purpose of their mutual benefit.

It should be noted that where we speak of a group determined by a relationship based on contract, we speak of the group eligible to benefit: it is no bar, if a group is sufficiently wide to satisfy the rule, that those who benefit are required to enter into a contract with the charity—for example, the contract between a parent and an independent school, a student and a university, a student and a students' union, a patient and a private hospital, an elderly person and a trust established to provide accommodation for old people[4].Those who benefit in these instances are linked by contract with the charity, but the group *eligible* is not determined by a relationship based on contract[5].

As a result of the application of the principle that groups determined by

1   [1951] AC 297, [1951] 1 All ER 31; (M & B).
2   [1945] Ch 123, [1945] 1 All ER 198, CA.
3   *Oppenheim v Tobacco Securities Trust Co Ltd,* ante; *Davies v Perpetual Trustee Co Ltd* [1959] AC 439, [1959] 2 All ER 128.
4   *Joseph Rowntree Memorial Trust Housing Association Ltd v A-G* [1983] Ch 159, [1983] 1 All ER 288; (1983) 46 MLR 782 (R. Nobles).
5   If a trust was established to provide, say, university education for children from one or more independent schools (whether the schools were charitable or not), then the group eligible would be determined by contract (the contracts between the parents and the schools concerned). Differing views have been expressed as to whether such a trust would infringe the public benefit rule. See *Oppenheim v Tobacco Securities Trust Co Ltd* ante, at 319 per Lord Macdermott (the trust would fail); at 306 per Lord Simonds (the trust would be valid).

family relationships or by contract are not sections of the public it was held in *Re Compton*[6], with regard to a trust to provide for the education of the descendants of three named persons; in *Davies v Perpetual Trustee Co Ltd*[7] with regard to a trust to establish a college for the religious instruction of 'the youth' of Presbyterian descendants of settlers from the North of Ireland in New South Wales, Australia; in *Oppenheim v Tobacco Securities Trust Co Ltd*[8] with regard to a trust to provide education for the children of employees or former employees of a certain company; in *Re Mead's Trust Deed*[9] with regard to a trust for the relief of sickness and old age among members of a trade union; in *Re Hobourn Aero Components Ltd's Air Raid Distress Fund*[10] with regard to a trust for the relief of distress caused by air raids among members of a mutual benefits club; in *Cunnack v Edwards*[11] with regard to a group established to provide for the care of the members' widows; in *Re Clark's Trust*[12] with regard to a friendly society; in *Lord Nuffield v IRC*[13] with regard to a trust to organise throughout a certain area mutual insurance associations to assist the members to meet expenditure incurred by illness— in all these cases it was held that the trusts (or institutions) concerned were not for the public benefit and so not charitable. And, similarly, in *Trustees of Sir Harold A Wernher's Charitable Trust v IRC*[14], it was held that money expended by a trust on putting up pavilions and laying out bowling greens and tennis-courts on land conveyed to be used as a playing field and for recreation by the employees of a certain company, was not money applied for charitable purposes only within the Income Tax Act 1918[15].

If a trust is for the benefit of a group that is sufficiently wide to satisfy the test of public benefit, then it has been held (in a decision that has been criticised[16] and interpreted narrowly[17]) that it is no bar to the charitable status of the trust that the settlor directs that preference should be given, out of the primary group, to members of a group which would not itself satisfy the public benefit rule. Thus in *Re Koettgen's Will Trusts*[18] a testatrix left property for the furtherance of commercial education among persons of either sex who were British born subjects and whose means were insufficient to allow them to obtain such education at their own expense. She directed that in selecting beneficiaries it was her wish that the trustees should give a preference to the employees of a certain company or members of their families. It was stipulated that not more than 75% of the income in any one year should be applied for the benefit of those in the preferred class. It was held that the terms of the trust did not infringe the public benefit rule. That the principle will not be extended was, however, illustrated in *Caffoor v I T Colombo*[19], in which property was directed to be held by trustees for the education of

6   [1945] Ch 123, [1945] 1 All ER 198, CA.
7   [1959] AC 439, [1959] 2 All ER 128.
8   [1951] AC 297, [1951] 1 All ER 31; (M & B).
9   [1961] 2 All ER 836, [1961] 1 WLR 1244.
10 [1946] Ch 194, [1946] 1 All ER 501.
11 [1896] 2 Ch 679.
12 (1875) 1 Ch D 497.
13 (1946) 175 LT 465.
14 [1937] 2 All ER 488.
15 Section 37(1)(b).
16 See *Theobald on Wills* (13th edn) p 376.
17 See infra.
18 [1954] Ch 252, [1954] 1 All ER 581.
19 [1961] AC 584, [1961] 2 All ER 436.

'deserving youths of the Islamic Faith', with a direction that recipients were to be selected first from male descendants of the settlor or his brothers or sisters and, failing them, from youths of the Islamic faith born of Muslim parents of the Moorish community resident in Sri Lanka. It was held that in view of what was in effect the absolute priority conferred on the settlor's family, the trust was not for the public benefit (and so was not charitable). And in *George Drexler Ofrex Foundation Trustees v IRC*[20] it was held that where there was a provision that the trustees were, on the settlor so directing, bound to apply up to 60% of the income from trust property for the benefit of a preferred class that did not satisfy the public benefit rule, then (notwithstanding that pending the making of the direction the trust was for the public benefit) the trust was not charitable. It will be noted that the distinction between this case and *Re Koettgen's Will Trusts* was that in *Re Koettgen's Will Trusts* the trustees were not obliged to apply any trust property for the benefit of the preferred class; in *Ofrex* the trustees would, on the settlor giving the direction provided for, be obliged to apply at least some property for the benefit of the preferred class. A restriction that exists in practice (in the sphere of tax) on the effectiveness of a direction such as that in *Re Koettgen's Will Trusts* will be noted later[1].

There is an important, and long established[2], exception to the rule that in order to have charitable status a trust must be for the public benefit (in the narrow sense of which we are speaking): trusts for the relief of poverty are not subject to the rule. Thus trusts which have had as their object the relief of poverty among the 'descendants' of the settlor's children[3], among the settlor's 'relatives'[4], among the employees of a company[5], among a particular category of employees of a certain company[6], among employees of a company and their families[7], and among members of a club[8], have all been held to be valid charitable trusts.

But even a trust for the relief of poverty will not have charitable status if the group to be benefited consists of no more than a group of named individuals (or, it would seem, a narrow class of individuals, such as a testator's brothers, which in effect (if not in every legal respect[9]) constituted no more than a group of named individuals). Otherwise the advantages of a charitable trust could be obtained for what in all essentials was a private trust. Thus in the case of a gift for the relief of poverty, it is necessary to determine (and may be a matter of construction) whether the gift is one 'for the relief of poverty amongst a particular *description* of poor people' (in which case the gift will be charitable) or is 'merely a gift to *particular* poor

---

20   [1966] Ch 675, [1965] 3 All ER 529.
1   See p 132, post.
2   *Isaac v Defriez* (1754) Amb 595.
3   *Re Scarisbrick* [1951] Ch 622, [1951] 1 All ER 822; (M & B).
4   *Re Cohen* [1973] 1 All ER 889, [1973] 1 WLR 416.
5   *Dingle v Turner* [1972] AC 601, [1972] 1 All ER 878; (M & B).
6   *Re Gosling* (1900) 48 WR 300 ('old and worn out clerks' of a specified company).
7   *Gibson v South American Stores (Gath and Chaves) Ltd* [1950] Ch 177, [1949] 2 All ER 985.
8   *Re Young* [1951] Ch 344, [1950] 2 All ER 1245; *Re Buck* [1896] 2 Ch 727 (members, and widows and children of members, of a friendly society); *IRC v Medical Charitable Society for West Riding of Yorkshire* (1926) 11 TC 1.
9   Eg as regards the class closing rules.

persons, the relief of poverty among them being the motive of the gift'[10] (in which case the gift will not be charitable).

The anomalies that may result from the application of the public benefit rule (in the sense under consideration) have been the subject of comment. Certainly, it might seem strange that as a result of the rule a gift of £½ million to build homes for lame kittens would be charitable, whilst a gift of the same money to assist in the education of children of those employed by British Railways would not. But whatever its shortcomings the rule does succeed in what has been accepted[11] as one of its major purposes, namely to prevent the fiscal advantages conferred on charities being obtained by what are in practice no more than groups established for the purpose of some form of private benefit.

PUBLIC BENEFIT IN THE GENERAL SENSE

The wider meaning of the term is that it must be in the interests of the public as a whole that the purposes of the trust should be carried out. This does not mean merely that the trust must not be contrary to public policy or to the national interest, or 'calamitous to the community'[12], though clearly, if the trust did have these effects, the rule would not be satisfied[13]. The requirement is not merely negative, it is positive in nature: there must be some discernable benefit to the public at large from the existence of a trust of the kind proposed[14]. And this benefit must be susceptible of proof: it must be possible to satisfy the court that some discernible benefit to the public will result from the existence of the trust.

The meaning of public benefit in its wider, general, sense can be illustrated by some cases in which it was held that the requirement was not met. In *Re Warre's Will Trusts*[15] it was held that no benefit to the public would accrue from the establishment of a 'retreat house' to which persons could retire for a time from the activities of the world for religious contemplation and cleansing of the soul. In *Re Hummeltenberg*[16] it was held that no public benefit would be obtained from a gift to the London Spiritualistic Alliance Ltd 'to form the nucleus of a fund for the purpose of establishing a college for the training and developing of suitable persons male and female as mediums ...' *Gilmour v Coats*[17] concerned a gift to a Carmelite convent. The convent consisted of a cloistered community of nuns who devoted themselves to prayer and contemplation and who engaged in no outside work. The court held that the benefit to the public of intercessory prayer and edifying example

10 Per Lord Cross, *Dingle v Turner* [1972] 1 All ER 878 at 883. The italics are added. See also *Re Scarisbrick* [1951] Ch 622 at 655, per Jenkins LJ.
11 *Dingle v Turner*, ante, at 889.
12 Per Lord Simonds, *National Anti-Vivisection Society v IRC* [1948] AC 31 at 63.
13 It was on the ground that its activities were contrary to public policy that pressure was brought to bear in 1981 on the Charity Commissioners to strike the Church of Scientology off the register. See also Report of the Charity Commissioners for 1976, para 131, regarding the certain activities of the 'Exclusive Brethren', activities which an enquiry under s 6 of the Act had found to cause dissension in, and a breaking up of, family life.
14 See *Re Pitt Rivers* [1902] 1 Ch 403.
15 [1953] 2 All ER 99, [1953] 1 WLR 725.
16 [1923] 1 Ch 237.
17 [1949] AC 426, [1949] 1 All ER 848; (M & B), following *Cocks v Manners* (1871) LR 12 Eq 574.

was too vague to be susceptible of legal proof that any benefit was conferred on the public at large. The gift to the convent was therefore held not to be for the public benefit and thus was not charitable[18].

Another illustration of the meaning of public benefit in the general sense is provided by *Re Hopkins Will Trusts*[19]. Here Wilberforce J said that research would be charitable (ie for a charitable purpose, under the heading of education) if it was one of the kinds which he specified[20]. But later in his judgment[1] he indicated that a trust for research would not be charitable if there was no intention to publish the results to the world. Since this intention did exist the trust was held to be for the public benefit and so was charitable.

The decision in *Gilmour v Coats* and *Re Hopkins* demonstrates another aspect of the nature of public benefit: namely that the requirement will not be satisfied unless, in addition to any benefit obtained by those undertaking the activity which the charity will cause to be undertaken (in the cases above, praying and research respectively), some advantage is also derived by *others*, charity by its nature being 'necessarily altruistic'[2].

We shall see shortly that a trust whose object is to secure a change in the law cannot be charitable. The reason for this has been attributed to the fact that such a trust cannot be regarded as satisfying the requirement of public benefit[3].

With regard to proof of public benefit, in the sense of which we speak, it has been held that trusts for the relief of poverty, for the advancement of education and for the advancement of religion will all be assumed to be for the public benefit 'unless the contrary is shown'[4]. From this it would seem that in the case of purposes under Lord Macnaghten's fourth head, evidence must be produced to satisfy the court that public benefit exists.

Whilst it is generally stated that trusts for the relief of poverty are not subject to the public benefit rule[5], it is suggested that the correct view is that such trusts are exempt only from the rule in the narrower sense, discussed above, and that such trusts are, like a trust for any other object, subject to the public benefit rule in its general sense—that it must be in the public

---

18   See also *Re Joy* (1888) 60 LT 175 (gift to a society whose members prayed privately for the suppression of cruelty, held not to be charitable). As to whether the requirement of public benefit in the case of trusts for religion has resulted in an anti-Roman Catholic bias in the law, see (1981) 2 Journal of Legal History 207 (M. Blakeney); [1990] Conv 34 (C. E. F. Rickett).

19   [1965] Ch 669, [1964] 3 All ER 46; (M & B).

20   See p 101, ante.

1   At 681.

2   Per Farwell J, *Re Delany* [1902] 2 Ch 642 at 648.

3   *Tyssen* on *Charitable Trusts* (1st edn) p 176; quoted with approval by Lord Simonds in *National Anti-Vivisection Society v IRC* [1948] AC 31 at 62: 'It is a common practice for a number of individuals amongst us to form an association for the purpose of promoting some change in the law, and it is worth our while to consider the effect of a gift to such an association ... However desirable the change may really be, the law could not stultify itself by holding that it was for the public benefit that the law itself should be changed. Each court in deciding on the validity of a gift must decide on the principle that the law is right as it stands.'

4   Per Lord Simonds, *National Anti-Vivisection Society v IRC* [1948] AC 31 at 651. See also *Holmes v A-G* (1981) *Times,* 12 February. In *Re Watson* [1973] 3 All ER 678, [1973] 1 WLR 1472; (M & B), it was held that in the case of trusts for the advancement of religion, the court will assume the existence of public benefit unless the objects of the religion to be advanced are subversive of all morality.

5   Eg Snell, *Principles of Equity* (28th edn) p 155.

interest that the trust should exist[6]. Almost invariably trusts for the relief of poverty will, in practice, satisfy this requirement, the benefit to the public consisting of the fact that the existence of the trust may avoid those eligible to benefit under it from becoming a charge on public funds. But it is possible to conceive of a trust for the relief of poverty which failed to satisfy the public benefit rule in its wider sense[7]. For example, a trust for the relief of destitution among children under five by placing them in a home (for the establishment of which the trust property was to be applied), separated from all contact with their families until they reached the age of 18. Such a trust, it is submitted, would not have charitable status by reason of failing the requirement of public benefit, notwithstanding that the trust was for the relief of poverty.

The distinction between the terms 'beneficial to the community' and 'public benefit' should be noted. The former, the fourth of Lord Macnaghten's four heads of charity, relates to the specific purpose of a trust, the latter refers to public benefit in the two senses that have been explained. Thus for a trust to be charitable under the fourth head it must be both beneficial to the community and for the public benefit.

Finally, it must be mentioned that a factor that does not assist in arriving with any confidence at a firm elucidation of the 'public benefit' rule is that the courts have on more than one occasion indicated that what may constitute public benefit in the context of a trust for one charitable purpose may not be a sufficient benefit in the context of a trust for some other charitable purpose. As Lord Simonds expressed the matter in 1949, 'It would not, therefore, be surprising to find that, while in every category of legal charity some element of public benefit must be present, the court had not adopted the same measure in regard to different categories, but had accepted one standard in regard to those gifts which are alleged to be for the advancement of education and another for those which are alleged to be for the advancement of religion, and it may be yet another in regard to the relief of poverty'[8].

And in the case of public benefit in the narrow sense of the term, discussed earlier, here too no certainty with regard to what section of the public will be accepted as being sufficient to satisfy the requirement can be regarded as existing, in view of the fact that the opinion has been judicially expressed that it could not be accepted that 'a section of the public sufficient to support a valid trust in one category must, as a matter of law, be sufficient to support a trust in any other category.... There might well be a valid trust for the promotion of religion benefiting a very small class. It would not follow at all that a recreation ground for the exclusive use of the same class would be a valid charity, though it is clear ... that a recreation ground for the public is a charitable purpose[9].' And in *Dingle v Turner*[10], Lord Cross said 'It may well be that, on the one hand, a trust to promote some purpose, prima facie

6 '... in every category of legal charity some element of public benefit must be present'. Per Lord Simonds, *Gilmour v Coats* [1949] AC 426 at 448–449.
7 'If today a testator made a bequest for the relief of the poor and required that it should be carried out in one way only and the court was satisfied by evidence that that way was injurious to the community, I should say that it was not a charitable gift, though three hundred years ago the court might upon different evidence or in the absence of any evidence have come to a different conclusion'. Per Lord Simonds, *National Anti-Vivisection Society v IRC* [1948] AC 31 at 69.
8 *Gilmour v Coats* [1949] AC 426 at 449.
9 Per Lord Somervell of Harrow, *IRC v Baddeley* [1955] AC 572 at 615, [1955] 1 All ER 525 at 549.
10 [1972] AC 601, [1972] 1 All ER 878; (M & B).

charitable, will constitute a charity even though the class of potential beneficiaries might fairly be called a private class and that, on the other hand, a
trust to promote another purpose, also prima facie charitable, will not
constitute a charity even though the class of potential beneficiaries might
seem to some people fairly describable as a section of the public'[11].

Factors affecting the validity of charitable trusts

Although generally not expressed as distinct conditions which a charitable
trust must satisfy, the three matters now to be mentioned can preclude a trust
from having charitable status.

1 PROFITS

If a body is established with the object of making (and distributing) profits,
then it cannot be charitable[12]. Thus a school may advance education, but if
it is run for profit, it cannot be charitable. On the other hand, if any excess
income over expenditure cannot be distributed, but must be applied for the
purpose of the school, then the school could operate under a charitable
trust[13]. The position is the same in the case of a hospital[14].

The fact that the making of profits cannot be the object of a charitable
trust does not, however, preclude a charity making charges (either of a
revenue or a capital[15] nature) for the services it provides, for example, a
school[16] operating under a charitable trust, or a home for the elderly[17], or a
hospital[18], charging fees; or the users of a bridge maintained by a charity
being charged tolls[19]. Nor is a body precluded from being charitable by
reason of the fact that its charges are at a level which prevents persons with
low incomes from taking advantage of its facilities[20].

11 [1972] 1 All ER 878 at 889.
12 *Re Satterthwaite's Will Trusts* [1966] 1 All ER 919, [1966] 1 WLR 277; and see *Re Girls'
    Public Day School Trust Ltd* [1951] Ch 400.
13 *Abbey Malvern Wells Ltd v Ministry of Local Government and Planning* [1951] Ch 728,
    [1951] 2 All ER 154.
14 *Re Smith's Will Trust* [1962] 2 All ER 563, [1962] 1 WLR 763; *Re Resch's Will Trusts*
    [1969] 1 AC 514, [1967] 3 All ER 915.
15 *Joseph Rowntree Memorial Trust Housing Association Ltd v A-G* [1983] Ch 159, [1983] 1
    All ER 288 (provision of dwellings, on long leases, for the elderly; 70% of cost of
    construction provided by the tenant, 30% by the trust).
16 *Brighton College v Marriott* [1926] AC 192.
17 *Re Cottam's Will Trusts* [1955] 3 All ER 704, [1955] 1 WLR 1299.
18 See *Re Adams* [1966] 3 All ER 825, [1967] 1 WLR 162; *Re Resch's Will Trusts* [1969] 1 AC
    514, [1967] 3 All ER 915.
19 As formerly was the case at the Long Bridge of Bideford.
20 *Re Resch, ante.* In *Re Clarke* [1923] 2 Ch 407, gift for a nursing home to provide for
    'persons of moderate means' held to be charitable.

2 MUTUAL BENEFIT

As a result of the existence of the public benefit rule, in the 'narrow' sense explained above, any form of 'self-help' group—any form of 'mutual benefit' association or club—made up of people bound together by the contract constituted by the group's rules, can only have charitable status if the object of the group is the relief of poverty amongst its members. If the group is directed to any other end[1] (or if relief of poverty is not the only object[2] or if poverty is not a requisite for entitlement to benefit in, eg sickness or old age[3]) then the group cannot be charitable[4]. Nor can a group be charitable if its rules provide that on its dissolution the assets are to be distributed between the members[5].

In *Neville Estates Ltd v Madden*[6] Cross J indicated[7] that the members of a congregation of a synagogue were to be regarded as constituting a self help group (an 'association which is supported by its members for the purposes of providing benefits for themselves') and that the members of the synagogue therefore did not constitute a section of the public for the purpose of the public benefit rule. He held[8], however, that the trust was charitable, the public benefit rule not applying to religious trusts in the same manner as trusts for other purposes. It is submitted that the judgment on this point is not helpful, and that the decision could better have been reached on the ground that members of a congregation are not in the position of members of a self help group, but are merely members of the group for whose potential benefit a religious trust exists, the fact that members of the congregation may support by their donation the work of the trust, and that they may have some control over the operation of the trust, being irrelevant. The section of public for the benefit of which a church exists consists, it is submitted, is not in the church's congregation, but all those eligible to attend the church if they so wish.

3 POLITICS

A trust for the attainment of political objects is not charitable[9]. A trust is for a political object if, firstly, its purpose is to secure an alteration in the law of the United Kingdom. The reason is not that such a purpose is illegal, 'for everyone is at liberty to advocate or promote by any means a change in the law'[10], but that 'First, the court will ordinarily have no sufficient means of judging, as a matter of evidence, whether the proposed change will or will not be for the public benefit. Second, even if the evidence suffices to enable it to form a prima facie opinion that a change in the law is desirable, it must still decide the case on the principle that the law is right as it stands, since to

---

1 As in *Lord Nuffield v IRC*, ante.
2 As is generally the position in the case of friendly societies. See, eg *Cunnack v Edwards* [1896] 2 Ch 679.
3 See *Re Clark's Trust* (1875) 1 Ch D 497 at 500.
4 *Hobourn Aero Components Ltd's Air Raid Distress Fund* [1946] Ch 86, [1945] 2 All ER 711.
5 *Neville Estates Ltd v Madden* [1962] Ch 832 at 849–850.
6 [1962] Ch 832, [1961] 3 All ER 769; (M & B).
7 [1962] Ch 832 at 853.
8 At 854–855.
9 *Bowman v Secular Society Ltd* [1917] AC 406, 442, [1916–17] All ER Rep 1, 18; *McGovern v A-G* [1982] Ch 321, [1981] 3 All ER 493, 505.
10 Per Lord Parker of Waddington, *Bowman v Secular Society*, supra, 442, 18.

do otherwise would be to usurp the functions of the legislature'[11]. Thus in
National Anti-Vivisection Society v IRC[12] a society which had as its object
the total suppression of vivisection, an object that could be achieved only by
legislation, was held not to be a charitable body. And in *McGovern v A-G*[13],
a body, the Amnesty International Trust, whose objects included the abolition
of torture or inhuman or degrading treatment or punishment, was held not
to be charitable, since this object would include the abolition of capital and
corporal punishment, an object that could only be secured by the passage of
legislation[14]. A trust is also for a political object if its purpose is to oppose a
change in the law, and here too the trust will not be charitable since 'the
court would have no means of judging whether the absence of change in the
law would or would not be for the public benefit[15]'. If the object of a trust is
not to obtain a change in the law, or to oppose a change, but to uphold the
enforcement of the existing law, it may be charitable under Lord Macnaghten's fourth head[16].

Secondly, a trust is for a political object if its object is to promote the
interests of a particular political party[17], or the principles propounded by a
particular political party[18], or one such principle (eg 'socialised medicine'[19]).
The reason is the same as in the case of political objects in the first category,
'but a fortiori'[20], because, since trusts with objects in the second category
would ex hypothesi be very controversial, the court could be faced with even
greater difficulties in determining whether the objects of the trust would be
for the public benefit; and it would be at even greater risk of encroaching on
the functions of the legislature and prejudicing its reputation for political
impartiality if it were to promote such objects by enforcing the trust[20].

Thirdly, a trust is for a political object if its purpose is to secure the
alteration of a law of a foreign country. The reason is that the court would
have no adequate means of judging whether the proposed change in the law
of the country concerned would be for the public benefit (ie the public benefit
of the United Kingdom[1]) nor would the court have any satisfactory means
of judging the probable effects of the change on the inhabitants of the foreign
country (which would doubtless have a history and social structure quite
different from that of the United Kingdom)[1]. Further the court would have
no satisfactory means of assessing the extent of the risk that the trust, if
enforced, would prejudice the relations of the UK with the foreign country
concerned, a risk to which the court ought on grounds of public policy to
have regard[1].

Fourthly, a trust is for a political purpose if its object is to procure the
reversal of government policy or of a particular administrative decision. The

11 Per Slade J, *McGovern v A-G* [1981] 3 All ER 493, 506.
12 [1948] AC 31, [1947] 2 All ER 217; (M & B).
13 [1982] Ch 321, [1981] 3 All ER 493; (M & B); (1982) 45 MLR 704 (R. Nobles); (1983) 46
    MLR 385 (F. Weiss); [1984] Conv 236 (C. J. Forder).
14 Capital punishment remaining a punishment in the UK for treason and piracy.
15 Per Vaisey J, *Re Hopkinson* [1949] 1 All ER 346.
16 *Re Vallance* (1876) Seton's Judgments and Orders 7th edn 1304.
17 *Re Jones* (1929) 45 TLR 259; *Bonar Law Memorial Trust v IRC* (1933) 17 TC 508.
18 *Re Ogden* [1933] Ch 678 (Liberal principles). It seems that *Re Scowcroft* [1898] 2 Ch 638,
    in which a trust 'for the furtherance of Conservative principles and religious and mental
    improvement' was held to be charitable, would now be unlikely to be followed.
19 *Re Bushnell* [1975] 1 All ER 721, [1975] 1 WLR 1596.
20 Per Slade J, *McGovern v A-G* [1981] 3 All ER 493, 507.
1   *McGovern v A-G* [1981] 3 All ER 493, 507.

reason is that 'If a trust of this nature is to be executed in England, the court will ordinarily have no sufficient means of determining whether the desired reversal would be beneficial to the public, and in any event could not properly encroach on the functions of the executive, acting intra vires, by holding that it should be acting in some other manner'[2]. Under this head can be placed trusts which have as their purpose the influence of government in a particular direction. For example in *Anglo-Swedish Society v IRC*[3] a trust for the promotion of friendship and understanding between nations, and in *Buxton v Public Trustee*[4] a trust to promote and aid the improvement of international relations by educating or informing public opinion, were held to be political in nature, and therefore not charitable. In *Re Koeppler Will Trusts*[5], on the other hand, a trust the purpose of which was held to be the formation of an informed international public opinion and the promotion of greater co-operation in Europe was held by the Court of Appeal to be educational in nature, and charitable.

Fifthly, a trust is for a political object if it has the same purpose in relation to the policies or decisions of a foreign country, since 'the court will not have sufficient means of satisfactorily judging, as a matter of evidence, whether the proposed reversal would be beneficial to the community in the relevant sense, after all its consequences, local and international, had been taken into account'[6].

If a trust for education, including a trust for research, is held to be primarily propagandist in its nature, with its real purpose being to promote the interests of a particular party, or the principles propounded by a particular party[7], or to further a particular cause of a political nature, or to secure a change entailing an alteration in the law[8], then the trust cannot be charitable, notwithstanding its educational wrappings. 'Political propaganda masquerading ... as education is not education'[9]. On the other hand, a trust that is for an educational purpose will not be prevented from being charitable by reason of the fact that political matters may be touched upon in discussion by participants during educational courses provided under the terms of the trust[10]; nor, in the case of a polytechnic established for educational purposes, by reason of the fact students are encouraged to develop political awareness and form views on political issues[11].

In the present century many trusts have come to recognise that their objects can only be achieved by government action. For example bodies seeking to protect the natural beauty of the countryside, to curb the growth of motorways, to obtain larger allocations of public money for housing, to reduce sexual or racial discrimination, to gain access for walkers to open country, to control pollution of the environment, to reduce the growth in world population, to protect endangered species of fauna and flora, to phase out

2 Ibid at p 508.
3 (1931) 47 TLR 295; see also *Re Strakosch* [1949] Ch 529, [1949] 2 All ER 6, CA; (M & B).
4 (1962) 41 TC 235.
5 [1986] Ch 423, [1985] 2 All ER 869, CA; [1985] Conv 412 (T. G. Watkin).
6 *McGovern v A-G* [1981] 3 All ER 493 at 508.
7 *Bonar Law Memorial Trust v IRC* (1933) 17 TC 508; *Re Hopkinson* [1949] 1 All ER 346.
8 *Re Shaw* [1957] 1 All ER 745, [1957] 1 WLR 729; (M & B).
9 Per Vaisey J, *Re Hopkinson* [1949] 1 All ER 346, 349.
10 *Re Koeppler Will Trusts* [1986] Ch 423, [1985] 2 All ER 869, CA.; [1985] Conv 412 (T. G. Watkin). See also *Re Trusts of Arthur McDougall Fund* [1956] 3 All ER 867, [1957] 1 WLR 81.
11 *A-G v Ross* [1985] 3 All ER 334, [1986] 1 WLR 252; see also p 127 infra.

reliance on nuclear power for electricity generation, can all only effectively pursue their objects by acting as a 'pressure group' to secure government support for their aims.

But to undertake the activities of a pressure group is to engage in a political activity. Commenting on this, the Charity Commissioners, in their report for 1969[12], said that it was 'very unlikely that it will lie within any charity's purposes and powers to sponsor action groups or bring pressure to bear on the government to adopt or alter a particular line of action'. Following the case of *McGovern v A-G*[13] the Charity Commissioners for England and Wales, in their report for the year 1981, gave the following guidance:

'53. The implications for charity trustees of the present state of the law—as confirmed by the Amnesty case—may be summarised as:

  (i) Trustees who stray too far into the field of political activity:

     (*a*) risk being in breach of trust;

     (*b*) risk being held personally liable to repay to the charity the funds spent on such activity; and

     (*c*) risk losing some tax relief for their charity, since this may be claimed only in respect of income applied to charitable purposes.

  (ii) Political activity by the trustees would not necessarily affect the charitable status of the institution or be a reason for removing it from the Central Register of Charities; *but*

  (iii) If the trustees could validly claim that the expressed purposes of the institution were wide enough to cover political activities, doubt would arise whether those purposes were exclusively charitable and, if the institution was registered as a charity, upon the correctness of the registration.

'54. The following guidelines may be of help for the general guidance of charity trustees:

  (i) A charity should undertake only those activities which can reasonably be said to be directed to achieving its purposes and which are within the powers conferred by its governing instrument.

  (ii) To avoid doubt being cast on the claim of an institution to be a charity, its governing instrument should not include power to exert political pressure except in a way that is merely ancillary to a charitable purpose. Whether a particular provision in the governing instrument of an institution is a substantive object or an ancillary object or power is a matter of the construction of the instrument. In general, what is ancillary is that which furthers the work of the institution, not something that will procure the performance of similar work by, for example, the Government of the day.

  (iii) The powers and purposes of a charity should not include power to bring pressure to bear on the Government to adopt, alter, or maintain a particular line of action. It is permissible for a charity, in furtherance of its purposes, to help the Government to reach a decision on a particular issue by providing information and argument, but the emphasis must be on rational persuasion.

  (iv) A charity can spend its funds on the promotion of public general

---

12   Paras 7–16. The Commission publishes guidance for charity trustees. (Revised draft, April, 1992.)

13   [1982] Ch 321, [1981] 3 All ER 493; (M & B).

legislation only if in doing so it is exercising a power which is ancillary to and in furtherance of its charitable purposes.

(v) If a charity's objects include the advancement of education, care should be taken not to overstep the boundary between education and propaganda in promoting that object: for example, the distribution of literature urging the Government to take a particular course, or urging sympathisers to apply pressure to Members of Parliament for that purpose, would not be education in the charitable sense.

(vi) A charity which includes the conduct of research as one of its objects must aim for objectivity and balance in the method of conducting research projects; and in publishing the results of the research must aim to inform and educate the public, rather than to influence political attitudes or inculcate a particular attitude of mind.

(vii) Charities, whether they operate in this country or overseas, must avoid:

(*a*) Seeking to influence or remedy those causes of poverty which lie in the social, economic and political structures of countries and communities.

(*b*) Bringing pressure to bear on a government to procure a change in policies or administrative practices (for example, on land reform, the recognition of local trade unions, human rights, etc).

(*c*) Seeking to eliminate social, economic, political or other injustice.

'55. Unless its governing instrument precludes it from doing so, a charity may, generally speaking, freely engage in activities of the following kinds:

(i) Where the Government or a governmental agency is considering or proposing changes in the law and invites comments or suggestions from charities, they can quite properly respond.

(ii) Where a Green or White Paper is published by the Government, a charity may justifiably comment.

(iii) Where a Parliamentary Bill has been published, a charity is justified in supplying to Members of either House such relevant information and arguments to be used in debate as it believes will assist the furtherance of its purposes.

(iv) Where a Bill would give a charity wider powers to carry out its purposes, it can quite properly support the passage of the Bill; and it can support or oppose any Private Bill relevant to its purposes, since private legislation does not normally have a political character.

(v) Where a question arises as to whether a Government grant is to be made or continued to a particular charity, the charity is entitled to seek to persuade Members of Parliament to support its cause.

(vi) Where such action is in furtherance of its purposes, a charity may present to a Government Department a reasoned memorandum advocating changes in the law.

'56. In suggesting these guidelines to trustees, we are not purporting to say that certain activities are morally, socially, or politically wrong or undesirable or that they ought not to be done; but that it is not permissible for them to be carried out by a charity, according to our understanding of the law. We are concerned only with the law and must seek to ensure that funds and other property impressed with charitable trusts are used for the purposes of those trusts and not for purposes which the law does not accept as charitable. We are always willing to give further advice on any specific problem a charity may have in this connection; for example, on the distinction between education and propaganda, or between an ancillary purpose and a main purpose, and to consider the drafts of any publications such as advertisements, appeals, newsletters, etc, on which trustees have doubts.'

Where a body wishes to undertake activities which do not come within the sphere which the Commissioners accept as being charitable (eg if it wishes to launch a campaign against some aspect of government policy) then it has become common for the body either to set up an independent, non-charitable body (eg as a company limited by guarantee) to carry out the political side of its activities, confining its own activities to those that are charitable; or, relinquishing any claim to charitable status, to make its own objects political, and set up an independent body to carry out those parts of its work that are charitable (and so attract the advantages of charitable status).

The trust must be exclusively charitable

For a trust to be charitable, the objects must be exclusively charitable. If the terms of the trust would enable the trustees to apply any part of the trust property, capital or income as the case may be, for a non-charitable purpose, the trust fails. For example, in *Williams' Trustees v IRC*[14] property was held by trustees to maintain an 'institute in London for the benefit of Welsh people resident in or near or visiting London with a view to creating a centre in London for promoting the moral, social, spiritual and educational welfare of the Welsh people and fostering the study of the Welsh language and Welsh history, literature, music and art'. The majority of the objects of the institute were for the advancement of education, and those intended to benefit from the trust constituted a section of the public. But promoting the 'social' welfare of the group concerned was not a charitable purpose, and thus the trust did not have charitable status. In *IRC v City of Glasgow Police Athletic Association*[15], the House of Lords held that although one of the purposes of the defendant association was to promote the efficiency of the city's police (a charitable object), the fact that its purpose was also to provide recreation for members of the force, which was not a charitable purpose, meant that the association did not exist for exclusively charitable purposes and so was not charitable.

In a number of cases trusts have been held not to be exclusively charitable by reason of the employment by the settlor of certain general words indicating purposes of a 'shadowy and indefinite nature' which may to the lay ear have a charitable ring but which are not sufficient to indicate a purpose that is exclusively charitable in law. For example, the adjective 'patriotic' might seem to have the flavour of charity under Lord Macnaghten's fourth head[16],

14   [1947] AC 447, [1947] 1 All ER 513; (M & B).
15   [1953] AC 380, [1953] 1 All ER 747; (M & B).
16   See p 97.

and the word 'philanthropic' might seem to indicate an intention to relieve poverty. But both patriotic[17] and philanthropic[18] purposes could include many that whilst respectively fostering patriotism (for example, providing Union Jacks for British Gas to hang outside its offices on the Queen's birthday) or philanthropy (for example, providing a free pint of beer for the inhabitants of Tideswell each mid-summer's day) are by no means charitable. Other words in the same category as these are—'benevolent'[19], 'utilitarian'[20], 'public'[1], and 'pious'[2]. The leading case in this field (and also the principal authority for the rule under consideration) is *Morice v Bishop of Durham*[3] in which it was held that a gift to the Bishop of Durham on trust 'to dispose of the ultimate residue to such objects of benevolence and liberality as the Bishop of Durham in his own discretion shall most approve of' was held, since it was not exclusively charitable, to fail.

Instances in which trusts (or organisations) have failed to attain charitable status by reason of not being exclusively charitable may be grouped into six categories.

1. In the first are those instances in which the words which express the objects may have a vague redolence of charity but are expressed in terms that are so wide as to include objects that are not necessarily charitable. In this category would be placed the gift in *Morice v Bishop of Durham*[4] referred to above for '... objects of benevolence and liberality'. Another example was the gift in *Farley v Westminster Bank Ltd*[5] to the vicars and churchwardens of two parishes 'for parish work'. And in *Re Clarke*[6] Romer J gave an example of a trust whose purposes would be too wide to be exclusively charitable when he cited a gift for 'undertakings of public utility'.

2. In the second group are those in which a body's objects (although perhaps primarily charitable) include objects that are not charitable. For example, where the objects of a quasi-religious body known as the Oxford Group were stated as being, inter alia:

'(A) The advancement of the Christian religion, and, in particular ... in accordance with the principles of the Oxford Group Movement ...
(B) The maintenance, support, development and assistance of the Oxford Group in every way ...
(C) To establish ... any charitable or benevolent associations ..., and to subscribe ... money for charitable or benevolent purposes in any way connected with the purposes of the association ...'

It was held that the words in (C) extended beyond purely religious activities and authorised the expenditure of funds on matters which were not charitable, and, therefore, the body was not formed for charitable purposes exclusively[7].

17 *A-G v National Provincial and Union Bank of England* [1924] AC 262.
18 *Re Macduff* [1896] 2 Ch 451.
19 *Re Barnett* (1908) 24 TLR 788.
20 *Re Woodgate* (1886) 2 TLR 674.
1 *Blair v Duncan* [1902] AC 37.
2 *Heath v Chapman* (1854) 2 Drew 417.
3 (1805) 10 Ves 522.
4 Ante.
5 [1939] AC 430, [1939] 3 All ER 491.
6 [1923] 2 Ch 407, 414.
7 *Oxford Group v IRC* [1949] 2 All ER 537; see also *IRC v City of Glasgow Police Athletic Association* [1953] AC 380, [1953] 1 All ER 747; (M & B), and *McGovern v A-G* [1982] Ch 321, [1981] 3 All ER 493; (M & B).

3. The third group consists of instances in which the charitable and the non-charitable purposes are expressed as alternatives, with the result that the trust property could be applied for both types of object, or wholly for the charitable purpose, or wholly for the non-charitable purpose. For example, in *Re Jackson*[8] a testatrix left property to 'the Archbishop of Wales for the time being to be applied by him towards the General Fund belonging to the Church in Wales, or in his discretion in any manner as he might think best for helping to carry on the work of the Church in Wales'.

Instances in which the purposes have been directed to be applied for charitable or non-charitable objects have included a number of cases in which the non-charitable alternative has been expressed in general terms, using one of the words, such as 'benevolent', mentioned earlier. Thus trusts employing the phrases 'such charitable or public purposes as ...'[9]; 'public, benevolent or charitable purposes'[10]; 'some one or more purposes charitable, philanthropic or [a blank]'[11]; 'charitable or benevolent'[12]; 'charitable or patriotic'[13]; 'charitable or other'[14] purposes, were all held to fail.

In some instances, however, the court has construed the word 'or' as meaning 'in other words' as in the phrase 'water, or H_2O', with the result that the trust did not fail. An example was a gift for 'charitable or other public objects'[15]. In other instances the word 'or' when used in conjunction with the word 'charitable' has been construed as restricting a purpose which was not exclusively charitable to being exclusively charitable. For example, in an Irish case, a gift for 'charitable or religious purposes'[16] was construed as indicating charitably religious purposes. But in the great majority of cases the use of the word 'or' between a charitable and a non-charitable purpose has been fatal.

4. In the fourth group are cases in which property is directed to be applied for charitable *and* non-charitable purposes, and the words used are construed disjunctively (ie as a gift for charitable purposes and for non-charitable purposes), the linking word 'and' 'being used ... by way of addition, for the purpose of enlarging the number of objects within the area of selection'[17]. For example, in *Re Eades*[18], a testator left property to be applied for 'such religious, charitable and philanthropic objects' as his trustees should decide. The gift was held not to be exclusively charitable. The result was the same where property was given for 'benevolent, charitable and religious purposes'[19], and where a testator left property for the 'education and welfare of Bahamian children'[20].

However, the general rule in cases such as these (where the word 'and'

---

8   [1930] 2 Ch 389.
9   *Blair v Duncan* [1902] AC 37.
10   *Houston v Burns* [1918] AC 337.
11   *Re Macduff* [1896] 2 Ch 451.
12   *Chichester Diocesan Fund and Board of Finance Inc v Simpson* [1944] AC 341, [1944] 2 All ER 60; (M & B); see also *Re Meyers* [1951] Ch 534, [1951] 1 All ER 538 ('charitable or benevolent institutions').
13   *A-G v National Provincial and Union Bank of England Ltd* [1924] AC 262.
14   *Re Davidson* [1909] 1 Ch 567.
15   *Re Bennett* [1920] 1 Ch 305.
16   *Re Salter* [1911] 1 IR 289.
17   Per Sargant J, *Re Eades* [1920] 2 Ch 353, 356.
18   [1920] 2 Ch 353.
19   *Williams v Kershaw* (1835) 5 Cl & Fin 111n.
20   *A-G of the Bahamas v Royal Trust Co* [1986] 3 All ER 423, [1986] 1 WLR 1001, PC.

links the word 'charitable' and some a word of non-charitable connotation) is that the word 'and' is prima facie to be construed conjunctively, thus having the effect of limiting an otherwise non-charitable object to an exclusively charitable one. For example, where property was given for 'charitable and public'[1] purposes, for 'charitable and deserving objects'[2], for 'charitable and benevolent' purposes then the gifts were construed as being for 'charitably public', 'charitably deserving', and 'charitably benevolent'[3] purposes respectively. Thus only where the word 'and' is construed disjunctively[4] (ie indicating an intention to make a gift for two or more distinct purposes[4]) will use of the word cause a trust to fail for the reason we are considering.

Where a gift is for two or more specific purposes, one of which is not charitable, then if the court finds itself able[5] to quantify the sum applicable to non-charitable purposes ('which is what ought to be done if possible'[6]) then the gift will only fail quoad that sum.

Further, where a disposition takes the form of a direction to apply a part of certain property for a charitable purpose (the size of the part being at the trustees' discretion) and the remainder for a non-charitable purpose, and the trustees are obliged by the terms of the trust to apply at least some part of the property for the charitable purpose (ie they would be in breach of trust if they applied the property solely for the non-charitable purpose), then under a rule for which *Salusbury v Denton*[7] is customarily given as authority, the court will apportion the fund between the charitable and the non-charitable purposes, the former standing and the latter failing.

Finally, under this head, we may note that 'if a testator gives a definite proportion of his property to such charitable objects as his executors may select, and the rest of his property to such non-charitable indefinite objects as his executors may select, the gift of the definite proportion would be a valid charitable gift and it would only be the gift of the rest of his property that would fail'[8].

5. In this fifth category are instances in which the trustees are required to apply property for a charitable purpose and any surplus remaining (ie after the charitable purpose has been fulfilled) for a non-charitable purpose. Here a distinction has to be made. If the donor has quantified the property applicable for the charitable purpose, or has provided some guide as to how this can be quantified, or the court finds itself able to quantify this sum, then the property so quantified is held for the charitable purpose, and the gift of the balance fails. But if the property applicable for the charitable purpose cannot be quantified, then the whole gift fails. In one situation, however, the gift may be saved. If the court accepts that the gift is to be construed as a gift of the whole fund, subject to a payment out of the fund to give effect to a non-charitable purpose[9], then the non-charitable gift fails, and the money

1 *Blair v Duncan* [1902] AC 37.
2 *Re Sutton* (1885) 28 Ch D 464.
3 *Re Best* [1904] 2 Ch 354.
4 As in *Re Eades, Williams v Kershaw* and *A-G of the Bahamas v Royal Trust Co, supra.*
5 Eg by receiving evidence on affidavit, as in *Re Vaughan* (1886) 33 Ch D 187.
6 Per North J, *Re Vaughan, ante,* at 193.
7 (1857) 3 K & J 529. See *Re Clarke* [1923] 2 Ch 407.
8 Per Romer J, *Re Clarke* [1923] 2 Ch 407 at 414.
9 Including, eg a purpose designed to promote the main charitable purpose, but one to which legal effect cannot be given, *Re Coxen, ante,* at 754.

set free is caught by, and passes under, the gift for charity[10].

6. In this group come gifts for a non-charitable purpose, with a direction that any surplus remaining is to be applied for a charitable purpose. If the sum applicable for the non-charitable purpose is quantifiable[11], then the trust fails quoad that sum and the balance is held for the charitable purpose[12]. If the sum applicable for the non-charitable purpose is not quantifiable, then the entire gift fails[13]. However, where the sum likely to be needed to meet the non-charitable purpose is small in comparison with the residue that would be available for the charitable purpose, the court may exert itself to find means to quantify the sum applicable to the invalid purpose[14].

A further qualification needs to be made. If the non-charitable purpose consists of the maintenance of a tomb (other than one in a church), and the direction to maintain the tomb is not confined to the perpetuity period, with the result (for reasons that will become apparent in the next chapter) that the trust for the maintenance of the tomb fails, then the whole fund is applied for the charitable purpose, which survives unscathed[15].

Having concluded this survey of the circumstances in which a trust may fail to be exclusively charitable we may at this point conveniently mention a principle that supplements the rule that to be charitable a trust must be exclusively charitable. In order to obtain the fiscal advantages accorded to a charity, not only must the objects of a trust be charitable, but, further, the property of the trust must be *applied* for charitable purposes only. Thus if a trust has objects that are exclusively charitable but it is held that trust property has in fact been applied for purposes other than charitable ones then the trust will be denied the tax advantages that would otherwise accrue in respect of the property so applied. For example, in *IRC v Educational Grants Association Ltd*[16] an association was established (and incorporated as a company limited by guarantee) for the advancement of education in general terms, inter alia, by making grants towards the cost of education of individuals. It was promoted by a director of Metal Box Co Ltd. The council of management were all connected with Metal Box and met at the company's premises. The income of the association consisted primarily of money paid under a deed of covenant by Metal Box and a letter was circulated to the company's senior employees inviting applications for grants. Between 76 and 85% of the income in the relevant years was applied for the children of persons connected with the company. The Inland Revenue Commissioners allowed exemption from income tax on income applied in grants to individuals and establishments not connected with Metal Box, but rejected exemption on the remainder. The Court of Appeal upheld the Commissioners' decision[17].

10 *Re Coxen, ante*, at 752; see also *Re Parnell* [1944] Ch 107 (a private trust, but involving the same principle).
11 The court may order an enquiry to determine the sum that would be required for the non-charitable purpose.
12 *Re Coxen* [1948] Ch 747 at 752.
13 *Re Porter* [1925] Ch 746; *Re Dalziel* [1943] Ch 277, [1943] 2 All ER 656; *Re Coxen* [1948] Ch 747 at 752.
14 *Re Birkett* (1878) 9 Ch D 576 at 578, 599; *Re Coxen* [1948] Ch 747 at 753.
15 *Fisk v A-G* (1867) LR 4 Eq 521; *Re Vaughan* (1886) 33 Ch D 187; *Re Rogerson* [1901] 1 Ch 715; *Re Coxen* [1948] Ch 747 at 752; *Hoare v Osborne* (1866) LR 1 Eq 585.
16 [1967] Ch 993, [1967] 2 All ER 893; (M & B). See also *IRC v Helen Slater Charitable Trust Ltd* [1982] Ch 49, [1981] 3 All ER 98, CA.
17 See also Finance Act 1986, s 31, Sch 7.

The principle that to obtain tax exemptions trust property must be applied for charitable purposes only provides a practical restriction (referred to earlier[18]) on the ability of a settlor to direct that preference should be given to a certain group without falling foul of the public benefit rule: if the group is not a sufficient section of the public to comply with the public benefit rule, then income applied for the benefit of the group will not enjoy the fiscal advantages accorded to a charity.

If a trust that has been established for a charitable purpose applies money for a non-charitable purpose, this action (although capable of being restrained, as *ultra vires*, by injunction at the suit of the Attorney General) does not affect the charitable status of the trust[19]. This matter, one concerning the control of a charitys activities, is treated at the end of the next chapter.

Application of money for a non-charitable purpose may, however, be relevant in determining whether the objects of a trust are exclusively charitable where the payments are made *intra vires* of the trust objects and, after the formation of the trust, doubts arise as to whether its objects are exclusively charitable[20].

EXCEPTIONS TO THE RULE

In the course of the above discussion a number of exceptions to the rule that to be charitable a trust must be for exclusively charitable purposes have been noted (eg that arising under the rule in *Salusbury v Denton*[1]). Four further exceptions, three of a general nature, and one arising as a result of statute, require attention.

1 Promotion of a primary charitable purpose by an ancillary non-charitable purpose[2]

Where a donor gives property for certain purposes, and the primary purpose is a charitable one, and one (or more) of the other purposes would not, considered by itself, be charitable, but this non-charitable purpose is ancillary to the main charitable purpose, that is, if both its aim and its effect are to promote the attainment of the primary, charitable purpose, then the entire gift will be charitable, including that part which would, in isolation, not be charitable[3].

For example, in *Re Coxen*[4] a testator gave the residue of his estate (amounting to some £200,000) to the Court of Aldermen of the City of London on trust (a) to apply annually a sum not exceeding £100 to a dinner

---

18   See p 118, ante.
19   *A-G v Ross* [1985] 3 All ER 334, [1986] 1 WLR 252. (Polytechnic Students' Union established for charitable purpose of furthering education applied money to assist striking miners and for famine relief in Africa; charitable status unaffected.)
20   On the expenditure of money by a students' union, see Report of the Charity Commissioners for 1983, Appx A.
1   (1857) 3 K & J 529. See p 131, ante.
2   See N. G. Gravells, 'Charitable Trusts and Ancillary Purposes' [1978] Conv 92.
3   *Incorporated Council of Law Reporting for England and Wales v A-G* [1972] Ch 73 at 84.
4   [1948] Ch 747, [1948] 2 All ER 492, following *Re Charlesworth* (1910) 101 LT 908.

for the Court of Aldermen upon their meeting upon the business of the trust, (b) to pay one guinea to each alderman who attended during the whole of a committee meeting, in connection with the trust, and (c) to apply the balance for the benefit of orthopaedic hospitals. He desired that the Court of Aldermen should from time to time appoint six of their number as a committee to administer the trust.

It was held that the first two dispositions were designed to promote the principal aim of the gift, the benefit of orthopaedic hospitals, by securing the better administration of the trust by providing an incentive to the trustees to attend meetings of the trust. The whole gift was therefore charitable.

Another example is provided by *Neville Estates v Madden*[5] in which the objects of a trust included the maintenance of a synagogue and a communal hall, associated with the synagogue, in which social functions took place. It was held that since the activities in the communal hall were ancillary to the primary, religious, charitable purpose, the trust was charitable[6].

2 Incidental promotion of a non-charitable purpose

In *Royal College of Surgeons of England v National Provincial Bank*[7] the court was required to decide whether the Royal College of Surgeons was a charitable body. The objects of the College, as set out in its charter, were the promotion and encouragement of the study and practice of the art and science of surgery. It was argued, however, that since individual practising surgeons derived certain benefits from the fact that the College existed, the body could not be charitable. It was held that this did not prevent the College having charitable status. Thus the fact that in carrying out a charitable purpose a non-charitable purpose is incidentally assisted will not affect the validity of the charitable purpose. As the matter has been expressed: 'it is clear that "purposes" are not the same as "results" and there is ample authority that a body of persons may be established for charitable purposes only although its establishment has results which are not charitable ...'[8].

Under this principle, it was held in *IRC v Yorkshire Agricultural Society*[9] that the fact that a trust for the promotion of high standards in agriculture incidentally conferred benefits on farmers did not prevent the trust from being charitable. In *Royal Choral Society v IRC*[10], it was held that the fact that the activities of the plaintiff Society provided entertainment to members of the public did not affect the Society's status as an educational charity.

In *Royal College of Nursing v St Marylebone Corpn*[11] it was held that the fact that the existence of the plaintiff College might advance the interests of

5 [1962] Ch 832, [1961] 3 All ER 769; (M & B).
6 See also *Brisbane City Council v A-G for Queensland* [1979] AC 411, [1978] 3 All ER 30, PC (trust for promotion of high standards in agriculture by, inter alia, the holding of annual shows not precluded from being charitable by the fact that the terms of the trust would permit commercial enterprises to have sites at the shows); and *Re Koeppler Will Trusts* [1986] Ch 423, [1985] 2 All ER 869, CA; p 120 above. Further, see *Wynn v Skegness UDC* [1966] 3 All ER 336, [1967] 1 WLR 52.
7 [1952] AC 631, [1952] 1 All ER 984.
8 Per Lord Oaksey, *IRC v City of Glasgow Police Athletic Association* [1953] AC 380 at 395.
9 [1928] 1 KB 611.
10 [1943] 2 All ER 101.
11 [1959] 3 All ER 663, [1959] 1 WLR 1077. See also *Re Bernstein's Will Trusts* (1971) 115 Sol Jo 808.

professional nurses did not prevent the College from having charitable status. And in *Re White's Will Trusts*[12] it was held that the purpose of a trust for the Royal Infirmary, Sheffield, to be applied for a home of rest for nurses of that hospital, was to increase the efficiency of the hospital, by providing a means of restoring the efficiency of the nurses; the fact that individual nurses obtained personal benefit did not affect the charitable status of the trust[13].

But the furtherance of the non-charitable purpose must be purely incidental. It must, as it were, be merely a by-product of carrying out the charitable purpose. What may perhaps represent the extreme limit to which this exception may be taken is illustrated by *Joseph Rowntree Memorial Trust Housing Association Ltd v A-G*[14]. An existing charitable trust proposed to build small self-contained dwellings for letting, on long leases, to elderly persons. Of the cost of the dwelling, 70% would be met by the tenant, and 30% by the trust. On a tenant's death the lease could be taken over by the tenant's spouse. The benefit of the trust's contribution might thus come to be enjoyed by a person who was not elderly. It was held that this fact did not prevent the expenditure proposed from being for a charitable purpose.

If the furtherance of a non-charitable purpose is one of the express purposes of a trust, however subsidiary and tucked away in the midst of other purely charitable purposes it may be, then the trust is not exclusively for a charitable purpose and so cannot have charitable status. Examples are provided by *Oxford Group v IRC*[15]; *IRC v City of Glasgow Police Athletic Association*[16] and *McGovern v A-G*[17].

We may note here that a settlor's motives are irrelevant in determining whether a trust is charitable[18]: the fact that a donor's motives are charitable will not convert a non-charitable purpose into a charitable one; and the charitable status of a trust will not be affected by the fact that the settlor's motives are non-charitable. For example, where money is given to provide some part of a church[19] or some accoutrement for a church (for example, a lectern) or to endow a prize in a certain subject at a school or university, the fact that the motive of the donor in creating the trust is to commemorate the memory of some person (a person with whose name the gift is perhaps to be associated) will not prevent the gift from being exclusively charitable.

3 Disaster funds

Suppose that after some disaster the local Mayor announces that a fund has been opened. People send money. The Mayor clearly holds the money as trustee. But on trust for what? If the objects of the appeal have been stated,

---

12 [1951] 1 All ER 528.
13 Further illustrations are provided by *Re Shakespeare Memorial Trust* [1923] 2 Ch 398; and *Incorporated Council of Law Reporting for England and Wales v A-G* [1971] Ch 626, [1971] 1 All ER 436, (M & B) (primary charitable purpose, dissemination of knowledge of the court's decisions, not prevented from being charitable by reason of the fact that the legal profession was incidentally assisted by the publication of law reports).
14 [1983] Ch 159, [1983] 1 All ER 288; (M & B); (1983) 46 MLR 782 (R. Nobles).
15 [1949] 2 All ER 537. See p 123.
16 [1953] AC 380, [1953] 1 All ER 747; (M & B). See p 122.
17 [1982] Ch 321, [1981] 3 All ER 493; (M & B). See p 119.
18 *Hoare v Osborne* (1866) LR 1 Eq 585 at 587.
19 Eg a stained glass window. *Re King* [1923] 1 Ch 243.

then the objects of the appeal are the objects of the trust. Whether the trust is charitable or not[20] will depend on how the objects were expressed. But what if no objects were expressly stated? It would seem that in such cases money is generally subscribed on the basis that donations are intended to provide financial assistance to those who have suffered physical loss; and where money can be no aid, as a means of expressing sympathy with those who have suffered disturbance or bereavement. But since the object of the appeal has not been defined, it could be argued that the trust is not necessarily for exclusively charitable purposes, and therefore is not charitable. If this were so, many disaster appeals might not have charitable status. How is the difficulty overcome?

The trust comes into existence when the first money is subscribed. Can the trustees subsequently decide on the terms of the trust so as retrospectively to bind property already donated? It is settled that this can be done. In *A-G v Mathieson*[1], Cozens-Hardy MR said 'When money is given by charitable persons for somewhat indefinite purposes a time comes when it is desirable, and indeed necessary, to prescribe accurately the terms of the charitable trust, and to prepare a scheme for that purpose. In the absence of evidence to the contrary, the individual or the committee entrusted with the money must be deemed to have implied authority, for and on behalf of the donors, to declare the trusts to which the sums contributed are to be subject. If the individual or the committee depart from the general objects of the original donors, any deed of trust thus transgressing reasonable limits might be set aside by proper proceedings instituted by the Attorney General, or possibly by one of the donors. But unless and until set aside or rectified, such a deed must be treated as in all respects decisive of the trusts which, by the authority of the donors, are to regulate the charity. And it is irrelevant to urge that the donors did not originally give any express directions on the subject . . .' It was under this principle that the trustees of money received following the disaster at Aberfan in 1966 subsequently executed a trust instrument, which the Charity Commissions recognised as creating a charity[2].

The problems that can arise with regard to the distribution of funds raised following a disaster were highlighted in 1981 following the loss of the Penlee lifeboat with all hands while attempting the rescue of the crew of a tanker wrecked on the Cornish coast. Donations to a fund set up for relief of the dependants of the crew amounted to over £2 million. For the fund to enjoy the tax advantages of a charity the fund would have had to have charitable status. Since the fund was for the relief of hardship it might well have been that the Charity Commissioners would have been prepared to consider registering the fund as a charity. But if the fund was charitable, then one consequence would have been that the trustees would have had to apply income from the fund for the assistance of the crew's dependants, giving them such sums as at their discretion they considered appropriate according to their reasonable needs: they would not, without acting in breach of their duty as charity trustees, have been able to divide the whole sum between the various dependants. The latter course could only have been adopted if the trust was treated as being private, not charitable. It was clear that it was the wish of the donors that all the money donated should go to the crew members'

20   As in *Re Gillingham Bus Disaster Fund* [1958] Ch 300, [1958] 1 All ER 37; (M & B).
 1   [1907] 2 Ch 383.
 2   Report for the Charity Commissioners for England and Wales for 1966, p 6.

families. The dilemma was overcome by the decision of the Charity Commissioners, reached after discussions with the Attorney General and the trustees, that the trust was private, not charitable. The number of individual donations to the fund which were over the limit of the exemption to Capital Transfer Tax (£3,000) was very small, the average individual donation being under £25, and the incidence to tax was therefore not considered to be a significant problem. The matter, however, showed the anomalies that could exist, and it was pointed out that in the case of the fishing boat Gaul, which sank in 1974, the fund raised after the disaster had been held under a charitable trust, the crew's dependants receiving weekly sums of only £3 or £4, and the capital being retained intact (presumably eventually to be applied *cy près*).

4 Charitable Trusts (Validation) Act 1954

The effect of this Act is that where property was held on trust under an instrument[3] taking effect before 16 December 1952[4] for charitable or non-charitable purposes[5], and under the terms of the instrument the property could validly have been applied exclusively for charitable purposes, then as regards the period before the commencement of the Act (30 July 1954) the trust was to be deemed to have been for wholly charitable purposes[6]. As regards the period following the commencement of the Act, the trust was to be deemed to be solely for those of its objects that were in law charitable. Thus if a settlor created a trust in 1950 for certain charitable purposes (A) or for certain non-charitable purposes (B), and the trustees applied money for purposes A and B in 1951, 1952 and 1953, and tax exemptions were allowed with regard to the trusts operating in these years, then as a result of the Act the trustees were not in breach of trust in executing a trust that, without the validation conferred by the Act, was void; and the tax exemptions could not be recovered by the Inland Revenue in respect of money applied for purpose B. After the Act the purposes of the trust were to be deemed to be solely for A. Thus with regard to the period before and after the commencement of the Act the trust was protected from the consequence of the rule that to be charitable a trust must be exclusively charitable (ie invalidity) but after the Act the trustees would only be acting within their powers if they applied money for A, and tax relief was only available in respect of money applied for A.

It should be noted that the Act applied retrospectively. Thus if a settlor created a trust for, to continue the example, purposes A or B, at any time from 16 December 1952 onwards the Act had no application and the trust was void under the general principles of law. In view of its retrospective

3 Including, eg a document appealing for funds. See s 1(3).
4 The date of publication of the Nathan Report on Charitable Trusts (Cmnd 8710) which recommended the passage of the Act.
5 Or for purposes described in a word such as 'public' or 'worthy' or 'benevolent' which could include both charitable and non-charitable purposes. *Re Wykes* [1961] Ch 229, [1961] 1 All ER 470; *Re Saxone Shoe Co Ltd's Trust Deed* [1962] 2 All ER 904, [1962] 1 WLR 943. The Act does not, however, apply where property is held on trust for two or more institutions, charitable and non-charitable. *Re Harpur's Will Trusts* [1962] Ch 78, [1961] 3 All ER 588, CA.
6 Section 1(1).

operation, the frequency with which resort is had to the Act decreases with time; but that the Act may still be relevant, and of assistance, continues to be demonstrated by occasional cases[7].

Other conditions

In order that a valid charitable trust may come into existence, not only must the requirements as to charitable status be satisfied, but also the requirements relating to the creation of a trust. For example, as in the case of a private trust, for a valid charitable trust to exist, there must be certainty of intention to create a trust. Not all, however, of the requirements of a private trust must be satisfied, since once charitable status has been attained, some of the conditions of a valid private trust are not required to be met.

We shall now set out the conditions for a valid private trust to exist and note the extent to which a charitable trust must comply with each.

1 There must be an intention to create a trust

As we have said, a charitable trust must satisfy this condition. Thus there is no need for the word 'trust' to be employed if the intention to create a trust is otherwise evident (as where property is given 'on condition'[8] that it is set aside permanently for a specified charitable purpose).

2 There must be certainty as to the property forming the subject matter of the trust

This condition must also be satisfied[9].

3 The trust must have beneficiaries

We have seen that a trust can be charitable if it is merely for a (charitable) purpose, eg the prevention of cruelty to animals. It is therefore clear that this condition is not required to be satisfied in the case of a charitable trust.

Although a charitable trust may have the effect of conferring benefits on members of a specified group, such persons are not beneficiaries in the legal sense of holding a proprietary interest in the trust property. Thus, not only is there no need for a charitable trust to satisfy this condition, but, further, any trust which does satisfy it (ie and has beneficiaries) cannot be a charitable trust.

---

7   Eg *Barralet v A-G* [1980] 3 All ER 918, [1980] 1 WLR 1565. See [1981] Conv 150 (St J. Robilliard).
8   *Brisbane City Council v A-G for Queensland* [1979] AC 411, [1978] 3 All ER 30, PC.
9   *Peek v Peek* (1869) 17 WR 1059.

4 There must be certainty as to the identity of the beneficiaries

Since the third condition does not apply, neither does this. (The question of certainty as to the purposes intended by the donor is considered separately below.)

5 There must be certainty as to the share of property each beneficiary is entitled to receive

For the same reason, neither does this condition apply. (The question of certainty as to the share of property to be taken when there is a gift for several charitable purposes, and the share is not specified by the donor, is considered separately below.)

6 The correct formalities must be observed

This condition applies to the creation of charitable trusts.

7 The trust must not infringe the rule against perpetuities

Except in one respect, gifts for charitable purposes are subject to the rule against perpetuities in the same way as are private trusts. Thus in *Re Lord Stratheden and Campbell*[10] a testator made a bequest to the 22nd Middlesex Rifle Volunteer Regiment 'on the appointment of the next lieutenant-colonel'. Since the gift was not bound to vest, if it vested at all, within the perpetuity period, the gift was void. The fact that the gift was for a charitable purpose was irrelevant.

The exception is that a gift over to a charity from another charity is not subject to the rule against perpetuities. For example, if a testator gives money to Charity A, until a specified event occurs[11], with a gift over (on the occurrence of the event) to Charity B, then although the gift over to Charity B might not vest until after the expiry of the perpetuity period, the gift to Charity B is not void[12]. But the exception only applies to a gift over to a charity which follows a gift to another charity. If a gift over to a charity follows a gift to an individual[13] or a non-charitable purpose[14] then the gift over to the charity would be subject to the rule against perpetuities. Similarly,

---

10 [1894] 3 Ch 265; *Re Wood* [1894] 3 Ch 381, CA. Cf *Re Swain* [1905] 1 Ch 669 (direction postponing operation of the trust until the trust fund reached a specified sum, designed to secure the better working of the charity held not to invalidate the trust); and *Chamberlayne v Brockett* (1872) 8 Ch App 206.

11 Or until the expiry of a specified time, eg 200 years; *Re Resch's Will Trusts* [1969] 1 AC 514, [1967] 3 All ER 915; (M & B).

12 *Christ's Hospital v Grainger* (1849) 1 Mac & G 460; *Re Tyler* [1891] 3 Ch 252; (M & B). *Royal College of Surgeons of England v National Provincial Bank* [1952] AC 631, [1952] 1 All ER 984; *Re Buzzacott* [1953] Ch 28, [1952] 2 All ER 1011.

13 *Re Bowen* [1893] 2 Ch 491; *Re Mills Declaration of Trust* [1950] 2 All ER 292.

14 *Re Dalziel* [1943] Ch 277, [1943] 2 All ER 656; *Re Wightwick's Will Trusts* [1950] Ch 260, [1950] 1 All ER 689; *Re Chamber's Will Trusts* [1950] Ch 267.

if there is a gift to a charity followed by a gift over to an individual[15] or to a non-charitable purpose[16] the gift over is subject to the rule.

8 A private trust must not infringe the rule against inalienability

Charitable trusts are not subject to the rule against inalienability. Thus if a testator left £10,000 on trust for the income to be applied for the upkeep of the graveyard of a certain church, then, since the trust is charitable, the trust is valid notwithstanding that the capital may be kept intact, and only the income used, for ever.

9 The trust must not infringe the rule against accumulations

It would be unusual for a charity to be directed to accumulate income. But if such a direction were made, it would seem that the direction would be subject to the provisions of the rule against accumulations.

10 The trust must not have been avoided under the Insolvency Act 1986

Here, too, charitable trusts are subject to the same rules as private trusts.
In order to be charitable a trust must thus comply with all but two of the requirements of a valid private trust and, in addition, must meet the requirements necessary for it to have charitable status. We can therefore envisage three 'levels' of status:

1. Valid charitable trust.
2. Valid private trust.
3. No trust at all.

It should therefore be noted that if a trust is found not to be charitable, this does not mean that the trust is necessarily void. Even if it does not attain charitable status, it can, if the necessary conditions are fulfilled, exist as a valid private trust.

'A charitable trust need not have certainty of objects'

This is a statement which is sometimes made. In the case of private trusts the statement that a trust must have certainty of objects refers to the requirements that the trust must have beneficiaries, and that their identity must be sufficiently certain[17]. We have seen[18] that in the case of a charitable trust there

15 *Re Cooper's Conveyance Trusts* [1956] 3 All ER 28, [1956] 1 WLR 1096; *Re Bowen* [1893] 2 Ch 491; *Re Peel's Release* [1921] 2 Ch 218. Cf *Re Blunt's Trusts* [1904] 2 Ch 767.
16 *Re Spensley's Will Trusts* [1954] Ch 233, [1954] 1 All ER 178; Replacing Bankruptcy Act 1914, ss 42, 44; Law of Property Act 1925, s 172.
17 Chap 4.
18 See p 114, ante.

are no beneficiaries in the sense of persons having a proprietary interest in the trust property. So the words 'certainty of objects' must refer to something different when used in the context of charitable trusts. The words in fact bear three meanings.

1. In the first place they indicate that if a donor fails to specify the purposes of a charitable trust with sufficient certainty, this deficiency may be made up by the court[19]. For example, suppose that a testator left money on trust 'for the relief of poverty in Peckham'. What do the trustees actually do with the money? Do they go out into the street and give £5 notes to those who look hard-up? It is important that the trustees act properly, otherwise they may be called upon by the Attorney General to replace any money incorrectly applied, out of their own pocket. To remove uncertainty as to what would constitute a proper means of carrying out the trust, the trustees may (there is no obligation on them to do so) seek directions from the court[19]. The court will look at the terms of the testator's gift and other information it considers relevant, and then set out in a 'scheme' directions specifying how the trust fund is to be applied, in terms which will leave the trustees in no doubt as to how they should act. For example, in *Re Gott*[20] a testatrix bequeathed money to found a scholarship at a university, open to 'male students of British and Christian parentage'. The validity of the bequest was challenged on the ground of the uncertainty of the class of students eligible. It was held that since the gift was charitable, any uncertainty as to its objects was no bar to its validity, and could be remedied by a scheme. The need for a scheme to supply certainty to the terms of a trust will readily be appreciated in the case of gifts such as those for 'my country England ...'[1]; for the 'benefit of the town of Kendall'[2] and for 'such of the charitable institutions in London or the neighbourhood as they may select'[3].

Even where a testator gives property to trustees for charitable purposes generally, with no indication whatsoever as to the charitable objects to be furthered, the uncertainty is no bar to the validity of the trust, and the court will draw up a scheme for the application of the property[4].

It is sometimes convenient for trustees to apply for a scheme in order to provide themselves with authority for applying property for a purpose which they believe to be within the terms of the trust, but which is not specifically referred to in the trust, thereby causing the trustees doubt[5].

2. Second, the words of which we speak indicate that whereas under a private trust, if a donor gives property on trust 'for A or B', the trust is void for uncertainty as to the identity of the beneficiary, in the case of a trust for 'charity X or charity Y'; or for 'charitable purpose X or charitable purpose Y', or even for such charitable purposes as his trustees (or executors) might select[6], then the gift is valid since 'a testator may validly leave it to his

---

19 Or the Charity Commissioners.
20 [1944] Ch 193, [1944] 1 All ER 293. See also *Re Mann* [1903] 1 Ch 232.
1 *Re Smith* [1932] 1 Ch 153.
2 *Re Allen* [1905] 2 Ch 400.
3 *Re Delmar Charitable Trust* [1897] 2 Ch 163.
4 See *Re Tyler's Fund Trusts* [1967] 3 All ER 389, [1967] 1 WLR 1269 (will be construed as showing an intention to create a trust for the benefit of charity generally; scheme ordered).
5 *Re Palatine Estate Charity* (1888) 39 Ch D 54 (scheme sanctioned to provide for the cost of a spire for a particular church, as being within the words 'other necessary occasions' of the church).
6 *Moggridge v Thackwell* (1803) 7 Ves 36; affd (1807) 13 Ves 416.

executors to determine what charitable objects shall benefit, so long as charitable and not other objects may benefit'[7].

3. Third, the words refer to the fact that whereas in the case of a private trust the amount of property to be held by each beneficiary must be ascertained (or made expressly subject to the discretion of the trustees), in the case of a charitable trust, if a donor gives property for a number of charitable purposes, without specifying how much is to be allocated to each, the court has power to order an inquiry as to what sum it would be appropriate to allocate to each[8] or, if this is not practicable, to order that the property should be divided equally between the charitable purposes[9].

It will therefore be seen that in the two statements:

> 'for a private trust to be valid there must be certainty of objects'; 'a charitable trust need not have certainty of objects';

the word 'objects' is used in different senses in each of the two statements. In the first, 'objects' refers to beneficiaries. In the second, 'objects' refers either to purposes or to institutions (including the share to be taken by two or more charitable purposes or institutions).

A statutory definition?

In 1989 the government considered, in response to a report by Sir Philip Woodfield[10], *Efficiency Scrutiny of the Supervision of Charities*[11], whether (inter alia) a definition of charity should be formulated and given statutory basis. The government's views were given in 1989 in a White Paper[12], *Charities: A Framework for the Future*.

'2.7 The loose framework, which was set by the 1601 preamble and clarified by Lord Macnaghten, has enabled the courts over the years to develop the law in a way which has been sensitive to changing needs whilst maintaining the fundamental principles on which the concept of charity rests. It has been argued that on the whole, given the increasing complexity of society, this development has been remarkably coherent and consistent. The scope of education, for example, has been gradually extended to cover not just free schooling but a whole range of objects of a broadly educational nature, such as research and information services, which are considered to be of public benefit.

'2.8 The scope of charity, as it applies to organisations concerned with the advancement of religion, has been similarly widened in response to increasing

---

7 Per Lord Simonds, *Chichester Diocesan Fund and Board of Finance Inc v Simpson* [1944] AC 341, [1944] 2 All ER 60; (M & B).
8 *Re Delmar Charitable Trust* [1897] 2 Ch 163.
9 As in *Hoare v Osborne* (1866) LR 1 Eq 585.
10 And certain other reports: National Audit Office, *Monitoring and Control of Charities* (HC Paper 380); Public Accounts Committee, *Monitoring and Control of Charities* (HC 116).
11 1987. Commissioned jointly by the Home Secretary and the Economic Secretary to the Treasury.
12 Cm 694; [1989] Conv 304.

religious toleration and to cultural diversity. Under the fourth head, in particular, the courts have admitted, under the umbrella of charity, a remarkable range of bodies which have been established by benefactors who have discerned new public needs and who have responded to them.

'2.9 If the main lines of the law's development are clear, it is fair to say that its results in detail are not always tidy and can sometimes be confusing, even to experts. It is perhaps not surprising that, as the threads reaching back to 1601 get longer and as the analogies which the courts employ become more extended, so the rationale for decisions on charitable status should not always be immediately apparent. This has undoubtedly led to a degree of uncertainty about the interpretation of the law which can inhibit innovative bodies from seeking charitable status. Some critics, however, go further. The law, they say, is now so complex and tangled that it is bound to lead to some decisions which can only be described as illogical or capricious.

'2.10 Against this background, it has been proposed from time to time, that a definition of charity should be formulated and given statutory effect. This might be achieved in one of the following ways:

i) by listing the purposes which are deemed to be charitable;

ii) by enacting a definition of charity based on Lord Macnaghten's classification; or

iii) by defining "charitable purposes" as "purposes beneficial to the community."

'2.11 The Government consider that an attempt to define charity by any of these means would be fraught with difficulty, and might put at risk the flexibility of the present law which is both its greatest strength and its most valuable feature. In particular, they consider that there would be great dangers in attempting to specify in statute those objects which are to be regarded as charitable.

'2.12 Even if it was possible to draw up a list which could command a reasonable measure of agreement it might well lead to the exclusion of trusts which have long been treated as charitable, depriving them of any means of enforcement. A list might be inflexible and quickly outdated by changing public opinion. Listing the details in statute would not evade for long the problems which are inherent in any system of case law. Disputes would undoubtedly quickly arise on which the courts would be asked to adjudicate. There is no reason to believe that a new body of case law would be any less complex than the old.

'2.13 In the Government's view, it would be scarcely less difficult to try to enact the whole of Lord Macnaghten's classification. As a classification, the formulation has proved of enduring use. As a definition, its advantages are much less compelling.

'2.14 Unless it were proposed to preserve the present case law, the incorporation of Lord Macnaghten's classification into statute would throw the law into confusion and uncertainty by depriving the courts of recourse to previous decisions when they were asked to interpret the new statutory provisions. On the other hand, if some form of words were to be found which would successfully preserve the present valuable case law, it is hard to see what the new definition would achieve.

'2.15 Defining "charitable purposes" as "purposes beneficial to the community" would have the merit of simplicity but this would also be open to major objections. Such a definition would allow the courts to admit to charitable status virtually any organisation which was not obviously for private benefit or profit. A definition on these simple lines, which was intended to supersede existing case law, would greatly expand the ambit of charity in ways which might be far from desirable. It would be notably subjective and would be likely to give rise to a great deal of litigation.

'2.16 An attempt might be made to make clearer exactly what is meant by "public benefit" by reference to existing case law and by incorporating the other heads of charity into the general formula. The more that detail becomes added in this way, however, the fewer appear the advantages of a new definition. Instead of being simplified the law would be ossified.

'2.17 There would appear, therefore, to be few advantages in attempting a wholesale redefinition of charitable status—and many real dangers in doing so.'

The Charities Act 1992, accordingly, contained no provision placing the definition of 'charity' or 'charitable purposes' on a statutory basis.

Chapter 8

Charitable trusts II:
Administration and control of charities

The *cy près* doctrine[1]

THE DOCTRINE

By way of introduction let us suppose that in 1700 a testator left £1,000 to
trustees on trust to apply the income for the relief of poverty among poor
widows resident in the Makepeace Almshouses at Longford. The trustees
invest the money and over the years apply the income as directed. The capital
is inalienable but, as we have seen, this does not invalidate the trust since
charitable trusts are not subject to the rule against inalienability. Thus the
trust may continue for ever. But what is the position if it later becomes
impossible for the trustees to carry out the purpose specified? For example,
what is the position if the income ceases to be sufficient to maintain the
almshouses, and they have to be closed down? It would still be possible to
apply the trust money for a purpose similar to that specified, for example by
applying the money for the relief of poverty among widows resident in the
parish of Longford. But such an application would depart from the terms of
the trust, and would thus constitute a breach of trust[2].

It may be that the donor conferred power on the trustees in the circumstances that have arisen to apply the trust property for other purposes
specified by him[3], or to close the trust and to apply the property in a specified
manner (eg by transferring the remaining capital to other appropriate
charities). Or it may be that power is conferred on the trustees to alter the
objects of the charity to other charitable objects[4]. In these cases the trustees
can act under the powers conferred on them, and no problem will exist.

In order to overcome the problem that would exist if no such power is
conferred on the trustees, it was early laid down that where it becomes
impossible for trustees to carry out the terms of a charitable trust, the court
has power, under its inherent jurisdiction, (a) to direct that the trust property
should be applied to some other charitable purpose which as nearly as
possible ('*cy près*') resembles the original purpose, and (b) to state (in a

---

1 See [1983] Conv 107 (P. Luxton).
2 Thus if property is left on trust for the purpose of building a new church, the trustees have
   no authority to use the property for enlarging an existing church and adding a chapel.
   Re Edwin Riley Charities (1930) 70 L Jo 409.
3 As in *Re Roberts* [1963] 1 All ER 674, [1963] 1 WLR 406.
4 As in *Re Bagshaw* [1954] 1 All ER 227, [1954] 1 WLR 238.

'scheme') the trusts on which the property should thenceforth be held. The Charity Commissioners now exercise a concurrent jurisdiction[5]. (The court also has power, under its inherent jurisdiction, to approve a scheme under which an administrative provision in the trust deed is varied[6].)

It should be noted that trustees themselves have no power to apply trust property *cy près,* and that this may be done only after application to, and direction by, the court or the Commissioners. (They certainly have no power to amend the terms of the trust so as to include non-charitable purposes[7].) Where, however, the circumstances indicate a need for property to be applied *cy près,* trustees are now under a duty, imposed by the Act[8], to enable it to be applied *cy près* (ie by making the necessary application).

It must be stressed that the *cy près* doctrine applies only to charities. If it becomes impossible for a non-charitable body to continue in existence then the outcome depends on, inter alia, the rules of the body concerned. But the property of the body is not subject to the *cy près* doctrine[9].

The distinction should be noted between a *cy près* scheme, and a scheme to provide certainty, considered earlier.

IMPOSSIBILITY

During the evolution of the *cy près* doctrine it came to be accepted that the circumstances in which property of a charitable trust might be applied *cy près* should include not only instances where it became impossible to carry out the trust but also where it became impracticable so to do.

Trusts have been held to be impossible ab initio where suitable land could not be found to build an institution intended by the donor[10]; where the money donated was insufficient for the achievement of the purpose proposed[11], or for all the purposes proposed[12], where money donated would be insufficient for the establishment of a proposed institution, but no money would be available for its maintenance[13]; where the consequences of observing the terms of the trust might tend to defeat the charity's main object[14]; where acceptance of the trust by the trustees named was an essential part of the donor's intention and these trustees declined to accept the trust, or to accept it on the terms of the trust[15]; where the purpose was not permitted by law[16];

5   Charities Act 1960, s 18.
6   *Re J W Laing Trust* [1984] Ch 143, [1984] 1 All ER 50; (M & B), [1984] Conv 319 (J. Warburton); [1984] All ER Rev 305 (P. J. Clarke).
7   *Baldry v Feintuck* [1972] 2 All ER 81, [1972] 1 WLR 552. Nor can the rules of a charitable association be altered, in the absence of an express power, by resolution of a general meeting. *Re Tobacco Trade Benevolent Association* [1958] 3 All ER 353, [1958] 1 WLR 1113.
8   Section 13(5).
9   *Re Jenkins* [1966] Ch 249, [1966] 1 All ER 926; (M & B).
10   *Re White's Trusts* (1886) 33 Ch D 449; *Biscoe v Jackson* (1887) 35 Ch D 460.
11   *Re Burton's Charity* [1938] 3 All ER 90; *Murray v Thomas* [1937] 4 All ER 545 (memorial hall); *Re Beck* (1926) 42 TLR 245.
12   *Rodwell v A-G* (1886) 2 TLR 712.
13   *Re White's Trusts* (1886) 33 Ch D 449.
14   *Re Dominion Students' Hall Trust* [1947] Ch 183; (M & B).
15   *Re Woodhams* [1981] 1 All ER 202, [1981] 1 WLR 493; [1981] Conv 231 (J. Warburton).
16   *A-G v Baxter* (1684) 1 Vern 248.

or the manner of attaining the object was illegal[17] or illegal in some respect (eg to the extent that a direction to accumulate income infringed the rule against accumulations[18]); where changing circumstances made it impracticable to proceed with the purpose intended[19]; where a person named by a testator to select charities to receive certain of the testator's property predeceased the testator[20]; and where a surplus existed after the attainment of a specified purpose (the trust being impossible quoad the surplus)[1]. In this last case the trust is treated as being impossible ab initio notwithstanding that it may not become evident until some time after the date of the gift that there will be a surplus after the object specified has been attained.

Subsisting trusts have been found to have become 'impossible' within the meaning of the *cy près* doctrine where a particular institution closed down due to lack of funds, or to a decline in, or cessation of, its need[2]; where the need ceased to exist[3]; where a trust's object was attained[4]; where a surplus accrued due to a decline in the group eligible to benefit[5]; where premises became inappropriate for the purpose intended[6]; where the purpose was provided for by other means[7]; where the group of persons for whose benefit a trust existed ceased to exist[8], or, at any rate, where applicants eligible to benefit ceased to come forward[9], and where it was shown that the terms of a trust had come to defeat, or tend to defeat, the trust's objective[10].

It became established[11], however, that no jurisdiction existed to order a *cy près* scheme merely because the original objects had ceased, because of changing circumstances, to serve a useful purpose; or because it would have been more expedient for the trust property to be applied in some manner different from that specified by the donor. A scheme could only be ordered

---

17 *A-G v Vint* (1850) 3 De G & Sm 704.
18 *Re Monk* [1927] 2 Ch 197; *Re Bradwell* [1952] Ch 575, [1952] 2 All ER 286.
19 *Re Hillier* [1954] 2 All ER 59, [1954] 1 WLR 700 (erection of voluntary hospital, delayed by onset of war, impracticable after National Health Service Act 1946 precluded erection of new voluntary hospitals).
20 *Re Willis* [1921] 1 Ch 44.
 1 *Re North Devon and West Somerset Relief Fund Trusts* [1953] 2 All ER 1032, [1953] 1 WLR 1260; *Re Robertson* [1930] 2 Ch 71; *Re Royce* [1940] Ch 514, [1940] 2 All ER 291; *Re Raine* [1929] 1 Ch 716.
 2 *Re Welsh Hospital (Netley) Fund* [1921] 1 Ch 655; *Re Hillier* [1954] 2 All ER 59, [1954] 1 WLR 700; *Re Peel's Release* [1921] 2 Ch 218.
 3 *Ironmongers' Co v A-G* (1844) 10 Cl & Fin 908 (a trust for, inter alia, the redemption of British slaves in Barbary and Turkey); *A-G v Earl of Craven* (1856) 21 Beav 392; *Re Prison Charities* (1873) LR 16 Eq 129.
 4 Eg a trust for the abolition of slavery in the colonies achieved by the passing of the relevant legislation. *A-G v Gibson* (1835) 2 Beav 317n.
 5 *Re Buck* [1896] 2 Ch 727.
 6 *Wallis v Solicitor-General for New Zealand* [1903] AC 173.
 7 Eg the need for a voluntary fire brigade superseded by introduction of a local authority service. *Re Wokingham Fire Brigade Trusts* [1951] Ch 373, [1951] 1 All ER 454.
 8 *A-G v London Corpn* (1790) 3 Bro CC 171 (infidels in Virginia); *A-G v Daugars* (1864) 33 Beav 621 (Huguenot refugees in London).
 9 *Philipps v A-G* [1932] WN 100.
10 *Re Robinson* [1923] 2 Ch 332 (condition attached to a gift endowing a particular church that a black gown should be worn in the pulpit found to alienate the congregation and defeat the testatrix's intention, namely the propagation of religious doctrines of the evangelical sort).
11 *Philpott v St George's Hospital* (1859) 27 Beav 107 at 111; *Re Weir Hospital* [1910] 2 Ch 124.

where the objects of the trust were impossible or impracticable[12].

The occasions on which property may be applied *cy près* were extended by s 13 of the Act of 1960. This provides (the italics are added) that 'the circumstances in which the original purposes[13] of a charitable gift can be altered to allow the property to be given or part of it to be applied *cy près* shall be as follows:

'(a) *where the original purposes*[14], in whole or in part,—
   (i) *have been* as far as may be *fulfilled*; or
   (ii) *cannot be carried out*, or not according to the directions given and to the spirit of the gift; or
(b) *where the original purposes provide a use for part only of the property* available by virtue of the gift; or
(c) *where the property available* by virtue of the gift *and other property* applicable for similar purposes *can be more effectively used in conjunction*, and to that end can suitably, regard being had to the spirit of the gift[15], be made applicable to common purposes; or
(d) *where the original purposes were laid down by references to an area which* then was but *has since ceased to be a unit* for some other purpose, *or by reference to a class of persons or to an area which has* for any reason since *ceased to be suitable*, regard being had to the spirit of the gift[16], or to be practical in administering the gift; or
(e) *where the original purposes*, in whole or in part, *have*, since they were laid down,—
   (i) *been adequately provided for by other means*; or
   (ii) *ceased*, as being useless or harmful to the community or for other reasons, *to be in law charitable*; or
   (iii) *ceased* in any other way *to provide a suitable and effective method*

---

12 Evidence is not altogether lacking, however, that schemes were ordered for the reasons of expedience. Witness the testament board in the parish church of Osgathorpe, Leicestershire. The notice is not dated but is in eighteenth century script. The italics are added, 'Mrs Margaret Mead of Osgathorpe bequeathed amongst other legacies LV yearly for ever issuing from profits of her Lands in Osgathorpe and Belton to buy 2s worth of bread every week (the two weeks at Christmas excepted) 1s worth of which to be given every Sunday to such poor of Osgathorpe as shall attend Divine Service that Day. The other 1s worth to be given every Friday between the hours of ten and twelve to such people of the Adjacent Parishes as shall come to the Church of Osgathorpe for the same. She likewise gave L yearly for ever to the Parishes of Osgathorpe and Belton and the village of Thirkstone arising out of the profits of the aforesaid Lands, to be paid alternatively to each Parish or Village in order to put out one poor Boy to be bound an apprentice to some good trade in London. *But by a Decree in Chancery since made to be within any other City, Town or place in the Kingdom of England.* The qualifications of the boys may be read in her Will without fee, which is in the custody of the Minister of this Parish'.
13 See [1985] Conv 313 (P. Luxton).
14 The phrase 'original purposes' refers to the objects on which the property given was to be applied. The phrase does not cover administrative provisions, for example, as in *Re J W Laing Trust* [1984] Ch 143, [1984] 1 All ER 50, a direction as to the period within which property was to be applied.
15 The phrase 'the spirit of the gift' has been held to mean 'the basic intention underlying the gift, that intention being ascertainable from the terms of the relevant instrument and in the light of the admissible evidence'. *Re Lepton's Charity* [1972] Ch 276 at 285.
16 See n 15 supra.

of using the property[17] available by virtue of the gift, regard being
had to the spirit of the gift[18].'

It will be seen that the 'section in part restates the principles applied under
the existing law, but also extends those principles'[19]. Further, it does not
supersede the earlier cases[20] concerning impossibility and these therefore
remain a guide to the circumstances in which jurisdiction exists for a *cy près*
order to be made.

It should be noted that a trust is not impossible merely because the trustee
named by the donor declines[1] to act (or is prohibited by law from acting[2]) as
trustee, since the court, acting under the maxim 'equity never wants for a
trustee' will, if necessary, appoint a trustee. However, if the language of the
gift indicates that the personality of the trustee appointed is essential to the
carrying out of the donor's intention, and the trustee named declines to
accept the trust, then the trust is impossible[3].

Where a trustee declines, or finds himself unable[4], to execute a trust
according to terms laid down by the settlor (eg because of difficulties in
observing the settlor's instructions) the court can either appoint a fresh
trustee (to carry out the existing terms of the trust); or it can make an order
directing that the property should be applied *cy près* (eg in a scheme removing
the difficulties that have arisen); or, where there is a gift over in the event of
the trustee failing to observe the terms of the trust, and there would be
difficulty in making a suitable *cy près* scheme, it can order that the gift over
should take effect[4].

Impossibility ab initio

At the beginning of this chapter we envisaged a situation in which a charity
came into existence and then later became impossible. What is the position
if the trust is impossible ab initio, ie at the time when the gift takes effect (eg
in the case of a trust established by will, at the death of the testator)? The
answer is that in this case in order that the property may be applied *cy près*,
not only must the trust be impossible, but a second condition must also be
satisfied. This second condition is that it must be shown that the donor, in
making the gift, manifested what is termed a 'general charitable intention'.
This is sometimes alternatively expressed by saying that he must be shown
to have had a 'paramount intention of charity', or to have given the property
'for charitable purposes generally'. (But it should be remembered that there
is no requirement of general charitable intention where the trust is impossible
subsequently[5].)

17 As in *Re Lepton's Charity* [1972] Ch 276, [1971] 1 All ER 799; (M & B).
18 See n 15 supra.
19 Per Pennycuick V-C. *Re Lepton's Charity,* ante, at 284.
20 Supra, p 147.
1 *Re Lawton* [1936] 3 All ER 378.
2 *Re Armitage's Will Trusts* [1972] 1 All ER 708.
3 *Re Lysaght* [1966] Ch 191, [1965] 2 All ER 888; *Re Woodhams* [1981] 1 All ER 202, [1981]
  1 WLR 493.
4 As in *Re Hanbey's Will Trusts* [1956] Ch 264, [1955] 3 All ER 874.
5 *Re Wright* [1954] Ch 347, [1954] 2 All ER 98, CA.

GENERAL CHARITABLE INTENTION[6]

The reason for the existence of this requirement may be appreciated by considering the facts in *Re Ulverston and District New Hospital Building Trusts*[7]. An appeal was launched, and donations were made, for the purpose of building a hospital to serve the needs of Ulverston and surrounding districts. The amount raised was insufficient to build the hospital. To carry out the trust was therefore impossible. The donations had been made for a specific purpose, and there was nothing to indicate that the donors had any intention wider than that of providing the hospital. There was no 'general charitable intention'. The money raised could therefore not be applied *cy près*. So the trustees held the money on a resulting trust for the donors, and all those who could be traced received their money back. The result accords with common sense. 'If the money is not used for the hospital', we can imagine a donor saying, 'I want it back'. Similarly in the case of a gift by will: if a testator leaves money for a specific charitable purpose, and this is impossible, it is reasonable that the money should pass to the residuary legatee, and not be used for some purpose other than that specified by the testator. Only if the testator had displayed the general charitable intention we are speaking of may the property be applied *cy près*. (It must be stressed that, for property to be applied *cy près* this general charitable intention need only be shown where the trust is impossible ab initio, ie at the date of the gift. If the trust is possible at the outset and only becomes impossible at a later date, then no general charitable intention need be shown in order that the property may be applied *cy près*.)

That a general charitable intention must be shown when a trust is impossible ab initio was confirmed by section 13(2) of the Charities Act 1960.

What is a 'general charitable intention'? How does it appear and how does it provide justification for the application of property in a way other than that specified by the donor? The matter can be explained in the following way. Suppose that, as in *Biscoe v Jackson*[8], a testator gives property on trust for the establishment of a soup kitchen in a particular parish, and that (as in this case[9]) the trust cannot be carried out. If the court finds that the object specified by the donor is no more than the mode of carrying out a charitable purpose, then the fact that the mode prescribed by the donor cannot be put into effect does not affect the intention that the property should be applied for the purpose the testator intended to achieve. As the matter was expressed by Kay J in *Re Taylor*[10], '... if upon the whole scope and intent of the will you discern the paramount object of the testator was to benefit ... a particular form of charity independently of any special institution or mode, then, although he may have indicated the mode in which he desires that to be carried out, you are to regard the primary paramount intention chiefly, and if the mode for any reason fails, the court ... will ... carry out the general paramount intention in some other way as nearly as possible the same as that in which the testator had particularly indicated ...'.

In *Biscoe v Jackson* the court held that the establishment of the soup

---

6   (1984) 128 SJ 760 (J. Warburton).
7   [1956] Ch 622, [1956] 3 All ER 164.
8   (1887) 35 Ch D 460; (M & B).
9   No suitable land could be found.
10   (1888) 58 LT 538, 543.

kitchen was merely the means adopted by the testator for achieving what the court found to be his real aim, the relief of poverty in the parish. Thus the gift was construed as being for the relief of poverty in Shoreditch, by the establishment there of a soup kitchen. The impossibility of setting up the soup kitchen did not affect the dedication of the property for the charitable purpose of relieving poverty in the parish, and the court therefore directed that the property should be applied *cy près* (with the result that the property was applied for the relief of poverty in the parish by some other means).

Thus for property to be applied *cy près* when a trust is impossible ab initio the court must find the existence of charitable purpose, albeit unexpressed by the testator, for the attainment of which the object specified by the testator was the means. It is this purpose, lying behind the purpose stipulated, that is termed a 'general charitable intention'. Seen in this light it will be appreciated that the word 'general' is misleading. The word is too wide. There is no need for the gift to be construed as showing an intention to benefit charity *generally*, or even to benefit a general, in the sense of wide, charitable purpose. The requirement may be satisfied when the primary purpose (of which the object specified is the means) is by any standards a narrow one. For example, in *Re King*[11] it was held that the primary purpose of a testator who had left property for provision of a stained glass window in a particular church was to benefit the church building as a whole. (Thus a surplus available after the erection of the window was ordered to be applied *cy près*, and would have been applied in some other way for the betterment of the building[12].) In *Re Royce*[13] property was bequeathed to the vicar and church wardens of Oakham church 'for the benefit of the choir'. The sum bequeathed being greater than could be used for the choir, the trust was impossible quoad the surplus. It was held that the primary purpose was the advancement of religion, the maintenance and improvement of musical services being the means of achieving this end. The surplus was therefore ordered to be applied *cy près*[14].

Where the court is unable to find that the terms of the gift constitute a means of achieving some charitable purpose, that the terms of the gift constitute the object, the *only* object, the testator intended to achieve, then no general charitable intention exists and the gift will fail[15]. As the matter has been expressed: 'If on the proper construction of the will the mode of application is such an essential part of the gift that you cannot distinguish any general purpose of charity but are obliged to say that the prescribed mode of doing the charitable act is the only one the testator intended or at all contemplated, then, the court cannot, if that mode fails, apply the money *cy près*[16]. For example in *Re White's Trusts*[17], a testator bequeathed property to build an almshouse for, inter alia, poor tinplate workers, and expressed the hope that someone else would endow it. No suitable site could be found and no one came forward to endow it. The trust was therefore impossible.

---

11 [1923] 1 Ch 243.
12 [1966] Ch 191, [1965] 2 All ER 888. See also *Re Raine* [1956] Ch 417, [1956] 1 All ER 355 (surplus after application of gifts of residue for seating in a parish church applied *cy près* for the church generally).
13 [1940] Ch 514, [1940] 2 All ER 291.
14 Other illustrations of general charitable intention are provided by *Re Hillier* [1954] 2 All ER 59, [1954] 1 WLR 700, and *Re Woodhams* [1981] 1 All ER 202, [1981] 1 WLR 493.
15 Per Younger LJ, *Re Willis* [1921] 1 Ch 44 at 54.
16 M. Chesterman, *Charities, Trusts and Social Welfare,* p 219.
17 (1886) 33 Ch D 449.

Since the court held that no general charitable intention existed, the property was not applied *cy près*, and fell into residue. In *Re Wilson*[18] property was given to provide income for a schoolmaster of a school that the testator hoped would be built by public subscriptions on a certain hill. The trust could not be carried out. It was held that no charitable intention wider than that for the purpose specified could be construed. The property fell into residue. In *Re Good's Will Trusts*[19] £2,300 was bequeathed for building certain rest homes. The fund was insufficient for the purpose specified. It was held that the language of the will was so particular as to exclude the possibility of finding any general charitable intention. The money fell into residue. In *Re Stanford*[20] a testator left money to a university in order to enable a dictionary which he had written to be published. There was a surplus after the book had been published. It was held that the will displayed no general charitable intention and the surplus was therefore not applied *cy près* and fell into residue.

In *Re White's Will Trust*[1], a testatrix devised two cottages to be used as rest homes for retired aged missionaries. At her death the trust could not be carried out as the cottages were occupied by tenants entitled to the protection of the Rent Acts and there was no indication that they proposed to leave. It was held that the will showed no general charitable intention, and that if an enquiry, which the court ordered to be carried out[2], found that there was no reasonable prospect that it would be practicable to carry out the trust, the gift would fail and the property pass to the residuary devisees[3].

Thus the decision which the court has to make is whether a donor's intention is specific, or is to further a purpose by a means which is not essential to his gift. As Parker J expressed the matter in *Re Wilson*[4]: 'I have to determine whether the gift in this will, which is in form a particular gift, is a gift really for a particular charitable purpose and for that purpose only, or whether there is a paramount intention to be gathered from the will that the money shall in any event be applied for some more general charitable purpose even if the particular mode of application which is prescribed cannot be carried into effect'. Thus what the court is seeking to decide is whether it is to be inferred that the donor would have wished, had he known that the gift would have been impossible (in whole or in part) to fulfil, that the property should be applied for some other purpose resembling as closely as possible that which he had specified. Whether or not this inference is to be made is a matter of construction. The decision was described in an Australian case as being reached by 'something approaching more nearly to divination, or intuition, than to interpretation in the accustomed sense'[5] and few guidelines exist[6].

---

18 [1913] 1 Ch 314.
19 [1950] 2 All ER 653.
20 [1924] 1 Ch 73.
 1 [1955] Ch 188, [1954] 2 All ER 620.
 2 An enquiry as to the practicability of carrying out a trust was ordered also in *Re James* [1932] 2 Ch 25, and in *Re Edwin Riley Charities* (1930) 70 L Jo 409.
 3 Examples of other cases in which no general charitable intention was found to exist include *Re University of London Medical Sciences Institute Fund* [1909] 2 Ch 1, and *Re Packe* [1918] 1 Ch 437.
 4 [1913] 1 Ch 314 at 324; see also *Re Willis* [1921] 1 Ch 44, 54.
 5 Per *Executor Trustee and Agency Co of South Australia Ltd v Warbey (No 2)* (1973) 6 SASR 336 at 345. Quoted by Picarda, op cit, p 245.
 6 It has been suggested that 'it is very necessary in these cases to remember that the

It has happened on occasions that the reason for a charitable trust being impossible to execute has been that a specific institution to which property has been given as the trustee has not been prepared to accept the property because of the existence of a particular term or condition in the gift. Acceptance by the institution being a necessary part of the testator's intention, the trust has been impossible. In such a case, in the event of a *cy près* order being made, the direction may take the form of an order deleting the term or condition concerned. In such a case it will be for the court, in deciding whether a general charitable intention exists, to determine whether the condition is an essential part of the testator's intention or whether the condition is one which the testator, had he known of the circumstances, would have wished, so that his general aim should be capable of being attained, to be deleted. For example, in *Re Lysaght*[7] a testatrix left property to the Royal College of Surgeons on trust to establish medical studentships for persons other than those of the Jewish or Roman Catholic faith. The College declined to accept the gift on these terms. It was held that it was of the essence of the gift that the College and no one else should undertake the trust. The trust was therefore impossible. However, since the testatrix's intention was construed as extending to the founding of medical studentships generally, the court directed a scheme under which the College held the property on the trusts in the will, omitting the words excluding those of the Jewish or Roman Catholic faith[8]. In *Re Woodhams*[9], a testator left residue to the London College of Music to fund annual scholarships for the musical education of 'a promising boy who is an absolute orphan and only of British nationality and birth from any one of Dr Barnardo's homes ...' The College was not prepared to accept the bequest with the restriction as to the class from which candidates for scholarships should be selected. The court[10] found that the restriction was not an essential part of the testator's intention and approved a modification deleting the restriction.

THE PRESUMPTIONS

We have seen that when a trust becomes impossible subsequently then, for the property to be applied *cy près*, no general charitable intention need be shown[11]. This is the general rule, but even here, if there is evidence to show that the donor did not intend the property to be applied *cy près* if the trust later became impossible (eg by the making of a gift over on the failure of the

---

application of the doctrine probably differs very much according to whether or not it is applied to residue or a share of residue. I think that where one finds a residuary gift out and out for a charitable purpose, and there is a surplus over and above what is required for that particular purpose, the overriding intention of a charitable disposition should still prevail, with the result that this surplus must be applied *cy près* for the benefit of [a particular church]'. Per Vaisey J, *Re Raine* [1956] Ch 417 at 423.

7 [1966] Ch 191, [1965] 2 All ER 888; (M & B).
8 See also *Re Robinson* [1923] 2 Ch 332; (M & B).
9 [1981] 1 All ER 202, [1981] 1 WLR 493.
10 Vinelott J.
11 This fact has sometimes not prevented the court from feeling an obligation to find a general charitable intention before making a *cy près* direction, notwithstanding that the trust became impossible subsequently. See *Re Welsh Hospital (Netley) Fund* [1921] 1 Ch 655.

charity) then the property will not be applied *cy près*[12]. The presumptions may therefore be summarised thus:

1. Where a trust becomes impossible subsequently, the presumption is that the property should be applied *cy près*, unless there is something to indicate that such an application was not intended.

2. Where the trust is impossible ab initio, the presumption is that the property should not be applied *cy près*, unless it is construed that this would have been the testator's wish (ie by finding a general charitable intention).

Deemed charitable intention

From the cases cited earlier it will have been seen that whether general charitable intention is to be inferred depends, inter alia, on how specific the donor was in framing his gift; the more specific the gift, the less room there is for construing the gift as manifesting a general charitable intention; the less specific the gift, the greater the likelihood of this intention being found. In two circumstances, however, a general charitable intention will be found notwithstanding that the gift is entirely specific.

1. One is where the gift which is impossible appears in a list of gifts all the rest of which are charitable[13]. (Of course, if the purpose specified is not of itself charitable then, since the *cy près* doctrine can only apply where a gift to a charity is or becomes impossible, the fact that the gift appears in a list of dispositions the rest of which are all charitable, is irrelevant. As Buckley J expressed the matter in *Re Jenkins Will Trusts*[14] 'If you meet seven men with black hair and one with red hair you are not entitled to say that there are eight men with black hair. Finding one gift for a non-charitable purpose among a number of gifts for charitable purposes the court cannot infer that the testator or testatrix meant the non-charitable gift to take effect as a charitable gift when in the terms it is not charitable, even though the non-charitable gift may have a close relation to the purposes for which the charitable gifts are made.' If the gift is impossible, since the *cy près* doctrine cannot be called in aid, the gift will fail and the share of property concerned will fall into residue[15].)

2. The other circumstance is where property is given on trust to a named institution, but an institution with that name has never existed. Provided that it is clear that the institution, if it had existed, would have been charitable, then a general charitable intention is inferred, and so the property applied *cy près*[16] (eg to an extant institution with similar objects). But here also it is the donor's intention which prevails, and if there are circumstances which counter an inference of general charitable intention (eg as where the residue is given to a named, existing charity[17]) then no such intention will

12　*Re Cooper's Conveyance Trusts* [1956] 3 All ER 28, [1956] 1 WLR 1096.
13　Or would be expected to be charitable by the average testator. *Re Satterthwaite's Will Trusts* [1966] 1 All ER 919, [1966] 1 WLR 277; (M & B).
14　*Re Jenkins Will Trusts* [1966] Ch 249, 256, [1966] 1 All ER 926, 929; (M & B).
15　*Re Jenkin's Will Trusts*, supra.
16　*Re Harwood* [1936] Ch 285 (the 'Peace Society of Belfast'); (M & B); *Re Satterthwaite's Will Trusts* [1966] 1 All ER 919, [1966] 1 WLR 277, CA; (M & B).
17　*Re Goldschmidt* [1957] 1 All ER 513, [1957] 1 WLR 524.

be found, and the gift to the body which never existed will not be applied *cy près*.

If a gift is made to an institution which has never existed, and the institution, if it had existed, might or might not have been charitable, then the fact that the gift appears in a list of gifts to other bodies which are charitable may be sufficient to show the existence of a general charitable intention and so enable the gift in question to be applied *cy près*[18].

Misdescription

A gift to an institution that never existed must be distinguished from a gift to a charity by an incorrect description. If the court finds on the evidence that the donor intended a particular body to receive his gift then the court will make an order giving effect to the donor's intention[19].

Time for determining impossibility

What is the position if a testator gives property to trustees on trust for A for life with remainder on trust for a charitable purpose, and the purpose is possible at the testator's death but impossible at A's death? Is the gift impossible ab initio or subsequently? It has been held[20] that the time for determining whether or not a trust is impossible is when the trustees acquire a vested interest, ie at the testator's death, and not when the interest for the charitable purpose falls into possession, ie at A's death. In the situation cited, therefore, since the trust was possible at the testator's death the trust became impossible subsequently and so no general charitable intention by the testator needed to be shown for the property to be applied *cy près* on A's death[1].

CHARITIES THAT CEASE TO EXIST BEFORE THE GIFT TAKES EFFECT

At this point it will be convenient to consider a particular form of impossibility, namely where a gift is made to trustees on trust to a charity which ceases to exist before the gift takes effect. For example, in his will made in 1970 T leaves £1,000 on trust for a named charitable body. The body ceases to exist in 1980. T dies in 1987. What result ensues? Since *Re Finger's Will Trusts*[2] it has been possible to make the following propositions.

1. If the gift is for a charity which had not been a corporate body (eg it had consisted merely of a set of trustees), and if the gift is to the charity on trust

---

18   *Re Knox* [1937] Ch 109, [1936] 3 All ER 623.
19   *Re Spence* [1979] Ch 483, [1978] 3 All ER 92; (M & B); *Re Meyers* [1951] Ch 534, [1951] 1 All ER 538.
20   *Re Moon's Will Trusts* [1948] 1 All ER 300; *Re Wright* [1954] Ch 347, [1954] 2 All ER 98; (M & B).
1   In the case of a gift vested in remainder which is liable to be defeated, the trust is possible at the testator's death if there is then a reasonable prospect that it will be practicable to give effect to the trust. *Re Tacon* [1958] Ch 447, [1958] 1 All ER 163, CA.
2   [1972] Ch 286, [1971] 3 All ER 1050; (M & B).

for its work (or 'purposes', or 'objects', etc), then the position will depend (i) on whether or not it is still possible for that work to be carried on, and (ii) on whether the continued existence of the institution named was a vital part of the donor's purpose.

If it is still possible for the work to be carried on (eg relieving poverty in a certain district), and the continued existence of the institution named by the donor is not construed as being a vital part of the donor's intention, then the gift is not impossible and so no question of *cy près* arises. The court will make a scheme[3] prescribing how the property is to be applied in order to carry on the work (eg it may direct that the property should be given to another, extant, charity with similar objects to the one which ceased to exist, and to which the funds of the charity named by the donor have been transferred[4]).

If it is impossible for the work to be carried on, or if the continued existence of the institution is construed as being a vital part of the testator's intention[5], the result will depend on whether or not a general charitable intention can be found. If it can, the property will be applied *cy près*, if not, the gift will fail[6].

2. If the gift is to a charity which (as in 1) had been a non-corporate body, but no words are added indicating that the gift is for the charity's work (or 'purposes' or 'objects', etc), then such words may nevertheless be construed[7], and the result is as in 1 above. Thus if it is still possible for the work to be carried on, and the continued existence of the named institution is not construed as being a vital part of the donor's intention, the gift is not impossible[8] and a scheme will be made setting out how the property is to be applied. If it is impossible for the work to be carried on[9], or if the continued existence of the institution is construed as being a vital part of the testator's intention[10], the result will depend on whether a general charitable intention can be inferred. If it can, the property will be applied *cy près*; if not, it will fail[11].

3. If the gift is to a charity which, before it ceased to exist, had been a corporate body (eg a company limited by guarantee) and words are added indicating that the gift is to the body on trust for its work (etc) then the result is as in 1 above.

4. If the gift is on trust for a charity which, before it ceased to exist, had been a corporate body and no words are added indicating that the gift is on trust for its work (and there is nothing to permit such an intention being construed), then the non-existence of the body makes the gift impossible. The gift is impossible ab initio. The outcome will therefore depend on whether

---

3 Not, it should be noted, a *cy près* scheme, but a scheme to provide certainty as to how the trust property should be applied.
4 As in *Re Roberts* [1963] 1 All ER 674, [1963] 1 WLR 406.
5 *Re Rymer* [1895] 1 Ch 19; (M & B).
6 *Re Rymer* [1895] 1 Ch 19; *Re Spence* [1979] Ch 483, [1978] 3 All ER 92; (M & B).
7 *Re Vernon's Will Trusts* [1972] Ch 300n, [1971] 3 All ER 1061n; *Re Finger's Will Trusts* [1972] Ch 286, [1971] 3 All ER 1050 (the gift to the National Radium Commission).
8 *Re Finger's Will Trusts*, ante.
9 *Re Slatter's Will Trusts* [1964] Ch 512, [1964] 2 All ER 469.
10 *Re Harwood* [1936] Ch 285; (M & B).
11 *Re Harwood*, ante; *Re Slatter's Will Trusts*, ante.

there is a general charitable intention. If there is, the property is applied *cy près*[12], if not, the gift fails[13].

It will be seen, therefore, that the above principles can be reduced to the rule that where a charity ceases to exist before a gift to it takes effect then the gift may nevertheless still be possible, but if it is impossible, then whether the gift is applied *cy près* depends on whether or not a general charitable intention is found to exist.

If a gift is made by a testator to a charity he was minded to found, but never did so, then the gift is treated as being for the purpose for which the charity would have existed, if it had been founded. If the purpose concerned still exists, then the trust is not impossible, and the court will direct, in a scheme, in what manner the property is to be applied[14].

CHANGE IN NAME

It should be noted that although a charity may cease to exist under a particular name, this does not necessarily indicate that the charity has ceased to exist. For example, where two or more charities are amalgamated under the name of one of them, or under a new name, the objects of the original charities may be incorporated, or substantially incorporated[15], into the trusts of the new, amalgamated, charity. In such a situation the objects of the original charity are not impossible merely because of the change of name, and so there cannot on this score alone be any question of property given to one of the original charities being applied *cy près*. The courts regard the original charities as still being in existence, albeit under a new name, and a gift to one of them by its original name passes to the consolidated charities under the new name[16].

Similarly, where, between the date of a will and the time when the gift takes effect, the objects of a charity, or its name, are altered (whether under a power conferred on the trustees by the trust instrument or under a scheme) provided that the change is 'merely in its mechanical aspect'[17], the change does not involve the charity ceasing to exist, and a gift to the charity by its earlier name takes effect as a gift to the charity under its new one[18].

CHARITIES WHICH CEASE TO EXIST AFTER THE GIFT TAKES EFFECT

Suppose that on his death a testator leaves a bequest to a particular charity. Before the executor has passed the money to the charity, it ceases to exist. To whom should the executor pass the money? There is no problem: the

12 *Re Finger's Will Trusts,* ante (the gift to National Council for Maternity and Child Care).
13 *Re Stemson's Will Trusts* [1970] Ch 16, [1969] 2 All ER 517; *Re Goldney* (1946) 115 LJ Ch 337; *Re Slatter's Will Trusts* [1964] Ch 512, [1964] 2 All ER 469.
14 *Re Mann* [1903] 1 Ch 232.
15 *Re Lucas* [1948] Ch 424, [1948] 2 All ER 22.
16 *Re Faraker* [1912] 2 Ch 488; (M & B); *Re Lucas,* ante; *Re Dawson's Will Trusts* [1957] 1 All ER 177, [1957] 1 WLR 391.
17 *Re Vernon's Will Trusts* [1972] Ch 300n, per Buckley J at 304, [1971] 3 All ER 1061n.
18 *Re Vernon's Will Trusts,* ante; *Re Bagshaw* [1954] 1 All ER 227, [1954] 1 WLR 238. See also *Re Waring* [1907] 1 Ch 166.

charity was in existence at the testator's death and so the bequest became the property of the charity at that moment. When the charity ceased to exist, in whatever way its funds were applied (eg under a *cy près* scheme), the bequest will be applied in the same manner[19].

THE ALTERNATIVE TO GENERAL CHARITABLE INTENTION PROVIDED BY SECTION 14

Suppose that in 1959 an appeal was launched to raise money for the relief of hardship caused by an earthquake in Bolivia. Funds were raised by collections in the streets and from the proceeds of raffles. Sums of money were also sent by post, some of them anonymously. Later it was found that the news was false and that no earthquake had occurred. How would the trustees hold the money which had been collected? The trust was impossible ab initio. No general charitable intention can be inferred. Therefore the money cannot be applied *cy près*. So the trustees would hold it on a resulting trust for the donors. But how could they return money to those who contributed by putting money in collecting boxes and by buying raffle tickets, and to those who sent money anonymously? And what should be done with the contributions of people who sent small sums, the cost of returning which might approach or even exceed the amounts contributed? Before the Charities Act 1960 no satisfactory answer existed to these questions and as a last resort trust money was sometimes paid into court. The Act resolved the matter by providing that in (inter alia) the circumstances set out above the property should be treated *as if* it had been given 'for charitable purposes generally'. The Act thus enabled the property to be applied *cy près*. The circumstances in which the Act enabled this to be done are set out in s 14[20], the words of which are given below. The italics are added.

> '14.—(1) *Property* given for specific charitable purposes which fail *shall be applicable cy près* as if given for charitable purposes generally, *where it belongs*—
> (a) *to a donor who, after,* (i) *the prescribed advertisements and inquiries have been published and made*, and; (ii) the prescribed period beginning with the publication of those advertisements, *cannot be identified or cannot be found*; or
> (b) *to a donor who has executed a written disclaimer* of his right to have the property returned.
> (2) For the purposes of this section *property shall be conclusively presumed* (without any advertisement or inquiry) *to belong to donors who cannot be identified, in so far as it consists*—
> (a) *of the proceeds of cash collections made by means of collecting boxes* or by other means not adapted for distinguishing one gift from another; or
> (b) *of the proceeds of any lottery, competition, entertainment, sale or*

---

19   *Re Slevin* [1891] 2 Ch 236; (M & B). It is not clear from the report of this case why the assets of the charity (which does not appear to have been a corporate body) passed to the Crown. Since the gift had become impossible, an application to the court for a direction that the property should be applied *cy près* would seem to have been the correct course.
20   As amended by the Charities Act 1992, s 15(2), (3). For difficulties inherent in the section, see [1983] Conv 40 (D. Wilson).

similar money-raising activity, after allowing for property given to provide prizes or articles for sale or otherwise to enable the activity to be undertaken.

(3) *The court may by order direct that property* not falling within subsection (2) above *shall* for the purposes of this section *be treated* (without any advertisement or inquiry) *as belonging to donors who cannot be identified, where it appears to the court either—*

(a) *that it would be unreasonable,* having regard to the amounts likely to be returned to the donors, *to incur expense with a view to returning the property;* or

(b) *that it would be unreasonable,* having regard to the nature, circumstances and amount of the gifts, and to the lapse of time since the gifts were made, *for the donors to expect the property to be returned'.*

The limits of s 14 should be noted, in particular that if a donor can be identified then unless he disclaims or unless the sum he donated is so small as to fall under s 14(3)(a) or (b), the section has no application and the money must be returned to the person who donated it[1].

Section 14 applies retrospectively and so enabled trust property held on resulting trusts at the date of the Act to be applied *cy près*[2].

It should be noted that since s 14 provides an alternative to the requirement of general charitable intention, the section has no relevance where a trust becomes impossible subsequently. (Here trust property may be applied *cy près* irrespective of how it was collected and irrespective of whether or not the donors can be identified.)

Finally, it should be noted that s 14 is of assistance only in the case of charities. Where a non-charitable trust becomes impossible (eg where there is a surplus after the object of an appeal for a non-charitable purpose has been attained[3]) s 14 has no application, and the property concerned is held on a resulting trust for the donors.

JURISDICTION TO MAKE *CY PRÈS* ORDERS

The jurisdiction of the court (and the Charity Commissioners) to direct that property should be applied *cy près* is exercisable where property is held on trust and, in the case of a corporate body, where under the terms of its constitution there is a strict obligation to apply its assets for objects that are exclusively charitable[4]. It follows that where property is given directly to a body that had never existed, ie without the employment of a trust[5], the court (and the Commissioners) have no jurisdiction to make a *cy près* scheme. Jurisdiction here rests with the Crown which, being guided by the same

1 See *Re Henry Wood National Memorial Trust* [1967] 1 All ER 238n, [1966] 1 WLR 1601.
2 Section 14(7).
3 As in *Re Gillingham Bus Disaster Fund* [1959] Ch 62, [1958] 2 All ER 749; (M & B).
4 *Liverpool and District Hospital for Diseases of the Heart v A-G* [1981] Ch 193, [1981] 1 All ER 994.
5 The fact that trustees are appointed in the instrument of gift will not cause the property to be deemed to be subject to a trust.

principles as courts, may make a *cy près* direction under the sign manual[6]. (Similarly, if no trust exists, the courts have no jurisdiction to make a scheme providing certainty[7], and an application must be made to the Crown for a scheme issued under the sign manual[8].)

Modification or termination of small charities under the Charities Act 1992

As an alternative to an application to the court or the Commissioners for a scheme under the *cy près* jurisdiction, the Charities Act 1992[9] provides means (replacing those previously existing under the Charities Act 1985) by which, in the case of certain categories of charity, certain alterations can be made.

1 TRANSFER OF ASSETS TO ANOTHER CHARITY[10]

Where (i) the gross income of a charity did not exceed £5,000 in its last financial year; (ii) the charity is neither an exempt nor a charitable company; and, (iii) the charity does not hold any land on trusts that stipulate that the land is to be used for the purposes of the charity, then if the trustees are satisfied that the existing purposes of the charity have ceased to be conducive to a suitable and effective application of the charity's resources and they pass (by a majority of not less than two-thirds) a resolution that all of the property of the charity should be transferred to another, specified, registered charity (or divided between two or more such charities), being one that they are satisfied has purposes as similar in character to those of the charity of which they are trustees as is reasonably practicable, then the trustees are required to give public notice of the resolution, and send a copy of the resolution to the Commissioners. The Commissioners, after taking into account any representations made to them, notify the trustees whether they concur, or do not concur, with the resolution. If they concur, the trustees are required to arrange for the property to be transferred in accordance with the resolution. Thereafter the property is held on the trusts of the charity to which it is transferred (but subject to any restrictions on expenditure to which it was subject before the transfer).

2 ALTERATION OF OBJECTS[11]

Where trustees of a charity (which complies with (i)–(iii) above) are satisfied that the existing purposes of the charity, or certain of those purposes, have ceased to be conducive to a suitable and effective application of the charity's

---

6   *Re Bennett* [1960] Ch 18, [1959] 3 All ER 295.
7   See p 141, ante.
8   *Moggridge v Thackwell* (1803) 7 Ves 36.
9   Sections 43–44.
10 Charities Act 1992, s 43.
11 Ibid.

resources and they pass (by a majority of not less than two-thirds) a resolution that the trusts of the charity should be modified by replacing all or any of those purposes with other such purposes as are charitable, being purposes that they are satisfied are as similar in character to the existing purposes as is practicable, then the procedure follows that given above: the trustees pass the relevant resolution, give public notice and send a copy to the Commissioners; the Commissioners notify the trustees whether or not they concur. In the event of the Commissioners notifying their concurrence, the trusts of the charity are deemed to be modified in accordance with the resolution from the date specified in the notification.

3 ALTERATION OF POWERS OR PROCEDURES[12]

The 1992 Act enables the powers or procedures contained in the trusts of a charity that complies with (i)–(iii) above to be modified by a corresponding procedure (ie passage of a resolution by a two-thirds majority, public notice, copy of the resolution being sent to the Commissioners, notification by the Commissioners as to whether or not they concur).

4 POWER TO SPEND CAPITAL[13]

Where (i) a charity has a permanent endowment that does not comprise any land; (ii) its gross income did not exceed £1,000 in its last financial year; (iii) it is neither exempt nor a company or other corporate body, and the trustees are of the opinion that the property of the charity is too small, in relation to its purposes, for any useful purpose to be achieved by the expenditure of income alone then, by following the procedure required in the case of (i)–(iii) above (passage of resolution by a two-thirds majority etc) the trustees can become entitled to expend property that forms part of the permanent endowment. (It will be appreciated that a charity may thereby exhaust its assets and as a consequence cease to exist.)

Forms of charity; charitable status

FORMS OF CHARITY[14]

1. A charity may be a trust; ie the trust property being held by trustees on trust for the purpose specified; or
2. A charity may take the form of an unincorporated association with officers, members and a rule book, the latter setting out the purposes and constitution of the association. The trust property may be vested in the members of a committee that has responsibility for running the association,

---

12 Ibid.
13 Charities Act 1992, s 44.
14 [1990] Conv 95 (J. Warburton).

or in a set of trustees, who may or may not be committee members; or

3. A charity may exist as a corporate body[15], for example as a limited company with a memorandum and articles of association. Commonly the form adopted is that of a company limited by guarantee, since it would not be possible for a body to have charitable status and at the same time distribute dividends on shares produced by profits on its activities. It is an advantage of this form of corporate status that the body can obtain exemption from the use of 'Ltd' or 'Plc' in its name[16].

4. Where a charity has a benevolent purpose[17] or a purpose authorised by the Treasury, it may exist as a friendly society by registration under the Friendly Societies Act 1974[18].

5. Where a charity is formed for the carrying on of an industrial trade or business[19] intended to be conducted for the benefit of the community, it may exist as an industrial and provident society by registration with the Chief Registrar of Friendly Societies[20].

Where a charity is established to achieve the fulfilment of an individual donor's particular purpose, then the charity commonly takes the first form. Where a charity is established in order to achieve what has come to be felt by a number of people to be a desirable end (eg the relief of destitution in the third world), then the charity is likely to take the second or third form described above.

With regard to finances, a charity may have a permanent endowment, from the investment of which its income is produced; or a charity may have no permanent endowment and instead rely on donations for its income; or a charity may have a permanent endowment and also receive donations. (Where a gift is made to a charity with a permanent endowment, the gift is treated as being intended to be applied as income unless an intention is shown by the donor that the money is to be added to the endowment.)

Where a donor directs that income from a fund is to be paid to a charity (ie indefinitely), this does not entitle the charity to receive the corpus of the fund[1]. Where it is unclear whether the intention is to make a gift of income from a fund or a gift of the corpus of the fund (ie a gift of capital), then the gift should take effect as a gift of the corpus, since an intention to make a gift only of income should not be imputed without an indication that an endowment fund was intended to be set up[2].

HOW THE QUESTION OF CHARITABLE STATUS MAY ARISE

The question of charitable status may arise in two ways:

1. Is a *particular gift* charitable? Eg is a gift for 'the advancement of education

---

15   [1984] Conv 112 (J. Warburton).
16   Companies Act 1985, s 30.
17   Ie, a purpose that is both charitable and benevolent.
18   Section 7(1).
19   Eg, under the Industrial Training Act 1964. *Construction Industry Training Board v A-G* [1973] Ch 173, [1972] 2 All ER 1339.
20   Industrial and Provident Societies Act 1965, s 1. [1990] Conv. 95 (J. Warburton).
 1   *Re Levy* [1960] Ch 346, [1960] 1 All ER 42, CA.
 2   *Re Beesty's Will Trusts* [1966] Ch 223, [1964] 3 All ER 82.

among the residents of Eyam' charitable? If the gift is charitable, then a charitable trust comes into existence. This is so whether the donor gave the property to trustees on trust for the purpose mentioned; or whether he did not do so. In the latter case the court will if necessary appoint trustees.

The outcome, as to whether the gift is or is not charitable, will decide such questions as (a) whether the gift is valid (since if it is not charitable, it may be void); and (b) whether concessions in the sphere of inheritance tax apply.

If a gift is made to an existing charitable institution, then the gift is necessarily charitable.

2. Is an *existing body*, eg an association, charitable? For example in *Oxford Group v IRC*[3], the court had to decide whether the Oxford Group was a charitable body. Here the outcome will decide such questions as (a) whether income from capital owned by the association is free of income tax; and (b) whether gifts made to the association in the future will prima facie[4] be automatically charitable.

DETERMINATION OF CHARITABLE STATUS

Most commonly the question whether a body is charitable is decided by the Charity Commissioners on the occasion of an application being made for registration. Appeal from a decision of the Commissioners lies to the Chancery Division of the High Court (as, for example, where the Inland Revenue maintains that the objects of a body registered are not charitable, or where a body refused registration maintains that its objects are charitable). Where a body is not registrable as a charity under the Act, the question whether it has charitable status will nevertheless require to be determined if the body seeks to benefit from the fiscal advantages enjoyed by a charity. In this event, the question whether the body is a charity will be determined, if tax relief is sought, by the Inland Revenue, whose jurisdiction in this sphere grew up in the nineteenth century, following the first granting of a tax advantage to charities (exemption from income tax) in 1799. Appeal from a decision of the Inland Revenue lies to the Special Commissioners of Inland Revenue and thence to the courts. Where relief from council tax is sought, the question of charitable status is determinable by the local authority concerned (which, in practice, may consult with and take advice from the Inland Revenue). The jurisdiction dates from the passing of the Rating and Valuation (Miscellaneous Provisions) Act 1955.

Alternatively, the question whether a body has charitable status may be determined by applying (by originating summons) to the Chancery Division, seeking a direction on the matter. This course—by-passing the Commissioners—may be adopted where there is a probability of an appeal from a decision of the Commissioners (eg where the property consists of a substantial legacy) and it seems likely that a decision that a body has charitable status will be contested by those who will receive the money if the trust is declared not to be charitable (ie the residuary legatees) and that a decision that the trust is not charitable will be contested on behalf of the Crown by the Attorney General. The application to the court may be made by the

3 [1949] 2 All ER 537.
4 *Re Vernon's Will Trusts* [1972] Ch 300n, [1971] 3 All ER 1061n.

trustees or by the persons to whom the property will pass if the trust is held not to be charitable (and so void), or by the Attorney General. The jurisdiction of the court to determine whether a trust has charitable status is part of the ancient jurisdiction of Chancery over the administration of trusts. (The court's jurisdiction exists only in relation to a trust. It has no jurisdiction to decide at first instance whether a corporation or association is charitable, though this question may reach the court in the shape of an appeal from a decision of the Commissioners[5].)

We noted above that in order for the tax advantages of charities to be enjoyed not only did the body have to have charitable status but, further, the body's income had to be applied to purposes that were exclusively charitable. Whether this latter requirement is satisfied falls to be decided by the Inland Revenue, from the decisions of which appeal lies to the Special Commissioners of Inland Revenue, and thence to the courts[6].

Control of charities

It will be recalled that it was the purpose of the Charities Act of 1601 to establish machinery for the supervision and control of charities. The primitive means of control introduced by the Act continued with little change into the last century. Reforms in this sphere were made by the Charities Act 1960, but these failed to provide adequate safeguards against maladministration or fraud by trustees, and the subject of the supervision of charities was examined in a number of reports[7], culminating in 1989 in a paper by the Home Secretary, 'Charities: A Framework for the Future'[8]. It was in large part to implement the recommendations of this paper that the Charities Act 1992 was passed. The Act made changes to the measures for the control of charities in the Act of 1960 and introduced certain new requirements. The system of control that exists following the 1992 Act may be set out under the eight heads below.

With regard to the various matters that follow it should be noted that (1) the Acts of 1960 and 1992 distinguish between, (a) 'trustees for a charity', ie those in whom the title to the trust property is vested; and, (b) 'charity trustees', who are defined[9] as 'the persons having general control and management of the administration of a charity'. 'Charity trustees' could therefore be the trustees of a charity, if it is they who control the administration of the charity, or members of a management committee appointed by the trustees, or the directors of a charity which is a company. (2) Not all the requirements of the Acts of 1960 and 1992 relating to the administration of and control

5   As in *Oxford Group v IRC* [1949] 2 All ER 537.
6   As in *IRC v Educational Grants Association* [1967] Ch 993, [1967] 2 All ER 893; (M & B); *IRC v Helen Slater Charitable Trust Ltd* [1981] Ch 79, [1980] 1 All ER 785; (1982) 98 LQR 1 (A. M. Tettenborn).
7   February 1987 Report of the Public Accounts Committee of the House of Commons, *Monitoring and Control of Charities* (HC 116); July 1987, report, commissioned by the Home Secretary and the Economic Secretary to the Treasury, of a committee chaired by Sir Philip Woodhead, *Efficiency Scrutiny of the Supervision of Charities*.
8   Cm 694.
9   Charities Act 1960, s 46; Charities Act 1992, s 1(2).

over charities (eg with regard to the preparation of accounts) apply to every category of charity: some categories of charities are exempted from the duty to comply with certain requirements. (3) The machinery for the control of charities in the Acts of 1960 and 1992 applies principally to charities other than those that are limited companies. Control over the latter is effected primarily (though not exclusively[9a]) through the legislation that regulates companies' affairs, in particular the Companies Acts 1985 and 1989.

1 REGISTRATION

The Charities Act 1960[10] requires the Commissioners to maintain a register of charities, in such manner as they think fit. Every charity, with specified exceptions, is required to be entered in the register. The duty to apply for registration rests with the charity trustees. Charity trustees are under a duty, also, to notify the Commissioners of changes in the trusts of the charity, and of the charity ceasing to exist. Where it appears to the Commissioners that an institution is no longer a charity (ie because the objects have been changed or the body has ceased to exist) they are required to remove the institution from the register. The register is open to public inspection, as also are copies of the trusts of any registered charity supplied to the Commissioners.

Charities that are not under a duty to register comprise[11]:

1. A charity, referred to in the Act as an 'exempt charity', which is included in the Second Schedule of the 1960 Act. 'Exempt charities' include, inter alia, the Universities of Oxford and Cambridge and their Colleges and Halls, the principal provincial universities, the Colleges of Eton and Winchester, the Church Commissioners, the British Museum, the Imperial War Museum, and Friendly Societies registered under the Friendly Societies Act 1896.

2. A charity which is excepted from the duty to register by order of the Charity Commissioners or by regulation made by the Home Secretary. Charities which have been 'excepted' from the duty to register include individual units of the Boy Scouts' and Girl Guides' Associations.

3. A charity (i) which has no permanent endowment; and (ii) which has no use or occupation of land; and (iii) whose income does not exceed £1,000 a year.

4. Further, no charity is required to be registered in respect of any place of worship registered under the Places of Worship Registration Act 1855.

Charities under 2, 3 and 4 above may be entered in the register if they so request.

A charity entered in the register is allotted a number which may be used as evidence (eg in connection with an application for fiscal relief) of charitable status.

It may be observed that with regard to registration the duty of the Commissioners is to determine whether the objects of the body seeking registration are charitable. Registration, contrary to what is perhaps sometimes believed, in no way marks approval of a charity's objectives or of its management. Thus the Commission 'cannot, for instance, refuse registration because it

9a See Charities Act, s 30, as amended by Companies Act 1989, s 111 and by Charities Act 1992, s 10, 40, 41 and 42.
10 Section 4, as amended by the Charities Act 1992, s 2.
11 Charities Act 1960, s 4(4).

believes that an applicant organisation is badly managed, or is proposing futile aims, or is engaged in an area of welfare provision adequately catered for by existing charities, or has a name that will duplicate that of an existing organisation or otherwise mislead the public'[12]. In short, it is not 'a licensing authority for charities'[13].

Where it appears to the Commissioners that the name of a registered charity is the same as, or too like, that of another charity (whether registered or not), or is likely to mislead the public as to the true nature of the purposes or activities of the charity, or is offensive, then they may direct that the name of the charity should be changed to such other name as the trustees, with the approval of the Commissioners, may determine.

2 OVERSIGHT BY THE ATTORNEY GENERAL; SUPERVISION BY THE COMMISSIONERS

The principle is that the Sovereign, as *parens patriae*, is the guardian of charity. The Crown has made the Attorney General responsible for exercising this function. It therefore falls to the Attorney General, acting on behalf of the Crown, to represent the public interest with regard to charities before the courts. It is accordingly the duty of the Attorney General to inform the courts if the trustees of a charitable trust fall short of their duty, and to propose a suitable remedy.

In practice, however, it is the Commissioners who play the most active part in the supervision of charities. It is the duty of the Commissioners to investigate and check abuses[14]. In order to promote the good management of charities, and to facilitate the supervision of charities by the Commissioners, statute provides that charity trustees are to maintain certain records, that certain information is to be regularly supplied to the Commissioners, that the Commissioners are to have power to make enquiries, and to take certain forms of action to correct deficiencies or abuses. These matters are considered below.

3 DISQUALIFICATION FOR ACTING AS A TRUSTEE

The Charities Act 1992[15] provides a person shall be disqualified for being the trustee for a charity or a charity trustee if, inter alia, (i) he has been convicted of any offence involving dishonesty or deception; (ii) he is an undischarged bankrupt; (iii) he has been removed from office as trustee of a charity by the Commissioners under their power to act for the protection of charities; (iv) he is subject to a disqualification order made under the Company Directors Disqualification Act 1986. A person who acts as a trustee for a charity or a charity trustee while disqualified commits an offence[16].

12   M. Chesterman, op cit, p 120.
13   Charities Act 1992, s 4.
14   See Report of the Charity Commissioners for 1966, paras 18–26.
15   Section 45.
16   Section 46.

4 INFORMATION ABOUT CHARITIES

(a) Status to be displayed

If a charity is registered and its gross income exceeds £5,000 in its last financial year, the fact that it is a registered charity is required to be stated 'in English in legible characters' in all notices or other documents soliciting money, and on cheques, orders for goods, invoices and receipts[17].

(b) Accounts

The Charities Act 1960[18] imposed on charity trustees a duty to keep 'proper books of accounts'. The provisions relating to accounts in the 1960 Act have been extended and strengthened by the Charities Act 1992[19]. Under this Act trustees of a charity[20] are required to keep accounting records that contain entries showing from day to day money received and expended, and the charity's assets and liabilities. The records must disclose at any time, with reasonable accuracy, the financial position of the charity.

Charity trustees must[1] prepare in respect of each financial year of the charity a statement of accounts complying with requirements prescribed by the Secretary of State. The day to day records and the annual statements must be preserved for six years from the end of the financial year to which they relate.

The annual accounts must[2] be audited[3], if the charity's gross income or total expenditure in a year exceeds £100,000, by a qualified auditor; in other cases by an independent examiner (an independent person who is reasonably believed by the trustees to have the requisite ability and practical experience to carry out a competent examination).

(c) Annual return

A registered charity must prepare in respect of each financial year an annual return containing such information as may be prescribed by regulations[4].

(d) Annual report

Charity trustees must prepare in respect of each financial year an annual

---

17 Charities Act 1992, s 3.
18 Section 32.
19 Section 19.
20 Other than an exempt charity or a charity which is a company. Charities Act 1992, ss 19(5), 24(1).
1 Section 20.
2 Except where the charity is a company, s 20(7); or is an exempt charity, s 24(1).
3 Section 21.
4 Section 26.

report on the activities of the charity during the year and such other information as may be prescribed by regulations[5].

(e) Submission to the Commissioners

The annual report, together with the annual statement of accounts and the annual return must, where these are required to be prepared, be sent to the Commissioners[6].

(f) Public inspection

The annual report of a charity must be open to public inspection at all reasonable times[7]. A charity must supply any person who so requests with a copy of its most recent accounts, subject to such reasonable fee (if any) that the charity requires[8].

(g) Offences

The Act of 1992[9] makes it an offence[10] (i) knowingly or recklessly to supply the Commissioners with information which is false or misleading in a material particular; (ii) wilfully to alter, suppress, conceal or destroy any document which one is under a duty to produce to the Commissioners.

5 RESTRICTIONS ON DISPOSITIONS

Before any land held by a charity is sold, leased or otherwise disposed of[11] the trustees must obtain a written report from a qualified surveyor, advertise the proposed disposition as advised by the surveyor, and conclude that the terms proposed for the disposition are the best that can reasonably be obtained[12]. A disposition to someone who is a 'connected person'[13] (eg a trustee, employee or agent of the charity, or the spouse of such a person) requires the consent of the Commissioners.

Where land is held by a charity on trusts that stipulate that it is to be used for the purposes of the charity, then, before disposing of the land, the trustees must[14] (unless the proposed disposition is with a view to acquiring other property by way of replacement) in addition to advertising and obtaining

---

5 Charities Act 1992, s 23. The requirement does not apply to an exempt charity, nor to a charity section 4(4)(c) which is not registered, nor to an excepted charity unless the Commissioners request that a report be submitted. Charities Act 1992, s 24.
6 Charities Act 1992, ss 23(3), 23(4), 26(2).
7 Section 25(1).
8 Section 25(3).
9 Section 54.
10 Punishable, on summary conviction, by a fine not exceeding the statutory maximum; on indictment, by imprisonment for a term not exceeding two years, or a fine, or both.
11 Other than by mortgage. See infra.
12 Section 32(1), (2), (3), (4).
13 Defined in Schedule 2.
14 Section 32(6), (7).

advice from a qualified surveyor, give public notice of the proposed disposition and consider any representations made to them about the proposal[15].

No land held by a charity may be mortgaged unless either the trustees have received written advice from an independent person who is qualified by his ability and practical experience to give such advice, or the mortgage is permitted by an order of the court or the Commissioners[16].

The Act of 1992[17] provides that any provision in the trusts of a charity (or in any Act of Parliament establishing or regulating a charity) that dispositions of land held by the charity require the consent of the Commissioners shall cease to have effect.

It is to be noted that the 1992 Act weakens the safeguard provided in the Charities Act 1960[18] (requirement of the Commissioner's consent) against trustees disposing of land that forms part of the permanent endowment of the charity. On the other hand, the Act does not alter the position that in order to sell property trustees of a charity must have power to do so. Thus in *Oldham Borough Council v A-G*[19] it was held that the court had no jurisdiction to authorise the sale by the plaintiff Borough Council of land which had been left to the Council by will expressly 'for the purposes of playing fields solely'. (The Council had disclaimed reliance on any circumstances that would entitle the court to proceed under the *cy près* doctrine.)

6 THE COMMISSIONERS' POWER TO INSTITUTE INQUIRIES

Under the Charities Act 1960[20] the Commissioners have power to institute inquiries with regard to a charity's affairs (or to those of a class of charities)[1]; to conduct an inquiry themselves or appoint a person to do so[2]; to direct any person to furnish information (including accounts and documents or copies of these); to direct any person to answer questions in writing, and to attend at a specified time and place to give evidence or produce documents; and to publish a report of the inquiries[3]. They have, further, power to order that the accounts of any charity should be investigated and audited by an auditor appointed by them[4].

7 THE COMMISSIONERS' POWERS TO TAKE ACTION

Under the Charities Act 1960[5], where at any time after having instituted an inquiry (see 6 above) the Commissioners are satisfied, following an inquiry, either that there has been misconduct or mismanagement[6], *or* that it is

---

15   The Commissioners have power to dispense with the requirement. Section 32(8).
16   Section 34.
17   Section 36.
18   Section 29, repealed by the 1992 Act.
19   (1992) *Times*, 13 April. The decision is the subject of an appeal.
20   Section 6, as amended by the Charities Act 1992, s 6.
 1   Other than those of an exempt charity. Section 6(1).
 2   Section 6(2).
 3   Sections 6(3), (7); 7.
 4   Section 8(3).
 5   Section 20, as amended by the Charities Act 1992, s 8 and Sch 1.
 6   'Misconduct or mismanagement' here (and below) includes the payment of remuneration that is excessive in relation to a charity's funds. Section 20(2).

necessary or desirable to act to protect the charity's property, they have power (i) to suspend a trustee, officer, agent or employee of the charity; (ii) to appoint additional trustees; (iii) to vest any of the charity's property in the official custodian for charities; (iv) to order any person who holds property of the trust not to part with it without their consent; (v) to restrict the transactions which may be entered into; (vi) to appoint a receiver to manage the property and affairs of the charity.

Where the Commissioners are satisfied that there has been both misconduct or mismanagement *and* that it is necessary or desirable to act to protect the charity's property, they have power[7] (i) to remove any trustee, officer, agent or employee of the charity who has been responsible for or privy to the mismanagement or misconduct; (ii) to appoint a person as trustee in place of the person removed; (iii) to establish a scheme for the charity's administration.

The Commissioners have power also to remove a charity trustee (i) who during the preceding five years has been discharged as a bankrupt; (ii) who is incapable of acting by reason of mental illness; (iii) who has not acted and will not declare whether or not he is willing to act; (iv) whose absence or failure to act impedes the proper administration of the charity; and to appoint a person in the place of the person so removed.

8 ENFORCEMENT

If a person fails to comply with any requirement imposed under the Acts of 1960 and 1992, the Commissioners may[8] by order give him such directions as they consider appropriate[9]. A person who is guilty of disobedience to an order of the Commissioners may, on the application of the Commissioners to the High Court, be dealt with as for disobedience to an order of the High Court[10].

Categories of charity

Charities are, as seen above, for certain purposes treated differently according to the category into which they fall. The principal categories of charity are set out below by way of summary.

1. If a body has charitable status (ie it exists for a charitable purpose and is for the public benefit) then it is a charity for the purpose of entitlement to the fiscal advantages referred to earlier, and for the purpose of the general law of the land (eg with regard to exemption from the rule against inalienability).

2. If, within 1 above, a body comes within the definition of a 'charity' in the Charities Acts of 1960 and 1992, it is subject to the terms of the Acts. A

---

7   Except in the case of an exempt charity.
8   Charities Act 1992, s 56.
9   Unless the failure to comply constitutes a criminal offence, in which case the relevant criminal penalty applies (eg knowingly or recklessly providing false information to the Commissioners; see p 168). Section 56(2).
10 Charities Act 1960, s 41.

'charity' is defined by the 1960 Act[11] as 'any institution, corporate or not, which is established for charitable purposes and is subject to the control of the High Court in the exercise of the court's jurisdiction with respect to charities'. (It is sufficient that an institution should be subject to the control of the court in some significant respect, eg that if it misapplied its funds the court in the exercise of its jurisdiction with respect to charities would be entitled to interfere and stop the misapplication[12]. The fact that an institution is under the control of a minister of the Crown does not mean that the body cannot also be subject to the control of the High Court[12].) The number of bodies which are charitable but not within the definition of the Act is very small.

3. If, within 2 above, a charity under the Act is an 'exempt charity'[13], then it is exempt (ie automatically exempt) from the duty to register[14], from the duties imposed with regard to the keeping of accounts, audit and annual report imposed by the Charities Act 1992[15] (but not from the general duty to keep 'proper books of account' imposed by the Charities Act 1960[16]), from inquiries carried out by the Commissioners under the Charities Act 1992[17], and from the forms of action that the Commissioners are empowered[18] to take (eg in the event of misconduct or mismanagement) under the 1992 Act.

4. If, within 2 above, a charity has been 'excepted' (by an order made by the Commissioners or a regulation made by the Home Secretary) then it is not under a duty to register[19]; and, if it is not registered, it is not under a duty to submit an annual report unless requested by the Commissioners to do so[20].

5. If a charity (within 2 above or otherwise) has no permanent endowment or use or occupation of land, and an income that does not exceed £1,000 a year, then it is under no duty to register[1]. If such a charity is not registered it is under no duty to comply with the requirements of the 1992 Act[2] relating to the keeping of accounts, audit and return[3].

Ex gratia payments

The case of *Re Snowden*[4] concerned a will in which a testator gave all his shares in a number of companies with which he had been connected to his

11 Section 45(1).
12 *Construction Industry Training Board v A-G* [1971] 3 All ER 449, [1971] 1 WLR 1303.
13 Charities Act 1960, Sch 2, as amended by the National Heritage Act 1983.
14 Charities Act 1960, s 4(4)(a).
15 Sections 19–23.
16 Section 32.
17 Charities Act 1960, s 6(1).
18 Charities Act 1960, s 20(12).
19 Charities Act 1960, s 4(4)(b).
20 Charities Act 1992, s 24(3).
 1 Charities Act 1960, s 4(4)(c).
 2 Sections 19–23.
 3 Section 24(2).
 4 [1970] Ch 700, [1969] 3 All ER 208. The case was heard with another, *Re Henderson*, in which the facts differed in that residue was given for charitable purposes generally, but the point at issue, whether or not a power existed to make *ex gratia* payments on moral grounds, was the same.

close relatives and, after other bequests, gave the residue of his estate to various charities. After the will had been made but before the testator's death the companies were taken over by another, larger, company; the testator received money for the shares that he had formerly held. Thus when he died there were no shares to pass to his relatives, the value of them passing under the residuary bequest to the charities. This had clearly not been the testator's intention and the trustees of the majority of the recipient charities felt that it was wrong that the relatives should, as a result of what had happened, get nothing. They were under a moral duty, they believed, to make a payment out of the monies they had received to the relatives. But were they entitled to do so? A payment to the relatives would constitute an application of trust money for a purpose outside the charities' objects, and so in breach of trust. On the other hand, the trustees argued, since charities rely on the moral duty felt by citizens to make donations for charitable causes, it would be wrong for charities to ignore what they believed were morally justified obligations— indeed, that it would not be in the interests of a charity for it to be seen to act otherwise than in a fair and responsible manner.

The trustees, with the encouragement of the Attorney General (so that clarification of the law could be obtained), sought a ruling from the court as to whether they were entitled to make a payment to the relatives. Cross J held that trustees of a charity had no power themselves to make a payment of the kind proposed, but that the court or the Attorney General, in appropriate circumstances, had power, on an application by the trustees, to authorise such a payment. He distinguished between instances in which a donor's intention had been carried out but his relatives thought that it was morally wrong that a charity should receive what it had (when only in exceptional circumstances would a power to authorise an *ex gratia* payment exist) and instances[5], like the one before the court, in which the testator's intention had not been fulfilled and a charity had received more than he had intended (when, at the discretion of the court or the Attorney General, such a power did exist).

The Charities Act 1992[6] confirms the jurisdiction of the court that Cross J in *Re Henderson* had held existed and provided that the jurisdiction should be exercisable also by the Commissioners, subject to the supervision of, and in accordance with any direction given by, the Attorney General. Refusal by the Commissioners to authorise a payment does not preclude permission being given by the Attorney General on application to him by the trustees.

Objects charitable; means undesirable

From time to time instances have arisen in which public concern has been expressed over the manner in which bodies of a religious nature, registered as charities, have acted in pursuance of their objectives. The government White Paper, *Charities: A Framework For The Future*[7] commented:

5   As an example Cross J cited an instance such as one where a testator had made a morally binding but legally unenforceable promise to leave a person a certain bequest in his will, but left the money to a charity instead.
6   Section 17, inserting s 23A into the Charities Act 1960.
7   1989. Cm 694.

'2.22 ... Anxieties have been expressed, in particular, about a number of organisations whose influence over their followers, especially the young, is seen as destructive of family life and, in some cases, as tantamount to brainwashing.

'2.23 The Government have considerable sympathies for these anxieties. They have considered whether it might be possible to amend the law in such a way as to exclude those religious organisations whose activities are deemed undesirable. Their conclusion is that there are great difficulties in the way of doing so....

'2.24 It has been suggested that the problem would be solved if charitable status were removed from all trusts which are established to advance religion—of whatever type and without exception. This proposal has, at least, the merit of simplicity. It would also avoid the need to make invidious comparisons between different religions....

'2.25 The Government finds the whole concept of removing charitable status from religious trusts unattractive and believes that it would be resisted vigorously, not just by the religious bodies who would be affected, but also by the great majority of the public. The removal of religion as a head of charity would leave many existing trusts, some of which are of considerable antiquity, in an impossible legal limbo. The legal difficulties of resolving the subsequent uncertainties would be immense and might well prove insuperable....

'2.27 For some critics the neutrality of the law is objectionable, and suggestions have been made from time to time that the presumption of public benefit should be removed and that it should be replaced with a positive test of worth. The Goodman Committee ... proposed that religions which were "considered detrimental to the community's moral welfare" should be excluded from charitable status....

'2.28 The difficulties of principle which the Goodman Committee encountered, in considering what criteria might be applied to religions, are formidable. So also are the practical difficulties which vary with the nature of the particular movement in question....

'2.29 In some cases the undesirability of a doctrine may be clear enough. Sometimes, however, the objectionable feature may be only one element in a complex body of doctrine. The question would then arise whether that one element alone should be enough to justify refusal to register, bearing in mind that, in religious matters, it is often a single doctrinal element which is the cause of controversy.

'2.30 Furthermore, with religious movements of the kind about which public anxiety has been expressed, it is not usually a question of whether their *objects* are contrary to the public interest. The question is whether, if the actual *conduct* of the movement causes harm, a trust which is set up to advance its beliefs should be deprived of charitable status on the grounds that they are not of public benefit....

'2.36 ... The Government will, therefore, be considering whether it would be possible ... to make it explicit that the Commissioners have the power to remove a body from the register where there is evidence that it is acting in pursuit of its objects in ways which are not for the public benefit.'

It was in order to confer such a power on the Commissioners that a clause[8] was included in the Bill that became the Charities Act 1992. The clause provided that notwithstanding that an institution's objects were in law charitable, in determining whether an institution was or was not established for charitable purposes, the manner and the circumstances in which these purposes had been, were being, or were intended to be, pursued by the institution were matters to which the Commission or the court might have regard. In the event, however, the clause was deleted during the passage of the Bill.

---

8 Clause 2.

Chapter 9

Trusts of imperfect obligation

NATURE

In his will the playwright George Bernard Shaw bequeathed his residuary estate to a trustee on trust for the purpose of carrying out certain inquiries connected with the use of a new alphabet, the use of which Shaw had long advocated. Shaw died in 1950 and the trustee took out a summons to determine the validity of the trust. It was held[1] that the trust was neither for the advancement of education nor for any other charitable purpose. Further, since there were no beneficiaries, the trust could not exist as a private trust, and so failed[2]. A trust of this kind—ie a trust for a non-charitable purpose and in which there are no beneficiaries—is termed a trust of *imperfect obligation*. Such a trust is imperfect in that no one exists who can oblige the trustees to carry out the trust. If the trust had had beneficiaries, they could have compelled the trustees to carry out the trust and the trust would have been a trust of perfect obligation[3]. If the purposes of the trust had been charitable then, as already seen[3], responsibility for enforcing the trust would rest with the Attorney General[4]. Charitable trusts and private trusts in which there are beneficiaries are therefore trusts of perfect obligation.

The general rule is that a trust of imperfect obligation is void[5]. Examples of trusts which have failed because they are trusts of imperfect obligation have been: a trust for the objects of the appeals broadcast weekly by the BBC in the series 'The Week's Good Cause'[6] (since these were not all necessarily charitable); a trust for the maintenance of good understanding between nations and the preservation of the independence of newspapers[7]; a trust 'for the purpose of providing some useful memorial' to the testator[8]; a trust for the establishment at Stratford-upon-Avon of a hotel for the benefit and

1 *Re Shaw* [1957] 1 All ER 745, [1957] 1 WLR 729; (M & B).
2 The property fell into residue.
3 See Chap 4.
4 Individuals who stand to benefit from a charitable trust do not have any entitlement to enforce the trust against the trustees, having no locus standi with regard to the trust. *Re Belling* [1967] Ch 425, [1967] 1 All ER 105.
5 *Re Astor's Settlement Trusts* [1952] Ch 534, [1952] 1 All ER 1067.
6 *Re Wood* [1949] Ch 498, [1949] 1 All ER 1100.
7 *Re Astor's Settlement Trusts*, ante.
8 *Re Endacott* [1960] Ch 232, [1959] 3 All ER 562; (M & B). See also *M'Caig's Trustees v Kirk Session of United Free Church of Lismore* 1915 SC 426; (M & B) (Bequest for the erection of eleven bronze statutes of the testatrix's parents and their nine children declared void.)

service of distinguished visitors from far countries[9]; and a trust for 'some worthy cause'[10]. Trusts in which property was left for purposes which have been held not to be charitable because they were not exclusively charitable (eg for 'charitable or benevolent'[11] purposes) and trusts which although for a charitable purpose are not for the public benefit also provide examples of trusts of imperfect obligation.

It is in accordance with common sense that such trusts should be void. If a person wishes to set up a trust for some charitable purpose, then it can be regarded as being in the public interest that the trust should be carried out. But if a person wishes to leave money for some non-charitable purpose, perhaps merely to satisfy some idiosyncrasy of his own, for example, training poodles to dance[12] or blocking up certain rooms in a house for 20 years[13], why should the State lend its aid to seeing that the purpose is carried out? No reason exists, and it is therefore reasonable that the trust should be void. Thus if a testator leaves property for one of the purposes instanced above the disposition is ineffective: the property is undisposed of and passes to the residuary legatee (or, if there is none, to those entitled under his intestacy).

Valid trusts of imperfect obligation

We have said that trusts of imperfect obligation are void. This is the general rule. In a limited number of instances, however, trusts for a limited range of non-charitable purposes are valid notwithstanding that they lack beneficiaries. Such trusts are thus *valid* trusts of imperfect obligation. For what purposes may such trusts exist?

In the first place, trusts for the erection or maintenance (or both) of tombs[14] or monuments[15] have been held to be valid. It will be recalled[16] that trusts for the maintenance of a tomb or a monument which forms part of the fabric of a church, or for the maintenance of a whole churchyard or cemetery, are charitable. It is therefore trusts for the maintenance of individual graves or monuments, not forming part of the fabric of a church, which exist as valid trusts of imperfect obligation.

In the second place, trusts for the maintenance of one or more specified animals have been held to be valid[17]. (It will be recalled that a trust for animals generally is charitable[18].)

Thirdly, in *Re Thompson*[19], it was held that a bequest for the furtherance of fox hunting was valid.

9　*Re Corelli* [1943] Ch 332, [1943] 2 All ER 519.
10　*Re Gillingham Bus Disaster Fund* [1958] Ch 300, [1958] 1 All ER 37; (M & B).
11　*Chichester Diocesan Fund and Board of Finance Inc v Simpson* [1944] AC 341, [1944] 2 All ER 60; (M & B).
12　Per Russell J, *Re Hummeltenberg* [1923] 1 Ch 237 at 242.
13　*Brown v Burdett* (1882) 21 Ch D 667; (M & B).
14　*Re Hooper* [1932] 1 Ch 38; (M & B); *Re Vaughan* (1886) 33 Ch D 187.
15　*Mussett v Bingle* [1876] WN 170: a trust for the erection of a monument to the testator's wife's first husband; *Mellick v Asylum President and Guardian* (1821) Jac 180.
16　See Chap 7.
17　*Re Dean* (1889) 41 Ch D 552.
18　See Chap 7.
19　[1934] Ch 342; (M & B).

It must be stressed that these three classes are 'anomalous and exceptional'[20]. They will not be extended. For example, where a testator left property on trust 'for the purpose of providing a useful memorial' to himself[1], this was held not to fall within the exception relating to specific monuments or tombs (and was therefore void).

POSITION OF THE TRUSTEE

What is the position if a trust of imperfect obligation is valid but the trustee is unwilling to assume responsibility for the trust? In a valid trust of perfect obligation (whether private or charitable) the maxim 'equity never wants for a trustee' will ensure that a trustee will always be found (if necessary, in the last resort, by appointment by the court[2]). But whether the maxim applies to valid trusts of imperfect obligation is uncertain. Some indication of the possible outcome is given by *Re Thompson*[3], where, if the trustee had not been willing to assume responsibility for applying the property for the purpose specified, it seems that the court might have held that the bequest was ineffective and directed that the property should pass to the residuary legatees. This might well be the course followed whenever a trustee of an otherwise valid trust of imperfect obligation declined to undertake the trust. (It is interesting to note, and indicative of the nature of the kind of trust of which we speak, that in certain[4] United States jurisdictions these trusts are termed 'honorary trusts'.)

What would be the position if a trust of imperfect obligation was valid, and the trustee expressed his willingness to carry out the trust, but later failed to do so? Could he be compelled to, eg use the trust money for the upkeep of the testator's tomb? The answer is that he cannot be compelled to carry out the trust. The trust is by definition one in which there is no one who can oblige the trustee to carry out the trust. But this does not mean that the trustee is free to spend the money on himself. A trust of imperfect obligation, valid or void, cannot be equated with a gift to the trustee beneficially[5] and money not applied for the purpose specified is held by the trustee on trust for the residuary legatee (or next of kin), who can apply to the court for a direction that it should be paid to him[6].

DURATION

Whilst a valid trust of imperfect obligation is an exception to the rule that a valid private trust must have beneficiaries, in other respects a trust of imper-

---

20 *Re Astor's Settlement Trusts* [1952] Ch 534 at 547.
1 *Re Endacott* [1960] Ch 232, [1959] 3 All ER 562; (M & B).
2 Trustee Act 1925, s 41.
3 [1934] Ch 342, following *Pettingall v Pettingall* (1842) 11 LJ Ch 176.
4 Eg Kentucky.
5 *Pettingall v Pettingall* (1842) 11 LJ Ch 176 might seem to some extent to be an exception to this principle. But the case is old and unsatisfactory and should perhaps best be regarded as having been decided on the construction of the particular words used by the testator. Evershed MR regarded the case as being 'anomalous' in *Re Endacott* [1960] Ch 232 at 245.
6 *Re Thompson* [1934] Ch 342; (M & B).

fect obligation must comply with the requirements of any other private trust. For example, the disposition must not infringe the rules against perpetuities[7] (ie the gift must vest within the perpetuity period).

Further, the disposition must not infringe the rule against inalienability[7]. This rule is of particular relevance in the case of trusts of imperfect obligation. Suppose that in his will a testator leaves £500 to a trustee on trust for the upkeep of his tomb. Here there is nothing to indicate that the £500 must be kept intact and only income used for the upkeep of the tomb. The money can be invested, if the trustee so decides, and only the income used. But there is nothing to prevent the trustee using 'bites' out of the capital for the purpose of maintaining the tomb. Thus although the capital could be kept intact indefinitely, it could equally well be used up (perhaps on some major repair) within a short time. The disposition therefore does not infringe the rule against inalienability (and so is valid.)[8] On the other hand, if the testator had left £500 to a trustee on trust to invest the money and to apply the income for the upkeep of the tomb, then the rule against inalienability would have been infringed, since the capital would have to be kept intact indefinitely and thus for a period longer than the perpetuity period. The disposition would therefore be void[9]. If the testator had directed that the income was to be applied for the upkeep of the tomb for a period of 21 years[10] (or for some shorter period) then the rule would not have been infringed and the trust would have been valid. Thus for a trust of imperfect obligation to be valid, not only must the purpose specified come within the limited group we have referred to[11], but it must also comply with the rule against inalienability[12]. (There is doubt as to whether the rule is affected by the Perpetuities and Accumulations Act 1964[13]. It is submitted that the rule is not affected by this Act and that therefore no question of a period of up to 80 years being available for the retention of capital arises.)

We have illustrated this principle in the context of trusts for the maintenance of a tomb, but the same principle applies in the context of a trust for a specified animal. In some cases which have come before the courts, however, the requirement that the duration of the trust must be limited to the perpetuity period has been overlooked, and the trust held to be valid notwithstanding that this requirement had not been complied with[14].

7   See p 46.
8   It seems that the absence of any provision preventing the trustees from using capital (thus by inference enabling the trustees to use capital) will not be sufficient to avoid the disposition infringing the rule if the real object is to set up a fund to be retained permanently. *Re Compton* [1946] 1 All ER 117.
9   *Re Vaughan* (1886) 33 Ch D 187; *Re Jones* (1898) 79 LT 154. See also *Yeap Cheah Neo v Ong Cheng Neo* (1875) LR 6 PC 381 (devise of land for use as family burial ground held to be void).
10   In *Re Hooper* [1932] 1 Ch 38; (M & B), a trust for the upkeep of graves 'so long as the trustees legally can do so' was construed as creating a trust for 21 years from the testator's death, and hence was valid. The result was the same where income was directed to be applied for the upkeep of a tomb for 'so long as the law for the time being permits'. *Pirbright v Salwey* [1896] WN 86.
11   See ante, p 176.
12   See supra.
13   See s 15(4).
14   As in *Re Dean* (1889) 41 Ch D 552; (M & B). In *Re Haines* (1952) *Times*, 7 November, a trust for two cats was held to be valid, the judge having recognised that the question of perpetuity was relevant, but being prepared to take judicial notice of the fact that 'sixteen

Tombs

If a testator wishes to provide for the upkeep of his (or someone else's) tomb there are four ways, using the machinery of a trust (as opposed to entering into a contract[15] for the maintenance of the tomb), in which this may be done:

1. The testator can leave property on trust for the upkeep of the whole churchyard in which the tomb stands. Since such a trust is charitable, it is valid notwithstanding that it is limited to continue for ever.

2. If the tomb forms part of the fabric of a church, the testator can leave property on trust for the upkeep of the tomb. This trust also is charitable and so can be limited to continue for ever.

3. The testator can create a trust of imperfect obligation and this will be valid if the capital is expendable; or, if only income is to be used, the duration of the trust is limited to the perpetuity period.

4. By way of introduction to the fourth method in which provision may be made for the upkeep of a tomb, let us consider a bequest of capital to the X Charity on trust to apply whatever is needed of the income for the upkeep of the tomb, with a direction that any surplus should belong to the X Charity, the trust to continue so long as the X Charity maintains the tomb, with a gift over to the Y Charity if the X Charity fails to maintain the tomb. Reduced to its essentials this is a gift to X on trust to maintain the tomb. The fact that X is a charity is irrelevant; X is a trustee, holding property on the trust specified. A trust of imperfect obligation has been created. But since the duration of the trust is not restricted to the perpetuity period, the trust is void[16]. Now consider a bequest to the X Charity *until* such time as the charity fails to maintain the tomb, with a gift over to the Y Charity; or a bequest to the X Charity, *but if* the X Charity ceases to maintain the tomb, then over to the Y Charity. In the first form, the X Charity holds a determinable interest; in the second, it holds a conditional interest. But in neither form is the X Charity under any obligation to apply all or any of the money for the upkeep of the tomb. No trust has been created. But the X Charity will only be able to retain the property while the tomb is maintained. This will clearly be an inducement to the X Charity to maintain the tomb. Further, because of the possibility that the day may come when the tomb (perhaps by an

---

years was a long life for a cat' and the trust therefore unlikely to exceed the perpetuity period. But this is a departure from the principle that, in dealing with questions relating to perpetuities, the law is concerned with possibilities (however remote), not with probabilities.

In *Re Howard* (1908) *Times*, 30 October, a testator gave an annuity of £10 to two of his servants on trust for the maintenance of a parrot. The court appears to have construed the gift as being limited in duration to the lives of the servants and the life of the survivor, and therefore limited to the perpetuity period. On this basis it was held that the trust was valid for the period of these lives, if the parrot should live so long. (Nothing was said as to the parrot's fate if it lived longer.)

15 See Parish Councils and Burial Authorities (Miscellaneous Provisions) Act 1970; (M & B).

16 Since the trust fails, the property might be thought to be held on trust for the settlor or his estate. But it is established that in the circumstances stated the property is held by the X Charity absolutely. *Re Dalziel* [1943] Ch 277, [1943] 2 All ER 656; *Re Coxen* [1948] Ch 747 at 752. See p 125, ante.

oversight) is no longer maintained, and the legal title becomes vested in[17] (or claimable by[18]) the Y Charity, the X Charity will be well advised to set the property concerned aside, in case the Y Charity ever becomes entitled. The X Charity may therefore decide to invest the money, and to apply the income, or so much of it as is needed, for the upkeep of the tomb. But they are under no obligation to retain the capital. The rule against inalienability is therefore not infringed and the disposition to the X Charity is valid.

But what, it might be asked, about the gift over to the Y Charity? The property might vest in the Y Charity long after the expiry of the perpetuity period. Does not the gift to the Y Charity therefore infringe the perpetuity rule (ie the perpetuity rule proper, as distinct from the rule against inalienability)? The answer is that since a gift over to a charity, following a previous gift to another charity, is not required to comply with the perpetuity rule[19] the gift over to the Y Charity is valid. The whole disposition is therefore valid[20], and thus provides a way in which an attempt, although no more than an attempt, can be made to ensure that a tomb will be maintained indefinitely.

What would be the position if there were a gift to a charity *until* a certain tomb ceased to be maintained, or *provided* that the tomb continued to be maintained (ie a gift to the charity for a determinable or a conditional interest) with a gift over, not, as considered above, to another charity, but to a private individual (or other non-charitable body)? In this case, at common law (irrespective of whether the gift to the X Charity was determinable or conditional in form) since the gift over might vest outside the perpetuity period, the interest was void. The X Charity's interest would therefore be absolute from the date of the gift (and thus no inducement to it would exist to maintain the tomb). Under the Perpetuities and Accumulations Act 1964[1], the gift over would not be void ab initio and it would be necessary to 'wait and see' for 21 years whether the determining event occurred before the end of that period. If it did, the gift over would take effect. If it did not, at the end of that period the gift to the X Charity would become absolute. After the Act, the disposition would therefore be an inducement to the X Charity to maintain the tomb for a period of 21 years. However, since the same result could be achieved by employing a trust (of imperfect obligation) limited in duration to this period, no advantage would accrue from employing this form of disposition.

If the gift to the X Charity had been determinable in form, and there had been no gift over (so that the possibility of reverter formed part of the testator's estate) then, at common law, on the occurrence of the determining event the title would pass from the X Charity to the person entitled to the testator's residue. The fact that the interest of that person might vest after the end of the perpetuity period did not invalidate his interest, because at common law the rule against perpetuities did not apply to a possibility of reverter. The whole disposition was therefore valid, and thus acted as an inducement to the X Charity to maintain the tomb[2]. Under the Perpetuities and Accumulations Act 1964[3], a possibility of reverter must be treated in the

17 Ie in the case of a determinable gift.
18 Ie in the case of a conditional gift.
19 *Christ's Hospital v Grainger* (1849) 1 Mac & G 460; see p 132, ante.
20 *Re Tyler* [1891] 3 Ch 252; (M & B).
 1 Section 3.
 2 *Re Chardon* [1928] Ch 464.
 3 Section 12.

same manner as a right of entry, ie it becomes subject to the common law rule against perpetuities, with the saving provision of the 'wait and see' principle introduced by the Act[4]. Thus after that Act no purpose would be achieved by using this method that would not be obtained more simply by setting up a trust for the maintenance of the tomb, limited in duration to 21 years. Before the Act, however, the method described constituted a fifth way by which provision might be made for the maintenance of a tomb[5].

'Purpose' trusts: trusts of perfect obligation for a specified purpose

In *Re Denley's Trust Deed*[6] land was conveyed to trustees who were directed to maintain the land for use as a sports ground for the benefit of (inter alia) employees of a certain company. The trust was not charitable since it was not for a charitable purpose and was not for the public benefit. Was it valid as a private trust? The trustees held the land on trust for a purpose; the purpose was not one within the limited class of exceptions in which trusts of imperfect obligation can be valid. Did the trust therefore fail? No, it did not. Goff J held that a distinction had to be drawn between 'purpose or object trusts which are abstract or impersonal', which (unless charitable) are void as being of imperfect obligation, and a trust which 'though expressed as a purpose, is directly or indirectly for the benefit of an individual or individuals', which, provided the class of beneficiaries is ascertainable at any one time and is not void for any other reason (eg as infringing the rule against inalienability) is valid. In *Re Denley* the trust was for the benefit of ascertainable individuals, ie the employees of the company, the terms of the trust did not infringe the rule against alienability[7], and so was valid.

This case was regarded by some as breaking new ground. It is submitted that it did nothing of the kind. It has long been accepted that in setting up a trust, a settlor can direct 'the mode of the enjoyment'[8] of the property (eg the education of certain children[9]), thus interposing, as it were, a purpose between the trustees and the beneficiaries. *Re Denley*[10] merely followed the same pattern.

What, it might be asked, would be the position in such a trust if the beneficiaries did not wish to have the trust property applied for the purpose specified? In *Re Denley* the settlor directed that if the land ceased to be required or used by the employees as a sports ground, it was to pass to a specified hospital. But what if no such direction had been given? The answer

---

4 Section 3.
5 *Re Chardon*, ante. See also *Re Chamber's Will Trusts* [1950] Ch 267.
6 [1969] 1 Ch 373, [1968] 3 All ER 65.
7 Since the duration of the trust was limited to the lives of specified persons plus 21 years.
8 Per Stirling J, *Re Jones* (1898) 79 LT 154, 154.
9 As in *Re Selby-Walker* [1949] 2 All ER 178, and *Re Andrew's Trust* [1905] 2 Ch 48.
10 Supra.

is illustrated by *Re Bowes*[11]. A testator left money in his will to be spent on the planting of trees on the estate of which he had been life tenant. On his death the land passed to S for life, with remainder to G in fee tail. S and G did not want trees to be planted. They wanted the money instead. The court held that where property is held on trust for a specified purpose for the benefit of specified beneficiaries, then provided the beneficiaries are of full age and between them absolutely entitled, they are entitled to call on the trustees to hand over the trust property to them. If G executed a disentailing assurance (thus converting his fee tail in remainder into a fee simple in remainder) he and S would then between them be absolutely entitled. The court therefore directed that on G doing so, S and G should be entitled to receive the money[12]. The same principle provided the grounds of the decision in *Re Andrew's Trust*[13]. A fund was subscribed by the friends of a deceased clergyman to pay for the education of his children. When they were all of full age there was money left in the fund. It was held that the money was to be divided equally among the children[14]. The principle was enunciated in *Re Smith*[15] in 1928, 'where there is what amounts to an absolute gift, that absolute gift cannot be fettered by prescribing a mode of enjoyment'[16]. Thus the existence of a direction as to the mode of enjoyment of a gift does not invalidate a gift, but where the beneficiaries are of full age and between them absolutely entitled, the direction has no binding force. Another example, in addition to those above, is provided by *Re Lipinski's Will Trusts*[17]. A testator left one half of his residuary estate on trust for the Hull Judeans (Maccabi) Association (an unincorporated association) to be used solely in constructing and improving new buildings for the association. It was held that since the trust was enforceable by the association's members (who were asertained or ascertainable) the trust was of perfect obligation. It was held, further, that the members were entitled either to enforce the purpose specified (and use the money for the buildings) or (notwithstanding the use of the word 'solely') to vary the purpose (and use the money for any other purpose for which the association existed)[18].

---

11 [1896] 1 Ch 507. The principle was enunciated in *Re Sanderson's Trust* (1857) 3 K & J 497. 'If a gross sum be given, or if the whole income of the property be given, and a special purpose be assigned for that gift, the court always regards the gift as absolute, and the purpose merely as the motive for the gift and therefore holds that the gift takes effect as to the whole sum or whole income as the case may be.' Per Page Wood V-C, p 503.
12 Which would be held for S for life with remainder to G; or the total divided between them in such shares as they agreed.
13 [1905] 2 Ch 48.
14 There was a corresponding outcome in *Re Osoba* [1979] 2 All ER 393, [1979] 1 WLR 247; (M & B).
15 [1928] Ch 915.
16 Per Swinfen Eady MR following *Younghusband v Gisborne* (1844) 1 Coll 400.
17 [1976] Ch 235, [1977] 1 All ER 33; (M & B).
18 See also *Re Turkington* [1937] 4 All ER 501 (gift of property to a masonic lodge to form a fund for the building of a temple in Stafford; held to be a gift to the members of the lodge to deal with as they pleased); and K. Widdows (1977) 41 Conv (NS) 179.

'Purpose trusts'

From what has been said in this and previous chapters, it will be seen that
the term 'purpose trust' could be applied

1. to some private trusts of perfect obligation (as in *Re Denley*[19]; *Re Bowes*[20]
and *Re Andrew's Trust*[1]);

2. to all charitable trusts;

3. to trusts of imperfect obligation which are valid (because they fall within
one of the three exceptional classes);

4. to trusts of imperfect obligation which are void (because they do not fall
within one of these classes).

To use the term 'purpose trust' as an alternative to 'trust of imperfect
obligation' is therefore clearly unsatisfactory: the term may have the merit
of brevity but, if used, requires elucidation as to the form of trust referred
to. The term 'trust of imperfect obligation' may appear clumsy, but it has
the merit that it immediately distinguishes the kind of trust intended. It is
therefore submitted that the term 'purpose trust' is best avoided.

Unincorporated associations

It will be convenient at this point to mention that a number of the principles
considered in this chapter are relevant in determining certain questions
relating to unincorporated associations.

The nature of an unincorporated association was considered by Lawton
LJ in *Conservative and Unionist Central Office v Burrell*[2]. In his judgment he
said, 'I infer that by "unincorporated association" in this context[3] Parliament
meant two or more persons bound together for one or more common purposes, not being business purposes, by mutual undertakings, each having
mutual duties and obligations, in an organisation which has rules which
identify in whom control of it and its funds rests and upon what terms and
which can be joined or left at will. The bond of union between the members
of an unincorporated association has to be contractual.[4]'

GIFTS TO UNINCORPORATED ASSOCIATIONS[5]

First we may consider the validity of gifts to such associations. The position
is as follows.

19 [1969] 1 Ch 373, [1968] 3 All ER 65.
20 [1896] 1 Ch 507.
 1 [1905] 2 Ch 48.
 2 [1982] 2 All ER 1, [1982] 1 WLR 522; (M & B), CA; [1983] Conv 150 (P. Creighton).
 3 In the context of s 526(5) of the Income and Corporation Taxes Act 1970, under s 238(1)
of which profits of an unincorporated association are chargeable to corporation tax.
 4 At p 525.
 5 On the methods by which unincorporated associations may hold property, see [1985] Conv
318 (J. Warburton), [1987] Conv 415 (P. J. Smart). See also [1992] Conv 41 (S. Gardner).

1. If (a) the gift to the association can (notwithstanding, perhaps, that a mode of enjoyment of the property is specified[6]) be construed as a gift to the present members beneficially; and, (b) there is nothing in the association's rules to prevent the association disposing of the property as it thinks fit[7], the gift is valid[8].

For example, in *Re Drummond*[9] a testator left his residuary estate to trustees on trust for the Old Bradfordian's Club, London (being a club for old boys of Bradford Grammar School) to be utilised as the committee of the club should think best in the interests of the club or the school. It was held, since the gift was not subject to any trust which would prevent the committee from spending the bequest in any manner they might decide for the benefit of the class intended, the gift was valid.

2. If (a) the gift can be construed as being in favour of the existing members of the association, not so as to entitle each member to an immediate distributive share, but as an accretion to the funds which form the subject matter of the contract by which the members, on joining, bind themselves together[10]; and (b) there is nothing in the rules to prevent the society from disposing of the property as it thinks fit (as by distributing the property among the existing members), then the gift is valid[11].

3. If (a) the gift is construed as being for the benefit of present and future members, or (b) the terms of the gift[12] or the society's rules preclude the society from disposing of the property as it thinks fit; then, in either case, since the capital must be kept intact and only income used,
(i) if the duration of the gift is confined to the perpetuity period (eg with a gift over thereafter) the gift is valid;
(ii) if it is not, it is void[13].

For example, in *Carne v Long*[14] a testator left certain land to the trustees of the Penzance Public Library and their successors to hold for ever for the maintenance and support of the library. The library was not charitable, books being available for loan only to subscribers to the library. The gift

---

6   As in *Re Denley's Trust Deed*, supra. See p 165.
7   It was the fact that this condition was held not to have been satisfied that caused the failure of the gift in *Re Grant's Will Trusts* [1979] 3 All ER 359, [1980] 1 WLR 360; (M & B). See B. Green (1980) 43 MLR 459.
8   *Re Taylor* [1940] Ch 481, [1940] 2 All ER 637; *Bowman v Secular Society Ltd* [1917] AC 406; *Re Clarke* [1901] 2 Ch 110.
9   [1914] 2 Ch 90.
10 See *Neville Estates Ltd v Madden* [1962] Ch 832, [1961] 3 All ER 769; (M & B). There 'may be a gift to the existing members ... subject to their respective contractual rights and liabilities towards one another as members of the association. In such case a member cannot sever his share. It would accrue to the other members on his death or resignation even though such members include persons who become members after the gift took effect.' Per Cross J at p 849.
11 *Re Recher's Will Trusts* [1972] Ch 526 at 535–540; (M & B); *Re Clarke* [1901] 2 Ch 110; *Re Prevost* [1930] 2 Ch 383; *Re Turkington* [1937] 4 All ER 501.
12 *Re Macaulay's Estate* [1943] Ch 435n (a gift for the 'maintenance and improvement of the Theosophical Lodge at Maidstone', the word 'maintenance' being held to indicate an intention of continuity).
13 *Leahy v A-G for New South Wales* [1959] AC 457, [1959] 2 All ER 300; (M & B); *Carne v Long* (1860) 2 De GF & J 75; *Re Recher's Will Trusts* [1972] Ch 526 at 535; *Re Grant's Will Trusts* [1979] 3 All ER 359 at 366–367; *Re Macaulay's Estate* [1943] Ch 435n; *Re Flavel's Will Trusts* [1969] 2 All ER 232, [1969] 1 WLR 444.
14 (1860) 2 De GF & J 75.

was thus for the benefit of present and future members of, in effect, an unincorporated association. It was held that as the land would have to be held indefinitely the gift was void.

4. If the gift is construed as being on trust for the purposes of the association then (unless the purpose falls within one of the three exceptions when a trust of imperfect obligation may be valid) the gift is void[15].

5. If the gift is stated to be for the purposes of the association (or for a specified purpose in furtherance of the association's objects, eg the construction of a meeting hall) and the words are construed as imposing no trust for the purpose or purposes specified but as merely expressing the motive for the gift, or indicating the mode of enjoyment intended (as in *Re Denley's Trust Deed*, considered earlier[16],) then the words are treated as mere surplusage and have no effect on the legal status of the gift, and the position is at (1), (2) or (3) above, according to the construction placed on the gift.

ACHIEVEMENT OF A NON-CHARITABLE PURPOSE BY A GIFT TO AN UNINCORPORATED ASSOCIATION

The fact that a gift on trust for a non-charitable purpose (eg a political purpose, such as anti-vivisection) is void does not mean that an association cannot exist with a non-charitable purpose. The matter was expressed by Brightman J in *Re Recher's Will Trusts*[17] thus: 'A trust for non-charitable purposes, as distinct from a trust for individuals, is clearly void because there is no beneficiary. It does not, however, follow that persons cannot band themselves together as an association or society, pay subscriptions and validly devote their funds in pursuit of some lawful non-charitable purpose. An obvious example is a members' social club. But it is not essential that the members should only intend to secure direct personal advantages to themselves. The association may be one in which personal advantages to members are combined with the pursuit of some outside purpose. Or the association may be one which offers no personal benefit at all to the members, the funds of the association being applied exclusively to the pursuit of some outside purpose. Such an association of persons is bound, I would think, to have some sort of constitution; that is to say, the rights and liabilities of the members of the association would inevitably depend upon some form of contract inter se, usually evidenced by a set of rules.'

A person who wishes to further a non-charitable purpose by making a gift to an association which has the objects he supports should, however, take care. If he gives the property to the association and he states that the property is given on trust for the purpose concerned (or on trust for the association's 'work', or 'aims', etc) and the words he uses are not construed as mere surplusage, then since a trust of imperfect obligation has been created the gift is void[18]. On the other hand, if he gives the property to the association[19],

---

15 *Leahy v A-G for New South Wales*, ante, at p 478. *Re Recher's Will Trusts*, ante, at p 537.
   Re Wightwick's Will Trusts [1950] Ch 260, [1950] 1 All ER 689 (a gift by will to the
   treasurer of an anti-vivisection society for the purposes of the society).
16 See p 181.
17 [1972] Ch 526, 538, [1971] 3 All ER 401.
18 *Re Recher's Will Trusts* [1972] Ch 526, [1971] 3 All ER 401; (M & B).
19 Or to such association of a specified kind as his trustees should select. *Re Ogden* [1933] Ch
   678.

without creating any form of trust, and if the gift complies with the conditions set out in 2(a) and (b) above, then the donor will have effectively achieved his aim. But the donor will suffer the disadvantage that his disposition does not have the security of a trust, as there can be no guarantee that the association will apply the property for the purpose the donor intended, since it may be that the association's rules empower the association to vary its objects, or authorise the association's property to be distributed among its members. As the matter has been stated[20], 'For the donor, the price of validity is unenforceability. All he has is the hope that the society's members will apply his contribution to secure his stated goal; though the chances of his intention being realised will be greatly improved where the proposed purpose is sanctified by the association's rules, for then the fate of his donation will be protected so long as the members' mutually enforceable contractual obligations survive'.

DISTRIBUTION OF THE PROPERTY OF AN UNINCORPORATED ASSOCIATION ON ITS DISSOLUTION

Finally, we may consider the question of entitlement to an association's property on its dissolution[1]. By way of illustration suppose that a gliding club is compelled, by the expiry of the lease of its airfield, to close down. Its aircraft are sold and realise £50,000. To whom should this money pass? If the distribution was to be made amongst the existing members at the date of the club's dissolution, this would be unlikely to be opposed by A, who had joined the club only six months previously, but would seem unfair to B, who had been a loyal member for 20 years, and who had done much to build up the club, and who had resigned two months before the dissolution, when his work had taken him to another part of the country. So, to meet the demands of B, should the assets be distributed among both existing and former members?

On the other hand, if the property is distributed amongst existing and former members, are all former members to benefit—including those who have ceased to be members many years previously? And if former members are to benefit, should the distribution also include the estates of former members who have died? Or should the property be treated as bona vacantia, and pass to the Crown? No course seems entirely to meet the needs of justice.

The position that has evolved in law is as follows. First, it is necessary to consider whether statute determines (or affects[2]) the outcome, either directly[3] (as by prescribing the nature of the organisation itself)[4] or indirectly (as by a statute prohibiting distribution of assets of a registered friendly society

---

20 B. Green (1980) 43 MLR 460 (commenting on *Re Grant's Will Trusts* [1979] 3 All ER 359, [1980] 1 WLR 360).
 1 See 'The Dissolution of Unincorporated Non-Profit Associations', B. Green (1980) 43 MLR 626; 'Unincorporated Associations and their Dissolution', C. E. F. Rickett [1980] CLJ 88.
 2 *Re Bucks Constabulary Widows' and Orphans' Fund Friendly Society* [1978] 2 All ER 571, [1978] 1 WLR 641.
 3 *Re Edis's Trusts* [1972] 2 All ER 769, [1972] 1 WLR 1135.
 4 *Ross v Lord Advocate* 1986 SLT 391 (Trustee Savings Bank held to be a statutory creature *sui generis*, not possessing any of the essential characteristics of a voluntary association of members, its assets therefore not being distributable among its members on the Bank's privatisation).

among its members, with the result that the only course open is for the property to pass as a bona vacantia to the Crown[5].

If no statute is relevant, it is necessary next to consider whether the group's rules lay down how its property is to be dealt with in the event of dissolution. If such provision exists, then this must be followed[6].

In the absence of any express rule on the matter, then a term is to be implied[7] into the contract constituted by the rules of an unincorporated association that on its dissolution the association's funds should belong to the members at the date of dissolution (and the estates of such members who have died since the dissolution), in equal shares[8]. No claim lies from former members (or their estates), the rights of such members being regarded as having been extinguished by their resignation or death[8].

If the association is moribund (a position that will be regarded as existing if only one member remains[8]) then the property will pass as bona vacantia to the Crown[8].

Where property falls to be distributed to members of an association at its dissolution, difficulties may arise in determining the precise moment that the dissolution occurred. An example is provided by *GKN Bolts and Nuts Ltd Sports and Social Club*[9]. The case concerned a social club formed for the benefit of employees of a company. In 1946 the trustees bought a sports ground. In 1970, as a result of financial difficulties, sale of the ground, which was no longer in use, was considered. In January 1975, membership cards ceased to be issued. In February the last annual general meeting of the club took place. In April the steward was dismissed and the club ceased to be registered for VAT. On 18 December a special general meeting was convened to consider an offer by a purchaser to buy the sports ground for £19,000. There was a unanimous decision to accept the offer. The sale did not take place. In May 1978, planning permission for development of the ground, which had earlier been refused, was granted. In July the trustees contracted to sell the land, and in August completion took place. The net proceeds amounted to £240,000. Two questions arose. First, had the club ceased to exist? (It will be noted that at no point had a resolution been passed formally winding up the club.) Secondly, if the club had ceased to exist, at what date did the cessation occur and on what basis should the assets be distributable among members? Sir Robert Megarry V-C held, 'As a matter of principle I would hold that it is perfectly possible for a club to be dissolved spontaneously. I do not think that mere inactivity is enough: a club may do little or nothing for a long period, and yet continue in existence. A cataleptic trance may look like death without being death. But inactivity may be so

---

5   *Cunnack v Edwards* [1896] 2 Ch 679; *Braithwaite v A-G* [1909] 1 Ch 510.

6   *Davis v Richards & Wallington Industries Ltd* [1991] 2 All ER 563, [1990] 1 WLR 1511.

7   A term that an association's funds should on its dissolution be held on trust for the members will not be inferred where the circumstances preclude such a finding. See *West Sussex Constabulary's Widows, Children and Benevolent (1930) Fund Trusts*, infra; *Davis v Richards and Wallington Industries Ltd* [1991] 2 All ER 563, [1990] 1 WLR 1511 (surplus of companies' pension scheme not held for employee contributors; [1992] Conv 41 (S. Gardner).

8   *Re Printers and Transferrers Amalgamated Trades Protection Society* [1899] 2 Ch 184; *Re Bucks Constabulary Widows' and Orphans' Fund Friendly Society (No 2)* [1979] 1 All ER 623, [1979] 1 WLR 936; (M & B). See C. E. F. Rickett [1980] CLJ 88. Cf *West Sussex Constabulary's Widows, Children and Benevolent (1930) Fund Trusts* [1971] Ch 1, [1970] 1 All ER 544; (M & B); (1971) 87 LQR 464 (M. J. Albery).

9   *GKN Bolts and Nuts Ltd Sports and Social Club* [1982] 2 All ER 855, [1982] 1 WLR 774; [1983] Conv 315 (R. Griffith).

prolonged or so circumstanced that the only reasonable inference is that the club has become dissolved. In such cases there may be difficulty in determining the *punctum temporis* of dissolution: the less activity there is, the greater the difficulty in fastening upon one date rather than another as the moment of dissolution. In such cases the court must do the best it can by picking a reasonable date somewhere between the time when the club could be said to exist,' and the time when its existence had clearly come to an end[10].' On the facts the court held that the club had ceased to exist on 18 December 1978, the date of the resolution to sell the sports ground. The rules of the club stated that the objects of the club were to promote sports and to provide facilities for recreation. By resolving to sell the ground, 'all must have recognised that the club had become incapable of carrying out any of its objects[11]'. The proceeds from the sale were therefore distributable among those who were members of the club at the date of the meeting.

A further matter for decision arose from the fact that the club's rules provided for various classes, comprising 'full', 'associate', 'temporary', and 'honorary' membership; and from the fact that some members had been members for a long time, and some had joined the club only in recent times. On what basis should the assets be distributed[12]? With regard to the classes of membership, it was held that[13] only 'full' members were entitled to receive a share of the assets. As between these the distribution should be on the basis of equality, irrespective of the length of membership.

The rule against inalienability: A postscript

We first met the rule in Chapter 4, when it was mentioned as a requirement with which a trust must comply. In Chapter 7 we learned that, as an exception, charitable trusts are not subject to the rule. In this chapter we have examined the application of the rule to trusts of imperfect obligation and noted the particular relevance of the rule to trusts for the upkeep of tombs and to gifts to unincorporated associations. A final point needs to be made.

The rule is that a trust is void if capital and income are incapable of being alienated for a period longer than the common law perpetuity period. What is the significance of the addition of the words 'and income'? The matter can be illustrated by an example. Consider a bequest:

'to my first grandson to attain 21 for his lifetime, and on his death to X.'

With regard to the rule against perpetuities (ie with regard to initial vesting) the contingent gift to the grandson is valid. (The gift is bound to vest, if it vests at all, within a life or lives in being at the testator's death plus a further

---

10   At p 779.
11   At p 282. *In Re William Denby & Sons Ltd Sick and Benevolent Fund* [1971] 2 All ER 1196, [1971] 1 WLR 973 it was held that a period of inactivity had not amounted to dissolution of a benevolent fund.
12   A similar question arose for decision in *Re St Andrew's Allotments Association's Trusts* [1969] 1 All ER 147, [1969] 1 WLR 229.
13   Following *Re Sick and Funeral Society of St John's Sunday School, Golcar* [1973] Ch 51, [1972] 2 All ER 439; (M & B), applied in *Re Bucks Constabulary Widows' and Orphans' Fund Friendly Society (No 2)* [1979] 1 All ER 623, [1979] 1 WLR 936; (M & B). See [1980] CLJ 88 (C. E. F. Rickett).

period of 21 years.) The gift in remainder to X is vested, not contingent, and so is not subject to the rule.

How long has the capital got to be kept intact? It would seem that it has got to be kept until the date of the death of the grandson who takes under the bequest (as being the first of the testator's grandsons to attain 21). Since this date is later than the end of the perpetuity period it would seem that the gift infringes the rule against inalienability and so is void. But this is in fact not the case. Consider the position when a grandson attains 21. At this point he becomes entitled in possession to a life interest in the property. This life interest is *his*—his to do what he likes with. So he could alienate it (eg sell it to an insurance company). Since the grandson is absolutely entitled to the income under his life interest and X is entitled to the remainder, between them they are entitled to the whole property. Thus they could, if they so wished, under the rule in *Saunders v Vautier*, put an end to the trust by directing the trustees to transfer the property in whatever manner they elect (eg to give one quarter to the grandson and three quarters to X). So, from the time when the grandson becomes entitled (when the perpetuity period ends) the capital becomes capable of being alienated[14]. It was because the income was not, by the terms of the gift, made inalienable for longer than the perpetuity period that the gift did not infringe the rule.

The result is the same, and for the same reason, in the case of a gift by a testator to trustees:

'on trust to pay the income to A until my grave ceases to be properly tended', with a gift over to X.

A, the holder of a determinable interest, and X are between them absolutely entitled and so could put an end to the trust. Thus the capital is not inalienable[15].

But where a testator leaves property to trustees:

'on trust for the upkeep of my tomb' (ie for ever, or for a period longer than 21 years),

since the capital must be kept intact for longer than the perpetuity period, the gift infringes the rule against inalienability and so is void. The result is the same in the case of a gift to the present and future members of a club: the capital must be kept intact for the benefit of the future members for an indefinite period and so the gift infringes the rule and is void[16].

Pension funds

Pension funds, which exist for the benefit of present and future members of pension schemes, have characteristics analogous to the form of gift set out under (3) on page 184 and so would, without protection by statute, fall foul of the rule against inalienability.

---

14 *Wainwright v Miller* [1897] 2 Ch 255; *Re Gage, Hill v Gage* [1898] 1 Ch 498.
15 *Re Chardon* [1928] Ch 464 at 470; *Re Chambers Will Trusts* [1950] Ch 267; *Re Wightwick's Will Trusts* [1950] Ch 260, [1950] 1 All ER 689.
16 *Re Flavel's Will Trusts* [1969] 2 All ER 232, [1969] 1 WLR 444.

The Superannuation and other Trust Funds (Validation) Act 1927[17] provided that 'The rule of law relating to perpetuities shall not apply' to superannuation funds registered under the Act. The uncertainty in this wording as to whether the Act exempted registered funds not only from the rule against perpetuity (ie the rule relating to initial vesting) but also from the rule against inalienability was removed when the Social Security Act 1973 repealed the 1927 Act and provided[18] that occupational pension schemes which satisfied certain conditions should be 'exempt from the operation of *any* rules of law relating to perpetuities which would otherwise invalidate, or might be taken to invalidate, any of the trusts of the scheme or any disposition made under it . . .'

---

17 Section 1.
18 Section 69(1). The italics are added.

Chapter 10

Implied trusts

The trusts which have been considered so far in this book, whether private or charitable, have been ones which arose as a result of the *express* intention of the settlor. A trust may also arise from the *implied* intention of a settlor. We can distinguish five situations in which this occurs.

1 Failure of the trust to take effect

We have in fact met some situations in which an implied trust arises. For example, in Chapter 3 we saw that if a settlor attempts to create a trust, but there are no beneficiaries, or there is lack of certainty as to the identity of the beneficiaries, or as to the amount of trust property to be distributed to each beneficiary, then the trustees hold the trust property on trust for the settlor. Thus, it will be noted, in these situations it is not correct to say that no trust exists; the trust which the settlor intended fails, but the property is held by the trustees on trust for the settlor. Such a trust is an implied trust, since it arises from what is regarded as having been the implied intention of the settlor: it is inferred that he would have intended, in the event of the trust he proposed failing, that the trustees should hold the trust property on trust for himself (or, if he is dead, his estate).

The result is the same if the trust fails for any other reason—for example if the gift to the beneficiaries is void for perpetuity, or because the necessary formality (eg under s 53(1)(b)) has not been complied with; or because the purpose of the trust is against public policy[1]; or because a condition precedent has not been fulfilled (as, for example, in *Barclays Bank Ltd v Quistclose Investments Ltd*[2], considered earlier[3]). Similarly, where property is given for a charitable purpose which proves to be impossible ab initio and there is no general charitable intention[4], the property is held on trust for the donor or donors[5]. And where a testator takes the first steps towards creating a half secret trust (ie by making the relevant disposition in his will) but fails to communicate the name of the beneficiary by the time of the making of the will, then the donee holds the property on a resulting trust for the testator's estate.

1 *Thrupp v Collett* (1858) 26 Beav 125.
2 [1970] AC 567, [1968] 3 All ER 651; (M & B); (1985) 101 LQR 269 (P. J. Millett).
3 See p 51, supra.
4 See Chap 8.
5 *Re Henry Wood National Memorial Trust* [1967] 1 All ER 238n, [1966] 1 WLR 1601; *Re Gillingham Bus Disaster Fund* [1958] Ch 300 at 310; (M & B).

In all these situations the beneficial interest reverts to the settlor. A trust in which the beneficial interest reverts to settlor (or his estate) is termed a 'resulting' trust. A resulting trust is one form of implied trust. (The word 'resulting' is obtained from the verb 'result', which is derived from the Latin *resultare*, to spring back. A resulting trust is thus one in which the beneficial interest springs back to the settlor.) As we shall see, all implied trusts, except those arising as a result of 'mutual wills' (considered later[6]), take the form of a resulting trust.

2   Failure to give away the entire beneficial interest

Another situation in which an implied trust arises is where the settlor does not give away the entire fee simple in realty or the absolute interest in personalty. For example, if a settlor conveys land to trustees for sale for A for life, with no remainder over, then on A's death the trustees hold the trust property on a resulting trust for the settlor (or his estate). Or there may be a gap in beneficial interests (ie a period of time after one interest ends and before another begins): during this period the property will be held on a resulting trust for the settlor (or his estate)[7]. Or there may be an interval of time before a gift vests. For example, if the testator leaves £1,000 'to my friend A if he attains 21', then until A attains 21 the income, from the £1,000 is held on a resulting trust for the testator's estate[8]. Or it may be that a settlor transfers property to trustees (as trustees) without specifying the beneficial interests. He declares these later. In the interval the trustees hold the income from the property on a resulting trust for the settlor[9].

In some cases the court may have to determine whether the settlor intended to convey an absolute interest in the property or whether a more limited interest, such as a life interest, was intended. In the latter case a resulting trust will arise on the expiry of the limited interest[10].

An example of a trust under this head is provided by *Re Ames' Settlement*[11]. In 1908 a settlor transferred £10,000 to trustees on trust for H for life with remainder to his wife W for life, with remainder to their children, or, if none, to those who would have been H's next of kin had he died without marrying. In 1926 the marriage was declared null on the ground of H's incapacity to consummate it. W married again and by deed released her interest under the settlement. H continued to receive the income until his death in 1945. It was held that since the marriage had been annulled, the settlement was ineffective and on H's death the trust fund was to be held on a resulting trust for the settlor's estate (ie and not for H's next of kin).

---

6   See p 207, post.
7   *Re Cochrane, Shaw v Cochrane* [1955] Ch 309, [1955] 1 All ER 222. *Re Vandervell's Trust (No 2)* [1974] 3 All ER 205 at 211; (M & B).
8   In some instances (though not the one cited) income arising during such an interval goes to the donee if he acquires a vested interest. This matter is dealt with in Chap 16.
9   *Vandervell v IRC* [1967] 2 AC 291, [1967] 1 All ER 1, HL; (M & B). See p 41, supra.
10   *Re Abbott Fund Trusts* [1900] 2 Ch 326; (M & B).
11   [1946] Ch 217, [1946] 1 All ER 689; (M & B).

3 Purchase in the name of another

Another situation in which an implied trust arises is where A provides money for the purchase of property from a vendor, V, but instructs V to convey the property, not to himself, but to B. Here it is inferred that since A provided the purchase money, he intended B to hold the property not beneficially but as trustee, on trust for himself, A[12].

Thus if A buys shares from V and directs V to have them registered in the company's books in the name of B, B holds the shares on an implied trust for A.

Where, however, the evidence shows that the transaction constitutes a loan of the purchase price by A to B, to enable B to buy the property, then no implied trust arises. B holds the property beneficially. A's position is that of a creditor and his remedy against B lies in contract[13].

(a) Joint purchasers

Or it may happen that more than one person provides the purchase money. For example, A and B may provide the purchase money and direct V to convey the legal title to C alone. C will hold the legal title on trust for A and B in proportion to their respective contributions[14]. (If A and B provide the purchase money in unequal shares, or if A and B are partners, these are situations in which equity presumes that A and B intend to hold the equitable interest as tenants in common. If they contribute the purchase money in equal shares, and are not partners, equity will normally presume them to hold as joint tenants.)

Or it may be that A and B provide the purchase money and the property is conveyed into the name of A. Here A will hold on trust for himself and B, in proportion to their contributions. (If the property is land, since A and B hold as co-owners, a trust for sale arises, A holding on trust for sale for himself and B[15].)

(b) Joint transferees

Or it may be that A alone provides the purchase money, and directs V to convey the legal title into the names of himself and B. Here A and B will hold the legal title on trust for A alone[16].

---

12 *Dyer v Dyer* (1788) 2 Cox Eq Cas 92 at 93.
13 *Re Sharpe (a bankrupt)* [1980] 1 All ER 198, [1980] 1 WLR 219.
14 *Wray v Steele* (1814) 2 Ves & B 388; *Heseltine v Heseltine* [1971] 1 All ER 952, [1971] 1 WLR 342.
15 *Bull v Bull* [1955] 1 QB 234, [1955] 1 All ER 253.
16 *Gross v French* (1975) 238 Estates Gazette 39, but cf *Re John's Assignment Trusts* [1970] 2 All ER 210n, [1970] 1 WLR 955.

(c) The trust based on a presumption

In all these examples of purchase in the name of another, the starting-point is that equity presumes that it was the intention of the person (or persons) who provided the purchase money that the person (or persons) to whom the legal title is conveyed should hold it on trust for him (or them). But this is only a presumption, and so, like any other presumption, it can be rebutted. Thus if A pays for shares and directs V to convey them to B, and B is able to produce evidence (for example a letter from A) which shows that the shares were intended as a gift, then the presumption of a trust is rebutted and B takes the shares absolutely[17].

In *Sekhon v Alissa*[18], in 1989, a mother and daughter bought a house. It was conveyed into the daughter's name alone. From the purchase price of £36,500, £15,000 was advanced to the daughter on mortgage. The balance was paid by the mother. The house was converted into two self-contained flats. The mother lived in the upstairs flat. The value of the whole property rose to £120,000. The daughter claimed that the mother's contribution to the purchase price was a gift and that she, the daughter, was therefore the sole beneficial owner. It was held that the circumstances indicated an intention that the mother was to have an interest in the property, the size of the interest being in proportion to the value of the contribution to the purchase price.

(d) Presumption of gift

Where A is regarded by equity as being under an obligation to provide for B, then the presumption is that a gift was intended. Thus if a husband, H, buys property and has it conveyed into the name of W, who is his wife or his fiancée whom he subsequently marries[19], then it is presumed that (subject to what is said later[20]) H intended to make a gift of the property to W, with the result that W will take the property absolutely, free from any trust[1]. Similarly if H and W have a child, C (who is legitimate), and H buys property and has it conveyed into the name of C, then it is presumed that H intended to make a gift of the property to C, who therefore takes the property absolutely. Further, if any person who stands *in loco parentis* to a child buys property and has it conveyed into the name of the child, then a gift to the child is presumed.

A person becomes *in loco parentis* to a child if he assumes the responsibilities of a father in providing for the child. For example, an uncle may take upon himself the duty of providing for a nephew, on the death of the father. But a person does not become *in loco parentis* merely because he undertakes some of the expenses of the child's upbringing, eg paying a child's school fees[2].

It should be noted that there is no presumption of gift where a man buys property and has it conveyed into the name of his mistress[3]. Nor is there a

17   As in *Fowkes v Pascoe* (1875) 10 Ch App 343; (M & B).
18   [1989] 2 FLR 94, [1990] Conv 213 (G. Kodilinye).
19   *Moate v Moate* [1948] 2 All ER 486.
20   See infra.
 1   *Gascoigne v Gascoigne* [1918] 1 KB 223.
 2   *Tucker v Burrow* (1865) 2 Hem & M 515.
 3   *Soar v Foster* (1858) 4 K & J 152.

presumption of gift where a wife, W, buys property and has it conveyed to the name of her husband, H: thus the presumption is that H holds the property on trust for W[4]. Nor is there a presumption of gift where a mother buys property and has it conveyed into the name of her child[5]. The presumption is therefore that the child holds the property on trust for the mother. (But if the mother places herself *in loco parentis* to the child, eg by assuming responsibility for the child on the death of the father, or on his desertion, then the presumption of gift would exist.) Nor is there a presumption of gift where a father buys property in the name of an illegitimate child, or a step child. (But here too, if the father[6] (or step father) has placed himself *in loco parentis* to the child, from this fact a presumption of gift to the child arises.)

(e) The onus of proof

Let us recapitulate: where A buys property and conveys it into the name of B, and no special relationship (of one of the kinds we have described) exists, B holds the property on trust for A, unless B can rebut the presumption of trust, in which case B holds the property absolutely. On the other hand, where one of the special relationships does exist, B holds the property absolutely, unless A can rebut the presumption of gift, in which case B holds on trust for A.

Thus it will be seen that where no special relationship exists, the onus is on B to show that no trust was intended[7]. Where one does exist, the onus is on A to show that a trust was intended.

(f) Evidence which may be adduced

Whether the onus is on A or B, the matter which the court must seek to establish is what had been A's intention in having the property transferred to B. The best evidence of this will be an express declaration in the document conveying the legal title to B (ie a declaration that B holds on trust, or that B takes beneficially).

In seeking to determine the intention of A (the person who provided the purchase money), the court will look at the circumstances of the transaction (eg whether A had retained the title deeds, or had passed them to B) and will take account of all the relevant factors, whether they are expressly pleaded or not[8].

In *Shephard v Cartwright*[9], Viscount Simonds accepted the following passage from Snell's, *Principles of Equity*[10] as a correct statement of the law: 'The acts and declarations of the parties before or at the time of the purchase, or so immediately after it as to constitute a part of the transaction, are admissible in evidence either for or against the party who did the act or made

4 *Mercier v Mercier* [1903] 2 Ch 98.
5 *Bennet v Bennet* (1879) 10 Ch D 474.
6 *Beckford v Beckford* (1774) Lofft 490.
7 As in *Fowkes v Pascoe* (1875) 10 Ch App 343; (M & B).
8 *Chettiar v Chettiar* [1962] AC 294, [1962] 1 All ER 494.
9 [1955] AC 431 at 445; (M & B).
10 Page 178 of the 27th edn.

the declaration; subsequent acts and declarations are only admissible as evidence against the party who made them, and not in his favour'.

We can illustrate this passage by an example. In January A writes to B, his brother, telling him that he intends to purchase certain shares and have them transferred into B's name. In February B replies to A's letter. In March A buys the shares in B's name. In April A writes to B about the transaction and in May B replies. A dispute later arises as to the beneficial ownership of the shares. The presumption is that a trust exists. Thus the onus is on B to rebut the presumption that he holds the shares on trust for A. In evidence, B can produce any letters[11] written by himself or A before the transaction took place to show (as he contends) that no trust was intended by A. As regards the correspondence after the transaction, he can use A's letter of April (against A) but he is not entitled to use his own letter of May (for himself). In seeking to defeat B's attempt to rebut the presumption, A is similarly entitled to use any letters written by himself or B before the transaction. He can use B's letter of May (against B); he cannot use his own letter of April (for himself). The effect of the rule is therefore that either party may produce any evidence of their own or their opponent's acts or declarations which came into existence before or at the time of the transaction, but they are not entitled to produce evidence of their own acts or declarations after the transaction has been completed[12].

It is for the court to decide whether the evidence produced is sufficient to rebut the presumption of a trust or a gift (as the case may be). If the evidence is not sufficient to rebut the presumption (for a trust or against a trust) the presumption prevails.

(g) Improper motive

A person (eg a husband) seeking to rebut a presumption of gift is not permitted to rely (in giving evidence of his intention to create a trust) on his purpose in purchasing property in the name of, eg his wife, if his purpose was legally an improper one. For example, if a husband, H, seeks to escape paying tax on certain shares, and to achieve this has the shares transferred into the name of his wife, W, with the intention that W should hold them on trust for him (so that H gets the best of both worlds, beneficial ownership of the shares, and reduced tax), H will not be allowed to use his motive in giving evidence of his intention to create a trust. He will thus fail to rebut the presumption of gift, and W will take the shares absolutely[13]. In *Gascoigne v Gascoigne*[14], H was in debt and feared that his property would pass to his creditors. When taking a lease of land, he therefore had the lease taken in the name of W, his wife. He later claimed (seeking to rebut the presumption of gift to W) that W held the lease on trust for him. Since his motive in

11   Or any other evidence, written or oral.
12   *Warren v Gurney* [1944] 2 All ER 472; (M & B).
13   *Re Emery's Investment Trusts* [1959] Ch 410, [1959] 1 All ER 577. Cf *Sekhon v Alissa* [1989] 2 FLR 94. (Mother contributed to purchase of property conveyed into name of daughter alone. Mother had been advised that transaction would have to be treated as a gift in order to gain exemption from capital gains tax. Mother not precluded from relying on evidence of intention that she was to be beneficially a co-owner since no scheme to avoid tax was prepared or carried out.) See also *Tinsley v Milligan* [1992] 2 All ER 391, [1992] 2 WLR 508.
14   [1918] 1 KB 223. Cf *Tinsley v Milligan* [1992] 2 All ER 391, [1992] 2 WLR 508.

having the lease taken in W's name was an improper one (seeking to defraud his creditors) he was not allowed to adduce his motive as evidence in rebutting the presumption of gift. So the presumption prevailed and W held the lease beneficially. (The outcome was not affected by the fact that W knew of H's motive in having the property conveyed into her name. To this extent W benefited from the fraudulent plan.) In *Tinker v Tinker*[15], in similar circumstances, the court decided that H had not acted with any improper motive. But the outcome was the same since the court held that as H had acted honestly, he must have intended W to have the property. So W took the property beneficially.

Similarly, where an attempt is being made to rebut a presumption of trust, evidence of the motive behind the transaction cannot be adduced if the motive is an improper one. For example, suppose that a wife (W) is expecting to become bankrupt. She buys property in the name of her husband (H). The presumption is that H holds on trust for W. W goes bankrupt. The trustee in bankruptcy claims the property (ie W's equitable interest). In seeking to rebut the presumption of trust, W cannot adduce in evidence her motive in transferring the property to H, ie her attempt to defeat her creditors. Thus the presumption of trust prevails, H holds on trust for W, and W's interest will pass to the trustee in bankruptcy.

(h) Matrimonial home[16]

The principles relating to purchase in the name of another are of special relevance in connection with ownership of the matrimonial home.

Contribution to the purchase price

Suppose that H and W contribute money for the purchase of their home. The house is conveyed into the name of H alone. Since W is not presumed to make a gift (ie of her contribution) to H, H will hold the house on trust for himself and W. This accords with what has been said earlier. On the other hand, if H and W provide money for the purchase of a house which is conveyed into the name of W alone, then since H is presumed to make a gift to W, it would seem that W would take the title to the house absolutely. And so she would according to the presumption laid down by equity in earlier times. More recently, however, with the increasing financial independence of women, the courts have held that in these circumstances the presumption of a gift by a husband to his wife is much weakened. The result is that, in the situation posed above, W would hold the legal title on trust for herself and H[17]. This is likely to be the outcome if the property purchased is the matrimonial home, and the result may be the same in the case of some other asset purchased for the joint use of H and W.

The most common situation, however, in which disputes have arisen is that in which H and W contribute to the purchase of the home, and the property is conveyed into the name of H alone. Here, as we have stated, H

---

15   [1970] P 136, [1970] 1 All ER 540.
16   *The Family Home*, W. T. Murphy and H. Clark (1983).
17   *Falconer v Falconer* [1970] 3 All ER 449, [1970] 1 WLR 1333, CA.

holds the legal title on an implied trust for himself and W. This may come about not only where W contributes to the purchase price, but also where the house is acquired by means of a mortgage. W may have contributed to the deposit, or if she has earnings of her own some of these she may use towards the mortgage repayments. Here also H will hold the property in trust for himself and W.

W may acquire a beneficial interest also by indirectly making a financial contribution to the purchase of the house. For example, in *Hargrave v Newton*[18] H and W were married in 1940. In 1960 W got a job and used her earnings for family expenses. In 1964 W received a reward of £5,045 for finding a large sum of money that had been stolen in the Great Train Robbery[19]. She used this for family expenses. The house in which they lived had been purchased in H's name alone. The marriage broke up in 1967 and H and W were divorced. The house was sold. It was held that W, by her contributions to the household expenses, had indirectly contributed to the purchase of the house (ie by enabling H to use his earnings to pay off more quickly the loan with which the house had been purchased). Thus H held the proceeds of sale on trust for himself and for W. In *Hazell v Hazell*[20] H and W in 1951 decided to move from rented accommodation that was too small for them into a house. W found a suitable house and the property was conveyed into H's name. The purchase price was £1,850. Of this, £370 was obtained from a loan from H's parents and the balance of £1,480 from a building society. In order to enable the repayments to be met W went out to work. She used her earnings to clothe herself and her children, and to supplement her housekeeping money, which H had reduced when she got a job. In 1970 the couple were divorced. The Court of Appeal held that W was entitled to a share in the beneficial ownership of the house. In *Ulrich v Ulrich and Felton*[1], W contributed some of her savings towards the deposit on the property (which was acquired before the marriage to H took place) and also went out to work, using her earnings for household expenses and improvements to the property. It was held that H held the legal title on trust for both himself and W.

But not every contribution by W will necessarily result in her acquiring a share in the beneficial ownership of the property. For example, in *Gissing v Gissing*[2], W acquired no beneficial interest in the house as a result of her having had a job and having paid £220 out of her savings for furnishings and the laying of a lawn. And in *Cowcher v Cowcher*[3] W obtained no increase in her beneficial interest (she already had a one-third interest by reason of an earlier contribution) by paying a single mortgage instalment properly payable by H. The contribution was too trifling to affect the beneficial interests in the property.

18 [1971] 3 All ER 866, [1971] 1 WLR 1611.
19 *R v Boal* [1965] 1 QB 402, [1964] 3 All ER 269, CCA.
20 [1972] 1 All ER 923, [1972] 1 WLR 301.
 1 [1968] 1 All ER 67, [1968] 1 WLR 180.
 2 [1971] AC 886, [1970] 2 All ER 780; *Midland Bank v Dobson and Dobson* [1986] 1 FLR 171, CA.
 3 [1972] 1 All ER 943, [1972] 1 WLR 425.

Improvements

W can acquire a beneficial interest not only by contributing, either directly or indirectly, to the purchase of the house, but also by contributing improvements to the property. Her contribution may take the form of paying, out of her own money, for improvements, such as the installation of central heating[4]; or it may take the form of her physically working on the property. For example, in *Smith v Baker*[5] H and W bought a plot of land for £95, mostly with W's money. The land was conveyed into H's name. H and W built a bungalow on the plot as their home. They did not employ a builder but did most of the work themselves. W gave up her job, which had brought her £10 a week, for about 16 months in order to help with the building work. Some years later the marriage broke up. Under the principle of purchase in the name of another, H would have held the legal title on trust for W no more than to the extent of her contribution to the purchase price. However, it was held that by virtue of her contribution to the building of the bungalow, H held the property on trust for W's estate (W having died during the proceedings) and himself equally.

It may happen that W acquires a beneficial interest in the house by reason of contributions by her which take the form of certain physical work, with which are coupled contributions in money towards the improvement or the purchase of property[6].

Acquisition of a beneficial interest by reason of physical work may accrue for the benefit of H where the property is in the name of W alone. For example, in *Jansen v Jansen*[7], W purchased a leasehold interest in a house. H, a student, decorated and repaired some of the rooms, and these were let furnished. The first and second floors were converted into two self-contained flats. H paid for materials out of his own money and did most of the work, abandoning his studies for a period to do so. Later, W left H and went to live with her children elsewhere. She sought an order for possession and a declaration that she was the sole beneficial owner. It was held that H, having worked to improve the property and having thereby enhanced its value, had an interest in the property amounting to £1,000.

Contributions in the form of work carried out will not, however, necessarily result in W (or H, as the case may be) acquiring (or increasing the share of) a beneficial interest in property the legal title to which is in the other spouse. For example, in *Pettitt v Pettitt*[8] W used her own money to purchase a cottage which was conveyed into her name. H improved the garden, made various internal modifications, and did some decorating. He claimed that the work he had done, which he valued at £725, had increased the value of the cottage by £1,000. The House of Lords held that H had acquired no beneficial interest in the property as a result of this work. This restrictive approach was followed in *Lloyd's Bank plc v Rossett*[9] in 1990. H purchased a semi-derelict farmhouse as a matrimonial home for himself and his wife, W. H provided the money

---

4 As in *Re Nicholson* [1974] 2 All ER 386, [1974] 1 WLR 476.
5 [1970] 2 All ER 826, [1970] 1 WLR 1160, CA.
6 As in *Davis v Vale* [1971] 2 All ER 1021, [1971] 1 WLR 1022, CA.
7 [1965] P 478, [1965] 3 All ER 363, CA.
8 [1970] AC 777, [1969] 2 All ER 385.
9 [1990] 1 AC 107, [1990] 1 All ER 1111, HL, [1990] Conv 314 (M. P. Thompson), [1990] Conv 370 (D. Hayton), [1991] CLJ 38 (M. Dixon). See also *Ungurian v Lesnoff* [1990] Ch 206, [1989] 3 WLR 840, [1991] Conv 596 (J. Hill).

for the purchase. W made no contribution to the purchase price but claimed that she held a beneficial interest in the home by virtue of express agreement between herself and H to this effect. At first instance it was held that W held a beneficial interest, not as a result of express agreement, but (under a constructive trust) as a result of a common intention that the property should be jointly owned, a common intention on reliance of which W had acted to her detriment by carrying out restoration work on the property prior to the date of completion. The House of Lords held that W had no interest in the property. In the absence of evidence of express discussion establishing an agreement, a common intention was only likely to be inferred from a direct contribution to the purchase price. W's work on restoration was not sufficient to raise an inference of a common intention that the property should be jointly held.

Matrimonial Proceedings and Property Act 1970

The cases prior to 1970 show that for H or W to acquire a beneficial interest by contributing (in money or by physical activity) to improvements the court must have been prepared to assume that it was impliedly the intention of the parties that the execution of the work by one should result in him or her acquiring a beneficial interest in the property the legal title to which was held by the other; and, further, that for this assumption to be made, the contribution must have been of a substantial nature[10]. The Matrimonial Proceedings and Property Act 1970 gives statutory force to these principles. Section 37 of the Act provides 'that where a husband or wife contributes in money or money's worth to the improvement of real or personal property in which or in the proceeds of sale of which either or both of them has or have a beneficial interest, the husband or wife so contributing shall, if the contribution is of a substantial nature and subject to any agreement between them to the contrary express or implied, be treated as having then acquired by virtue of his or her contribution a share or an enlarged share, as the case may be, in that beneficial interest of such an extent as may have been then agreed or, in default of such agreement, as may seem in all the circumstances just to any court before which the question of the existence or extent of the beneficial interest of the husband or wife arises (whether in proceedings between them or in any other proceedings)'.

The following points call for attention:

(a) The section applies irrespective of whether the legal estate is in H or W, or in them both.

(b) The section applies to any property, not necessarily the matrimonial home (eg it could apply to a shop or some other business premises).

(c) As previously had been the principle of the courts, the contribution must be 'substantial'[11].

(d) The section relates both to the position where H or W carries out some work on the property (a contribution in 'money's worth') and also where H[12]

---

10   *Button v Button* [1968] 1 All ER 1064 at 1067.
11   See *Harnett v Harnett* [1973] Fam 156, [1973] 2 All ER 593.
12   As in *Griffiths v Griffiths* [1974] 1 All ER 932, [1974] 1 WLR 1350.

or W[13] makes a financial contribution ('in money') to the work concerned.

(e) The section would apply where the improvement took the form of building a house or other premises, the improvement in this case being to the land.

(f) The section applies to personal as well as real property, and so would apply, eg to an improvement by W to premises held by H on lease.

Ownership of property other than the matrimonial home

We have discussed the principles of law by which beneficial ownership of the matrimonial home can be determined. But in law the matrimonial home is not a distinct species of property. It is merely an asset which is commonly the most valuable item of property owned by a married couple (or one of them) and, partly for this reason, the item over which disputes often arise. The principles of law which we have discussed with regard to beneficial ownership of the matrimonial home are therefore, in the main[14], no more than general principles of law applied to this particular item of property.

The principles we have discussed are equally applicable in the case of disputes between H and W over items of property other than the house which is, or has been, their home. These principles are thus equally applicable in determining who owns, for example, a grocery business and sub-post office[15], or a fruit, vegetable and fish shop[16], run by H and W. Or the dispute may be over the title not to freehold or leasehold property, but to pure personalty; for example, furniture[17].

It should be noted, further, that neither s 17 of the Married Women's Property Act 1882 (which provides a procedure for resolving disputes between H and W as to rights in property) nor s 37 of the Matrimonial Proceedings and Property Act 1970 (which relates to improvements by H or W) are confined to, or indeed refer to, issues concerning the matrimonial home. Both sections are thus applicable in the case of issues concerning any form of property owned by H or W (or by them both).

It may be added here that the courts have sometimes used the phrase 'family assets'[18]. Whilst this may be a convenient term to describe the property owned in some manner by a family as a family, it does not indicate that there is any separate body of law to which the property so described is subject[19].

Homes other than those of a married couple[20]

Not only are the principles we have discussed relevant in determining disputes

---

13 As in *Davis v Vale* [1971] 2 All ER 1021, [1971] 1 WLR 1022.
14 The matrimonial home is distinguished from other species of property in that it is subject to the Matrimonial Homes Act 1983. See p 183, post.
15 *Bothe v Amos* [1976] Fam 46, [1975] 2 All ER 321.
16 *Re Cummins* [1972] Ch 62, [1971] 3 All ER 782, CA.
17 As in *Hoddinott v Hoddinott* [1949] 2 KB 406.
18 See Miller, 'Family Assets' (1970) 86 LQR 98.
19 See Viscount Dilhorne in *Gissing v Gissing* [1971] AC 886, [1970] 2 All ER 780; and Ormrod LJ in *P v P* [1978] 1 WLR 483 at 490.
20 See M. A. Richards, 'The Mistress and the Family Home' (1976) 40 Conv (NS) 351; [1984] Conv 103 (M. P. Thompson).

between spouses over forms of property other than the matrimonial home, they may be relevant also in determining disputes over the ownership of a home, but not one established by a married couple[1]. For example in *Cooke v Head*[2], H and C met in 1962 and C became H's mistress. A piece of land was bought and conveyed into H's name. With the help of some labour, they together built a bungalow. C did a great deal of heavy work, including mixing and carting cement. She also contributed some of her earnings towards paying mortgage instalments. Later H and C separated, and the property was sold. It was held that the principles applied by the courts in the case of a husband and wife who by their joint efforts acquire property for their joint benefit applied equally to a man and his mistress who acquire property by their joint efforts with the intention of setting up home together. C was held to be entitled to one-third of the proceeds of sale. In *Eves v Eves*[3], the mistress, who had done much work, some of it very heavy, to the house and garden was held to be entitled to a quarter interest in the property[4]. In *Hussey v Palmer*[5], the parties were a widow and her son-in-law. The son-in-law owned a house which he occupied with his wife. The couple invited the widow to live with them. The widow paid £607 for a bedroom to be added to the house. After living there for 15 months, the widow left. She claimed the £607. It was held that the £607 has not been intended as a gift, and the son-in-law held the house on trust for the widow proportionate to her payment[6].

In other cases, a mistress has been held to have acquired a right to remain on property not by reason of her having acquired some interest in the property under an implied trust but as a result of the application of certain other principles. For example, in *Tanner v Tanner*[7] a mistress who had helped furnish the house but who had contributed nothing to its purchase and had done no improvements was held not to have acquired any interest in the property. She was, however, held to be a contractual licensee and to be entitled to have accommodation in the house for herself and the children so long as the children were of school age and reasonably required the accommodation. In *Pascoe v Turner*[8] a mistress, the defendant, stayed on in the plaintiff's house and, in reliance on the plaintiff's assurance that he had given her the house and its contents, spent money, with the plaintiff's encouragement, on repairing, redecorating and improving the house. The house was never conveyed to her, and the plaintiff later sought to get her out. It was held that although the defendant acquired no interest under a constructive trust and occupied the property under a licence revocable at will, the plaintiff was[9] by his conduct estopped from asserting his title to the house, and that equity would be achieved only by the plaintiff being ordered

1 *Gordon v Douce* [1983] 2 All ER 228, [1983] 1 WLR 563, CA. (1984) 47 MLR 735 (J. Dewar); *Stokes v Anderson* [1991] FCR 539, [1991] 1 FLR 391, CA.
2 [1972] 2 All ER 38, [1972] 1 WLR 518.
3 [1975] 3 All ER 768, [1975] 1 WLR 1338; (M & B); *Robinson v Robinson* (1976) 241 Estates Gazette 153. (Co-habitee entitled to one fifth.)
4 Cf *Tanner v Tanner*, infra.
5 [1972] 3 All ER 744, [1972] 1 WLR 1286; (M & B).
6 See also *Grant v Edwards* [1986] Ch 638, [1986] 2 All ER 426, CA; [1986] Conv 291 (J. Walburton).
7 [1975] 3 All ER 776, [1975] 1 WLR 1346.
8 [1979] 2 All ER 945, [1979] 1 WLR 431, CA.
9 Following *Inwards v Baker* [1965] 2 QB 29, [1965] 1 All ER 446, CA.

to execute a conveyance of the property to the defendant[10].

However, the court will by no means, invariably make an order in favour of a mistress plaintiff. In *Burns v Burns*[11], for example, a mistress used her earnings as a driving instructor to pay household expenses, including the rates and the telephone bills, and fixtures and fittings. But the court found no evidence of a common intention that she should acquire a beneficial interest in the house and so declined the order sought[12].

Rights of occupation[13]

It should be noted that the question of the right of a spouse to occupy the matrimonial home is a matter distinct from the question of the ownership of the home. It is true that a spouse, say W, who is a beneficial owner of the matrimonial home has a right of occupation arising from her proprietary interest. But a spouse who has no beneficial interest in the home does not necessarily lack a legal right of occupation. A spouse has a right to occupy the matrimonial home conferred both by common law and by statute (under the Matrimonial Homes Act 1983[14]). The right is in addition to any right that a spouse may have by virtue of having a beneficial interest in the property. Spouses' rights of occupation, in particular the statutory right (which is registrable as a Class F Land Charge), are matters that are properly dealt with in land law (or family law) rather than in the law relating to trusts.

Disputes over the matrimonial home in the context of divorce proceedings

Where divorce proceedings have been commenced, the court has jurisdiction under the Matrimonial Causes Act 1973[15] to make such order as it considers just with regard, inter alia, to the matrimonial home. In the exercise of this jurisdiction the court is under a duty to consider the relevant circumstances and bear in mind certain guidelines prescribed by statute[16]. It is in no way bound by the matter of title.

Continued relevance of principles of property law

Since disputes between H and W concerning the matrimonial home are most likely to occur in the context of a breakdown of the marriage, and since, in the event of a divorce, the court can disregard matters of title, have the

---

10 On the other hand, in *Horrocks v Forray* [1976] 1 All ER 737, [1976] 1 WLR 230, in which a man had bought a house for use by his mistress and their daughter, the mistress failed to secure any right to occupy the house after the man had been killed.
11 [1984] Ch 317, [1984] 1 All ER 244, CA; [1984] Conv 381 (S. Coneys); (1984) 47 MLR 341 (N. V. Lowe, A. Smith).
12 See also *Coombes v Smith* [1986] 1 WLR 808; *Layton v Martin* [1986] Fam Law 212.
13 [1984] Conv 198 (R. Cocks).
14 Section 1.
15 Section 24.
16 Section 25; [1981] Conv 404 (M. Hayes and G. Battersby); *Clutton v Clutton* [1991] 1 WLR 359.

principles discussed earlier with regard to the ownership of the home ceased to be of practical relevance? By no means. For example, (1) if H (or W) is adjudicated bankrupt it will be necessary to determine his (or her) interest in the matrimonial home: only that part which is his (or hers) will be available for the creditors; (2) if H or W dies leaving his or her interest in the home otherwise than to the other, it will be necessary to determine what that interest is; (3) if H and W separate but divorce proceedings are not commenced, then in the case of a dispute over, for example, whether the house should be sold, the principles governing trusts for sale will be those which determine the outcome; and (4) if property is owned by couples who are not married, it is the basic principles of property law that will be applied in the resolution of any dispute.

Thus although the jurisdiction conferred by the Matrimonial Causes Act 1973 may produce an outcome different from that obtainable by applying the principles of property law, these principles have by no means ceased to be of relevance.

4 Voluntary transfer

It might be thought that if A transferred property to B without receiving consideration from B, then the presumption was that A intended to make a gift of the property to B. This is certainly the position at the present day (formerly it was not[17]) with regard to transfers of realty and of leaseholds.

In the case of voluntary transfers of other forms of property, however, the law appears to be that A is presumed to have intended B to hold the property on trust for him[18]. The principle is the same where A pays money into a bank account in the name of B: there is a presumption that B holds the money on trust for A[19].

Similarly, if A transfers his own property into the name of himself and B (or into a bank account in the names of himself and B) the presumption is that A and B hold on trust for A.

The presumption of trust can be rebutted by evidence of A's intention derived from the circumstances. For example, in one case, the evidence showed that when A (a woman) paid money into a joint banking account in

---

17 Before 1926, if A transferred the fee simple in *land* to B, without consideration from B, B held the land on an implied trust for A. The Statute of Uses 1535 executed the trust, with the result that legal estate was transferred from the trustee B to the beneficiary A. So the fee simple ended back where it started, with A; and B got nothing. Thus if A wished B to receive the fee simple, the conveyance to B would employ one of the means devised to evade the effects of the Statute, eg land would be conveyed 'unto and to the use of' B. The effect of this would be to convey the legal fee simple to B free from any trust. Section 60(3) of the Law of Property Act 1925 now provides that on a voluntary conveyance of land (including, it seems, leaseholds) a resulting trust is not to be implied merely because the land is not conveyed, eg 'unto and to the use of B'. So, since the Act, if A transfers land (including leaseholds) merely 'to B', no implied trust for A arises. By repealing the Statute of Uses, the Act removed the need to use formulae such as 'unto and to the use of' B in order to avoid the effects of the Statute. But the removal of the presumption of a trust was achieved by s 60(3), not by the repeal of the Statute of Uses.

18 *Fowkes v Pascoe* (1875) 10 Ch App 343 at 348.

19 *Re Howes* (1905) 21 TLR 501.

the names of herself and her nephew, B, she intended B to have any money in the account when she died[20].

The presumption of a trust in the case of a voluntary transfer can lead to absurd results. For example, in *Re Vinogradoff*[1] A transferred some government stock into the name of herself and B, her granddaughter, who was four years old. A was not *in loco parentis* to B. It was held that A and B held the stock on trust for A. (A person under 18 cannot, as we shall see[2], be appointed a trustee, but they can, by operation of law, as here, become a trustee.) But why should A wish a girl of four to be a trustee of the stock for her? It would have been open to the court to have held that the circumstances rebutted the presumption of trust. It is submitted that the law would be more in accord with reality if, on a voluntary transfer of all property, the presumption was that no trust existed, the transferee taking absolutely, unless the transferor could rebut the presumption of gift by showing that a trust was in fact intended.

(a) Presumption of gift

Following the principles considered under the heading of purchase in the name of another, if A is the husband or father of B, or stands *in loco parentis* to him, then there is a presumption that the transfer was intended as a gift[3]. The presumption will be rebutted if A can show that he intended B to hold on trust for him[4].

(b) Improper motive

The principles are the same as in the case of purchase in the name of another. Thus if A makes a voluntary transfer of property to B and his motive is an improper one, he cannot claim that he intended B to hold on trust for him[5].

(c) Joint bank accounts

Suppose that A and B have a joint bank account. Sometimes the arrangement is that money may be withdrawn, and cheques paid, on the authority of one signature; sometimes both signatures are required. It is for A and B to decide how they wish to operate the account and to instruct the bank accordingly. But who does any money belong to if one, say A, dies? The principles relating to voluntary transfers and the presumption of gift may provide the solution[6]. For example, if a husband, H, pays money into a bank account opened in the name of himself and his wife, W, and H dies, because of the presumption of gift, the money will belong to W[7], unless the presumption is rebutted (as

20 *Young v Sealey* [1949] Ch 278, [1949] 1 All ER 92.
1   [1935] WN 68.
2   Chap 13.
3   *Re Figgis* [1969] 1 Ch 123, [1968] 1 All ER 999.
4   *Hoddinott v Hoddinott* [1949] 2 KB 406.
5   *Chettiar v Chettiar* [1962] AC 294, [1962] 1 All ER 494.
6   See M. C. Cullity (1969) 85 LQR 530.
7   *Re Figgis* [1969] 1 Ch 123, [1968] 1 All ER 999.

by showing that the account had been opened in joint names as a matter of convenience, it being easier for W than for H to get to the bank[8]) in which case the money will belong to H's estate[9]. Alternatively, the solution may take the form of a finding by the court that the parties intended the money in the account to be held by them as joint tenants, with the result that on the death of one party, the sum standing in the account vests solely in the survivor[10].

(d) Loan

We have seen that if A makes a voluntary transfer, say of £100, to B, the transaction may be construed as a gift or the creation of a trust. There is a third possibility. A may have intended neither a gift nor a trust, but a loan. It might seem that if a loan was intended the result would be the same as if a trust had been created—A could demand back the money. If B is solvent, this is so. But if B is insolvent the difference is crucial. If a trust is shown to have been created, B's trustee in bankruptcy will pass £100[11] to A. If a loan was made, A will rank *pari passu* with B's creditors and take whatever percentage B's trustee in bankruptcy distributes.

Whether a voluntary transfer is construed as a gift, a trust or a loan depends on the circumstances, taking into account the presumptions of gift. As between a gift and a loan, the presumption is that a loan was intended[12].

(e) Formalities

In Chapter 4 we saw that s 53(1)(b) of the Law of Property Act 1925 requires a declaration of trust of land to be evidenced in writing. In this chapter we have met many situations in which property was held on a resulting trust for the settlor, but there was no evidence in writing of a declaration of trust. The reason why s 53(1)(b) need not be complied with is that s 53(2) expressly provides that s 53 does not effect the operation of implied or resulting trusts[13].

(f) Presumption of 'advancement'

We have said (in the context of both purchase in the name of another and of voluntary transfer) that where A is regarded by equity as being under an obligation to provide for B (eg where A is the father of B), there is apresumption of a gift to B. The legal name for this presumption is a 'presumption of advancement'. The word 'advancement' might seem to imply that there was a requirement that B should, by the purchase or transfer, in some way be advanced in life (the meaning attached to the word in the term

---

8   *Marshal v Crutwell* (1875) LR 20 Eq 328.
9   *Re Bishop* [1965] Ch 450, [1965] 1 All ER 249.
10 Or whatever money B has up to this amount.
11 *Seldon v Davidson* [1968] 2 All ER 755, [1968] 1 WLR 1083. See pp 49–50, supra.
12 See *Sekhon v Alissa* [1989] 2 FLR 94, [1990] Conv 213 (G. Kodilinye).
13 See *Hodgson v Marks* [1971] Ch 892, [1970] 3 All ER 513.

'power of advancement'[14]). The word advancement carries no such meaning here and the nature of the presumption is better indicated, it is submitted, by the term 'presumption of gift'.

5 Mutual wills[15]

The implied trusts which have been considered so far have been resulting trusts. The final form of implied trust to be considered, a trust arising from the making of 'mutual wills', is not a resulting trust. The property under this form of trust is held on trust, not for the settlor, but for a third party.

If two people execute wills in which they each leave certain of their property in identical ways, eg to the other for life with remainder to a third person, then they are said to make 'mutual wills'. The same result may be achieved when (in practice, a rare event) two people execute a joint will, ie a single document which each signs[16].

How a trust may arise from the execution of mutual wills can be explained by an example.

Let us suppose that a husband, H, and his wife, W, each own property. They have an unmarried daughter, D, for whom they wish to provide when they are both dead. H and W therefore make an agreement by which H undertakes that in his will he will leave his £10,000 in ICI shares to W for her life, with remainder to D. W undertakes that in her will she will leave certain government stocks to H for life, with remainder to D. H dies. It is found that in his will he has left the shares as agreed. At that moment a trust comes into existence, under which W is obligated to carry out her side of the agreement, ie to leave the stocks on her death to D. Later she revokes her will and makes a fresh one in which she leaves the stocks to Z. W dies. The gift of the stocks to Z is ineffective: W's executor holds the stocks on trust for D[17].

The following matters now call for attention.

(a) Intention

The basis of the trust is the implied promise of H and W, when they agree to make mutual wills, that if one party observes the agreement, so will the other. Thus, in our example, when H dies without having departed from the arrangements, he dies with the implied promise of W that she will leave her will in the form agreed. But for a trust of this kind to come into existence there must be evidence of an intention by the parties that the survivor should be bound; and the fact that the two wills are made simultaneously and to the same effect, although a relevant circumstance, is not by itself sufficient proof of an agreement between the parties that the survivor should not depart from the relevant terms of his or her will: other evidence must be adduced to

14   See Chap 17.
15   See R. Burgess (1970) 3 Conv (NS) 230; (1989) 105 LQR 534 (C. E. F. Rickett).
16   *Dufour v Pereira* (1769) 1 Dick 419.
17   *Re Green* [1951] Ch 148, [1950] 2 All ER 913.

show the existence of an agreement to be bound by the arrangement[18]. Sometimes the intention that the survivor should be bound is stated expressly: for example in *Re Hagger*[19] H and W executed a joint will in which it was agreed that neither party should revoke or alter the will without the consent of the other.

(b) When the trust arises

The trust does not come into existence at the time of the agreement (or at the time of the execution of the mutual wills), but when the first party to the agreement dies, having left the property concerned in the way specified in the agreement.

(c) Conditions to be satisfied

From what has been said, it will be seen that for a trust under this head to come into existence three conditions must thus be satisfied:

1. There must be an agreement between the parties that they will leave property in their wills in a certain way, with an intention that the survivor should be bound by the arrangement.

2. They must execute wills leaving property in the way agreed.

3. On the death of the first to die, his or her will must leave the property in the way agreed (ie he or she must not have departed from the agreement by altering or revoking his or her will).

(d) Revocation

Since the trust does not come into existence until one of the parties dies, either party may withdraw from the agreement until that time. Thus if either party alters his will (ie with regard to the mutually agreed part), or revokes his will, while the other is still alive, the arrangement is terminated and no trust under this head can arise[20]. The arrangement may also be terminated by agreement between the parties. But once one party has died leaving a will in the agreed form, the other party cannot withdraw from the arrangement (even, it seems[1], if they renounce any benefit under the will of the party who has died).

---

18   *Re Oldham* [1925] Ch 75; *Gray v Perpetual Trustee Co Ltd* [1928] AC 391; *Re Cleaver* [1981] 2 All ER 1018, [1981] 1 WLR 939; (M & B); [1982] Conv 228 (K. Hodkinson).
19   [1930] 2 Ch 190.
20   *Stone v Hoskins* [1905] P 194.
 1   *Re Hagger* [1930] 2 Ch 190 at 195.

(e) Co-ownership

It may be that H and W are co-owners of their home, and that they each agree to leave their interest in the house to the other for life with remainder to D. If H and W are beneficial tenants in common then on H's death his share in the house will pass under his will to W for life with remainder to D. From H's death, W will hold *her* share in the house on trust to leave it in her will to D[2]. If H and W are beneficial joint tenants, on H's death his interest will vest in W absolutely, by virtue of the right of survivorship. W will then hold the house on trust to leave it to D in her will: in effect she will hold it on trust for herself for life with remainder to D[3].

(f) No lapse

Suppose that H and W agree to make mutual wills, each leaving certain of their property to the other for life, with remainder to D. H dies, leaving his will in the agreed form. D then dies. Later W dies, leaving the property concerned, as agreed, to D. It is a rule of the law of succession that if a testator leaves property in his will to a beneficiary, and the beneficiary dies before the testator, then the gift lapses and the property falls into the residue of the testator's estate[4]. From this it might be thought that (D having died before W) the gift to D would lapse and the property fall into the residue of W's estate. But this is not so. The reason is that D acquired her interest not at the time of W's death but when the trust came into existence, namely, at H's death. Thus from H's death D has a vested interest (albeit in remainder) in the property. Therefore, when D dies, this vested interest forms part of her estate and passes under her will or intestacy. Let us suppose that she dies testate leaving everything to her husband E. In this case, from D's death, W will hold the property on trust for herself for life, with remainder to E. (If in her will W leaves the property to, say, X, the gift is ineffective: her executor must pass the property to E[5].)

(g) Forms of disposition

We have envisaged H and W giving each other a life interest with remainder to D. This is the most common form of disposition giving rise to the creation of a trust under the heading of mutual wills. Alternatively, it may be that the

---

2 H and W will have held the legal estate as joint tenants on trust for sale for themselves as beneficial tenants in common. On H's death W will hold the legal estate on trust for herself for life with remainder to D. If the house is to be sold (to P), a second trustee (X) will have to be appointed. If P obtains a receipt signed by W and X, D's equitable interest is overreached, and the trustees will hold the purchase money on trust for W for life with remainder to D.
3 The legal estate will have been held by H and W as joint tenants on trust for sale for themselves as beneficial joint tenants. On H's death W will hold the legal estate on trust for sale for herself with remainder to D. Assuming that no memorandum of severance had been entered in the title deeds, if W sells the house to P, P will take the legal title free of D's equitable interest. (Law of Property (Joint Tenants) Act 1964.) W will hold the purchase money on trust for herself for life with remainder to D.
4 See Chap 2, p 12.
5 *Re Hagger* [1930] 2 Ch 190; (M & B).

mutual wills take the form of a bequest of property by H to W, subject to the promise of W to leave it on her death to X, and a bequest by W to H, subject to the promise of H to leave it on his death to Y. This was the form taken by the mutual wills in *Re Green*[6].

(h) Property subject to the trust

We envisaged H and W each leaving specified assets (H's shares and W's stocks) in mutual wills. Where this is the position there can be no uncertainty as to what property is subject to the trust. But what if H and W agree to leave *all* their property to the other, with remainder to D? If H dies leaving all his property to W, is W bound from that moment to hold all H's property and all her own on trust to leave it to D in her will?—with the result that she cannot dispose of any of it during her lifetime? Further, would she be bound to hold any property she acquired subsequently to H's death on the same trust? The position is uncertain[7]. In *Re Oldham*[8], Astbury J declined in these circumstances to find that the survivor was bound by any trust, on the ground that the uncertainty as to what would be subject to the trust precluded any intention that the arrangement should be irrevocable. In *Re Hagger*[9], on the other hand, the fact that the mutual wills bound all the properties of the parties was not held to be a bar to a trust arising.

(i) Parties other than spouses

We have envisaged mutual wills being made by a husband and wife, with their child as the ultimate beneficiary. The parties to mutual wills most commonly are husband and wife, but they do not have to bear this relationship[10]; nor need the ultimate beneficiary be a child of the parties.

(j) Classification of trusts arising under mutual wills

We have considered trusts arising as a result of the making of mutual wills under the head of 'Implied trusts'. It should be mentioned that trusts arising from the making of mutual wills are considered by some to be a species of constructive trust. For example, in *Re Cleaver*[11] Nourse J said '. . . a court of equity will not permit a person to whom property is transferred by way of gift, but on the faith of an agreement or clear understanding that it is to be dealt with in a particular way for the benefit of a third person, to deal with that property inconsistently with that agreement or understanding. If he attempts to do so after having received the benefit of the gift equity will intervene by imposing a constructive trust on the property which is the subject matter of the agreement or understanding'. It is suggested, however, that

---

6   [1951] Ch 148, [1950] 2 All ER 913.
7   See Snell, *Principles of Equity* (28th edn), p 191.
8   [1925] Ch 75.
9   [1930] 2 Ch 190; (M & B).
10 *Walpole v Orford* (1797) 3 Ves 402.
11 [1981] 1 WLR 939 at 947.

since a constructive trust is generally regarded as one which is imposed by equity on a certain party irrespective of his (or anybody else's), intention, a trust arising from mutual wills, which does arise from the parties' intention, is best placed in the category of implied trusts.

Chapter 11

Trusts and powers[1]

Introduction

In this chapter we compare trusts and powers. What kind of powers are we speaking of when making this comparison? We shall meet powers at many points in this book. For example, we shall be considering trustees' powers of investment[2], their power to make advancements of capital[3]; their power to maintain infant beneficiaries out of income from trust property[3] and their power to appoint new trustees[4]. And a student of land law will have learned of the powers of a tenant for life (who is in the position of a trustee with regard to the legal estate in the settled land) to sell the settled land, to grant leases, to mortgage the land and so on; and of the powers of trustees of a trust for sale, including the statutory power to postpone sale. These are all 'powers'. But none of them is the kind of power which it is pertinent to compare with a trust. All the powers we have mentioned are powers which assist the administration of a trust, and they are for this reason classified as *administrative* powers. Some are conferred by statute, some may be conferred expressly by the settlor. Such powers are (or may be), ancillary to a trust: but there is nothing to 'compare' between such powers and a trust—they are part and parcel of the operation of a trust. And, we may mention here (and as will be stated again[5]) in relation to such powers trustees are in fiduciary position: they are under a duty to exercise the power in a proper manner, according to the character of the power concerned.

When we compare a trust and a power, the power to which we refer is a power to appoint property: a power of appointment. For example, if T dies leaving certain property among such of his children, A, B and C as his widow W should appoint, then here W has a power of appointment: she has a power to decide which child or children should (and in what shares they should) get the property. Such a power is not concerned with mere matters of administration: it is a power to decide who gets the property concerned.

The terminology relating to powers of appointment should be noted. In the example above, the testator is the *donor* of the power, the widow is the *donee* of the power, and the children are the *objects* of the power. If the widow exercises the power she becomes the *appointor*, and the child (or children) in whose favour the power is exercised becomes the *appointee* (or

---

1 *Farewell on Powers* (3rd edn, 1916); D. M. Maclean, *Trusts and Powers*, (1989).
2 See Chap 15.
3 See Chap 17.
4 See Chap 13.
5 See Chap 20.

appointees). A power may be made exercisable *inter vivos* (eg by deed), or by will, or by either method. If a donee of a power dies without exercising the power, the gift vests in the *persons entitled in default of appointment*. Who these persons are will depend on the terms of the gift. If the donor specifies who are to take in default of appointment, then these people take. If there is no gift over in default of appointment, then in some circumstances the court may, exceptionally, infer an intention by the donor that in default of appointment the property should be distributed among the objects of the class equally[6]. Generally this intention has been found where the objects consist of a class of relatives, eg children, or nephews and nieces. It would seem that no such intention could be inferred where the objects consisted of a class that is not ascertainable. In the absence of a gift over in default if appointment, express or implied, the property reverts to the settlor or his estate.

A power may be made exercisable among specified individuals, or among a specified class (who, in either case, may include the donee of the power). In these cases the power is termed a *special* power. Or a power can be made exercisable in favour of anyone in the world, in which case, it is termed a *general* power. The donee of a general power can exercise it in his own favour. (Thus, to confer a general power, exercisable by deed, comes close to making an outright gift[7].) Or a power may be made exercisable in favour of anyone in the world except for one or more specified persons (eg the donee[8]), or except for a class of persons. A power of this kind is termed a *hybrid*, or *intermediate* power[9].

Suppose that a settlor leaves property to his widow for life, with remainder to such of his sons, A, B and C, as the widow should appoint, with a gift over in default of appointment to Z. Who holds the legal title to the property? In such a situation it would be normal for the settlor to appoint trustees to hold the legal title. They would hold the property on trust for W for life, and on trust to pass the property to whichever son or sons (if any) the widow appointed, and if no appointment was made, on trust for Z. Thus a power of appointment may, and in fact most commonly does, exist within the framework of a trust. (And, indeed, if the property subject to the power is land, since the end of 1925, the power can only exist under a trust[10].) But the actual disposition in favour of A, B and C is a power of appointment not a trust; A, B and C are objects of a power, not beneficiaries under a trust; W is a donee of a power, not a trustee. (If W made an appointment in favour of say, A, at that point A would become a beneficiary, with an absolute interest in remainder, and the trustees would hold the property concerned on trust for him accordingly.)

Further, it sometimes happens that a power of appointment is conferred on the trustees of a settlement. For example, a testator may leave property to T_1 and T_2 on trust for W for life with remainder to such of the testator's

---

6 We shall see later that where this intention is found to exist, the character of the disposition may become transmogrified. See p 220 et seq, post.

7 But the two forms of disposition are not identical, eg if the donee of such a power dies without making an appointment, the property passes not under his will or intestacy but to the person entitled in default of appointment.

8 *Re Park* [1932] 1 Ch 580.

9 *Re Hay's Settlement Trusts* [1981] 3 All ER 786, [1982] 1 WLR 202; [1982] Conv 432 (A. Grubb).

10 LPA 1925, s 1(7): 'Every power of appointment over ... land ... operates only in equity'.

sons, A, B and C, as the trustees should appoint, with a gift over in default of appointment to Z. In their capacity as holders of the legal title to the property, T_1 and T_2 are trustees; and in respect of W's life interest, and the gift over to Z, T_1 and T_2 are trustees. But with regard to the disposition in favour of A, B and C, T_1 and T_2 are donees of a power of appointment.

What resemblance, it might be asked, can there be between the position where W has a power of appointment, such as that set out above, and that where a testator leaves property to trustees on trust for his children A, B and C, the property being divided equally between them? The answer is that such a trust bears no resemblance to a power of appointment. But if the testator had left the property to trustees on trust for such of his children, A, B and C as the trustees should at their discretion decide, ie under a *discretionary* trust, then it will be seen at once that a resemblance does exist. In each case, no child can be certain of obtaining any trust property: who gets the property depends on someone making a decision. Under a power of appointment the decision rests with the person on whom the power is conferred, ie the donee of the power; under a discretionary trust, the decision rests with the trustees.

A power of appointment may be conferred on more than one person. So it may be that a testator's children know that the decision as to which of them is to become entitled to their father's property rests with their two uncles X and Y. Why does it matter to the children whether they are beneficiaries under a discretionary trust of which X and Y are the trustees, or objects of a power of appointment, of which X and Y are the donees? What, in short, are the differences between a discretionary trust and a power of appointment? There are ten differences, and these are set out below.

Differences between trusts and powers of appointment

1 Intention

The first difference we may note concerns the intention which underlies each form of disposition. In the case of a discretionary trust the purpose of the disposition is the benefit of the beneficiaries. Where the settlor confers a discretion to allocate property to such members of a class as the person exercising the discretion 'sees fit', the intention is that the discretion should be exercised in the potential beneficiaries' interests, ie as he 'sees fit' *in the best interests of the beneficiaries*; not as he 'sees fit' according to his own personal whims or preferences—a liking for people with freckles or a dislike of people who empty their car ashtrays in the gutter. Further, in the case of a discretionary trust it is generally the intention that, come what may, the beneficiaries should benefit and that no one else should do so. (We say 'generally' because under a discretionary trust it is possible that a settlor may provide that if no distribution has occurred within, say, two years[11], the property is to pass to, eg, his residual estate[11].)

In the case of a power of appointment, on the other hand, neither of the above two intentions exist. The focus is not on the benefit of the objects but on the freedom of choice of the donee of the power. The absence of an

---

11   *Re Beatty, Hinves v Brooke* [1990] 1 WLR 1503.

intention that the interests of the objects (or one or more of them) are paramount, is indicated by the fact that part and parcel of the standard form of a power of appointment is an express gift over in default of appointment to a specified donee or donees. Hence the existence of a gift over in default of appointment is a strong, indeed, in the overwhelming majority of cases a conclusive[12], pointer to an intention that the disposition takes the form of the grant of a power of appointment[13].

2 Failure to exercise

Next, we may ask, what happens if trustees fail to exercise their discretion, or a donee of a power of appointment fails to make an appointment? In the case of a power, the answer follows from what was said above. If a testator leaves property to such of his sons A, B and C as his widow, W, should appoint, with a gift over in default of appointment to Z, then the sons can do nothing if W makes no appointment[14]. The sons may find that W leaves the power unexercised for 50 years and that it is only on her death that, in her will, the power is exercised, in favour of, say A. In the meantime, the sons can do nothing about W's non-exercise of the power. Or it may be that on W's death the will is found to be silent as to the exercise of the power, which thus remains unexercised by W. In this case the property will pass to the person entitled in default, or if there is no such person named, it will (unless exceptionally, as we shall see later[15], the court finds an implied gift over to the members of the class equally) revert to the testator's estate and pass to his residuary legatee or devisee; or, if there was no gift of residue, to the person entitled under the testator's intestacy.

In the case of a discretionary trust, on the other hand, the trustees are under a duty to consider whether their discretion should be exercised and, if so, in what way[16]. If the trustees fail in this duty the beneficiaries may seek the aid of the court. The court will take whatever course seems appropriate, eg the court may appoint fresh trustees or it may, applying the maxim 'equality is equity', order that the property should be divided equally[17], or it may even itself direct how the property is to be distributed[18].

Since trustees of a discretionary trust are under a duty to consider in what way the discretion should be exercised, if trustees of a discretionary trust exercise the discretion without giving their mind to the matter, as by acting without a proper understanding of what is involved, at the direction of some other person, for example the settlor, or his solicitor, then the exercise of the discretion is void[19].

---

12 *Re Mills* [1930] 1 Ch 654.
13 The position is no different if the gift in default is for some reason void. *Re Sprague, Miley v Cape* (1880) 43 LT 236.
14 *Whishaw v Stephens* [1970] AC 508 at 525, [1968] 3 All ER 785 at 793.
15 See post.
16 *Re Locker's Settlement* [1978] 1 All ER 216, [1977] 1 WLR 1323; *Re Vestey v IRC (No 2)* [1979] Ch 198, [1979] 2 All ER 225; *Re Hay's Settlement Trusts* [1981] 3 All ER 786, [1982] 1 WLR 202; (M & B).
17 *Re Douglas* (1887) 35 Ch D 472, 485.
18 *Mosely v Mosely* (1673) Cas temp Finch 53; *McPhail v Doulton* [1971] AC 424, [1970] 2 All ER 228.
19 *Turner v Turner* [1984] Ch 100, [1983] 2 All ER 745.

3 Interests in the property

Beneficiaries under a discretionary trust have an interest in the trust property. Whether their interest is vested, or contingent, or vested but liable to divesting, or is of some other nature, is debatable. But, it is submitted, and will be argued later[20], they do have an interest of some kind. The objects of a power on the other hand, have no interest whatsoever in the property subject to the power. Those entitled in default of appointment have a vested interest, but since they will lose the interest in the event of the power being exercised, they have an interest that is *vested but liable to defeasance*[1] (or, *vested but liable to divesting*).

4 Death during a testator's lifetime of donees of a power and of trustees

If T in his will confers on A a power to appoint among a specified class, with a gift over in default of appointment to Z, and A dies before T, then the conferment of the power lapses, and on T's death the property concerned passes to Z[2]. On the other hand, if T had left property to A on trust for the specified class, and A had predeceased T, then, since equity does not want for a trustee, the trust will not fail and, if necessary, the court will appoint a trustee in place of A[3].

5 Death of one of two donees, and death of one of two trustees

If S confers a power of appointment on two persons, and one dies then, unless the settlor has indicated an intention to the contrary[4] (eg by the power being conferred on each successive holder of the position of donee[5]), the power is not exercisable by the survivor, and the gift over takes effect[6]. On the other hand, if two trustees hold property on a discretionary trust and one dies, the survivor continues to be able to exercise the discretion.

6 Formalities

When a donor confers a power of appointment on a donee, it is customary for the donor to stipulate in what way the power may be exercised, eg that the power may be exercised by deed, or by will, or by either method. If a particular method is stipulated, an exercise of the power by any other method is invalid. Thus if A confers a power on B which is exercisable by deed, and B dies without having exercised the power by deed during his lifetime, but his will contains an appointment, the appointment is void and the property goes to the person entitled in default.

It has never been the practice, in the case of a discretionary trust, for the

20 See Chap 12.
1   *Re Brooks' Settlement Trusts* [1939] Ch 993 at 997.
2   *Brown v Higgs* (1803) 8 Ves 561 at 570; *Down v Worrall* (1833) 1 My & K 561.
3   *Brown v Higgs*, ante.
4   *Re Beesty's Will Trusts* [1966] Ch 223, [1964] 3 All ER 82.
5   *Re Wills' Trust Deeds* [1964] Ch 219, [1963] 1 All ER 390.
6   Halsbury (4th edn) Vol 30, Chap 422.

decision to be required to be exercised by the execution of particular formality, eg by the execution of a deed.

Thus a power of appointment is exercised when the donee or donees comply with the formality stipulated by the donor; a discretion is exercised by the making of a mental decision. (There may, of course, be evidence of the decision in the shape of a minute of the trustees' meeting and the transfer of the property to the beneficiary will have to comply with any formality that is relevant, eg the registration of the transfer of the title to registered land.)

In the case of the exercise of both a power of appointment and a discretion, if the settlor stipulates that the consents of certain persons are required then these consents must be obtained for the exercise to be valid.

7 Perpetuities

Within the rule against perpetuities, the rules relating to powers of appointment differ from those which relate to the interests of a beneficiary under a discretionary trust.

8 Revocation

A power of appointment (ie the exercise of the power) may be revocable. For example, suppose that in his will T leaves certain property to his widow W for life with remainder to such of their sons, A, B and C as she should by will appoint, with a gift over to Z, and the exercise of the power is made revocable. After T's death W makes an appointment by deed in favour of A. Later in her life W decides that B will be more in need of the property on her death than A. Since the power is revocable, W may (by deed) revoke the appointment in favour of A and make a fresh appointment in favour of B. If T had made the power irrevocable, or, it seems, if there is no express or implied indication as to whether the power was or was not intended to be revocable, then the power could not have been revoked, and the appointment in favour of A, once made, would have stood.

Where a power of appointment is made revocable, it can only be revoked prior to an appointment being made. For example, if in his will T had left property to such of his sons as W should by deed or will appoint (with no life interest to W), with a gift over to Z, and W had made an appointment in favour of A, then A would acquire a vested title to the property and, the property having become A's, the appointment could not be revoked.

In the case of a discretionary trust, on the other hand, once a discretion has been exercised, in no circumstances can it be revoked. Normally the exercise of the discretion will give the beneficiary an interest which is vested in possession, with the result that he will be able to require the property to be passed to him. But even if the exercise of the discretion gives him only an interest in remainder (eg after the death of a prior life interest), once the discretion is exercised the beneficiary acquires a vested interest which cannot be taken from him.

9 Certainty

When dealing, in Chapter 4, with the conditions for a valid express private trust to exist, we saw that in the case of a discretionary trust, the rule with regard to certainty of objects was that, for the trust to be valid, it must be possible to postulate of any given person that he is or he is not a member of the class. If it is not possible so to do, then the trust is void for uncertainty. This test for discretionary trusts was established by the House of Lords in *McPhail v Doulton*[7]. Before this case, for a discretionary trust to have certainty of objects, the beneficiaries of the trust had to be ascertained or capable of ascertainment.

In the case of powers of appointment, in order to be certain, the rule has for long been that it must be possible to say 'with certainty whether any given individual is or is not a member of the class and [the power of appointment] does not fail simply because it is impossible to ascertain every member of the class'[8]. This rule was applied in *Re Gestetner's Settlement*[9] and in *Re Wootton's Will Trusts*[10] and confirmed by the House of Lords in *Re Gulbenkian's Settlement Trusts*[11]. The test, as was noted in Chapter 4, is the same as that which, since *McPhail v Doulton*[12], applies in the case of discretionary trusts. The effect of the decision in *McPhail v Doulton*[12] was, therefore, the application to discretionary trusts of the rule as to certainty which had hitherto applied to powers of appointment.

The fact that before *McPhail v Doulton*[12] the rules as to certainty were different for trusts and for powers had the result that one form of wording might be valid if the disposition which the words created was a power, but void if it was a trust. For example, a disposition for the benefit, inter alia, of 'dependants' was void in *Re Saxone Shoe Co's Trust Deed*[13] since the disposition was construed as being a trust; but a disposition for the benefit of 'dependants' in *Re Sayer Trust*[14] was valid, since the disposition was construed as being a power of appointment. Many dispositions which were valid since they took the form of powers of appointment (eg for the benefit of the settlor's 'friends' in *Re Coates' Trusts*[15]) would almost certainly have been void if the disposition had taken the form of a trust.

The outcome of a case involving the issue of certainty therefore depended, before the decision in *McPhail v Doulton*[16], on whether the disposition was construed as creating a trust or a power. In seeking to determine whether a trust or a power had been created, the courts looked to see whether there was an obligation to make a distribution of the property (whether the disposition was mandatory) or whether no such obligation existed. If the

7   [1971] AC 424, [1970] 2 All ER 228; (M & B). See p 27.
8   Per Lord Wilberforce in *McPhail v Doulton* [1971] AC 424 at 450.
9   [1953] Ch 672, [1953] 1 All ER 1150.
10 [1968] 2 All ER 618, [1968] 1 WLR 681.
11 [1970] AC 508, [1968] 3 All ER 785, sub nom *Whishaw v Stephens*. In *Re Gibbard* [1966] 1 All ER 273, [1967] 1 WLR 42. Plowman J held that a power of appointment was valid for certainty if it could be shown that any *particular* claimant came within the description. This, wider test, was rejected by the House of Lords in *Re Gulbenkian's Settlement* [1970] AC 508, [1968] 3 All ER 785.
12 [1971] AC 424, [1970] 2 All ER 228.
13 [1962] 2 All ER 904, [1962] 1 WLR 943.
14 [1957] Ch 423, [1956] 3 All ER 600.
15 [1959] 2 All ER 47n, [1959] 1 WLR 375.
16 [1971] AC 424, [1970] 2 All ER 228.

former was the case, a trust existed; if the latter, a power. For example, in *McPhail v Doulton*[17] the House of Lords held that the word 'shall' in the phrase '... shall apply the net income of the trust fund in making at their absolute discretion grants to or for the benefit of ...' was mandatory, and so resulted in the creation of a trust. (It was therefore only because the House of Lords changed the rule as to certainty for discretionary trusts that the trust was subsequently held to be valid.)

So, before *McPhail v Doulton*[17] abolished the distinction between trusts and powers as regards the test of certainty, the validity of a disposition in a settlement could hinge on the drafter's choice of a single word, eg whether the word 'shall' or 'may' was used. Thus whether a trust or a power was construed might depend on 'mere straws in the wind'[18]. Such a position was 'absurd and embarrassing'[19] and the decision in *McPhail v Doulton*[20] has generally been welcomed.

Finally under the head of certainty we may note that notwithstanding the decision in *McPhail v Doulton* one difference between trusts and powers in the sphere of certainty remains: when dealing (in Chapter 4) with certainty we saw that a trust might be void due to the class of beneficiaries being so wide as to render the trust 'administratively unworkable'. No such factor can affect the validity of a power of appointment, since a power of appointment can be made exercisable in favour of the whole world.

10 Release

We have seen that if T confers a power on W to appoint among A, B and C, with a gift over to Z, W is under no obligation to exercise the power. If she dies without exercising the power, the property will go to Z. Thus W has it in her power to give Z the property on her death. In order to avoid the need for her to live out her life before attaining this end the law permits W to *release* the power. If a donee releases a power, any gift over thereupon takes effect. If there is no gift over, the property reverts to the testator's estate. In the above example, if W releases the power, Z immediately becomes entitled to the property.

There is only one situation in which a power of appointment cannot be released: this is when the power is conferred on trustees *virtute officii*[1] (ie in their capacity as trustees of the trust under which the property concerned is held) and there is nothing in the settlement authorising them to release the power. If there is, they may do so[2].

Trustees cannot, of course, 'release' their trust. (Trustees can retire, but this is a different matter[3].)

17 Ibid.
18 Per Harman LJ in *Re Baden's Deed Trusts* [1969] 2 Ch 388, [1969] 1 All ER 1016, 1020.
19 Per Harman LJ, ibid at p 1019.
20 [1971] AC 424, [1970] 2 All ER 228.
 1 *Re Wills' Trust Deeds* [1964] Ch 219, 236.
 2 *Muir v IRC* [1966] 3 All ER 38, [1966] 1 WLR 1269.
 3 See Chap 13.

Fiduciary powers

Suppose that a testator leaves property to trustees on trust for his widow, W, for life with remainder to such of their sons, A, B and C as W should appoint. The disposition in favour of A, B and C is clearly a power of appointment. But suppose that there was no gift over, and the wording was unclear as to whether T intended to create a power of appointment in favour of A, B and C, or a trust for A, B and C, as, for example, where property is left to W for her life and on her death 'on trust for such of my sons, A, B and C as my widow at her absolute discretion may appoint'. Has a trust or a power been created? The word 'trust' points to a trust; the word 'appoint' towards a power. And sometimes the difficulty of deciding whether a trust or a power has been created is compounded by the fact that the decision falls to be made by the settlor's trustees, when what otherwise would appear to be a power assumes the flavour of a trust. Another pointer towards an intention to create a trust can be the existence of a gift over in default of appointment to the members of the class of objects equally. In such a situation it may happen that the question as to whether the disposition is a trust or a power is never raised. A decision may be made in favour of A, and there the matter ends. But if no decision is made (eg if, in the above example, the widow dies without making any decision) then whether a trust or a power has been created becomes pertinent: if the disposition was a trust, the property will be divided between A, B and C. If it was a power, the property will revert to the settlor's estate.

Further, under the law prior to *McPhail v Doulton*[4], if the class of beneficiaries was not ascertainable (eg if the gift had been for A, B and C and their dependants) then the question as to whether a trust or a power existed was crucial: if there was a power, the disposition was valid; if there was a trust it was void. In the latter case, if the settlement was created by will, the property would fall into residue; or if the property was itself residue, it would pass to the testator's next of kin. (It is for this reason that in cases prior to *McPhail v Doulton* we find the residuary legatees or next of kin claiming that the disposition was a trust not a power[5].)

Where the wording of a settlement is unclear as to whether a trust or a power is intended, the courts may be called upon to determine the matter. In the cases in this field, the courts have described some dispositions, not as a 'trust' or a 'power', but as a 'trust power', or a 'power in the nature of a trust', or a 'power coupled with a duty', or a 'power imperative', or a 'fiduciary power', or a 'fiduciary power of appointment', or a 'power of a fiduciary character'. A fiduciary power, as we shall call this creature, is a disposition which at first sight has the appearances of being a power of appointment (perhaps because of the use of the word 'appoint' or 'appointment') but which the court construes as imposing a duty. The courts will hold that a disposition has this character where it finds that, whilst the disposition may have the outward appearances of a power, it is the settlor's intention that the persons in the class he has specified should get the property concerned or, at the least, that the person authorised to make the decision is under a *duty* to turn his mind to the question of the exercise of the discretion:

4   [1971] AC 424, [1970] 2 All ER 228.
5   See, eg *Re Leek* [1969] 1 Ch 563, [1968] 1 All ER 793.

he is not, as is the donee of a power of appointment, entitled to yawn and dismiss the whole matter from his mind. Thus a fiduciary power is a wolf in sheep's clothing. At first sight it may have the sheepish characteristics of a power; but beneath the sheep's clothing lie the teeth of a trust.

Since fiduciary powers partake of the nature of a trust they are subject to the rules of law relating to trusts. As Lord Eldon said in *Brown v Higgs*[6], 'But there are not only a mere trust and a mere power, but there is also known to this Court a power, which the party, to whom it is given, is intrusted and required to execute; and with regard to that species of power the Court consider it as partaking so much of the nature and qualities of a trust, that if the person, who has that duty imposed upon him, does not discharge it, the Court will, to a certain extent, discharge the duty in his room and place ...'. He went on to say[7] that if the power is a fiduciary power, the donee of the power 'is a trustee for the exercise of the power, and not as having a discretion whether he will exercise it or not; and the Court adopts the principle as to trusts; and will not permit his negligence, accident, or other circumstances, to disappoint the interests of those for whose benefit he is called upon to execute it'.

Thus, under a fiduciary power the donee of the power cannot release the power[8]. If the donee of a fiduciary power declines to exercise the power, the court may intervene[9]. And, as seen above, when the rules relating to certainty were different for discretionary trusts and for powers, dispositions which were construed as being fiduciary powers had, to be valid, to comply with the narrower, more stringent, test for discretionary trusts.

An example of a gift that was held to constitute a fiduciary power is provided by *Burrough v Philcox*[10] (in 1840) in which a testator, after giving life interests to his two children, directed that the survivor of the two children should have power to dispose by will of the property 'amongst my nephews and nieces or their children, either all to one of them or to as many of them as my surviving child shall think proper'. The surviving child died without having made any selection. It was held that 'when there appears a general intention in favour of a class, and a particular intention in favour of individuals of a class to be selected by another person, and the particular intention fails, from that selection not being made, the Court will carry into effect the general intention in favour of the class'[11]. The intention referred to being held to be present, the court held that the disposition constituted a gift to the 'nephews and nieces, and their children, subject to the selection and distribution of the survivor of the son and daughter; and that they all constitute the class to take all the property as to which no such selection and distribution has been made'[12]. Thus where a disposition appears to create a power of appointment, but the court finds an intention that the members of a class are intended, come what may, to benefit, then one course (ie, as in *Burrough v Philcox*) has been to construe the disposition as a gift *to* the class, subject to the power of selection. Where this course is adopted each member

---

6 (1803) 8 Ves 561 at 570.
7 At 574.
8 *Re Wills' Trust Deeds* [1964] Ch 219, [1963] 1 All ER 390.
9 Ibid. See p 215 ante.
10 (1840) 5 My & Cr 72; (M & B).
11 At 92.
12 At 95. The result was the same in *Brown v Pocock* (1833) 6 Sim 257, explained in *Lambert v Thwaites* (1866) LR 2 Eq 151 at 157.

222 Chapter 11 Trusts and powers

of the class has an interest that is vested but liable to divesting.

Another means of giving effect to an intention that the class should benefit notwithstanding that no selection has been made is for the court to construe a gift as conferring a power of appointment among members of the class, with an implied gift over to the members of the class equally[13]. Where in default of appointment the power of selection is exercisable by will only, then only those living at the date when the power could have been exercised (eg at the death of a life tenant who is donee of the power) will be members of the class entitled in default[14]. Where the power of selection is exercisable inter vivos or by will, then since the power could have been exercised immediately after the grant of the power, all members of the class alive at that time become entitled in default of appointment (with the result that, in the event of a member of the class predeceasing the donee, his interest under the gift over will pass to his estate[15]). Thus in *Wilson v Duguid*[16] leasehold property was assigned to trustees on trust for a life tenant with remainder to such of his children as he should by any writing appoint. The life tenant died without making an appointment. It was held that there was a plain implication from the wording of the will of a gift in default of appointment for the children equally. Since the power was exercisable by 'any writing', all children alive at the date when the power became exercisable were members of the class (notwithstanding that three had predeceased the donee). Generally, the courts have been more willing to find an implied gift over in default of appointment to the objects of a power where the class consists of the settlor's children, or other particular members of his family, rather than some larger group[17]. It will, of course, only be possible for an implied gift over to a class of objects equally to be found where the class is ascertainable. (Where there is a power of appointment among a class, with an *express* gift over to members of the same class, then in some instances the disposition has been treated as creating a power of appointment, and thus subject to the normal rules relating to this form of disposition[18]; in others[19], it has been treated as constituting a fiduciary power, and thus subject to the rules of a discretionary trust, in particular with regard to the duty to consider whether to exercise the discretion, and with regard to the inability of the person or persons having the discretion to release the discretion. It is the latter treatment which seems to be in accordance with the present tendency in the law.)

It is, however, by no means the case that where a power is given to decide how property should be distributed that the disposition will necessarily be construed either as a gift to the class, subject to the power of selection, or as containing an implied gift over in default of appointment to the members of the class. If the necessary intention on the part of the settlor that the class is intended to benefit is lacking, then neither course will be followed. For example, in *Re Weekes' Settlement*[20] a testatrix bequeathed certain real property to her husband for life, and gave him 'power to dispose of all such property by will amongst our children'. There was no gift over in default of

13   *Wilson v Duguid* (1883) 24 Ch D 244; *Re Llewellyn's Settlement* [1921] 2 Ch 281.
14   *Walsh v Wallinger* (1830) 2 Russ & M 78 at 81; *Kennedy v Kingston* (1821) 2 Jac & W 431.
15   *Lambert v Thwaites* (1866) LR 2 Eq 151.
16   (1883) 24 Ch D 244.
17   *Re Combe* [1925] Ch 210; *Re Perowne* [1951] Ch 785 at 790.
18   See *Smith v Houblon* (1859) 26 Beav 482.
19   See *Re Wills' Trust Deeds* [1964] Ch 219, [1963] 1 All ER 390.
20   [1897] 1 Ch 289; (M & B).

appointment. There were children, but the husband died intestate without having exercised the power. It was held that there was no evidence in the will to indicate that the disposition was intended to be more than a power of appointment. Consequently the property was not to be divided amongst the children equally, but went to the testatrix's heir. In *Re Combe*[1], a testator left residue to trustees on trust for his wife for life, with remainder to his son for life, with remainder 'in trust for such person or persons as my said son ... shall by will appoint but I direct that such appointment must be confined to any relation or relations of mine of the whole blood'. There was no gift over in default of appointment. The son took out a summons to ascertain what would be the result of his releasing the power of appointment. It was held that the disposition was a pure power (ie a power of appointment) and since there was nothing in the will to indicate an intention on the part of the testator to create a trust in favour of the objects, the son could release the power, and if he did so the property would be held on (a resulting) trust for the testator's next of kin.

Terminology

In reading the cases it should be borne in mind that there is considerable variation in the terms used to refer to powers of appointment and fiduciary powers. We have noted already that a fiduciary power is sometimes called 'a power in the nature of a trust', or a 'trust power', or a 'power coupled with a duty', or a 'power imperative', or a 'power of a fiduciary character' and further, that much uncertainty attaches to the use of these terms[2]. A power of appointment is sometimes termed a 'mere power' or a 'pure power', or a 'power collateral', or a 'bare power'.

These variations can be a source of confusion. And matters are not helped by the fact that trustees of a discretionary trust are often spoken of as having a 'power to appoint' the property among the beneficiaries[3]. Indeed, so loosely has the word 'power' on occasions been used that it is sometimes not possible to determine whether a proposition of law is intended to refer to a power in the sense of a power of appointment, or a power in the sense that that word is (confusingly) used to describe a discretion conferred on trustees[4].

Attempts have from time to time been made to sort out the muddle by proposing fresh ways of categorising the various forms of disposition that can exist in this field. It is submitted here that at the end of the road there are, basically, only two creatures, a power (a 'pure' power) of appointment and a trust (within which term we include fiduciary powers). Each of these two can be divided into subcategories according to whatever system of classification may be preferred. But every form of disposition that involves a choice being made as to the destination of property falls, it is submitted, on one side of the basic dividing line or the other.

1 [1925] Ch 210.
2 For the different meanings that have been attached to the term 'trust power' and proposals for rationalising the terminology, see R. Bartlett and C. Stebbings [1984] Conv 227.
3 The difficulties caused by the blurring of the distinction between discretionary trusts and powers of appointment is illustrated by *Re Gestetner Settlement* [1953] Ch 672 at 688, and by *Re Wills' Trust Deeds* [1964] Ch 219, [1963] 1 All ER 390.
4 [1964] Ch 219; [1981] 3 All ER 786, [1982] 1 WLR 202.

The distinguishing characteristics
In the previous edition of this book it was proposed that one distinguishing characteristic of a trust was an intention that the beneficiaries were intended to benefit, and no one else. Thus the presence of a gift over to other persons in the event of an election not being made established, it was said, that the disposition was a power of appointment. A case heard in 1990, however, demands a reconsideration. In *Re Beatty*[5] a testatrix bequeathed property to trustees directing that they 'shall ... within ... two years following [her] death [distribute the property] ... among such ... persons ... as they think fit and any [remaining property] shall fall into [the] residuary estate'. Was the effect of the disposition to confer a power of appointment or to create a trust? The presence of the gift over is a pointer to a power of appointment. But the terms of the bequest were mandatory: the word '*shall*', not 'may', was used. It was, we can infer, the testatrix's intention to impose on the trustees a duty to give effect to her wishes of which they were aware. Seen in this light the disposition takes on the colour of a trust. And it was on this side of the line that the court held that the disposition fell. (That this makes sense is demonstrated if we ask the question 'Are we to construe the gift as showing an intention that the trustees should be able, after the death of the testatrix, to execute a deed of release that resulted in the property concerned passing immediately to the residuary estate?' Clearly this was not the intention. But only if the gift had fallen on the power of appointment side of the dividing line could this construction be found to be the one that had been intended.)

The case shows that the presence of a gift over cannot be taken as establishing conclusively that the disposition is a power of appointment. In determining the question as to which side of the line a disposition falls we are driven to fall back solely on the issue of intention: was it the settlor's intention that the person with the authority to make a decision should be in breach of no duty if he failed even to turn his mind to the matter (if, as we said earlier, he was free to yawn and turn away) or was it the settlor's intention that this person should be under a duty to give his attention to the matter and make a conscious decision whether or not a distribution of property ought properly to be made (and if it should, to make it)?

The distinction between trusts and powers—some practicalities
The question as to whether a particular disposition confers a power or creates a duty is not one of mere idle speculation. As we saw at the beginning of this chapter, the consequences of a disposition falling on one side of the line or the other can be crucial. That this is so has been demonstrated recently in a number of cases involving company pension funds, in particular in *Mettoy Pension Trustees Ltd v Evans*[6]. The funds of a company's pension scheme were held by trustees. Under the rules of the scheme, decisions as to the distribution of benefits to pensioners rested with the company. Any surplus not distributed was to belong to the company. The company went into liquidation. Thus the liquidator assumed control of the company's affairs, including authority to make decisions with regard to the pension fund. If this authority was a power of appointment, it would be open to him to release the power, thus passing the fund to the company, and so making the money

5   [1990] 1 WLR 1503.
6   [1990] 1 WLR 1587; (1991) 107 LQR 214 (S. Gardner); [1991] Conv 364 (J. Martin).

available to the company's creditors—to whom the liquidator's duty lay. The court held that the arrangement was not in the form of a power. Thus the liquidator was not able to execute a deed of release that secured the fund for the creditors. The fund was held for members of the scheme, who were entitled (in the same way as beneficiaries of a discretionary trust) to enforce the trust.

But who was to make decisions as to the distribution of benefits? The directors could not (the company being in liquidation) do so. Neither could the liquidator, in view of the conflict that would arise if he did so between his duty to the creditors and his duty to pensioners. The court held that in the absence of anyone to make the relevant decisions, the court could itself intervene. As to the means of so doing, the court (Warner J) followed the judgment of Lord Wilberforce in *McPhail v Doulton*[7], when he said that where no trustees were available to make decisions, or existing trustees failed to carry out their duty with regard to the exercise of a discretion, the court could execute a trust 'by appointing new trustees, or by authorising or directing representative persons of the classes of beneficiaries to prepare a scheme of distribution, or even, should the proper basis for distribution not appear, by itself direct the trustees so to distribute'. (As to the proper means to be adopted in the circumstances of the case, the court deferred a decision until further evidence and submissions had been heard.)

In the *Mettoy* case, the judge termed the discretion exercisable under the pension scheme a 'fiduciary power'. The use of this term has become increasingly common (and hence its adoption earlier in this chapter for dispositions of this kind). Its use is, however, unfortunate in view of the fact that it combines the element of duty, importing the existence of a trust, with a word ('power') that is traditionally used for a form of disposition that is of a kind the very opposite to that of a trust, as in a 'power of appointment'. (Few distinctions in English law run more deeply, or in so many different fields, than that between a duty and a power.)

Settlements of income

So far in this chapter we have considered situations in which donees of a power of appointment had power to appoint capital among certain objects of the power, and in which trustees of a discretionary trust held capital on trust for a class of beneficiaries. However, it may be that the property subject to the power or the trust is not capital, but income[8]. For example, a testator may leave capital to trustees, with a direction that the income is to be paid to such of his sons as the trustees should at their discretion appoint, and that on the death of the last son the capital should go to Z. Although here we are concerned with income, not capital, the same principles in the main apply as if it had been capital which was being disposed of. Thus if the disposition is construed as constituting a trust (or a trust power), then:

(a) the trustees are under a duty to exercise their discretion. If they fail to

7 [1971] AC 424 at 457.
8 As in *Re Park* [1932] 1 Ch 580.

do so, the sons can apply to the court which may order that income which has arisen should be distributed equally;

(b) before *McPhail v Doulton*[9], in order that the trust should have certainty of objects, the beneficiaries would have had to be ascertainable[10];

(c) there can be no question of the trust being released.

If the disposition were construed as constituting a power of appointment:

(a) if the trustees failed to make an appointment of the income, the sons could take no action. Any income not appointed would be undisposed of and revert to the settlor's estate;

(b) the disposition would not (either before or after *McPhail v Doulton*[11]) have been void if the class had not been ascertainable, provided that the disposition complied with the rules as to certainty for powers of appointment;

(c) if the power had not been conferred on trustees, but had been conferred on, for example, the testator's widow, she would have been free to release the power with the result that the income would be undisposed of and would go to Z. (Since, in our example, the power is conferred on trustees *virtute officii* they could not release the power.)

In one respect, however, there is an important difference between a discretionary trust and a power of appointment when the trust property is income. In the case of a discretionary trust, the discretion exists each time income arises. Thus if a testator left certain shares to trustees on trust to apply the income for such of the testator's sons A, B and C, and in such shares as the trustees should decide, then each time a dividend was received the trustees would have to decide which of the sons was to receive the money. In the case of a power of appointment, on the other hand, the appointment of the income operates once and for all. Thus if the testator confers a power of appointment on trustees, with his sons as objects, and the trustees make an appointment of the income in favour of A, then A is entitled to all income, present and future, produced by the shares. However, if the power is revocable, the position can be assimilated to that under a discretionary trust by the donee of the power making an appointment in favour of, say, A; paying him a dividend when it is received; revoking the appointment; making a fresh appointment in favour of, say, C; paying him a dividend received; then revoking the appointment; and so on.

General

Trusts, powers of appointment, trust powers and administrative powers within one settlement
It should be noted that in a settlement trustees (a) may hold some property on non-discretionary trusts; (b) may hold other property on discretionary trusts; (c) may hold other property subject to a power of appointment, the

---

9   [1971] AC 424, [1970] 2 All ER 228.
10   *Re Saxone Shoe Co's Trust Deed* [1962] 2 All ER 904, [1962] 1 WLR 943.
11   Supra.

power to appoint being conferred on themselves; (d) may hold other property subject to a power of appointment, the power to appoint being conferred on some other person (eg the settlor's widow); (e) may hold other property subject to a trust power; (f) may hold other property which is subject to a combination, at different times, of various forms of disposition, eg subject first to a power to appoint income among a class of persons for their life and then subject to a non-discretionary trust, of the capital in favour of remaindermen; (g) will[12] have powers conferred by statute relating to the administration of the trust, eg relating to the investment of trust money; (h) may have further similar powers conferred expressly by the trust instrument; (i) will be subject to the duties imposed by equity and statute; (j) may be subject to other duties imposed expressly by the trust instrument.

Delegation
In Chapter 14 we shall see that a trustee is not permitted to delegate responsibility for taking decisions to another (unless they have authority to do so). The rule applies equally in the case of a power of appointment. Thus if S confers a power of appointment on W to appoint among a class, and W purports to appoint to such members of the class as certain named persons (eg the trustees by whom the legal title to the property in the settlement is held) shall select, since W has sought to delegate responsibility for the exercise of the power, the appointment by her is void[13].

Attempted achievement of a non-charitable purpose
In Chapter 9 we saw that if a person gives property on trust for a purpose other than a charitable purpose (and other than for one of the three forms of valid trust of imperfect obligation, and other than for a purpose enforceable by human beneficiaries) then the trust is void. A question which arises is whether a person can give property subject to a power of appointment for such a purpose—eg in a disposition 'for such purposes as will further the cause of anti-vivisection as my widow shall select'. It has been suggested[14] that no bar to the validity of the grant of such a power exists[15]. It is submitted[15], however, that a power of appointment for a non-charitable purpose is void, and that *Re Clarke*[16] is authority for this view.

A further suggestion[17] has been that, if a non-charitable purpose *can* be made the object of a power of appointment, an invalid trust for a noncharitable purpose should be allowed to take effect as a valid power of appointment. This suggestion, however, has been decisively rejected by the courts[18].

---

12 Unless excluded by the settlement.
13 *Re Hay's Settlement Trusts*, supra; [1982] Conv 432 (A. Grubb).
14 Maudsley and Burn, *Trusts and Trustees, Cases and Materials*, 4th ed, p 315.
15 Morris and Leach *The Rule against Perpetuities* (2nd edn) pp 320–321; (M & B).
16 [1923] 2 Ch 407.
17 Morris and Leach, *The Rule against Perpetuities* (1st edn) pp 306–311; L. A. Sheridan (1953) 17 Conv (NS) 46.
18 *IRC v Broadway Cottages Trust* [1955] Ch 20 at 36; *Re Shaw* [1957] 1 WLR 729 at 746; *Re Endacott* [1960] Ch 232 at 246. See Morris and Leach, *The Rule against Perpetuities* (2nd edn) pp 319–321.

Chapter 12

Discretionary and protective trusts

Discretionary trusts[1]

A discretionary trust is one under which discretion is conferred by the settlor on the trustees to decide which member or members of a class of beneficiaries should be entitled to the trust property. We have learnt a number of matters about discretionary trusts from the previous chapter. Thus we have seen that if trustees of a discretionary trust fail to exercise their discretion, the beneficiaries can seek the aid of the court[2]; that (unlike donees of a power of appointment) trustees of a discretionary trust are under a duty to consider periodically whether the discretion should be exercised and, if so, in what way[3], that since *McPhail v Doulton* the rule for determining whether the objects of a discretionary trust are described with sufficient certainty, corresponds with the rule which governs powers of appointment in this regard[4]; that property subject to a discretionary trust may take the form of capital or income[5]; and that where the property is income, then the discretion is exercisable each time that income arises[5]. A number of further matters now call for attention.

1. The terms of a discretionary trust may give trustees discretion not only as to which beneficiary or beneficiaries should take, but also as to whether to make any distribution of trust property (capital or income as the case may be) at all. If the discretion is of this nature the trust is said to be 'non-exhaustive'. If the trust is non-exhaustive any income not distributed will be accumulated and will be available for subsequent distribution. In the absence of the express conferment of a discretion not to make any distribution at all, the trustees are under a duty to distribute trust property to those entitled (eg to distribute income from capital to beneficiaries with life interests)[6]. In this case the trust is said to be 'exhaustive'.

2. Whether a trust is exhaustive or non-exhaustive, trustees of a discretionary trust are always under a duty to exercise their discretion with regard to the distribution of any trust property, capital or income, which comes into their hands. But it will be noted, from what has been said above, that if the trust

---

1 L. A. Sheridan (1957) 21 Conv (NS) 55; Hadingham and Best, *Discretionary Trusts* (1975).
2 See p 215.
3 See ibid.
4 See p 218.
5 See p 225.
6 The fact that the trustees' discretion is expressed to be 'absolute and uncontrolled' is not sufficient to make the trust non-exhaustive. *Re Locker's Settlement* [1978] 1 All ER 216, [1977] 1 WLR 1323.

is non-exhaustive the exercise of a discretion will not necessarily mean that property is distributed (since the exercise of the discretion may take the form of a decision to make no distribution).

3. If the trust is exhaustive, then trustees are under a duty to distribute the trust property within a reasonable time of its becoming available for distribution[7] (and this is so notwithstanding that their discretion was expressed to be 'absolute and uncontrolled', and that it had been the known wish of the settlor that no distribution should be made[8]).

4. A beneficiary who receives nothing under the trust has no grounds for attacking the trustees' exercise of their discretion unless he can show that the trustees have acted capriciously (eg if they selected beneficiaries according to their height or complexion[9]), or corruptly or otherwise in bad faith. If the trustees have acted in good faith then the court will not interfere with their decision.

5. What is the position if the trustees fail to make any allocation of property available for distribution to beneficiaries under the trust?[10] If the trust is non-exhaustive and the trustees fail to make any distribution, then whether the beneficiaries have any remedy will depend on whether the trustees have exercised their discretion, ie turned their mind to the matter and made a decision. If it is found that the trustees have validly exercised their discretion (ie and decided to make no distribution) then the court will not intervene unless it can be shown that the trustees have acted in bad faith, eg under the influence of an improper motive. If it is found that the trustees have failed to address themselves to the exercise of the discretion then the court has power to order them to do so[11]. If they persist in their refusal to make a valid exercise of the discretion (even if only to decide against any distribution) then the court can remove them and appoint new trustees. But what the court is extremely reluctant to do is to exercise the discretion on behalf of the trustees, and it has only been in very rare instances that it has done so[12]. If the trust is exhaustive and the trustees fail to make any distribution (and thus cannot have exercised their discretion) then the beneficiaries can apply to the court which has power to, and normally will, order that the property should be divided equally[13].

6. Does a beneficiary under a discretionary trust have any interest in the trust property? From one viewpoint he has no interest, since he has no right to demand any benefit under the trust: he has no more than 'a hope that the discretion will be exercised in his favour'[14]. Thus if a beneficiary goes bankrupt, nothing passes to the trustee in bankruptcy, with regard to the beneficiary's position under the trust.

From another viewpoint, however, it can be argued that a beneficiary

---

7 *Re Gourju's Will Trusts* [1943] Ch 24, [1942] 2 All ER 605; (M & B); *Re Gulbenkian's Settlement Trusts (No 2)* [1969] 3 WLR 450 at 457.
8 *Re Locker's Settlement* [1978] 1 All ER 216, [1977] 1 WLR 1323.
9 *Re Manisty's Settlement* [1973] 2 All ER 1203 at 1210.
10 A. J. Hawkins (1967) Conv (NS) 117.
11 *Wain v Earl of Egmont* (1843) 3 My & K 445.
12 *Gower v Mainwaring* (1750) 2 Ves Sen 87; *Liley v Hey* (1842) 1 Hare 580.
13 *Jones v Clough* (1751) 2 Ves Sen 365; *Longmore v Broom* (1802) 7 Ves 124. See also *McPhail v Doulton* [1971] AC 424 at 475 (per Lord Wilberforce).
14 Snell, *Principles of Equity* (28th edn) p 138, cited with approval by Salmon J in *Gartside v IRC* [1968] AC 553, 574.

under a discretionary trust does hold some proprietary interest, albeit a slender one, in the trust property. A beneficiary can assign his interest under the trust. The assignee will hold no more than the original beneficiary (a hope that he will benefit), and a right to require the trustees to bear him in mind when considering in whose favour the discretion should be exercised. But if an assignment is made, the assignment must be of something and, it is submitted, it is proper to regard this something as being an interest in the trust property. A more positive argument in support of the view that a beneficiary holds some form of interest under a discretionary trust rests on the fact that if all the beneficiaries are sui juris and together absolutely entitled, then they may, under the rule in *Saunders v Vautier*[15], bring the trust to an end and direct the trustees as to how the trust property is to be applied (eg divided equally between them)[16]. Thus it is suggested that even if it is doubted whether the beneficiaries have any interest under the trust with regard to their hope of benefiting from the exercise of the trustees' discretion, they have certainly an interest in the trust property by virtue of their holding a right, contingent on their all attaining full age and becoming absolutely entitled, to demand the trust property. However, since during the continuation of the trust a beneficiary has no quantifiable interest in the property, he has no 'interest' within the meaning of s 43 of the Finance Act 1943 (which amended the operation of the estate duty provisions of the Finance Act 1894)[17].

Protective trusts

It will now be convenient, having considered the nature of discretionary trusts, to deal with a form of trust which includes in its operation the machinery of a discretionary trust: the trust concerned is a *protective trust*. In the United States a trust with the objectives of a protective trust is termed a 'spendthrift trust' and this describes part of its purpose well: to guard a beneficiary's interest against his own folly or mismanagement.

Consider an example. Suppose that T settles property on his son A for life with remainder to any children born to him. After T's death A assigns his life interest to X in consideration of a lump sum of £10,000. A spends the money and is left without income from the trust. To guard against this, T could settle the fund on A for life until he attempts to alienate his interest, thus conferring on A a determinable life interest. In this case, if A purported to alienate his interest, the interest would terminate (with the consequence that in practice no assignee would agree to purchase the interest). Another risk which T may foresee is that A might become bankrupt, with the result that his life interest in the fund would pass (with his other property) to his trustee in bankruptcy. To guard against this eventuality, T could settle the fund on A for life until he either attempts to alienate his interest, or has a

15   (1841) 4 Beav 115; (M & B).
16   *Re Smith* [1928] Ch 915.
17   *Gartside v IRC* [1968] AC 553, [1968] 1 All ER 121; *Sainsbury v IRC* [1970] Ch 712, [1969] 3 All ER 919.

bankruptcy order made against him under the Insolvency Act 1986[18]. Then, if A committed an act of bankruptcy, his life interest would terminate and there would be nothing, as regards the life interest, to pass to the trustee in bankruptcy.

Provided that the life interest created by T is determinable in form (ie by using words which delimit the duration of the interest, eg 'until ...') then the grant is valid. In the case of a conditional interest (ie one created by words which cut short the interest before it reaches its natural boundary, eg 'provided that ...'; 'on condition that ...') a proviso against alienation or for forfeiture on bankruptcy is void[19]. If T is to achieve his end, he must therefore confer on A a determinable, not a conditional, interest.

Let us assume that T confers on A a life interest determinable on attempted alienation or on his committing an act of bankruptcy. What will happen to the property in the event of attempted alienation by A, or of his bankruptcy? This will depend on what direction T gives in his will. T could, for example, direct that on the termination of the life interest, the fund was to be held by the trustees of the settlement for the remainder of A's life on discretionary trusts for the maintenance or support or otherwise for the benefit of A, any wife of his, and their issue. The trustees would then have discretion as to how the income was to be distributed between these persons. If A married, the trustees might, for example, in one year pay a quarter of the income to A, pass one half to A's wife to assist in housekeeping expenses, and use the rest to assist in the education of A's son. In another year the allocation of income might be different, depending on the circumstances. A trust in this form, ie one which couples a life interest determinable on bankruptcy or attempted alienation with a discretionary trust for the life tenant and certain other persons for the remainder of the life tenant's life is termed a *protective trust*.

Such a trust may be created by setting out the terms expressly. In order to avoid the need for this, however, s 33 of the Trustee Act 1925 provides that where (after 1925) income is directed to be held on 'protective trusts' for the benefit of any person for his life (or any shorter period), then the income is to be held subject to trusts which are set out in the section. These, in essence, create a determinable interest coupled with a discretionary trust in the form which we have considered above. The section refers to the life tenant, whom we have called A, as 'the principal beneficiary'.

Under the trusts set out in the section, income is to be held (i) on trust for the principal beneficiary (A) until he 'does or attempts to do or suffers any act or thing, or until any event happens ... whereby, if the said income were payable during the trust period to the principal beneficiary absolutely ..., he would be deprived of the right to receive the same or any part thereof'. This creates the determinable interest. In the event of the interest terminating, the income is then to be held (ii) on trust for the maintenance or support or otherwise for the benefit of all or any of the following persons, namely,

(a) the principal beneficiary and his or her spouse and their issue; or

(b) if the principal beneficiary has no spouse or issue, the principal beneficiary and the persons who, if the principal beneficiary were dead, would be entitled to the trust property or the income.

18 Section 278.
19 *Brandon v Robinson* (1811) 18 Ves 429.

Certain matters call for attention. These can be illustrated by supposing a settlement by T on trust for A on protective trusts for life with remainder to B absolutely.

(a) T may if he wishes stipulate a shorter period than that of A's life for the duration of the protective trusts; eg the settlement could be to A until he is thirty on protective trusts, and then to A for the remainder of his life (ie not on protective trusts), with remainder to B.

(b) The protective trusts set out in s 33 and incorporated by a direction to hold 'on protective trusts', may be modified by the instrument creating the trust[20], eg T may vary the membership of the class of persons entitled under the discretionary trust.

(c) Unless and until a terminating event occurs, A is entitled to receive all the income under the trust: thus he has a normal life interest at the outset of his interest and this will continue for the rest of his life, provided that nothing occurs which determines the interest. If A's determinable life interest terminates and the discretionary trust arises, then the trustees are obliged (within reasonable limits) to apply the whole of the income for the benefit of the beneficiaries specified[1]. Thus if A has a wife and one child, and the trustees for some reason do not think fit to apply the income for the benefit of A, then the trustees are obliged to apply the income for the benefit of the wife or child (or both of them). If A has no wife or issue, the trustees hold the income on trust for A and B (the person who would, if A were dead, be entitled to the property).

(d) It seems that if A is already bankrupt at the time of the creation of the trust, this fact operates immediately to bring the discretionary trust into force[2].

(e) If X confers on Y a power to appoint property among a specified class of persons and in exercise of the power Y appoints the property to trustees on protective trusts for Z (who is one of the objects of the power) the appointment is invalid for two reasons: (i) the appointment infringes the rule that the donee of a special power cannot delegate his authority to another (ie to the trustees of the discretionary trust, if this comes into existence)[3]; (ii) the appointment may benefit persons who will usually be outside the class of objects (ie if the discretionary trust comes into existence, Z's spouse and issue)[4].

(f) If, as part of a settlement, income is held on protective trusts for A for life and the court makes an order varying the effect of the terms of the trust (eg under s 57 of the Trustee Act 1925[5]) this will not operate as an event which terminates A's determinable life interest[6].

(g) If the trustees wish to exercise a power of advancement[7] in favour of B, then the giving of consent by A will not operate to terminate his determinable

---

20 Section 33(2).
1   *Re Gourju's Will Trusts* [1943] Ch 24, [1942] 2 All ER 605; (M & B).
2   See *Re Walker* [1939] Ch 974, [1939] 3 All ER 902.
3   *Re Hunters' Will Trusts* [1963] Ch 372, [1962] 3 All ER 1050.
4   *Re Boulton's Settlement Trust* [1928] Ch 703.
5   See Chap 18.
6   *Re Mair* [1935] Ch 562.
7   See Chap 17.

interest since s 33 expressly excludes this event as a happening which will terminate the interest[8].

(h) Section 33 resembles ss 31 and 32[9] in that, like them, it is a 'word saving' section. It differs from these sections in that whilst ss 31 and 32 confer powers on trustees unless the sections are excluded, the trusts in s 33 come into operation only if the settlor expressly directs (ie by directing that property is to be held on 'protective trusts').

(i) We have seen[10] that if S attempts to escape his creditors by conveying his property to trustees, the trust is liable to be set aside. S cannot take advantage of s 33 (ie by conveying his property to trustees on trust for himself on protective trusts) to achieve the same end. Section 33 expressly provides that nothing in the section is to have the effect of validating a trust which would be liable to be set aside[11].

(j) The circumstances that will operate to determine A's interest (and bring into existence the trust for the beneficiaries specified in the section) include the impounding[12] of part of A's income by the trustees to make good a sum paid to A in breach of trust[13].

(k) An assignment by A in the form of a release of his life interest, made in the mistaken belief that the effect would be to make the remaindermen absolutely entitled (A being unaware that the legal effect would in fact be to bring into operation a discretionary trust for persons specified in the terms of the protective trust) has been held, where the persons who would become beneficiaries under the discretionary trust were volunteers, not to be sufficient to determine A's determinable life interest. (The court ordered that the deed of release should be set aside[14].)

Safeguards against prodigality
It will be seen that a settlor may guard against a beneficiary's prodigality (a) by creating a discretionary trust; (b) by making the beneficiary's interest determinable, eg on his committing an act of bankruptcy; or (c) by creating a protective trust.

'Determinable trusts'
It may be added that a trust under which the interest of a beneficiary is determinable is sometimes termed a 'determinable trust'. No purpose, it is submitted, is served by the use of this term. Discretionary trusts and protective trusts have special characteristics which warrant their receiving a distinct appellation. But to speak of a determinable trust as if it were a distinct form of trust is, we believe, misleading: we do not speak of a 'life trust' merely because a beneficial interest under it happens to be a life interest.

---

8 Section 33(1).
9 See Chap 16.
10 See Chap 4.
11 Section 33(3).
12 See Chap 22.
13 *Re Richardsons' Will Trusts* [1958] Ch 504, [1958] 1 All ER 538.
14 *Gibbon v Mitchell* [1990] 3 All ER 338, [1990] 1 WLR 1304.

Chapter 13

Appointment of trustees

INTRODUCTION

In the earlier chapters we were concerned with how trusts are created and with the various types of trust which can exist. These chapters (together with the discussion of trusts and powers in Chapter 10) may be regarded as constituting the first half of the subject matter which goes to make up the law of trusts. The second half is concerned primarily with trustees—their appointment, their duties, their powers, their liability and so on. In this chapter we are concerned with how trustees are appointed and how they may cease to be trustees. The chapter is divided into three parts. In the first part we follow the story of a trust from the appointment of the first trustees through to the time when, after a number of changes in trustees, the trust comes to an end. In the second part of the chapter we summarise the points of law met in the first part. In the final part of the chapter we deal with some points of law not previously covered.

Part 1

Let us suppose that in his will a testator, S, wishes to leave certain shares to his wife, W, for her lifetime, with remainder to his only daughter, Z. To this end, in his will, S creates a trust with the wife and daughter as the beneficiaries. How are the trustees appointed?

FIRST TRUSTEES

The most common arrangement would be for S expressly to appoint the trustees in the will. He could do this in a separate clause in his will, for example, 'I appoint A, B and C to be trustees of this my will' (ie of any trusts set up in his will, including that for W for life with remainder to Z). Or S could merely leave the shares 'to A, B and C on trust for W for life, with remainder to Z'. In either case there is a valid appointment of A, B and C as trustees.

At this point, to explain what follows, it must be noted that when a testator dies leaving property either by a direct bequest to a named legatee, or to trustees on specified trusts, in neither case does the title to the property vest immediately on the testator's death in the legatee or in the trustees. On the testator's death all[1] his property vests in his 'personal representative', ie if he has appointed an executor, in the executor. If the will appoints no executor, then (as seen in Chapter 2) the court appoints the personal representative who, in this case, is termed an 'administrator'.

A testator's property is held by his personal representative on trust to pay the testator's debts and funeral and testamentary expenses and then to give effect to the provisions of the testator's will.

From this, it will be clear that if our testator appoints X his executor, it will be necessary for X to transfer the property to the trustees, A, B and C. (Similarly, if the testator appoints no executor, the administrator, when appointed, will have to transfer the property to the trustees.)

What is the position prior to this transfer? Suppose that X does not transfer the property to A, B and C until 18 months after the testator's death. How is the property held in the meantime, assuming that the property is not needed for paying the testator's debts? The answer is that during this interim period, X, having completed the administration of the estate (ie collecting in the deceased's assets and paying his debts) himself holds the property on trust to give effect to the terms of the will; ie on trust for W for life, with remainder to Z. So if a dividend is received, X must pass the money to W. If W dies, X must arrange for the shares to be transferred to Z.

Since X will not wish to be saddled with the responsibilities of his office for longer than necessary, it is likely that, on completing the administration of the estate, he will forthwith transfer the trust property to the trustees. So X will complete a share transfer form and send this together with the share certificates to the company. The company will register A, B and C as the legal owners of the shares. X gives A, B and C a written assent which states how they are to hold the shares—ie on trust for W for life with remainder to Z.

(We may note here that if the trust property had been land, for A, B and C to hold the legal title, the trust must have been a trust for sale[2]. If the testator imposed no trust for sale, so that the settlement took the form of a strict settlement, under the Settled Land Act 1925, X would have to transfer the legal title to W, as tenant for life, by means of a vesting assent. If a trust for sale was created, the document used to transfer the legal title to A, B and C would be a simple assent.)

If X is ready to transfer the property (in our example, shares) to the trustees but he finds that A has by this time died (either before or after the death of the testator) he must convey the property to B and C. If A and B had died, he would transfer the property to C alone.

What is the position if X finds that A, B and C are all alive, but A declines to accept the position of trustee? What if, as we say, A 'disclaims' the trusteeship? In this case, X should transfer the trust property to B and C. If A and B both disclaim, he will transfer it to C alone.

It may be, however, that X finds that there are no trustees available, either because none were appointed in the will or because those appointed by the will have all died, or have all disclaimed. In this case it is necessary for X to ascertain whether the will gave power to any person or persons to appoint new trustees. If the will did confer such a power, the person nominated may appoint the necessary trustees. If the will did not confer such a power, then

1 With limited exceptions. Eg, a fee tail vests immediately in the heir.
2 Law of Property Act 1925, ss 34–36.

X may ask the court to appoint trustees, and the court has power to do so[3]. Thus, by one means or another, trustees come into existence. It should be noted that X, as personal representative, does not himself have power to appoint fresh trustees (unless, of course, this power happened to be expressly conferred on him by the testator). Pending the appointment of trustees, X, as personal representative, holds the property on the trusts declared by the testator[4].

It is, in fact, an ancient principle that equity will not allow a trust to fail for lack of a trustee. Hence the dictum 'Equity does not want for a trustee'. There is only one exception to the rule that the lack of a trustee will not cause a trust to fail. This is where it is construed as being a settlor's intention that the trustee named by him, and no one else, should act: the acceptance of the trust by the trustee named thus forming a condition precedent to the existence of the trust. In such a situation, if the trust is private, the trust will fail. If it is charitable, the trust may be saved by the *cy près* doctrine[5].

SUBSEQUENT TRUSTEES

Let us assume that our testator appointed A, B and C trustees in his will; that these were all alive and willing to act, and that X therefore transfers the shares to them by the procedure already explained. A, B and C will then hold the legal title to the shares on trust for W for life with remainder to Z. The following events then occur.

1 Death of a trustee

A dies. Since trustees hold trust property always as joint tenants, on A's death the legal title vests in B and C. Section 36(1) of the Trustee Act 1925[6] confers power on B and C, as surviving trustees, to appoint a new trustee in place of A. We shall see that s 36(1) confers on existing trustees power to appoint a new trustee or trustees in a variety of situations, but in each case the power exists only if there is no contrary provision in the will, either by an express exclusion of the section, or by implied exclusion of the section, eg by the nomination of a person or persons to have power to appoint fresh trustees.

B and C decide to appoint D. They therefore execute a deed of appointment, and D becomes a trustee. (Section 36(1) in fact only requires the appointment to be in writing, but in practice a deed is generally used.)

But what about the trust property? Since the trust property takes the form of shares, it will be necessary for B and C to execute a share transfer form and send this, together with the share certificates[7] to the company, which will enter the names of B, C and D as the holders of the shares. Similarly, if the trust property took the form of money in a bank account, the existing trustees must notify the bank so that the bank's books can be amended accordingly.

---

3   Trustee Act 1925, s 41.
4   *Re Cockburn's Will Trusts* [1957] Ch 438, [1957] 2 All ER 522.
5   See Chap 7.
6   Replacing Trustee Act 1893, s 10.
7   And evidence of the death of A, eg a certified copy of the death certificate.

Whenever, in fact, property is only transferable by making an alteration in the books kept by a company or other body (or in a manner directed by, or under an Act of Parliament), it is necessary for a separate transaction (ie separate from the appointment itself) to be carried out in order to secure the vesting of the trust property in the new set of trustees. (What happens in other cases, where no such entry is required, is considered later.)

2 Retirement

B decides that he wishes to retire as trustee. Provided that certain conditions are satisfied, B has power, conferred on him by s 39 of the Trustee Act 1925, to retire by executing a deed of retirement. The conditions are two-fold: (1) B's co-trustees[8] (C and D) must consent by deed to his retirement. (Their consent may be given in the deed which B executes in order to retire.) (2) On B's retirement there must remain a trust corporation to act as trustee or at least two individuals to act as trustees. Since, in our example, two trustees would remain, this condition is satisfied. Thus if C and D consent, B may retire under the power conferred by s 39.

There is another section which may be employed to enable B to retire. Under s 36(1), if a trustee 'desires to be discharged', the other trustee or trustees[9] may appoint a trustee in his place. Thus if C and D intend to appoint someone in place of B, s 36(1) will enable both B to be released, and the new appointment to be made. It will be noted that if there are only two trustees, and one of them wishes to cease to be a trustee, he may do so under s 36(1), but not under s 39.

Let us suppose that C and D wish to appoint E in place of B. They therefore use their power under section 36(1) and appoint E in B's place[10].

3 Refusal to act

The trustees are now C, D and E. A meeting of the trustees is arranged. C does not attend, and he fails to answer any letters about trust business. He also declines to sign any papers connected with trust business. In such a situation, where a trustee 'refuses to act', s 36(1) provides that the other trustees may appoint a fresh trustee in his place. D and E therefore appoint F trustee in place of C.

4 Disclaimer

Shortly after his appointment, F decides that, because a change in his job requires him to go to live in Truro, he does not wish to accept the appointment as trustee. In this situation, since F has not done anything to indicate his acceptance of the trusteeship (eg signing a document as a trustee), he may disclaim the trusteeship. He may do this notwithstanding that before the appointment he had expressed willingness to be a trustee. F may effect the

8 And the person, if any, empowered in the will to appoint new trustees.
9 Or, if the testator nominated someone to appoint trustees, that person.
10 B may join in making the appointment if he is willing; s 36(8).

disclaimer in writing or by word of mouth. The best practice, however, in order to avoid doubt, is for F to make the disclaimer by deed.

The effect of the disclaimer by F is to nullify his appointment as trustee. Thus after the disclaimer the trustees remain D and E.

If F does not expressly disclaim the trusteeship, but a long time passes after the appointment without his taking any part in the administration of the trust, he may be taken to have impliedly disclaimed the trusteeship[11]. A person may also be held by his conduct to have impliedly disclaimed the trusteeship[12].

On F disclaiming, the other trustees, D and E, appoint G as new trustee[13]. If F disclaims expressly, the disclaimer by F and the appointment by D and E may both be contained in the same deed.

We have now met two situations in which a trustee has disclaimed. The first[14] was where an original trustee disclaims (in which case the appointment by the testator of that trustee had no effect and the trust property was transferred to the other trustees); the second is where a trustee appointed subsequently to the testator's death disclaims. The principles are the same in each situation. For example, in either case the disclaimer may be express or implied; and in either case, the person appointed may not disclaim if he has done any act indicating acceptance of the appointment. Thus if a trustee has done something which indicates his acceptance of the trusteeship it is too late for him to disclaim. If he wishes to give up his position, he can only do so by retiring under the power conferred by, and in accordance with the requirements of, s 39; or by being replaced under s 36(1) as a trustee who 'desires to be discharged'.

5 Additional trustees

The trustees (D, E and G) decide that it would be wise to appoint an additional trustee, bringing the total of trustees up to four. Section 36(6) confers power on existing trustees to appoint an additional trustee or trustees, provided that the appointment does not increase the number of trustees beyond four. D, E and G therefore appoint H.

6 Remaining outside the United Kingdom

H accepts an offer of employment in Canada and goes to live in Toronto. It is inconvenient for the administration of a trust that a trustee should be away from the country for a prolonged period, and where a trustee remains outside the United Kingdom for a continuous (ie uninterrupted) period exceeding 12 months, s 36(1) confers power on the other trustees to appoint a new trustee in his place[15]. D, E and G therefore appoint I as a new trustee.

---

11 *Re Clout and Frewer's Contract* [1924] 2 Ch 230, (executor trustee survived the testator for 30 years without taking any action in either capacity held to have disclaimed his position).
12 *Re Birchall* (1889) 40 Ch D 436, CA.
13 Ie, they again exercise their power to replace C.
14 See p 235, ante.
15 The power exists even if the trustee returns to the United Kingdom after the expiry of his period of absence.

7 Unfitness to act

E is declared bankrupt and absconds to Brazil. Section 36(1) provides that where a trustee is 'unfit' to act, the other trustees may appoint a new trustee in his place. The Act does not define the meaning of 'unfit' but it has been held that one who is bankrupt and absconds comes within this description[16]; and it may be that one who is merely bankrupt also is 'unfit'[17], but this is uncertain. Since E is clearly 'unfit', D, G and I appoint J as trustee.

8 Incapacity

Years pass and D enters senility. He becomes confused over simple things and has difficulty in signing his name. Section 36(1) provides that where a trustee is 'incapable of acting', the other trustees may appoint a new trustee in his place. The incapacity referred to in the section has been held[18] to include personal incapacity, such as that attendant on senility. G, I and J therefore appoint K Ltd, a bank, as trustee in D's place. (There is nothing to prevent a corporation acting as a trustee jointly with individual trustees, or with another corporation.)

9 Mental disorder

G is detained in a mental hospital. It has been held[19] that mental disorder makes a trustee 'incapable of acting' under s 36(1). The other trustees have power to appoint a new trustee in his place. I, J and K Ltd appoint L.

10 Dissolution

K Ltd is wound up. Section 36(3) provides that where a corporation is a trustee and the corporation is dissolved, the corporation shall be deemed, under s 36(1), to be 'incapable of acting' as a trustee from the date of the dissolution. Thus under the section the other trustees have power to appoint a new trustee in the place of the dissolved corporation.

Since s 36(1) confers merely a *power* to appoint a new trustee or trustees, there is no *duty* on existing trustees to appoint a fresh trustee[20]. Let us suppose that I, J and L do nothing for a number of years.

11 Removal under an express power

I then goes to live in Cornwall. The other trustees, J and L, know that the testator had envisaged the trustees holding meetings in Edale, and on re-reading the testator's will they discover a clause which provides that if any

16 *Re Wheeler and De Rochow* [1896] 1 Ch 315.
17 *Re Hopkins* (1881) 19 Ch D 61 at 63.
18 *Re Lemann's Trusts* (1883) 22 Ch D 633.
19 *Re East* (1873) 8 Ch App 735.
20 TA 1925, s 37(1)(c).

trustee ceases to have his permanent home within 5 miles of the centre of Edale, the other trustees shall have power, by deed, to remove him. Section 36(1) provides that where a trustee is removed under a power in the trust instrument, the other trustees shall have power to appoint a fresh trustee in the place of the trustee removed. J and L therefore execute a deed which removes I and appoints M.

12 Death of a sole trustee

J and L are killed in a car accident. M is left as a sole trustee. M would have power to appoint fresh trustees under s 36(1) but he does nothing and later he himself dies.

In his will it is found that he has purported to appoint N and O as trustees of the trust. The appointment is a nullity. M could, under s 36(1), have appointed N and O trustees during his lifetime. But he cannot do so by will[1]. So now no trustees exist.

In this situation, under the Administration of Estates Act 1925[2], the trust property vests in M's personal representatives. In his will M appointed P his executor. Thus the trust property vests in P. P has power, under s 36(1), to appoint fresh trustees. (He has this power, incidentally, notwithstanding that he may be intending to decline to accept the position of executor.)

What is the position between P becoming executor (on M's death) and his appointing fresh trustees? The answer is that during this time P has two courses open to him: (a) he can, if he wishes, accept the position of trustee (eg by performing a duty carried by a trustee). In this case he is empowered[3] to exercise any power which could have been exercised by M; (b) he can decline to act as trustee. He will then have none of the responsibilities of the trusteeship.

We have said that M appointed P his executor in his will: if P predeceased M, the appointment of new trustees may be made by the court. If M had appointed no executor, or had died intestate, the court would appoint an administrator, and it would seem that the administrator, by virtue of being M's personal representative, would be in the same position as P, the executor appointed by M (and so could appoint fresh trustees).

Whether M's executor, P, accepts the position of trustee, or declines to do so, in either case he has the power[4] to appoint fresh trustees. P therefore appoints Q, R and S trustees.

13 The trust ends

W, who holds the life interest under the trust, dies. The testator's daughter Z thus becomes absolutely entitled. If Z is of full age, the trust becomes a bare trust. The trustees, Q, R and S convey the legal title to the trust property to Z, ie they execute a share transfer form and send this, together with the

---

1 Because s 36(1) confers powers which are exercisable inter vivos, not by will.
2 Sections 1–3.
3 TA 1925, s 18(2).
4 TA 1925, s 36(1). If the settlor had nominated a person to appoint trustees, the power would rest with that person, not P.

share certificates, to the company. The company enters the name of Z as the holder of the shares in its register of shareholders, and sends the share certificates to Z. The trust thus comes to an end. (It should be noted that at each change of the trustees which has occurred in the events set out at (1) to (12) the names of the holders of the legal title to the shares will have had to be amended in the company's register.)

Part 2

RECAPITULATION

At this point it may be helpful to set out the principal points of law which we have dealt with so far.

1. If a testator fails to appoint trustees, or the trustees appointed by him have died or are unwilling to act, and he does not confer power on any person to appoint trustees, the court has power to appoint the trustees.

2. On the death of a trustee the trust property vests in the surviving trustee or trustees. On the death of a sole surviving trustee the trust property vests in his personal representative.

3. Under s 36(1)
(a) a new trustee may be appointed in place of one who:
    (i) is dead ((1) above);
    (ii) remains outside the United Kingdom for more than 12 months ((6) above);
    (iii) desires to be discharged ((2) above);
    (iv) refuses to act ((3) above);
    (v) is unfit to act ((7) above);
    (vi) is incapable of acting ((8), (9), (10) above);
    (vii) is removed under a power contained in the trust instrument ((11) above).
(b) If the settlor conferred power on a named person to appoint new trustees, the appointment is made by that person.
(c) If no such person was nominated, the appointment is made by the other trustee or trustees.
(d) On the death of a sole surviving trustee, the appointment may be made by his personal representative.

4. Under s 36(6), existing trustees have power to appoint an additional trustee or trustees, provided that the number of trustees is not thereby increased above four ((5) above).

5. The powers conferred by s 36 may be excluded or extended (eg (11) above) by the settlor[5].

---

5 TA 1925, s 69(2).

Part 3

GENERAL MATTERS

The following further matters now call for attention.

1 Beneficiaries not entitled to appoint trustees

Beneficiaries are not entitled to appoint new trustees. Even when Z was of full age and absolutely entitled, and Q, R and S[6] held on a bare trust for her, she could not appoint a fresh trustee in addition to, or in substitution for Q, R and S. She could, if Q, R and S declined, or merely failed, to convey the legal title to her, require them to do so. But this was the limit of her power[7].

2 Person nominated to appoint trustees

We have seen[8] that a settlor may, if he wishes, confer a power of appointing new trustees on a named person. For example, in his will the testator may provide that his brother Y should have power to appoint new trustees. Or the power could be conferred on a beneficiary, eg W. In this case the power conferred by s 36 on continuing or surviving trustees or trustee to appoint new trustees is excluded. Thus when (at 1 above), A dies, it would be the person nominated, not B and C, who would have power to appoint a new trustee. But even if the testator had expressly conferred power on, say Y, to appoint new trustees, s 36(1) remains of relevance, since the section provides that a person on whom the settlor had conferred power to appoint new trustees may do so in any of the situations set out in s 36(1). Thus, if (as at 9 above), G became mentally ill, Y could, by virtue of s 36, exercise the power conferred on him by the testator, and appoint a new trustee in place of G. Similarly, if the testator conferred power to appoint trustees on Y, it is Y, not the existing trustees, who has power to appoint additional trustees under s 36(6). (An anomalous difference exists between the exercise by Y of his power under s 36(1) and the exercise of his power under s 36(6): under the former he can appoint himself a trustee; under the latter it has been held[9] that, because of the wording of the section, he cannot. He may only appoint another person.[10])

If the testator confers power to appoint trustees on Y, and Y dies, the power then comes to an end. (The power does not, for example, devolve on Y's personal representative.) At this point the statutory power conferred by s 36 on the existing trustees arises, and from then on it is they who may appoint new trustees.

If the person on whom the settlor confers power to appoint new trustees

---

6 *Re Brockbank* [1948] Ch 206, [1948] 1 All ER 287; (M & B).
7 See Chap 21.
8 See p 236, ante.
9 *Re Power's Settlement Trusts* [1951] Ch 1074, [1951] 2 All ER 513.
10 The Law Reform Committee, 23rd Report, recommended that this anomaly should be removed and that a person with power to appoint additional trustees should have power to appoint himself. (Para 2.6.)

is an infant, this fact will not invalidate an appointment made by him, or her, but the appointment 'will be closely scrutinised'[11].

If the settlor had conferred power to appoint new trustees on two or more named persons, then,

(a) if they cannot agree (or cannot be found) the power to appoint new trustees vests in the existing trustee or trustees;

(b) if one out of the persons nominated dies, the power does not vest in the survivor but vests in the existing trustees[12].

3 Capacity to be a trustee

Any legal person (with one exception) who has capacity to hold the legal title to property may be a trustee or co-trustee[13]. An alien may not hold an interest in a British ship[14], and may therefore not be a trustee of such property, though he may be a trustee of any other property.

The exception referred to exists in the case of an infant. An infant cannot hold a legal title to land[15]. For this reason an infant is not capable of being a trustee of land. An infant can hold legal title to personalty but statute[16] expressly provides that the appointment of an infant as a trustee shall be void. An infant is thus prevented from being appointed a trustee of personalty or realty. But it has been held[17] that this provision will not prevent an infant from becoming a trustee under an implied (including resulting) or constructive trust. For example, if P, an infant, acquires trust property otherwise than as a bona fide purchaser without notice of the trust, he will become a constructive trustee of the property. Thus an infant may not be *appointed* trustee, but he may (by application of a principle of law) *become* a trustee.

The Charities Act 1992[18] provides that certain categories of persons shall be disqualified from acting as trustee of a charitable trust. These include those who (a) have been convicted of any offence involving dishonesty or deception; (b) are bankrupts; (c) have been removed from the office of trustee of a charity by order of the Commission or the High Court on grounds of misconduct or mismanagement.

---

11 Snell, *Principles of Equity*, 28th edn, p 203.
12 Unless the trust instrument indicates an intention that the power should continue to be exercised by the survivor or survivors; or unless the power is conferred on a class of which at least two members are still alive.
13 The former statutory restrictions on the authority of corporations to hold land have now been removed. Charities Act 1960, s 38. The previous requirement that a married woman must have her husband's consent to her becoming a trustee or disposing of trust property has also been removed. Married Women's Property Act 1882, ss 1(2), 18, 24; LPA 1925, s 170.
14 Status of Aliens Act 1914, s 17, as amended by British Nationality Act 1948.
15 LPA 1925, s 1(6).
16 LPA 1925, s 20.
17 *Re Vinogradoff* [1935] WN 68.
18 Section 45.

4 Maximum number of trustees[19]

TRUSTS OF PERSONALITY

It will be seen that in the story of the trust set out in Part 1 of this chapter initially there were three trustees. There is no reason, however, why the number appointed should not have been larger, since, in the case of a trust of pure personalty, there is no upper limit to the number of trustees whom a settlor can appoint.

As regards trustees appointed subsequently, as noted earlier, under s 36 existing trustees have power to appoint a trustee to fill the place of one who falls into one of the categories specified in s 36(1) (eg in place of one who dies, who becomes 'incapable', etc), and also (under s 36(6)) to appoint an additional trustee or trustees. But, as we have noted, they only have power under s 36(6) to appoint additional trustees if the number of trustees is thereby not raised above four. (We saw an example of the exercise of this power at 5 above, when D, E and G appointed H an additional trustee.) It might seem that the effect of this proviso is that whilst the trustees of a trust of pure personalty may initially number more than four, and may continue to number more than four, their number may never be increased above the number (in excess of four) initially appointed.

This may have been the intention of the Trustee Act; but if so the intention is not achieved. The reason is that s 36(1) confers a power to appoint 'one *or more persons* ... to be a trustee or trustees in place of' a trustee who falls into one or other of the categories listed in the sub-section. Thus if there were seven trustees and one died, the remaining six could, it seems, appoint an unlimited number of trustees in the place of the one who had died. Thus in the case of a trust of personalty the Act imposes no limit on the number of trustees, either initially or subsequently, who may be appointed.

CERTAIN TRUSTS OF LAND

If the trust property is land held on trust for sale or under a 'settlement' (ie presumably whenever the land is settled under the Settled Land Act 1925) it is expressly provided[20] that the number of trustees can never (ie either initially or subsequently) exceed four. If the settlor purports to appoint more than four trustees, the first four who are willing and able to act become the trustees. There are certain exceptions to the rule that the number of trustees holding land must not exceed four. For example, the limit does not apply to trustees who hold land on trust, or on trust for sale, for a charitable or public[1] purpose[2].

---

19   The Law Reform Committee, 23rd Report, recommended that in the case of a private trust the number of trustees should be limited to four. (Para 2.2.)
20   TA 1925, s 34(2).
 1   Eg a trust of land belonging to an unincorporated association within the provisions of the Literary and Scientific Institutions Act 1854. *Re Cleveland Literary and Philosophical Society's Land* [1931] 2 Ch 247.
 2   TA 1925, s 34(3).

5 Minimum number of trustees

The minimum number of trustees who may be appointed, in the case of trusts of land or personalty, is one. But if the trust property is land held on trust for sale or by way of settlement under the Settled Land Act, a purchaser does not receive a valid receipt for capital money (ie so as to overreach the equitable interests of the beneficiaries under the trust) unless the receipt is signed by at least two trustees or a trust corporation. Thus, unless a trust corporation is appointed sole trustee, there is no purpose in a settlor appointing a sole individual as trustee since, if the land is to be sold (or otherwise disposed of, eg leased), the sole trustee will have to appoint an additional trustee in order that the transaction may be effected.

6 Appointment of trustees by the court

We have met certain instances when the court may appoint new trustees; for example, (a) where the settlor appoints no trustees and nominates no one to appoint trustees; or (b) where the trustees whom the settlor appointed have died or disclaimed; or (c) where the personal representative of a sole surviving trustee predeceases that trustee, or survives him but dies before having appointed a new trustee or trustees. The power to appoint trustees is conferred on the court by s 41 of the Trustee Act 1925. Section 41 extends further than the situations set out above and enables the court to appoint a trustee or trustees—

(i) whenever no trustee exists (eg where a corporation which is a sole trustee is wound up);

(ii) in addition to an existing trustee or trustees;

(iii) in place of an existing trustee or trustees.

The court may exercise its power under s 41 to appoint a new trustee or trustees 'whenever it is expedient' to do so 'and it is inexpedient, difficult or impracticable so to do without the assistance of the court'. The section goes on to provide that the court should specifically have power to appoint a trustee in place of a trustee who (a) is mentally defective; or, (b) is bankrupt; or, (c) is a corporation which is in liquidation; or, (d) is a corporation which has been dissolved.

It will be noted that in some of these situations, existing trustees might have power under s 36(1) to appoint a new trustee. However, there may well be difficulty, and in this case it might be expedient, and would be likely to be convenient, for the appointment to be made, not by the other trustees, but by the court. The application to the court may be made by a beneficiary or an existing trustee.

The power of the court under s 41 to appoint new trustees thus sometimes:

(a) exists in the absence of anyone else to make the appointment (eg where the sole trustee is a corporation which is wound up; or where the personal representative of a deceased sole surviving trustee dies without appointing trustees);

(b) exists in situations where it may be expedient for a new trustee to be appointed in place of an existing trustee, but the other trustees have no power under s 36(1) to appoint a fresh trustee (eg where a trustee was, as far as was known, in enemy occupied territory[3]; where there was friction between the existing trustees[4]; where a trustee had gone to live in Tahiti and intended to stay there permanently[5]);

(c) exists co-terminously with a power conferred on existing trustees to appoint a fresh trustee.

JUDICIAL TRUSTEE

In addition to the power conferred by s 41 of the Trustee Act 1925, a power to appoint trustees is conferred on the court by certain other statutes. For example, under the Judicial Trustees Act 1896 the court may appoint a 'judicial trustee'. The position of a judicial trustee differs from that of an ordinary trustee in the following ways. A judicial trustee, (i) is an officer of the court, and thus subject to the court's supervision and control; (ii) can obtain directions from the court as to the way in which he should act without needing to make a formal application by way of summons; (iii) must have his accounts audited each year; (iv) cannot appoint a successor (as can an ordinary trustee under s 36(1)); (v) is entitled to such remuneration as the court specifies.

An application for the appointment of a judicial trustee is likely to be made in cases where the administration of the trust by the ordinary trustees has broken down but it is not wished to incur the expense of having the trust administered by the court itself.

An application for the appointment of a judicial trustee may be made by the settlor, or by a trustee, or by a beneficiary. The person appointed may be the person nominated in the application, or an official of the court (usually the official solicitor).

A judicial trustee may act alone or jointly with other trustees. If the court so directs, he may act in place of all or any existing trustees.

Under the Public Trustee Act 1906[6] the court has power, on the application of a trustee or beneficiary, to appoint the Public Trustee to be a trustee in addition to or in substitution for an existing trustee or trustees.

7 Same persons appointed personal representatives and trustees

We saw when dealing with the initial trustees that it is the duty of the personal representative to transfer the trust property to the trustees. What is the position if the testator had appointed, say, three persons (X, Y and Z) as his executors, and that he had appointed the same three persons as his trustees, eg under a trust for sale? In this case, at the moment when X, Y and Z

---

3 *Re May's Will Trusts* [1941] Ch 109.
4 *Re Henderson* [1940] Ch 764, [1940] 3 All ER 295.
5 *Re Bignold's Settlement Trusts* (1872) 7 Ch App 223.
6 Section 1. The functions of the Public Trustee were extended by the Public Trustee and Administration of Funds Act 1986.

complete the administration of the estate they undergo an automatic change of capacity[7] and become trustees[8].

With regard to the trust property, must X, Y and Z, as personal representatives, make out an assent to themselves as trustees?—ie is the validity of the title to property incomplete if they fail to execute this document? If the trust property takes the form of shares, then if X, Y and Z are recorded as the owners in the company's books, no further step is necessary. But if the trust property is land, X, Y and Z, as personal representatives, must make a written assent to themselves as trustees[9].

8 Termination of trusteeship

From what has already been said it will be seen that trusteeship may be determined in the following ways:

1. Death of a trustee.
2. Replacement of a trustee in any circumstances set out in s 36(1).
3. Retirement of the trustee under s 39.
4. Replacement of a trustee by the court under s 41.

To this list we may, for convenience, add:

5. Disclaimer by a person appointed trustee (though disclaimer does not so much terminate a trusteeship as prevent an appointment as trustee from taking effect).

9 Section 40

On page 236, we saw that when A died, it was necessary for the remaining trustees, B and C, to transfer the title to the trust property from themselves alone, to themselves and the new trustee, D; and for them to do this by obtaining an alteration in the company's register of shareholders.

What is the position with regard to the transfer of the legal title to trust property in cases where no such alteration in a company's (or other body's) books is necessary in order to effect a transfer of the legal title to the property? (For example, where the trust property is land or chattels.) The answer is that there is then generally no need for a separate transaction to be carried out in order to vest the legal title in the new set of trustees. The reason is that s 40 of the Trustee Act 1925 provides that when a new trustee is appointed by deed, and the deed contains a declaration (a 'vesting declaration') that the trust property should vest in the persons who are in future to be the trustees (ie the existing trustees and the new trustee) then the deed of appointment operates to vest the trust property in those persons. Further, s 40 provides that if the deed of appointment is made after 1925, the deed is to operate as if it contained such a declaration, even if no such declaration is in fact included. Thus, under s 40, the legal title to the trust property vests

7 See 'The Transition from Personal Representative to Trustee', C. Stebbings [1984] Conv 423.
8 *Attenborough v Solomon* [1913] AC 76, HL.
9 *Re King's Will Trusts* [1964] Ch 542, [1964] 1 All ER 833.

automatically in the new trustee or trustees (together with the existing trustees) without any separate document needing to be executed.

Similarly, if a trustee retires, and the deed of retirement contains a vesting declaration by the retiring and the continuing trustees, the trust property becomes vested in the continuing trustees. Similarly again, if the deed of retirement is executed after 1925, the deed operates as if it contained such a declaration, even if no such declaration is in fact included.

This provision is particularly convenient in the case of trusts of land[10]. For example, if A, B and C are trustees holding land on trust for sale, and A dies, and B and C appoint D as a new trustee, there is no need for a conveyance to be drawn up conveying the land from B and C to B, C and D. The deed of appointment (containing the 'vesting declaration') suffices.

It will be noted that whilst under s 36(1) a trustee may be appointed in writing, if advantage is to be taken of s 40, the appointment must be by deed.

It will also be noted that, of the three most common forms of trust property today, ie land, money in a bank account, and investments, it is only with regard to transfers of the first of these that s 40 applies[11].

Since s 40 applies only with regard to the vesting of trust property in newly appointed trustees, the section therefore has no application in connection with the vesting of trust property in first trustees. This must be done by the testator's personal representative transferring the property to the first trustees by whatever formality is required, according to the nature of the property (eg if the property is land to be held on trust for sale the personal representative must execute a written assent). On the other hand, where a sole surviving trustee dies, and the trust property vests in his personal representative, X, and X appoints fresh trustees, then s 40 does operate, and vests the trust property in the new trustees, provided, as we have noted, that the trust property is not of a kind which requires an alteration in a company's books[12].

10 Protection of purchasers: s 38

Suppose that A, B and C are trustees of a trust for sale of land. C remains outside the United Kingdom for more than 12 months. A and B execute a deed which appoints D as trustee in C's place. Section 40 operates to vest the legal title to the land in A, B and D. Later A, B and D agree to sell the land to P. P investigates their title to the land. P knows that A and B had power to appoint D in place of C, provided that C was outside the United Kingdom for more than twelve months. Does P need to obtain evidence of this fact before he can be satisfied that A, B and D have a good title to the

---

10 Section 40 does not, however, apply in two situations. (a) Where trustees hold a mortgage of land as security for a loan of trust money. In this case, if A, B and C hold a mortgage of land (as security for a loan of trust money), and A dies, and B and C appoint D a trustee, B and C must execute a deed conveying the mortgage from themselves, to themselves and D. (b) Nor does s 40 apply where the trust property is a lease which contains a condition prohibiting disposition of the land without consent, unless, prior to the execution of the deed containing (expressly or impliedly) the vesting declaration, the necessary consent has been obtained; or, unless, by reason of any statute or rule of law, the vesting of the property in the new trustees would not constitute a breach of the condition.
11 And then with the exceptions stated in footnote 10, ante.
12 Subject to the exceptions stated in footnote 10, ante.

land? Does he, in fact, whenever a new trustee is appointed under the power conferred by s 36(1), need to obtain evidence of the circumstances (eg refusal to act, unfitness to act, etc) on the basis of which the power was exercised? The answer is that if the power conferred by s 36(1) was exercised by reason of the death of a trustee, P must obtain evidence of the death (eg in the form of a certified copy of the death certificate). But where the power is exercised by reason of a trustee remaining out of the United Kingdom for more than 12 months, or his refusing or being unfit to act or being incapable of acting, and the instrument appointing the new trustee contains a statement to the effect that the trustee replaced had remained out of the United Kingdom for more than 12 months, or had refused to act, etc, then P is entitled, by s 38(1), to treat this statement as conclusive proof of the matter stated, and is thus relieved of the need to obtain further evidence.

11 Appointment of trustees by personal representatives

The differences should be noted between the position of a personal representative of a *testator* who creates a trust without appointing trustees (or who appoints trustees but they die before the trust property is transferred to them) and that of a personal representative of a deceased *sole or sole surviving trustee*. The former has no power[13] (subject to what is said below) to appoint trustees and the appointment can be made only by the person nominated by the testator or, if there is no such person, by the court. The latter has power, under s 36, to appoint fresh trustees.

The only circumstance in which the personal representative of the original testator can appoint trustees arises where a testator leaves property (whether a specific bequest or devise, or a gift of residue) to an infant absolutely. In this case the executor[14] may appoint two or more individuals[15] not exceeding four, to be trustees for the infant, and vest the property in them. On so doing he is freed from further liability in respect of the property[16].

12 Trustees and personal representatives compared

There are similarities between the position of a trustee and a personal representative. Both hold property in a fiduciary capacity, on trust to deal with it, in the case of a trustee, for the beneficiaries, in the case of a personal representative, for those entitled under the deceased's will or intestacy. With only a few exceptions the rules that govern trustees apply equally to personal representatives[17] as do the provisions of the Trustees Act 1925 (unless a contrary intention appears)[18]. The principal differences that exist are as follows:

13 Unless of course, the testator appoints him a trustee as well as personal representative, or he is subsequently appointed a trustee by the other trustees. But in these situations he makes any appointment in his capacity as a trustee, not as a personal representative. See *Re Cockburn* [1957] Ch 438, [1957] 2 All ER 522.
14 An administrator under an intestacy has the same power.
15 Or a trust corporation.
16 Administration of Estates Act 1925, s 42.
17 *Re Speight* (1883) 22 Ch D 727, 742, CA; affd sub nom *Speight v Gaunt* 9 App Cas 1, HL.
18 Section 68(17).

1. The primary duty of a trustee is to retain property, that of a personal representative is to distribute it.

2. Trustees can only act jointly. Thus a good title can be passed only by trustees acting together in making a transfer: one or more out of a group cannot pass a good title (even if the purchaser is a bona fide purchaser without notice). Personal representatives can act only jointly with regard to a conveyance of land, but one or more out of a group can, without the authority of the others, pass a good title to pure personalty[19] to a bona fide purchaser.

3. Where land is held on trust, a purchaser will take free of equitable interests only where the receipt for the purchase money is signed by at least two trustees or a trust corporation. A sole personal representative can give a valid receipt for such proceeds of sale.

Where a testator appoints the same persons to be his executors and to be trustees of property under his will, then the persons appointed hold the property first as personal representatives. When the administration of the estate is complete their capacity changes to that of trustees[20]. However, where the property concerned is land, it has been held[1] that where the same persons are appointed executors and trustees, they must (as personal representatives) make a written assent[2] to themselves (as trustees) in order to take advantage of s 40 of the Trustee Act 1925[3].

We may note here that whilst beneficiaries under a trust have an interest in the trust property, beneficiaries under a will of a testator, the administration of whose estate has not been completed, have no interest in the property forming the estate. This is because, until administration is complete, there can be no knowledge as to what the property available for the beneficiaries will consist of. Pending completion of administration, beneficiaries have no more than a right to have the will duly administered[4]. At the moment that administration is complete, the beneficiaries acquire an interest in the property available for distribution to them according to the terms of the will.

13 Trusts created inter vivos

In this chapter we have so far envisaged a trust which was established by a testator in his will. The principles we have set out apply equally to a trust created inter vivos, with the following exceptions:

(a) The transfer of the trust property to the initial trustees will be made by the settlor himself, not by his personal representative.

(b) The settlor may appoint himself one of the trustees.

(c) Alternatively, instead of transferring the trust property to trustees, a

---

19 Ie personalty excluding leaseholds.
20 *Attenborough v Solomon* [1913] AC 76, HL.
1   *Re King's Will Trusts* [1964] Ch 542, [1964] 1 All ER 833. [1976] CLP 60 (E. C. Ryder). Followed in *Re Edwards' Will Trusts* [1982] Ch 30, [1981] 2 All ER 941, CA. [1981] Conv 450 (G. Shindler), [1982] Conv 4 (P. W. Smith).
2   By an assent a personal representative vests property in the person named in the assent, eg a purchaser, or a person entitled under the will or intestacy. By AEA 1925 s 36(2), (4) an assent of land must be in writing, signed by the personal representative.
3   See p 247.
4   *Stamp Duties Comr (Queensland) v Livingston* [1965] AC 694, [1964] 3 All ER 692, PC.

settlor may constitute a trust by declaring himself (sole) trustee of the trust property.

(d) The settlor can reserve to himself the power to appoint fresh trustees. (In the absence of such reservation he has no such power.)

(e) If the trustees appointed by the settlor die (or cease to exist) before receiving the title to the trust property or are incapable of taking the trust property (eg because of infancy) the trust is incompletely constituted. If the trust was created for value, the settlor himself holds the property on the trust he has specified[5].

It will be seen that the difference between the appointment of trustees in the case of trusts created inter vivos and on death relate, in the main, to the initial appointment of trustees.

5   See Chap 6.

Chapter 14

Duties on appointment; agents; delegation; expenses; remuneration

Duties on appointment

Let us suppose that a testator, T, decides to appoint his two brothers A and B as his trustees. When T dies, his wife, W, telephones the news to T's solicitor X, and it is arranged that A, B and W should meet at X's office in a fortnight's time. At the meeting X reads T's will and in the discussion which follows B says 'T has made A and myself trustees of this trust which T has set up. What happens now? What do we do?'

'Well', replies X, 'for the time being most of the things to be done rest with me, since T has appointed me his executor[1]. First, I will have to get probate of the will. This means that I have to get the will approved by the court. In practice, the will will be examined by officials of the principal registry of the Family Division of the High Court. They will check that the will has been properly signed and witnessed. If they are satisfied that the will has been validly made, they will stamp it with the Registry stamp, file it and then send me a "grant of probate". This is a document signed by the Registrar of the Family Division and sealed with the Registry seal which declares that T's will has been "proved" (ie shown to be valid) and registered in the registry of the Family Division, and that "administration of all the estate" (ie responsibility for winding up T's affairs and distributing his property according to the will) has been granted to me. (The grant of probate will have a photocopy of the will attached to it. The original will be retained by the Registry.)

On 'T's death', X continues, 'all his property vested automatically in me, as his personal representative, by virtue of the Administration of Estates Act 1925[2]. But I shall not be able to begin my work of paying T's debts and distributing his estate until probate has been granted. This is because, although I am appointed executor by the will, my authority to begin acting as executor is the grant of probate.

'Having obtained probate', X goes on, 'my first job will be to collect all T's property into my hands. It is true that legally the title to all T's property is vested in me at the moment of T's death: but some property may still be in T's name. For example, T's shares in ICI will still be registered in his name. So I must notify ICI and have the shares transferred into my name. Similarly with Redacre: T's name will still be recorded as the registered proprietor in

---

1 X, as T's solicitor will probably only have agreed to act as executor if the will authorised him to charge for his services.
2 Section 1(1). There are limited exceptions: for example, if T had had an interest in land in fee tail, on his death the land would vest immediately in T's heir.

the Land Registry. I must have myself registered as the proprietor. I must also collect money which was owed to T and if necessary sue debtors who do not pay. Then, having collected all T's assets into my hands, I will pay out any money he owed at his death and any money which has become payable by his estate since his death, including the cost of his funeral and of obtaining probate. When I have done this I will know how much T's estate is worth, and I shall have to work out the Inheritance Tax which is due to the Inland Revenue. Then I will pay the specific bequests which T made in his will. Whatever is left is the "residuary estate", and this I will transfer to you. For example, I shall arrange for the shares (assuming I have not had to sell them to pay T's debts) to be registered in your names; money will be transferred into a new account in your names at a bank; I shall make out an assent to you in respect of Redacre, and I shall have the land registered in your name at the Land Registry. When all these things have been done, you will hold all the trust property. You are trustees now, by virtue of the appointment in T's will; but your responsibilities do not in practice begin until some property is transferred to you'.

'And what are our responsibilities?' asks A.

'They can be put under seven heads', X explains. 'First, you must check that you have been validly appointed. You can do this by examining the terms of the will. (I will let you each have a copy after this meeting.) Second, you must acquaint yourselves with the interests of the beneficiaries under the trust. You can study these from the will. Third, you must satisfy yourselves that all the property due to the trust has been transferred to you and that you have received all the relevant documents of title (for example, the land certificate of Redacre, the share certificates for the ICI shares and so on). Fourth, you must consider whether you are under any duty, express or implied, to sell any part of the trust property. Fifth, you must give your attention to the investment of the trust fund. In particular you must satisfy yourselves that those parts of the trust fund which already consist of shares or other securities are properly invested, according to the provisions of the will and the Trustee Investment Act 1961; and you must decide how trust money which is not already invested should be invested. Sixth, you must manage those parts of the trust fund which require management. For example, in the case of the flats on Redacre, you must see that rents continue to be paid, and repairs done where necessary, and so on. Seventh, when income becomes available (for example, if a dividend is received from ICI) you must see that it is applied according to the terms of the trust. But initially your responsibilities will be confined to the first three: checking your appointment, acquainting yourselves with the beneficial interests, and getting the trust property into your hands'.

The responsibilities of trustees under a trust created inter vivos are broadly the same as those set out above. There may, however, be minor differences arising from the different circumstances. For example, in the case of a trust created by will, much of the work involved with getting in the property which is to be trust property (eg collecting debts to the estate) will be done by the executor: the trustees will merely have to ensure that it is properly transferred to them by him. In the case of a trust created inter vivos, work of this kind may fall to the trustees. For example, in the case of an ante-nuptial settlement, responsibility for getting in the trust property (eg enforcing a covenant to settle existing or after acquired property) would rest with the trustees.

Employment of agents

A and B leave X's office, pondering on what he has told them. 'We can't handle all those things X told us about', A says to B, 'we shall need a lot of advice. Let's go to see my own solicitor, Y'. B agrees and together they consult Y. Y tells them that he will be glad to act as solicitor to the trust (not as 'solicitor-trustee', as Y is not a trustee).

'So we can leave everything in your hands?' B asks.

'No', Y replies, 'you can leave it to me to handle a great deal of the work, letter writing and so on. But if any decision has to be made (for example, whether to make a change in the investments or whether to sell Redacre) I shall have to come to you. You can appoint me as your agent to undertake work on your behalf, but responsibility for making decisions will remain with you'.

The power of trustees to appoint agents to undertake work on their behalf is conferred by s 23 of the Trustee Act 1925. The section provides that 'trustees . . . may, instead of acting personally, employ and pay' (ie out of trust money) 'an agent, whether solicitor, banker, stockbroker, or other person to transact any business . . . including the receipt and payment of money . . .'. The section (which is subject to any provision to the contrary in the trust instrument) confers the same power on personal representatives.

Under s 23, if a trustee appoints an agent and a loss results due to the fault of the agent then, provided that the trustee employed the agent 'in good faith', he is not responsible for the agent's default[3].

Before the 1925 Act, a trustee had power to employ agents (and pay them from the trust fund) only if the employment of the agent was 'conformible to the common usage of mankind'[4] (eg the employment of a broker to sell a quantity of tobacco[4], or to invest trust money[5]) or was legally necessary (eg the employment of a solicitor to undertake conveyancing work). A trustee who appointed an agent was liable for the agent's default unless he could show that he had acted in a reasonable manner both in appointing the agent, and in his subsequent supervision of him.

The 1925 Act thus now not only permits an agent to be employed for any work on behalf of the trust, but may also make it easier for a trustee to escape liability for an agent's default. The trustee does not now have to show that he acted reasonably, only that he acted in good faith. We shall see later[6], however, that a trustee may become liable for an agent's default if the trustee was himself in some way at fault, for example in failing properly to supervise the agent's conduct.

---

3 See Chap 23.
4 *Re Parsons* (1754) Amb 218.
5 *Re Speight* (1883) 22 Ch D 727, CA; affd sub nom *Speight v Gaunt* 9 App Cas 1, HL.
6 See Chap 22.

Appointment of delegates[7]

If a trustee employs someone as his agent, he employs that person to under-take certain work, but he cannot (subject to the exceptions to be considered shortly) delegate to another person his responsibility for taking decisions[8]. This is because the trustee is himself a delegate (responsibility for handling the trust property having been delegated to him by the settlor) and the rule is that a delegate cannot delegate, ie a person to whom responsibility has been delegated cannot 'sub-delegate' that responsibility to someone else[9]. (The maxim is: 'Delegatus non potest delegare'.) The matter is neatly expressed by Snell[10]: '... power to employ agents to do specified acts is not power to authorise agents to decide what acts to do'.

There are only a limited number of instances in which a trustee can delegate his powers to another. These are as follows:

1. If the trust property, or part of it, is outside the United Kingdom (eg if at T's death he owned a cottage in France, or had money in a Swiss bank account), then under s 23(2) of the Trustee Act 1925 a trustee has power to appoint an agent with authority to act on his behalf with regard to the management and administration (including sale) of the property concerned. If a loss occurs as a result of the appointment, the trustee is not liable.

2. Under s 25 of the Trustee Act 1925 as amended by the Powers of Attorney Act 1971[11], a trustee may delegate all or any of his powers to another for a period of up to one year. (Before the 1971 Act the power to delegate under s 25 existed only if the trustee intended to remain outside the United Kingdom for over a month.)[12] The delegation may be to any person except to a sole remaining co-trustee who is not a trust corporation[13].

A person who authorises another to act in his place is said to grant the other 'a power of attorney'. To be valid under s 25 the instrument containing the grant of a power of attorney by a trustee must be signed by the trustee and at least one witness[14], and written notice containing details of the grant[15] must be given[16] to the other trustees[17].

A person to whom power is delegated under s 25 of the Trustee Act can

---

1 X, as T's solicitor will probably only have agreed to act as executor if the will authorised him to charge for his services.

8 Hence the principle that a trustee on selling (or leasing) trust property cannot sell (or lease) at a price (or rent) to be determined by a third party or in accordance with a specified formula (as can a beneficial owner on the sale or lease of his own property). *Peters v Lewes and East Grinstead Rly Co* (1880) 16 Ch D 703; on appeal, (1881) 18 Ch D 429; *Re Earl of Wilton's Settled Estates* [1907] 1 Ch 50. But see [1985] Conv 44 (G. Lightman).

9 See *Re Hay's Settlement Trusts* [1981] 3 All ER 786, [1982] 1 WLR 202.

10 *Principles of Equity*, 28th edn, p 264.

11 Section 9.

12 Distinct from a power of attorney granted under s 25 of the Trustee Act 1925 is a power of attorney, termed an 'enduring power of attorney', granted under the Enduring Powers of Attorney Act 1985. Such a power may last indefinitely (ie until the death of the donor). It has the further advantage over a power under s 25 of the Trustee Act 1925 that it is not automatically revoked by the mental incapacity of the donor.

13 Section 25(2).

14 Trustee Act 1925, s 25(3).

15 Including its date of commencement, duration, the reason for it being granted; and, where only some powers are delegated, what these are.

16 Before the grant, or within seven days after it.

17 And any person having power to appoint new trustees.

exercise any of the powers which were exercisable by the trustee who appointed him. There is one exception: s 25 does not give him power to delegate (ie to sub-delegate) to someone else the powers which were delegated to him[18]. (This does not, of course, prevent him from employing an agent to carry out work for the trust.) If a loss arises, then the trustee is liable as if the default had been his own.

It will be seen that (1) a trustee is not liable for the default of a delegate appointed under s 23(2) to act in connection with property abroad; (2) he is not liable for the default of an agent appointed under s 23(1), if the appointment was made honestly. But, (3), he is liable for the default of a delegate appointed under s 25. Therefore, since a trustee remains liable for the default of a delegate appointed under s 25, this power of delegation is seldom in practice used. A trustee is more likely to retain his responsibility for taking decisions and, where necessary, appoint an agent under s 23(1).

It should be noted that in the two instances set out at (1) and (2) above, the person to whom power is delegated may sometimes in practice and in legal textbooks be referred to as an 'agent'. But such a person is more than an agent in the sense in which that word is used when speaking, for example, of a solicitor employed by a trustee to undertake conveyancing work. For example, if a purchaser offers to buy Redacre from A and B, they may employ C to prepare the contract and the conveyance. But the decision to sell, and the act of selling (ie the signing of the documents) must be that of A and B. If B goes abroad and delegates his powers to D, then the decision to sell rests with A and D, and D's signature is valid in place of B's in the execution of documents. Thus whilst C is an agent and no more, D is a delegate. It may happen that C is both appointed delegate for B and employed to undertake certain conveyancing work: in this case C is both an agent (for the trust) and a delegate (for B).

In the two instances considered so far, at (1) and (2) above, a trustee may delegate all or any of his powers to another. In the next two instances, only certain powers may be delegated.

3. If A and B hold land on trust for sale for W for life with remainder to Z, then, under s 29 of the Law of Property Act 1925, until the land is sold, A and B may delegate to W (the person[19] beneficially entitled for the time being to the income from the land) their powers of managing the land and granting (and accepting surrenders of) leases of the land. If this delegation occurs, A and B are not liable for the acts or defaults of W. The court has power (for example, on an application by W) to compel A and B to delegate these powers to W. It will be noted that A and B cannot delegate responsibility for deciding whether the land should be retained (ie their power to postpone sale). This decision remains with A and B.

4. The effect of s 8 of the Trustee Act 1925 is to enable trustees in certain circumstances to delegate their responsibility for valuing land. This section will be considered later when dealing with the duties and powers of trustees in relation to the investment of trust money[20].

---

18 Section 25(6). It seems that a person to whom power is delegated under s 23 to act in connection with land outside the UK can 'sub-delegate' his powers. See s 23(2).
19 Being of full age and not merely an annuitant.
20 See Chap 15.

Expenses of administering a trust[1]

Expenses incurred in administering a trust are payable out of the trust property. If a trustee pays such expenses out of his own pocket, he can recover the sums spent from the trust[2]. Further, as already noted[3], if trustees employ an agent to conduct trust business, they have power to pay the agent out of the trust money.

Remuneration[4]

Trustees are not, however, permitted to receive payment for acting as trustees: they are not entitled to any remuneration[5].

This is the general rule. There are, however, the following exceptions, when a trustee is entitled to receive payment.

1. If the instrument creating the trust authorises payment to a trustee (if the instrument includes a 'charging clause') then a trustee (or a personal representative) is entitled to be paid accordingly[6].

If the instrument creating the trust includes a charging clause authorising a solicitor-trustee to charge for his services, and the clause is in general terms, for example, authorising payment for 'all professional and other charges for his time and trouble'[7], this will be construed narrowly as authorising him to charge for his professional services only, and not for carrying out duties which could be performed by a layman (for example, attending weekly meetings held by trustees for the purpose of carrying on a deceased testator's business[8]).[9] In order to enable a solicitor-trustee to charge for time and trouble spent on trust work which could be done by someone other than a solicitor, the charging clause must contain words such as 'including acts which a trustee not being in any profession or business could have done personally'.

If a charging clause is included, then a solicitor-trustee may charge reasonable fees[10]. The safest method for determining whether fees charged are

---

1   X, as T's solicitor will probably only have agreed to act as executor if the will authorised him to charge for his services.
2   Trustee Act 1925, s 30(2). *Holding and Management Ltd v Property Holding and Investment Trust plc* [1990] 1 All ER 938, [1989] 1 WLR 1313.
3   See p 254, ante.
5   *Bray v Ford* [1896] AC 44.
6   *Willis v Kibble* (1839) 1 Beav 559.
7   *Re Chalinder and Herington* [1907] 1 Ch 58.
8   *Clarkson v Robinson* [1900] 2 Ch 722.
9   The Law Reform Committee, 23rd Report, recommended that a trustee who is allowed to charge for his professional services should be presumed to be able to charge for all work that could reasonably be done by a person of his expertise, even though it could be done by a layman, if an ordinary prudent man of business would expect a trustee to do this work. (Para 3.52.)
10   The Law Reform Committee, 23rd Report, recommended that a beneficiary under a trust should be entitled to obtain a remuneration certificate from the Law Society in order to establish that the charges made by a solicitor-trustee under a charging clause are reasonable. (Para 3.50.)

reasonable is for them to be approved by an official of the court termed a 'taxing master'. (This is known as having the fees 'taxed'.) An alternative method is for the trust instrument to give the non-professional trustees authority to determine whether fees charged are reasonable. If a charging clause stipulates a rate of payment and this ceases to be adequate in the light of the work undertaken the court has power to authorise an increase[11], but this jurisdiction is exercised sparingly, and only in exceptional circumstances, as where there has been a fundamental change in the nature of the assets of the trust[12]. The fact that the rate of remuneration is lower than that currently charged for the work of the kind undertaken will not of itself warrant the exercise of the jurisdiction[12]. However, where the jurisdiction to authorise an increase is exercised, the court may sanction not only an increase in respect of work already performed, but also prospectively, in respect of future levels of work[13].

2. Even if there is no charging clause in the instrument creating the trust, under the rule in *Cradock v Piper*[14] a solicitor-trustee may charge his professional fees (known as 'profit costs') for work done by him on behalf of himself and one or more co-trustees in connection with legal proceedings brought by or against the trustees, including non-contentious proceedings (for example an application to the court in connection with maintenance of an infant[15]). Under the rule, however, no charge may be made in respect of any cost attributable to the solicitor-trustee having represented *himself* as well as a co-trustee. Thus the fees will be limited to the costs which would have been incurred if the co-trustee had been the sole party to the action.

The rule in *Cradock v Piper*[16] is not only an exception to the general rule; it is without any satisfactory rational basis. If a solicitor-trustee is not entitled (in the absence of a charging clause) to be paid for non-litigious work, there seems no valid reason why he should be paid for work in connection with litigation.

It will be convenient to note here that a solicitor trustee is at liberty to employ his partner as solicitor to the trust, and his partner may then charge for his services, provided the arrangement is clearly made that the partner alone receives the costs[17]. If a trustee who is a solicitor employs his firm for work in connection with the trust no charge may be made, even if the trustee solicitor receives no share of the charges (ie either by arrangement[18] or because he is merely a salaried partner[19]).

3. If all the beneficiaries are sui juris and between them absolutely entitled to the trust property, and they enter into a contract with a trustee (whether professionally qualified or not) under which he is authorised to receive payment for performing the duties of trustee, then the trustee is entitled to receive payment accordingly. The courts will be on the watch for any undue

11 *Re Codd Will Trusts* [1975] 2 All ER 1051n, [1975] 1 WLR 1139.
12 *Re Duke of Norfolk's Settlement Trusts* [1979] Ch 37, [1978] 3 All ER 907; (M & B); (1979) 95 LQR 55 (H. W. Wilkinson); (1982) 98 LQR 181 (JMT); (1982) 45 MLR 211 (B. Green).
13 *Re Duke of Norfolk's Settlement Trusts* [1982] Ch 61, [1981] 3 All ER 220, CA.
14 (1850) 1 Mac & G 664.
15 *Re Corsellis* (1887) 34 Ch D 675.
16 (1850) 1 Mac & G 664.
17 *Clack v Carlon* (1861) 30 LJ Ch 639.
18 *Re Gates* [1933] Ch 913.
19 *Re Hill* [1934] Ch 623.

influence by the trustee on the beneficiaries in making such a contract, and if this is found the contract will be set aside.

4. If the Public Trustee is appointed as trustee, then (irrespective of whether or not there is a charging clause in the will) he may charge for work carried out[20]. The Treasury lays down a scale of fees which are set out in Statutory Instruments[1].

5. In certain circumstances the court has power to authorise a trustee to receive payment for his services. Thus:

(a) if the court appoints a corporation (other than the Public Trustee) then the court may authorise the corporation to receive remuneration[2];

(b) if the court appoints a judicial trustee[3] then he is entitled to the remuneration which the court lays down[4];

(c) if the court considers that a trustee has done work for the trust which has been exceptionally onerous or which has, as a result of the trustees' exceptional skills, produced a significant profit, then it has an inherent jurisdiction[5] to direct that he should be compensated for the work involved[6]. The jurisdiction is wholly exceptional[7] and will only be exercised where (a) the circumstances are such as to indicate an implied promise by the beneficiaries that remuneration would be paid; or, (b) where it is necessary to obtain the services of a particular kind of trustee; or, (c) where it is necessary to obtain a particular individual trustee whose services are of special value to the trust[8].

Where trustees are not entitled to receive remuneration under any of the foregoing heads, and it is considered expedient in the interests of the trust that remuneration should be paid to them, then it is open for an application to be made to the court for an order under the Variation of Trusts Act 1958 authorising the inclusion of a term in the trust instrument permitting the payment of remuneration to the trustees[9].

If a trustee is appointed a director of a company by virtue of the voting rights in shares which are trust property, the question arises as to whether he is entitled to retain remuneration paid to him as a director. This matter is considered later, when dealing with the principle that a trustee is not entitled to derive a profit from his position[10].

---

20 Public Trustee Act 1906, s 9.
 1 Made under the Public Trustee Act 1906 as amended by the Public Trustee (Fees) Act 1957.
 2 Trustee Act 1925, s 42.
 3 See p 246.
 4 Judicial Trustees Act 1896, s 1(5).
 5 *O'Sullivan v Management Agency & Music Ltd* [1985] QB 428, [1985] 3 All ER 351. For the exercise of the court's inherent jurisdiction for the purpose of authorising payment to a liquidator of a company who had done work for the benefit of beneficiaries under a trust fund, see *Re Berkeley Applegate (Investment Consultants) Ltd* [1989] Ch 32, [1988] 3 All ER 71. For the court's refusal of a payment based on *quantum meruit* to a company director who had performed valuable services but not (as the director claimed) in a professional capacity (merely in his capacity as a director) see *Guinness plc v Saunders* [1990] 2 AC 663, [1990] 1 All ER 652; [1990] Conv 296 (S. Goulding), [1990] CLJ 220 (J. Hopkins).
 6 See *Re Worthington* [1954] 1 All ER 677; *Re Duke of Norfolk's Settlement Trusts* [1979] Ch 37, [1978] 3 All ER 907.
 7 *Re Freeman's Settlement Trusts* (1887) 37 Ch D 148; *Re Masters* [1953] 1 All ER 19, [1953] 1 WLR 81.
 8 *Re Duke of Norfolk's Settlement Trusts* [1979] Ch 37, [1978] 3 All ER 907; (M & B).
 9 See Chap 18.
10 See Chap 19.

Professional and non-professional trustees

Suppose that in his will a testator, T, wishes to leave all his property on trust for his wife for her lifetime, with remainder to their children. Who should he appoint as the trustees? One course would be for T to appoint an institution which is authorised to carry out trust business, a 'trust corporation', as trustee. All the major banks are trust corporations and have their own executor and trustee departments. But such a body will only accept the position of trustee if it is permitted to charge for the work it does, and it can only do this if the testator's will so authorises.

Let us suppose that T, whilst recognising the experience and reliability which a trust corporation will have, decides that such a body might be somewhat impersonal in its approach, and would have to be more inflexible in its application of the law, and its interpretation of his will, than he would wish. Therefore, instead, T considers appointing as trustees two of his professional advisers, his solicitor and his accountant. Such professionally qualified persons are commonly appointed trustees, but in this case also they will only be willing to accept the trusteeship if they can charge for their services, and to be able to do this there must be provision for their remuneration in the will.

T then considers appointing two of his brothers as trustees. At first he thinks that this will avoid the cost of the remuneration which his solicitor and accountant would require if they were to be the trustees. But he quickly realises that even if his brothers were appointed trustees they would, being unqualified in law, have to employ a solicitor (and perhaps also an accountant) to advise them on how to administer the business of the trust. So either way, T rightly concludes, there will be no escaping bills for professional advice.

Another course which T considers is appointing as his trustees his two brothers and his solicitor. 'The solicitor will be able to advise on technical matters', T thinks, 'and his office will be able to do most of the actual work, but the decisions will be shared between him and my brothers, and the latter will provide the family link'. Such a course, to appoint professional and non-professional trustees (with express authority for the professional trustee to charge for his services), is commonly followed.

'On the other hand', T thinks, 'if my solicitor is one of the trustees, and my brothers consider that his charges are too high, they would not be able to get rid of him as a trustee (at least, not on this ground alone) and they might find it awkward to get the work transferred to another solicitor. Perhaps my best course', T decides 'is to appoint my brothers alone as trustees. They can then employ (and pay) who they wish as solicitor, and if they find the charges of whoever they employ too high, they can always transfer the work to another firm'. So T may decide to appoint his brothers A and B to be the trustees of his will. However, in order to enable A and B, or later trustees, if they wish, to appoint a solicitor or accountant as a trustee, T may include in his will a charging clause authorising any solicitor-trustee (or accountant-trustee) to charge for work done for the trust.

Chapter 15

Investment

Introduction

THE DUTY TO INVEST

It has for long been regarded as the duty of a trustee to invest trust money so that income may be produced for the beneficiaries[1]. Pending the purchase of an investment, a trustee has power to pay the trust money into a current or a deposit account at a bank. If a trustee delays for an unreasonable length of[2] time before investing the trust money, then he is chargeable with interest[3]. The rate of interest charged is at the discretion of the court.

FORMS OF INVESTMENT

Originally a trustee was permitted to invest in a very limited number of types of investment. Today his choice is wider. Before considering the present position, it will be helpful, by way of introduction, to consider the principal forms of investment which are available today to a private person, A.

1. A could put his money into the National Savings Bank (formerly the Post Office Savings Bank) at any post office. He would receive a fixed rate of interest.

2. A could buy National Savings Certificates at a post office. Here too there is a fixed rate of interest, but the interest is added to the capital and is payable, together with the capital, after a certain number of years.

3. A could buy National Development Bonds. There is a fixed rate of interest on these. A will receive a small bonus if he retains the Bonds for longer than a certain period.

4. A could buy one of the various forms of stocks issued (or guaranteed) by the government. For example, he could buy £1,000 1994 5% Treasury stock. The '£1,000' refers to the nominal value of the stock. '1994' indicates that the government will pay this sum to the holder of the stock in 1994. (Such stock is termed 'redeemable' or 'dated' stock.) The '5%' indicates the annual interest payable.

   A could buy undated stock, for example £1,000 $4\frac{1}{2}$% Consols. In this case

---

1   *Stone v Stone* (1869) 5 Ch App 74.
2   Trustee Act 1925, s 11(1).
3   *Holgate v Haworth* (1853) 17 Beav 259; *Re Jones* (1883) 49 LT 91.

the government is not obliged (but in the case of some undated stocks has power) to redeem the stock, ie pay the holder the nominal value.

Dated and undated government stock is bought and sold on the Stock Exchange. A may buy the £1,000 1994 5% Treasury stock for £600. Why £600, when the nominal value is £1,000? The answer is that if the rate of interest offered (ie 5%) is below that which is generally obtainable at the time elsewhere (eg from a building society) then the price of the stock will be below the nominal value. So if A buys the £1,000 stock for £600, and he receives 5% interest on the nominal £1,000, this is equivalent to 8.3% on the £600 which he actually paid. And 8.3% will be closer to the general level of interest. As the stock is dated 1994, then as 1994 approaches the price will gradually increase up to the nominal value—the sum which will be paid by the government in that year. Conversely, if the general level of interest was below 5%, the price of the stock on the Stock Exchange would be more than the nominal value of £1,000.

5. A could buy (on the Stock Exchange) various stocks issued by nationalised industries or local authorities. These may be either dated or undated. (4 and 5 are known as 'gilt-edged' securities.)

6. A could buy (on the Stock Exchange) debentures in a commercial company, X Ltd. When a person buys a debenture in a company, he lends money to the company, at a certain rate of interest. Normally a debenture is secured by a 'floating charge' on the company's assets. The charge 'floats' in the sense that the charge is on whatever assets the company possesses, the company being free to buy and sell its assets without restraint. If the company goes into liquidation, then the charge becomes fixed on the particular assets owned by the company at the time of liquidation. Debentures may be redeemable or unredeemable. They have a nominal value and, for the same reasons which were explained in the case of government stocks, their price may differ from their nominal value.

7. A could buy 'ordinary' shares in X Ltd. A person who buys an ordinary share in a company becomes a part owner of the company. He is not entitled to any fixed rate of interest on the money he has invested, but he is entitled to whatever rate of dividend is declared by the company from the profits which it makes. Shares have a nominal value, based on the value of the assets of the company at the time of the issue of the shares. If the dividends declared represent a rate of interest (on the nominal value) higher than the interest rate generally obtainable, then this will, for the reasons we have seen, raise the market price above the nominal price. Further, if the actual value of the company's assets increase in value (eg if the company's land increases in value) this will be reflected in a rise in the value of the company's shares. So it may be that if A buys 100 £1 shares in X Ltd he may have to pay, not £100 (the nominal value) but, say £400. However, if the dividends declared are 32%, this will mean that he is in fact obtaining 8% on the £400 which he paid.

8. Some companies also issue 'preference' shares. A preference share is closer in nature to a debenture than to an ordinary share, since it carries a fixed rate of interest. Further, preference shares may, like debentures, be either redeemable or unredeemable. But, unlike debentures, preference shares usually entitle their holder to some limited voting rights at meetings. They

are bought and sold on the Stock Exchange and their market price fluctuates. If the company goes into liquidation its assets are used first to pay debenture holders, then preference shareholders, and finally ordinary shareholders. Since preference shares rank after debentures (and since they give no charge on the company's assets) the rate of interest on preference shares is likely to be slightly higher than that on debentures. Thus A's investment may take the form of purchasing preference shares in X Ltd.

9. A may buy units in a unit trust. A unit trust provides an example of the machinery of a trust being employed for a new purpose in this century. A unit trust works like this: individual investors subscribe money to the managers of the unit trust; the managers use the money subscribed to buy a wide range of investments. The investments are registered in the name of the trustees of the trust, often a trust corporation such as a bank. From the dividends received, the managers' salaries and the administration expenses are paid. The surplus is paid to the unit holders, according to the number of units they each hold. Units of each unit trust have a price which fluctuates according to the amount distributed to unit holders (which will depend on the dividends received by the managers) and the market value of the securities held by the trust. Thus units in a unit trust, like shares, have a nominal value and a market value. So A may buy 1,000 50p units in the Z Unit Trust for £750. Units in a unit trust are purchased direct from the managers, not on the Stock Exchange. (Ordinary shares and units in a unit trust are together colloquially termed 'equities'.)

10. A may deposit his money with the Y Building Society. He can do this by taking (or posting) his money to a branch of the society. He will be given an account book, in which will be recorded all his deposits and withdrawals. A deposit with a building society is a loan to the society. The society pays a stated rate of interest, which the society may occasionally vary in order to keep the rate in line with interest rates currently paid by other bodies (in particular, the Bank of England). The society lends the money it receives from investors to house buyers, who mortgage their house to the society as security for the loan.

11. Alternatively, A may buy shares in a building society. He can do this by taking (or posting) his money to any branch of the society. He will be given a different account book, and the sum invested will be recorded in it. A share account is sometimes termed a 'subscription account' since the person is in fact 'subscribing' for shares in the society. Normally, a person who wishes to open a subscription account has to undertake to subscribe a fixed sum every month. A person who has subscribed for shares becomes a member of the society and has voting rights at the annual general meeting. He receives a stated rate of interest, which the society may vary. If the society becomes insolvent its assets are used first to pay off loans from people who had deposited money with the society, and other creditors. Any surplus is distributed among the shareholders. Because of this fractionally higher risk, shareholders receive a slightly higher rate of interest than depositors.

12. A could lend money to a borrower who agreed to pay him a certain rate of interest. If A considered that he could rely on the borrower paying the interest and repaying the loan, A may not demand any security. A loan to a

company without any security is termed (like a loan secured by a floating charge on its assets) a 'debenture'.

13. Or A may only be prepared to lend money if the loan is secured by certain property. (We met one such form of security when considering debentures secured by a floating charge.) A common form of security for a loan is land: A may lend money to B at a certain rate of interest on the security of B's land Blackacre, A thus becoming mortgagee, and B mortgagor. In this situation A is sometimes said to be 'investing in a mortgage'. This phrase is misleading since the investment is the loan in return for interest: the mortgage is merely the security.

14. A's investment may take the form of the purchase of the freehold of a piece of land. The land could then be let to a tenant, and the rent would provide the income. Alternatively, A might buy an assignment of an existing lease. A could then sub-let the land and the rent from the sub-lease (after paying rent due under the head-lease) would provide the income. In either case, whether A buys a freehold or leasehold interest, he is said to 'invest in land'. (It should be noted that investing in a mortgage and investing in land are different forms of investment.)

15. A could invest in Government Index-linked Certificates. Under the fourth issue of the scheme, A can invest any sum between £25 and £5,000. At the end of each year the money invested will earn (i) an amount equivalent to the difference between the value of the money invested at the beginning of the year and the value of the money at the end of the year, measured by the reference to the change in the Retail Price Index during the intervening period[4] (thus if the rate of inflation measured by the Retail Price Index increased at 4.5% during the year, the sum would earn 4.5% interest); and (ii) an additional amount of interest that increases each year, from 3% at the end of the first year to 6% at the end of the fifth year (over the five years adding up to a rate of 4.04%). Money may be withdrawn at any time, but interest is earned only if the money has remained invested for one year. Repayments are free of income tax and capital gains tax. The investment is 'index-linked' in that the rate of return is linked to changes in the Retail Price Index. The investment is thus protected against the effects of inflation.

It will be seen that of the 15 examples of investment set out above—

(a) some are *loans* to a particular body (1–6, 8, 10, 12, 13 and 15); others take the form of acquiring an *interest* in certain property (7, 9, 11 and 14);
(b) some provide a set rate of interest (1–6, 8, 10–13); others provide a rate of interest which can fluctuate according to market forces (7, 9 and 14); one provides no interest (15);
(c) in some the price of the investment remains constant (1, 2, 10, 11, 12 and 13); in others, the price fluctuates according to market forces (3–9 and 14); in one there is no 'price' (15).

This last consideration (ie (c)) is of particular importance to any investor. For example, if A deposited £1,000 with the X Building Society in 1976 and he withdrew the money in 1986, he would get back £1,000. But because of

---

4   If A takes his money out before the five years is up he gets back what he has put in, but nothing more.

the decline in the value of money during this period the effect of A's investment would be that in real terms the £1,000 he received back might be
worth only £500. Furthermore, the income produced (in the form of interest
payments) would[5] be half the value of the income produced at the time of
the original investment. On the other hand, if A invested money in shares in
a company, then, as we have seen, he becomes a part owner of the company,
acquiring a share of the assets of the company concerned. Suppose that A
invested £500 in X Ltd in 1976, the company's assets at that time being worth
£1 million. In 1986 the company has, let us suppose, the same physical assets.
Because of the decline in the value of money, if the assets retain their original
real value, the assets will be worth £2 million. Since a share in a company
represents a proportion of the company's assets, on the Stock Exchange A's
shares will now be worth £1,000. He is, of course, in fact no better off, since
if he sold the shares the £1,000 he would receive in cash would only buy the
same value of goods as he could have bought for his £500 in 1976. But he
would at least be no worse off. Furthermore, assuming that the company
continued to make the same level of profits, the real value of the dividends
would be the same in 1986 as in 1976.

So an investment which takes the form of the acquisition of an asset which
retains its value in real terms will protect the investment against the effects
of the decline in the value of money.

If an asset is in increased demand, then the value of an investment in the
asset may rise at a faster rate than the rate at which the value of money
declines, with the result that the value of the investment, in real terms, may
actually increase. For example, because of the shortage of building land in
Britain, a piece of such land may have more than doubled in value between
1976 and 1986, and thus to have more than offset the fall in the value of
money during this period.

But there is no certainty that the price of shares (or land) will rise in value
as the value of money falls. The price of a share is governed in large part by
the level of dividends which the company pays, and this in turn is governed
by what profits the company is able to make. If the company's profitability
falls, so will the level of dividends, and consequently the price of the share.
The company may even go bankrupt and the shares become almost, or even
completely, valueless.

If the investment had been in a fixed interest security such as a deposit in
a building society or a purchase of government stock, then this risk would
have been largely avoided.

What we have said with regard to the advantages and disadvantages of
fixed interest securities and of shares in commercial undertakings helps us to
understand the dilemma which faces anyone with money to invest. If he
invests money in an institution such as a building society, the institution is
unlikely to become insolvent. In this sense the investment is 'safe'. But
because of the decline in the value of money, the value of the investment will
be eroded with the passing of time. On the other hand, if he invests money
in shares in a commercial concern, the rise in share prices may offset, or help
to offset, the decline in the value of money. But there can be no certainty
that the value of the investment may not be lost completely.

But the protection of his capital is only one of the two main factors that
an investor must bear in mind: the other is the rate of interest which he seeks.

5 Disregarding changes in the interest rates.

Generally, the rate of interest on fixed interest securities is higher than on equities. Thus if an investor is interested more in the short-term fruits of his investment, he may wish to select the former rather than the latter type of investment.

The dilemma may therefore be stated thus: if an investor opts for fixed interest securities he is likely to have a high degree of security; he will receive a relatively high rate of interest, but he will see the value of his capital diminish. If he invests in equities he has a lower degree of security; he is likely to receive a lower rate of interest, but he has a better chance of seeing the real value of his capital protected.

With these factors in mind we can turn to consider the law relating to the investment by trustees of trust money.

EXPRESS POWERS OF INVESTMENT

In what investments may a trustee invest trust money? In answering this question the starting-point, both in the past and at the present day, is to consider any directions which the settlor may have given in the instrument creating the trust. For example, in his will T may have included a clause authorising his trustees to invest trust money in any government security or company whose shares are quoted on the Stock Exchange. However widely or narrowly the trustees' powers are drawn by the settlor, the settlor's express directions apply.

But what is the position if the trust instrument contains no express direction as to the form which the investment of trust money may take? Originally, in this event trustees were regarded as being permitted to invest either in mortgages (ie by making a loan at a certain rate of interest on the security of a mortgage of the borrower's land) or in government securities in the form of 'Consols'. (In 1759 various loans raised by the government were consolidated into a single investment which subsequently came to be known as Consols.)

STATUTORY POWERS OF INVESTMENT PRIOR TO THE TRUSTEE INVESTMENT ACTS 1961

In 1859 the Law of Property Amendment Act authorised trustees, in the event of the trust instrument being silent on the point, to invest (in addition to investing in Consols and mortgages) in various government securities, and loans raised by various public bodies. The range of investments in which trustees were authorised to invest was widened further by subsequent statutes, in particular by the Trustee Act 1925. Section 1 of this Act contained 18 heads of authorised investment. These did not, however, include investment in equities.

The investments permitted by the 1925 Act reflected the attitude of the previous century, when the safety of the trust property was regarded as paramount, and when the value of money had remained steady over long periods. In the period of economic depression in the late 1920s and early 1930s, when share prices sank to low levels and many companies were forced into liquidation, it seemed that the type of investment permitted by the 1925 Act was correct.

However, with the gathering rate of inflation witnessed in the years following the 1939–45 war, the range of investments permitted by the 1925 Act came to be regarded as being too narrow, and it was considered that trustees ought to have power to invest some of the trust fund in equities. These less restrictive notions were embodied in the Trustee Investments Act 1961, the statute which currently controls trustees' powers of investment.

The Trustee Investments Act 1961

The Trustee Investments Act 1961 repealed s 1 of the Trustee Act 1925, but retained the principle that the statutory powers contained in the Act were subject to any express provisions in the trust instrument.[6] (The Law Reform Committee, in its 23rd Report, recommended radical changes in trustees' powers of investment. The Committee recommended that the Act of 1961 should be repealed and new powers conferred on trustees. A summary of the Committee's recommendations is given at the end of this chapter.)

PRINCIPAL PROVISIONS OF THE ACT

The major innovation of the 1961 Act is that it permits trustees to invest trust money in shares of certain commercial concerns, provided that not more than half the trust fund is invested in this way. The Act permits trustees (subject to what is said below about the division of the fund) to invest in the shares of any company which:

(a) has a total share capital of not less than £1 million; and
(b) had paid a dividend on all its shares which are entitled to a dividend in each of the five years preceding the year in which the investment is made; and
(c) has its shares quoted on the stock exchange[7], and
(d) has shares which are fully paid for (or which are required by the terms of the issue to be fully paid for within nine months of the date of issue); and
(e) is incorporated in the United Kingdom.

It will be seen that the conditions are intended to ensure that trustees invest only in the shares of large British companies which have a safe record in recent years.

Investments permitted by the Act are divided into three categories which are set out in Parts I, II and III of the First Schedule of the Act. Investment in shares of commercial concerns which satisfy the conditions set out at (a) to (e) above is included in Part III, 'Wider Range Investments'.

The Act provides that not more than half of the trust fund may be invested in Part III, 'Wider Range Investments'. This requirement is contained in s 2 which provides that (a) trustees are not permitted to invest in any Part III investment unless the trust fund has first been divided into two parts, equal in value, called the 'narrower range part' and the 'wider range part'; and

---

6 Section 1(3).
7 Ie the London Stock Exchange or other recognised stock exchange.

(b) only property in the wider range part may be used for the purpose of purchasing Part III (wider range) investments.

The narrower range part of the trust fund may be invested in securities set out in Parts I and II of the First Schedule. The investments in Parts I and II represent the kind of investments which were accepted as satisfactory by the Trustee Act 1925. Those in Part I represent what are regarded as the safest forms of investment of all (safe, that is, except from the ravages of inflation) and include, for example, National Savings Certificates and deposits in the National Savings Bank. Those in Part II in the main represent other investments authorised by the Trustee Act 1925 and include, for example, deposits in building societies, securities issued by the nationalised industries and debentures[8] issued in the United Kingdom by companies incorporated in the United Kingdom.

The distinction between investments in Part I and Part II is that whereas in the case of Part II investments a trustee must obtain advice on whether the investment is satisfactory (as he must also for Part III investments), he is not required to obtain advice before investing in Part I investments.

CONTENTS OF THE FIRST SCHEDULE

Having explained in outline the principal provisions of the Act, we shall now set out the principal types of investment in Parts I, II and III of the First Schedule of the 1961 Act. The Act[9] provides that further types of investment may be added to any of the three parts by Order[10] in Council[11].

Part I
Para 1 Defence Bonds, National Savings Certificates.
      2 Deposits in the National Savings Bank[12], deposits in a trustee savings bank.

Part II
Para 1 Fixed interest securities issued by the government of the United Kingdom (other than those in Part I).
      2 Securities, the payment of interest on which is guaranteed by the government.
      3 Fixed-interest securities issued by any public authority or nationalised industry or undertaking in the United Kingdom.
      4 Fixed-interest securities issued by the government of any overseas territory within the Commonwealth or by any public or local authority within such a territory, being securities registered in the United Kingdom.

---

8   Not *shares.*
9   Section 12.
10 The Order is subject to disapproval by either House of Parliament.
11 Eg additions have been made by Trustee Investments (Additional Powers) Orders in 1962 (SI 1962 No 658; SI 1962 No 2611); 1964 (SI 1964 No 703; SI 1964 No 1404); 1966 (SI 1966 No 401); 1968 (SI 1968 No 470); 1972 (SI 1972 No 1818); 1973 (SI 1973 No 1332); 1975 (SI 1975 No 1710); 1977 (SI 1977 No 831; SI 1977 No 1878); 1982 (SI 1982 No 1086); 1983 (SI 1983 No 772; SI 1983 No 1525); 1986 (SI 1986 No 601) and 1988 (SI 1988 No 2254).
12 Prior to 1969 the Post Office Savings Bank. (Post Office Act 1969, s 94.)

5 Fixed-interest securities issued in the United Kingdom by the International Bank for Reconstruction and Development.
6 Debentures issued in the United Kingdom by a company incorporated in the United Kingdom.
7 Stock of the Bank of Ireland.
8 Debentures issued by the Agricultural Mortgage Corporation Limited or the Scottish Agricultural Securities Corporation Limited.
9 Loans to a local authority. Fixed-interest securities issued in the United Kingdom by any such authority.
10 Debentures or guaranteed or preference stock of any statutory water undertakers within the meaning of the Water Act 1945.
11 Deposits by way of special investment in a trustee savings bank.
12 Deposits in a building society designated under s 1 of the House Purchase and Housing Act 1959.
13 Mortgages of freehold property in England and Wales or Northern Ireland and of leasehold property in those countries of which the unexpired term at the time of investment is not less than 60 years.
14 Perpetual rentcharges on land in England and Wales or Northern Ireland[13].

Part III
Para 1 Shares in companies which comply with the conditions set out at (a) to (e) on page 267.
2 Shares in authorised[14] building societies.
3 Units in authorised[15] unit trusts.

RECAPITULATION

At this point it may be helpful to recapitulate the position described so far:

Narrower range part of the fund may be invested in:	Investments in Part I	Advice need not be obtained. Example: National Savings Certificates
	Investments in Part II	Advice must be obtained. Example: deposit in Bakewell Building Society.
Wider range part of the fund may be invested in:	Investments in Part III	Advice must be obtained. Example: shares in ICI

13 Under the Rentcharges Act 1977 (a) with certain exceptions, no new rentcharges have been capable of being created after 22 August 1977; (b) with certain exceptions, existing rentcharges are to be extinguished at the expiry of 60 years from the passing of the Act (22 July 1977) or the date on which the rentcharge became payable, whichever was later; ss 2 and 3.
14 Under s 1 of the House Purchase and Housing Act 1959.
15 By an order made under s 17 of the Prevention of Fraud (Investments) Act 1958.

Mortgages

One particular type of investment in Part II calls for special attention, namely, mortgages.

Paragraph 13 of Part II of the First Schedule permits investment in the form of a loan secured by the mortgage of freehold land, or of leasehold land of which the lease has 60 years or more unexpired.

Mortgages have since early times been accepted as a suitable form of investment for trust money. They were approved by the courts prior to 1859 and were included among authorised investments in the Law of Property Amendment Act 1859 (under the name of 'real subsequent securities') and in other statutes up to and including the Trustee Act 1925.

What forms of mortgage may be taken as security? In the last century it was held that only a legal first mortgage (or sub-mortgage) could be taken. A second mortgage or an equitable mortgage was not suitable. It is not certain whether these restrictions apply to the mortgages specified in the 1961 Act, but the better view is that they do[16], and a trustee would be wise to act accordingly.[17] The Trustee Act 1925[18] permitted a mortgage taken as security to be in either of the two forms permitted by s 85 of the Law of Property Act 1925 and it seems that this provision (which was not altered by the 1961 Act) applies to mortgages under Part II of the 1961 Act.

What kind of land should a trustee accept as security? A trustee should remember that what he has authority to accept as security is land; not the additional value of a business which is being run on a piece of land. But this does not mean that he should not accept a mortgage of business premises, if the value of the land and buildings constitute adequate security.

How much money should a trustee lend on the security of a mortgage? This will depend on the value of the land concerned. Before deciding how much money to lend, a trustee will therefore need to know the value of the land being offered as security. This is an important matter. For example, suppose that a trustee values the land at, say, £10,000 and lends £7,000 on the security of this. The mortgagor, let us suppose, fails to pay the interest due and the trustee forecloses (or exercises the statutory power of sale). The land proves to be worth only £6,000. There is thus a loss to the trust fund of £1,000 due to an incorrect valuation having been made. A trustee will therefore need to employ a professional valuer to advise him on the value of land offered as security before he makes the loan. But without some additional protection, since a trustee is not permitted to delegate his responsibility for taking decisions[19] (and if he exercises the power to delegate under s 25 of the Trustee Act 1925 he remains liable[19]), he would not be able to escape liability for an incorrect valuation. (His only remedy might be to seek damages in tort from the valuer for negligence.) In order to protect a trustee in this situation, s 8 of the Trustee Act 1925 provides that if certain conditions are satisfied a trustee will not be liable for breach of trust if the value of the security taken proves to be too low in relation to the sum lent. The conditions are as follows:

(i)   The trustee must obtain a report on the value of the property.

---

16   Snell, *Principles of Equity* (28th edn) p 220.
17   The Law Reform Committee, 23rd Report, recommended that trustees should be authorised to invest in second mortgages. (Para 3.11.)
18   Section 5(2).
19   See Chap 14.

(ii) The report must be made by a person whom the trustee 'reasonably believed to be an able practical surveyor or valuer instructed and employed independently of any owner of the property'; not, for example, someone employed by the mortgagor as his rent collector[20]. But it has been held that the trustee is not under a duty to inquire whether the valuer has acted at any time for the mortgagor[1].

(iii) The trustee must have made the loan in reliance on the advice in the report.

(iv) The amount lent must not exceed two-thirds of the value of the property as stated in the report.

(v) The interest in land taken as security must be authorised; ie since 1961 it must fall within para 13 of Part II of the First Schedule of the 1961 Act.

If these conditions are satisfied, then not only will a trustee escape liability in the event of the valuation proving too low but, further, he is freed from any responsibility for making inquiries about the property concerned, or the credentials of the mortgagor[2].

If the condition at (v) above is not complied with (eg if the property mortgaged consists of a lease with only seven years to run), and the value of the property does not cover the amount lent, the trustee is liable for the difference.

If the conditions at (i) to (v) are all complied with, but the value of the land proves to be insufficient to cover the money lent, then the trustee escapes liability and the loss falls on the trust fund. In this case, in addition to a loss of capital there is likely to have been also a loss of income (ie from the mortgagor having failed to pay interest). Therefore, when the land is sold, part of the proceeds are given to the tenant for life to make up for any loss of income. To this end the proceeds are apportioned between the life tenant and the trust fund in the same proportion that the total of the arrears of interest bears to the total deficiency (of capital and income).

In one situation trustees escape liability for a deficiency without the need to obtain a report (ie under s 8 of the Trustee Act 1925). This is where (i) trustees[3] hold land for an estate in fee simple or for a lease having 500 years or more to run; (ii) they propose to sell the land; (iii) a purchaser wishes to raise part of the purchase money by means of a mortgage of the land; (iv) the trustees agree to lend the purchaser not more than two-thirds of the money needed on the security of a mortgage of the land; (v) the purchaser agrees to covenant to keep any buildings on the land insured for their full value, and (vi) the conveyance to the purchaser and the mortgage back to the trustees are drawn up accordingly[4].

Purchase of land
In the introduction to this chapter we saw that purchase of a freehold or leasehold land is a form of investment. But it will be noted that the purchase of land does not appear in any of the three parts of the First Schedule and

20 *Shaw v Cates* [1909] 1 Ch 389; (M & B).
1 *Re Solomon* [1912] 1 Ch 261; (M & B).
2 *Re Solomon* [1912] 1 Ch 261; (M & B).
3 Including a tenant for life or statutory owner under the Settled Land Act 1925.
4 Trustee Act 1925, s 10(2).

is thus not authorised by the Act as a form of investment available to trustees[5].

This being so, a trustee may only invest money in the purchase of land either if he is expressly authorised to do so by the trust instrument[6], or by some Act of Parliament. For example, if land subject to a settlement under the Settled Land Act 1925[7] is sold, the trustees of the settlement may invest the proceeds of sale by purchasing freehold land or leasehold land with at least 60 years unexpired[8]. And under the Law of Property Act 1925[9] trustees for sale who have sold some (but not all[10]) of the land may use the proceeds of sale (or the proceeds of sale of investments purchased with the proceeds of sale of the land) for the purchase of other land by way of investment[11].

THE TWO PARTS OF THE TRUST FUND

We have seen that only that part of the trust fund set aside as the wider range part may be invested in Part III investments. However, this does not mean that the wider range part has got to be invested in Part III investments. The trustees may, if they decide that such is the wisest course, invest all the trust money in Part I and Part II investments. Or they may invest a quarter of the trust money in Part III investments and the other three-quarters in Part I and II investments. But if *any* investment in Part III is to be purchased then there *must* be a division of the fund into two parts, a narrower range part and a wider range part, and only money from the latter may be employed for the purchase of Part III investments.

The 1961 Act contains provisions designed to ensure that not more than half of the fund is invested in Part III investments. Notwithstanding these provisions, it may happen (perhaps because of an oversight when the Act was drafted) that the two parts become unequal with the result that the trustees will be able to invest more than half the trust moneys in Part III investments. We can see how this may happen, and explain the operation of these provisions generally, by means of an illustration.

Let us suppose that when T dies he leaves his residuary estate on trust for sale for A for life with remainder to B. The residuary estate consists of: £500 in a bank account; £500 in the National Savings Bank; £10,000 of Treasury stock (value £1,500); £1,000 deposited in the Bakewell Building Society; 4,000 shares in T's small family business (value £2,000); 500 shares in PVC Ltd

---

5 The Law Reform Committee, 23rd Report, recommended that trustees should be authorised to invest in freehold and leasehold land subject to their first obtaining professional advice on the investment. (Paras 3.1–3.14.)

6 In this event, although he may purchase land for the purpose of producing an income, an express power to invest in 'land' does not extend to the purchase of land for any other purpose, such as providing a house for a tenant for life. *Re Power* [1947] Ch 572, [1947] 2 All ER 282. The Law Reform Committee, 23rd Report, recommended that the decision in *Re Power* should be reversed and that trustees should have power to purchase a residence for occupation by the person entitled to the income on the money used for the purchase. (Para 3.5.)

7 SLA 1925, s 73(1)(xi).

8 The Law Reform Committee, 23rd Report, recommended the abolition of this limit.

9 Section 28(1).

10 If they have sold all the land, they cease to be trustees for sale under the statutory definition in s 205(1)(xxix) and so no longer have the power under s 28(1) to invest in land. *Re Wakeman* [1945] Ch 177, [1945] 1 All ER 421.

11 *Re Wellsted's Will Trusts* [1949] Ch 296, [1949] 1 All ER 577.

(value £1,500). 20,000 £1 shares in ICI (value £3,000); 1,000 units in the Fortune Unit Trust (value £2,000).

The trustees wish to retain the shares in ICI and PVC and the units in the Fortune Unit Trust. These are Part III investments. So the fund must be divided. The total value of the trust property is £12,000, so the two parts, the narrower range part and the wider range part (which from now on we shall call part A and part B) will each contain £6,000. The trustees then add up the value of the Part III investments (the shares in PVC Ltd and ICI Ltd and the unit trusts) and find that the total comes to £6,500. This tells them that £500 worth out of these investments must be sold. So they sell £500 worth of the PVC Ltd shares. This reduces the value of the Part III investments to the maximum sum permitted, namely £6,000.

What about the shares in T's family business? This is not an investment authorised by Part I, II or III of the First Schedule, and so the trustees must (since the trust is a trust for sale[12]) sell these shares. They do so. The £2,000 they obtain, added to the £500 which T had in the bank and the £500 they received from the sale of the shares in PVC Ltd gives a total of £3,000 available in cash. When deciding what this money should be invested in, the trustees know that since part B of the fund is fully utilised, they can only select investments from Part I or Part II of the First Schedule. They decide to add the money to the deposit in the Bradford Building Society, bringing this to £4,000.

Now the following events occur:

1. A reversionary interest (T having been a remainderman under a trust) falls in and brings £2,000 into T's residuary estate. The trustees must divide the property (and likewise with any other after-acquired property) between the two parts of the fund. The notional total of each part thus now amounts to £7,000. The trustees invest the whole of the £2,000 in a special investment account of the Trustee Savings Bank. This is an investment in Part II of the First Schedule (para 11). The result is that part A of the fund still includes only Part I and Part II investments; the money in part B now includes £6,000 invested in Part III investments and £1,000 in Part II investments. (The Act is not infringed as no sum out of part A is invested in a Part III investment.)

2. Later, a further £2,000 accrues to the trust fund, this time from the payment of a debt which had been owed to T. Again, the money is divided between the two parts of the fund, each part now totalling £8,000. The trustees would like to invest the whole £2,000 in the Rainbow Unit Trust (a Part III investment), but there is only £1,000 available in part B of the fund. Trustees are permitted[13], however, to transfer property from one part of the fund to the other if a compensating transfer is made the other way. This being so, the trustees transfer the £1,000 which they have just allocated to part A over to part B. By way of compensating transfer, they transfer £1,000 of the £2,000 in the Trustee Savings Bank from part B over to part A, with the result that the whole of the £2,000 of this investment is now in part A. The trustees now have £2,000 available in part B with which to buy units in the Rainbow Unit Trust, and this they do. The two parts of the fund remain equal at £8,000.

---

12 For the position where there is no trust for sale, see p. 277.
13 Section 2(1).

3. ICI announce that they are making a bonus issue of shares to ordinary shareholders. The value of the issue is £1,000. Under the Act[14], since this accrual arises from a particular item of property, the bonus shares are added to that part (part B) of the fund in which the property concerned lay. So the value of part B is increased by £1,000 to £9,000[15]. Since part A remains at £8,000, the two parts of the fund are no longer equal.

4. At the request of a beneficiary entitled in remainder, and with the consent of the life tenant, the trustees exercise their power of advancement under s 32 of the Trustee Act 1925, and advance £3,000 to the beneficiary concerned. In this situation (and wherever the trustees take money from the fund in exercise of any power or duty) the Act[16] permits them to select from which part of the fund the money is provided. The trustees decide to take the money out of the Bradford Building Society. The effect of their so doing is to reduce the value of part A to £5,000. The value of part B remains at £9,000.

It is strange that the 1961 Act, whilst laying down elaborate provisions designed to ensure that not more than half the trust fund should be invested in Part III investments (provisions which in practice may entail complex accounting) provides no guard against the two parts of the fund becoming unequal.

Because of the complications involved in administering the fund in the two parts required by the Act, it is now common for settlors to exclude the provisions of the Act entirely by the inclusion of an express investment clause.

LAW REFORM COMMITTEE PROPOSALS

It was a major recommendation of the Law Reform Committee, in its 23rd Report (paras 3.15–3.25) that the Trustee Investments Act 1961 should be repealed and fresh, wider, powers of investment conferred on trustees. The recommendations are set out at the end of this chapter.

Express investment clauses

Since the provisions of the Trustee Investments Act 1961[17] are subject to any contrary intention expressed by the settlor, a settlor can widen or restrict the scope of investments permitted by the Act. He could, for example, if he wished to widen the statutory power,

(a) authorise the trustees to invest more than half the trust property in Part III investments;

(b) release the trustees from the duty to obtain advice in the case of Part II and III investments;

(c) relax the conditions which must be fulfilled for a security to come within

---

14 Section 2(3).
15 For the sake of simplicity we are ignoring the fact that the bonus issue might reduce the market value of the existing shares.
16 Section 2(4).
17 Section 1(3).

either Part III (eg by waiving the requirement that a company must have a capital of £1 million or over, or must have declared dividends during the preceding five years), or Part II (eg by waiving the requirement that for a lease to be accepted as security it must have 60 years or more to run);

(d) authorise the trustees to invest in a form of security which does not (even with conditions attached) appear in any form in Parts I, II or III of the First Schedule; for example, by authorising the trustees to invest trust money in the purchase of land;

(e) authorise the trustees to invest in a particular named security which is not authorised under the Act, eg in the shares of the settlor's small family business;

(f) give the trustees discretion as to the securities in which trust money is invested, as by authorising them to invest in 'such investments as to them may seem fit'.

Formerly, express investment clauses conferring discretion on trustees were construed narrowly. For example, in 1882 a clause in terms similar to that at (f) above was construed as giving the trustees power to invest only in such *authorised* securities as they should think fit[18]. More recently such forms of wording have been construed less restrictively, and more in accord with their natural meaning. For example, in 1949 the words 'in such investments as to them may seem fit' were construed[19] as empowering the trustees to invest in any type of investment, whether authorised by statute or not. But we may note here that if a trustee is given absolute discretion as to the 'investments' or 'shares, stocks, property or property holding company'[20] in which trust money should be invested, such words will be construed as extending only to investments in types of property which are normally treated as an investment, and thus will not extend to the making of a personal loan without any security[1] or to the retention of the settlor's assets in a family business. (Thus the latter could only be retained if there was an express authorisation to this effect.)

'Special powers'

We have noted that a trustee may be permitted to invest in securities outside the Act by the express authorisation of the settlor. Trustees may also be permitted to hold investments otherwise than according to the 1961 Act by statute: we met two instances when dealing with the power of a trustee to invest in land. We saw[2] then that trustees of a settlement under the Settled Land Act 1925 and trustees of a trust for sale have, subject to certain conditions, power to invest in land—a form of investment not authorised by the 1961 Act. A private Act may similarly give authority to trustees to invest outside the 1961 Act. For example, the Baptist and Congregational Trusts

---

18 *Re Braithwaite* (1882) 21 Ch D 121.
19 As in *Re Harari's Settlement Trusts* [1949] 1 All ER 430; (M & B).
20 *Re Peczenik's Settlement* [1964] 2 All ER 339, [1964] 1 WLR 720.
 1 Ibid.
 2 See p 272, ante.

Act 1951 gives trustees of Baptist or Congregational trusts absolute discretion as to the investment of trust money[3]. The 1961 Act calls a power (whether conferred by a settlor or by statute) to invest otherwise than under the Act, a 'special power'.

It may happen that a trustee is authorised to invest the entire trust fund by a special power. But what is the position if a trustee is permitted to invest only part of the trust fund by a special power? For example, what if the settlor gives the trustee absolute discretion as to the investment of one-half of the trust fund? What about the other half? Or what if trustees for sale have power to invest certain proceeds of sale in the purchase of land[4]: what about other capital money held by the trustees for sale—how may this be invested? The answer is that any part of the trust fund which is not authorised to be invested under a special power is subject to the provisions of the 1961 Act, including the provision as to the division of the fund into two parts. Thus if a settlor gives a trustee absolute discretion as to one half of the trust fund, the fund will have to be divided into three parts: one half will be that which may be invested under the special power; one quarter will be the narrower range part and the other quarter will be the wider range part. The effect of the Act[5], however, is that if a trustee makes any investment, other than a narrower range investment, this must be reckoned as first absorbing that much of the entitlement to invest under the special power. Thus if a trustee wishes to invest up to the limit of, say, half the fund in investments outside the Act and also to acquire some Part III investments, he should at the outset invest the whole of that half of the fund outside the Act. Any Part III investments he then purchases will fall within the (part B) quarter of the fund allocated to Part III investments, and will not absorb any of the part of the fund which may be invested, under the special power, in investments outside the Act.

Variation of the power of investment

Where trustees consider that their existing powers of investment (whether arising under the 1961 Act or from an express investment clause) are not suitable, an application may be made to the court for an order extending (or otherwise varying) the power of investment. Where the trust is charitable, the application will be for a scheme made under the court's *cy près* jurisdiction[6] or for an order under s 57 of the Trustee Act 1925[7]. Where the trust is private, the application will be for an order under s 57 of the Trustee Act 1925[7] or for an order under the Variation of Trusts Act 1958[8].

---

3   Section 4, which enables trustees of Baptist or Congregational trusts to adopt a model
    form of trust instrument which confers absolute discretion with regard to investment.
4   See p 272, ante.
5   Section 3(2), Sch 2.
6   Chap 8. *Trustees of the British Museum v A-G* [1984] 1 All ER 337, [1984] 1 WLR 418;
    (M & B) (not following *Re Kolb's Will Trusts* [1962] Ch 531, [1961] 3 All ER 811 and *Re
    Cooper's Settlement* [1962] Ch 826, [1961] 3 All ER 636); [1984] Conv 373 (H. E. Norman);
    Steel v Wellcome Custodian Trustees Ltd [1988] 1 WLR 167 (scheme conferring wide
    powers of investment including power to delegate to professional fund managers approved);
    (M & B); [1988] Conv 380 (B. Dale).
7   Chap 18. *Mason v Farbrother* [1983] 2 All ER 1078; (M & B).
8   Chap 18.

Variation of investments within a trust fund

The Act authorises trustees to vary investments in the trust fund—by selling one security and buying another in its place[9] (subject, of course, to the provisions regarding the two parts of the fund).

If trustees' powers of investment are defined by an express investment clause, then, in the absence of an express power to vary the investments, there is an implied power to do so[10].

Investments forming part of the initial trust property

Suppose that a testator left his 1,000 shares in X plc to trustees on trust for certain beneficiaries. No express power of sale is conferred. Since the trust is not a trust for sale there is no express duty to sell. If the trustees wish to sell the shares (to invest in another security), do they have power to do so? The answer is, Yes. Under s 1(1) of the 1961 Act 'a trustee may invest any property in his hands, whether at the time in a state of investment or not, in any manner specified' under the Act. Since the power exists with regard to 'any property' and since the only way that trustees could 'invest' the shares in X plc would be to sell them and invest in another security, the effect of the section is to confer power on the trustees to sell the shares and re-invest the proceeds (ie, under the Act)[11].

If the shares in X plc are not authorised by the 1961 Act is the trustee obliged to sell the shares? No. The trustee is not *investing* in X plc. He receives the shares as trust property. The shares can therefore be retained[12].

If the shares in X plc had been left to the trustee on trust *for sale*, then the position is as follows: if the shares in X plc were an investment which was not authorised by the 1961 Act, the whole of the shares would have to be sold and the proceeds invested under the Act. If the shares fell within Part I or II of the Act, then the shares could be retained (provided that, if the shares fell within Part II, advice was obtained), since retention of the shares is equivalent to carrying out the duty to sell the shares and then investing the proceeds in purchasing fresh shares in the same company. If the shares fell within Part III of the Act, then[13] one half of the shares could be retained and the rest would have to be sold (this being the equivalent of selling the whole of the shares and investing half the proceeds in X plc).

---

9 Section 1(1).
10 *Hume v Lopes* [1892] AC 112.
11 *Re Pratt's Will Trusts* [1943] Ch 326, [1943] 2 All ER 375, following *Hume v Lopes* [1892] AC 112.
12 Subject to what is said below with regard to the duties of trustees to have regard to the suitability of any investment.
13 Assuming that the shares in X plc were the only securities bequeathed. For an illustration of the position where authorised and unauthorised instruments are left on trust for sale, see p 272.

Advice

We have seen that a trustee must obtain, and consider, advice before investing in a security in Parts II or III of the First Schedule. The Act provides[14] that the advice which he obtains must be as to whether the investment proposed is 'satisfactory' with regard to:

(i) the 'suitability' of the investment, both—
(a) as to the 'suitability' of the actual investment proposed, eg whether a company has had a good record and sound prospects;
(b) as to the 'suitability' to the trust of investments of the description of the investment proposed, eg if what is needed is a high income (as opposed to capital appreciation), whether the investment proposed is of a kind which is likely to produce this;
(ii) the need for 'diversification' of investments in the trust fund 'so far as is appropriate to the circumstances'.

Trustees are, however, under no duty to obtain advice as to the suitability of a mortgage as an investment[15]. (But, as already seen[16], for a trustee to rely on the protection afforded by s 8 of the Trustee Act 1925, he must obtain an independent report on the property proposed as security.)

The Act provides[17] that the advice obtained must be 'proper advice', and the Act defines[18] this as 'the advice of a person who is reasonably believed by the trustee to be qualified by his ability in and practical experience of financial matters'. (The advice must be given in writing or must be subsequently confirmed in writing[19].)

The duty to seek advice on Part II and Part III investments is a continuing one since what may have been a suitable investment initially may cease to be suitable later. It is up to the trustee to decide, in the light of the circumstances and the nature of the investment, at what intervals he should seek advice[19]. In practice it is prudent for a trustee to obtain a report from a stockbroker on all the trust investments once a year.

The duty of trustees in investing trust money[20]

The duty to obtain advice in connection with Parts II and III investments is in addition to, and supplementary to, a general duty imposed by the Act[1] on trustees to have regard to the 'suitability'[2] of, and to the need for 'diversification' of, *all* investments in the trust fund, ie including investments made

14   Section 6(2).
15   Section 6(7).
16   See p 270.
17   Section 6(4).
18   Section 6(5).
19   Section 6(3).
20   [1983] Conv 127, 'Negligent investment by trustees', P. Pearce and A. Samuels. For the duty of trustees of a charitable trust, see H. Beynon, (1982) 45 MLR 268.
1   Section 6(1).
2   The word having the same meaning as above, see supra.

under a special power. In the exercise of this general duty, it is for the trustees to decide whether or not they should seek advice.

The general duty imposed by the Act itself supplements a general duty of care imposed by equity on trustees in the investment of trust money. Equity requires a trustee who is investing trust money to act with prudence. And the degree of prudence required is higher than that to be expected from a person investing his own money: the 'duty of a trustee is not to take such care only as a prudent man would take if he had only himself to consider; the duty rather is to take such care as an ordinary prudent man would take if he were minded to make an investment for the benefit of other people for whom he felt morally bound to provide. That is the kind of business the ordinary prudent man is supposed to be engaged in; and unless this is borne in mind the standard of a trustee's duty will be fixed too low[3]'.

Where the trustee is a body which holds itself out as having specialised skills and knowledge for the business of trust management (such as a trust corporation, eg the trustee department of a bank), then the standard of care required from the trustee is higher than that required from a trustee without such specialised knowledge. In *Bartlett v Barclays Bank Trust Co Ltd (No 2)*[4] the trustee was a trust corporation. The trust property consisted of a 99.8% shareholding in a private company. In 1961 the board of directors decided that the company should become involved in speculative property development. The trustee was not consulted, and did not ask for information about the change in policy, or the company's subsequent activities. In 1974 the property boom ended and this fact, together with an earlier ill-judged and ill-managed scheme for development of a site opposite the Central Criminal Court (the 'Old Bailey Project') resulted in a substantial loss to the trust. It was held that the trustee should not have relied only on information given at annual general meetings of the company but should have required the board to inform it and consult it so that it could have intervened, if it thought necessary, to protect the interests of the beneficiaries. The beneficiaries claimed that the trustee was liable for all losses resulting from the company's involvement in property development. It was held that the trustee was liable for the loss arising from the Old Bailey project, but that against this loss the trustee was entitled to set off a profit that had (by 'sheer luck'[5]) been made on another property development scheme ('which exemplified the same folly as the Old Bailey disaster[6]').

It will be seen that as a result of both the general duty imposed on a trustee by the Act[7] to consider the 'suitability' of an investment, and the duty of prudence imposed by equity, a trustee will not necessarily escape liability for breach of trust by investing trust money solely in authorised investments. An investment may be made within a trustee's power, but (however wide the discretion given to the trustee) this alone will not necessarily make it a suitable or prudent investment. For example in *Re Whiteley*[8], trustees invested trust money in a loan secured by a mortgage of a brick works and quarry. The investment was made within the trustees' powers, but the trustees were held

---

3 Per Lindley LJ, *Re Whiteley* (1886) 33 Ch D 347 at 355.
4 [1980] Ch 515, [1980] 2 All ER 92; (M & B).
5 Ibid, at p 538.
6 Ibid.
7 Section 6(1); see p 278, ante.
8 (1886) 33 Ch D 347 at 355.

to be in breach of trust since the land mortgaged, being a wasting asset, was an inadequate security for the loan, which had therefore not been a proper investment for the trust money. Thus an investment is not necessarily a proper one merely because it happens to be authorised[9].

Further, it would seem that trustees will not escape liability if, due to lack of prudence, they retain an unsatisfactory investment that came to them as part of the initial trust property. The reason is this. Assuming that (as indicated above) trustees have power to sell an investment notwithstanding it formed part of the initial trust property, and taking account of the fact that trustees are under a duty to consider whether their powers should be exercised[10], it would appear that they would be liable if they failed to give consideration to the matter and, if prudence dictated sale of such an investment, they failed to sell and re-invest the proceeds suitably.

The wishes of the beneficiaries[11]

If trustees are minded to invest trust money in a particular investment, may they, in reaching a decision, allow themselves to be influenced by what they believe to be the views of the beneficiaries regarding the nature of the investment concerned? The issue came before the court in *Cowan v Scargill*[12]. The case concerned the management of the pension scheme set up by the National Coal Board for mineworkers. Management of the scheme rested with a committee of the trustees, five appointed by the Board and five by the National Union of Mineworkers. In 1982 a revised investment plan was proposed. The five Union trustees on the committee refused to concur in the adoption of the plan because of their objection to the investments that would be made in oil, and in investments overseas. They asserted that their position was in accordance with Union policy determined at the Union's annual conference, and that they were acting solely for the benefit of the beneficiaries under the scheme. The Board's nominees on the committee sought directions from the court as to whether the Union trustees were acting in breach of their fiduciary duty in declining to agree the investment plan. The court held that the duty of trustees towards their beneficiaries was paramount. 'They must, of course, obey the law; but subject to that, they must put the interests of their beneficiaries first. When the purpose of the trust is to provide financial benefits for the beneficiaries, as is usually the case, the best interests of the beneficiaries are normally their best financial interests.'[13]

In considering what investments to make trustees must put on one side their own personal interests and views. This did not mean that trustees could not take account of the known views of beneficiaries. 'Thus if the only actual or potential beneficiaries of a trust are all adults with very strict views on moral and social matters, condemning all forms of alcohol, tobacco and popular entertainment, as well as armaments, I can well understand that it

---

9   But cf *Nestle v National Westminster Bank plc*, (1992) *Times*, 11 May, CA. (Bank which had failed to inform itself of the true scope of its investment powers and invested only in certain (authorised) bank and insurance shares held not liable for loss due to not investing more widely.)
10   See Chap 20.
11   See Middleton and Phillips, *Charity Investment Law and Practice* (1988).
12   [1985] Ch 270, [1984] 2 All ER 750; [1985] Conv 52 (P. Pearce and A. Samuels).
13   Per Sir Robert Megarry V-C, at p 513.

might not be for the "benefit" of such beneficiaries to know that they are obtaining rather larger financial returns under the trust by reason of investments in those activities than they would have received if the trustees had invested the trust funds in other investments. The beneficiaries might well consider that it was far better to receive less than to receive more money from what they consider to be evil and tainted sources. "Benefit" is a word with a very wide meaning, and there are circumstances in which arrangements which work to the financial disadvantage of a beneficiary may yet be for his benefit ... But I would emphasise that such cases are likely to be very rare ...'[14]. The present case was not one of this rare type. The duties owed by trustees of a pension fund were governed by the same principles as those which applied to other forms of trust. The motivation behind the Union's trustees' opposition to the investment plan was a wish to carry out Union policy, '... the broad economic arguments of the defendants provide no justification for the restrictions that they wish to impose. Any possible benefits from imposing the restrictions that would accrue to the beneficiaries under the scheme (as distinct from the general public) are far too speculative and remote. Large though the fund is, I cannot see how the adoption of the restrictions can make any material impact on the national economy, or bring any appreciable benefit to the beneficiaries under the scheme[15].' Taking into account this conclusion, together with the duty of trustees to obtain advice, the advice that the committee of management had received, and the duty of trustees to consider the need to diversify investments in the fund, the court found that the Union's trustees were in breach of their fiduciary duty in refusing to agree the investment plan proposed.

An issue of a nature similar to that in *Cowan v Scargill* arose in 1991 in *Harries v Church Comrs for England*[16]. The Church Commissioners, a charity, constituted the trustees of a fund established principally for the purpose of providing income for the payment of the stipends of clergy of the Church of England. The plaintiff (who was one of the Commissioners) sought a declaration that the Commissioners, in their investment policy, were in legal error in attaching overriding importance to financial considerations (ie the maximisation of income and capital growth) and that they ought properly to have in mind the underlying purpose for which they held the assets that made up the fund, namely promotion of the Christian faith through the instrument of the Church of England. Ethical considerations should, the plaintiff contended, be among the considerations taken into account in deciding investment policy, notwithstanding that significant financial detriment might be incurred. The court found that the Commissioners already had an investment policy that took into account ethical considerations: this policy stated (in a recent annual report) 'We do not invest in companies whose main business is armaments, gambling, tobacco and newspapers'. This policy did not infringe the legal duty of the Commissioners with regard to investment since there remained open to them an adequate range of satisfactory alternative investments. For the Commissioners to adopt a policy of basing investment decisions on non-financial considerations, when, by so doing, financial benefits might be jeopardised, would be a departure from their legal duty with regard to investment. The declaration sought was therefore refused.

14   Ibid, at p 514.
15   Ibid, at p 512.
16   (1991) Times, 30 October 1991; [1992] Conv 115 (R. Nobles).

Investment in chattels

A person is sometimes said to have 'invested' in the purchase of a particular chattel, for example a valuable painting, an antique piece of furniture, a diamond bracelet, or a collection of postage stamps. The purpose of such a purchase as an investment is to acquire an asset the value of which is expected to rise at least as fast as any fall in the value of money, by this means offsetting the effect of inflation. But since an 'investment' in the context of investments made by trustees denotes the acquisition of property which produces an income[17], purchases of the kind mentioned are not merely unauthorised by the 1961 Act, but would not be authorised by an investment clause giving absolute discretion as to the type of 'investment' selected.

Law Reform Committee

Paragraph 10 of the summary of the recommendations of the Committee's 23rd Report states:

The statutory powers contained in the Trustee Investments Act 1961 are out of date and ought now to be revised. We recommend that the 1961 Act be repealed and the following new powers be conferred upon trustees:

(i) investments should be divided into those which can be made without advice and those which can be made only with advice; (para 3.21)

(ii) the former category should comprise those investments presently known as narrower-range securities and listed in Parts I and II of the 1961 Act and also unit trusts and investment trusts, as defined in s 359 of the Income and Corporation Taxes Act 1970; (para 3.21)

(iii) the latter category should comprise any other investment quoted on the English Stock Exchange; (para 3.21)

(iv) trustees should be free to invest in such proportions as they choose; (para 3.21)

(v) the provisions on advice presently contained in s 6 of the 1961 Act should be retained; (para 3.22)

(vi) express reference should be made in the new statutory provision to the duty of trustees to maintain a balance between income and capital so as to protect all those interested under the trust fund; (para 3.22)

(vii) the requirement in s 6(1)(a) of the 1961 Act which compels trustees to have regard to the need for diversification of investments in so far as is appropriate to the circumstances of the trust is sufficient and further restrictions on the trustees' discretion are not required; (para 3.23)

(viii) investments in foreign securities should not be made unless expressly authorised by the trust instrument. (para 3.24)

---

17   See Lawrence J in *Re Wragg* [1919] 2 Ch 58 at 64, 65.

Chapter 16

Apportionment: the rules in *Howe v Dartmouth*

Introduction

It is the duty of a trustee to act impartially as between the beneficiaries, administering the trust in a manner that ensures that (unless the settlor so intended) one beneficiary does not benefit at the expense of another[1]. For example, where a testator left 46/80ths of the total of 999 shares that he owned in a company to his widow and the balance to other beneficiaries, and by virtue of 46/80ths of the shares conferring a controlling interest in the company, the value of the widow's interest was greater than 46/80ths of the total value of the 999 shares, the executors were directed to sell the shares and pay the widow 46/80ths of the proceeds of the sale[2].

In pursuance of his duty to act impartially between the beneficiaries a trustee may be required to sell certain forms of trust property and invest the proceeds in authorised investments; he may be required to apportion income between a life tenant (to whom income would normally wholly belong) and a remainderman; or to apportion capital between a remainderman (to whom it would normally pass in its entirety) and a life tenant. The principal authority for the rules governing these matters is the case of *Howe v Dartmouth*[3]. In this chapter we examine the operation of these rules. It should be borne in mind throughout that the rules we shall be dealing with constitute various applications of the principle that a trustee must administer the trust equitably as between the various beneficiaries[4].

The Law Reform Committee, in its 23rd Report[5], recommended that the apportionment rules treated in this chapter should be subsumed in a new statutory duty to hold a fair balance between beneficiaries, in particular between those entitled to capital and those entitled to income.

---

1 *Cowan v Scargill* [1984] 3 WLR 501, 513.
2 *Lloyds Bank plc v Duker* [1987] 3 All ER 193, [1987] 1 WLR 1324.
3 (1802) 7 Ves 137.
4 *Stannard v Fisons Pension Trust Ltd* (1991) Times, 19 November. (Trustees required to act equitably with regard to the valuation of property as it affected two pension schemes of which they were the trustees.)
5 Paras 3.20–3.41.

Sale of wasting assets and unauthorised investments

Let us suppose that in his will a testator, T, left a car to A for his lifetime and directed that on A's death the car was to go to B. 'That's all very well', we can imagine B saying, 'but by the time A dies, the car will be worn out. All the benefits from the gift will go to A. The car ought to be sold and the money invested. The income from the money would go to A, and when he dies the capital would be intact to come to me.'

The law does not support B's contention. Since T had referred to the car specifically, it is assumed that T had given his attention to the matter and that he must have realised that the effect of the gift would be that the tenant for life, A, would benefit and that the remainderman, B, would lose. Since the law seeks to give effect to the intentions of a testator, and the testator's intention is clear, there is no reason for equity to intervene.

Now suppose that in his will, after making a number of specific gifts, T left the residue of all his property to A for life with remainder to B; and that amongst the various items of T's residuary estate was a car. Here there is nothing to indicate that T had considered the effect of the car being given to A for life with remainder to B—that the outcome would be that A would benefit at the expense of B.

When property is given to a person for life with a remainder to another person absolutely, the understanding is normally that the person with the life interest should have the use of the property during his lifetime, and that on his death the property should pass undiminished in value to the remainderman.

When T left the residue of his property to A for life with remainder to B, it is reasonable to assume that T intended the same principle to apply—that the whole of the value of the residue should be available to pass to B on A's death. But if A was allowed to have the use of the car, this result would not be achieved: on A's death B would not obtain the value which the car had had at T's death.

In this situation, therefore, equity does intervene. It does so by requiring the trustees of T's will to sell the car, to invest the proceeds in authorised investments, to pass the income from these investments to A during his lifetime, and on A's death to hand over the investments to B.

This duty to sell the car arises under the rule in *Howe v Dartmouth*[6]. The rule lays down (inter alia) that:

1. where a testator
2. leaves residuary
3. personalty
4. to persons by way of succession
5. and the residue includes a wasting asset;

then the trustee must

(a) sell the property concerned, and

(b) invest the proceeds in authorised investments (and pass the income from these to the tenant for life).

6　(1802) 7 Ves 137.

It will be seen that the rule applies to all 'wasting' assets. Any item of property the value of which will waste away is therefore subject to the rule—ships[7], shoes, wine, watches, garden tools, golf clubs, carpets and canaries—all these must be sold and the proceeds invested. Further, suppose that T had written a book and, by holding the copyright, received royalties from the sale of the book. A copyright lasts for 50 years. So with each year that passes its value declines. So a copyright is a wasting asset, and if T's residue included a copyright, it must, as a 'wasting asset', be sold.

Similarly, suppose that T held a lease of Blackacre. The lease was for 40 years and he bought it for £27,000 in 1970, and paid an annual rent of £100. There were thus 30 years unexpired at his death in 1980. With each year that passes the value of the lease (ie its saleable value) decreases. Thus a lease is a wasting asset, and if a lease is included amongst T's residue, it must be sold. There is an exception: a lease of which 60 years or more is unexpired is not subject to the rule and therefore need not be sold[8]. The reason is that if a lease is held for persons by way of succession then it is either settled land or subject to a trust for sale; if the lease is sold the trustees of a strict settlement and of a trust for sale are authorised[9] to invest the proceeds of sale in the purchase of a lease with 60 or more years unexpired. (To produce income for the trust the land would, of course, have to be sub-let.) It would be nonsense for trustees to be under a duty under the rule in *Howe v Dartmouth* to sell a lease having more than 60 years unexpired, and then to be authorised to purchase such a lease (perhaps the same one as they had just sold) as an authorised investment. So it is only leases with less than 60 years to run which must be sold as wasting assets under the rule in *Howe v Dartmouth*.

The rule in *Howe v Dartmouth* lays down that not only must items of residue which consist of wasting assets be sold, but also any items of residue which consist of 'hazardous or otherwise unauthorised investments'. For example, suppose that T's property included shares in a South American gold-mining company. Whilst the shares might for a while yield a high dividend, the company's fortunes might change and value of the shares decline. Here, as in the case of the car, any benefit from the gift might go to A, and B might get nothing.

To recapitulate, the rule in *Howe v Dartmouth* states that where a testator leaves residue to persons by way of succession, any items of residuary personalty which consist of wasting assets or of hazardous or unauthorised investments must be sold and the proceeds invested in authorised investments. (The rule imposes a duty to sell residue which consists of one other form of property: this will be considered later.)

Contrary intention

We have said that the rule in *Howe v Dartmouth* operates in order to give effect to the presumed intention of the testator—that A should not benefit at the expense of B. Since the rule is designed to give effect to the presumed intention of the testator, it follows that if there is anything in the will to

7   As in *Brown v Gellatly* (1867) 2 Ch App 751.
8   *Re Gough* [1957] Ch 323, [1957] 2 All ER 193.
9   Settled Land Act 1925, s 73(1)(xi); Law of Property Act 1925, s 28(1).

indicate that it is the testator's wish that the property should not be sold, (and that, eg the car should be used by A during his lifetime and that B should get what is left of it), then the presumption on which the rule rests is rebutted, and the rule thereby excluded. In this situation the trustees must give effect to the testator's actual wishes (ie that A should have the use of the car during his lifetime).

The rule is thus always subject to any contrary intention shown by the testator. Such a contrary intention may be indicated in (inter alia) the following ways:

1. by express provision in the will that the rule in *Howe v Dartmouth* is not to apply;

2. by a direction that no items of residue are to be sold;

3. by a clause in the will which authorises the trustees to retain unauthorised investments[10];

4. by a clause which gives the trustees discretion to sell if and when they consider it expedient[11] or gives the trustees power to retain or sell and convert, at their discretion[12];

5. by a direction or by an intention shown by the will[13] that the tenant for life is to receive the income 'in specie'; ie in the actual form in which it arises. For example, income in specie from the shares in the gold-mining company would be the dividends paid by the company; income in specie from a herd of cows would be the milk they produced (or the value of the milk when sold); income in specie from leasehold land would be the use of the land or the rent produced by sub-letting it.

The rule is excluded as regards the whole residue where there is a general direction (or an intention shown) that the income is to be paid in specie. It may be excluded as regards a particular item of the residue if there is a direction (or an intention shown) that a certain form of income should be paid in specie to the tenant for life. For example, if the residue includes leasehold land, and there is a direction that the tenant for life is to be paid the 'rents' (ie from sub-letting the land) then this excludes the rule from applying to the leasehold land, which need not be sold. (If the residue includes freehold and leasehold land, and there is a direction to the trustees to pay the 'rents' to the tenant for life, it has been held that since the word 'rents' could refer to rents received from letting freehold land, it was not to be taken that the testator necessarily intended the tenant for life to receive the rents from (sub-letting) the leasehold land. Thus, since there was nothing to exclude the rule, the leasehold land had to be sold[14].)

Position pending sale

Suppose that in a will residue was left to A for life with remainder to B, and that the residuary estate included certain shares in a gold-mining company.

---

10   *Brown v Gellatly* (1867) 2 Ch App 751.
11   *Re Pitcairn* [1896] 2 Ch 199.
12   *Gray v Siggers* (1880) 15 Ch D 74.
13   *Re Gough* [1957] Ch 323, [1957] 2 All ER 193; *Alcock v Sloper* (1833) 2 My & K 699.
14   *Re Wareham* [1912] 2 Ch 312.

Under the rule in *Howe v Dartmouth*, the trustees, as we have seen, are (in the absence of any contrary intention) under a duty to sell the shares. Suppose that they do not do so immediately and later receive a dividend from the company representing 27% of the value of the shares. What should the trustees do with the money? If the shares had been sold immediately on the testator's death (when the duty arose) and the proceeds invested in authorised investments, the income produced would be unlikely to have been at anywhere near so high a level. Is it fair that A should receive a high income merely because of a delay by the trustees in selling the shares? Equity considers that it is not, and therefore requires the trustees to give to A (out of, in our example, the 27% dividend), a sum which represents 4% of the value of the shares. (If the shares are sold within a year of the testator's death, the value of the shares is taken at the time of the sale. If they are not sold by the end of one year from the testator's death, the value of the shares is taken as at the first anniversary of the testator's death.)

The balance is treated as capital. This must be invested. The income will be paid to A during his lifetime, and the capital will pass (together with the rest of the capital ie the proceeds of the sale of the shares) to B on A's death.

It will be seen that this apportionment of the income received prior to the sale of the shares not only prevents A receiving an unjustifiably high income, but also creates a sum of capital which may go towards compensating B for any decline in the value of the shares between the testator's death and the time when the trustees get around to selling the shares.

The rule is the same in the case of income received (prior to sale) from any wasting assets or hazardous or otherwise unauthorised investments which trustees are under a duty to sell under the rule in *Howe v Dartmouth*. The income is not paid to A in specie, but is apportioned, A receiving 4% of the value of the property (ascertained either at testator's death or one year thereafter, as explained above) any balance going to capital.

There is only one exception to this principle. If trustees are under a duty (under the rule in *Howe v Dartmouth*) to sell leaseholds, then pending sale, any income produced by the properties (ie rents received from sub-leases) is paid to the tenant for life in specie, ie he gets the rents themselves.

If the income received pending sale does not amount to 4% of the value of the property, A receives whatever income is in fact produced. If the income produced later exceeds 4% A is entitled to have the previous short-fall made up[15]. If any short-fall has not been made up by the time the property is sold, A is entitled to have this made up out of the proceeds of sale, ie out of capital[15]. (If there is a short-fall in any one year A is not entitled to have this made up out of a surplus which arose in a previous year[15].)

Sale of reversionary interests

By way of introduction of this fresh aspect of the rule in *Howe v Dartmouth* suppose that someone called X made a will in which he left certain shares on trust for Y for life with remainder to T absolutely. Here T has a vested interest under the trust. The interest forms part of his property. T can wait

---

15   *Re Fawcett* [1940] Ch 402; (M & B).

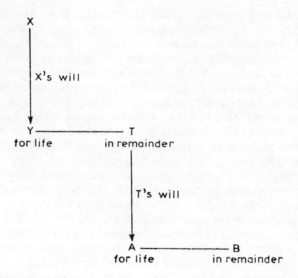

for Y to die; or, if he wishes, he can dispose of the interest in remainder during Y's lifetime, eg by selling it. Or T can leave the interest in remainder in his will, say to A. (A would then hold the interest in remainder and, in turn, could wait for Y to die and the property to fall into possession, or he could dispose of it.)

Suppose that T specifically bequeathed this interest in remainder (which, rather confusingly, is termed a 'reversionary interest') to A for life with remainder to B. The position will then be as shown above.

'That's all very well', we can imagine A saying on T's death, 'but T intended me to benefit from this gift for the *whole* of the rest of my life. But I will have to wait until Y dies before there is any property available for me to enjoy. And the longer Y lives, the fewer years I will have to benefit from the gift. B is the one who will stand to gain: if Y dies before I do, he (B) will take the property on my death; if Y dies after me, I get nothing, but in the end B (or his estate) will get the property. The arrangement is unfair. The reversionary interest ought to be sold now, so that the proceeds of sale can be invested, and so produce an income for me. Why should I have to wait until Y dies before I get any benefit?'

Before considering whether equity supports A's contention, we may at this point explain that it would be quite possible (as A urges) for the reversionary interest to be sold. The trustees of T's will could approach, for example, an insurance company. The company would want to know, inter alia, the current value of the property concerned (say £20,000) and Y's age. If Y were 60, then the company might buy the reversion for, say £15,000. When Y died, the property would pass to the company. The company would lose the interest which £15,000 would earn during the remainder of Y's life, but would obtain the full value of the property on his death, and by this stand to make their profit.

But should, as A contends, the reversionary interest be sold? The answer is that, since T gave the interest to A for life with remainder to B in a specific gift, it is to be presumed that he realised the result of so doing. The gift is therefore allowed to take effect as it stands. A must wait until Y dies before any capital becomes available from which he may derive income. No duty to sell arises.

However, if the reversionary interest had formed part of T's residuary estate, it may be assumed that T did not give his attention to the effect of the gift. In this case equity regards T as having intended that the value of the residuary estate should be enjoyed by A for the whole of the rest of his life (and not merely from Y's death). Thus if the reversionary interest is included in the testator's residuary estate, the trustees must sell it, in order to obtain a capital sum which, when invested, will produce income for A.

We are now in a position to state the whole of the rule in *Howe v Dartmouth*: Where a testator leaves residuary personalty to persons by way of succession then the trustees must, unless there is a contrary intention in the will, sell any items which are wasting assets or unauthorised investments, or are reversionary interests.

We have said that T's interest in remainder (under X's will) is a reversionary interest: this is only one example of a reversionary interest. This term includes any interest in property which is not immediately available on T's death and which will only become available at some time in the future. For example, if T had taken out an insurance policy on Q's life, under which T (or his estate) would be entitled to £10,000 on Q's death, T would hold a reversionary interest, ie the right to £10,000 on Q's death[16]. Again, suppose that T had made a contract with D under which D agreed, in exchange for goods, to pay T a certain sum in six years' time, the right to this sum would be a reversionary interest, since the money would not be available until six years had elapsed[17]. All such reversionary interests must, if part of residuary personalty left to persons by way of succession, be sold under the rule in *Howe v Dartmouth*[18].

It should be noted that the rule, both as regards (a) wasting assets and unauthorised investments, and (b) reversionary interests, applies only to items of personalty. It does not apply to residuary realty. Why not?

As regards (a) above, land is generally not a wasting asset (its value generally rises) and further, it is capable of being an authorised investment[19]. Therefore there is no reason why it should be sold. (If the land concerned is in fact likely to decline in value, eg because it consists of a quarry that is being worked, or a plantation of trees, that may be felled, then the interests of the remainderman are protected by the doctrine of waste[20] and so do not need protection by the rule in *Howe v Dartmouth*.)

As regards (b) above, if X left land on trust for sale for Y for life with remainder to T, T's reversionary interest would (because of the doctrine of conversion) be personalty, and so T's bequest to A for life with remainder to B would be subject to the rule in *Howe v Dartmouth*, and so the reversionary interest[1] would be sold. If the land left by X to Y for life with remainder to T was not subject to a trust for sale, then it would be subject to the Settled Land Act 1925. Since the item of residue is realty, not personalty, no duty

16 *Re Morley* [1895] 2 Ch 738.
17 See *Re Duke of Cleveland's Estate* [1895] 2 Ch 542.
18 Another illustration of an interest subject to the rule is provided by *Re Chance's Will Trusts* [1962] Ch 593, [1962] 1 All ER 942.
19 Ie if purchased by trustees of a settlement under the Settled Land Act 1925 or of a trust for sale. See Chap 15.
20 As modified by the Settled Land Act 1925, ss 47 and 66.
1 Not the land, which will be held, if it has not been sold, by the trustees for sale of X's will.

to sell under the rule under *Howe v Dartmouth* would arise. It might seem harsh that in this case A would have to wait until Y died before any property became available, but this nevertheless is the position[2].

Contrary intention

Since the duty to sell reversionary interests which consist of personalty is a part of the rule in *Howe v Dartmouth*, it follows that any contrary intention shown by the testator will exclude the duty to sell reversionary interests. The ways in which a contrary intention may be shown have already[3] been explained[4].

Position pending sale

Suppose that T's residuary estate, which is left to A for life with remainder to B, includes a reversionary interest in personalty. The trustees, as we have seen, are (in the absence of any contrary intention) under a duty to sell the interest. When they do, the proceeds will be invested and the income passed to A. Suppose that the trustees do not get round to selling the interest for, say, three years after T's death. 'What', we can imagine A asking, 'about the position in the meantime? If the interest had been sold, as it should have been, on T's death, there would have been capital available from that moment from which income would be produced for me. Why should I lose merely because the interest is not sold immediately on T's death? I ought to be compensated in some way for not having received any income during the period between T's death and the sale.'

Equity agrees with A's contention. The solution which it adopts is to require the trustees to pass part of the proceeds of sale of the reversionary interest to A in order to make up for his not having received any income prior to the sale. The sum produced by the sale of the reversionary interest is thus apportioned between A and the capital fund. How is the apportionment made? The formula to be used was laid down in *Re Earl of Chesterfield's Trusts*[5]. What the trustees must do is to calculate[6] what sum, if (a) it had been available at T's death, and (b) it had been invested, and (c) had produced an income of 4% a year, and (d) this income (less tax at the current rate) had been re-invested, would have risen up (by reason of reinvesting the income) to the sum which was actually produced by the sale of the reversionary interest. For example, suppose that £10,000 is produced by the sale of the interest. The trustees calculate what sum, if it had been invested at 4% pa at compound interest at T's death, would have mounted up to £10,000. They find that the answer is, say, £9,400[7]. This £9,400 is treated as capital, and invested so as to produce income for A during the remainder of his life. The balance (in our example, £600) is handed to A in place of the income he had

2   *Re Woodhouse* [1941] Ch 332, [1941] 2 All ER 265.
3   See p 285, ante.
4   See also *Re Guinness Settlement* [1966] 2 All ER 497, [1966] 1 WLR 1355.
5   (1883) 24 Ch D 643.
6   In practice they, or their accountants, will obtain the answer from actuarial tables.
7   With tax at 5% and three years elapsing between T's death and the sale.

failed to receive in the period between T's death and the sale.

It will be noted that this apportionment is of capital (ie the proceeds of sale of the reversionary interest), and is for the benefit of A. By way of contrast, it may be useful here to point out the following differences:

In the case of a wasting asset or an unauthorised investment:	In the case of a reversionary interest:
1. the duty to sell is imposed for the benefit of the *remainderman*;	1. the duty to sell is imposed for the benefit of the *tenant for life*;
2. the apportionment is—	2. the apportionment is—
(a) of *income* (that is actually received prior to the sale);	(a) of *capital* (ie the proceeds of sale);
(b) for the benefit of the *remainderman*.	(b) for the benefit of the *tenant for life*.

Apportionments of income and capital under express trusts for sale

The rule in *Howe v Dartmouth* imposes a duty to sell certain forms of residuary personalty which is left to persons by way of succession. We must now consider the position where there is an *express* trust[8] for sale of residue for persons by way of succession. In this case, as regards wasting assets and unauthorised investments, the remainderman's interest is protected by the fact that trustees are under an express duty to sell the property concerned. In the case of reversionary interests, the tenant for life's interest is likewise protected by the express duty to sell.

But what about the position prior to sale? Here the same question arises as arose in the case of (a) wasting assets and unauthorised investments and (b) reversionary interests, which the trustees were under a duty to sell under the rule in *Howe v Dartmouth*. In the case of (a), is the tenant for life, A, entitled to the income in specie or does the 4% rule apply? In the case of (b), does A get no income prior to the sale, or is he to be compensated out of the proceeds of sale, under the principle in *Re Earl of Chesterfield's Trusts*?

The answer is that, subject to one minor modification, the same rules apply in determining the position as regards the income which A receives pending the sale under an express trust for sale, as apply in the case of a duty to sell imposed under the rule in *Howe v Dartmouth*. Thus if the wasting asset consisted of a lease, A would receive the income in specie pending sale[9]; if it consisted of a cow, the 4% rule would apply; if it was an unauthorised investment, the 4% rule would likewise apply[10]; if it was a reversionary interest, on the sale of the interest, the proceeds would be apportioned under the principle in *Re Earl of Chesterfield's Trusts*[11].

The modification is that if, under the express trust for sale, the trustees are

---

8 If the settlor gives the trustees mere power to sell, or to 'convert', this is not sufficient to create a trust to sell and so no express duty to sell arises. *Re Pitcairn* [1896] 2 Ch 199.
9 *Re Brooker* [1926] WN 93.
10 *Re Chaytor* [1905] 1 Ch 233 (The percentage at that time was 3%); *Re Berry* [1962] Ch 97, [1961] 1 All ER 529.
11 *Re Chance* [1962] Ch 593, [1962] 1 All ER 942.

given a power to postpone sale indefinitely (or are given discretion to sell
when they can get the best price) then the date at which the wasting assets
or unauthorised investments are valued (for the purpose of calculating the
4% which A is entitled to receive as income) is that of the testator's death[12].
(If there is no power to postpone sale, the position is as described[13] when
dealing with an implied duty to sell[14].)

Thus apportionment may be required in the case of an express trust for
sale as well as where there is an implied duty to sell under *Howe v Dartmouth*[15].
But, as where there is an implied trust, the duty to apportion is subject to
any contrary intention shown by the testator. For example, if the testator's
residuary personalty (left on trust for sale) included an unauthorised
investment, and he directed that the tenant for life should receive income in
specie, then the 4% rule would be excluded and prior to the sale the income
would be paid in specie as directed. Broadly the same indications of contrary
intention are sufficient to exclude apportionment in the case of an express
trust as exclude apportionment in the case of an implied trust. But the mere
giving of a power or a discretion to trustees to postpone sale is not in itself
sufficient to exclude the apportionment rules[16].

The rule in *Howe v Dartmouth* applies only where the residuary personalty
consists of certain forms of property (wasting assets, etc). But an express
trust for sale may exist in relation to any form of property. What is the
position pending sale in the case of forms of property other than those
governed by the rule in *Howe v Dartmouth?* The answers are set out below.

1. If the property subject to the express trust for sale consists of realty, then
pending sale the tenant for life is entitled to the income[17] in specie[18].

2. If the property consists of a lease the income is enjoyed in specie.

3. If the property consists of authorised investments, the trustees are not
under a duty to sell and the investments may be retained. (There would be
no point in the investments being sold and the proceeds used to buy other,
or the same, authorised investments.) The income would be enjoyed in specie.
(If the investments retained are ones in Part III of the First Schedule of the
Trustee Investments Act 1961, then the fund must be divided into two parts
as required by the Act.)

4. Reversionary interest in realty. It is uncertain whether the trustees would
be under a duty to apportion the proceeds of sale according to the rule in *Re
Earl of Chesterfield's Trusts*. Probably they are not.

---

12   *Re Owen* [1912] 1 Ch 519; *Re Parry* [1947] Ch 23, [1946] 2 All ER 412.
13   See p 287, ante.
14   *Re Fawcett* [1940] Ch 402 at 407 and 409. *Re Parry* [1947] Ch 23, [1946] 2 All ER 412.
15   (1802) 7 Ves 137. It is also required in the case of a statutory trust for sale imposed by the
    Administration of Estates Act 1925 in the case of an intestacy, where the intestate's
    property includes a reversionary interest. *Re Fisher* [1943] Ch 377, [1943] 2 All ER 615.
16   *Re Berry* [1962] Ch 97, [1961] 1 All ER 529 (not following *Re Fisher* [1943] Ch 377, [1943]
    2 All ER 615 on this point).
17   Ie after meeting the cost of insurance, repairs and other outgoings. LPA 1925, s 28(2).
18   *Re Searle* [1900] 2 Ch 829; *Re Oliver* [1908] 2 Ch 74.

CONTRARY INTENTION

We have spoken in this chapter in various places of a testator showing a contrary intention. It may be helpful to mention here that—

1. In the case of the rule in *Howe v Dartmouth*, where we speak of the testator showing a contrary intention, this refers to an intention that the rule should not be applied (with the result that the property is not sold, and the apportionment rules are not applied).

2. In the case of an express trust for sale, the contrary intention which may be shown relates to an intention that the apportionment rules (ie the 4% rule) should not apply (with the result that the tenant for life receives income in specie).

INCOME IN SPECIE

It may be helpful to point out that the notion of income being enjoyed in specie is relevant in two ways in the context of the subject matter of this chapter.

1. If the conditions necessary for the rule in *Howe v Dartmouth* to apply would exist, but the testator has indicated that the tenant for life is to receive income in specie, this is sufficient to show an intention that the rule should not be applied. No duty to sell therefore exists and the property is retained in its existing form.

2. If a trust for sale is imposed expressly, and the settlor has indicated that the tenant for life is, pending the sale, to receive income in specie, this is sufficient to exclude the application of the 4% rule in the case of wasting assets or unauthorised investments, and the rule in the *Earl of Chesterfield's Trusts* in the case of reversionary interests in personalty.

LEASES

We have been concerned with leases at various points in this chapter. We can recapitulate how they are affected as follows:

1. If a testator's residuary estate, left to persons in succession, includes a lease with less than 60 years to run, the trustees are under a duty (under the rule in *Howe v Dartmouth*) to sell it. Pending sale, the income received (ie rents received from sub-letting) is paid to the tenant for life in specie.

2. If a testator's residuary estate, left to persons in succession, includes a lease with 60 years or more to run, the trustees are under no duty under *Howe v Dartmouth* to sell the lease. They therefore retain the lease, and the income received is paid in specie to the tenant for life.

3. If a testator leaves a lease with any number of years unexpired expressly on trust for sale for persons by way of succession, then pending sale, the income received is paid to the tenant for life, in specie.

THE ELEMENTS OF THE RULE IN *HOWE V DARTMOUTH* AND OF THE RULE IN THE *EARL OF CHESTERFIELD'S TRUSTS*

It may be useful to point out here that the case of *Howe v Dartmouth* is the authority for three rules:

1. That (a) wasting assets and unauthorised investments and (b) reversionary interests (which form part of a residuary personalty left to persons in succession) must be sold.

2. That on the sale, under 1(a), of wasting assets and unauthorised investments, the income must be apportioned (ie the 4% rule applied).

3. That on the sale, under an express trust for sale, of wasting assets and unauthorised investments (forming part of residue left to persons in succession) the income must be apportioned (ie the 4% rule applied).

The case of the *Earl of Chesterfield's Trusts* is authority for two rules.

A. That on the sale of a reversionary interest under a trust for sale arising under the rule in *Howe v Dartmouth* (1(b) above), the proceeds of sale must be apportioned.

B. That on the sale, under an express trust for sale, of a reversionary interest in personalty (which forms part of residue left to persons in succession) the proceeds of sale must be apportioned.

It is not always appreciated that the rules in *Howe v Dartmouth* and in the *Earl of Chesterfield's Trusts* may arise in the context of express trusts for sale (ie at 3 and at B above respectively) as well as relating to implied trusts for sale.

THE FOUR PER CENT RULE OF TODAY

When dealing with the duty of trustees (under an implied or express trust for sale) to apportion income, prior to sale, from wasting assets and unauthorised investments, we stated that A was entitled to receive a sum representing 4% of the value of the property. The rule, as was explained, was intended to ensure that the tenant for life received no more than a fair yield.

Originally, a 'fair yield' was taken as being the interest which would have been obtainable by an investment in Consols. By 1852[19], 4% of the value of the property was accepted as representing a fair yield. In 1904 this was reduced to 3%[20] and in 1912 restored to 4%[1]. Since 1912 the level of interest obtainable on authorised fixed rate investments (such as government securities or loans to building societies) has risen to a much higher level than 4%. But no change in the figure of 4% has followed this rise. Thus, at the present day, instead of striking a fair balance between the tenant for life and the remainderman, the rule does not do justice to the tenant for life. (The fact that the rate reckoned as a fair yield has remained at 4% works an equal injustice on the tenant for life in the case of the apportionment of capital on

19   *Meyer v Simonsen* (1852) 5 De G & Sm 723.
20   *Re Woods* [1904] 2 Ch 4.
1   *Re Owen* [1912] 1 Ch 519.

the sale of a reversionary interest, sold either under the rule in *Howe v Dartmouth* or under an express trust for sale.)

The reasoning behind the imposition of an implied trust for sale under *Howe v Dartmouth* retains its validity, but for the apportionment rules to retain their original fairness some arrangement would have to be introduced under which the present fixed rate of 4% was replaced by a rate which could be varied according to the current average level of interest produced by authorised investments.

Chapter 17

Powers of advancement and maintenance

A. Power of advancement

Introduction

Suppose that in his will A leaves £1,000 to trustees on trust for his niece, B. When A dies, B, who is 15, asks the trustees for the money which A has left her. 'We cannot give you money until you are 18', the trustees explain. 'As an infant you are not capable of giving us a valid receipt[1]. If we handed over the money to you now, you might demand the money again when you were 18, and we should have nothing effective in law to prove that you had already been paid. So we might be obliged to pay you again, out of our own pockets.'

Whilst it is sensible that a trustee (or executor) should in this way be effectively prevented from passing money to someone too young to be capable of handling it responsibly, there are situations when it would clearly be equally sensible that someone younger than 18 should be able to obtain the benefit of property to which they had become entitled.

Express powers of advancement

Originally this difficulty was met by expressly conferring on trustees a power to apply the whole or a specified proportion of the property for the 'advancement' of the beneficiary concerned. ('Advancement' means the establishment or preferment in life of the beneficiary and has been held to include such matters as buying a commission in the army[2], purchasing a house for a doctor[3], paying for a passage to a colony[4], assisting a person in starting a career at the Bar[5], and establishing a person in business[6].) Under such an express power trustees were able to allow the beneficiary to benefit from property in advance of the time when the beneficiary would become entitled to call on the trustees to hand over the property to him. Thus although the word 'advancement' strictly connotes the application of trust property for the *advancement* of the beneficiary, it may also perhaps be regarded as bearing

1 Nor can an infant's parents or guardian, or spouse, give a valid receipt for a legacy. *Harvell v Foster* [1954] 2 QB 367, [1954] 2 All ER 736.
2 *Lawrie v Bankes* (1857) 4 K & J 142.
3 *Re Williams' Will Trusts* [1953] Ch 138, [1953] 1 All ER 536.
4 *Re Long's Settlement* (1868) 38 LJ Ch 125.
5 *Roper-Curzon v Roper-Curzon* (1871) LR 11 Eq 452.
6 *Re Kershaw's Trusts* (1868) LR 6 Eq 322.

the separate[7] meaning of making money available in *advance* of the time when this would otherwise be possible.

The statutory power of advancement

Section 32 of the Trustee Act 1925 now[8] provides that trustees[9] shall have a power to advance up to one half[10] of capital money held on trust for a beneficiary.

Section 32 enables trustees to advance capital to a beneficiary who has a vested interest in property but because he is below the age of majority could not otherwise receive it—the situation envisaged at the beginning of this chapter. But the section has a wider application than this: the section also authorises trustees to advance capital to a beneficiary who (irrespective of his age) has a contingent interest in the property. Thus if a testator leaves £1,000 to A when he marries, A has a contingent interest. Notwithstanding that A is still single (and perhaps has no intention of marrying) the trustee may, by virtue of s 32, advance up to one half of the £1,000.

Similarly, if a testator leaves £1,000 to the first of A's sons to be called to the Bar, and A has three sons, B, C and D, each son has a contingent interest. Under s 32, the trustees have power to advance up to one half of the presumptive share of the property held by each son. Since there are three sons the presumptive share of each son is taken as one third. Thus the trustees can advance up to one sixth to each son[11]. If the trustees advance a sixth of the property to each son, and then one son, say B, is called to the Bar, he would be entitled to all the remainder of the property. But C and D would not be required to hand over to him the property they had received by way of advancement[12].

As a further illustration of s 32, suppose that a testator leaves £900 to be divided between all A's sons who are called to the Bar before attaining the age of 30. A is living at the testator's death and has three sons B, C and D. The trustees advance £100 to B. B later is called to the Bar. His interest in one third of the money (£300) then vests. But the sum he has already received is taken into account, and so he will receive £200, ie £300 less £100[13]. The further distribution of the money will depend on whether any advances are made to C and D, and on whether C and D qualify. It will be noted that if A is still living at the time of the advance to B, the size of B's interest is liable

---

7 *Pilkington v IRC* [1964] AC 612 at 635.
8 No power was conferred by earlier legislation.
9 And personal representatives.
10 If one half of the fund is advanced, then the power is exhausted, irrespective of the fact that subsequently the value of the remaining half increases in value. *Re Marquess of Abergavenny's Estate Act Trusts* [1981] 2 All ER 643, [1981] 1 WLR 843; [1982] Conv 158 (J. W. Price). The Law Reform Committee, 23rd Report, recommended that trustees should no longer be bound to use the cash basis of accounting when bringing advances into account, but should be permitted to account for such sums at their value at the time of advance multiplied by any increase in the retail price index up to the time of the final division (paras 4.42–4.47).
11 It could be argued that each son has a presumptive share in the whole of the property, since the first son to be called to the Bar would be entitled to the whole property. But this is not how the Act is interpreted.
12 *Re Fox* [1904] 1 Ch 480 (a case concerning an express power of advancement).
13 Section 32(1)(b).

to be diminished by the birth of a further son to A who is called to the Bar before attaining the age of 30. Notwithstanding this fact, the trustees may advance up to one half of B's presumptive share (ie one third) at the time of the advancement.

Section 32 goes further. Suppose that a testator leaves property to such of his sons as his widow should appoint, with a gift over in default of appointment to X. X's interest is vested (since X does not have to fulfil any condition in order to become entitled), but his interest is one which is liable to become divested, ie if the widow makes an appointment in favour of one of the sons. (The sons, being merely the objects of a power, have no interest in the property, either vested or contingent[14].) Section 32 authorises the trustees to make an advancement to X. Such an advancement might seem to be contrary to the testator's intention but the widow can, if she wishes, prevent the exercise of the power of advancement by making an appointment to one of the sons. (And, as we have seen, it is always open to the settlor to exclude the statutory power if he so wishes.)

Section 32 therefore enables trustees to advance capital held on trust for a beneficiary, infant or adult, with *any* interest in the property, whether vested or contingent, and irrespective of the fact that the size of the share is liable to be diminished, and of the fact that the interest is liable to be defeated by the exercise of a power of appointment.

Contrary intention

This power exists only if there is no contrary intention expressed by the settlor[15]. The settlor can exclude the power either expressly, ie by directing that the trustees should not have the statutory power, or by implication, eg by stating that the trustees should have a power to advance up to a specified sum which is more, or is less, than the statutory half share[16]; or by directing that pending the vesting of the gift the income from the property is to be accumulated[17]; or by authorising the trustees to advance up to the whole of a beneficiary's interest (instead of the half permitted under the statutory power). But the fact that a settlor includes a power of advancement in a settlement will not of itself exclude the statutory power: the statutory power and an express power may co-exist[18]. The statutory power is excluded only where (as in the instances cited above) the express power is inconsistent with the statutory power.

Prior interests

Now consider a situation where a testator leaves property to trustees on trust for A for life with remainder to B when he attains 18. B has a contingent interest in remainder. If the trustees make an advancement to B, this would

14   See Chap 11.
15   Section 69(2).
16   *Re Evans' Settlement* [1967] 3 All ER 343, [1967] 1 WLR 1294.
17   *IRC v Bernstein* [1960] Ch 444, [1960] 1 All ER 697.
18   *Re Evans' Settlement*, supra.

reduce the income available for A. In such a situation the Act[19] provides that the trustees may only make an advancement to B if A is of full age and gives his written consent. But this provision, too, is subject to contrary intention being expressed by the settlor who can, if he so wishes, direct that the consent of A need not be obtained by the trustees before making an advancement to B.

Purposes for which the statutory power may be exercised

We have said that before the Trustee Act 1925 it was common for trustees to be given a power to apply capital for the advancement of beneficiaries. The power conferred by the Trustee Act 1925 is one to pay or apply capital money for a beneficiary's 'advancement or benefit'. The addition of the word 'benefit' extends the circumstances in which the power may be exercised. 'Benefit' has been held to include not only the use of money for the immediate personal benefit of the beneficiary, but also where the result is of only indirect benefit to him, eg as where an advance was made to enable a beneficiary to contribute to a charity which he felt an obligation to support, and where it would have been a great burden on him to do so out of his taxed income[20].

Further, the power can be exercised even if the result is to benefit, in addition, persons other than the beneficiary himself, provided always that the prime purpose is the benefit of the beneficiary. Thus it has been held that the power was validly exercised when money was advanced for the purpose of enabling a beneficiary (a wife) to make a loan to her husband so that he could set up a business in England and so prevent the family separating[1]; and for the purpose of enabling the beneficiary to set up a trust (sometimes referred to as a 'sub-trust') for the benefit of himself and his children[2]; or for the benefit of his wife and children[3]. In the last two instances the benefit to the beneficiary may consist of the relief from anxiety obtained by the beneficiary from the knowledge that his family was provided for[4]. Or the benefit may take the form of minimising estate duty[5].

The word 'advancement' in the section has been interpreted widely and has been held to mean 'any use of the money which will improve the material situation of the beneficiary'[6]. Where the purpose of the advancement is to set up a sub-trust for the benefit of, for example, the beneficiary and his family, some doubt exists as to whether the advancement may validly be made if the trustees of the new trust are to hold the property on discretionary trusts. This is because, if such a trust were set up, the trustees of the original trust (the trustees making the advancement) would be delegating to the trustees of the new trust responsibility for determining who should receive the property advanced. The advancement would thus infringe the principle that a trustee may not delegate the exercise of his powers. Thus, unless the original trust instrument conferred on the trustees a power to advance property on

---

19 Section 32(1)(c).
20 *Re Clore's Settlement Trusts* [1966] 2 All ER 272, [1966] 1 WLR 955.
1 *Re Kershaw's Trusts* (1868) LR 6 Eq 322.
2 *Re Pilkington's Will Trusts* [1961] Ch 466, [1961] 2 All ER 330; (M & B).
3 *Re Halsted's Will Trusts* [1937] 2 All ER 570.
4 Ibid.
5 *Re Pilkington's Will Trusts*, ante.
6 Per Viscount Radcliffe, *Pilkington v IRC* [1964] AC 612, [1962] 3 All ER 622.

discretionary trusts, an advancement on discretionary trusts would therefore probably be void.

Where the effect of the exercise of the power of advancement is to create a sub-trust, the limitations contained in the sub-trust must comply with the rule against perpetuities. The creation of the sub-trust by the exercise of the power of advancement is subject to the same rules in this regard as apply to the exercise of a special power of appointment[7]. If an advancement by way of the creation of a sub-trust in some way infringes the rule against perpetuities, any part of the sub-trust that does not infringe the rule is permitted to take effect[8].

It is clear that the power is not validly exercised where the prime purpose is the benefit of someone other than the beneficiary, eg the trustees themselves[9], or a member of the beneficiary's family whom the beneficiary has no obligation to make provision for, eg the beneficiary's father[10].

The duty of the trustees

The Act provides that trustees may 'pay or apply' the trust money. The trustees can therefore, at their discretion, either hand over money to a beneficiary or apply it on his behalf. If they pass the money to the beneficiary, stipulating the purpose for which the money is advanced, they are not entitled to leave it to the beneficiary to apply the money for the purpose stipulated or spend it as he chooses. If the beneficiary fails to apply the money as stipulated the trustees must make no further advance to the beneficiary unless they can be sure that the money will be applied in the way they stipulated. If they fail in this duty they are in breach of trust and may be required to account for the money improperly advanced. *Re Pauling's Settlement Trust*[11], in which a bank, acting as trustee, made a series of advances to the children of a family, provides a good illustration of proper and improper exercises of the power of advancement and the factors taken into account by the court in deciding whether trustees will be liable for breach of trust in connection with the exercise of a power of advancement. The facts and the decision in this case will be considered further in Chapter 22.

Since s 32 confers a power of advancement, and does not impose a duty to advance, if trustees elect not to exercise the power, the beneficiaries cannot compel them to do so.

Property out of which advances may be made

Section 32 enables trustees to make advances out of any capital which consists of money or securities or which consists of property (including land) which is held on trust for sale. But the section[12] does not extend to capital which takes the form of land subject to a settlement under the Settled Land Act

7 For an example of an exercise of a power of advancement which was void for perpetuity, see *Spens v IRC* [1970] 3 All ER 295, [1970] 1 WLR 1173.
8 *Re Hastings-Bass* [1975] Ch 25, [1974] 2 All ER 193.
9 *Molyneux v Fletcher* [1898] 1 QB 648.
10 *Re Pauling's Settlement Trusts* [1964] Ch 303, [1963] 3 All ER 1; (M & B).
11 [1964] Ch 303, [1963] 3 All ER 1.
12 Section 32(2).

1925, nor to capital money applicable under that Act (eg the proceeds of sale of settled land)[13]. There is, however, nothing to prevent a settlor conferring an express power of advancement on trustees of a settlement under the Settled Land Act 1925.

Trusts in which the statutory power applies

The statutory power of advancement conferred by s 32 is (subject, as mentioned earlier[14], to any contrary intention) incorporated into all trusts created after 1925, whether created inter vivos or by will, including trusts in a will made before 1926 by a testator who dies after 1925.

B. Power of maintenance

Introduction: 'intermediate income'

Let us suppose that in his will a testator leaves all his shares in a particular company to his son A if he attains the age of 18. A has a contingent interest in the property. A is seven years old at the testator's death. The trustees retain the shares and wait to see whether A will fulfil the condition and so enable them to pass the shares to him. (We know from what has gone earlier that in this situation the trustees would have power to advance up to half the capital to A. But, as will shortly be seen, we are not now concerned with the capital.) Six months later the trustees receive a dividend of £30 from the company. To whom does this money belong? The general rule is that when a person has a contingent interest in property, any income earned by the property (eg dividends from shares) between the date of the gift and the time when the interest vests, belongs to the donee, provided that he attains a vested interest. When this is the position we express the matter by saying that the gift 'carries the intermediate income', ie the gift of capital carries with it income earned up to the time when the gift vests. Thus, in our example, assuming the gift to A carries the intermediate income, when A attains 18 the trustees will pass to him not only the shares but also the accumulation of money from dividends.

Not all gifts, however, do carry the intermediate income. For example, a testator might leave shares to A if he attains 25 and direct that in the meantime any dividends from the shares should be paid to B. In this case the income, as it arises, will be paid to B. When A attains 25, he will receive the capital only.

---

13 Nor to any money or securities which by any other statute or by a rule of equity are deemed to be land.
14 See p 298, ante.

GIFTS WHICH CARRY THE INTERMEDIATE INCOME

When do gifts carry the intermediate income, and when do they not? We
have seen that if the donor directs that the intermediate income is to be paid
to someone other than the donee then the gift does not carry the intermediate
income. But what is the position if the donor makes no such direction? The
answer is that in the absence of any direction by the donor, certain types of
gift are deemed to be intended to carry the intermediate income and others
are deemed not to be so intended. The law on this subject is contained in
s 31(3) of the Trustee Act 1925 and s 175 of the Law of Property Act 1925.
The effects of these provisions as regards instruments coming into operation
after 1925 are set out below in the following five propositions:

1. With one exception, which will be considered shortly, a deferred gift of
residue does not carry the intermediate income[15]. A deferred gift is one which
is limited to take effect at a specified time, or on the occurrence of a specified
event, at some time in the future. (Such gifts are therefore sometimes termed
'future' gifts.) Examples of deferred gifts are 'to A on the death of B'; or 'to
A two years after the date of my death'. Note that these two gifts are not
contingent: their taking effect is not dependent, in the first case, on A surviving
B, or, in the second case, on A being alive at the expiry of two years from
the testator's death. Since the gifts are not contingent, they are vested. (The
result in each case will be that if A dies before the occurrence of the future
event, the interest forms part of A's estate and passes under his will or
intestacy). A deferred gift may also be contingent[16], eg 'the residue of my
personality to A five years after the date of my death, if he attains 21'. (If A
attains 21 before the five years elapse the gift vests but the property does not
pass to A until the end of the five years. If he has not attained 21 when the
five years expire, the gift remains contingent until he attains 21. If he dies
before attaining 21 then, whether this occurs before or after the expiry of the
five years, the gift fails.) In each of these three examples, provided the gift
was of residue, the gift would not carry the intermediate income[17]. The
exception to the rule that deferred gifts of residue do not carry the intermediate income is that a deferred *contingent* gift of residuary *realty*[18] does
carry the intermediate income; eg a gift of 'the residue of my land to A on
the death of B, if A attains 21'.

2. A deferred pecuniary legacy (eg '£1,000 to A one year after my death')
does not carry the intermediate income[19] (subject to what is said under 5
below).

3. A contingent pecuniary legacy (eg '£1,000 to A when he is called to the
Bar') does not carry the intermediate income[20] (subject to what is said under
5 below).

15 *Re Gillett's Will Trusts* [1950] Ch 102, [1949] 2 All ER 893; *Re Geering* [1964] Ch 136,
    [1962] 3 All ER 1043; *Re Oliver* [1947] 2 All ER 162 at 166; *Re Lord's Estate* (1867) 2 Ch
    App 782.
16 As in *Re Cohn* [1974] 3 All ER 928, [1974] 1 WLR 1378.
17 The income is therefore undisposed of and so would pass to the next of kin.
18 This is due to the wording of LPA, s 175, the anomalous effect of which (with regard to
    this form of gift) was perhaps neither foreseen nor intended.
19 *Re Lord's Estate* (1867) 2 Ch App 782.
20 *Re George* (1877) 5 Ch D 837; *Re Raine* [1929] 1 Ch 716; (M & B).

4. All other gifts carry the intermediate income[1].

5. The above rules give the prima facie position, and are subject to the expression of an intention to the contrary. Further, in some instances the courts will infer that it was the intention of the testator that the gift should carry the intermediate income. Thus in the case of a contingent (or deferred[2]) pecuniary legacy[3] if:

(a) the testator is the father of, or is some other person *in loco parentis* to, an infant beneficiary, and no other 'proper provision'[4] is set aside for the maintenance of the beneficiary, then a presumption arises that it was the testator's intention that the gift was intended to carry the intermediate income[5]. This inference is based on the assumption that the testator intended the gift to provide for the child during its infancy[6]. In earlier cases it was held to follow from this that the presumption that the gift carried the intermediate income was rebutted if the gift was limited to vest not on the child attaining the age of majority (then 21) or marrying under that age, but on some event which had no reference to the infancy of the legatee, for example, the child attaining the age of 25[7], or the age of 30[7]. In *Re Jones*, however, in 1925, it was held that the fact that the gift was made contingent on an event that would happen after the age of 21 was not of itself sufficient to preclude an inference that the gift was intended to carry the intermediate income, and in a 'proper case' the court might be able, although it would 'always be difficult', to find an intention that the intermediate income was intended to be carried. In a case where the contingency was some event happening long after the child attained 21, the court would be very slow to draw any such inference[8]. In the case before the court it was held that a gift contingent on a child attaining the age of 25 should carry the intermediate income. Thus where the contingency is other than attaining full age, whether the gift carries the intermediate income is a matter for the court;

(b) the gift is to an infant to whom the testator is not *in loco parentis*, but the will shows an intention that the income should be used for the child's maintenance[9] or education[10], then the gift carries the intermediate income;

(c) the will directs, expressly or impliedly, that the legacy should be set aside from the rest of the estate for the benefit of the legatee (with the result that the money will be available for the legatee as soon as the contingency occurs), then the gift carries the intermediate income. For example in *Re Medlock*[11] the gift was for three grandchildren, A, B and C, on their attaining 21. But the gift was not merely in the form 'to A, B and C on attaining 21'. The money was given to trustees to be held by them on trust for A, B and C

---

1 Eg a deferred specific gift of realty (*Re McGeorge* [1963] Ch 544, [1963] 1 All ER 519); or a pecuniary legacy in which those entitled had a vested interest subject (on the exercise of a power of appointment) to divesting (*Re Master's Settlement* [1911] 1 Ch 321).
2 *Re Bowlby* [1904] 2 Ch 685, 697–698.
3 But not, it seems, in the case of deferred gifts of residue.
4 Per Farwell J, *Re Jones* [1932] 1 Ch 642 at 651.
5 *Re Moody* [1895] 1 Ch 101.
6 The income in this case is interest on the legacy at 5%. Section 31(1).
7 *Re Abrahams* [1911] 1 Ch 108.
8 Per Farwell J, *Re Jones,* ante, at 652.
9 *Re Churchill* [1909] 2 Ch 431.
10 *Re Selby-Walker* [1949] 2 All ER 178.
11 (1886) 55 LJ Ch 738.

contingently on their attaining 21. It was held that the gift carried the intermediate income[12].

Maintenance out of income

We have seen that if a gift does carry the intermediate income, then the trustees, in addition to holding the capital on trust for the beneficiary, also hold on trust for him the income produced by that capital. The question we must now consider is whether, instead of accumulating the income (ie reinvesting the income and adding it to the capital) the trustees can use it for the benefit of the beneficiary, eg to pay for his everyday needs such as clothes, food, accommodation, education, and for his maintenance generally.

Without special authority trustees would have no power to apply the income in this way. There are two reasons for this.

(1) A beneficiary who is under 18 and who is unmarried[13] cannot give a valid receipt. So if trustees used income for, eg buying clothes for a beneficiary who was, say, seven, the trustees would not get a valid receipt from the beneficiary for the expenditure. When the beneficiary became of age he could demand the money again from the trustees. Thus even if a beneficiary's interest is vested, if he is under 18 (and unmarried) trustees cannot without additional authority apply the income for the maintenance of the beneficiary.

(2) If a beneficiary's interest is contingent, the trustees cannot apply the income for the beneficiary's maintenance as they do not know whether the beneficiary will, by fulfilling the condition which makes the gift contingent, become entitled to the capital and the income which goes with it. If the trustees applied income for the beneficiary's maintenance while his interest was still contingent, and the beneficiary died before attaining a vested interest, then the gift would fail and the trustees would hold the property (capital and income) on trust for, if the gift had been by will, the residuary legatee. The residuary legatee could then demand the money which the trustee had applied for the beneficiary's maintenance.

Express powers of maintenance

Where it was a settlor's intention that income should in fact be used for a beneficiary's maintenance it was originally the practice for a power so to apply income (a 'power of maintenance') to be expressly conferred on the trustees in the instrument creating the trust.

---

12   '... if it is clear upon the testator's will that he has directed the contingent legacy to be immediately set apart for the benefit of the objects of the gift when the contingency which he has indicated happens, when that contingency does happen the fund set apart with all its accretions belongs to the contingent legatees'. Per Kay J at p 739.

13   By s 21 of the Law of Property Act 1925 a married infant may give a valid receipt for income.

The statutory power

Section 31 of the Trustee Act 1925[14] now confers a power on trustees[15] to apply income for the 'maintenance, education or benefit' of an infant beneficiary. The statutory power exists only in the absence of any indication of a contrary intention in the will[16]. If the will directs that the income from a gift is to be accumulated, until the beneficiary attains full age[17], or some greater age[18], then generally[19] this is regarded as showing an intention that the income is not to be available for the infant's maintenance. The effect of a direction to accumulate is considered further below.

For the statutory power of maintenance to exist three conditions must be satisfied:

1. The beneficiary must be an infant. If the instrument which created the trust was executed after 1969, the age of 18 is substituted for the age of 21 in s 31[20].

2. The trustee must hold *property* on trust for the beneficiary. It is immaterial what kind of interest in the property the beneficiary holds: the interest may be vested, or contingent, or vested but liable to divesting[1] (as where he is entitled in default of an exercise of a power of appointment). It is also immaterial whether the trust was created inter vivos or by will.

3. The trustees must hold *income* from that property on trust for the beneficiary: income must be *'available'*. From what has been said earlier we know that in order for income to be available the gift must carry the intermediate income, and that certain types of gifts are deemed to be intended to carry the intermediate income.

By way of illustration let us consider whether trustees may exercise the statutory power of maintenance in favour of A in each of the following instances.

1. T leaves certain shares to trustees on trust for A when he marries. A has a contingent interest. The gift carries the intermediate income. So the trustees may use the income for the maintenance of A while he is an infant.

2. T leaves certain shares to trustees on trust for X for life with remainder to A when he marries. A has a contingent interest in remainder. The gift carries the intermediate income. But while X is alive the income must be paid to X. So while X is alive no income is available for A. So the trustees cannot use the income for A's maintenance while X is alive. When X dies, if A is still an infant, the statutory power then becomes exercisable. (If X is an infant at the testator's death, the trustees can exercise the statutory power for X's maintenance during his, X's infancy.)

---

14 Section 43 of the Conveyancing Act 1881 conferred a similar power. This Act continues to apply to instruments coming into operation after 1881 and before 1926.
15 Including personal representatives.
16 TA 1925, s 69(2).
17 *Re Reade-Revell* [1930] 1 Ch 52.
18 *Re Turner's Wills Trusts* [1937] Ch 15, [1936] 2 All ER 1435; (M & B).
19 But not necessarily invariably. *Re Thatcher's Trusts* (1884) 26 Ch D 426.
20 Family Law Reform Act 1969, s 1(3) and Sch 1.
1 *Re Sharp's Settlement Trusts* [1973] Ch 331, 339, [1972] 3 All ER 151; *Re Delamere's Settlement* [1984] 1 All ER 584, [1984] 1 WLR 813, CA.

3. After making certain specific bequests and after devising the whole of his realty, T directs that the residue of his estate should go to A on the death of B. The gift is of residue, and is a deferred gift. Such a gift does not carry the intermediate income. Therefore no income is available. So no power of maintenance is exercisable. (If T has not stated to whom the income should be paid, the income is undisposed of and, being residue, is paid to T's next of kin.)

4. T leaves £1,000 to his niece A when she is 18. A is five at T's death. A has a contingent interest in the capital. But the gift being a contingent pecuniary legacy, does not carry the intermediate income (which, in the absence of any direction by T, falls into residue). No statutory power of maintenance is therefore exercisable.

5. T leaves £100 'to A'. A is five at T's death. A has a vested interest in the property. It is only A's inability to give a valid receipt which prevents the trustees passing the capital to him. The trustees hold capital until A is eighteen. In the meantime the trustees may apply the income for A's maintenance. (If A dies before attaining 18, since A had a vested interest, the capital passes under his intestacy.)

6. T leaves £1,000 to his son A if he attains 18. A is seven at T's death. No other provision for A is made in T's will. The gift is a contingent pecuniary legacy. Normally such a gift does not carry the intermediate income. But in the case of the gift to A an intention is inferred that the gift should carry the intermediate income. The trustees can therefore apply income for the maintenance of A.

7. T leaves his farm Greenacre to A when he is 18 and directs that the income should be accumulated. The gift carries the intermediate income, but T's direction that the income should be accumulated excludes the statutory power. So no income may be applied for A's maintenance. All income must be accumulated and passed to A, with the land, when he is 18.

8. T leaves Blackacre Farm to A if he attains 18. There is no direction to accumulate the income. The gift carries the intermediate income and this may therefore be applied for the maintenance of A. (Since the land is settled land under the Settled Land Act 1925, the trustees have no power of advancement.)

9. After making certain specific bequests T leaves the residue of his estate among such of his children A, B, C and D as his widow should by deed or will appoint, with a gift over in default of appointment to C and D equally. C and D hold an interest that is vested but liable to divesting[2]. The gift carries the intermediate income. Thus the trustees of T's will can apply the income for the maintenance of C and D during their infancy.

The exercise of the statutory power

In exercising the statutory power of maintenance, the income may be paid to a beneficiary's parent or guardian, or applied by the trustees themselves[3]. Section 31 provides that in exercising the statutory power trustees should

---

2 See p 216, ante.
3 Section 31(1)(i).

'have regard to the age of the infant and his requirements and generally to the circumstances of the case, and in particular to what other income, if any, is applicable for the same purposes ...' The court will not interfere with the manner in which trustees exercise the statutory power provided that the trustees can show that they have acted in good faith and have given their minds to the way in which the power should be exercised. But if the trustees merely make automatic payments of income, eg to a beneficiary's father[4], without considering whether they were exercising their discretion wisely, the court may order the trustees to refund out of their own pockets the money they have paid.

Section 31 confers on trustees a *power* of maintenance. The trustees therefore exercise the power at their discretion; they cannot be compelled to apply income for a beneficiary's maintenance.

Failure to fulfil a condition

If the trustees apply income for the beneficiary's maintenance, and later the beneficiary fails to fulfil a condition which made the gift contingent (eg by dying before attaining a specified age), the income applied by way of maintenance is not recoverable, eg from the beneficiary's estate.

Effect of a direction to accumulate

It is a common error to suppose that a direction to accumulate indicates that the gift does not carry the intermediate income. The contrary is in fact the case: a direction to accumulate indicates that the gift does carry the intermediate income. Such a direction would for example be sufficient to make a gift carry the intermediate income where the gift was of a kind (eg a contingent pecuniary legacy) which otherwise would not carry the intermediate income. But the direction to accumulate does preclude the income from being used for the beneficiary's maintenance[5] (and this is so even if the direction is void as infringing s 164 of the Law of Property Act 1925[6]). The court has jurisdiction, however, to authorise income which is directed to be accumulated to be used for maintenance[7].

What part of income may be used?

The whole or part of any income may be applied for the beneficiary's maintenance. Any income not so applied is accumulated. Income not used in one year (and therefore accumulated) may be used for a beneficiary's maintenance in a subsequent year (in addition to the income in that year)[8].

---

4 *Wilson v Turner* (1883) 22 Ch D 521.
5 Such a direction is sufficient also to exclude the statutory power of advancement. (See p 298, supra.)
6 *Re Ransome* [1957] Ch 348, [1957] 1 All ER 690; *Re Erskine's Settlement Trusts* [1971] 1 All ER 572, [1971] 1 WLR 162.
7 *Havelock v Havelock, Re Allan* (1881) 17 Ch D 807.
8 Section 31(2).

Forms of property from which income may be applied

Section 31 enables trustees to apply income arising from any form of property including land whether subject to a trust for sale, or a settlement under the Settled Land Act 1925.

Maintenance out of capital

The power of advancement, as noted earlier, was originally intended as a means of enabling trustees to advance capital for the purpose of bringing about some substantial preferment in life of a beneficiary, and that maintenance was concerned more with his day-to-day needs. Since the end of 1925, however, because the statutory power of maintenance enables income to be applied for the 'maintenance *or benefit*' of the beneficiary, and the statutory power of advancement enables capital to be advanced for his 'advancement *or benefit*', the line dividing the purposes appropriate for the exercise of each power is no longer as distinct as formerly. For example, if trustees wished to provide a regular sum for the maintenance of an infant beneficiary but the income produced was insufficient, or if no income was available (eg because the gift did not carry the intermediate income), the trustees might decide to find the sum needed by advancing a series of sums of capital for the purpose intended. Whether in the absence of express authorisation by the settlor they can legally do so is, however, unclear. But the court has jurisdiction to authorise the use of capital for maintenance, and so it is open to trustees to apply to the court for a direction authorising them to apply capital in this way[9].

What happens when a beneficiary is 18?

We have seen that the statutory power of maintenance is exercisable only in favour of a beneficiary who is under 18. What happens when a beneficiary reaches 18? Suppose, for example, that a testator leaves property 'to A when he attains 21'. It would seem illogical that trustees should be able to apply income for A's benefit up to his 18th birthday, but that he should not be able to benefit from the income after that time. To meet this point, s 31(1)(ii)[10] provides that where a beneficiary attains the age of 18 and his interest has by then still not become vested, from that time on the trustees must (assuming, of course, that the gift does carry the intermediate income) pass the income to him as it arises (ie notwithstanding that his interest in the capital is still contingent)[11]. Any accumulation of income held by the trustees at the time when the beneficiary attains 18 (ie any income which has arisen previously and which has not been used for maintenance), is added to the capital. The

---

9   Payments for maintenance purposes out of capital may, according to the circumstances, be treated as payments of a capital nature (and so giving rise to no liability for income tax) *Stevenson v Wishart* [1987] 2 All ER 428, [1987] 1 WLR 1204 or as payments of income (so giving rise to a liability for payment of income tax).

10   As amended by the Family Law Reform Act 1969, s 1, Sch 1.

11   The sub-section applies equally where the beneficiary to whom the contingent gift is made has attained 18 at the time of the gift. (So he will be entitled to the income from the date of the gift.)

beneficiary will receive the income produced from this accretion to capital, but will not be entitled to the accretion itself unless and until his interest vests. When that time comes he will become entitled to the original capital plus the accumulation of income held by the trustees at the date when he became 18. But this provision, like the rest of s 31, is subject to any contrary intention expressed by the settlor[12]. Thus, for example, if the settlor directs that income arising after the beneficiary attains 18 should be accumulated[13], or paid to someone named, or applied in some other way, then the settlor's direction must be followed.

It will be noted that if trustees hold an accumulation of income for a beneficiary who is, say 17, they can apply the whole of this sum for his maintenance or benefit under their statutory power under s 31. But once the beneficiary attains 18 and the accumulation becomes part of capital, the trustees (by exercising their statutory power of advancement) can make available only half this sum.

Matters relating to the application of s 31(1)(ii) arose in *Re McGeorge*[14]. A testator devised land to his daughter and declared that the devise was not to 'take effect until after the death of my wife should she survive me'. The testator further directed 'Should my daughter die in the lifetime of the survivor of myself and my said wife leaving issue living at the death of such survivor such issue ... shall take by substitution ... the aforesaid devise ...' The testator died in 1960, survived by his wife and by his daughter, who was of full age. The question arose as to the disposition of the income from the land between the time of the testator's death and the death of his wife. It was held that (i) the gift was a deferred ('future') specific devise. As such, under s 175 of the Law of Property Act 1925, it carried the intermediate income. (ii) The gift was vested (since no contingency had to be satisfied for the daughter to take) but was liable to be divested (ie in the event of the daughter dying during her mother's lifetime without leaving issue). (iii) On the question whether s 31(1)(ii) entitled the daughter to require the trustees to pay her the income arising between the date of the gift and her mother's death, the court held that the section had no application, for two reasons: (a) the section applied to a person who, on attaining full age 'has not a vested interest in such income'. The daughter did have a vested interest in the income and therefore the section did not apply; (b) s 31(1)(ii) (like the rest of s 31) applies only in the absence of a contrary intention. By 'deferring the enjoyment of the devise until after the widow's death the testator has expressed the intention that the daughter shall not have the immediate income'[15] (ie should not have the income immediately). Thus the terms of the gift constituted a contrary intention and so excluded s 31(1)(ii). (iv) The income was ordered to be accumulated 'to see who eventually becomes entitled to it'[15] (for a period of 21 years or until the mother's death).

12 *Re Turner's Will Trusts* [1937] Ch 15, [1936] 2 All ER 1435; (M & B).
13 A direction to accumulate will exclude s 31(1)(ii) even if the direction infringes s 164 of the LPA 1925. *Re Ransome* [1957] Ch 348, [1957] 1 All ER 690. See [1979] Conv 423 (J. G. Riddall).
14 [1963] Ch 544, [1963] 1 All ER 519.
15 Ibid, at p 552.

ACCUMULATIONS

It will be convenient at this point to set out the principal situations in which accumulations of income may arise and to state in each case how such accumulations are to be treated. The treatment of accumulations is provided for in s 31(2). Like the rest of the section, the sub-section is subject to a contrary intention[16].

We shall suppose that in every case (1) trustees hold property on trust for an infant, A; and (2) the gift carries the intermediate income. The sections quoted are of the Trustee Act 1925, unless otherwise stated. ('Surplus income' refers to income remaining after some income has been applied for maintenance.)

1. A gift 'to A' (a vested gift).
(a) Prior to A attaining 18 or marrying under that age the trustees accumulate any surplus income. The accumulation may be used for A's maintenance (s 31(2))[17].
(b) If A marries under 18 the trustees must pay A the accumulation (s 31(2)(i)(a)). From the date of his marriage until he is 18 the trustees must pay A the income as it arises. This is because A's interest is vested and by s 21 of the Law of Property Act 1925 a married infant may give a valid receipt for income. When A is 18 the trustees pass the capital to him[18].
(c) If A attains 18 without having married, the trustees pass him the accumulation (s 31(2)(i)(a)) and the capital[19].
(d) If A dies under 18 his interest in the original capital and the accumulation[20] pass under his intestacy[1].

2. A gift 'to A if he attains 18' (a contingent gift).
(a) Prior to A attaining 18 or marrying under that age the trustees accumulate any surplus income. The accumulation may be used for A's maintenance (s 31(2))[2].
(b) If A marries under 18, the position remains unchanged[3].
(c) When A attains 18, the trustees pass him any accumulated income (s 31(2)(i)(b)) and the original capital[4].

---

16 *Re Delamere's Settlement Trusts* [1984] 1 All ER 584, [1984] 1 WLR 813, CA. (Gift of income to six named beneficiaries 'absolutely' showed intention to exclude s 31(2).) [1985] Conv 153 (R. Griffith).
17 If A held merely a life interest, the position would be the same.
18 If A held merely a life interest, the capital would continue to be held by the trustees, and A would receive the income for the remainder of his life.
19 If A held a life interest the trustees would pass him the accumulation; the capital would be held on trust for him for the remainder of his life.
20 If not already passed to him because he married under 18.
1 If A held merely a life interest, his interest in the capital would end and would then be held on trust for whoever was next entitled (eg a remainderman). It might be thought that the accumulation would form part of A's estate and pass under his intestacy, but this is not so; the accumulation becomes an accretion to capital. Section 31(2)(ii). *Stanley v IRC* [1944] KB 255, [1944] 1 All ER 230; (M & B).
2 If A held a life interest the position would be the same.
3 If A held a life interest the position would be the same.
4 If A had been granted merely a life interest, the accumulation (s 31(2)(ii)) and the original capital would continue to be held by the trustees, A receiving the income for the remainder of his life.
  If the gift to A were to take effect in default of the exercise of a power of appointment, then the capital cannot be passed to A on his attaining 18 as it remains subject to exercise

(d) If A dies before attaining 18, the gift to A (both as to capital and any accumulation of income) fails[5].

3. A gift 'to A if he attains 18 or marries under that age' (a contingent gift).

(a) Prior to A attaining 18 or marrying under that age the trustees accumulate any surplus income. The accumulation may be used for A's maintenance (s 31(2))[6].

(b) If A marries under 18, the trustees must pay A the accumulation (s 31(2)(i)(b))[7]. From the date of his marriage until he is 18 the trustees must pay A the income as it arises. This is because A's interest has vested and by s 21 of the Law of Property Act 1925 a married infant may give a valid receipt for income. When A is 18 the trustees pass the capital to him[8].

(c) If A attains 18 without having married, the trustees pass him the accumulation (s 31(2)(i)(b)), and the original capital[9].

(d) If A dies under 18 without having married, the gift (as to accumulation and capital) fails[10]. If A dies under 18, but having married since the gift was vested, the capital passes under A's intestacy[11].

4. A gift 'to A if he attains 25' (a contingent gift).

(a) Prior to A attaining 18 or marrying under that age the trustees accumulate any surplus income. The accumulation may be used for A's maintenance (s 31(2))[12].

(b) If A marries under 18 the position remains the same[13].

(c) When A attains 18 the trustees must from then on pay A the income as it arises (s 31(1)(ii)). The accumulation at the date A attains 18 becomes a permanent accretion to capital (s 31(2)(ii)). A will receive the income produced from this until he is 25[14].

(d) When A attains 25, the trustees pass him the capital (including the accumulation)[15].

---

of the power. Nor can the accumulations of income be passed to A on his attaining 18, since A does not hold his interest 'absolutely' within the meaning of s 31(2)(i)(b). The accumulation thus (like the capital) remains subject to the exercise of the power of appointment. A will only receive the accumulation (and the capital) if the power is never exercised. *Re Sharp's Settlement Trusts* [1972] Ch 331, [1972] 3 All ER 151. However, the income produced by the capital (including the accumulated income) will be paid to A under s 31(1)(ii) and the power of advancement may be exercised in respect of the capital.

5 *Re Bowlby* [1904] 2 Ch 685. If A had been granted a life interest, the property would be held on trust for whoever was next entitled.
6 If A held a life interest, the position would be the same.
7 If A had been granted merely a life interest, the accumulation (s 31(2)(ii)) would continue to be held by the trustees.
8 If A had been granted merely a life interest, the trustees would continue to hold the capital and accumulation (s 31(2)(ii)), A receiving the income for the remainder of his life.
9 If A had been granted merely a life interest, the trustees would continue to hold the capital and accumulation (s 31(2)(ii)), A receiving the income for the remainder of his life.
10 If A had been granted merely a life interest, the position would be the same.
11 If A had been granted merely a life interest, the property (accumulation and capital) would be held on trust for whoever was next entitled.
12 If A held a life interest the position would be the same.
13 If A held a life interest the position would be the same.
14 If A held a life interest the position would be the same.
15 If A had been granted a life interest, the trustees would continue to hold the capital (and accumulation), A receiving the income for the remainder of his life.

(e) If A dies before attaining 25 the gift (as to both the capital and the accumulation) fails[16].

MAINTENANCE BUT NO ADVANCEMENT, AND VICE VERSA

Are there any situations in which trustees can exercise powers of maintenance, but not of advancement? There is at least one such situation: if trust property consists of land which is settled land under the Settled Land Act 1925 no advancement may be made, but income from the land may be applied for maintenance under s 31.

Are there any situations in which trustees can exercise powers of advancement, but not maintenance? There are at least two such situations. (1) If there is a prior life interest, provided the life tenant consents, an advancement can be made. But no income is available and so no maintenance is possible. (2) If a gift does not carry the intermediate income no maintenance is possible but this does not prevent an advancement being made, provided that the person entitled to the income gives his consent[17].

POWERS OF MAINTENANCE AND ADVANCEMENT OF PERSONAL REPRESENTATIVES

Under the Trustee Act 1925[18], personal representatives have the same powers of maintenance and advancement as trustees.

16   If A held merely a life interest, the property would be held on trust for whoever was next entitled.
17   TA 1925, s 32(1)(c).
18   Section 68(17).

Chapter 18

Variation of trusts[1]

INTRODUCTION

In 1944 a husband and wife conveyed certain property to trustees on trust for any children born to their son Robert who should attain 21. By clause 3, until the youngest child attained 25 the trustees were to hold the property on discretionary trusts for all or any of the children. The settlors were later advised that, because of the wording of clause 3, on the death of the survivor of the two settlors estate duty would be likely to be payable on the trust property. In order to avoid such a claim arising the settlors wished to have clause 3 removed from the terms of the trust: they wished to *vary* the terms of the trust. Could this be done? Did the court have jurisdiction to sanction such a variation in the terms of the trust? The case came before the court as *Chapman v Chapman*[2]. Before considering the outcome, it will be convenient first to set out the various forms of jurisdiction existing at that time which empowered the court, in certain circumstances, to effect variations in the terms of a trust.

Power to order maintenance

We saw in Chapter 17 that the court has power to order that income which a settlor had directed to be accumulated should be used for a beneficiary's maintenance[3].

Saunders v Vautier

Under the rule in *Saunders v Vautier*[4], where all the beneficiaries are *sui juris* and absolutely entitled they can by unanimous direction either direct the trustees to hand over the trust property to them, or direct the trustees to hold the trust property on fresh trusts (thus, in effect, varying the terms of the original trust).

---

1 See J. W. Harris, *Variation of Trusts*.
2 [1954] AC 429, [1954] 1 All ER 798.
3 *Havelock v Havelock, Re Allan* (1881) 17 Ch D 807.
4 (1841) 4 Beav 115.

Trustee Act 1925, s 57

The court has a statutory jurisdiction, under s 57 of the Trustee Act 1925, to confer on trustees power to effect a particular transaction which in the opinion of the court is 'expedient', but which the trustees do not otherwise have power to carry out. The purpose of the section is to ensure that 'the trust property should be managed as advantageously as possible in the interest of the beneficiaries'[5]. For example, the jurisdiction has been used to sanction a sale of land where a necessary consent could not be obtained[6], to sanction sale of settled chattels[7] and to sanction the substitution of a new investment clause[8] giving wider powers than an existing clause[9]. But the section does not permit the court to vary the beneficial interests under the trust; it is concerned solely with the administration of the trust property.

Settled Land Act 1925, s 64

Section 64 of the Settled Land Act 1925 confers jurisdiction on the court to make an order authorising a tenant for life of settled land to effect any transaction concerning the settled land[10] which could have been validly carried out by an absolute owner and which, in the opinion of the court, would be for the benefit of the land or the beneficiaries under the settlement. Section 64 thus confers a wider jurisdiction on the court than does s 57 of the Trustee Act 1925, since s 64 not only empowers the court to authorise transactions concerning the trust property (eg a lease of the settled land for a period longer than that authorised by s 41 of the Settled Land Act 1925), but also empowers the court to authorise the variation of the beneficial interests under the trust. This is because s 64(2) defines 'transaction' as including any '... disposition ... or arrangement'. Thus the court could by order authorise a tenant for life to make an arrangement with the trustees and with other adult beneficiaries which remodelled the beneficial interests under the settlement. For example in *Re Downshire's Settled Estates*[11] the court approved a scheme under which land was resettled under fresh trusts in order to avoid a claim for estate duty arising on the tenant for life's death.

Trustee Act 1925, s 53

Another statutory provision which confers jurisdiction on the court to vary the beneficial interests under a trust is s 53 of the Trustee Act 1925. This section enables the court, where an infant is beneficially entitled to property, to make an order, with a view to the application of the trust property for the maintenance, education or benefit of the infant, 'appointing a person to

---

5   Per Evershed MR, *Re Downshire's Settled Estates* [1953] Ch 218 at 248.
6   *Re Cockerell's Settlement Trusts* [1956] Ch 372, [1956] 2 All ER 172.
7   *Re Hope's Will Trust* [1929] 2 Ch 136.
8   See p 276, supra.
9   *Mason v Farbrother* [1983] 2 All ER 1078; (M & B).
10   This has been held (in the context of s 64) to include land held on trust for sale. *Re Simmons* [1956] Ch 125, [1955] 3 All ER 818.
11   [1953] Ch 218, [1953] 1 All ER 103. See also *Raikes v Lygon* [1988] 1 All ER 884, [1988] 1 WLR 281.

convey such property'. Thus in *Re Meux*[12], property was settled on A for life with remainder to B (an infant) in tail. The court granted an application under the section for the appointment of a person to convey B's interest to A absolutely in consideration of a sum to be paid by A to trustees on trust for the benefit of B. It will be seen that this arrangement varied the terms of the trust not only with regard to the interests of A and B, but also with regard to those of B's heirs, whose interests were by the arrangement struck out.

Approval of compromises

Finally, in this review of the court's jurisdiction to vary the terms of trusts, we must add that, at the time when *Chapman v Chapman*[13] was heard, it had long been accepted that the court had power, under its inherent jurisdiction, to approve an arrangement which constituted a compromise of a dispute between the beneficiaries as to their rights under the trust. In exercising this jurisdiction the court gave approval on behalf of beneficiaries who were not *sui juris* (eg infants or unascertained beneficiaries) to arrangements proposed by beneficiaries who were *sui juris*.

In the course of time it became the practice[14] for applications to be made to judges in chambers for approval of arrangements which varied the terms of trusts for the benefit of infants and unascertained beneficiaries, but which did not constitute a compromise of any real dispute. Such arrangements were, however, approved by judges on the basis that they had jurisdiction to do so.

Chapman v Chapman

But did such jurisdiction exist? This was the question for decision in *Chapman v Chapman*. The House of Lords decided that the courts had no such general jurisdiction. They held that the court had power to approve an arrangement only where there was a genuine dispute about the rights of beneficiaries. In *Chapman v Chapman* no such dispute existed. The application was therefore rejected. The decision in *Chapman v Chapman* meant that those who wished to vary the terms of trusts from time to time in order to avoid the effects of current tax legislation (or for other purposes) would in future be likely to find it impossible to achieve this end. In 1954 the matter was referred to in the Law Reform Committee which reported to Parliament in November 1957. The Committee recommended that the court should be given the 'unlimited jurisdiction to sanction such changes which it in fact exercised in the years immediately preceding the decision in *Chapman v Chapman*'[15]. A bill to implement the Committee's recommendation was introduced into Parliament in December 1957 and enacted the following July as the Variation of Trusts Act 1958.

The decision in *Chapman v Chapman* did not affect the jurisdiction to approve compromises which might have the effect of varying the terms of a

12 [1958] Ch 154, [1957] 2 All ER 630.
13 [1954] AC 429, [1954] 1 All ER 798, HL.
14 *Chapman v Chapman* [1954] AC 429 at 464.
15 (1957) Cmnd 310; para 13.

trust. The court's decision was, as stated above, that there had to be some real dispute, and that on the facts of the case no such dispute existed. A gloss on the matter was added by *Mason v Farbrother*[16], in 1983, when the court held that whilst there had to be genuine points of difference which were required to be settled by a compromise in order that the court should have jurisdiction to determine the issue, the points of difference did not have to amount to a contested dispute. They might concern such a matter as the interpretation of the trust deed. In the case before the court there was a genuine difference of opinion over the construction of the investment clause in the trust deed. The court therefore had jurisdiction to approve a compromise. The court did not, however, consider that its jurisdiction extended so far as to give it power to approve, not some form of compromise, but the substitution of an entirely new investment clause for the existing one. (A new clause was approved instead under s 57 of the Trustee Act 1925.)

Variation of Trusts Act 1958

Effect of Act

The effect of the Act is to authorise the court to approve, on behalf of certain specified categories of persons, an 'arrangement' which varies the terms of the original trust. The Act thus confers on the court the wide jurisdiction that was in practice exercised prior to *Chapman v Chapman*. But the Act expressly provides that the court has power to approve an arrangement only where it is satisfied that it is for the benefit[17] of the person or persons on whose behalf approval is sought.

The term 'arrangement' in the Act is not confined to one that is 'in some sense *inter partes*, some kind of scheme which two or more people have worked out'[18]. The word 'arrangement' is 'deliberately used in the widest possible sense so as to cover any proposal which any person may put forward for varying or revoking the trusts'[18].

Persons on whose behalf arrangements may be approved

Since it is the purpose of the Act to permit the court to approve arrangements on behalf of beneficiaries who cannot give their own consent, it follows that the court has no power to approve an arrangement on behalf of a beneficiary who is *sui juris*[19]. Thus, before an application is made to the court for the approval of an arrangement, the consent of all beneficiaries who are *sui juris* should be obtained. For example, suppose that trustees hold funds on trust for A and B for life with remainder to C. B is an infant. The trustees wish to divide the trust fund, giving C three-quarters absolutely. The court has power to approve the scheme only on behalf of B. It is for A and C to decide

---

16   [1983] 2 All ER 1078; (M & B).
17   Subject to what is said below. See p 322, post.
18   Per Lord Evershed MR, *Re Steed's Will Trusts* [1960] Ch 407 at 419.
19   With one exception. See infra.

whether they wish to support the scheme. (We will consider later the position if the consent of a beneficiary who is *sui juris* is not in fact obtained.)

On behalf of what categories of beneficiary may the court approve an arrangement? The Act lists four such categories. These are as follows. The court has power to approve an arrangement on behalf of—

1. Any person who is *unborn*[20], for example under a trust for A for life, with remainder to A's first son to marry, where A has no children. (Section 1(1)(c).)

2. Any person who is an *infant*[1] or who is incapable of assenting to the proposed arrangement by reason of any *other incapacity*, eg insanity; for example under a trust for A for life with remainder to B, where A or B (or both) are infants (or are insane). (Section 1(1)(a).)

3. Any person who has a *discretionary interest under a protective trust*[2], where the interest of the principal beneficiary (eg a life tenant) still subsists[3]. (Section 1(1)(d).) For example, where a settlor leaves property to A for life on protective trusts, and A has a wife B, the court may approve on behalf of B an arrangement varying the terms of the trust. Since there is no requirement that the person in this category must be an infant, the court may give its approval notwithstanding that B is an adult, and notwithstanding the fact that B does not concur with the arrangement proposed. (This is an exception to the general position under the Act that the court has no power to override the wishes of an adult beneficiary.)

4. Any 'person (whether ascertained or not) who may become entitled directly or indirectly to an interest under the trusts as being at a future date or on the happening of a future event a person of any specified description or member of any specified class of persons ...'. (Section 1(1)(b).)

However, from this class (in what has become termed 'the proviso to s 1(1)(b)') certain persons are excluded. The wording of the proviso is: '... so however that this paragraph does not include any person who would be of that description, or a member of that class, as the case may be, if the said date had fallen or the said event had happened at the date of the application to the court'.

Guidance as to the effects of s 1(1) can be obtained from the cases. In *Re Moncrieff's Settlement Trusts*[4], in 1938 property was assigned by a settlor, a woman, to trustees to be held on trust for the settlor for life with remainder to such of her children as she should by deed or will appoint; and in default of appointment on trust ultimately for the persons who would be the settlor's next of kin had she died a widow and intestate. At the time of the application the settlor had one child, an adopted son, who was an adult. The settlor was past the age of child-bearing. By virtue of the Adoption Act[5], the adopted son would be entitled to participate in any property as to which S died intestate as if he had been born her own child. If the settlor survived her son, her next of kin in the event of her dying a widow would be four cousins of

---

20 As in *Re Whittall* [1973] 3 All ER 35, [1973] 1 WLR 1027.
1 As in *Re Whittall*, supra.
2 See Chap 12.
3 Ie before an event, eg an act of bankruptcy by the principal beneficiary, has brought the beneficiary's (sole) life interest to an end and the discretionary trust into being. (See p 169.)
4 [1962] 3 All ER 838n, [1962] 1 WLR 1344; (M & B).
5 Section 16.

hers. An application was made by the settlor for approval by the court of an arrangement on behalf of the son and the four cousins. The cousins were persons who might 'become entitled ... as being ... on the happening of a future event' (S's death after surviving the adopted son) persons of a specified description (S's next of kin). But they were *not* persons who would be of the specified description (S's next of kin) if she had died intestate and a widow if the said event (S's death) had occurred at the date of the application to the court—*S's adopted son would be*. So the cousins were not within the proviso to s 1(1)(b) and the court therefore could (and did) give consent on their behalf. But the son did come within the proviso to s 1(1)(b) and therefore the court was not able to give consent on his behalf. (The arrangement could therefore only be made with the son's approval.)

The outcome in *Re Moncrieff's Settlement Trusts* may be contrasted with that in *Re Suffert's Settlement*[6]. Under a settlement by S, personalty was held on trust for S's daughter, D, for life with remainder to D's children; if D had no children, the property was to go to whomsoever D appointed by will (ie under a general power of appointment) with a gift over in default of appointment on trust for the persons who would be D's statutory next of kin if she died intestate and unmarried. D was 61 and unmarried. If she died unmarried her next of kin would be three cousins. D and one of the cousins applied to the court for a variation of the trust which would have divided the trust fund between D and the three cousins. Could the court give approval on behalf of the two cousins who were not a party to the application? Buckley J held that it could not. Each cousin was 'a person who would be of that description [D's statutory next of kin] ... if the said ... event [D's death] had happened at the date of the application to the court.' Therefore approval could not be given on their behalf[7].

In *Knocker v Youle*[8] property was held on trust for the settlor's daughter for life, with remainder to appointees under her will with a gift over in default of appointment to the settlor's son or, if he were dead, to the settlor's four married sisters living at the son's death or, if then dead, their issue who should attain 21. The settlor's wife and four sisters were dead. Approval of an arrangement was sought on behalf of the numerous issue of the four sisters. Warner J held that the issue of the sisters did not come within s 1(1)(b). Para (b) referred to persons who 'may' become entitled. It therefore did not include persons who at the date of the application *were* entitled to an interest. The issue were entitled to a contingent interest. (The fact that the contingency was remote was irrelevant.) Therefore approval could not be given on their behalf. For a variation to be made their consent was necessary. Alternatively, he held that 'even if this difficulty could be overcome', ie and the cousins brought within the first part of s 1(1)(b), since some of them would fall within the proviso the consent sought on their behalf could not be given.

It should be noted that the proviso to s 1(1)(b) does not operate in relation to the other sub-clauses of s 1(1). Thus the fact that the proviso

6   [1961] Ch 1, [1960] 3 All ER 561; (M & B).
7   No consent needed to be given by the objects of the power of appointment since it was open to the donee of the power to exclude the objects by releasing the power. But where an arrangement will exclude the objects of a power of appointment it has been held that before approval is given by the court, the donee should expressly release the power. *Re Ball's Settlement* [1968] 2 All ER 438, [1968] 1 WLR 899.
8   [1986] 2 All ER 914, [1986] 1 WLR 934; (M & B); (1986) 136 NLJ 1057 (P. Luxton); [1987] Conv 144 (J. G. Riddall).

precludes consent being given under s 1(1)(b) on behalf of a certain person will not bar consent being given on his behalf if he can be brought within one of the other heads of s 1(1), eg if he is an infant or a person unborn.

Suppose that a settlor settles property on A for life, with remainder to A's wife, with remainders over. A is unmarried. Can the court approve an arrangement on behalf of A's future wife? It would seem that the proviso to s 1(1)(b) prevents the court from approving an arrangement. (Any woman in the world would be 'a person of that description [A's wife] ... if the ... said event [marriage to A] had happened at the date of the application to the court'.) In a number of cases, however, the courts have approved arrangements on behalf of future wives of beneficiaries who were unmarried[9]. It would clearly be inconvenient if the court was not able to give approval on behalf of the future wife of a beneficiary who was unmarried and over 17, since without the approval of the court no variation of the trust could be achieved. It has been suggested[10] that the difficulty could be avoided if the wording of the proviso to s 1(1)(b) was construed as being intended to be read with the word 'person' being restricted to an 'ascertained' person. The proviso would then read: 'this paragraph shall not include any ascertained person who would be of that description ... if the ... said event had happened at the date of the application'[11]. With this interpretation, the court could approve an arrangement on behalf of a future wife of an unmarried beneficiary who was over 17, since any future wife of his would be a person who was unascertained, and so not within the proviso to s 1(1)(b), with the result that the paragraph would give the court the jurisdiction necessary to approve the arrangement.

Benefit

The court has jurisdiction under the Act to approve an arrangement varying the terms of the trust only if it is satisfied (subject to one exception[12]) that the proposed arrangement is for the benefit of those on whose behalf the application is made. What factors should the court take into account in deciding whether the proposed scheme is for these persons' benefit? The Act does not say, but the cases show that the following matters have been accepted as constituting a sufficient benefit for the court to exercise the jurisdiction conferred on it by the Act[13].

---

9 *Re Clitheroe's Settlement Trusts* [1959] 3 All ER 789, [1959] 1 WLR 1159; *Re Steed's Will Trusts* [1960] Ch 407, [1960] 1 All ER 487; (M & B); *Re Lister's Will Trusts* [1962] 3 All ER 737, [1962] 1 WLR 1441.
10 J. W. Harris, *Variation of Trusts*, pp 39–40.
11 It has been pointed out (J. W. Harris, op cit, p 40) that 'Such an interpretation can be supported on constructional grounds. The words "any person" in the earlier part of the paragraph are followed by the words "whether ascertained or not". No such qualifying words follow "any person" in the later part of the paragraph, so that it can be read as removing from the approval umbrella only "ascertained" persons'.
12 See p 322, post.
13 The Law Reform Committee, 23rd Report, recommended that trustees should be entitled to make application under the Variation of Trusts Act 1958 to ask the court to widen their powers of investment. (Para 3.25).

TAX AVOIDANCE

The majority of applications to the court for variation of trusts under the
Act have been made with a view to reducing the tax which would become
due if the trusts remained unaltered. For example, prior to 1974 if property
were settled on A for life with remainder to his son B, then on A's death
estate duty would be payable. If the trusts were varied so as to divide the
fund between A and B absolutely, then this liability would be reduced.
Liability for capital gains tax and income tax could also in some circumstances
be avoided or reduced by variations being made to the terms of a trust. (It
has been observed[14] that the main object of the 1958 Act 'was to give
relief from estate duty liability in the case of settlements which contained
beneficiaries who were infant or unborn or under other disability ... [o]n the
argument that, because relief could be obtained if all the beneficiaries were
adult, it was unreasonable to deny relief to those who were in law incapable
of consenting'.)

Although doubts have from time to time been expressed[15] as to whether it
is in the public interest for the courts to enable the legislature's tax enactments
to be sidestepped, the general attitude of the courts[16] has been that tax
avoidance is a legitimate purpose for a proposed variation[17].

The mere fact, however, that financial gain by tax avoidance would be
obtained from the proposed variation does not mean that the court will in
all cases necessarily sanction the arrangement. The court must be satisfied
that the scheme, taken as a whole, is for the benefit of those on whose behalf
the application is made. If the court considers that the overall effect on these
persons is, notwithstanding the financial advantage, not for their benefit,
then the arrangement will not be approved. For example, in *Re Weston's
Settlements*[18] a settlor sought approval for an arrangement under which
property settled by him on his sons and their issue would be transferred from
certain English settlements to settlements in Jersey. The transfer would have
avoided a capital gains tax liability of about £163,000. The arrangement
would have entailed the settlor's sons, who until a few months before the
application had lived in England, living in Jersey. It was held that the
arrangement was not for their benefit: 'I do not believe that it is for the
benefit of children to be uprooted from England and transported to another
country simply to avoid tax'[19]. It has been suggested[20] that the decision of

14 R. M. Maudsley, *The Modern Law of Perpetuities*, p 216.
15 Lord Morton of Henryton, *Chapman v Chapman* [1954] AC 429 at 448.
16 *Re Tinker's Settlement* [1960] 1 WLR 1011 at 1013; *Re Holmden's Settlement Trusts* [1966]
    Ch 511 at 527, on appeal [1968] AC 685 at 699; *Re Holt's Settlement* [1969] 1 Ch 100 at
    120–121. See also *Re Drewe's Settlement* [1966] 2 All ER 844n, [1966] 1 WLR 1518
    (arrangement approved subject to the addition of a clause providing that a power of
    appointment included in the variation should not be exercisable without the consent of
    the trustees after advice from counsel that the exercise of the power would not give rise
    to an estate duty liability) and *Re Clitheroe's Settlement Trusts* [1959] 3 All ER 789, [1959]
    1 WLR 1159.
17 This also was the view expressed in the Sixth Report of the Law Reform Committee ((1957)
    Cmnd 310, para 16) which lead to the passing of the Variation of Trusts Act 1958.
18 [1969] 1 Ch 223, [1968] 1 All ER 338; (M & B).
19 Per Lord Denning. Cf *Re Seale's Marriage Settlement* [1961] Ch 574, [1961] 3 All ER 136
    (arrangement for the transfer of the trust property to the trustee of a Canadian settlement
    with terms as similar as possible to those of the English settlement, the beneficiaries having
    emigrated to Canada, approved).
20 J. W. Harris, *Variation of Trusts*, pp 85–92.

the Court of Appeal in this case was not entirely free from a degree of opposition on moral grounds to certain forms of tax avoidance. Whether the courts may in the future come to draw a distinction[1] between legitimate and illegitimate forms of tax avoidance remains to be seen[2].

OTHER FORMS OF BENEFIT

The courts have accepted a wide variety of other matters as constituting a benefit for the purpose of the Act. Some illustrations of these follow.

1. Where a life tenant under a protective trust was a mental patient, approval was given to an arrangement under which the life tenant gave up her life interest in favour of the remaindermen, her two adopted daughters. It was held that this was for the benefit of the life tenant as this was in all probability what she would have wanted if she had been of full mind[3]. The benefit here was thus a moral one.

2. Where an infant beneficiary, who would become absolutely entitled on attaining her majority, was shown by the evidence to be irresponsible and immature, approval was given to an arrangement under which the date on which her interest vested absolutely was postponed until a later age, the property in the meantime being held on protective trusts[4].

3. Where the terms of a settlement provided that specified beneficiaries in remainder should forfeit their interest if, on the death of the life tenant, they were 'practising Roman Catholicism' (which was defined to include being married to a Roman Catholic), an arrangement was approved under which the interests in remainder were accelerated and the forfeiture clause was struck out. The deletion of the clause was held to be a benefit to the children in that the clause might have tended to deter them from marrying the person of their choice, and might have proved 'a source of possible family dissension'[5].

4. Under the will of a testatrix who died in 1923 property was left to her two sons with remainder, if a son died without issue, to any widow he might leave unless the son 'shall in writing direct otherwise', with remainders over. No power of advancement was contained in the will and in 1962 an application was made to vary the trust so as to incorporate into the trusts of the will the statutory power of advancement contained in s 32 of the Trustee Act 1925. The insertion of a power of advancement would not be to the benefit of a possible widow of either of the sons, but an arrangement was proposed in which the incorporation of a power of advancement was coupled with a variation striking out the discretion given to the sons to exclude their widows from taking under the trust. It was held that this was a sufficient benefit to a possible widow for the court to be justified in approving the arrangement on behalf of such a widow[6].

---

1 A distinction drawn by Stamp J in *Re Weston* in the hearing at first instance. [1968] 1 All ER 720 at 725.
2 For full discussion see J. W. Harris, op cit.
3 *Re CL* [1969] 1 Ch 587, [1968] 1 All ER 1104.
4 *Re T's Settlement Trusts* [1964] Ch 158, [1963] 3 All ER 759.
5 *Re Remnant's Settlement Trusts* [1970] Ch 560, [1970] 2 All ER 554; (M & B).
6 *Re Lister's Will Trusts* [1962] 3 All ER 737, [1962] 1 WLR 1441.

NO BENEFIT

By way of contrast we may consider two instances in which the court found that the requirement of benefit was not satisfied.

1. A settlor gave property on certain trusts for his son and daughter. Under the trusts, if the son died under 30 then his share passed to the daughter for life with remainder to her children. The settlor had intended that if the son died under 30 leaving issue, the property should pass to them. The settlor applied to the court for a variation to give effect to what had been his intention. The application was made on behalf of the unborn children of the daughter. It was held that the proposed variation was not in any way for their benefit and the application was therefore refused[7].

2. Under a settlement, income was directed to be held on certain trusts until the settlor's last surviving son died, when it was to be divided between the settlor's grandchildren and the issue then living of any grandchild who should then have died. In 1965 one son survived. He applied for a variation which would enable the property to be distributed on 30 June 1973, instead of on his death. The application was refused as it would have deprived of benefit any issue of a grandchild born between 30 June 1973 and the son's death[8].

We may note here that where there is little[9] or no chance[10] of a future beneficiary coming into existence (eg as when property was left to D for life with remainder to her children and, as D was 50, it was unlikely that she would have another child[11]) the court has power under its inherent jurisdiction, after hearing the evidence, to authorise the trustees to deal with the trust property on the basis that no further beneficiaries will come into existence. (Such an order may be coupled with an order giving approval to an arrangement under the 1958 Act.)

PROTECTIVE TRUSTS

The exception referred to above[12], when the court is not required to be satisfied that an arrangement is for the benefit of those on whose behalf the application is made, exists in the case of applications made on behalf of persons with a discretionary interest under a protective trust. Thus an arrangement may be approved notwithstanding that it confers no benefit on such a person, and even if it deprives him of his interest[13]. (It will be seen that protective trusts in two respects form exceptions within the provisions of the Act, as regards benefit and as regards consent being given on behalf of an adult beneficiary.)

If a person has an interest under a discretionary trust, and so falls under

7   *Re Tinker's Settlement* [1960] 3 All ER 85n, [1960] 1 WLR 1011.
8   *Re Cohen's Settlement Trusts* [1965] 3 All ER 139, [1965] 1 WLR 1229.
9   *Re Westminster Bank Ltd's Declaration of Trust* [1963] 2 All ER 400n, [1963] 1 WLR 820.
10   *Re Pettifor's Will Trusts* [1966] Ch 257, [1966] 1 All ER 913.
11   *Re Westminster Bank Ltd's Declaration of Trusts*, ante.
12   See p 319, ante.
13   Variation of Trusts Act 1958, s 1(1). In *Re Steed's Will Trusts* [1960] Ch 407, [1960] 1 All ER 487, however, the court (in reaching a decision not to approve a proposed arrangement) took into account the interest of any future husband of a woman for whom property was held on protective trusts, thus seemingly failing to observe that part of the proviso of s 1(1) of the Act relating to para 1(1)(d).

s 1(1)(d), and he also comes within another head of s 1(1), for example if he is an infant (under s 1(1)(a)) or is unborn (under s 1(1)(c)), approval may be given on his behalf solely in respect of his falling within s 1(1)(d), and therefore no benefit need be shown to accrue to him[14].

INTENTION OF THE SETTLOR

In addition to considering whether a proposed variation is in the interests of the persons on whose behalf the court is asked to approve the arrangement, the court, in exercising its discretion, should 'look at the (proposed) scheme as a whole, and when it does so, to consider, as surely it must, what really was the intention of the benefactor'[15]. (Where the settlor is living, he is required to be made a party to the proceedings[16].) Even so, in practice, it seems that the overriding consideration is the benefit of the persons on whose behalf consent is given. That this is the case is apparent when one considers instances (eg *Re Remnants' Settlement Trusts*[17]) in which the variation approved constitutes a clear departure from what the settlor had expressly stipulated.

The effect of an order approving an arrangement

The variation of a trust under the Act is not effected by the order of the court. The order merely gives approval to the arrangement on behalf of those persons who (because, for example, they are infants or are unborn) are incapable of giving their own consent to the arrangement. The variation is made, not by the court order, but by the arrangement itself[18]. The consent provided by adult beneficiaries with vested interests[19], when coupled with the consent given by the court on behalf of other beneficiaries, enables the trust property to be dealt with according to the arrangement. The variation is thus made under the rule in *Saunders v Vautier*[20]. The Act does no more than make the variation possible by conferring on the court power to give consent on behalf of beneficiaries who are not *sui juris* and absolutely entitled. Thus each beneficiary is bound by the arrangement, not because the court has varied the trust, but because he has consented (or consent has been given on his behalf) to the variation. So 'the arrangement must be regarded as being an arrangement made by the beneficiaries themselves'[1].

Non-consenting adult beneficiary

What is the position if an adult beneficiary does not consent to the proposed arrangement? It is not the court's responsibility to ensure that adults have

14 *Re Turner's Will Trusts* [1960] Ch 122 at 127.
15 Per Lord Evershed MR, *Re Steed's Will Trusts* [1960] Ch 407 at 421.
16 RSC Ord 55, r 14A (3A).
17 [1970] Ch 560, [1970] 2 All ER 554. See p 297, supra.
18 *Re Holt's Settlement* [1969] 1 Ch 100 at 115; (M & B).
19 And those within the proviso to s 1(1)(b); see p 317, ante.
20 (1841) 4 Beav 115.
 1 Per Lord Reid, *IRC v Holmden* [1968] AC 685 at 701.

consented: its concern is for the beneficiaries on whose behalf it is asked to give consent. However, if the court discovered that an adult beneficiary had not been consulted it might exercise its discretion and defer approving the arrangement until the necessary consent had been obtained. If it learned that an adult beneficiary had refused to consent, it seems probable that the court would decline to approve the arrangement.

What would be the position if an adult beneficiary had not given his consent and the court, unaware of this, approved the arrangement? Is there a valid variation of the trust? It seems that the validity of the court's order would not be affected, but that since all the beneficiaries had not consented, the arrangement would not be effective to vary the trust. The non-consenting adult beneficiary would certainly not be bound by the arrangement[2]. If the trustees acted according to the terms of the arrangement, it would seem that the non-consenting adult beneficiary, on discovering what had happened, could bring proceedings to enjoin the trustees from acting otherwise than in accordance with the original trust, and claim damages for any loss which he suffered. If he discovered what had happened and took no action in the matter then it is possible (especially if his interests were not affected by the arrangement) that the court would, if he brought proceedings at some subsequent time, hold that he had, by his silence, impliedly consented to the arrangement, and decline to disturb the arrangement by making any order against the trustees.

Miscellaneous

1. The Act empowers the court to approve an arrangement 'varying' the terms of a trust. The court thus has no jurisdiction to approve an arrangement 'resettling' the trust property[3]. However, an arrangement may be approved which might be regarded as being in effect a resettlement, provided that the 'substratum'[4] of the old trusts remain and that the arrangement is described in the summons as 'varying' the trusts (and not 'resettling' the trust property)[5].

2. *Law of Property Act 1925, s 53(1)(c)*. After the Variation of Trusts Act 1958 was passed, in the case of many arrangements the consent of adult beneficiaries was given, not by their signing any document, but by their counsel stating on their behalf in court that they gave their consent to the arrangement proposed. Many applications under the Act involve a reshuffle of the beneficial interests under the trust. Such an arrangement thus involves a disposition of equitable interests—from those previously entitled, to those entitled under the varied trusts. Section 53(1)(c) of the Law of Property Act 1925 provides that any disposition of an equitable interest must be made in writing, signed by the transferor[6]. Does this mean that where the consent of adult beneficiaries was merely given by their counsel in court, no variation of the trust ever in fact took place—that hundreds of variations, assumed to

---

2   *IRC v Holmden* [1968] AC 685 at 701.
3   *Re Ball's Settlement* [1968] 2 All ER 438, [1968] 1 WLR 899; (M & B); see also *Allen v Distillers Co (Biochemicals) Ltd* [1974] QB 384, [1974] 2 All ER 365.
4   Per Megarry J, *Re Ball's Settlement*, ante, at p 442; 905.
5   *Re Ball's Settlement*, ante.
6   Not merely, in the alternative, by his agent.

be valid, were void? In order to seek a means of avoiding a conclusion with such inconvenient results, in *Re Holt's Settlement*[7] Megarry J accepted two arguments put forward by counsel to show that compliance with s 53(1)(c) was not required for a valid variation to have been made. These were as follows. (i) The arrangement constituted an agreement between the parties. All had given consideration. Therefore (by analogy with the principle in *Walsh v Lonsdale*[8]) the agreement was enforceable in equity (notwithstanding that the correct formalities had not been complied with). Thus the beneficiaries under the rearrangement held under a constructive trust. Section 53(2) excluded constructive trusts from the requirements of s 53 and thus there was no call for s 53(1)(c) to be complied with. (ii) Parliament, in conferring a power on the court to do something by order had impliedly provided an exception to the requirements of s 53(1)(c)[9].

3. *Perpetuities and Accumulations Act 1964*. In the case of many variations, new limitations replace those in the original trust. In framing these limitations, can advantage be taken of the provisions of the Perpetuities and Accumulations Act 1964? In *Re Holt's Settlement*[10] it was held that, as the 'arrangement' under the Variation of Trusts Act constituted an 'instrument' as defined in s 15(5) of the 1964 Act, advantage could be taken of the 1964 Act in framing the limitations in an arrangement under the 1958 Act (eg the trusts as varied could employ the fixed perpetuity period not exceeding 80 years[11]).

4. The provisions of the Act relate to trusts of both real and personal property; and to trusts arising under a will or an inter vivos settlement or disposition.

5. Normally an application should be made by one or more beneficiaries and not by the trustees, who should stand aside in order to be able to act as watch-dogs for all future possible beneficiaries. But the application can be made by the trustees if no beneficiary is willing to make it and if they are satisfied that it is in the interests of the trust for them to do so[12].

6. The jurisdiction conferred by the Act is generally wider than the forms of jurisdiction considered at the beginning of this chapter and resort to these forms of jurisdiction is now likely to be infrequent. However, in a few situations the other forms of jurisdiction may still be of assistance. For example:

(a) Under s 53 of the Trustee Act 1925 an application can be made for an order which will enable the interest of an infant tenant in tail to be barred, thus cutting out the interests of his heirs. Such an order could not be made under the 1958 Act since the variation would not be for their benefit.

(b) Under s 57 of the Trustee Act 1925 there is no need for it to be shown that the order applied for (eg vesting additional powers in the trustees) is for the benefit of each beneficiary who is not *sui juris*: it is sufficient if it is 'expedient' for the operation of the trust as a whole.

---

7   [1969] 1 Ch 100, [1968] 1 All ER 470; (M & B); (1968) 84 LQR 162 (PVB).
8   (1882) 21 Ch D 9.
9   Both arguments are criticised by J. W. Harris, *Variation of Trusts*, pp 104–109.
10 [1969] 1 Ch 100, [1968] 1 All ER 470.
11 Perpetuities and Accumulations Act 1964, s 1; (M & B).
12 *Re Druce's Settlement Trusts* [1962] 1 All ER 563, [1962] 1 WLR 363.

Applications may be made to the court at the same time for orders under the 1958 Act and under another form of jurisdiction, eg under s 53 of the Trustee Act 1925[13].

Where no jurisdiction exists for the court to approve an arrangement under the Act, it may be possible for the court to approve the arrangement under its jurisdiction, noted at the beginning of this chapter, to approve a compromise reached between the parties to an action[14].

7. What may amount to an express power of variation may be conferred on trustees. For example, a settlor may direct, (a) that capital or income (or both) is to be held on trust for a specified class; (b) that the class is to comprise certain persons; (c) that the trustees are to have power (perhaps subject to certain conditions) to make another person a member of the specified class. (Such a direction does not entail an infringement of the rule with regard to certainty of beneficiaries[15], nor of the rule with regard to non-delegation by trustees[16].)

CONCLUSION

In this chapter it will be seen that the issues discussed raise the question: which should prevail, a settlor's expressed intentions (in which case, no variation should be allowed) or the notion of 'equitable property' (ie that the trust property is the property of the beneficiaries and should be applied in whatever way is most beneficial to them, variation being permitted if it is for their benefit)? It will be seen that in *Chapman v Chapman* the pendulum swung towards adherence to a settlor's intentions, and that under the 1958 Act it was swung a long back towards the notion of 'equitable property'.

---

13 *Re Bristol's Settled Estates* [1964] 3 All ER 939, [1965] 1 WLR 469.
14 As in *Allen v Distillers Co (Biochemicals) Ltd* [1974] QB 384, [1974] 2 All ER 365.
15 *Blausten v IRC* [1972] Ch 256, [1972] 1 All ER 41; *Re Manisty's Settlement* [1974] Ch 17, [1973] 2 All ER 1203.
16 *Re Manisty's Settlement* [1974] Ch 17, [1973] 2 All ER 1203.

Chapter 19

The duties of trustees

It is the duty of a trustee to administer the trust in accordance with the terms expressed by the settlor and the principles of equity[1]. In addition to this general duty a trustee has a number of specific duties. Some of these, because of their importance or their complexity, have been the subject of separate chapters earlier in this book. Thus we have seen that:

1. A trustee has various duties which must be performed at the outset of the trust[2].

2. A trustee is under a duty to invest the trust property prudently and in accordance with statute and the terms of the trust[3].

3. A trustee is under a duty to protect the interests of beneficiaries as between the beneficiaries themselves and in the execution of this duty he may be under a duty to sell the trust property and convert the proceeds into authorised investments. He may also be under a duty to apportion income or capital[4].

In this chapter certain further duties remain to be considered: the duty to keep accounts and records, the duty not to make a profit from the trust, and the duty to distribute the property to those entitled.

1 Duty to maintain accounts and records

It is the duty of a trustee to keep accounts and records relating to the trust's administration and a beneficiary has a right to inspect these[5]. This duty is imposed on charity trustees by statute[6].

Trustees are not under any duty with regard to the audit of the trust's accounts but they have power[7], at their discretion, to have the accounts audited by an independent accountant. An audit must not be carried out

---

1 For an example of a dispute as to whether trustees had failed to administer a trust in accordance with the terms, and intentions, of the trust, see *Baron Wentworth v National Trust for Places of Historic Interest or Natural Beauty* unreported; [1985] Conv 134 (A. Samuels).
2 See Chap 14.
3 See Chap 15.
4 See Chap 16.
5 Subject to what is said later, see p 344, post.
6 Charities Act 1960, s 32.
7 Trustee Act 1925, s 22(4).

more than once every three years unless the nature of the trust or any special dealings with the trust property make a more frequent audit reasonable[8].

2 The duty not to profit from a trust

It is 'a principle founded on no technical rule of law, but on the highest principles of morality'[9] that a trustee may not make any profit from the fact that he acts as trustee: '... equity ... prohibits a trustee from making any profit by his management directly or indirectly. For however innocent an act of this nature may be in itself, it is poisonous with regard to its consequences. If any opportunity be given for making profit in this manner, a trustee will lose sight of his duty, and soon learn to direct his management chiefly or solely for his own profit'[10].

One effect of this rule, treated earlier[11], is that a trustee is not entitled to receive remuneration. But the rule has a wider application in that it ordains that a trustee is not permitted (unless expressly or impliedly[12] so authorised by the settlor) to obtain any indirect or incidental profit or gain by reason of the fact that he is a trustee. Equity provides that if a trustee does in fact make such a profit, he holds this on a constructive[13] trust for the beneficiaries entitled under the trust.

We shall now consider certain instances which demonstrate the working of this rule.

A REMUNERATION

As we saw earlier[14], a person who accepts appointment as a trustee is not entitled to claim payment for acting as trustee: 'he is to have nothing for his labour and pains, though some have thought this a great hardship'[15]. Thus when we say that a trustee is not entitled to make any 'profit' from the trust, this does not merely mean that he must obtain no unjust or unearned gain, but that he must receive no gain whatsoever from the trust, even if, by commercial standards, the time and attention which he gives would warrant payment. The exceptions to this rule, when remuneration is permitted, were noted earlier[16].

---

8 Trustee Act 1925, s 22(4).
9 *Aberdeen Town Council v Aberdeen University* (1877) 2 App Cas 544 at 549, per Lord Cairns LC.
10 Home, *Principles of Equity* (1760) p 176.
11 Chap 14.
12 *Re Sykes* [1909] 2 Ch 241.
13 See Chap 24.
14 See Chap 14.
15 H. Ballow, *Treatise of Equity* (5th edn, 1822), Vol 2, p 176.
16 See Chap 14.

B PROFIT FROM THE EXERCISE OF A TRUSTEE'S POWER

If a trustee exercises one of his powers in order to obtain advantage for himself, then any profit he obtains belongs to the trust. For example, in *Sugden v Crosland*[17], X was a trustee of a will. Y wished to become a trustee and paid X a bribe of £75 to exercise his power as trustee to retire and appoint him, Y, in his place. It was held that the retirement of X and the appointment of Y were void, and that X held the £75 for the trust. Another example is provided by *Molyneux v Fletcher*[18]. Here the husband of B, a beneficiary, owed a trustee, T, a large sum of money. T exercised a power of advancement to advance £250 to B, on the understanding that the money would be used to repay in part the money owed to him. It was held that the advancement was void as it had been made by T with a view to securing a personal benefit for himself—the repayment of the money he was owed[19].

C PROFIT FROM THE EXERCISE OF RIGHTS ATTACHING TO LEGAL OWNERSHIP

Attaching to a title to property held by a trustee may be certain rights. If a trustee exercises one of these rights he must do so for the benefit of the trust, not for his own personal gain. If he exercises the right for his own advantage, then any profit he makes must be held by him for the trust (or the exercise of the right may be directed by the court to be set aside[20]).

For example, in 1801 the Aberdeen Town Council held certain land on the sea coast on trust for the purpose of endowing two professorships at Aberdeen University. The Council applied to the Crown for, and obtained, a grant of the right to fish for salmon in the sea opposite the land it held. The Council then granted fishing licences to individuals and applied the income received for municipal purposes. It was held that the Council held the rents so received for the purpose of the trust, and so were liable to restore the income they had received[1].

DIRECTORS' FEES

An important application of the rule against a trustee profiting from rights attaching to legal ownership of the trust property concerns directors' fees. Suppose that trust property includes shares in X Ltd. The shares confer on the registered holders the right to vote at the company's annual general meeting. At an annual general meeting, T, a trustee, uses this voting right to secure his election as a director. As a director he receives a fee of £10,000 a year. Since this money comes to him as a result of his exercise of powers

---

17 (1856) 3 Sm & G 192.
18 [1898] 1 QB 648.
19 In an earlier case, *Butler v Butler* (1877) 7 Ch D 116, where an advancement was made to a beneficiary who owed money to a trustee, but there was no understanding that the money was to be used for repaying the loan, the court allowed the advancement to stand.
20 *Richardson v Chapman* (1760) 7 Bro Parl Cas 318, HL. (Executor entrusted with advowson; made presentation to a living under a secret condition for his own benefit; presentation set aside and executor directed to present to a more suitable person.)
1 *Aberdeen Town Council v Aberdeen University* (1877) 2 App Cas 544.

which are his by reason of his holding the legal title to the trust property, T must hold the fees he receives as director on trust for the beneficiaries. This principle was established in *Re Francis*[2] and confirmed by *Re Macadam*[3]. Later cases have shown, however, that there are exceptions to this rule, and that in certain circumstances fees received by a trustee as a director may be retained by him. Thus, fees may be retained,

(a) where the settlor expressly so authorises, or impliedly does so, as by providing that trustees may use their shareholding to secure appointment as directors[4];

(b) where the shares held by a trustee qualify him to be a director of the company issuing the shares, but his appointment as director is made by the other shareholders and without the trustee exercising any voting rights to secure his own election[5];

(c) where, although the trustee votes in support of his own election, he would have been elected by the other votes even if he himself had voted for someone else[6];

(d) where the effort and skill required of the trustee have been over and above those ordinarily required of a director representing the interests of a substantial shareholder, and the court, in the exercise of its inherent jurisdiction in such circumstances, allows the fees and remuneration paid to the trustee to be retained by him[7]. The court also has an anticipatory jurisdiction to authorise a director trustee to retain remuneration payable to him in the future. An application for the retention of future remuneration should ordinarily be made as soon as a trustee is elected a director. The jurisdiction will be exercised sparingly and only if it is in the interests of the trust that the trustee should be a director, and if the additional duties imposed on him by being a director are such that he cannot fairly be expected to undertake them without receiving appropriate remuneration[8].

It will be recognised that where a trustee director is entitled to retain fees paid to him as a director, and the company's articles empower the directors to fix their own remuneration, then a trustee director will be in a position in which his duty to the trust and his personal interest are in conflict. It has been held, however, at any rate in the case of (a) above, that this is a result that must inevitably ensue, and will not preclude a trustee retaining fees due to him as a director[9].

D PROFIT FROM USE OF KNOWLEDGE OR POSITION

It may happen that a trustee, because of his position as trustee or his knowledge of the trust property, has the opportunity to do himself a good turn. In so doing he may not act with any dishonest motive, and his action

2   (1905) 74 LJ Ch 198.
3   [1946] Ch 73, [1945] 2 All ER 664; (M & B).
4   *Re Llewellin's Will Trusts* [1949] Ch 225, [1949] 1 All ER 487.
5   *Re Dover Coalfield Extension* [1908] 1 Ch 65.
6   *Re Gee* [1948] Ch 284, [1948] 1 All ER 498.
7   *Re Keeler's Settlement Trusts* [1981] Ch 156, [1981] 1 All ER 888; (M & B); [1981] CLJ 243 (C. M. G. Ockelton).
8   Ibid.
9   *Re Llewellin's Will Trusts*, ante.

may not result in the trust being any the poorer. Nonetheless, equity requires that if any such advantage is gained by a trustee (or any other person in a fiduciary position, eg a company director[10]) then the benefit concerned must not be retained by the trustee personally but must be held by him for the trust: the trustee is made constructive trustee of the profit he has obtained[11].

For example, in *Williams v Barton*[12], X was employed as a clerk by a stockbroker. He was paid commission for business which he brought to the firm. X was also trustee of a trust. The assets of the trust were to be valued and X arranged for his employer's firm to do the work. X accordingly received commission from his employer. It was held that, since the gain to X was attributable not merely to his position as an employee but also to his position as trustee, he held the money he had received on trust for the beneficiaries.

We may note here that the principle that any profit acquired by use of knowledge of the trust's affairs or the exercise of a trustee's position is held on trust for the beneficiaries, relates not only to a profit acquired by a trustee but also to any such profit acquired by an agent of the trust, for example by a solicitor acting for the trust. For example, in *Boardman v Phipps*[13] B was solicitor to a trust which held 8,000 shares in a private company. The trustees had no power to purchase further shares in the company. B resolved, with the knowledge of the trustees, to acquire the other 22,000 shares in the company. He waged a prolonged fight for control of the company by the purchase of these shares and eventually succeeded in acquiring almost all the company's shares other than those held by the trust. In the take-over battle B was assisted by information which he obtained from the company by purporting to act on behalf of the trustees, as shareholders in the company. B paid between £3 and £3.50 for the shares he acquired. After he had gained control of the company, and as a result of changes made by him, the price of the shares rose to £8. A substantial profit thus accrued both to B and to the trust. One of the beneficiaries claimed that B held the profit he had made for the trust. It was held, on the facts, that as he would not have been able successfully to secure control of the company without the information he obtained as solicitor to the trust, B held the profit he had made on trust for the beneficiaries. However, as B had acted honestly and openly, he was to be allowed liberal payment for his work and skill during the negotiations[14].

RENEWAL OF LEASES: THE RULE IN *KEECH v SANDFORD*

An important illustration of the principle that if a trustee derives personal benefit from his position he holds this benefit for the trust is provided by what has become known as the rule in *Keech v Sandford*[15]. In this case T was

10 *Regal (Hastings) Ltd v Gulliver* (1942) [1967] 2 AC 134n, [1942] 1 All ER 378, HL.
11 *Ex p Lacey* (1802) 6 Ves 625 at 626, 627.
12 [1927] 2 Ch 9; (M & B).
13 [1967] 2 AC 46, [1966] 3 All ER 721; (M & B); (1968) 84 LQR 472 (G. H. Jones); see also *Industrial Development Consultants Ltd v Cooley* [1972] 2 All ER 162, [1972] 1 WLR 443, (1973) 89 LQR 187 (A. Yoran), (1972) 35 MLR 655 (H. Rajak). Cf *Swain v Law Society* [1983] 1 AC 598, [1982] 2 All ER 827, HL. (No duty to account as defendant held not to be in a fiduciary position.) See [1982] Conv 447 (A. M. Kenny).
14 See *O'Sullivan v Management Agency & Music Ltd* [1985] QB 428, [1985] 3 All ER 351, CA; (M & B).
15 (1726) Sel Cas Ch 61; (M & B).

trustee of a trust the property of which included a lease of Romford Market. When the lease expired T applied on behalf of the trust to the fee simple owner, L, for a renewal of the lease. L declined to grant a renewed lease to T as trustee. His reason for so doing was that the beneficiary under the trust was, by virtue of his infancy, not able to contract to observe the usual covenants. T thereupon sought, and obtained, a grant of a lease to himself beneficially. It was held[16] that although T had not acted fraudulently, as he had secured the lease by virtue of the knowledge which he had acquired as a trustee, he held the fresh lease on a constructive trust for the infant beneficiary. (It will be noted that with regard to the original lease, T held as an express trustee; with regard to the new lease, he held as a constructive trustee.)

The rule might seem hard on L in that he might not (and in *Keech v Sandford* did not) wish to grant a lease to the trust, but was willing to grant one to T beneficially; and hard on T in that T had not acted dishonestly and in that he was the only person in the world to whom a lease could not be granted beneficially. The fact that the rule pays no heed to these considerations illustrates the strength of equity's adherence to the principle that if a trustee obtains any advantage from his position, he must hold this for the trust.

In *Keech v Sandford* it was a trustee who obtained a fresh lease for himself in place of an expired lease to the trust. The rule applies also to a personal representative[17]. Further, the rule has been applied where several persons together have an interest in a lease: if one of them obtains a renewal of the lease for his own benefit then a presumption arises that he holds the new lease on trust for himself and the others. For example, in *Featherstonhaugh v Fenwick*[18], the plaintiff and three others formed a partnership to manufacture glass. They took a lease of certain premises. On the expiry of the lease, the plaintiff, unknown to the other partners, approached the lessor and secured a fresh lease in his own name. It was held that he must hold the lease on trust for the partnership. Similarly, if R mortgages a lease to E, both R and E have an interest in the lease. If the lease expires and R then acquires a fresh lease, there is a presumption that R holds the new lease subject to the mortgage[19].

Where a fresh lease is granted to a person who is not in any fiduciary position, and who is not one of a group who were together interested in the previous lease, then he will not be subject to the rule. For example in *Re Biss*[20], S.B., who was a yearly tenant of a shop, died intestate. His widow was appointed executrix and, with her son and daughter, both adults, continued to carry on the business. The lessor refused to grant a new lease for the benefit of the estate, but later he granted a new lease to the son. The widow sought a declaration that the son held the new lease as constructive trustee for the estate. The Court of Appeal held that the son was entitled to retain the lease beneficially: any hope of renewal to the estate had been extinguished by refusal of the widow's application. The son had in no way abused his

16   Following *Holt v Holt* (1670) 1 Cas in Ch 190.
17   *Holt v Holt* (1670) 1 Cas in Ch 190.
18   (1810) 17 Ves 298.
19   *Rakestraw v Brewer* (1728) 2 P Wms 511.
20   [1903] 2 Ch 40; (M & B).

position, nor did he stand in a fiduciary position to the other interested persons.

The limits to the rule in *Keech v Sandford* are further illustrated by *Savage v Dunningham*[1]. In this case, A, B and C decided to rent an unfurnished flat. The flat was leased, without a premium, to A. All three contributed equally towards the outgoings (including the rent) and a common housekeeping pool. A television was rented, and a telephone installed, in the name of A. Various items of furniture were bought by the three separately, and some were bought jointly. Seven months later the landlord offered to grant A a long lease of the property. A did not tell B or C of the offer. Some months later A informed B and C of the proposal and told them that he would not be inviting them to join in the taking of the lease. The landlord subsequently granted A a 62-year lease, at a premium which A paid. A paid the rent; B and C contributed to this. A year later A decided to sell the flat and asked B and C to leave. B and C sought a declaration that A held the lease on trust for the three of them. It was held that if B and C had contributed to the payment of the premium, then A would have held the lease on an implied trust for the three. But since the rent to which B and C had contributed was paid for the use of the property (which B and C had enjoyed) and not for the acquisition of a capital asset, A held the lease free of any trust. It will be noted that a trust did not arise under the principle of purchase in the name of another, since B and C had not contributed to the payment of the premium; and that neither did a trust arise under the rule in *Keech v Sandford*, since A was not in a fiduciary position in relation to B and C, as B and C did not have any interest in the original lease, which had been taken out in A's name alone.

What is the position if L grants a lease to a trustee, T, and T subsequently purchases the freehold[2] from L? Does T hold the freehold on a constructive trust for the beneficiaries? It will be noted that after the purchase, T, instead of paying rents to the original lessor, pays them to himself. The trust has not suffered any loss and originally it was held that, except in certain circumstances, T was entitled to retain the freehold beneficially. (T was obliged to hold the freehold on trust, when, inter alia, (i) T only obtained the freehold by virtue of the fact that he held the lease, as where L offered to sell the reversion to all his tenants; or (ii) the lease from L to T was one which had been renewable by contract or custom, so that the purchase of the freehold by T would put an end to the automatic right of renewal by the trust; (iii) where T acted fraudulently.) However, although the trust may not have lost, the trustee has obtained an advantage and in *Protheroe v Protheroe*[3], the Court of Appeal held that it was 'a long established rule of equity' that T should hold the freehold for the trust. This decision has, however, been criticised[4].

E AVOIDANCE OF CONFLICT OF INTEREST

There is a rule that a trustee must not place himself in a position in which his private interest and his duty as a trustee may conflict.

1 [1974] Ch 181, [1973] 3 All ER 429.
2 Or, eg the head lease.
3 [1968] 1 All ER 1111, [1968] 1 WLR 519.
4 See L. Megarry (1968) 84 LQR 309.

'It is an inflexible rule of a Court of Equity that a person in a fiduciary position, ... is not allowed to put himself in a position where his interest and duty conflict. It does not appear to me that this rule is, as has been said, founded on principles of morality. I regard it rather as based on the consideration that, human nature being what it is, there is danger, in such circumstances, of the person holding a fiduciary position being swayed by interest rather than by duty, and thus prejudicing those whom he was bound to protect[5].' In a sense, of course, any person who accepts appointment as a trustee finds himself in a position in which his duty and his private interests may conflict: temptation to abuse his position for his own benefit may never be absent. The principle of which we speak relates, however, to the actions of a person after he has been appointed a trustee: once someone has become a trustee he must not then so act as to place himself in a position in which his duty as a trustee may direct him one way, and his own interests pull him another. For example, if a testator requires his trustees to carry on his business, and then one of the trustees opens up in the very same business, and thus in competition with the business being conducted by the trust, he has placed himself in a position in which his duty as trustee (to promote the trust business) and his personal interest (to promote his own) conflict. This is what occurred in *Re Thomson*[6]. The testator's business was that of a yacht broker in London. One of the trustees started up in the same business on his own account close by. The court confirmed[7] that the trustee had acted in breach of his duty to avoid a conflict between his own and the trust's interests[8]. The principle that a person in a fiduciary position must not put himself in a position in which his interest and his duty are in conflict has in recent years had special application to company directors, in relation to their personal interests and the interests of the company[9].

Purchase by a trustee of trust property

Does the rule that a trustee must not allow his duty and his private interests to conflict prohibit a trustee from purchasing trust property (or taking a lease of trust land)? For example, if the trust fund consists of certain shares, does the rule prevent a trustee purchasing the shares from the trust? The danger is, of course, that the trustee might be tempted to pay less than the full value of the shares. This danger arises from the fact that if a trustee purchases trust property he places himself in a position in which his duty as a trustee (which calls for a high price) and his interest as a private person (which would prefer a lower one) conflict. Another danger could be that although the trustee paid

---

5   Per Lord Herschell, *Bray v Ford* [1896] AC 44 at 51.
6   [1930] 1 Ch 203; cf *Moore v McGlynn* [1894] 1 IR 74.
7   The trustee conceded before the hearing that he had acted in breach of his duty and the case was concerned with the payment of costs, which were awarded against the trustee.
8   For the potential conflict of interest that may be faced by an employee of a company who is a trustee of the company's pension fund (between operating the scheme in a manner satisfactory to his employer, and the interests of the beneficiaries), see (1985) 14 ILJ 1 (R. Nobles). For the obligation imposed by law on a company not to withhold consent to an amendment to the rules of the company's contributory pension scheme for the purpose of forcing members of the scheme to give up their accrued rights in the fund in order that the company should obtain a benefit for itself, see *Imperial Group Pension Trust Ltd v Imperial Tobacco Ltd* [1991] 2 All ER 597, [1991] 1 WLR 589.
9   *Guinness plc v Saunders* [1990] 2 AC 663, [1990] 1 All ER 652, HL; [1990] Conv 296 (S. Goulding), [1990] CLJ 220 (J. Hopkins).

the full current market value, he might have acquired knowledge that the shares would shortly rise in value and, if this rise occurred, the benefit would accrue to himself and not the trust. On the other hand there might be advantages in permitting a trustee to purchase trust property. For example, if trust land was to be sold, and a trustee was willing to pay above the market value in order to acquire the land, it would be of benefit to the trust for the land to be bought by the trustee. Equity has therefore never prohibited the purchase of trust property by a trustee but, because of the kinds of risk we have mentioned, has laid down the rule that if a trustee purchases trust property, any beneficiary can within a reasonable time of discovering the circumstances, have the transaction set aside[10]. (The rule is sometimes referred to as the 'self-dealing rule'.) Purchases of trust property are therefore not void, but are voidable at the instance of any beneficiary. A beneficiary wishing to exercise this right does not have to show any fraud on the part of the purchasing trustee, and the right exists even if the price paid was higher than the market value (even to the extent of being generous to the trust[11]), or the sale was by auction at which the trustee was the successful bidder[12], or the sale was made to the purchasing trustee by his co-trustees[13]. The rule has been applied so as to set aside a grant of a lease to a company of which one trustee was a director and majority shareholder[14]. If a beneficiary exercises the right to have a sale to a trustee set aside, then the property revests in the trust and the trustee receives back the price he paid with interest.

What is the position if trust property is sold to a stranger, S: can one of the trustees then purchase the trust property from S? The answer here is that whilst the contract for the resale to the trustee is still executory (ie in the case of land, before the date of completion), the beneficiaries have the same right to avoid the transaction that they have if the sale had been to the trustee direct. But once the sale is complete, then provided that the sale to S was bona fide (eg there was no agreement that S would resell to the trustee) the sale to the trustee will not be disturbed.

There are a limited number of exceptions to the rule that a purchase of trust property is voidable at the instance of a beneficiary. For example (1) the purchase will not be voidable if the trust instrument expressly permits such purchases; (2) the Settled Land Act 1925[15] provides machinery by which a tenant for life may purchase (and, eg take a lease of) the settled land; (3) the court has power under its inherent jurisdiction to authorise such purchases; or to authorise a trustee to bid at an auction[16].

Purchase by a trustee of a beneficiary's interest

Does the rule that a trustee must not allow his duty and his private interest to conflict prohibit him from purchasing the interest of a beneficiary under the trust? For example, if trustees hold property on trust for A for life with remainder to B, can one trustee purchase B's interest in remainder? Here, unlike the previous position, where the trustee was both vendor and pur-

10 *Ex p Lacey* (1802) 6 Ves 625 at 629.
11 *Re Thompson's Settlement* [1986] Ch 99, [1985] 2 All ER 720.
12 *Holder v Holder* [1968] Ch 353 at 398.
13 *Wright v Morgan* [1926] AC 788, PC.
14 *Re Thompson's Settlement*, supra.
15 Section 68.
16 *Holder v Holder* [1968] Ch 353 at 398.

chaser, the trustee is solely in the position of purchaser. A danger to the interests of the trust may, however, lie in the fact that the trustee may be in a position to bring influence on the beneficiary to persuade him to sell, or to accept less than a proper value, or that the trustee would be able in some way to take unfair advantage of his position, for example, by having information about the value of the property which he withheld from the beneficiary.

Equity does not, however, regard these risks as sufficiently great to prohibit a purchase by a trustee of a beneficiary's interest. But such purchases are subject to the closest scrutiny by the court. If the court finds that the beneficiary was a willing seller and that there was 'no fraud, no concealment, no advantage taken by the trustee of information acquired by him in the character of trustee'[17], then the transaction will not be disturbed[18]. But if there is any indication that the trustee in any way took unfair advantage of his position, the sale will be set aside. (The principle is sometimes referred to as the 'fair dealing rule'[19].)

Disclosure
It is possible that where a trustee finds himself in a position in which his personal interests and those of the trust are, or may be, in conflict, breach by the trustee of his duty may be avoided by full disclosure[20] of all the circumstances to his co-trustees, and any relevant decision being taken, or confirmed, by the co-trustees alone. But where no disclosure is made then a breach occurs and any gain is held by the trustee concerned as constructive trustee for the trust[1].

3 Duty to distribute the trust property to those entitled

It might perhaps seem almost to go without saying that trustees are under a duty to ensure that trust property, whether income or capital, is passed to those entitled. Some points regarding this duty nonetheless need to be made.

In the execution of the duty the trustees must ensure that no one who is not entitled receives any trust property. *Eaves v Hickson*[2] provides an illustration.

A testatrix, who died in 1843, devised land to trustees, S and H, on trust for sale for the children of one William Knibb. The land was sold. In 1856, the youngest of Knibb's children having attained 21, S distributed the fund between Knibb's children. He did so on the strength of a marriage certificate produced to him by Knibb which showed that Knibb had been married on 14 March 1826, a date prior to the birth of any of his children. In fact Knibb had not been married until 14 March 1846, a date subsequent to the birth of

---

17 *Coles v Trecothick* (1804) 9 Ves 234 at 247, per Lord Eldon LC.
18 *Morse v Royal* (1806) 12 Ves 355.
19 See *Re Thompson's Settlement* [1986] Ch 99, [1985] 2 All ER 720.
20 *Hanson v Lorenz* [1987] 1 FTLR 23, CA.
1   *Guinness plc v Saunders* [1990] 2 AC 663, [1990] 1 All ER 652, HL; [1990] CLJ 220 (J. Hopkins).
2   (1861) 30 Beav 136.

all his children, the figure '1846' having been altered by him on the certificate to '1826'. Knibb's children were thus illegitimate and so not entitled to take as beneficiaries under the will ('children' being construed as legitimate children). It was held that the payment to the children constituted a breach of trust. The loss was caused to any children of Knibb yet to be born by his present or any future wife. The money therefore had to be restored to the trust to be held contingently on their birth. Although the forgery could not have been detected except by someone who was looking out for a forgery, the trustees were liable for the breach since 'where a forgery is committed, and a person wrongfully gets trust money which cannot be recovered from him, on whom is the loss to fall? I am of opinion, that it falls on the person who paid the money. Here the loss falls on the trustees, and the persons to whom the fund really belongs are not to be deprived of it. The trustee is bound to pay the trust fund to the right person'[3]. The court held that the children were bound to restore the money they had received to the trust, with interest at 4%; Knibb was bound to restore so much of the trust fund as could not be recovered from his children; and H and the personal representatives of S (who had died) were bound to restore so much of the fund as had not been recovered from the children and from Knibb. In *Ministry of Health v Simpson*[4] a testator left property 'for such charitable institutions or other charitable or benevolent ... objects' as the trustees should select. Unaware that the trust was void[5], and that the residuary legatees were therefore entitled, the trustees distributed the property among certain charities. They were held to be liable for breach of trust.

In the execution of this duty trustees must also ensure that *all* those who are entitled receive their entitlement. It is here that practical problems may be faced. For example, if a testator leaves property on trust for his widow for life with remainder to all his sons and grandsons living at her death, on the widow's death the trustees may have difficulty in drawing up a list of all those entitled. (One son may have gone to Australia and not been heard of since. Is he still alive? Has he had children?) A similar difficulty may arise in locating all the statutory next of kin of an intestate. If the trustees distribute the fund among all those known to be entitled and later there appears a beneficiary (or next of kin, as the case may be) of whose existence the trustees were unaware, he can bring an action against them for breach of trust; ie for failing to pay him his entitlement. Further, under the Family Law Reform Act 1969[6] such words as 'child', 'children', 'son' are to be construed as including illegitimate children. If a testator leaves property to his 'sons', how can trustees satisfy themselves that they have located all of the testator's illegitimate sons, if any? Further, under the same Act[7], illegitimate children become entitled to take on a parent's intestacy[8]. How can an administrator be sure that he has traced all an intestate's illegitimate issue, if any[9]? The duty to distribute the trust property to all those entitled, and only to those

---

3 Per Sir John Romilly MR, at 141.
4 [1951] AC 251, [1950] 2 All ER 1137.
5 See Chap 7.
6 Section 15.
7 Section 14.
8 And both parents of an illegitimate child become entitled to take on the intestacy of the child.
9 Or traced both parents of an intestate illegitimate child.

entitled, can thus confront trustees (and personal representatives) with formidable problems. Assistance is provided in the following ways[10].

1 Application for directions

If trustees are in any doubt over the correct construction of the terms of the trust they may apply to the court for directions. If they follow these they are protected against any claims.

2 Persons born of unmarried parents

Regarding the locating of illegitimate issue[11], if trustees (or personal representatives) know of the existence of an illegitimate child[12] who is entitled under a settlement or will or intestacy then they are under the same duty to ensure that he receives his entitlement as they are with regard to someone who is legitimate.

In order to overcome the difficulty that may exist in tracing the father of illegitimate issue, the Family Law Reform Act 1987[13] creates a presumption that, for the purpose of the intestacy rules, the father of a person whose parents were not married to each other at the time of his birth predeceased that person unless the contrary is shown.

3 Section 27

If trustees are seeking to distribute property among a class of persons and wish to protect themselves against a later claim by a beneficiary of whose existence they were unaware, they may take advantage of s 27 of the Trustee Act 1925. This section authorises trustees and personal representatives to advertise for claimants[14]. The advertisement must state that the trustees are intending to distribute the trust property (or estate) and require any claimant to send particulars of his claim within a specified period, being not less than two months from the date of the notice. The advertisement must be placed in the *London Gazette* and, if the property is land, in a newspaper in the district in which the land is situated[15]. If the property does not include land, then it is the practice to place an advertisement in a newspaper circulating in the district most likely to be concerned (eg where the testator had lived). It is also necessary to place 'such other like notices' (of their intention to distribute) 'including notices elsewhere than in England and Wales, as would, in any special case, have been directed by a court of competent jurisdiction

---

10 The Law Reform Committee, 23rd Report, recommended that trustees should be
     empowered to distribute trust property on the strength of opinion from counsel that
     distribution should be made, subject to certain conditions. (Para 5.1.)
11 Or father of an intestate illegitimate child.
12 Or of the existence of the father of an intestate illegitimate child; s 14(3)(a).
13 Section 18.
14 There is of course no need to advertise for claimants who are entitled by virtue of ss 14
     and 15 of the Family Law Reform Act 1969 because of the protection afforded by s 17 of
     the Act. See 2, ante.
15 LP (Am) A 1926, Sch.

in an action for administration[16]. If the trustees are uncertain as to where notices should be placed, they should apply to the court for directions[17]. If the trustees place the necessary notices, wait until the expiry of the time stated in the notices and then distribute the property to those entitled, they will not be liable if at some later date another beneficiary whose entitlement was unknown to them, claims a share of the property. Section 27 does not, however, disentitle such a claimant from claiming his share of the property from those among whom the property has been distributed. The right of an unpaid beneficiary to 'follow' or 'trace' property is considered later[18].

4 Benjamin Order

If trustees (here including personal representatives) know that a beneficiary existed, but are unable to find out whether he is still alive, they may apply to the court. If the court is satisfied that all practical inquiries have been made, it has power to grant a 'Benjamin Order'[19]. This authorises the trustees to distribute the trust property on the basis that the missing beneficiary is dead. The order may also authorise distribution on the basis that all beneficiaries have been located (or on any other basis stated in the order) and an application for the order may thus provide an alternative to proceeding under s 27. The effect of the order is the same as that of s 27: trustees are protected against subsequent claims, but claimants may seek their share from assets distributed to other beneficiaries.

5 Payment into court

In cases of great difficulty it may be advisable for the trustees to exercise the right conferred on them by statute[20] to pay the trust money into court. But payment into court is regarded as being appropriate only when all other means of overcoming a problem have failed[1]. If trustees pay trust money into court when some other means could have been adopted for solving a problem (eg advertising under s 27) they may be made liable for the costs of any subsequent payment out[2].

---

16 Trustee Act 1925, s 27(1).
17 *Re Holden* [1935] WN 52.
18 See Chap 22.
19 *Re Benjamin* [1902] 1 Ch 723; (M & B).
20 Trustee Act 1925, s 63(1), as amended by the Administration of Justice Act 1965, s 36 and Sch 3.
 1 Eg the undisposed part of the trust fund in *Re Gillingham Bus Disaster Fund* [1959] Ch 62, [1958] 2 All ER 749; (M & B), was paid into court.
 2 *Re Elliot's Trusts* (1873) LR 15 Eq 194.

Chapter 20

Trustees' powers

To facilitate the administration of a trust certain powers are conferred on trustees by statute, principally the Trustee Act 1925. Other powers may be conferred by the trust instrument. Some of these powers, because of their importance, have been the subject of separate chapters earlier in this book. Thus in Chapter 13 we saw that trustees have power to appoint agents; in Chapter 15 that they have power to invest in certain types of security; in Chapter 17 that they have certain powers to advance capital to beneficiaries and to apply income for the maintenance of infant beneficiaries; in Chapter 18 that they have power to seek the approval of the court for the variation of the terms of the trust. In this chapter it remains to mention two other powers not hitherto dealt with, and to consider certain matters relating to trustees' powers generally.

1 Power to sell

LAND

Trustees may have power to sell land by virtue of the fact that the land is held by them subject to an express or statutory trust for sale, or subject to an express power of sale. In addition, a power to sell the land exists in the following situations: (1) If trustees of a trust for sale sell the land and use the proceeds of sale to purchase other land, they hold that other land on trust for sale also[1]. (2) If trustees of personalty exercise an express power to sell the personalty, and use the proceeds to buy land, they hold the land on trust for sale[1]. (3) If trustees lend money on the security of land and the land becomes vested in them (eg because the borrower fails to repay and they foreclose) then they hold the land on trust for sale[2]. (4) If trustees purchase land in breach of trust they hold the land on trust for sale[3]. (5) If trustees (other than Settled Land Act trustees[4] or trustees of a charity) are authorised by the trust instrument to apply capital money for any purpose (eg the maintenance of an infant) or are authorised by law so to do, then they have power[5] to obtain the money required by selling (or mortgaging) the land, or part of it[6].

---

1 Unless the settlement provides otherwise.
2 LPA 1925, s 31.
3 *Re Patten and Edmonton Union* (1883) 52 LJ Ch 787.
4 Unless they are also the statutory owners.
5 Notwithstanding anything in the instrument to the contrary, Trustee Act 1925, s 16(2).
6 Trustee Act 1925, s 16(1).

Apart from these instances, and subject to what is said below, no other power exists which enables trustees to sell land. There are, however, likely to be few cases today when land which is subject to a private trust cannot be brought within one or other of the headings above.

CHATTELS

Trustees have power to sell chattels where this power is conferred expressly, and where they are authorised by the trust instrument or by law to apply capital money for any purpose[7].

It is generally stated that otherwise no power to sell chattels exists. But it is suggested that a power may possibly in fact exist. When dealing with trustees' powers of investment in Chapter 15 we saw that (notwithstanding the absence of an express duty to sell or an express power of sale) trustees have, by virtue of s 1(1) of the Trustee Investments Act 1961, a power to sell an investment that they receive as part of the initial trust property (and invest the proceeds under the Act).

This being so, is the result that the effect of the section is to enable a trustee to sell chattels and invest the proceeds? For example if a testator leaves his gold watch to trustees on trust for his infant son when he attains 18, would the trustees be acting within their powers if they sold the watch and invested the proceeds? It could be argued that the history of the section points to an answer in the affirmative. The predecessor of the section was s 1 of the Trustee Act 1925. This provided that 'A trustee may invest any trust funds in his hands, whether in a state of investment or not, in any manner specified' in the Act. The words 'any trust funds' became, in the 1961 Act, 'any property', with 'property' being defined to include 'real and personal property', and so to include the watch posited in the example (and, it seems, land in respect of which a power of sale does not otherwise exist).

Further, whilst the provisions of the Act are subject to any contrary intention, the Act speaks only of a contrary intention expressed in 'any instrument'. There is no reference to an implied contrary intention (such as might be likely to be thought to exist in the case of the watch). Certainly, if the trustees sold the watch, in the knowledge that the testator had wanted it to go to his son, they would be acting contrary to the spirit and intendment of the gift, and possibly to that of the Act. But whether they would be in breach of trust if, in reliance on s 1, they sold the watch (and, if they were held to be in breach, what the measure of damages would be) is uncertain.

APPLICATION TO THE COURT

If trustees of land or chattels wish to sell the trust property but have no power to do so, they may apply to the court under s 57 of the Trustee Act 1925 for an order conferring this power. The court has jurisdiction under the section, where it considers it expedient, to confer on trustees power to effect any transaction, including sale, lease, mortgage or purchase. The court may confer the power subject to such terms as it sees fit.

---

7   Trustee Act 1925, s 16(1). Another statutory power is conferred by LPA 1925, s 130(5).

2 Power to insure

Trustees have power under the Trustee Act 1925[8] to insure any building or
other insurable property and to pay premiums out of income from any
property subject to the trust. They may not insure the property for more
than three-quarters of its value. The power does not exist if the trust instrument excludes it[9], or if the trustees are bound to convey the property to any
beneficiary upon being requested to do so. It will be noted that in the absence
of any express direction in the trust instrument trustees are, surprisingly, not
under any duty to insure the trust property, and so will not be liable for
failing to insure in the event of the property being damaged or destroyed[10].
If insured trust property is damaged or destroyed then the money received
under the policy may be applied in rebuilding, replacing, or repairing the
property, provided that any person whose consent to the investment of trust
money is required by the trust instrument consents to this application of the
money[11]. If the money is not so applied it is to be treated as capital money,
and held upon trusts corresponding as nearly as may be with trusts affecting
the property in respect of which the claim was made[12].

The Law Reform Committee, in its 23rd Report, recommended that
trustees' power to insure trust property should become a duty[13].

Trustees' powers—general

Exclusion
Most of the powers held by trustees by virtue of statute are conferred on
them by the Trustee Act 1925, eg advancement[14], maintenance[15], insurance[16],
employment of agents[17], advertisement for claims[18], payment into court[19]. It
should be noted that all these powers may be excluded or varied by the trust
instrument[20]. Powers of investment conferred by the Trustee Investments Act
1961 may likewise be excluded or varied by the trust instrument[1], as may

---

8   Section 19.
9   Section 69(2).
10 *Re McEacharn* (1911) 103 LT 900.
11 Section 20(4).
12 Section 20(3).
13 The Committee's recommendations were (a) that trustees be placed under a duty to insure
    against any risk in all the circumstances in which an ordinary prudent man of business
    would so insure, but that this should not be imposed on existing trusts (para 4.33); (b) that
    trustees should have the power to insure the trust property up to its full replacement value
    in all cases in which it would be sensible to do that, and in other cases up to its market
    value (para 4.31); (c) that trustees should be empowered to pay insurance premiums out
    of capital as well as income but should make the payments in such a way as to maintain
    the balance between the interests of the life tenant and the interests of the remainderman
    (para 4.36).
14 Section 32.
15 Section 31.
16 Section 19.
17 Section 23.
18 Section 27.
19 Sections 63, 68(17).
20 Section 69(2).
 1 Trustee Investments Act 1961, s 1(3).

also the power conferred by the Law of Property Act 1925 on trustees for sale to postpone sale[2].

'Power'; 'discretion'

It is possible that confusion may arise from the fact that the word 'power' can be used in the context of equity to refer to two different things. The word can refer to an administrative power, eg the power conferred by statute to advance capital or to insure trust property; or it can be used as an abbreviation of the term 'power of appointment'. It is important that the meaning intended should be understood in every instance where the word is met. A power in the former sense is something conferred on trustees of a trust; a donee of a power of appointment has a power to appoint (ie select out of the objects of the power) and no more: he does not have the powers of a trustee. (A donee of a power of appointment may, of course, be a trustee and in this case will, in his capacity as a trustee, have a trustee's powers with regard to the trust.) Any confusion can be avoided if, when we intend 'power' to mean a power of appointment, the term 'power of appointment' is used in full.

Care should also be exercised with regard to the words 'power' and 'discretion'. Sometimes the words are used as if they were interchangeable, eg in a reference to a trustee exercising a 'discretion' to advance capital; or in a reference to a trustee exercising a 'power' to select beneficiaries under a discretionary trust. It is suggested that clarity is best served if the usage of the words is kept distinct: that 'discretion' should be reserved for use in connection with the function of a trustee of a discretionary trust—a discretion to select which beneficiary or beneficiaries, if any, should take; and that 'power' should be reserved for use in connection with those powers conferred on trustees to facilitate the administration of the trust. If these usages are borne in mind we shall be able to distinguish:

—a power of appointment, exercised by the donee of the power;

—an administrative power, conferred on trustees;

—a discretion, held by trustees of a discretionary trust.

One difficulty will remain: into which of these categories should we place the function conferred under a trust power? As we saw in Chapter 8 this is a disposition which bears the outward marks of a power of appointment, but is to be treated as a discretionary trust. Here we may feel compelled to use the word 'power' for what is referred to, but no harm will result if we remember that it is a power which is to be treated as corresponding to the discretion conferred on trustees of an (exhaustive[3]) discretionary trust.

Unanimity

Trustees may only exercise a power (ie an administrative power) or a discretion (ie under a discretionary trust) (and donees of a power of appointment may only exercise the power of appointment) if they are unanimous[4]. There are limited exceptions to this rule. Thus, trustees of a charitable trust need

2 Section 25(1).
3 See Chap 12.
4 *Luke v South Kensington Hotel Co* (1879) 11 Ch D 121 at 125. For a discussion of the rationale of the rule and an argument that decisions should be made on a majority basis, see [1991] Conv 30 (J. Jaconelli).

not be unanimous, and a majority will bind the minority[5]. If a majority of trustees of a private trust wish the trust money to be paid into court, they may seek an order of the court on an originating summons[6]. (If they are unanimous, payment may be made on affidavit[7].)

Reasons for decisions

Trustees need not give reasons why they have exercised a power or a discretion in a particular way (or declined to exercise the power or discretion). Trustees are therefore under no duty to keep minutes of their meetings. If minutes are kept, they are under no duty to disclose any parts which show their reasons for the exercise of a power or discretion[8].

Interference by the court[9]

The court is reluctant to interfere with the exercise of a power or a discretion[10]. Thus if trustees consider exercising a power of advancement in favour of a particular beneficiary, and make a decision in good faith against doing so, the court will not interfere. But where the exercise of a power (eg of maintenance or advancement) will confer some benefit on a beneficiary, then, as in the case of the exercise of a discretion by trustees of a discretionary trust[11], the court does require that they should within a reasonable time[12] give their attention to the matter. If there is evidence that they have failed to do so then the court may intervene[13]. The court will also intervene if it appears that the power has been exercised improperly, as where a trustee exercises a power to advance capital without taking sufficient care to ensure that the money is applied for the beneficiary's advancement or benefit[14]. Wherever, in fact, it can be shown that the trustees have acted unreasonably, or in bad faith, or for an improper motive, then the court may, despite its reluctance to intervene in the management of a trust, grant a remedy to a beneficiary, on the grounds that the trustees have acted in breach of trust[15].

Powers of charity trustees

Charity trustees who hold land have, with regard to the management and disposition of the land, the powers of a tenant for life and the trustees of a settlement under the Settled Land Act 1925[16]. In other respects charity trustees have the same powers as those of the trustees of a private trust, ie they have the powers, if any, conferred on them expressly in the trust instrument, and (unless varied or excluded by trust instrument) the powers conferred on trustees by statute, in particular, the Trustee Act 1925 and the Trustee Investments Act 1961.

5   *Re Whiteley* [1910] 1 Ch 600.
6   TA 1925, s 63(3); RSC Ord 5, r 3.
7   RSC Ord 92, r 2.
8   See *Re Londonderry's Settlement* [1965] Ch 918, [1964] 3 All ER 855; (M & B).
9   See *Control of Trustee Discretions*, [1989] Conv 244 (N. D. M. Parry).
10 *Tempest v Lord Camoys* (1882) 21 Ch D 571; (M & B).
11 See Chap 11.
12 *Re Allen-Meyrick's Will Trusts* [1966] 1 All ER 740, [1966] 1 WLR 499; (M & B).
13 *Prendergast v Prendergast* (1850) 3 HL Cas 195.
14 *Re Pauling's Settlement Trusts* [1964] Ch 303, [1963] 3 All ER 1; (M & B).
15 *Klug v Klug* [1918] 2 Ch 67; (M & B).
16 SLA 1925, s 29.

Where trustees of a charity do not have power to carry out a proposed action in the administration of a charity, the Commissioners have jurisdiction under the Charities Act 1960[17] by order to authorise the action, provided that it appears to the Commissioners that the action proposed is 'expedient in the interests of the charity'[17] (ie not merely convenient for other purposes) and provided that the act is not expressly prohibited by Act of Parliament or by the terms of the trust[18]. (Nor, in the absence of jurisdiction under the *cy près* doctrine, will the court sanction a transaction that is precluded by the express terms of the trust[19].)

Powers and duties

The duties of a trustee are distinct in nature from a trustee's powers (and from his discretion under a discretionary trust). But throughout much of the law of trusts we find that a trustee's duties and his powers are in many instances closely linked: thus, a trustee is under a *duty* to invest trust money[20], he has *power* to select investments under the Trustee Investments Act 1961[20] (or the settlement), he is under a *duty* to make the investment with due prudence[20]. If a trustee has a *power* to sell trust property[1], he is under a *duty* to get the best price reasonably obtainable[2]. A trustee is under a *duty* to pass trust property to the right person[3], he has *power* to protect himself against claims by untraced claimants[3]. In the exercise of their *powers*, trustees are under a *duty* to act unanimously[4]. Further, as we have just seen, they are under a *duty* to consider whether a *power* or discretion should be exercised. And, in the exercise of a *power* or discretion they are under a *duty* to act impartially and without being influenced by improper motives. Wherever, in fact, a power exists, a duty exists—the duty to exercise the power in a proper manner.

---

17 Section 23(1).
18 Section 23(5).
19 *Oldham Borough Council v A-G* (1992) *Times,* 13 April (specific land devised 'for the purposes of playing fields solely'). An appeal has been lodged.
20 See Chap 14.
 1 See p 340, ante.
 2 See A. Samuels, 'The Duty of Trustees to obtain the best price' (1975) 39 Conv (NS) 177.
 3 See Chap 19.
 4 See p 343, ante.

Chapter 21

Rights of beneficiaries

In general, every duty imposed on a trustee represents a right conferred on a beneficiary. Thus a beneficiary has a right to have the trust's affairs conducted prudently, to have the trust administered, and the beneficial interests distributed, according to the terms of the trust instrument, and so on. In the enforcement of these rights a beneficiary can bring proceedings to restrain a trustee from committing a breach, or to recover any loss caused by a breach.

Further, a beneficiary has a right to require a trustee to provide him with information which will enable him to determine whether the trust is being administered correctly. Thus he has a right to see the trust's accounts, to know how trust money is invested, to inspect title deeds and the trust instrument[1] and to obtain all reasonable information regarding the management of the trust property[2]. And at the time of his attaining full age he must be told of his interest under the trust. Further, a beneficiary has a right to apply to the Public Trustee to have the accounts investigated and audited[3]. (There is, however, we may note here, no duty on the part of trustees to give legal advice to a beneficiary[4].)

The rights we have referred to are rights of a negative nature, in that they are concerned with ensuring that a trustee does not fail in his duty. Does a beneficiary have any rights of a more positive kind—rights which enable him to have some say in the running of the trust? Or, in the absence of any wrongdoing by a trustee, is it for a beneficiary merely to sit back and wait for whatever is due to him? In general, with a few exceptions which we shall be noting, this last does represent a beneficiary's position: in the absence of any breach of trust, a beneficiary is entitled to benefit and, generally, no more.

A beneficiary thus has no right to share in the running of the trust. He can, of course, bring to the notice of the trustees information which may influence them in the execution of their duties or the exercise of their discretions. He can, for example, say 'X plc is a good investment'; or 'I am desperately in need of money'[5]. But in general the beneficiary has no right to control or participate in the making of decisions, and he has no right to

---

1 *O'Rourke v Darbishire* [1920] AC 581, at 626 [1920] All ER Rep 1, at 17.
2 *Hawkesley v May* [1956] 1 QB 304, [1955] 3 All ER 353. But, as noted in Chap 20, he has no right to inspect documents which disclose the trustee's reasons for exercising a power or a discretion. *Re Londonderry's Settlement* [1965] Ch 918, [1964] 3 All ER 855; (M & B).
3 Public Trustee Act 1906, s 13. A trustee has the same right under the section. The Law Reform Committee, 23rd Report, para 4.48, recommended the repeal of the section.
4 *Hawkesley v May*, ante. See also *Low v Bouverie* [1891] 3 Ch 82; *Toronto-Dominion Bank v Wong* (1985) 65 BCLR 243, BCCA.
5 See Chap 17.

determine who should be appointed a trustee[6]. And since liability for failure to administer the trust prudently rests with the trustees, it is reasonable that their authority should not be fettered by the need to abide by the wishes of a beneficiary.

In the following two situations, however, the general rule gives way.

1. If the trust instrument directs the trustees to abide by the wishes of the beneficiaries over a particular matter, then they must do so. For example a settlor may convey land to A and B on trust for sale for X, Y and Z, with a direction that the land should not be sold without the consent of Z.

Where a trust for sale of land is imposed by statute (eg where land is conveyed to co-owners and there is no express creation of a trust for sale) then the Law of Property Act 1925[7] requires the trustees, so far as is practicable, to consult the beneficiaries who are of full age and absolutely entitled and, so far as is consistent with the general interest of the trust, give effect to their wishes, or in the event of a dispute, the wishes of the majority (by interest) of them. They must give effect to the wishes of the beneficiaries, not only with regard to the sale or retention of the land, but also with regard to the exercise of all other powers and duties conferred on them by statute or by the trust instrument[8].

If a trust for sale is created not by statute but expressly, then the requirement of the statute (that the trustees should have regard to the wishes of the beneficiaries) does not apply unless the instrument creating the trust shows an intention that it should.

Where the purpose of the trust is to conceal the identity of the real owner of property, as where shares are registered in the name of a nominee, the instrument creating the trust (which will normally take the form of a contract between the nominee and the real owner) will direct the nominee to act according to the directions of the true owner. In this case, the trustee (the nominee) will be subject to the total control of the beneficiary (the real owner).

2. Under the rule in *Saunders v Vautier*[9], where all the beneficiaries under a trust are *sui juris* and are together absolutely entitled, they can put an end to the trust and require the trustees to hand over the trust property as they direct. It is under this rule that trusts normally come to an end. For example, S settles property on A for life with remainder to B. If, when A dies, B is *sui juris* the trustees will transfer the legal title to the trust property to him, and the trust will come to an end. The following matters call for attention.

(a) For the rule to apply it is not necessary that the beneficiaries should each have an absolute interest: the rule applies whenever the sum total of the interests of all beneficiaries (who are *sui juris*) amounts to an absolute interest. Thus if property is held for A for life with remainder to B, neither A nor B has an absolute interest, but their interests, when combined, amount to an absolute interest, and so entitle them, if they are both *sui juris*, to bring the

6 *Re Brockbank* [1948] Ch 206, [1948] 1 All ER 287; (M & B).
7 Section 26(3) as amended by LP (Am.) A 1926, Sch.
8 *Re Jones* [1931] 1 Ch 375.
9 (1841) Cr & Ph 240; A. Samuels (1970) 34 Conv (NS) 29. For the implications of the rule with regard to liability for Capital Gains Tax, *see Stephenson (Inspector of Taxes) v Barclays Bank Trust Co Ltd* [1975] 1 All ER 625, [1975] 1 WLR 88; (M & B).

trust to an end[10]. Thus in the case of *Saunders v Vautier*[11] itself a benefactor left property on trust to accumulate the income until the sole beneficiary reached 25, and then transfer to him the capital and accumulated income. It was held that on becoming *sui juris* (then 21), the beneficiary was entitled to have the fund transferred to him. It should be noted that the beneficiary had an absolute vested interest, payable on a future date. If the interest had been subject to a condition precedent, eg a gift of the capital and accumulated income to the beneficiary if he attained 25, then the beneficiary would not (prior to attaining 25) be absolutely entitled and so would have had no right to put an end to the trust. But such a beneficiary and the person entitled in default of his attaining 25 would together be absolutely entitled and so these two, if both *sui juris*, could direct the trustees to hand over the trust property as they directed[12].

(b) The rule applies not only where the beneficiaries are between them absolutely entitled to capital (when they can terminate the trust) but also where they are between them absolutely entitled to income. For example, trustees are directed to apply the whole or part of the income of a fund for the benefit of A during his life, and are directed to apply whatever is not applied for A, for the benefit of B during his lifetime, with remainder to C absolutely on the deaths of A and B. Here A and B are between them absolutely entitled to the whole of the income and may therefore direct the trustees as to how the income is to be applied[13]—eg the whole of the income to be passed to A (ie and not merely 'applied for his benefit'), or divided between A and B equally, or passed to a stranger. But the application of the rule will not at this point terminate the trust: the capital will continue to be held by the trustees until the deaths of A and B. (If A, B and C are all *sui juris* they can terminate the trust forthwith.)

(c) Where trust property is divisible, and one or more beneficiaries are *sui juris* and absolutely entitled, they can call on the trustees to transfer to them their share of the property. This is so notwithstanding that the division of the property would cause some reduction in the value of the rest of the property[14], and the entitlement exists notwithstanding that the property is held on trust for sale with a power to postpone sale. But there is no entitlement to call for a division if the trustees consider that, because of special circumstances, the division would operate an undue hardship on the other beneficiaries[15], and it is probably for this reason that there is no entitlement to call for a division if the trust property is land[16].

(d) Where all the beneficiaries are *sui juris* and together are absolutely entitled, but they decline to accept from the trustees the transfer of the title to the trust property, then the trustees may pay the trust fund into court[17].

(e) Since the rule enables the beneficiaries to direct the trustees how to apply the trust property, they can, if they so wish, direct the trustees to settle the property on fresh trusts, eg by ordering them to transfer it to new trustees

10   *Re White* [1901] 1 Ch 570. See also *Re Smith* [1928] Ch 915; (M & B).
11   Ante.
12   *Gosling v Gosling* (1859) John 265.
13   *Re Smith* [1928] Ch 915.
14   *Re Marshall* [1914] 1 Ch 192.
15   *Re Sandeman* [1937] 1 All ER 368.
16   *Re Horsnaill* [1909] 1 Ch 631.
17   *IRC v Hamilton-Russell Executors* [1943] 1 All ER 474.

subject to terms dictated by them or by directing the existing trustees to hold it subject to fresh trusts. (The existing trustees could, of course, if they wish, decline to act as trustees of the new trust.) Beneficiaries can in this way in effect vary the terms of an existing trust.

(f) The rule extends no further than entitling the beneficiaries to direct the trustees as to the handing over (or resettlement of) the trust property: it does not empower beneficiaries to leave a trust in existence and interfere in its administration (eg with regard to the investment of the trust fund[18]); nor does it give beneficiaries power to direct who should be appointed a trustee of the trust[19].

18 See *Stephenson (Inspector of Taxes) v Barclays Bank Trust Co Ltd* [1975] 1 All ER 625, [1975] 1 WLR 88; cf *Hayim v Citibank NA* [1987] AC 730, [1987] 3 WLR 83, ([1988] Conv 60 (P. McLoughlin)), in which the Privy Council took no account of the principle that a beneficiary has no entitlement to give directions with regard to the administration of a trust.
19 *Re Brockbank* [1948] Ch 206, [1948] 1 All ER 287; (M & B).

Chapter 22

Remedies of a beneficiary

We have seen that a beneficiary has a right to have the trust administered according to the terms laid down by the settlor. If a trustee departs from the terms of the trust, or if he is in breach of a duty imposed on him by equity or by statute, the beneficiary can bring an action against him. In this chapter we shall consider the forms of remedy which may be available to a beneficiary. These are: an order for an account; an injunction; damages; a tracing order. It should be noted that here 'damages' is used in the sense of money compensation ordered for breach of trust. An award of damages at common law (as for breach of contract) is, of course, a separate, and distinct, remedy.

1 Account

A beneficiary has a right to seek an order from the court requiring the trustee to account for his conduct of the trust's affairs. The order may require the trustee to provide specific information[1], or to produce accounts for all the financial transactions conducted on behalf of the trust. Further, the trustee can be required to answer on oath questions put to him in court relating to the trust's affairs.

2 Injunction[2]

If a beneficiary finds that a trustee is intending to act in a way which the beneficiary considers will be in breach of trust, he can seek an injunction from the court enjoining the trustee from committing the act concerned. If a trustee has already committed the breach, the beneficiary can seek an injunction to restrain further breaches by the trustee.

---

1 As in *Re Tebbs, Redfern v Tebbs* [1976] 2 All ER 858, [1976] 1 WLR 924.
2 See Pettit, *Equity and the Law of Trusts*, Chaps 25–27.

3 Damages for breach of trust, and tracing[3]

For convenience, as these two remedies are in many cases closely related, we shall deal with them under one head.

A. ACTIONS AGAINST TRUSTEES

Where a trustee has acted in breach of trust and this has caused a loss to the trust an action for an injunction is unlikely to be a sufficient remedy, and the beneficiary will probably wish to bring an action for breach of trust. Where a beneficiary brings an action for breach of trust, and the action is successful, and the trustee pays the sum awarded against him, no problem arises. (It may be decided that it would be expedient for the trustee who has committed the breach of trust to be replaced, but this is a separate matter[4].) But what is the position if the trustee does not have enough money of his own to pay the sum awarded? What, for example, if the sum claimed by the trust and the sum owed to other creditors together exceed his total assets—what if the trustee is insolvent? This is where problems arise, and it is this situation, where the trustee is insolvent, that must now be considered.

1 Separate bank accounts

(a) NO MONEY TAKEN OUT

Let us suppose that a trustee holds £10,000 trust money in a bank account. He has £3,000 of his own money in a separate bank account. He becomes insolvent with creditors claiming debts of £20,000. On the trustee's bankruptcy the £10,000 remains inviolate as trust money[5], and the creditors can recover only the trustee's own £3,000[6].

(b) TRUST MONEY TAKEN OUT AND DISSIPATED

Now suppose that the facts are as before, but the trustee takes out the £10,000 from the trust account and dissipates the money. As before, the trustee becomes insolvent with creditors claiming debts of £20,000. Who gets the trustee's £3,000, the beneficiaries or the creditors? The answer is that in this case the beneficiaries, in their claim for £10,000, rank pari passu with the other creditors[7]. They get no priority by reason of the fact that their claim is

---

3 See R. H. Maudsley, 'Proprietary Remedies for the Recovery of Money' (1959) 75 LQR 234. This article has been overtaken by later cases, but it remains a valuable discussion of the issues involved. See also, (1976) 40 Conv (NS) 277 (R. A. Pearce); [1983] Conv 135 (K. Hodkinson); *An Introduction to the Law of Restitution*, P. Birks.
4 See Chap 13.
5 Insolvency Act 1986, s 283.
6 *Re Hallett's Estate* (1880) 13 Ch D 696; (M & B).
7 *Space Investments Ltd v Canadian Imperial Bank of Commerce Trust Co (Bahamas) Ltd* [1986] 3 All ER 75, [1986] 1 WLR 1072, PC.

for the replacement of trust money. So the trustee's £3,000 is divided pro rata[8] according to the two claims. £1,000 going to the beneficiaries (ie the money is replaced in the trust account), and £2,000 going to the creditors. Where a beneficiary takes his place in the queue with other creditors, ranking pari passu with them and taking pro rata according to the sums claimed, we say that the beneficiary has an action in personam against the trustee[9].

(c) TRUST MONEY USED FOR PURCHASE OF SPECIFIC ITEM

Now let us suppose that the facts were as before, but that when the trustee took £10,000 out of the trust account, he did not dissipate it, but used it for the purchase of a specific identifiable item of property, such as a piece of land, or an antique shotgun or some shares in a company. As before, the trustee is insolvent. Here the trustee's assets will consist of £3,000 of his own money and the item valued at £10,000, a total of £13,000. The claims against him are for £10,000 by the beneficiaries and for £20,000 by the creditors. How is the £13,000 of assets divided? In this situation the beneficiaries are entitled to claim that the item purchased, let us say the fee simple in Blackacre, represents the trust money and that the land has thus now become trust property[10]. They are entitled, we say, to *trace* the trust money into the land. The result is that the beneficiaries can elect to have the land treated as security for their £10,000 or, if they wish, to take the land itself[11]. The other creditors have to be content with the £3,000 of the trustee's own money.

Where beneficiaries are able to point to a piece of property purchased with trust money and show that this has become trust property, where they are entitled to trace, then we say that the beneficiaries have an action in rem; against the 'thing', ie against the property purchased. The beneficiaries' action is thus not against the trustee personally, it is not a claim (along with other creditors) for a share of the trustee's property, it is a claim in which the beneficiaries say 'that thing is *ours*: that thing is *trust property*'.

An action in rem has important advantages over an action in personam. As we have said, an action in rem enables beneficiaries to take priority over other creditors. Further, if the item of property has increased[12] in value since it was purchased then the increase in value accrues to the trust. Another advantage of an action in rem is that in the case of the action in personam the period of limitation under the Limitation Act 1980[13] applicable to the claim is six years[14]; in the case of the action in rem no statutory period of

8   Ie one-third and two-thirds.
9   If the trustee had dissipated only part of the trust money, what was left in the trust account would remain trust money and the beneficiaries would have to claim against the trustee for whatever had been lost, in an action in personam.
10   *Pullan v Koe* [1913] 1 Ch 9; (M & B).
11   *Sinclair v Brougham* [1914] AC 398, 442.
12   If the value of the property has decreased, say from £10,000 to £9,000, then the beneficiaries could claim the property in an action in rem, and would have to claim for the loss to the trust fund, ie £1,000, in an action in personam against the trustee, ranking pari passu with the other creditors, with regard to the claim for £1,000.
13   Section 21(3).
14   If the claim is in respect of the personal estate of a deceased person the period is 12 years. Limitation Act 1980, s 22.

limitation applies[15] (although the claim will be subject to the equitable doctrine of laches).

2 Mixed bank account

(a) NO MONEY TAKEN OUT

Suppose that a trustee has £3,000 of his own money in a bank account. He then places £10,000 trust money in the bank account. (Whether such mixing of trust money and a trustee's own money constitutes a breach of trust is uncertain. It seems that in some circumstances it might do so. For a solicitor, whether acting as a solicitor/trustee or as solicitor to the trust, to mix trust money with other money, eg that of his firm, is contrary to Rule 4 of the Solicitors' Accounts Rules[16] and would render the solicitor liable to disciplinary action by the Law Society.) He then goes bankrupt, with the beneficiaries claiming the £10,000 and other creditors claiming £20,000. Here, since the trust money is intact and no money has been taken out of the account, the beneficiaries can claim the whole £10,000. They have a 'first charge', sometimes referred to as a 'lien' on the mixed account for their £10,000[17]. Thus they take priority over the creditors, who are left with £3,000[18]. In that the right to a first charge gives the beneficiaries priority over the creditors, the right partakes of the nature of a right to claim the property in rem; but it is not identical to a claim in rem, since there is no one identifiable item or fund to which the beneficiaries can point and say '*That*, the *whole* of that, is trust property'. Further, a practical difference lies in the fact that if the property in respect of which the claim is brought has increased in value, then if a beneficiary has a claim in rem, he will obtain the benefit of the increase. If his right is to a first charge he may obtain only part of any amount by which the property has increased in value.

(b) MONEY TAKEN OUT AND DISSIPATED

Now suppose that, in the last example, after adding £10,000 of trust money to the £3,000 in his own account, the trustee had drawn out £11,000 and dissipated it, leaving a balance of £2,000. What is this £2,000? Is it trust money? If so, the beneficiaries can claim it to the exclusion of the other creditors. Or is it the trustee's own money? If so the beneficiaries will merely rank pari passu with the other creditors and receive only a proportion of it. The answer to this question is obtained by applying the rule in *Hallett's Case*[19]. This rule states that where a trustee mixes trust money with his own money in one account, and then draws out money from the account, he is presumed to draw out his own money first. Applying this rule to the facts

---

15 Limitation Act 1980, s 21(1)(b).
16 Made by the Law Society, under s 29 of the Solicitors Act 1957.
17 *Re Hallett's Estate* (1880) 13 Ch D 696 at 708–709.
18 The position would be no different if it had been trust money which had been in the account first, with the trustee's own money added later.
19 (1880) 13 Ch D 696; (M & B).

above, it will be seen that when the trustee drew out £11,000 he is presumed to have first drawn out his own £3,000. The remaining £8,000 will have come from the trust money. The result is that what is left in the account (ie £2,000) is trust money. The beneficiaries can therefore claim this to the exclusion of the other creditors, who will receive nothing.

It will be seen that the rule in *Hallett's Case* works to the advantage of the beneficiaries and to the disadvantage of other creditors. Is there any reason why beneficiaries should be favoured over other creditors in this way? It is a matter of opinion. But the rule is logical: the rule assumes that the trustee is honest; it assumes that when the trustee took money out of the account he was first taking out and dissipating his own, not trust, money. In defence of the rule it could also be argued that creditors can generally decide with whom they will do business; they must watch the creditworthiness of people with whom they deal; they must stand on their own feet. Beneficiaries, on the other hand, have no choice as to their trustee, and so need protection.

Equity, however, is not unaware of the claims of creditors, and a proviso to the rule in *Hallett's Case* may operate in their favour. Under this proviso, where, as in the above example, a trustee mixes trust money and his own money in an account, takes money out of the account and spends it, *and then puts more money of his own into the account* (perhaps a cheque for his salary, or income from his business), the money which he adds to the account is to be regarded as remaining his own, and not as being a replacement of trust money (unless the beneficiaries can show that the trustee intended to replace trust money[20].) By way of illustration, let us suppose that after putting £10,000 of trust money and £3,000 of his own into the account and after taking out £11,000 and spending it (leaving a balance of £2,000), the trustee puts into the account £3,000 which he has received as a fee. This will increase the balance in the account to £5,000. Of this, applying the rule in *Hallett's Case*, £2,000 is trust money and the beneficiaries can claim this in an action in rem to the exclusion of the creditors. But the balance of £3,000 is the trustee's own money. This is therefore available towards meeting the claims of the creditors. But the beneficiaries still have a claim—for £8,000, being the difference between the £2,000 they can claim in rem and the original £10,000 in the trust fund. With regard to their claim for the £8,000 the beneficiaries and the creditors rank pari passu. Since the beneficiaries claim £8,000 and the creditors, let us say, claim £32,000, the beneficiaries will receive £600 and the creditors £2,400. The beneficiaries thus have a claim in rem to the £2,000 and a claim in personam to the £8,000, and in the latter claim will receive £600.

It will be seen that the beneficiaries' claim in rem is for the sum which was the lowest balance in the account (£2,000). Thus the more the trustee takes out and dissipates then, regardless of how much he puts into the account, the lower will be the sum which the beneficiaries are entitled to claim in rem: 'in short, beneficiaries can usually claim no more than the lowest balance in the account during the period in question'[1].

20   *James Roscoe (Bolton) Ltd v Winder* [1915] 1 Ch 62; (M & B).
 1   *Snell, Principles of Equity* (28th edn) p 299.

(c) MONEY TAKEN OUT AND USED FOR PURCHASE OF A SPECIFIC ITEM

Here quicksands begin. The area is one in which there is uncertainty not only as to what the law is, but uncertainty in many minds as to what it would be equitable for the law to be. It is submitted that, since *Re Tilley's Will Trusts* in 1967[2], the law is as set out in the following paragraphs[3].

A. A trustee mixes £1,000 of his own money and £500 of trust money in a bank account. He takes out all the money and purchases certain property, say some land.

(a) The beneficiary has a first charge on the property for the recovery of the £500 of trust money[4].

(b) Further, if the property has increased in value, then according to the view of Ungoed-Thomas J in *Re Tilley's Will Trusts*[5], the beneficiary can claim that part of the increase which is proportionate to the amount of trust money employed in the purchase. Thus, if the land has increased from £1,500 to £1,800, he can claim £100 of the increase (ie one-third of the increase of £300). This result is logical since if the trustees took the whole increase they would[6] be profiting by the trust. The part of the decision which forms authority for this proposition was, however, obiter, but strong endorsement is provided by the Australian case of *Scott v Scott*[7]. The contrary view, supported by the late Professor Maudsley[8], on the authority of the judgment of Jessel MR in *Re Hallett's Estate*[9], is that the existing law entitles the beneficiary only to a first charge for the recovery of trust money, and not to any part of the increase in value.

Alternatively, it is possible that in some circumstances the proper course might be found to be to order the trustee to hold the whole of the increase on trust for the beneficiary. For example, if the trustee would not have been able to acquire the property without using trust money in the purchase, then to allow the trustee to retain any proportion of the increase in value would be to permit him to obtain a profit from the trust.

(c) If the value of the land has declined in value, say, to £300, then it seems that the beneficiary would have a charge on the land for its value of £300 and would have to fall back on an action in personam with regard to the deficiency of £200 and be content to rank pari passu with other creditors in respect of this claim.

---

2 [1967] Ch 1179.
3 See P. H. Pettit, *Equity and the Law of Trusts* (5th edn), pp 455–458.
4 *Re Oatway* [1903] 2 Ch 356 at 359 per Joyce J; *Re Tilley's Will Trusts* [1967] Ch 1179 at 1189.
5 [1967] Ch 1179 at 1188.
6 As pointed out by Professor Pettit, op cit, p 451.
7 (1963) 109 CLR 649. Support is also to be derived from *Wedderburn v Wedderburn* (1838) 4 My & Cr 41. In *Sinclair v Brougham* [1914] AC 398 Lord Parker of Waddington said (at 442) that where a trustee makes a purchase partly with trust money and partly with his own money, the beneficiary 'can only claim a charge on the property for the amount of the trust money expended in the purchase'. It is submitted, however, that by this Lord Parker meant that the beneficiary could not *either* take the property itself *or* claim a charge on it (as he had stated, two lines earlier, could be done where solely trust money has been used for the purchase), and that Lord Parker was not here directing his attention to the question whether a proportion of any increase in value could be claimed by the beneficiary.
8 (1959) 75 LQR 234, 246.
9 (1880) 13 Ch D 696 at 709; (M & B).

B. A trustee mixes £3,000 of his own money with £2,000 of trust money in a bank account. He takes out £4,000 and purchases some land. The balance is thus £1,000.

(a) The beneficiary can claim a first charge on the land for the recovery of the £2,000 of the trust money[10].

(b) Further, if the land has increased in value he can[11] claim that part of the increase which is proportionate to the amount of trust money employed in the purchase. Thus if the land had increased in value to £5,000 he can claim £500, ie one half of the increase of £1,000. It might be argued that under the rule in *Hallett's Case*[12] the £1,000 balance in the account is trust money. Thus only £1,000 has been employed in purchasing the land. Therefore only one quarter of the increase should be claimable by the beneficiary. The flaw in this argument is, however, that if this solution were adopted the trustee would have been permitted to make a profit from the trust, since he had used trust money to enable him to acquire the land. The approach has, in any case, been decisively rejected. In *Re Tilley's Will Trusts*[13] it was held that there was no presumption that a trustee's drawings from a mixed fund were to be treated as withdrawals of his own money (thus leaving trust money in the account) where the beneficiary's claim was against property bought by such drawings.

(c) If the land has declined in value to an extent which precludes him recovering all the money due to the trust, say to £1,500, the beneficiary has a charge on the land for £1,500 and has an action in rem (as a result of applying the rule in *Hallett's Case*) against the balance in the account to recover the deficiency of £500[14].

C. A trustee mixes £1,000 of his own money with £1,000 of trust money in a bank account. He takes out £500 and purchases some land. He later takes out the balance of £1,500 and dissipates it.

(a) The beneficiary has a first charge on the land towards the recovery of the £1,000 trust money[15].

(b) If the land has increased in value, the beneficiary can, adopting the purchase, claim the land[16]. With regard to any remaining deficiency, the beneficiary will have to rely on an action in personam against the trustee.

(c) If the land has declined in value, then, likewise, the beneficiary can adopt the purchase, and will have to rely on an action in personam for the deficiency.

D. A trustee mixes £1,000 of his own money with £1,000 of trust money in a bank account. He takes out £500 and purchases some land. The balance is left at £1,500.

(a) The outcome will depend on whether the court holds that the trustee had relied on his own money, or on trust money in purchasing the land[17].

(b) If, on the facts, the court finds that the trustee had laid out trust money

---

10   *Re Tilley's Will Trusts* [1967] Ch 1179, [1967] 2 All ER 303.
11   Assuming acceptance of the proposition at A (b) above.
12   (1880) 13 Ch D 696.
13   Ante, at 1185.
14   *Re Hallett's Estate* (1880) 13 Ch D 696.
15   *Re Oatway* [1903] 2 Ch 356 at 360–361; *Re Tilley's Will Trusts* [1967] Ch 1179 at 1189.
16   *Wright v Morgan* [1926] AC 788 at 799. See also *Re Lake* [1903] 1 KB 439.
17   *Re Tilley's Will Trusts* [1967] Ch 1179 at 1193.

on the purchase, then the beneficiaries are entitled to claim the land (including any increase in its value)[18].

(c) If it finds that the trustee laid out his own money, the beneficiary can claim his £1,000 from the balance in the account but he has no claim to the land[18]. Thus if the land has increased in value, any increase accrues to the trustee; if the land has declined in value, the loss would fall on the trustee.

It should be noted that the rule in *Hallett's Case*[19], under which the trustee would be assumed to have used his own money in the purchase of the land (with the result that any increase in its value would necessarily accrue to the trustee (or his creditors)) is relevant only where a claim is made against a balance in an account. It has no relevance in determining claims to property purchased with money from a mixed account[20].

3 Sale of trust property

Suppose that a trustee, in breach of trust, parts with a certain item of trust property, say a piece of land, to a purchaser who pays the trustee £10,000 for it. The trustee pays the money into a separate bank account. The trustee is insolvent with other creditors claiming £20,000. Here the beneficiary is entitled to trace the trust property into the purchase money and claim this in an action in rem, and thus take the £10,000 in priority to the other creditors[1].

In the hands of the trustee, the £10,000 becomes trust money. Therefore if the trustee later dissipates the money or mixes the money with other money of his own and then makes withdrawals, the results are the same as discussed above in situations where from the start what the trustee held was trust money.

4 Mixed trust funds: the rule in *Clayton's Case*

It will be convenient at this point to make a digression to consider the position where a trustee mixes in one active bank account funds from two separate trusts, say those from Trust A and Trust B, and then takes money from the account which he dissipates. Does what remains in the account belong to Trust A or Trust B? Here, it will be noted, there is no reason for the law to have special regard for Trust A or Trust B. The 'equities are equal'.

The outcome is decided by applying the rule in *Clayton's Case*[2]. The rule is that, as between the two trust funds, the trustee is regarded as having taken out of the fund whatever money had first been puts in it. The rule is summed up by the words 'First in, first out'. Consider an example. Suppose that the trustee received £1,000 of Trust A money and puts it in a newly opened bank account. Then he receives £500 of Trust B money, and adds it to the account.

18 Ibid.
9 (1880) 13 Ch D 696.
20 *Re Tilley's Will Trusts* [1967] Ch 1179 at 1193.
1 *Re Hallett's Estate* (1880) 13 Ch D 696, 708–709; *Aluminium Industrie Vaassen BV v Romalpa Aluminium Ltd* [1976] 2 All ER 552, [1976] 1 WLR 676.
2 (1816) 1 Mer 572. *Re Stenning* [1895] 2 Ch 433; *Re Diplock* [1948] Ch 465, [1948] 2 All ER 318; (M & B); cf *Vaughan v Barlow Clowes International Ltd* (1992) *Times*, 6 March, CA.

Next he takes out £1,200 and spends it. Does the balance of £300 belong to Trust A or Trust B? Since Trust A money was in the account first, this is the money the trustee is regarded as having taken out first. So the balance of £300 belongs to Trust B. The outcome is thus a matter of chance, depending on when money from the two trusts was entered in the account. The rule has little to commend it except convenience. It is arguable that equity would be better served if the two trusts ranked pari passu, sharing the balance of £300 between them in proportion to the sums originally placed in the account from the two trusts. Where the money from Trust B was added to the account many years after that from Trust A the operation of the rule would seem to work a particular injustice on Trust A.

Where the application of *Clayton's Case* determines that the final balance in an account consists of, say, Trust B money, then the beneficiaries of Trust A would have to rely on a claim in personam against the trustee (as would the beneficiaries of Trust B in respect of any difference between the final balance in the account and the original sum of Trust B money).

PURCHASE OF A SPECIFIC ITEM

If a trustee takes money from an account in which has been mixed funds from two separate trusts, and uses the money for the purchase of a specific item, then the item is held by the trustee on trust for the two trusts in proportion to the sums of money in each trust fund account at the time of the purchase[3]. Any increase in the value of the item is thus shared pro rata between the two trusts[4].

B. ACTIONS AGAINST TRANSFEREES[5]

So far we have been concerned with a position in which there were three parties, the trustee, the beneficiary, and the trustee's other creditors. We must now turn to consider the position where the same three parties are present but with the addition of a fourth—a person to whom trust property is passed. For example, suppose that a trustee, in breach of trust, conveys an item of trust property to P. Here the beneficiary can bring an action for breach of trust against the trustee for the loss which the trust has suffered. If the trustee is solvent, he will be required to make good the loss. And, as we have seen, if the trustee is insolvent, and the purchase money is identifiable, the beneficiary can claim this in an action in rem, in priority to other creditors. But if the trustee is insolvent and the beneficiaries have no action in rem (for example, because the purchase money has been dissipated) is the beneficiary's only remedy that of an action in personam against the trustee, taking pari passu with the trustee's other creditors? Or can the beneficiary in any circumstances claim back the item of trust property from the person to whom it was transferred? If so, this will offset the fact that the trustee, against whom the beneficiary's claim primarily lies, is insolvent. And such a claim will also be an advantage if the beneficiaries wish to secure the recovery of the

---

3 *Sinclair v Brougham* [1914] AC 398 at 442.
4 *Edinburgh (Lord Provost) v Lord Advocate* (1879) 4 App Cas 823.
5 102 LQR 267 (C. Harpum), 27 Mal LR (D. Hayton).

particular property because of some unique characteristic which it has. Whether the beneficiaries can successfully claim back trust property from a transferee will depend into which of three categories the transferee falls. These will now be considered.

1 The transferee is a bona fide purchaser without notice

Suppose that a trustee, in breach of trust, sells the legal title in trust property, say the legal fee simple in Blackacre, to P. If P can show that he purchased the property in good faith and without knowledge of the breach of trust, then, since P is a bona fide purchaser for value of the legal estate[6] without notice, P takes Blackacre free of any claim by the beneficiary[7].

Similarly, if a trustee, in breach of trust, uses trust money to purchase some item, say the legal fee simple in Redacre, from P, then if P can show that he took the purchase money in good faith and without knowledge of the breach of trust, he will take the purchase money free of any claims by the beneficiary. (Here P is a purchaser of the money, and the value he gave was the land.)

If, in the first case, the trustee retains the purchase money, and keeps this distinct then, as explained above, the beneficiary will have an action in rem in respect of that money. Similarly, if, in the second case, he retains the land, the beneficiary will have an action in rem in respect of the land. But in either case, and this is the point with which we are concerned here, the beneficiary has no claim to the property conveyed to the purchaser who, being a bona fide purchaser, takes free of the equitable interests under the trust. (The beneficiary's only remedy will thus lie against the trustee.)

2 The transferee takes with notice

If a trustee, in breach of trust, transfers trust property to a person who takes with notice[8] that the transfer is in breach of trust then the transferee (irrespective of whether he is a purchaser for value[9] or gives no consideration) takes the property (ie whether goods, land, money, or any other property) subject to the claims of the beneficiary. The purchaser becomes a constructive trustee[10] of the property and the beneficiary can claim the land in an action in rem. (This remedy would be of special value if the value of the property had increased, or if the trustee was insolvent.) The beneficiary's rights against the constructive trustee, eg with regard to tracing the trust money into a mixed account, are the same as they would be if the action was brought against the (original) trustee.

---

6 If the trust property consists of an equitable interest, then the purchaser will, under the rule in *Dearle v Hall* (1823–28) 3 Russ 1, take the property subject to the interest of the beneficiary.
7 *Thorndike v Hunt* (1859) 3 De GF & J 563; *Thomson v Clydesdale Bank Ltd* [1893] AC 282; *Lipkin Gorman v Karpnale Ltd* [1989] 1 WLR 1340; [1992] Conv 124 (M. Halliwell).
8 Or who is unable to establish that he took the property for value and without notice of the breach of trust. *GL Baker Ltd v Medway Building and Supplies Ltd* [1958] 3 All ER 540, [1958] 1 WLR 1216.
9 *Nelson v Larholt* [1948] 1 KB 339, [1947] 2 All ER 751.
10 See Chap 24.

3 The transferee is an innocent volunteer
Suppose that a trustee, in breach of trust, transfers trust property to a third person who takes without notice of the breach of trust, and who gives no consideration to the trustee. Such a person is not a purchaser for value of the property and so, according to the basic rule of equity, takes the property subject to the trust. It will be noted that this person, unlike the purchaser with notice, is not guilty of any fault, he is as innocent as the beneficiary: he is an innocent volunteer. As one means of mitigating the hardship imposed on an innocent volunteer as a result of his finding himself bound by the equitable interests under the trust, equity provides that before a beneficiary is entitled to make any claim against an innocent volunteer, he must first bring an action against the trustee. Thus if the trustee is solvent, the beneficiary will recover from the trustee, and the innocent volunteer will keep the property. But if a claim against the trustee is of no avail (eg because the trustee is bankrupt), then equity allows the beneficiary to recover the property from the innocent volunteer. This, at any rate, is the position where the fiduciary relationship between the persons we have referred to as trustee and beneficiary is that between executor and those entitled to a deceased's estate (ie an unpaid or under-paid creditor, legatee or next of kin). For example, in a major case in this field a testator directed his executors to apply the residue of his estate 'for such charitable institutions or other charitable or benevolent objects in England' as they should select. The executor distributed a large part of the residue among various charities. The next of kin of the testator then challenged the validity of the bequest. In *Chichester Diocesan Board of Finance v Simpson*[11], it was held that the gift failed for uncertainty. The next of kin therefore claimed the amounts paid to the charities from the executors. With the approval of the court, these claims were compromised. The next of kin claimed the balance (ie the difference between what they received from the executors and the total due to them) from the charities which had received money from the estate. The case came before the courts as *Re Diplock*[12]. The Court of Appeal held that the next of kin were entitled to recover the money which had been paid to the charities in good faith but by an error of law.

Did the claim by the next of kin against the charities lie in rem or in personam? The Court of Appeal held that if in these circumstances the innocent volunteer has retained the property in an identifiable form then the beneficiary can claim the property in an action in rem, with the consequence that if the property has increased in value, that increase accrues to the beneficiary, and with the further consequence that interest will be payable in respect of the period during which the property was held by the innocent volunteer. If the property is not identifiable, the beneficiary's claim will lie merely in personam.

Whether the beneficiary's claim to the property against the innocent volunteer is in rem or in personam becomes of particular importance if the innocent volunteer is bankrupt. In this event, if the beneficiary's claim is in rem, he takes priority over the innocent volunteer's other creditors. If his claim is merely in personam, he ranks pari passu with the other creditors.

In *Re Diplock*[13] the Court of Appeal considered when property was to be

11 [1944] AC 341, [1944] 2 All ER 60.
12 [1948] Ch 465, [1948] 2 All ER 318; (M & B). For the historical background, see (1983) LJLH (S. J. Whittaker).
13 Ante.

regarded as being identifiable for the purpose of giving rise to an action in rem. If a specific item of property has been purchased, then clearly it is identifiable. But in *Re Diplock* money had been expended on alterations to buildings and on the erection of a new building. It was held that no action in rem lay in respect of the new or altered buildings. Similarly, money used to discharge a charity's debts was held to be no longer traceable. (It must be stressed here that the fact that the trust money is not traceable does not necessarily mean that it is not recoverable: it means that no action in rem lies for the recovery of the trust money. As we have stated, if no action in rem lies, then the claimant can fall back on an action in personam, although, as we have also seen, this action has the disadvantage that in it a claimant ranks pari passu with other creditors[14].)

If trust money is retained by an innocent volunteer in a separate bank account, or if it has been placed in a bank account with other money of the innocent volunteer's, and no withdrawals are subsequently made, then the money is traceable; ie an action in rem lies in respect of the sum concerned[15]. But what is the position if the trust money is mixed in an account with the innocent volunteer's own money and withdrawals are then made from the account? Is the balance trust money (in which case an action in rem lies) or the innocent volunteer's own money (in which case only an action in personam lies)? We saw that where a trustee mixes trust money with his own and makes withdrawals, he is presumed, under the rule in *Hallett's Case*[16], to withdraw his own money first, with the result that the balance will consist of trust money[17]. Does the same principle apply where an innocent volunteer mixes his own with trust money? In *Re Diplock* it was held that the rule in *Hallett's Case* did not apply here. Since no fiduciary relationship existed between the beneficiary and the innocent volunteer, there was no reason for the special protection conferred on a beneficiary by the rule in *Hallett's Case* to be conferred on a beneficiary in this different situation. The Court of Appeal therefore held that in determining whether the balance in the account was trust money or the innocent volunteer's money, the rule in *Clayton's Case* was to be applied. Thus if the account contains trust money before the innocent volunteer's own money is added, the trust money is regarded as being expended first, with the result that the balance is the innocent volunteer's (and vice versa).

If the innocent volunteer mixed the trust money with his own in a bank account and then made a withdrawal from the account and used the money for a particular purpose, then if it can be shown that it had been the innocent volunteer's intention to use trust money for the purpose concerned, and if the money so used is traceable (eg used for the purchase of some identifiable object), then the beneficiaries can trace their money in an action in rem[18].

The case before the Court of Appeal in *Re Diplock* occupied nearly three weeks. Much of the time was spent in argument as to whether the claim of the beneficiaries lay in rem or in personam. But, it may be asked, if the charities would be obliged to repay the money, did it make all that great a

---

14 See *Space Investments Ltd v Canadian Imperial Bank of Commerce Trust Co (Bahamas) Ltd* [1986] 3 All ER 75, [1986] 1 WLR 1072, PC; p 50, ante.

15 *Banque Belge pour l'Etranger v Hambrouck* [1921] 1 KB 321, CA.

16 Ante.

17 Subject to the proviso to this rule explained on p 354, ante.

8 *Re Diplock* [1948] Ch 465 at 551–554. See [1983] Conv 135 (K. Hodkinson).

362   *Chapter 22   Remedies of a beneficiary*

difference (since they were not bankrupt) whether the claims lay in rem or in personam? Why was the matter not settled out of court? The answer is that, while the charities may have realised that they would have to repay (with interest) the money which was identifiable, they hoped to persuade the court that where the money had been spent, and thus was no longer traceable, they would not have to find an equivalent sum from their own funds. They hoped, in fact, that the court would hold that no claim in personam lay against them. But that hope was not fulfilled: the Court of Appeal held that the beneficiaries had an action in rem for property which was traceable, and an action in personam for the balance. The charities appealed to the House of Lords with regard to the action in personam, but the Lords confirmed the judgment of the Court of Appeal[19]. The decision could well have inflicted a hardship on the charities concerned, and charities that accept large legacies should perhaps insure themselves against the risk of claims for the recovery of gifts they have received.

It is important to note that an action lies against an innocent volunteer for recovery of trust property only to the extent that the beneficiary has attempted, and failed, to recover from the trustee. In *Re Diplock*, if the next of kin had recovered in full from the executors, no claim against the charities would have lain.

It should further be noted that in the case of an action against an innocent volunteer in rem, an action lies at the suit not only of a beneficiary under a trust and a legatee under a will, but wherever the property concerned was, before it passed into the hands of the innocent volunteer, held by a person in a fiduciary position, for example, by an agent with regard to his principal's property[20], and by a person who has received property as a result of a factual mistake[1]. In the case of an action against an innocent volunteer in personam, on the other hand, the decision in *Re Diplock* that such an action lay rested on the fact that the property, before the transfer, had been held by a person whose fiduciary position was that of an executor and the judgment of Lord Simonds indicated[2] that under the existing law no corresponding right was to be regarded as existing where the fiduciary was a trustee. Whether the principles enunciated in *Re Diplock* with regard to an action in personam will ever be extended to cover the position where the fiduciary is a trustee remains to be seen.

19   *Ministry of Health v Simpson* [1951] AC 251, [1950] 2 All ER 1137.
20   See [1975] CLP 39 (J. D. Stephens).
 1   *Chase Manhattan Bank NA v Israel–British Bank (London) Ltd* [1981] Ch 105, [1979] 3 All ER 1025; (M & B).
 2   At 1140.

Chapter 23

Liability and defences of trustees

Liability of trustees[1]

1 LIABILITY OF THE TRUSTEE WHO COMMITS THE BREACH

If a trustee commits a breach of trust, then he is answerable to the beneficiaries. It is irrelevant that a trustee acted without knowledge that he was
acting in breach of trust, or that he acted with 'best motives'[2], or 'thought
that there might be more profit by this mode of dealing'[2]: as a defence
'inadvertence and good nature'[2] are not enough. Thus regardless of the moral
blamelessness of the trustee, and regardless of the fact the breach may in fact
have benefited the trust, if a breach was committed the trustee is answerable
for it. This does not mean, however, that the trustee will necessarily be found
liable by the court to pay damages. It may be that the trustee can offer a
defence for his action, and if the court finds that the defence avails, then the
trustee, although *answerable* for the breach, will not be found *liable* for it.
The word 'liable', it will therefore be noted, needs to be read with care. In
some contexts the word is used to indicate a breach has been committed; in
others that not only has a breach been committed but also that there is no
defence; and in others it refers to the fact that there is responsibility for the
acts of another. Conversely, 'not liable' is sometimes used to indicate the
absence of any breach; in others the existence of a valid defence; in others
the absence of responsibility for the acts of another.

2 LIABILITY[3] OF THE TRUSTEE FOR A BREACH COMMITTED BY ANOTHER

If a trustee does not himself commit a particular breach of trust, he will not
be answerable for the breach unless he was himself in some way at fault. This
principle of equity has had statutory basis since 1859[4], and is now contained
in s 30(1) of the Trustee Act 1925. 'A trustee shall be answerable ... only for
his own acts, receipts, neglects and defaults, and not those of any other

1 A. J. Hawkins, 'Personal Liability of Charity Trustees' (1979) 95 LQR 99.
2 Per Lord Langdale, *Booth v Booth* (1838) 1 Beav 125 at 129.
3 Ie answerability.
4 Law of Property (Amendment) Act 1859, s 31.

trustee nor any banker, broker, or other person with whom trust money or securities may be deposited, ... nor for any other loss, unless the same happens through his own wilful default'[5]. Some cases will provide illustrations.

1. Trust land was leased to a tenant who paid rent to the trustees, A and B, and obtained a receipt from them. The money was received by A. B took no steps to ensure that the money was safeguarded (eg by investment) and A later misappropriated it. B was held to be answerable (along with A) for the loss as he was at fault in allowing the money to remain in A's hands without watching over what he did with it[6].

2. A testator left property which included an earthenware manufacturing business to two executors, A and B, on certain trusts. The business should have been sold and the proceeds invested but instead A carried on the business for his own benefit. Later he became insolvent, and the business was lost. It was held that B was answerable for the loss as he had known of, and acquiesced in, the breach which A had committed[7].

3. Trust property included certain company stock. Trustee A, in breach of trust, held the stock. Co-trustee B concealed the sale from a beneficiary. (When money was advanced to the beneficiary, B said that the money had been borrowed rather than selling the stock.) It was held that B was answerable, along with A, for the breach[8].

4. A and B, the latter a solicitor, were trustees of a will. In order to provide cash for distribution to a beneficiary certain stock, part of the trust property, was sold at B's direction by B's broker. The proceeds were paid in to B's firm's account at the X Bank. A thought that the money had been paid into the trust's account at the Y Bank, where B later told him it was still deposited. A did not see the pass book of the trust account, or ask to see it, or make any inquiries at the Y Bank. A year later B died insolvent. It was held that, by reason of his negligence, A was answerable for the loss to the trust[9].

If a new trustee has no reason to suspect that the existing trustees (and any trustees who have retired) have failed to carry out their duties, then he is entitled to assume that they have performed their duties in a proper manner[10]. If a breach has in fact been committed, he will not be liable. But if a new trustee discovers that a breach has occurred then he must[11] take steps to ensure that the loss is made good: if he fails to do so he will himself become liable[12].

A trustee who has retired remains liable for breaches of trust (for which he is answerable) committed during the period while he was trustee. As regards breaches of trust which occur after his retirement, the general rule is that he will not be liable. However, if it can be shown that he retired in order to facilitate the commission of a particular breach, then he will be liable

5 For the meaning of 'wilful default' in various contexts, see J. E. Stannard [1979] Conv 345.
6 *Townley v Sherborne* (1633) J Bridg 35.
7 *Booth v Booth* (1838) 1 Beav 125.
8 *Boardman v Mosman* (1779) 1 Bro CC 68.
9 *Wynne v Tempest* (1897) 13 TLR 360.
10 *Re Strahan* (1856) 8 De GM & G 291.
11 Unless he can show that it would be useless to bring proceedings against a retired trustee. *Re Forest of Dean Coal Mining Co* (1878) 10 Ch D 450.
12 *Hobday v Peters (No 3)* (1860) 28 Beav 603.

(along with those by whom the breach was actually committed)[13]. It will be enough, however, to show merely that the retirement of the trustee made it possible for the breach to be committed; or that the trustee, when he retired, knew that some breach was likely[13].

It will be seen that the wording of s 30 expressly confirms the liability of a trustee for loss caused by his negligence (his 'neglects'). It sometimes happens that a trustee is exempted from liability for negligence by a term in the trust instrument which provides that a trustee is to be exonerated from liability for any matter other than 'wilful and individual fraud or wrongdoing on the part of the trustee who is sought to be made so liable'[14].

3 FAULTLESS TRUSTEE

If a trustee does not himself commit a breach, and if the breach is not due to or assisted by his own default, then he is not answerable for the breach. This is so notwithstanding that he has signed a receipt 'for conformity'[15]. The meaning of this term can be explained by an illustration. A, B, and C are trustees for sale of land. The land is sold to P. In order that the beneficial interests should be overreached, P requires a receipt signed by two trustees. A signs a receipt and gets B to sign it also. A goes to P, gives him the receipt, and receives the purchase money. P is under no duty to see that the money is paid (whether by cash, by banker's draft or by cheque) to the persons whom he knows to be the vendors of the land, or to the persons named on the receipt[16]. So A can tell P to hand over cash to him, or to make a banker's draft or cheque payable to him. By this means a trustee may be able to keep trust money in his own hands. In these circumstances, if A misapplies the money, B is not answerable solely on the grounds that he signed the receipt, since statute expressly frees him from liability on this ground[17]. But he may become answerable on some other ground, a likely one being that, having knowledge that P had paid money to the trust, he failed to satisfy himself that A had handled the money in a proper manner eg by placing it in the trust's account at a bank, or investing it (in the name of all the trustees) in an authorised investment.

4 THE JOINT AND SEVERAL LIABILITY OF TRUSTEES

Suppose that a trust has three trustees A, B and C. A commits a breach which causes a loss to the trust of £10,000. B is answerable along with A because he had knowledge which should have prompted to him to inquire what A was doing with the money. C is in no way implicated in the breach. A beneficiary, Z, has an action to recover the £10,000 from the trustees who are answerable, namely A and B. If one (or both) of them has died, the action can be brought against his estate (or their estates). But what if A is insolvent,

13 *Head v Gould* [1898] 2 Ch 250.
14 For the position of such an exemption clause under the Unfair Contract Terms Act 1977, see W. Goodhart [1980] Conv 333.
15 Trustee Act 1925, s 30(1).
16 Ibid, s 14(1).
17 Ibid, s 30(1).

or has disappeared? Does this mean that if B alone is sued Z recovers only £5,000? No, the position is that each trustee who is answerable for the breach is liable for the *whole* of the loss. Thus if A is insolvent and Z sues B alone, B must pay the whole £10,000 (notwithstanding that his own default may have been secondary to that of A, who committed the breach which caused the actual loss). Further, even if both trustees are solvent, and can be found, a beneficiary can, if he wishes (perhaps for convenience), bring his action against only one of them. If it is found that a breach has occurred, then the trustee will have to pay the whole of the damages awarded. The action can thus be brought against all the trustees answerable or against any one of them. (The beneficiary cannot, of course, obtain more in total than the sum awarded by the court.)

Further, if the action is brought against two or more trustees and the court awards damages against them, the plaintiff can proceed to execute judgment against (ie take proceedings to obtain the damages awarded from) any one or more out of those found liable. For example, the plaintiff may have found it the best course to bring the action against all the trustees in any way answerable, but only one of them may have sufficient money to pay the damages, and it will be against him that the plaintiff executes judgment.

These principles are sometimes expressed by saying that the liability of trustees is 'joint and several', ie they can be sued and held liable jointly, or any one of them can be sued, or any one of them can be held liable to pay the damages. It should be noted, however, that it is only the liability of trustees answerable for the breach which is joint and several; a trustee who is innocent is not liable at all.

5 THE POSITION OF TRUSTEES INTER SE

CONTRIBUTION AND INDEMNITY

The reason why the liability of trustees is several as well as joint is the convenience of the beneficiary: it improves his chances of being able to recover. But if A and B are both answerable for a breach and B finds himself having to pay the whole of the damages awarded, although this may be satisfactory to a beneficiary, it would result in an injustice as between A and B. Equity therefore provided that, whilst any one trustee might be liable, as between themselves all the trustees answerable for the breach had to share the loss equally. Thus if A and B were answerable, and B paid the whole loss, B could recover one half from A: B had a right to claim *contribution* from A.[18]

In certain instances a trustee, B, who had had to pay damages was able to recover from a co-trustee, A, the whole (and not merely a share) of the sum he had paid. Where B had this right to recover what amounts to 100% contribution from his co-trustee he is said to have had a right to be indemnified, or a right to *indemnity*. The instances in which this right existed included:

18   *Jackson v Dickinson* [1903] 1 Ch 947.

1. Where A acted as solicitor to the trust, and the breach was committed solely in reliance on his advice[19].

2. Where A alone was morally guilty and B was free of moral guilt; as where A received trust property and misappropriated it. But the fact that one trustee, B, was less directly responsible than another, A, did not of itself enable B to obtain indemnity from A. For example, in *Bahin v Hughes*[20] a trustee, A, made an improper investment and a loss to the trust resulted. But since A had not acted dishonestly, the two co-trustees were unable to obtain an indemnity from A. All three trustees shared the payment of damages equally.

3. The third instance will be explained within the framework of a matter to be considered, impounding.

The rules evolved by equity with regard to contribution and indemnity, whilst providing a measure of justice, were unsatisfactory in their rigidity: where A and B were answerable for a breach of trust and a beneficiary sued A and recovered against him, then A could recover from B one half (by way of contribution) or the whole (by way of indemnity) of what he had had to pay the beneficiary, but the court had no power to award A any other fraction.

The flexibility lacking under the old rules was introduced by the Civil Liability (Contribution) Act 1978, under which, in our example, A can (where the loss caused by the breach occurs after 1978) recover from B such amount as may be found by the court to be just and equitable having regard to the extent of B's responsibility for the damage caused by the breach of trust.[1] In making an award under the Act, the court has power to direct that the sum recovered by A should amount to a complete indemnity by B[1]. In deciding when such indemnity should be ordered, it seems likely that the court will be guided by the instances in which, under the previous rules of equity,[2] the court would order A to be indemnified by B.

IMPOUNDING

If a trustee has a beneficial interest under a trust and the trustee commits a breach of trust, then the trustee in breach is not entitled to receive any part of his beneficial interest until he has made good the whole of the loss to the trust[3]: his interest is *impounded*. Thus if B, a trustee who is also a beneficiary, has an interest of £2,000 under the trust and he commits a breach causing a loss of £1,000, then the result is that he loses £1,000 out of his equitable interest. The reasoning is that equity treats the trustee as if he has paid himself his entitlement out of the trust fund[4]. Even if another trustee, A, is answerable along with B for the breach, the loss is met wholly out of B's beneficial interest. Thus, B will not be entitled to obtain any contribution

19 *Re Partington* (1887) 57 LT 654.
20 (1886) 31 Ch D 390.
1 Sections 1, 2(1), 2(2).
2 Supra.
3 *Chillingworth v Chambers* [1896] 1 Ch 685.
4 *Re Dacre* [1916] 1 Ch 344 at 348.

from A towards the cost of making good the loss. Further, if proceedings are brought with regard to the loss against A and he is compelled to make good the loss, he can recover the £1,000 he has had to pay from B's beneficial interest under the fund. (This is the third instance in which one trustee can obtain an indemnity from another.)

If the facts had been that B's interest under the fund was £1,000, and the loss he had caused by his breach was £2,000, then the whole of his beneficial interest would go towards making good the loss and he would be liable to find the balance of £1,000. As regards this £1,000, which he has actually had to pay out in damages, he could obtain a contribution from a co-trustee who was answerable with him for the loss. Further, if proceedings with regard to the loss were brought against A, the co-trustee, and A had to pay the £2,000 loss, then A could require to be indemnified to the extent of B's beneficial interest (ie £1,000) and he could require a contribution (ie of £500) from B with regard to the balance of £1,000.

Where a person is a trustee of two distinct trust funds, and has a beneficial interest in one of them, then his beneficial interest cannot be impounded to make good a loss caused to the other trust by a breach committed by him[5].

6 LIABILITY FOR[6] AGENTS

When dealing with the power of trustees to appoint agents we saw[7] that under s 23 of the Trustee Act 1925, if an agent is employed 'in good faith', the trustee is not responsible for the agent's default[8]. It will be noted, however, that under s 30(1) a trustee is not answerable for the defaults of any banker, broker or other person unless the same happens through his own *wilful default*. Thus, notwithstanding that the original appointment was made 'in good faith', the trustee may become liable if subsequently he is guilty of some 'wilful default', for example, failing adequately to supervise the agent's handling of the trust's business[9]. The words 'wilful default' are thus relevant both when considering the liability of a trustee for acts of a co-trustee[10] and when considering the liability of a trustee for acts of an agent. *Re Vickery*[11] provides an illustration of the latter. A testatrix, who died in December 1926, appointed S as sole executor of her will. S went to J, a solicitor, for assistance in winding up the estate. J obtained a grant of probate to S in May 1927. In July, V, a son of the testatrix, who was entitled to a half share in the residuary estate, informed S that J had previously been suspended for six months from acting as a solicitor for assaulting another solicitor. But S had no reason at that time for believing J to be dishonest. Not long afterwards V told S that on a previous occasion J had been suspended by the Law Society for five years. In August, V wrote to S saying that he had discovered that he, S, had

5 *Re Towndrow* [1911] 1 Ch 662.
6 For the possible liability *of* agents. See p 385 et seq.
7 See Chap 14.
8 The Law Reform Committee, 23rd Report, recommended that a trustee should be liable for the default of his agent unless it is shown that he took reasonable steps to ensure that the agent was competent and that he took reasonable steps to ensure that the agent's work was done competently. (Para 4.11.)
9 See Gareth H. Jones, 'Delegation by Trustees' (1959) 22 MLR 385.
10 See p 363, ante.
11 [1931] 1 Ch 572; (M & B).

authorised a payment of £62 to J from Savings Certificates, part of the estate. V objected to this having been done but did not suggest that the administration of the estate should be taken out of J's hands. In September V went to see S, accompanied by N, a solicitor's managing clerk. N advised that the matter should be taken out of J's hands. (The court found that it was not until this time that S was told of charges of dishonesty which had been made in the past against J.) S wrote to J urging him to complete the winding up. In December S placed the matter in the hands of X, another solicitor, who pressed J for a settlement. In January 1928 S took out an originating summons against J, but J absconded. V sued S for the money lost, claiming that the loss had been due to S's breach of trust. It was held that although S had been guilty of an error of judgment, in the circumstances this did not amount to a wilful default under s 30(1) of the Trustee Act 1925. S was therefore not liable.

Another illustration is provided by *Re Speight*[12]. Here a broker was employed by a trustee for the purpose of investing trust money. At the request of the broker, the cheque for the sum to be invested was made payable to the broker. The broker appropriated the money for his own use and a month later became bankrupt. The beneficiaries claimed that the trustee was personally liable to make good the loss. It was held that the trustee, having acted as in the ordinary course of business, was not liable to make good the loss. The decision provides a yardstick by which the conduct of a trustee may be judged for the purpose of determining whether he should be held liable for the acts of an agent[13]. 'It seems to me that on general principles a trustee ought to conduct the business of the trust in the same manner that an ordinary prudent man of business would conduct his own, and that beyond that there is no liability or obligation on the trustee. In other words, a trustee is not bound because he is a trustee to conduct business in other than the ordinary and usual way in which similar business is conducted by mankind in transactions of their own. It never could be reasonable to make a trustee adopt further and better precautions than an ordinary prudent man of business would adopt, or to conduct the business in any other way. If it were otherwise, no one would be a trustee at all'[14].

7 LIABILITY IN CRIMINAL LAW

In this chapter we have considered the liability of trustees in civil law. A breach of trust may also constitute a crime. Under s 5(1) of the Theft Act 1968[15] a trustee is liable for theft 'if he dishonestly appropriates property belonging to another with the intention of permanently depriving the other of it'[16].

---

12 (1883) 22 Ch D 727.
13 The test was applied in *Re Lucking's Will Trusts* [1967] 3 All ER 726, [1968] 1 WLR 866; (M & B).
14 Per Jessel MR at 739.
15 Repealing the Larceny Act 1916, under s 21 of which fraudulent conversion by a trustee was an offence.
16 See A. T. H. Smith, 'Constructive trusts in the law of theft' [1977] Crim LR 395.

Defences of trustees

The clearest defence to an action for breach of trust will be, of course, for the defendant to show that no breach was committed. But even if it is established (or admitted) that a breach occurred, certain defences may operate to free the defendant from liability.

Where all the trustees can show that they have a good defence (or that they were not in breach) then the beneficiary will fail in his action. Where one or more out of several trustees can show a valid defence the effect will be to cast a heavier burden of damages on to the trustee or trustees who are without defence.

1 RELIEF UNDER SECTION 61 OF THE TRUSTEE ACT 1925[17]

If a trustee has acted dishonestly then clearly he does not deserve relief. But what if his breach was committed in error or by inadvertence? For example, if a trustee invests trust money in a mortgage, and the security proves to be inadequate (a situation more likely before the introduction of statutory safeguards[18]), should he be liable for the loss? Or if a trustee in error pays the wrong beneficiary, or if he passes money to an agent who absconds, should he be liable for a loss which the breach has caused?

If a trustee was in all cases freed from liability on the ground that he had not been dishonest, the result could not only cause hardship to the beneficiaries, but might also tend to lead other trustees to believe that they could, provided they were not dishonest, safely relax their standards of care. On the other hand, to impose absolute liability for every breach could not only produce injustice but might also tend to make people reluctant to accept the position of voluntary trustee.

The law strikes a compromise: lack of dishonest motive is alone no defence[19], but the court has power, under s 61 of the Trustee Act 1925[20], to relieve a trustee of liability if it appears to the court that the trustee has not only acted 'honestly' but also has acted 'reasonably' and, further, that he 'ought fairly to be excused for the breach of trust and for omitting to obtain the directions of the court in the matter in which he committed such a breach'. The onus is on the trustee to show that he acted honestly and reasonably[1].

The courts have declined to lay down any guidelines for determining the precise circumstances in which the section will operate to confer relief. Decisions will depend on the facts in each case[2]. With regard to the require-ment that the trustee must have acted 'honestly', there have been no cases which hinged solely on the definition of this word, but it has been suggested that a trustee should be regarded as having acted honestly, not merely when he has acted without selfish motive, but 'when, in deciding whether or not to act in a certain way, the predominant reason for his decision was that he

---

17 See L. A. Sheridan (1955) 19 Conv NS 420.
18 See Chap 15.
19 See *Re Rosenthal* [1972] 3 All ER 552, [1972] 1 WLR 1273; executor, in error and without dishonesty, paid estate duty, properly payable by devisee, out of residue; held liable.
20 Replacing Judicial Trustees Act 1896, s 3.
 1 *Re Stuart* [1897] 2 Ch 583.
 2 *Re Kay* [1897] 2 Ch 518 at 524.

thought it would further the interests of the trust'. With regard to the requirement that the trustee 'ought fairly to be excused', the word 'fairly' here means in fairness both to the trustee and to the other persons who may be affected[3]. This condition will not be satisfied where, although the trustee acted honestly, some other conduct by him (other than that constituting the breach) counted against him, for example his failure to do all he could to mitigate the loss which his breach had caused[4].

There remains the requirement that the trustee must have acted 'reasonably'. Let us first consider some cases in which this requirement has been satisfied and relief granted. In *Re Smith*[5] a trustee who lived in Surrey employed solicitors in London to act as her agents. When the need arose the solicitors made out cheques and sent them to the trustee for signature. A clerk employed by the solicitors, and well known to the trustee, fraudulently obtained the trustee's signature to cheques which he cashed, and absconded with the proceeds. It was held that the trustee had in the circumstances acted reasonably and was granted relief. In *Re Lord De Clifford's Estate*[6] solicitors to the trustees informed the trustees that money was required for certain purposes including the payment of debts. The trustees paid the money to the solicitors who applied all but £530 for trust purposes. The solicitors went bankrupt and the £530 was lost to the trust. The trustees were granted relief[7]. In *Re Grindey*[8] the executors and trustees of a will were a bank manager and two farmers. The will contained no express provision as to calling in debts. The estate included a debt of £116, payable by a seemingly creditworthy debtor. The executors did not call for payment of the debt and the debtor later died insolvent. It was held that it was reasonable for them, on reading the will, to think that they did not have to call in the debt. Further, it was reasonable for them not to have applied to the court for directions over such a small sum. *Perrins v Bellamy*[9] also concerned an error. The trustees of a settlement mistakenly thought that they had a power of sale and sold certain leaseholds which resulted in a reduction in income. The sale would have been proper if the usual power had existed, and the trustee's solicitor had advised them that they had the power to make the sale. They were relieved from liability[10].

Reliance on the advice of another (whether a solicitor or some other person) is, however, no sure way of showing that trustees have acted reasonably, as will be seen in the course of considering the following instances in which it was held that trustees did not act reasonably and relief was refused. In *Re Barker*[11], an executrix and trustee failed to sell unauthorised investments for 14 years after the testator's death, relying on the advice of a commission agent who had been a friend and adviser of her husband. In *Re Turner*[12] a trustee, who was a draper, relied in connection with the investment of trust

3 *Marsden v Regan* [1954] 1 All ER 475, [1954] 1 WLR 423.
4 *National Trustees Co of Australasia Ltd v General Finance Co of Australasia Ltd* [1905] AC 373.
5 (1902) 86 LT 401.
6 [1900] 2 Ch 707.
7 See also *Re Mackay* [1911] 1 Ch 300.
8 [1898] 2 Ch 593.
9 [1899] 1 Ch 797; (M & B).
10 The fact that trustees had relied on the advice of a solicitor was a defence also in *Hawkesley v May* [1956] 1 QB 304, [1955] 3 All ER 353.
11 (1898) 77 LT 712.
12 [1897] 1 Ch 536.

money on the advice of his co-trustee who was a solicitor. In both cases relief was denied on the ground that the trustee had failed to exercise the degree of prudence which could be expected from a reasonable man of business in the handling of his own affairs.

It is the failure to show this degree of prudence[13] either in the trustee's own acts, or in his reliance on advice, or in his employment of agents, or in his reliance in the honesty of a co-trustee, which provides the basis for the decisions in cases in which relief has been denied. For example, in *Wynne v Tempest*[14], considered earlier[15], the defendant failed to exercise a sufficient degree of prudence when he allowed the trust fund to remain under the control of his co-trustee who later died insolvent. In *Re Jebb*[16], trustees made payments of trust money in the erroneous belief that the recipient was entitled by virtue of the Adoption of Children Act 1949. It was clear from the Act that its provisions were not applicable. Relief was refused. In *Shaw v Cates*[17], the trustees failed to obtain a satisfactory valuation of property before lending trust money on mortgage: not only was the valuer employed by the mortgagor, but the trustees did not give him full instructions. Further, the trustees did not comply with the valuer's advice in making the loan. Relief was denied.

Where a trustee relies on the advice of a solicitor it might seem hard that he can be found liable for a breach committed in acting on the advice received[18]. Could a reasonable man of business be expected to do more in the handling of his own affairs? It is clear that the courts consider that, in certain circumstances, he could. For example, if the construction of a trust deed is in doubt and a substantial sum is involved, the opinion of counsel ought to be sought. But the hardship on the trustee may not be as great as at first sight appears, since it may be open to the trustee to sue the solicitor for negligence and recover the damages and costs he has had to pay. Further, if the solicitor was a trustee and solicitor to the trust, then the trustee found liable may be able to claim an indemnity from him[19].

Paid trustees are expected to show higher standards of knowledge and attention than are unpaid trustees[20]. Thus where a trustee is paid, as where a solicitor or a bank acts as an executor, the court is less ready to grant relief under the section than it would be where the trustee is unpaid[1]. (Of course a paid trustee can, and a solicitor normally will, allocate a part of all the fees he receives for the purpose of providing insurance against claims for negligence.)

If a trustee can show that he has transacted certain trust business honestly and reasonably, and as prudently as he would have been likely to do in his own affairs, this may result, not merely in the trustee having a defence, but in the trustee being held not to have committed any breach of trust in the first place[2].

13   *Re Turner* [1897] 1 Ch 536.
14   (1897) 13 TLR 360.
15   See p 364, ante.
16   [1966] Ch 666, [1965] 3 All ER 358.
17   [1909] 1 Ch 389; (M & B).
18   See *Davis v Hutchings* [1907] 1 Ch 356.
19   See p 366, ante.
20   *Re Waterman's Will Trusts* [1952] 2 All ER 1054, 1055.
 1   *Re Pauling's Settlement Trusts* [1964] Ch 303, [1963] 3 All ER 1, CA; (M & B).
 2   *Peffer v Rigg* [1978] 3 All ER 745, [1977] 1 WLR 285.

2 BANKRUPTCY

Where a trustee goes bankrupt[3] and obtains his discharge, then he is freed from any existing liability for breach of trust. His liability will continue, however, if the breach was fraudulent and he was a party to the fraud.

3 ACQUIESCENCE BY THE BENEFICIARY

It will be a defence to a trustee to show that the beneficiary who brings the action consented to, or acquiesced in, the breach. For this defence to avail the trustee must be able to show that the beneficiary was *sui juris*, and that he consented to, or acquiesced in, the breach freely and without pressure or undue influence. Delay by a beneficiary in bringing proceedings does not of itself necessarily constitute evidence of acquiescence by the beneficiary in a breach[4].

In *Re Pauling's Settlement*[5] a beneficiary agreed that a bank, which was the trustee of the settlement, should make certain advances of capital to her. The money advanced in fact benefited her parents. It was held that the presumption of undue influence by a parent over a child continues to exist for a period after the child attains his majority. The presumption was held not to have been rebutted and since the child's consent was thus negatived, the bank's defence that the beneficiary had consented to the breach did not avail.

The defendant trustee must be able to show that the beneficiary had full knowledge of the circumstances. Thus the beneficiary must know the nature of the act to which his consent is given or in which he is acquiescing[6], and he must also know of its consequences[7]. But it need not be shown that the beneficiary concerned benefited from the breach, nor is it necessary that he should have known that the act concerned constituted a breach of trust[8].

4 IMPOUNDING

Consent by a beneficiary may be not only a defence to a trustee but may provide the trustee with a form of counter-attack. If the beneficiary's consent was in writing or if it took the form of actually requesting or instigating the breach (whether this was done orally or in writing), then the court has power under s 62 of the Trustee Act 1925[9] to make an order 'for impounding all or any part of the interest of the beneficiary ... by way of indemnity to the trustee' who is sued: the beneficiary's interest is used to make good the loss that has occurred. Thus if T holds on trust for X and Y; a breach occurs to which X consented in writing; there is a loss to the fund of £1,000; Y sues T; X's interest under that fund amounts to £2,000; then the court has discretion to order that X's interest should be impounded to indemnify T. If the order

---

3 Under the procedure laid down in the Insolvency Act 1986.
4 *Re Freeston's Charity* [1979] 1 All ER 51, [1978] 1 WLR 741.
5 [1961] 3 All ER 713, [1962] 1 WLR 86.
6 *Strange v Fooks* (1863) 4 Giff 408 at 413.
7 *Cockerell v Cholmeley* (1830) 1 Russ & M 418.
8 *Re Pauling's Settlement*, ante; *Holder v Holder* [1968] Ch 353; (M & B).
9 Replacing and enlarging the former jurisdiction under the Trustee Act 1893, s 45.

is made the result will be that X loses £1,000[10], the loss to Y is made good, and T pays no damages. If the loss to the fund was greater than X's interest, T would be liable for the difference. If, after the breach, X (perhaps fearing the worst) assigned his equitable interest to Z, an order of the court under s 62 impounding X's interest would take priority over the right of Z[11].

In exercising its discretion under s 62 the court will make an order under the section only if it is satisfied that, even if the beneficiary did not know that what he had requested, instigated or consented to in writing amounted to a breach, he was nevertheless fully aware of the circumstances constituting the breach.

Distinct from, and in addition to, the jurisdiction conferred on the court by s 62, the court has an inherent jurisdiction to order that a beneficiary's interest should be impounded by way of indemnity to a trustee where it finds that the beneficiary either requested or instigated the breach. The court may also so order where it finds that a beneficiary consented to the breach and derived personal gain from it, though the amount ordered to be impounded will be limited to the amount of the gain[12]. It will be seen that the inherent jurisdiction is only likely to be called in aid where the beneficiary concurred in the breach orally since here s 62 would not apply.

5 CONFIRMATION OR RELEASE

If a trustee commits a breach of trust and the beneficiaries then either confirm his action, or release him from liability, the trustee is protected against any subsequent action brought in respect of the breach. For the defence to avail, the trustee must show that the beneficiaries were *sui juris* and were in possession of the facts[13].

6 LIMITATION ACT 1980

If a trustee commits a breach of trust and no proceedings are brought against him, then after the lapse of a certain period of time, an action may become statute barred under the Limitation Act 1980[14]. Under the Act the general rule is that a beneficiary has six years from the date when the breach was committed in which to bring his action. The following matters call for attention.

1. The Act applies to actions for breach of trust brought not only against express trustees, but also against implied and constructive trustees[15].

2. Even if the beneficiary was unaware of the breach, in general the six-year period begins to run nonetheless[16].

---

10 Or what ever part the court orders.
11 *Bolton v Curre* [1895] 1 Ch 544.
12 *Chillingworth v Chambers* [1896] 1 Ch 685.
13 *Burrows v Walls* (1855) 5 De GM & G 233.
14 Section 21, replacing and varying Trustee Act 1888, s 8. Previously an action against an express trustee was not barred merely by lapse of time.
15 Section 38(1).
16 *Re Somerset* [1894] 1 Ch 231.

3. If the beneficiary was under a disability at the date of the breach, the six-year period does not begin until the disability ends[17].

4. If the beneficiary's interest was reversionary at the time of the breach, the period does not begin until his interest falls into possession[18].

5. If the breach of trust was fraudulent and the trustee was a party, or was privy, to the fraud or if the action is against defendants who claim through a fraudulent trustee[19], then no statutory period of limitation applies[20], and an action may thus be brought at any time until the trustee has died and his estate wound up. Nor does any statutory period apply with reference to an action brought by a beneficiary against a trustee in connection with a purchase by a trustee of trust property or of an equitable interest under the trust[1].

6. If the action is brought, not against the trustee personally, but is an action in rem brought to recover trust property 'or the proceeds thereof in the possession of the trustee, or previously received by the trustee and converted[2] to his use[3]', then no period of limitation applies and trustees and those who have received trust property from them (other than bona fide purchasers) will remain liable to the beneficiaries indefinitely[4].

7. The provision[5] that a beneficiary must bring proceedings against trustees within six years has no application to an action brought by the Attorney General to enforce a charitable trust (for there is not, in any meaningful sense, any beneficiary in whom property might vest who can bring an action in relation to the trust)[6]. If a beneficiary has a claim against a trustee in respect of which time has begun to run, and the trust then does some act that amounts to fraudulent concealment of the beneficiary's claim, that act does not start time running afresh.[7]

GENERAL

'INDEMNITY'

It will be noted that the word 'indemnity' may be used with reference to:

1. the right of one trustee, who has been found liable in an action for breach of trust, to recover from a co-trustee the damages he has had to pay (eg, where the co-trustee is solicitor to the trust)[8];

---

17 Section 28.
18 Section 21(3). And see *Re Pauling's Settlement Trusts* [1964] Ch 303, [1963] 3 All ER 1, CA; and p 351 post.
19 Section 32. *GL Baker Ltd v Medway Building and Supplies Ltd* [1958] 3 All ER 540, [1958] 1 WLR 1216.
20 Section 21(1).
 1 *Tito v Waddell (No 2); Tito v A-G* [1977] Ch 106, [1977] 3 All ER 129.
 2 Section 21(1). *Re Howlett, Howlett v Howlett* [1949] Ch 767, [1949] 2 All ER 490.
 3 See *Re Sharp* [1906] 1 Ch 793.
 4 For an argument that the passage of time should in certain circumstances be a defence, see [1989] CLJ 472 (H. M. McLean).
 5 Under s 21(3).
 6 *A-G v Cocke* [1988] Ch 414, [1988] 2 All ER 391; [1988] Conv 292.
 7 *Tito v Waddell (No 2)*, ante.
 8 See p 366, ante.

2. the right of a trustee to have the interest of a beneficiary who has, eg, instigated a breach of trust, impounded[9];

3. the right of a trustee to have the interest of a co-trustee, who is also a beneficiary, impounded[10];

4. the right of a trustee to recover out of pocket expenses from the trust fund[11].

MORE THAN ONE DEFENCE

Where an action is brought against a trustee by several beneficiaries, different defences may be available against each one; thus the trustee may plead that beneficiary A acquiesced in the breach; that B had given a release, that C's action was statute barred, that D had instigated the breach and should have his beneficial interest impounded by way of indemnity. If there is a fifth beneficiary against whom the trustee has no defence, then the trustee will be liable to that beneficiary, but his liability will be limited to the loss caused to that one beneficiary. A useful illustration of a case in which a variety of defences were pleaded is provided by *Re Pauling's Settlement Trust*[12]. As mentioned in an earlier chapter[13] the case also provides a good illustration of the improper exercise of a trustee's powers of advancement. In this case income from a trust fund was held on trust, under a settlement made in 1919, for a mother for life with remainder to her children or remoter issue. There were three sons of the marriage, F, G and A; and one daughter. By clause 11 of the settlement, C & Co, a bank, who were the trustees, were empowered with the written consent of the mother to raise any part 'not exceeding in the whole one half ... share of any child ... and to pay the same to him or her for his or her absolute use or pay or apply the same for his or her advancement or otherwise for his or her benefit in such manner as the trustees shall think fit'. After the war of 1939–45, the family lived above their means, and the father was always in need of money. In 1948 the father was seeking a means of obtaining a house in the Isle of Man, and counsel advised him that advances could be made to F and G, who could then if they wished settle the property purchased on the mother for life and on themselves after her death. F and G were then over 21. The bank advanced £8,450 ('advance A'), the price of the house, to F and G on a written request from the mother and with the written authority of F and G, who chose not to be separately advised. Contrary to the legal advice previously given, and without the consent of F and G, but with the knowledge of the bank, the house purchased was conveyed to the father and the mother absolutely. It was subsequently mortgaged by the father for £5,000 and ultimately was sold for less than that sum, so that the sons lost the whole of the £8,450. On the advice of the bank's solicitor, a sum of £1,000 was advanced ('advance B'), in respect of F's and G's shares, with their assent, for the purchase of furniture. This was credited to the mother's account with the bank. At that time the bank did not know that the house would not be settled. Subsequently £2,600 was advanced

9   See p 367, ante.
10   See p 373, ante.
11   See p 257, ante.
12   [1964] Ch 303, [1963] 3 All ER 1; (M & B).
13   Chap 17.

('advance C') to F and G and applied in paying off a loan which the bank as trustees of another settlement had advanced to the mother, the two sons being assigned insurance policies on the mother's life, these policies having a surrender value of £650. The sons had separate advice, but the transaction as carried out was not as originally advised, the difference being to the sons' disadvantage. In 1949, at the father's instance, the bank advanced to F and G £2,000 ('advance D'), which was paid to the mother's account; this was done with the written consent of the sons, stating that they appreciated that the money was being used for improvements to the property in the Isle of Man belonging to the mother. The sons had no separate advice.

At that time G was 23; F was 28 but mentally ill (though the bank did not know this) and was living with his grandmother. Subsequently sums amounting to £3,360 ('advance E') were advanced by the bank in respect of the daughter's share, nominally for furnishing a house which had been bought for the family in Chelsea, but in fact the money was spent on the property in the Isle of Man or was applied to reduce the mother's overdraft. The daughter, who was under 21, requested that the advances should be made, well knowing that only £300 was being used for furniture. She conceded that the £300 was not recoverable by her. Later, a total of £6,500 ('advance F') was advanced by the bank to the youngest son, A, and was paid into his mother's account. A was then just 21. He consented to this step, but had no proper separate advice. In 1958 the four children brought an action against the bank for breach of trust, each suing to recover advances purported to have been made to him or her for his or her benefit. In addition to pleading by way of defence the consent of beneficiaries, the bank pleaded the Limitation Act 1939, and the defences of laches[14] and acquiescence, and claimed relief under s 61 of the Trustee Act 1925. The Court of Appeal held as follows.

(1) The bank's liability was to be determined according to the following principles. (a) The power under clause 11 to raise a part of the share of a child and to pay it to the child 'for his or her absolute use' could only be exercised for the benefit of the child to be advanced, viz if there were a good reason for the advance and if it would be beneficial to the child. (b) When making an advance for a particular stated purpose, the bank could properly pay it to the child advanced if the bank reasonably thought that the child could be trusted to carry out the prescribed purpose, but that the bank could not properly leave the child entirely free, legally and morally, to apply the sum for that purpose or to spend it in any way that he or she chose, without any responsibility on their part to inquire as to its application. (c) If trust money were advanced for an express purpose, the child advanced was under a duty to carry out the purpose and could not properly apply it to another purpose, and, if any misapplication came to the bank's notice, they could not safely make further advances for a particular purpose without making sure that the money was applied for that purpose. (d) A trustee who carried out a transaction in breach of trust with the beneficiary's apparent consent might nonetheless be liable if the trustee knew or ought to have known that the beneficiary was acting under the undue influence of another, or might be presumed to have been so acting. (e) For the purpose of (d) above, the presumption of undue influence of a parent over his child endures for a short time after the child has attained 21, the duration being in each case a question

---

14 The equitable principle that undue delay disentitles a plaintiff to a remedy.

of fact. (f) Where a bank undertook to act as a paid trustee, and placed itself in a position where its duty as trustee conflicted with its interest as banker, the court should be very slow to grant relief under s 61 of the Trustee Act 1925.

(2) The bank were in breach of trust in making all the advances. Relief under s 61 of the Trustee Act 1925 was granted in respect of advance C above. The consent of the beneficiaries afforded a defence in the case of advance D. The bank was liable in the cases of advances A, B, E and F.

(3) The Limitation Act 1939 did not afford a defence because the plaintiffs' interest was a future interest within the proviso to s 19(2) and did not fall into possession when an invalid advance was made; accordingly the plaintiffs' rights were preserved by the proviso to s 19(2).

(4) In view of the express statutory provision of a period of limitation for the plaintiffs' claim there was no room for the equitable doctrine of laches. (The equitable doctrine, from which comes the maxim 'delay defeats equity', that if a plaintiff delays for an unreasonable length of time in bringing his action, a court of equity will refuse him a remedy.)

(5) Having regard to the many matters to be explored before instituting an action, the four years that had elapsed between the plaintiffs' discovery of what their rights were and the issue of the writ did not establish the defence of acquiescence on their part.

EXEMPTION CLAUSES

It is the practice for wills and settlements drafted by professional advisers to contain a clause exempting the trustees from liability for breach of trust, the protection extending well beyond that afforded by statute, under s 30(1) or s 61 of the Trustee Act 1925. To what extent can trustees by this means validly be exempted from the duties imposed on them by law? In a valuable examination of this question the following conclusions were drawn.[15]

(1) It is unclear whether section 30(1) of the Trustee Act 1925 goes so far as to protect a trustee against liability for want of ordinary prudence: it does if *Re Vickery* is correct.

(2) It is not free from doubt whether an exemption clause may confer protection greater than that contained in section 30.

(3) It is clear that neither liability for fraud or intentional wrongdoing nor duties leading to such liability can be validly excluded, nor powers to commit acts otherwise giving rise to such liability validly included.

(4) It is very likely that neither liability for gross negligence nor duties leading to such liability can be validly excluded, nor powers to commit acts otherwise giving rise to such liability validly included (Scots law and American law are clear on this point, and may even go further).

(5) It is arguable that any otherwise effective exemption clause is, in cases of

---

15   *The Efficacy of Trustee Exemption Clauses in English Law*, P. Matthews [1989] Conv 42.

professional trustees appointed by the settlor, subject to the provisions of the Unfair Contract Terms Act 1977, and in particular to the test of 'reasonableness'.

(6) It will not be easy for a professional trustee to demonstrate the 'reasonableness' of his exemption clause, should he be called upon to do so.

(7) An otherwise enforceable exemption clause may still fail to have effect, if imposed in breach of fiduciary duty or through undue influence.

(8) In any event such exemption clauses are always construed strictly against trustees.

Chapter 24

Constructive trusts[1]

We have seen[2] that a trust may be created by the express intention of a settlor and in Chapter 3 we considered the conditions which must be satisfied for an express trust to come into existence. We have seen also that in some circumstances equity infers that a person intended that a trust should come into existence and in Chapter 8 we considered when such implied trusts arose. We know too from the brief mention in Chapter 1 and from various references in later chapters that in some circumstances a person may find himself required to hold property as trustee: where, in order to achieve the ends of equity, the law constructs a trust where none existed before, no intention, express or implied, having been indicated by a settlor. In this chapter we shall consider certain situations in which constructive trusts have arisen. Then we shall explore the nature of a constructive trust in English law.

1 WRONGFUL TRANSFER OF TRUST PROPERTY

By way of introduction to trusts under this head it is necessary to explain that the term constructive trust can be used in two ways.

The constructive trust—actions in rem

Suppose that a trustee, in breach of trust, conveys the legal title to property to a purchaser. The purchaser pays for the property. But his solicitor had failed to make the enquiries that should have been made and so had not discovered that the property was held on trust, and that the transfer was in breach of the terms of the trust. Since the purchaser, although a purchaser of the legal estate, and for value, is fixed with constructive notice of the trust (having imputed notice—ie notice imputed to him of what his solicitor should have discovered) he does not qualify as a bona fide purchaser of the legal estate without notice and so takes the property subject to the trust. The result is that the purchaser holds the legal estate in the property on trust for the beneficial interests under the trust. The beneficiaries are entitled to say '*That* property is *ours*. You hold it for us.' In Chapter 22 we learned that we can express this by saying that the beneficiaries have an action *in rem* against the property. Since the purchaser holds the property on trust, he must hold it under some kind of trust. Since the trust is not an express or an implied trust

1 A. J. Oakley, *Constructive Trusts.*
2 See Chap 2.

but one imposed by law (equity requiring the purchaser to hold the property for the beneficiaries), it is consistent with reason to consider that the purchaser holds it under a constructive trust.

The constructive trust—actions *in personam*

The second meaning of the term is one that arises in connection with providing redress against fraud or other forms of unconscionable conduct. Where a person becomes a constructive trustee in this way, he becomes personally liable to make good any loss (for example in the event of the trust property having been dissipated), or to hand over to the trust some profit that he has improperly obtained. Here the action that lies against the constructive trustee is one *in personam*. It is in this sense that the term constructive trustee will be used hereafter in this chapter.

It would be understandable if, when reading Chapter 22, on the remedies of beneficiaries, the impression was gained that what a beneficiary was usually most interested in obtaining was the right to trace the trust property—that what he wanted most was an action in rem. And so, in certain circumstances, he might. In particular, he would want a right to trace the trust property where the person holding it was bankrupt, with creditors at his door wanting everything they could lay their hands on for the satisfaction of their debts. As we know from Chapter 22, where an action in rem lies, the beneficiary takes the property concerned to the exclusion of the creditors.

But if the property is not traceable, then it is in the beneficiary's interests that he should have an action in personam, against the defendant personally. If the holder was not bankrupt, the beneficiary would recover the amount of his loss. If the holder was bankrupt, the beneficiary would (assuming that the defendant was not penniless) at least get something, ie in his claim pari passu with the creditors.

So which remedy he will seek, one in rem or one in personam, will depend on the circumstances.

The defendant

Now consider matters from the point of view of the defendant in an action by a beneficiary. If an award in rem is made against him this will mean that the trust property is still in an identifiable form in his hands. If he had given no consideration for the property—if he was a volunteer—then on returning the property to the original trustee (or to the beneficiary) he would (if we disregard here the costs of the action) be no worse off in pecuniary terms than at the outset. If he had given consideration—if he was a purchaser for value—he would be able to recover what he had paid for the property from the trustee, on the ground of failure of consideration. So here too he would be restored to his original position.

But suppose that the defendant against whom a claim is made has disposed of the property—given it away or, if it is money, spent it. Imagine his consternation if in these circumstances he finds that an action in personam lies against him—that he has to find the value of the trust property out of his own pocket. 'This is terrible!' he will exclaim. 'To find the money I shall have to sell my house. My family will be homeless. I appreciate that the beneficiary has suffered loss. But does the fact that he has suffered loss automatically entail that I should be ruined?'

What answer would the reader give? One answer might be to rely on the most fundamental principle of English property law: the doctrine of notice under the bona fide purchaser rule. If we apply this rule the conclusion we reach is that if the purchaser is fixed with notice (actual or constructive, the latter including imputed notice) that the transfer was in breach of trust he will be liable to make good the loss, the possibility of the purchaser's ruin in having so to do being irrelevant. A certain unease, though, might be felt at such a finding. Surely, it might be thought, there is more to the matter than the rigid application of what in essence is a conveyancing rule?

The point arose in 1984 in *Re Montagu's Settlement Trusts*[3]. Under a family trust certain furniture, pictures and other chattels were held on trust for the ninth Duke of Manchester with the remainder to his successor to the title. In 1923 there was a re-settlement of the property under the trust. By clause 14 of the re-settlement the future tenth Duke of Manchester assigned his interest in remainder to trustees who were directed, after the death of the ninth Duke or, if and so far as practicable and convenient, during his lifetime, to select and make an inventory of such of the chattels as the trustees might consider suitable for inclusion in the settlement (ie so that these would pass to future holders of the title) and to hold the remainder on trust for the tenth Duke absolutely. The trustees made no inventory. The ninth Duke died in 1947. In 1948 the trustees released the chattels to the tenth Duke who later disposed of a number of items. He died in 1977. The eleventh Duke sought a declaration that the tenth Duke had become a constructive trustee of the chattels that he had disposed of (with the result, if the declaration was granted, that his estate would be liable to make good the loss).

Since the property was no longer traceable in the hands of the defendant estate, the remedy sought was one in personam, not in rem. In reaching a conclusion the court, the Vice-Chancellor, Sir Robert Megarry, considered whether the tenth Duke had had notice of the breach of trust—viz the transfer to him of the chattels by the trustees without reserving, in the inventory they were required to draw up, chattels to be maintained within the family settlement. The tenth Duke's solicitor had known at an earlier stage of the effect of clause 14 of the re-settlement of 1923. But in November 1948 they had written to the Duke informing him that he was free to sell the items that had been released to him.

If the claim had been in rem the outcome would have depended on whether the tenth Duke could have been shown to have been a bona fide purchaser of the legal estate without notice, actual or constructive. Clearly, he could not be shown to have been such a purchaser. His solicitors had had knowledge of clause 14, and this knowledge was to be imputed to the Duke, thus fixing him with constructive notice. What the court had to decide, however, was whether the rules that governed actions in rem (ie the doctrine of notice under the bona fide purchaser rules—rules to which 'centuries of equity jurisprudence have attached a detailed and technical meaning[4]'—applied with equal rigidity to an action in personam, so as to make the tenth Duke (ie his estate) liable for the loss to the trust. As Sir Robert, in the course of his judgment expressed the matter—'The core of the question ... is what suffices

---

3 [1987] Ch 264, [1987] 2 WLR 1192.
4 At p 1196.

to constitute a recipient of trust property a constructive trustee of it. I can leave on one side the equitable doctrine of tracing: if the recipient of trust property still has the property or its traceable proceeds in his possession, he is liable to restore it unless he is a purchaser without notice. But liability as a constructive trustee is wider, and does not depend upon the recipient still having the property or its traceable proceeds. Does it suffice if the recipient had "notice" that the property he was receiving was trust property, or must he have not merely notice of this, but knowledge, or "cognizance," as it has been put?'[5]

The court held that the latter was correct. For a person to be fixed with liability as a constructive trustee it was necessary to show more than that he had notice in the technical, conveyancing sense. To be fixed with liability as constructive trustee the defendant had to be shown to have had *knowledge*, at the time of the transfer, of the breach of trust. '... the fundamental question is whether the conscience of the recipient is bound in such a way as to justify equity in imposing a trust upon him[6].' 'The cold calculus of constructive and imputed notice does not seem to me to be an appropriate instrument for deciding whether a man's conscience is sufficiently affected for it to be right to bind him by the obligations of a constructive trustee ...'[7] What mattered was 'whether or not the Duke's conscience was affected in such a way as to require him to hold any or all of the chattels that he received on a constructive trust.[8]'

On the facts the court found that there was 'no suggestion that anyone concerned in the matter was dishonest. There was a muddle, but however careless it was, it was an honest muddle[9].' The letter to the Duke from his solicitors of 15 November 1948 was 'perfectly capable of conveying to him that ... he could have all the chattels, and I think that it did convey this to him. Furthermore, everyone concerned acted at the time as if that were the position[10].' So the Duke was not at any relevant time conscious of the fact that he was not entitled to receive the chattels and deal with them as beneficial owner. Thus the Duke had not been fixed with liability as a constructive trustee and the claim against his estate failed.

Summary

It was common ground between the parties, Sir Robert said, 'that it was impossible to contend that the law to be found in the cases was clear and not in something of a muddle[11].' In order to 'find a path through the wood'[12] he summarised his conclusions[13].

'(1) The equitable doctrine of tracing [in an action in rem] and the imposition of a constructive trust [in an action in personam] by reason of the knowing receipt of trust property are governed by different rules and must be kept

5   Ibid.
6   At p 1197.
7   At p 1198.
8   Ibid.
9   At p 1195.
10 At p 1202.
11 At p 1196.
12 At p 1204.
13 Ibid.

distinct. Tracing is primarily a means of determining the rights of property, whereas the imposition of a constructive trust creates personal obligations that go beyond mere property rights.

'(2) In considering whether a constructive trust has arisen in a case of the knowing receipt of trust property, the basic question is whether the conscience of the recipient is sufficiently affected to justify the imposition of such a trust.

'(3) Whether a constructive trust arises in such a case primarily depends on the knowledge of the recipient, and not on notice to him; and for clarity it is desirable to use the "knowledge" and avoid the word "notice" in such cases.

'(4) For this purpose, knowledge is not confined to actual knowledge, but includes ... actual knowledge that would have been acquired but for shutting one's eyes to the obvious, or wilfully and recklessly failing to make such inquiries as a reasonable and honest man would make; for in such cases there is a want of probity which justifies imposing a constructive trust.

'(5) Whether knowledge [that takes the form of knowledge of circumstances that would indicate the facts to an honest and reasonable man, or which would put an honest and reasonable man on inquiry] suffices for this purpose is at best doubtful; in my view it does not, for I cannot see that the carelessness involved will normally amount to a want of probity.

'(6) For these purposes, a person is not to be taken to have knowledge of a fact that he once knew but has genuinely forgotten: the test (or a test) is whether the knowledge continues to operate on that person's mind at the time in question.'

This is a valuable and welcome summary. From it we conclude that where the recipient of trust property is innocent of any moral guilt, where he is an innocent volunteer, no action in personam lies against him: he is not fixed with the liability of a constructive trustee. There is, though, more to be said.

Receipt of property from an executor

In *Re Diplock*[14] property was transferred to an innocent volunteer—the charity that received the legacy in ignorance of the fact that the bequest was void on the ground that the gift was not exclusively charitable. Notwithstanding the innocence of the transferee (in the language of *Re Montagu's Settlement Trusts*[15], that the recipient had no knowledge of the breach of trust) the House of Lords held that an action in personam lay against the charity with regard to any property that was no longer traceable. The fiduciary transferor concerned was an executor, and in his judgment Lord Simonds indicated that the finding was limited to this circumstance, and that no corresponding right of action was to be regarded as existing where the fiduciary transferor was a trustee.

There is therefore no inconsistency in law between the decision in *Re Diplock* and *Re Montagu*. Whether there is, with regard to justice and common sense, inconsistency between the two decisions is a matter of opinion. It could, on the one hand, be contended that if a recipient has no knowledge of the breach, if he is wholly innocent, it is anomalous that he should be bound in an action in personam if he receives property from an

14   [1948] Ch 465, [1948] 2 All ER 318; (M & B); see p 360, supra.
15   [1987] Ch 264, [1987] 2 WLR 1192.

executor, but not so bound if he receives property from a trustee. Against this view it could be argued that a person who receives property from an executor should be expected to have regard to the need to satisfy himself that the terms of the bequest are valid; that the larger the bequest the greater the care that should be taken in this respect; that the recipient of a bequest of a size that would make it worthwhile the residuary estate contesting the validity of the gift would be likely to be professionally advised; and that the professional adviser of such a recipient could be expected to advise the recipient that, if he intends to dissipate the bequest, he should consider the advisability of taking out insurance against the eventuality of the gift being overturned and an action in personam lying against him.

2 WRONGFUL ACTS BY A STRANGER WHO HOLDS TRUST PROPERTY: CASES OF 'KNOWING DEALING'[16]

If trust property is transferred to an agent for the trustees, for example to a solicitor, or to a bank, then, since trustees are entitled to employ agents, there is nothing improper about such a transfer. If a breach of trust then occurs the beneficiaries become entitled to bring an action to recover the loss to the trust. Against whom does their action lie? If the breach was committed by the trustees, then it is they who are liable. In certain circumstances, however, an agent of the trust may find himself fixed with liability as a constructive trustee and thus liable for any loss[17]. He will place himself in this position if the property that he has received is trust property and he deals with the property, or enables the property to be dealt with, or fails to take adequate steps to prevent the property being dealt with[18], in a manner inconsistent with the trust. For example, in *Soar v Ashwell*[19] a trust fund was entrusted by trustees to a solicitor who dealt with the fund without reference to the trustees, investing the money in his own name and later distributing one half to the beneficiaries entitled and retaining the other half in his own hands. It was held that since he had knowledge that the fund was trust property and since, by assuming to act, and by acting, as a trustee, he had acted inconsistently with the trust, he was liable to account as a constructive trustee to the beneficiaries. In *Lee v Sankey*[20] money from the sale of trust property was paid to a firm of solicitors as agents of G and L, the two trustees of a will. The solicitors should have handed the money to both trustees, and obtained a receipt signed by both. Without authority, they handed the money to G, and obtained a receipt from him alone. G died insolvent. The beneficiaries brought an action against the solicitors. It was held that they were liable to make good the loss: 'It is ... established that a person who

16 Per Sir Robert Megarry V-C, *Re Montagu's Settlement Trusts*, supra, at p 1196.
17 A solicitor acting honestly in his capacity as a solicitor for his client is in no different position from any other agent acting for his principal and is not to be imputed with knowledge of a trust merely because, in acting for his client, he knew that it was claimed against his client that there was a trust, and such knowledge cannot be notice of a trust or notice of misapplication of trust funds. *Carl-Zeiss-Stiftung v Herbert Smith & Co (a firm) (No 2)* [1969] 2 Ch 276, [1969] 2 All ER 367.
18 *Rowlandson v National Westminster Bank Ltd* [1978] 3 All ER 370, [1978] 1 WLR 798; [1979] Conv 222.
19 [1893] 2 QB 390.
20 (1872) LR 15 Eq 204.

receives[1] into his hands trust moneys, and who deals with them in a manner inconsistent with the performance of trusts of which he is cognisant, is personally liable for the consequences which may ensue upon his so dealing[2].'

In *Rowlandson v National Westminster Bank Ltd*[3], in 1967, a grandmother deposited four cheques for £500 each at a branch of the defendant bank in favour of four of her grandchildren, the plaintiffs in the action. No paying in slip or other documents were made out at that time. No accounts at that branch existed for the grandmother or the four plaintiffs. A trust account, no 608, was opened by an official of the bank in the names of the plaintiffs' two uncles, A and G, who had accounts at the branch, and the four cheques were paid into this account. The grandmother died later in the year. There was another account at the branch, no 357, which was in A's name, but which was for the benefit of his two children. A took a cheque, no 997, from a cheque book issued by the bank for drawing on account no 357, altered '357' to '608' and drew £1,529 6s from the latter account to pay a firm of stockbrokers for certain shares. Shortly afterwards the balance in account no 608 was transferred to account no 357. A died in 1970. None of the £2,000 reached the plaintiffs and in 1974 they issued a writ seeking to recover the £2,000, and interest, from the bank. It was held that, since the money had been in a trust account, the bank was in a fiduciary position in relation to the beneficiaries. The circumstances attending the withdrawal of cheque no 997 should have put a reasonable banker on his enquiry, and since the bank had failed to prevent, or question, the withdrawal, it was liable to make good the £2,000, with interest at the rate paid by the bank on its deposit accounts.

The limits of this principle must be noted. If an agent receives property with the knowledge that it is trust property, but he acts honestly and does not intermeddle in the trust by doing acts characteristic of a trustee, confining himself solely to acts within his duties as an agent, then he will not be liable for any loss that has occurred[4]. For example, in *Re Bell's Indenture*[5] it was held that where a solicitor to a trust assisted in a breach of trust (the sale of certain land) and the trust money passed through his firm's client's account, whilst the solicitor was liable as a constructive trustee, his partner, who had no knowledge of the breach of trust, was not fixed with liability as a constructive trustee[6].

3   WRONGFUL ASSISTANCE BY A STRANGER WHO HOLDS NO TRUST PROPERTY[7]: CASES OF 'KNOWING ASSISTANCE'[8]

Even though an agent of a trustee does not himself hold any trust property he may nonetheless incur liability as a constructive trustee if, with knowledge

---

1   The wrongful act of one partner, if he acted within the scope of his authority as a partner, may implicate all the members of the firm. *Blyth v Fladgate* [1891] 1 Ch 337.
2   *Lee v Sankey* (1872) LR 15 Eq 204. Per Sir James Bacon at 211.
3   [1978] 3 All ER 370, [1978] 1 WLR 798.
4   *Barnes v Addy* (1874) 9 Ch App 244; *Mara v Browne* [1896] 1 Ch 199; *Williams-Ashman v Price and Williams* [1942] Ch 219, [1942] 1 All ER 310; *Competitive Insurance Co Ltd v Davies Investments Ltd* [1975] 3 All ER 254, [1975] 1 WLR 1240.
5   [1980] 3 All ER 425, [1980] 1 WLR 1217; (M & B).
6   Or under ss 10 and 11 of the Partnership Act 1890.
7   (1989) 9 OJLS 260 (P. L. Loughlan), [1989] Conv 328 (M. Halliwell).
8   Per Sir Robert Megarry, V-C, *Re Montagu's Settlement*, supra, at p 1196.

of what is afoot (or failing to make enquires that, in the circumstances, he should have made as to what is afoot) he assists in a dishonest and fraudulent design carried out by a trustee.[9] For example, in *Karak Rubber Co Ltd v Burden*[10], K Ltd was a dormant rubber company with a balance of over £115,000 at the C Bank. B took over the company by acquiring a majority shareholding. He arranged for the shares he had obtained to be paid for by a series of transactions carried out through an account at a branch of the X Bank, the net result of which was that the company's own money was used (contrary to the Companies Act 1948[11]) to purchase its own shares (ie from those who had assented to the take-over). Four months after the take-over the company's cash balance was £3 odd. An action was brought by the company and the Board of Trade against B and the branch manager of the X Bank, H, who had handled the matter, for replacement of the money illegally used for the purchase of the shares. B died, bankrupt, during the hearing. Was H (and through him, the X Bank) liable to make good the loss? It was held that B, as a director of K Ltd, was to be treated as a trustee of the money paid into the X Bank. H was to be treated as his agent. Although H had not acted dishonestly at any stage it was held that since he had had knowledge of facts which should have indicated to an honest and reasonable[12] banker the existence of a dishonest and fraudulent design, or that he ought to have made enquiries (which H had failed to make), he was to be treated as having constructive notice of what was being done. It was held that H was on this basis liable, as a constructive trustee, for the loss that had been incurred.

For a stranger to a trust to incur liability it is essential that he should have sufficient knowledge of the breach: the cases have been referred to as ones of 'knowing assistance'[13]. There has been discussion as to what constitutes sufficient knowledge in this context. For the court to require too detailed a knowledge, places the plaintiff at a disadvantage. But for the court to be satisfied with the haziest suspicion could ensnare third parties who were innocent of any moral guilt, and the court will therefore be cautious in imputing knowledge of fraudulent design. A bank is not expected to play the detective[14]. Mere suspicion would not place a duty on a bank to refuse to comply with instructions from a customer, and it is under no duty to make enquiries when these are unlikely to disclose what is going on[15].

Guidance on the matter of the nature of the knowledge required was provided at first instance in *Lipkin Gorman v Karpnale Ltd*[16] by Alliott J, 'the stranger to the trust must be proved subjectively to know of the fraudulent scheme of the trustee when rendering assistance, or to shut his eyes to the obvious, or to have wilfully and recklessly failed to make such enquiries as

---

9   See *Agip (Africa) Ltd v Jackson* [1991] Ch 547, [1991] 3 WLR 116, CA; (M & B).
10   [1972] 1 All ER 1210, [1972] 1 WLR 602; (M & B); following *Selangor United Rubber Estates Ltd v Cradock (No 3)* [1968] 2 All ER 1073, [1968] 1 WLR 1555.
11   Sections 27, 54, 66. *Trevor v Whitworth* (1887) 12 App Cas 409.
12   *Carl-Zeiss-Stiftung v Herbert Smith & Co (a firm) (No 2)* [1968] 2 All ER 1233.
13   See n 16, p 385.
14   *Baden, Delvaux and Lecuit v Société Générale pour Favoriser le Développement du Commerce de l'Industrie en France SA* [1983] BCLC 325; (M & B); All ER Review 1983, p 251 (P. J. Clarke).
15   Ibid.
16   [1987] 1 WLR 987.

a reasonable and honest man would make'. And in the Court of Appeal[17] it was held that, with regard to a bank's duty to a customer, a bank would be in breach of this duty where it knew of facts (note, *facts*) which would have led a reasonable and honest banker to consider that there was a serious or real possibility that the customer might be being defrauded by the drawing of a cheque. If an agent has no trust property vested in him, or placed under his control, and he is not guilty of any misconduct or lack of care then he will not be fixed with liability as a constructive trustee by virtue merely of his position as an agent[18].

4 FRAUD

If A, by some fraudulent or unconscionable act, acquires title to B's property, equity will require him to hold the property on a constructive trust for the person deprived. For example, in *Bannister v Bannister*[19], a woman, D, owned a cottage. She made an oral agreement to sell the cottage to P; D was to be allowed to continue to live in the cottage for as long as she wished; the price agreed was less than the full value of the property. The cottage was conveyed to P. In the conveyance there was no mention of D being allowed to live in the cottage. P later sought, relying on the absolute title vested in him by the conveyance, to evict D from the cottage. It was held that, since it was fraudulent of P, in all the circumstances, to attempt to rely on the absolute character of the conveyance, P held the property on a constructive trust to allow D to remain there as long as she wished. (P had argued that no trust of the land could have come into existence as s 53(1)(b) of the Law of Property Act 1925[20] had not been complied with. The court rejected this argument on the ground that the section could not be used so as to uphold a fraud. Further, since the trust which the court decided had come into existence was constructive, s 53(1)(b) was no bar to its existence[1]. The result was that P held the legal fee simple on a constructive trust[2] for D for an equitable determinable life interest in the land. It was of this latter interest which P, by his fraudulent, or at any rate unconscionable, conduct had attempted to deprive D[3].

5 PROFIT FROM A TRUST

We saw in Chapter 19 that the rule against a trustee making a profit from his trust has two aspects: the rule prohibits a trustee from making such a profit; and it provides that if any such profit is made, then the profit must

17 [1989] 1 WLR 1340, (1991) 107 LQR 521 (P. Watts); [1992] Conv 124 (M. Halliwell).
18 *Re Barney* [1892] 2 Ch 265; *Barnes v Addy* (1874) 9 Ch App 244.
19 [1948] 2 All ER 133.
20 See Chap 3.
 1 LPA 1925, s 53(2).
 2 For the difficulties arising from the fact that the land became subject to the Settled Land Act 1925, see A. J. Oakley, 'Has Constructive Trust become a general equitable remedy?' (1973) 26 CLP 17.
 3 There was a similar outcome in *Hodgson v Marks* [1971] Ch 892, [1970] 3 All ER 513 and in *Binions v Evans* [1972] Ch 359, [1972] 2 All ER 70.

be held for the trust, the trustee being made constructive trustee of the profit he has obtained. Thus, as we saw in that chapter, a bribe accepted by a trustee[4], income earned as a result of the exercise of a power attaching to the legal title[5], fees received by a director of a company who is appointed by his use of voting rights in shares held by him as a trustee[6], commission received by an employee for introducing business from a trust of which he is trustee[7], and a renewal of a lease, previously held for the trust, obtained by a trustee for his own benefit[8], are all examples of a profit which equity requires to be held on a constructive trust for the beneficiaries.

6 PROFIT BY A FIDUCIARY OTHER THAN A TRUSTEE: UNJUST ENRICHMENT

In Chapter 19, when dealing with the duty of a trustee not to profit from his trust, we saw that in *Boardman v Phipps*[9] a solicitor to a trust was required to hold certain profits he had obtained from the trust. The reason for the solicitor being required to hold the gain he had made as constructive trustee can be regarded as being based on an extension, to agents, of the rule against a trustee making a profit from his use of knowledge of the trust property. But the ground of the decision goes deeper than this, and is founded on the principle that equity will not allow any fiduciary to obtain an unjustified benefit from his position. Thus a director who concluded in his own name a profitable contract, knowing that he should have made it on behalf of his company[10] an employee who exploited a trade secret belonging to his employer[11], an agent who was commissioned to buy a house for his principal, and bought it for himself[12], a partner in a business who secretly renewed a lease of partnership premises for his own benefit[13], have all been required either to desist in their activity, or to hold the enrichment they have obtained for their principal. Similarly a purchaser (a property development company) who prior to a contract for the sale of land sought and obtained planning permission for development of the land in the vendor's name, purportedly acting as the vendor's agent, but without disclosing to the vendor what had been done, was required to account to the vendor for the profits ultimately received as a result of the successful planning application[14].

The principle that a fiduciary may not obtain unjustified benefit from his position may be regarded as resting, in turn, on the principle that equity will make a person who obtains unjust enrichment at another's expense disgorge his gain, by requiring him to hold it as constructive trustee. (Fraud, which, for convenience, we have treated as being under a distinct head, can be

---

4 *Sugden v Crossland* (1856) 3 Sm & G 192.
5 *Aberdeen Town Council v Aberdeen University* (1877) 2 App Cas 544.
6 *Re Francis* (1905) 74 LJ Ch 198.
7 *Williams v Barton* [1927] 2 Ch 9; (M & B).
8 *Keech v Sandford* (1726) Sel Cas Ch 61.
9 [1967] 2 AC 46, [1966] 3 All ER 721; (M & B).
10 *Cook v Deeks* [1916] 1 AC 554.
11 *Hivac Ltd v Park Royal Scientific Instruments Ltd* [1946] Ch 169, [1946] 1 All ER 350.
12 And then sold the house to the principal at a higher price than he had paid. *Regier v Campbell-Stuart* [1939] Ch 766, [1939] 3 All ER 235.
13 *Featherstonhaugh v Fenwick* (1810) 17 Ves 298. See Chap 18.
14 *English v Dedham Vale Properties Ltd* [1978] 1 All ER 382, [1978] 1 WLR 93.

regarded as constituting one example of a type of unjust enrichment for which equity will provide redress.)

7 VENDOR AND PURCHASER

If (i) V enters a contract to sell certain land to P; (ii) the contract is evidenced in writing as required by s 40 of the Law of Property Act 1925 (or is evidenced by a sufficient act of part performance); and (iii) P contracts to give consideration to V for the land, then, from the date of the contract until the conveyance by V of the legal estate to P, P holds an equitable title to the land, and V holds the legal estate on trust for him as constructive trustee[15]. But in this situation V is not in the full sense a trustee. For example, rents from the land between the contract and the conveyance go to V, not to P. But V is nevertheless a trustee to the extent that (a) he must not deal with the land inconsistently with P's interests[16], and must take reasonable care of the property[17] (b) P holds an equitable interest in the land (which, since 1925, is registrable as an estate contract); (c) as holder of the beneficial interest in the land, P bears the risk of damage to the land and is therefore responsible for insuring against the risk of damage, for example by fire.

The nature of a constructive trust

When a plaintiff seeks a decree that property is held on a constructive trust, or that a particular person is a constructive trustee, he is seeking a remedy[18] from the court. This being so, should a constructive trust be regarded not as a substantive institution—a thing with its own existence—but rather as a remedy granted by the court, just as an injunction is not an institution, but merely a remedy? This is how the constructive trust is regarded in Canada[19], and in some quarters in the United States: 'The subject of constructive trusts is a part of the law of restitution. The constructive trust is a remedial device that is employed to correct unjust enrichment. It has the effect of taking title to property from one person whose title unjustly enriches him, and transferring it to another person who has been unjustly deprived of it ... To correct the injustice, the court of equity declares that the unjustly enriched person shall be a constructive trustee for the benefit of the unjustly deprived person, and the court directs that legal title be transferred by the unjustly enriched person to the unjustly deprived person. The constructive trustee is not regarded as a fiduciary with respect to the constructive trust property; his only function is to act to place the title where it belongs. The equity court merely uses the trust analogy to achieve a restitutional result'[20]. This view of

---

15 *Lysaght v Edwards* (1876) 2 Ch D 499; *Walsh v Lonsdale* (1882) 21 Ch D 9.
16 *Abdulla v Shah* [1959] AC 124, [1959] 2 WLR 12.
17 *Phillips v Silvester* (1872) 8 Ch App 173.
18 An action for breach of trust is not a 'tort' within the meaning of Order 11, r 1(l)(f) of the Rules of the Supreme Court. *Metall und Rohstoff v Donaldson Lukin & Jenrette Inc* [1990] 1 QB 391, [1989] 3 All ER 14, CA.
19 [1991] Conv 125 (C. E. F. Rickett).
20 P. G. Haskell, *Preface to the Law of Trusts*, p 145.

the nature of a trust, which we shall refer to as the American view (but which is by no means held universally in the United States[1]) has been both supported[2] and opposed[3] in England.

It is true that a constructive trust can in many instances be explained in terms of the granting of a remedy. For example, instead of describing a vendor as a constructive trustee for the purchaser, we could say that equity gives the purchaser a remedy that will prevent the vendor from dealing with the property inconsistently with the purchaser's rights under the contract. Again, instead of saying that if a trustee makes a profit from the trust, he holds this on a constructive trust for the beneficiary, we could say that equity gives the beneficiary a remedy which takes the form of requiring the trustee to hand over the profit to the trust fund. Time and again we shall find that when the court makes a decree which declares that a constructive trust exists, the effect is no more than that one person is required to hand over some property to another. This being so, is the term 'constructive trust' no more than a phrase adopted by equity for want of a better, and having the disadvantage that it conceals rather than clarifies the nature of what is referred to?

Let us put the question another way. Suppose that A seeks to recover land from B. If A sues at common law and succeeds, he will obtain an order for possession. The court says in effect, 'The land is A's. B must hand over the land to A'. If A brings his action in equity and succeeds the court will in effect say 'B must hold the property on trust for A'. Was the reason for the adoption of this form of redress the influence of a structure of ideas evolved by equity over the centuries[4]? If this is so, are the Americans therefore in fact correct when they say that a constructive trust is merely a name for a particular restitutional remedy? Or are there grounds for supporting the view generally held in England, that a constructive trust is something which does have a substantive existence: that it is something which actually exists, as one form of trust[5]? If a constructive trust is to be viewed in the latter light, we

---

1   For example, in *Chase Manhattan Bank NA v Israel-British Bank (London) Ltd* [1980] 2 WLR 202; (M & B), Golding J held that, on the written and oral evidence of US law before the court, a defendant bank which had received property by a mistake was required, under the law of New York State, to hold the property as a constructive trustee by the application of 'a rule of substantive law' and not as 'the mere result of a remedial or procedural rule'; (at 218).
2   A constructive trust 'is an equitable remedy by which the court can enable an aggrieved party to obtain restitution'. Per Lord Denning MR *Hussey v Palmer* [1972] 3 All ER 744 at 747. D. W. M. Waters, *The Constructive Trust* (1964).
3   R. H. Maudsley, 'Proprietary remedies for the recovery of money' (1959) 75 LQR 234.
4   This is the view of Waters, op cit, p 39: 'The truth of the matter is that the constructive trust was coined as a term because Chancery was invited to adjudicate in disputes where the relationship of the parties was rooted in the common law, and upon which Chancery imposed the language of trust. The language of trust came naturally, moreover, when Chancery was invited to impose the rudiments of trust obligation upon persons who were not trustees by express or implied creation. But, ... there was never a theme behind the use of constructive trust by Chancery. It was never any more than a convenient and available language medium through which for the Chancery mind the obligations of parties might be expressed or determined. Whereas the divided jurisdictions of law and Equity gave rise to the ready use of trust language where common law language might equally well have served, the dominance of the trust in all Chancery thinking after the seventeenth century brought about the process of ready thinking by analogy. In short, a separated Court of Chancery gave us the term constructive trust, and the application of the term by analogy with the express trust was Chancery's practice from the beginning.'
5   See A. J. Oakley, *Constructive Trusts* (2nd edn).

would expect it to bear at least some, however remote, resemblance to a trust in a form which undoubtedly has a substantive existence, namely an express private trust.

So let us make a comparison between an express and a constructive trust.

1. In the case of an express trust the trustee normally has certain powers with regard to the trust property, eg the power to apply income for maintenance, and to advance capital. A constructive trustee is not generally regarded as having these powers.

2. In an express trust, the trustee has certain powers with regard to his trusteeship, eg to retire, to appoint fresh trustees. A constructive trustee does not appear to have these powers.

3. In an express trust, the trustee may have certain duties, eg to sell and convert the property, to apportion income, to invest the trust fund according to the terms of the trust instrument or under the Trustee Investments Act 1961. Generally, a constructive trustee is not regarded as having duties of this kind.

In the majority of instances, the only duty binding a constructive trustee will be to hand over the trust property—to a beneficiary or to the trustees of an express trust, or to a fund of which he is already an express trustee. Where he is under a duty to hand over to a beneficiary (including a principal to whom an agent is obliged to restore property) his duty is limited to that of a trustee under a bare trust, ie to hand over the trust property to the person entitled (under the rule in *Saunders v Vautier*[6]).

4. In an express trust, the lack of a trustee will not cause the trust to fail[7]. In the case of a constructive trust, unless there is a constructive trustee, no trust of this kind can exist.

5. In the case of an express trust, there is generally some clearly identified item of property which forms the corpus of the trust. In a constructive trust, on the other hand, there may not be any equivalent certainty of subject matter, and the property subject to the constructive trust may only become identifiable from the judgment of the court. (Indeed, where the trust is created in order to impose liability, it might seem that there is no trust property to be held on trust by a constructive trustee. For example in the *Karak Rubber*[8] case the defendant, H, was found to be liable both in tort and as a constructive trustee. But H at no stage held any trust property. This being so, of what was he constructive trustee? If the additional ground of liability is to have any meaning, he presumably became constructive trustee of the sum for which he was found liable, with the result that if he was bankrupt that sum would go to the plaintiff company and not to his creditors. Unless this was intended to be the effect of the decision it is submitted that no purpose was served by making H liable as a constructive trustee as well as in tort.)

6. An express trust is normally intended to have some continuing existence, even if it is of short duration. In the case of a vendor of land, the trust will endure for a certain period (between the contract and conveyance), but in most instances a constructive trust arises only in order to compel the trustee to take certain action—to hand over some property or to make good some

---

6 (1841) 4 Beav 115. See Chap 20.
7 See Chap 13.
8 [1972] 1 All ER 1210, [1972] 1 WLR 602; (M & B).

loss, and when this is done the trust ends. The trust is thus brought into the world with a view to its dying as soon as possible.

We could look at other attributes of an express trust and compare them with those of a constructive trust, but already it would appear that the resemblances between the two are so slender and the differences so great that we must feel driven to ask again, are the Americans not right? Is a constructive trust not more of a remedy than a substantive institution? It is possible that we might be driven to accept the American view were it not for the fact that we have so far failed to take into account one vital characteristic of any trust—the nature of trust property. Once property becomes subject to a trust its nature is changed: a transubstantiation occurs. (In the hands of the priest the bread may look the same but its essence is altered.)

Let us give some illustrations of this phenomenon. If T holds the legal title to various items of property, holding some beneficially and some absolutely, then (a) if T becomes bankrupt, the trust property will remain sacrosanct, and will be held by T's trustee in bankruptcy on trust for the beneficiaries, who will take priority over T's creditors; (b) if T mixes trust money with his own, and it becomes necessary to disentangle the account, the rule in *Hallett's Case*[9] not *Clayton's Case*[10] applies; (c) if the trust property rises in value, the increase belongs to the trust, not to T. Further, and of special significance here, trust property, if it continues in an indentifiable form, retains its character as trust property after it has passed into the hands of a person who receives it in breach of trust. Only if trust property passes into the hands of a bona fide purchaser for value without notice, will it cease to bear the special hallmark of trust property.

It is because the consequences of the property being trust property are the same whether the property is held under an express or a constructive trust that we are, it is submitted, correct to regard a constructive trust as a form of *trust*, not merely a form of remedy[11].

It is true that the notion that a constructive trust is a substantive institution can become inter-mixed with the notion that it is merely a remedy[12]: for example, we can say that if a constructive trust is declared to exist, the plaintiff obtains a remedy; and conversely, that it is because the plaintiff ought to have a remedy that the court decrees that a constructive trust exists. But nonetheless it is submitted that the two notions are distinct: the granting of the remedy (the declaration that a constructive trust exists) is no more than a recognition of an existing state of affairs—the existence of the trust. Thus if T transfers trust property to S who takes with notice, S holds under a constructive trust, a trust whose existence started at the moment of the transfer. The trust exists irrespective of whether or not a beneficiary ever seeks a remedy from the court requiring S to perform his duty, eg to hand the property to him (or to T, or to a fresh trustee); to make good any loss; or to disgorge any gain. (Those who contend that a constructive trust is in

---

9 (1880) 13 Ch D 696. See Chap 21; (M & B).
10 (1816) 1 Mer 572. See Chap 21.
11 See *Re Sharpe (A bankrupt)* [1980] 1 All ER 198, [1980] 1 WLR 219.
12 For the function of the constructive trust as a remedy, and the basis on which such a trust should exist, see P. T. Evans *The Fall and Rise of the Remedial Constructive Trust*, [1989] Conv 418.

essence a remedy would consider such a view as far fetched. Unless a declaration is made, they would say, the beneficiary acquires nothing; the potential constructive trustee keeps what he has got, the notion that a constructive
trust exists irrespective of whether a remedy is granted being no more than
a myth with no legal meaning.

If a constructive trust is a substantive institution does it have any identifying characteristics? No satisfactory definition has yet been given and it
may be that we are confronted by no more than 'a pot pourri of uncertain
situations'[13] and that there is no 'golden thread'[14], linking the instances in
which a constructive trust has been found to arise[15]. But the fact that no
satisfactory definition of a thing has ever been given has never been a bar to
the recognition by the law that the thing concerned exists. (Throughout
English law, we find that if we ask 'What is X?' the court will reply 'You tell
us the facts and we will tell you whether X exists'.) At most, we can say that
there are certain situations in which a constructive trust can be expected
almost without question to arise. These are the constructive trusts which
arise out of an existing fiduciary relationship, as where there is an extension
of an existing trust to other property (eg to a profit made by a trustee) or
there is an extension of an existing trust to another person (eg to a purchaser
of trust property with notice of the trust or to an agent who acts inconsistently
with the trust). Outside this zone we enter an area where the incidence of
constructive trusts cannot be predicted with the same certainty. It is not a
matter of the categories of constructive trust not being closed. There are,
despite our attempt in this chapter to group the circumstances in which a
constructive trust arises under certain heads, no real *categories* of constructive
trust, unless (always an admission of defeat when seeking to categorise) we
add to any list a category marked 'Others'[16], to include any new circumstances
that occur in which a constructive trust is found to exist.

---

13 Waters, op cit, p 20.
14 A. J. Oakley, 'Has the constructive trust become a general equitable remedy?' (1973) 26
   CLP 17, 19.
15 But cf (1981) 97 LQR 51 (J. C. Shepherd).
16 It would be into such a category that we would have to place the constructive trust found
   to exist in *Barclays Bank plc v Willowbrook International* [1987] 1 FTLR 386, [1987] BCLC
   717n, CA (Debt used by a creditor as security for a loan from a third party. Monies paid
   by debtor to creditor in repayment of the loan held by the creditor on trust for the third
   party.)

Chapter 25

The relevance of the law of trusts at the present day

By way of conclusion to this book we shall set out some of the purposes served by trusts today, and some contributions made by the law of trusts to English law generally.

PENSION FUNDS

This century has seen a growing tendency for employers to provide retirement pensions for their employees and their dependants. Sometimes the fund from which pensions are paid comes from contributions paid by the employer alone; sometimes both employer and employee make contributions to the fund.

Pension funds are commonly vested in trustees on trust for the persons entitled under the scheme. There are two advantages in this arrangement. In the first place substantial tax reliefs[1] are obtainable in the sphere of capital gains tax where the scheme is approved by the Superannuation Funds Office of the Inland Revenue as an 'exempt approved scheme'. For such approval, the fund must be established under an irrevocable trust. Second, where the terms of the settlement (the constitution of the pension fund) ensures that the assets of the fund are kept distinct from those of, and in no circumstances are recoverable or disposable by, the employer, and the management of the fund is independent of the employer, then the fund is protected from being available for distribution among the employer's creditors in the event of the employer's bankruptcy. The events following the death of Robert Maxwell, chairman of Maxwell Communications, in 1991 demonstrated, however, that the assets of no trust fund are safe against the kind of theft[2] that was subsequently revealed in the case of the pension fund of the Mirror Group's employees[3].

UNIT TRUSTS

It has been possible since the last century for a person to invest his money among a wide range of companies by buying shares in an investment company, one which itself exists for the purpose of investing, and speculating, in the shares of other companies.

---

1 The total cost of such reliefs in 1991–2 amounted to £91 billion.
2 Approximately £4m was stolen.
3 See Report of the House of Commons Social Security Committee, March 1992, HC 61-II and the Preface to this book.

Another and in some respects simpler means of achieving the same purpose is for the investor to buy units in a unit trust. A unit trust, like an investment company, buys shares in various companies. The management of the unit trust rests with managers; the title to the shares is vested in trustees, who hold the shares on trust for the persons who have bought units. Unit holders are thus beneficiaries under the trust, the size of their interest corresponding to the size of their holding of units in the scheme.

TRADE UNION FUNDS

Under the Trade Union Act of 1871[4] the property of all unions which were registered under the Act was required to be vested in trustees. The property of unions which did not so register was commonly also vested in trustees. The Industrial Relations Act 1971 repealed the Act of 1871[5], provided that unions registered under the Act were to become corporate bodies, and that the property of such unions was to vest in them accordingly[6]. The property of unions which did not register under the 1871 Act remained unaffected, and so commonly remained vested in trustees. The 1971 Act was repealed by the Trade Union and Labour Relations Act 1974[7], which made provision for property of trade unions which had registered under the 1971 Act to be vested in trustees[8].

LAND HELD BY CO-OWNERS

Where land is held by more than one person it is subject[9] to a trust for sale. In the absence of an express trust for sale, statute imposes such a trust[10]. Thus wherever the title to a matrimonial home is held by the husband and wife, then the land is subject to a trust for sale. Similarly, where partners own business premises the title (freehold or leasehold) to the property will be vested in two or more of the partners on trust for sale for all the members of the partnership.

PROPERTY OF CLUBS[11]

There are few clubs which do not hold some property. If a club has not been incorporated, it ranks as an unincorporated association. As such, it is convenient, and common, for its property to be vested in one or more trustees, as where a club's funds are held by a club's treasurer. (If the club's property is land, then, as mentioned above, since the beneficial ownership is in more than one person, the land will be held subject to a trust for sale, the trustees commonly being certain members of the club's committee.)

4   Section 8.
5   Section 169, Sch 9.
6   Section 74.
7   Section 1.
8   Section 19.
9   If it is not settled land.
10   Law of Property Act 1925, ss 31–36.
11   See J. F. Gosling and Lionel Alexander, *The Law of Clubs*.

CHARITABLE AND CERTAIN OTHER PURPOSES

It has always been possible for property to be given to an institution which has charitable objectives, but it was not until the development of the use[12] in the later Middle Ages that it became possible for property to be given for some charitable purpose specified by the donor.

The trust is also the means by which property can be applied for certain non-charitable purposes, for example the upkeep of the testator's tomb or the maintenance of his dog[13].

PROPERTY HELD BY AN INFANT

The Law of Property Act 1925[14] provides that no legal estate in land may be held by an infant. Thus an infant can only hold a beneficial interest in land under a trust. (Unless the trust is a trust for sale, the trust will take effect under the Settled Land Act 1925[15].)

There is nothing in law to prevent an infant holding a legal title to personalty. But there may be inconveniences and risks in permitting an infant to hold the legal title to personalty of more than a trifling value[16]. (And the younger the infant, the greater may be the risks.) In many cases it is therefore safer and more convenient for personalty to be held for an infant by trustees until he attains full age.

PROVISION FOR A SETTLOR'S FAMILY AND DEPENDANTS

Among the oldest types of trust are those created by a settlor in order to provide for his family after his death. A trust created by a testator for the benefit of his widow for her lifetime, with remainder to their children, is perhaps the classic form of trust in this category. (Coupled with a settlor's desire to provide for his family after his death may have been a desire to attempt to ensure that his property, in the past particularly his land, remained within the family for as long a period into the future as the law would permit him to prescribe.) The machinery evolved by equity and statute for the administration of a trust enables a settlor to include terms to meet his particular wishes. Thus the settlor can guard against the loss of the trust property through the prodigality of one of his children by the creation of a protective trust[17]; he can vary the powers of maintenance and advancement now conferred by statute[18]; he can confer special powers on trustees, and impose particular duties on them. The trust can thus be tailor-made to meet the settlor's requirements.

---

12 See Chap 8.
13 See Chap 9.
14 Section 1(6).
15 Section 1(1)(ii)(d).
16 Further, an infant cannot give to, eg a personal representative, a valid receipt for property to which he has become entitled. See Chap 17.
17 See Chap 12.
18 See Chap 17.

REDUCTION OF TAX LIABILITY

In making provision for his family, a testator is likely to be concerned with arranging his estate so that the amount of tax payable on and after his death is reduced to a minimum. Many schemes were devised to avoid or to minimise the incidence of estate duty and these commonly made use of the machinery of a trust, in particular that of a discretionary trust[19]. A report by the Royal Commission on the Distribution of Income and Wealth[20] published in 1975 stated[1] that in 1960 63.1% of the total wealth of England and Wales was owned by 10% of the population. With no means of avoiding the payment of estate duty it is clear that this tax (which was levied at rates of up to 80% during this period) would have been likely to have affected a substantial redistribution of wealth within the country. The Commission found, however, that in 1973 10% of the population still owned 50.9% of the wealth of the country. If it is accepted that the distribution of wealth is a matter which affects the nature of any society, then the role which the trust has played in the shaping of our present society will be evident.

CONTRIBUTION TO THE RESOLUTION OF DISPUTES OVER TITLE TO PROPERTY

The principles evolved by equity for determining whether a trust exists have in some circumstances provided a pattern of reasoning which enables disputes over the title to property to be resolved in a consistent and logical manner.

In some disputes the position may be that A holds certain property, the beneficial title to which is claimed by B. A may have obtained some gain; B claims he made it from his position as trustee and that the beneficial ownership belongs to him, B. Again, A may have acquired certain property and claims to hold it beneficially; B claims that the property is trust property and that since A took it with notice, he holds it as constructive trustee. In disputes such as these the holder, A, claims a right to retain property as his own, and B claims to have the beneficial title. If A is bankrupt the dispute will lie between B and A's creditors, B claiming that the trustee in bankruptcy holds the property on trust for him, the creditors claiming that B has no title and that the property is therefore available towards meeting their claims. Whether A is bankrupt or not, the question in dispute is the same—did A hold on trust for B or did he not: is there a trust or is there not?[2]

In other circumstances (as mentioned in Chapter 4) the issue may be not whether A or B has the beneficial title to property, but whether A owes property, say a sum of £1,000, to B, or whether he holds it on trust for B. In this situation if A is solvent the question whether the relationship is one of contract or one of trust may never arise: if A passes the property to B, that may well be the end of the matter. But if A is insolvent[3] then the relationship between A and B becomes critical. If, as B will claim, A holds on trust for

19   See Chap 12.
20   Cmnd 6171.
 1   At p 102.
 2   See *Competitive Insurance Co Ltd v Davies Investment Ltd* [1975] 3 All ER 254, [1975] 1 WLR 1240.
 3   Or if B seeks to trace the property into the hands of a transferee from A *Lister & Co v Stubbs* (1890) 45 Ch D 1; (M & B).

him, B will take the property to the exclusion of A's creditors. But if A owes B the £1,000, B will rank pari passu with the creditors and take whatever percentage the trustee in bankruptcy declares. Thus here the dispute is not: is there a trust or is there no trust? but: is the relationship one of trust (as B will claim) or is it one of contract (as A's creditors will claim)[4]?

B will also be concerned to show that the relationship is one of trust and not one of contract where he has failed to bring his action within the time prescribed by statute before which the action becomes statute barred[5]. Thus, if B brings his action more than six years after his claim arises and A can show that the relationship was one of contract, B's claim will be statute barred[6]. If B can show that the relationship was one of trust (and that A had been fraudulent) then there will be no bar to his action[7].

MATRIMONIAL HOME

The concept of the trust has played a major part in determining disputes relating to the beneficial ownership of the matrimonial home. The relevant principles were treated when dealing with implied trusts in Chapter 10.

CONTRIBUTION OF IDEAS TO OTHER AREAS OF LAW

A major contribution of equity to English law has lain in the way that certain ideas, originating within the trust, have made their way into, and been found to serve valuably, in areas of law where otherwise common law and statute have held primary sway. An illustration is provided by the way in which the standards required of a director of a company have come to be accepted as being closely analogous to those required of a trustee. A trustee and a company director are in important respects in very different positions. But both are in a fiduciary position in that both owe a special duty, one to the beneficiary, the other to his company. The law of trusts has in this way come to provide a set of standards by which the actions and omissions of directors may be judged[8]. (Conversely, cases which have come before the courts concerning the exercise by a director of his fiduciary duty have added to our knowledge of the nature of the duty owed by trustees to beneficiaries[9].) Thus we find that directors must avoid a conflict of interest, that they must not make a profit from their position, that if they do so they hold the profit for the company[10], and so on. The fact that the control of companies has for

---

4   *Barclays Bank Ltd v Quistclose Investments Ltd* [1970] AC 567, [1968] 3 All ER 651; (M & B); *Re Kayford Ltd* [1975] 1 All ER 604, [1975] 1 WLR 279.
5   As in *Burdick v Garrick* (1870) 5 Ch App 233.
6   Limitation Act 1980, s 2.
7   Ibid, s 19. See Chap 23.
8   See *Belmont Finance Corpn Ltd v Williams Furniture Ltd* [1979] Ch 250, [1979] 1 All ER 118; *Thomas Marshall (Exports) Ltd v Guinle* [1979] Ch 227, [1978] 3 All ER 193; *International Sales and Agencies Ltd v Marcus* [1982] 3 All ER 551, [1982] 2 CMLR 46; (M & B); [1982] CLJ 244 (J. McMullen); (1983) 46 MLR 204 (W).
9   See *Re City Equitable Fire Insurance Co Ltd* [1925] Ch 407.
10 *Parker v McKenna* (1874) 10 Ch App 96 at 124.

long been within the jurisdiction of the Chancery courts helps to explain how this has come about; but it does not affect the fact that the trust has in this and in other matters provided a fertile seedbed of ideas which have been transplanted to, and taken firm root in, other fields of law.

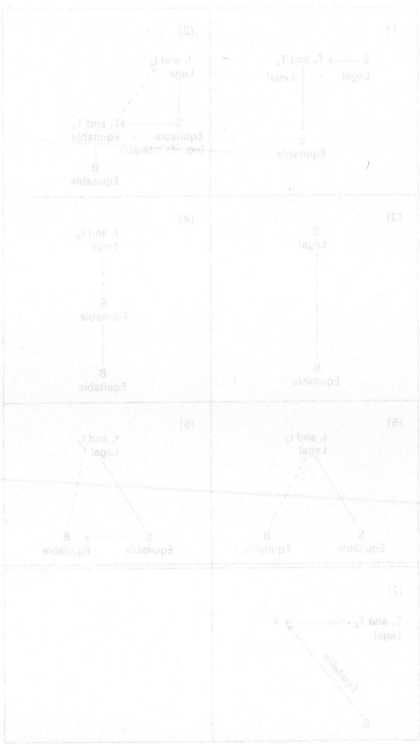

Appendix: Ways in which a trust may be created (see p 35)

(1)
S → T1 and T2
Legal
Legal
B
Equitable
(2)
T1 and T2
Legal
S → T1 and T2
Equitable
(eg, life interest)
Equitable
B
Equitable
(3)
S
Legal
B
Equitable
(4)
T1 and T2
Legal
S
Equitable
B
Equitable
(5)
T1 and T2
Legal
S
Equitable
B
Equitable
(6)
T1 and T2
Legal
S
Equitable
Equitable
(7)
X

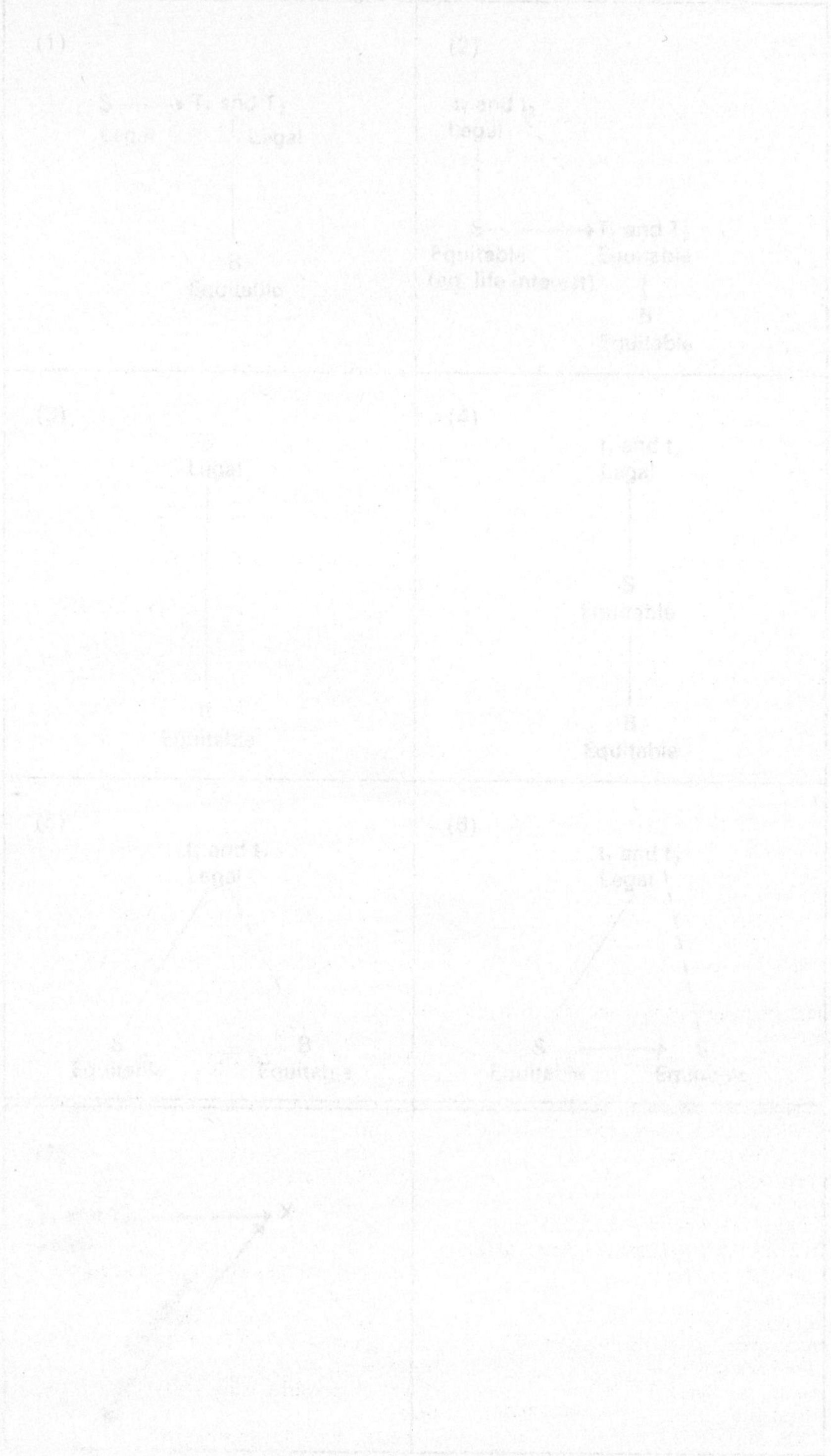

Index